HARRY S. TRUMAN:
A Bibliography of
His Times and Presidency

HARRY S. TRUMAN:
A Bibliography of
His Times and Presidency

Compiled for the
HARRY S. TRUMAN LIBRARY INSTITUTE
by
Richard Dean Burns

SR *Scholarly Resources Inc.*
Wilmington, Delaware

© 1984 by the Harry S. Truman Library Institute
All rights reserved
First published 1984
Printed and bound in the United States of America

Scholarly Resources Inc.
104 Greenhill Avenue
Wilmington, Delaware 19805

Library of Congress Cataloging in Publication Data

Burns, Richard Dean.
   Harry S. Truman: a bibliography of his times
and presidency.

   Includes index.
   1. Truman, Harry S., 1884–1972—Bibliography.
2. United States—Politics and government—1945–1953—
Bibliography. I. Title.
Z8888.9.B87   1984   016.973918′092′4   84-20223
[E814]
ISBN 0-8420-2219-8

Contents

Chapter 3   Administration Personalities: Political, Military, and Diplomatic   27

Contents

Chapter 6   Domestic Affairs: Civil Rights, Internal Security and Civil Liberties, Politics and Public Opinion, and the Supreme Court   99

Chapter 8   Foreign Affairs: Bilateral Relations 183

Chapter 9 Military Affairs: Atomic Weapons, Defense Policies, and Arms Control   239

Preface

More than three decades have passed since Harry S. Truman finished his second and final term as president. In the intervening years, literally thousands of scholarly books, articles, monographs, dissertations, and theses have been written documenting the history of the Truman administration and Truman's public career. As more and more Truman-related publications have become available, there has been a growing need for a full-scale bibliographic guide to materials written by chroniclers of the Truman era. This volume is designed to fill that need. Its publication in 1984, when we are celebrating the centennial of President Truman's birth, is a happy circumstance, especially in view of Truman's lifelong interest in the study of history, and in the lives of great men and women.

The Truman Library Institute, a private, nonprofit corporation, was established in 1957 to lend support to the Truman Library and to promote its interests. The development of the library as a major research center has been its principal goal. Since the library opened for research in 1959, it has sponsored scholarly conferences, supported special research projects, underwritten the publication of scholarly works, and administered a grant-in-aid program designed to assist students working in the Truman period. This publication adds another dimension to the institute's activities. We hope that in future years, scholars investigating the Truman era will find this volume to be a basic and perhaps even indispensable tool as they proceed with their research.

JAMES C. OLSON, President
Harry S. Truman Library Institute
Independence, Missouri

6 February 1984

Acknowledgments

This volume owes its comprehensiveness and its prompt completion to many people. Foremost among these is Dr. Benedict K. Zobrist, director of the Harry S. Truman Library and secretary of the Harry S. Truman Library Institute. Dr. Zobrist's recognition of the need for a guide to the literature of the Truman era and, subsequently, his enthusiasm for the project—even when others wearied—were vital ingredients in the completion of this volume. I appreciate his advice and encouragement, both of which contributed significantly to the shape this project has taken. I would also like to acknowledge the financial support of the Harry S. Truman Library Institute, for without this assistance it would not have been possible for me to have finished a comprehensive examination of the historical literature in time for this volume to appear during the Truman centennial year.

Staff members of the Harry S. Truman Library at Independence, Missouri were most generous in their support. Dr. George H. Curtis, assistant director of the library, was helpful in resolving administrative matters and, additionally, read most of the draft manuscript. Philip D. Lagerquist, Niel M. Johnson, Harry Clark, Elizabeth Safly, and Pauline Testerman located materials, wrote a number of annotations, and read parts, or all, of the final draft. Their comments were very useful and most of them have found their way into the present volume. Additionally, they made my visit to the library a pleasant and useful experience.

I am exceedingly grateful to the many Truman scholars who responded to my plea for specialists to comment on my draft chapters. While it was not possible to utilize all of these volunteers, I do appreciate their warm letters of encouragement and hope this volume lives up to their expectations. Francis H. Heller and Richard W. Leopold undertook the tedious task of reviewing the entire manuscript. Others who read various chapters and subsections include Richard M. Fried, Alonzo L. Hamby, Thomas J. Heed, Michael J. Hogan, R. Alton Lee, Donald R. McCoy, Robert Matray, Robert Messer, Richard L. Miller, and Robert L. Zangrando. The suggestions, criticisms, and corrections returned by these exceptionally generous and prompt colleagues greatly improved the final version of the bibliography. My thanks also go to Robert J. Donovan, Truman biographer, who in his perceptive and wide-ranging introduction to this volume sets the scene for the many decisions and events of this period.

In Southern California, Susan Hutson assisted me during the early stages by preparing many of the annotations. The reference librarians at the Kennedy Library, California State University, Los Angeles, were most generous with their time, advice, and energy. The most overworked of all the librarians was Christine J. Caldwell of Interlibrary Loan who quickly processed my inordinately large number of requests for books and articles.

Margaret Davis, a student assistant, showed remarkable abilities in tracking down errant titles and locating the proper books.

To the production staff at Scholarly Resources, I would like to express my admiration for their ability to transfer such a bulky manuscript so promptly into the present useful volume. To Philip G. Johnson, James L. Preston, and the many unsung people who contributed to the final attractive product, thank you.

As usual the final paragraph is devoted to my coworker and companion, Frances R. Burns. Her unflagging assistance made this unusually demanding undertaking bearable and kept it on schedule. I would like here to acknowledge Frances's past assistance with this, and so many similar, academic projects and to express my continuing amazement at her forbearance. How she managed through all of this and still extended thirty-five years of affectionate companionship is beyond my ken, but not my deepest love, appreciation, and gratitude.

Richard Dean Burns

Introduction

Harry S. Truman was a man of redoubtable character and humane disposition as well as a president of high historical importance. One need only know the era of the Truman administration (1945–53) to understand and appreciate his qualities and significance.

The Second World War destroyed much of the old order. The concluding year of that war, 1945, also brought the dawn of the nuclear age, altering the terms on which human beings live. For nearly eight years Truman was the president who was responsible for the initial adjustment of U.S. policy to a new balance of power in the world. He was the president who had to lay out the paths for relations with a new order in Europe, Asia, the Middle East, and the Third World. He was the first president to have to decide whether to use the atomic bomb and how to compete with the Soviet Union in the development of nuclear weapons. That is to say, he was the first president in the epoch of the superpowers.

Truman's approach to the new world order left the United States with a foreign policy drastically changed from what it had been in peacetime in the past. Perhaps the change was best illustrated by the North Atlantic Treaty, which clearly ended the old isolationism. Truman's foreign policy endured under other presidents in the critical postwar years. It forms the matrix of much of the policy that still guides the United States in foreign affairs.

For a man thrust into a position in which some of his decisions made a large impact on the history of the time, Truman was cast in anything but the image of a statesman. On the contrary, he was simple and informal, appealing rather than imposing, a pleasant-looking Missourian with a flat voice, a neighborly air, and rather old-fashioned virtues. While the future diplomats of his generation studied at Harvard and Yale, he worked for some years as a farmer after graduation from high school. While they went on to prestigious Eastern law firms, he became a partner in a Kansas City haberdashery. While they were moving up in society, he went broke in the depression of 1920–21. While they were making themselves at home in the capitals of the world, he turned to politics and became a judge (commissioner) of Jackson County, Missouri and worked on local problems until he was elected to the U.S. Senate in 1934.

It tells something about Truman that when he was in the Senate for ten years he was one of its best-liked members. And when he and his wife, Bess, were in the White House, they were held in probably greater affection by the people who worked in and around the place than any other president and first lady who come to mind. It tells something, too, that thirty years after the end of his term, Truman surely ranks among the most likeable men who ever held the office. This is particularly interesting because, largely as a result of the Korean War and the bitterness it engendered, he departed the White House with his popularity in shreds. The rebound that is still strong in 1984, the centennial of his birth, demonstrated that his character has had an enduring appeal to the American people.

Truman was no saint, least of all one who foreswore bourbon and cussing. He was not an angel, least of all one incapable of indignation and anger. He was not one whose mind worked like a computer, certainly not on the day when he wrote a blistering letter to the publisher of *The New York Times* to complain of an editorial which had appeared in *The New York Herald Tribune*. Truman was not in the front pew of the Baptist church every Sunday. Somehow he managed to get through life without too many sermons but not without a lot of poker. On the other hand, he was not a ladies' man, except when the ladies were his wife Bess and daughter Margaret. He did not overindulge in the company of artists and intellectuals. His taste in companionship ran to professional politicians, fellows with yarns that reminded him of life on the farm, and men who knew a one-eyed jack when they saw one.

The character that has appealed to the American people over the years was built on very familiar foundations. By friend and foe alike, Truman's honesty was never questioned. His directness made him a pleasure to deal with. He was marvelously free of the emotional hang-ups that entangled some of his successors. Even in the presidency, he had a basic humility that was often obscured by his combativeness when put on the defensive. He once asked reporters to stop describing him as cocky. He was not cocky, he said. It was a fair point. Cockiness and humility do not go together.

In this age of greed and quick and easy money for the politically powerful, it was to Truman's credit, if not to his comfort, that he left the White House low on cash. He was the last president we have had, perhaps excluding Gerald R. Ford, who did not have money and luxury of his own or access to them because of his position. He was the only president since Grover Cleveland who did not go to college, and possibly only one or two of the other presidents since Cleveland read as much as Truman, especially as much history and biography.

At his best he was a president who stood up to challenges as he saw them, tackling questions in a practical way without immersing himself in the philosophy of a subject. Common sense was his forte, though not always powerful enough to save him from impulsive acts. He was apt to lunge at what seemed right without always calculating the cost.

A partisan Democrat who often put able Republicans in vital positions and who owed his greatest accomplishments to a bipartisan foreign policy, Truman was deeply influenced by Andrew Jackson, Woodrow Wilson, and Franklin D. Roosevelt. When he took office, Truman strove to carry on and enlarge the New Deal. His efforts fell short, in no small measure because Congress and the people were rather uninterested in domestic reform after the war. But he did keep the Republicans from turning back the New Deal.

Truman mixed caution with boldness in his approach to civil rights. He established a Civil Rights Committee and, based on its findings, issued orders to prohibit discrimination in the hiring of federal employees and to end segregation in the armed forces. Truman may also be remembered for standing up to Southern critics who led a walkout in the 1948 Democratic National Convention over the issue of civil rights. Perhaps most notably, he became the first president to submit a comprehensive civil rights program to

Congress. His proposals, though not acted upon then, foreshadowed practically all of the civil rights measures of the next quarter of a century.

On other domestic matters, Truman presided over the successful reconversion of the American economy after World War II. Inflation caused concern and numerous strikes over wages aroused some alarm, but unemployment did not become a problem and wage settlements began keeping pace with rises in the cost-of-living. The Employment Act of 1946, although weaker than Truman wanted, committed the federal government to a policy of supporting full employment of the nation's work force. Although delayed in bringing them about, the Truman administration managed to broaden Social Security coverage, to raise the minimum wage, and to obtain passage of the Housing Act of 1949 that established a national housing policy and provided federal assistance for slum clearance and low-cost housing projects. A large measure of the success of reconversion may be attributed to the "G. I. Bill" of 1944. In the postwar period it furnished millions of war veterans with low-cost home loans and educational subsidies on an unprecedented scale.

In the area of public power, Truman tried and failed to establish TVA-type authorities in other large river valleys, but power and reclamation projects, mostly in the West, did consume more federal dollars than in any previous decade. The administration also failed to convince Congress of the need for a national health insurance program and for a new cabinet-level department to administer health and welfare programs, but its efforts in this field presaged the "Great Society" programs of the 1960s.

Only two major new pieces of domestic legislation—the above-mentioned Employment Act of 1946 and the National Housing Act of 1949—were enacted during Truman's tenure. But in nearly eight years of historic activity in foreign affairs, Truman never lost a single piece of major foreign policy legislation. Moreover, all those victories were won with votes to spare, even while the Republicans were in control of the Eightieth Congress of 1947 and 1948.

The steps that were taken under Truman with the support of the great consensus, including Senator Arthur H. Vandenberg of Michigan, the senior Republican on the Senate Foreign Relations Committee, are familiar. In contrast to the rejection by the Senate of American membership in the League of Nations after the First World War, the United States joined the United Nations in 1945. Following that, Truman extended a $3.75 billion loan to stave off economic collapse in Great Britain. Then came the Truman Doctrine, in effect making containment of communism the basis of American policy. In the face of the Soviet blockade of Berlin, Truman preserved the American position in Germany with an airlift. Thereafter, the administration fostered the formation of an independent West German government, and its alliance with the victorious Western powers.

The Marshall Plan and the North Atlantic Treaty were landmarks, the latter ending the historic policy of no permanent alliances outside the Western Hemisphere. Together, the purposes of the Marshall Plan and NATO were to put Western Europe back on its feet after the ravages of war, while providing a military shield against possible attack from the East. The Marshall Plan gave assistance to the economies of allied countries on an unprecedented scale in peacetime. Congress was receptive partly because a great deal of the money was spent on goods from the United States, thereby helping the postwar American economy.

With almost unanimous support in favor of drawing the line against further Communist encroachment anywhere, Truman committed American forces to war in Korea in 1950. Without a murmur of disapproval from Congress or the public, he also made the first commitment by the United States aimed at preventing a Communist takeover of Vietnam. He extended diplomatic recognition, political support, and arms to the pro-French Bao Dai government. The commitment was to flourish beyond belief under Eisenhower, Kennedy, Johnson, and Nixon.

As part of the process of containment in Asia, Truman concluded an enlightened, nonpunitive treaty with Japan. Under the Truman administration, therefore, our deadly enemies in the Second World War, Japan and Germany (West Germany at least), were brought into a constructive friendly relationship with the United States.

In the midst of these developments, Truman recognized the new state of Israel in 1948, an act that led to a lasting special relationship between the two countries.

Needless to say, President Truman's war policies and foreign policy initiatives are not something that could be wrapped up and placed on a shelf in expectation of universal approval by history. Many of them are still hotly debated, none more than his decision to drop atomic bombs on Japan. Among his contemporaries that decision was perfectly understandable and overwhelmingly approved. He used the bombs to end the war quickly and save American and Japanese lives that might otherwise have been lost in the planned allied invasion of the Japanese islands. Among later generations who never experienced the Second World War and who are appalled at the proliferation of nuclear weapons, it is much harder to find understanding of the problems and pressures that led Truman to use the atomic bomb and to build the hydrogen bomb. That trend of opinion is likely to continue in the future.

While Truman's foreign policies were lastingly successful in Europe, his worst troubles as president flowed from the Far East. Although there was no feasible action Truman could have taken to prevent the Chinese Communists from winning the civil war against Chiang Kai-shek's Nationalist government, the outcome was looked upon by large numbers of Americans as a disaster for the United States. The event paved the way for Senator Joe McCarthy's anti-Communist rampage. Republicans turned the Communist victory into an issue against the Democrats, permanently damaging Truman's leadership.

On top of the China trouble, North Korea invaded South Korea, catching the American intelligence community completely by surprise and the Truman administration unprepared for a large war. For weeks it was all U.S. troops and their U.N. allies could do to keep from being overrun. When the fighting was at last turned around with the help of General of the Army Douglas A. MacArthur's brilliant amphibious landing at Inchon, a still more serious dilemma confronted Truman. His aim when he entered the war was to drive the North Koreans back to the 38th parallel, the boundary between north and south, across which they had made their invasion. Despite Inchon, many of them had been able to retreat to North Korea to fight another day. Tempted to stamp out Soviet influence in Korea and urged by public pressure to end the Korean problem once and for all, Truman authorized MacArthur to cross the parallel to smash the North Korean army as a step toward unification of the country. China warned that it would intervene if American troops crossed the line. Truman and his advisers would not listen. MacArthur launched a reckless drive north to the Yalu River, the boundary with China. In overwhelming force, China struck and drove U.N. forces back across the 38th parallel.

Facing a possible ghastly defeat, MacArthur demanded that the United States bomb and blockade China. Truman refused, fearing such acts would lead to a third world war. MacArthur persisted. Truman relieved him of his command. Although political upheaval swept the United States, Truman's decision is generally accepted today as inevitable and proper. The United States was forced to settle for a truce near the 38th parallel, but the war dragged on into the Eisenhower administration. The hostile relationship with China persisted for two decades. Fear of China had a great deal to do with America's fighting a disastrous war in Vietnam to keep Southeast Asia out of China's hands. As for Korea, it remains divided, and American troops still stand guard near the 38th parallel. As a result of Truman's decision, however, South Korea still stands and flourishes, its independence contributing to the security of Japan.

Undoubtedly, the doctrine of anticommunism led Truman and his successors farther afield than American power could support. Truman was the first president to have the ultimate power in his hands and realize that he no longer could use it without blowing up the world. He had to accept use of limited power and its concomitant: limited success. The story of presidents in the nuclear age will always begin with Truman.

Robert J. Donovan

Use of the Period after "S" in Harry S. Truman's Name

In recent years the question of using a period after the "S" in Harry S. Truman's name has become a subject of controversy, especially for editors. The evidence provided by Truman's own practice argues strongly for the use of a period. While, as many people do, Truman often ran his signature together in a single stroke, the archives of the Harry S. Truman Library has numerous examples of his signature throughout his lifetime where the use of the period is very obvious.

Truman apparently initiated the "period" controversy himself in 1962 when he told newspapermen, probably in jest, that the period should be omitted. In explanation he said that the "S" did not stand for any name but a compromise between the names of his grandfathers, Anderson Shippe Truman and Solomon Young. He was later heard to say that the use of the period did not matter and many examples of him using the period appear after 1962 as well as before. Moreover, according to the University of Chicago Press *Manual of Style*, all initials given with a name should "for convenience and consistency" be followed by a period, even if they are not abbreviations of names. The U.S. Government *Style Manual* states that the period should be used after the "S" in Harry S. Truman's name.

Most published works that use the name employ the period. One of the difficulties is that if one chooses to omit the period in his own writing, to be accurate he must use it in citing other works that do use it, and in citing the names of organizations that employ the period in their legal titles, such as the Harry S. Truman Library, the Harry S. Truman Library Institute, the Harry S. Truman Historic District, the Harry S. Truman Sports Complex, and the Harry S. Truman Dam. Thus an editor following that policy would have to decide in each instance whether to use it or not.

Authoritative publications produced by the Government Printing Office consistently use the period in Truman's name, notably the Department of State's documentary series *Foreign Relations of the United States, Diplomatic Papers*, the Department of the Army's *United States Army in World War II*, and two major publications of the Office of the Federal Register, *Public Papers of the Presidents—Harry S. Truman* and the *United States Government Organization Manual*.

Chronology–Harry S. Truman

Prepresidential—1840s–1945

1840s —The families of Solomon Young and Anderson Shippe Truman moved from Kentucky to the vicinity of Westport, Missouri, on the American frontier. Young and Truman were grandparents of Harry S. Truman. His father, John Anderson Truman, was born in 1851, and his mother, Martha Ellen Young, was born in 1852.

1884 —8 May: Harry S. Truman was born in Lamar, Missouri.

1885 —Family moved to a farm near Harrisonville, Missouri.

1887 —Moved to a farm owned by Solomon Young near present-day Grandview, Missouri.

1890 —Moved to 619 Crysler Street in Independence, Missouri.

—Young Harry met Bess Wallace for the first time in First Presbyterian Church's Sunday school.

1892 —Entered elementary school (Noland School) in Independence.

1896 —Moved to 909 West Waldo Avenue in Independence.

1900 —Served as a page at the Democratic National Convention in Kansas City, Missouri. Heard William Jennings Bryan speak.

1901 —Graduated from Independence High School with forty other students.

—Visited aunts in Illinois and St. Louis.

—Attended Spalding's Business College.

—His father, John Anderson Truman, lost his savings in grain-futures market.

1902 —Worked for two weeks in mailing room of Kansas City *Star*.

1902–3 —Worked as timekeeper for L. J. Smith on Santa Fe Railroad construction project.

1903 —Joined Baptist church at age eighteen (Benton Boulevard Baptist in Kansas City).

—Moved with family to 902 N. Liberty Street in Independence, and then to 2108 Park Avenue in Kansas City, Missouri.

1903–5 —Worked as clerk for National Bank of Commerce in Kansas City, Missouri.

1905–6 —Worked as bookkeeper for Union National Bank in Kansas City.

1905 —Moved to rooming house at 1314 Troost Avenue in Kansas City.

1905–11—Served in Battery B of Missouri National Guard. Entered as a private, but was soon promoted to corporal.

1906 —Moved to 600-acre family farm near Grandview, Missouri to help parents and brother, Vivian, manage and operate it.

1909 —Joined Masonic Order, Lodge No. 450, Belton, Missouri.

1910 —Began courting Bess Wallace.

1911 —Organized the first Masonic lodge in Grandview, Missouri.

1913 —Purchased his first automobile, a 1911 Stafford.

1914 —2 November: His father died.

—Appointed road overseer in southern half of Washington Township.

1915 —Appointed postmaster in Grandview.

—Invested and lost money in a zinc-mining venture.

1916 —Helped organize an oil-drilling company, later named the Morgan Oil and Refining Company, and invested $10,000 in it, managing perhaps to break even before the company was dissolved in 1919. Served as its treasurer.

—Joined Grandview Baptist Church, Grandview, Missouri.

1917 —June: Rejoined National Guard and was elected first lieutenant of Battery F, 2nd Missouri Artillery.

—August: Sworn into regular army service as a member of 129th Field Artillery regiment.

—September: Assigned to Camp Doniphan, Fort Sill, Oklahoma, and appointed canteen officer, with Sgt. Edward Jacobson as assistant.

1918 —13 April: Arrived in Brest, France, on board U.S.S. *George Washington*.

—May: Promoted to captain, although he did not receive official notification until October.

—11 July: Assigned command of Battery D, 129th Field Artillery regiment, 35th Division. Battery was composed of 188 men, 167 horses, and a complement of French-designed 75-mm guns.

—6 September: Engaged in first combat operation in Vosges Mountains.

—11 November: Battery D fired last round at 10:45 A.M.

1919 —9 April: Sailed from Brest aboard liner U.S.S. *Zeppelin*.

—6 May: Discharged from the army.

—28 June: Married Elizabeth (Bess) Virginia Wallace at the bride's church, Trinity Episcopal, in Independence, and moved into home at 219 N. Delaware, Independence, the residence of his mother-in-law, Madge Gates Wallace.

—November: Opened men's haberdashery store, in partnership with Edward Jacobson, at 104 West 12th Street, Kansas City, Missouri.

1920 —Appointed major in Field Artillery, Officers Reserve Corps.

1921 —Helped form the first Reserve Officers Association unit in the United States, in Kansas City. Became a chapter in new national association in 1922.

1922 —Haberdashery business failed as a result of business recession, but Truman refused to file a petition of bankruptcy and paid off his share of the firm's debts during the ensuing fifteen years.

—With the endorsement of county Democratic party leader, T. J. Pendergast, won election as eastern judge on the Jackson County Court, an executive body that administered affairs of the county.

1923–25 —Attended Kansas City School of Law.

1924 —Defeated for reelection by Henry Rummel, the only election Truman ever lost.

—With Spencer Salisbury, established the Community Savings and Loan Association in Independence, and served as general manager until 1932.

1925–26 —Worked as a membership salesman for the Kansas City Automobile Club.

1926 —Elected president of the National Old Trails Association.

—Elected presiding judge of the Jackson County Court.

1927 —January: Sworn in as presiding judge of the Jackson County Court. Served two four-year terms, 1927–34.

1928 —Led successful campaign resulting in approval of a bond issue for $6.5 million to build 224 miles of paved highways in the county, and additional funds for building a county hospital.

1931 —Obtained voter approval of bond issues to complete the road system, build a new courthouse and jail in Kansas City, remodel the Independence courthouse, and construct a detention home.

1932 —Promoted to colonel in the Field Artillery Reserve.

1933 —Appointed federal reemployment director for Missouri.

1934 —May: Filed as a Democratic candidate for the U.S. Senate.

—7 August: Won Democratic primary election with 276,850 votes; John Cochran received 236,105; and Jacob Milligan, 147,614.

1934 —6 November: Defeated incumbent Republican Roscoe C. Patterson by 262,000 votes.

—27 December: Participated in the dedication of new courthouse in Kansas City.

1935 —3 January: Sworn in as U.S. senator, along with twelve other new Democratic senators.

—Assigned as a member of the Appropriations Committee and the Interstate Commerce Committee. Also served on Public Buildings and Grounds Committee and the Committee on Printing in his first term.

—15 May: Introduced his first public bill—"A bill to provide for insurance by the Farm Credit Administration of mortgages on farm property, and for other purposes." Bill died later in committee.

1937 —Named as vice-chairman of a subcommittee of the Interstate Commerce Committee to investigate American railroad finances.

—Met with Justice Louis D. Brandeis on several social occasions and discussed transportation regulation.

1938 —Helped draft the Civil Aeronautics Act of 1938.

1939 —With Senator Burton Wheeler, introduced bill to reorganize the railroads and place them under the regulation of the Interstate Commerce Commission.

—As member of Military Subcommittee of the Appropriations Committee, visited defense installations in the United States, Panama, Cuba, and Puerto Rico.

1940 —15 June: Launched reelection campaign at courthouse in Sedalia, Missouri.

—Summer: Mortgage foreclosed on Truman farm near Grandview; mother Martha Ellen Truman and sister Mary Jane moved to town. (Farm was purchased by Truman friends and sold back to the Truman family several years later.)

—6 August: Won Democratic senatorial primary election, garnering 268,557 votes; Lloyd Stark received 260,581; and Maurice Milligan, 127,363.

—18 September: Transportation Act of 1940, also known as the Wheeler-Truman Act, was signed by President Roosevelt.

—September: Elevated to Grand Master of the Grand Lodge of Missouri, Masonic Order.

—5 November: Won reelection to the Senate, with 930,773 votes; Manvel Davis received 886,376.

1941 —10 and 13 February: Proposed that the Senate create a special committee to investigate defense contracts.

—1 March: The Senate, by unanimous vote, created the Senate Special Committee to Investigate the National Defense Program. Became known as the Truman Committee, after Senator Truman was appointed chairman (8 March).

—15 April: First hearing of the Truman Committee was conducted, with Secretary of War Henry L. Stimson as first witness.

1942   —15 January: Truman Committee presented its First Annual Report to the Senate. Helped induce President Roosevelt to replace the Office of Production Management with a new, more powerful War Production Board.

1943   —8 February: Reported that savings attributable to the work of the Truman Committee were being estimated in a range up to $11 billion.

—8 March: His portrait appeared on cover of *Time* magazine.

1944   —29 January: Spoke at ceremony launching the battleship U.S.S. *Missouri*. Daughter Margaret christened the ship with a bottle of champagne.

—May: Selected as one of the ten most useful officials in Washington, D.C. in a poll of fifty-two correspondents conducted by *Look* magazine.

—21 July: Nominated for the office of vice-president at the Democratic National Convention, Chicago, Illinois.

—3 August: Resigned chairmanship of Truman Committee. During his tenure, the committee received funding of $400,000 and grew to a staff of about twenty-five, in addition to senatorial members.

—18 August: Had first meeting with President Roosevelt as his running mate.

—31 August: Launched his vice-presidential campaign at his birthplace, Lamar, Missouri.

—4 September: Delivered Labor Day speeches to AF of L and CIO audiences in Detroit, Michigan.

—12 October: Began official campaign tour, by railroad, with speech in New Orleans. Used railroad car "Henry Stanley."

—7 November: Elected as vice-president of the United States.

1945   —20 January: Sworn in as vice-president in inauguration ceremony at White House.

—29 January: Attended funeral of Thomas J. Pendergast in Kansas City, Missouri.

Presidential—First Term, 1945–49

1945   —12 April: Sworn in as thirty-third president of the United States upon the death of President Roosevelt.

1945 —25 April: Delivered radio address from Washington, DC, opening U.N. conference being held in San Francisco to create the charter for a new, permanent world organization.

—8 May: Announced the end of the war in Europe over radio at 9 A.M. (V–E Day).

—11 May: Visited at the White House by mother Martha Ellen and sister Mary Jane.

—19 June: Flew to Washington State, becoming the first president in office to use air travel within the country.

—26 June: Delivered address at the closing session of the U.N. Charter Conference in San Francisco.

—17 July–2 August: Attended conference at Potsdam, Germany to discuss postwar treatment of Germany with Premier Joseph Stalin of Russia and Prime Minister Winston Churchill of Great Britain, latter being replaced by Prime Minister Clement Attlee on 29 July.

—6 August: Announced dropping of the first atomic bomb on Hiroshima, Japan by a B–29 bomber of the U.S. Army Air Force. (Second atomic bomb dropped on Nagasaki, Japan on 9 August.)

—14 August: Announced end of war with Japan at press conference held at 7 P.M. (V–J Day).

—6 September: Presented twenty-one-point legislative program to Congress for the reconversion period as a continuation and expansion of Roosevelt's New Deal, contrary to popular expectations that the policies of the new president would be more conservative than that of his predecessor.

—23 October: Delivered message to Congress calling for enactment of a peacetime universal military training program.

—15 November: Issued joint statement in Washington with Prime Ministers Clement Attlee of Great Britain and Mackenzie King of Canada calling for a U.N. Atomic Energy Commission.

1946 —17 January: Proposed that the dispute between U.S. Steel and the United Steel Workers union be settled by an 18½ cents per hour wage increase. A walkout was not prevented, but it and most major strikes in 1946 were settled on the basis of an 18½ cent increase.

—15 February: Accepted resignation of Harold L. Ickes as secretary of the interior. Ickes, who left cabinet in protest against proposed appointment of Edwin W. Pauley as undersecretary of the navy, was replaced by Julius Krug on 18 March.

—20 February: Signed Employment Act of 1946 which established Council of Economic Advisers.

—21 February: Reestablished Office of Economic Stabilization under Chester Bowles in an attempt to control mounting prices.

—24 May: Announced he would end strike of railroad trainmen and engineer brotherhoods, which had started the day before, by the following day. On 25 May the strike ended with the unions accepting the president's recommendations.

—29 May: Attended graduation exercises of his daughter Margaret at George Washington University, on which occasion he received the degree of LL.D.

—15 July: Signed bill authorizing loan of $3.75 billion to Great Britain.

—25 July: Signed new price control act reviving the Office of Price Administration which had gone out of existence on 29 June when the president vetoed a compromise price control measure.

—20 September: Requested the resignation of Secretary of Commerce Henry A. Wallace as a result of a speech delivered by Wallace on 12 September criticizing Secretary of State James F. Byrnes and U.S. policy toward Russia. Wallace was replaced by W. Averell Harriman.

—15 October: Ended price controls on meat.

—5 November: Received political setback when, in midterm congressional elections, Republican majorities were returned to the Senate and House of Representatives.

—9 November: Signed executive order ending all wage and price controls except on rents, sugar, and rice. As a result prices rose sharply.

—21 November: Ordered contempt proceedings against John L. Lewis when mine leader, defying a government injunction, called members of the United Mine Workers union out on strike. On 5 December Lewis sent the miners back to work after a federal district court had fined him $10 thousand and the union $3.5 million.

—31 December: Signed proclamation declaring end of hostilities for World War II.

1947   —7 January: Accepted resignation of Byrnes as secretary of state.

—21 January: Sworn in as new secretary of state was Gen. George C. Marshall, World War II chief of staff of the U.S. Army.

—22 January: Asked former President Herbert Hoover to undertake mission to study critical food problem in Central Europe and make recommendations for its solution.

—3 March: Arrived in Mexico on a state visit. Reaffirmed his predecessor's Good Neighbor Policy.

1947 —12 March: Requested appropriation for $400 million before a joint session of Congress to fight the spread of communism in Greece and Turkey (Truman Doctrine). The doctrine received the backing of most of the Republican members of Congress in accordance with the bipartisan foreign policy which was in effect during most of the Truman administration.

—21 March: Ordered loyalty investigation of all federal government employees.

—22 May: Approved bill providing $400 million in assistance to Greece and Turkey.

—11 June: Addressed Canadian Parliament in Ottawa, outlining U.S. foreign policy.

—14 June: Signed peace treaty ratifications with Italy, Hungary, Romania, and Bulgaria.

—16 June: Vetoed $4 billion income tax reduction bill as being unfair to small taxpayer.

—20 June: Vetoed Taft-Hartley Bill (Labor-Management Relations Act of 1947) on grounds that it was discriminatory against labor. Bill passed by Congress over the veto on 23 June.

—26 July: Signed National Security Act of 1947 unifying the armed forces in one department, a measure long advocated by him. Appointed James V. Forrestal as first secretary of the unified National Military Establishment (later realigned as Department of Defense). Act also established the Central Intelligence Agency and the National Security Council.

—28 July: Attended funeral of mother in Grandview, Missouri.

—2 September: Addressed final session of Inter-American Conference for the Maintenance of Continental Peace and Security. Treaty of Rio de Janeiro signed.

1948 —2 February: Sent message to Congress asking for civil rights legislation to secure the rights of the country's minority groups.

—1 April: Vetoed income tax reduction act. Bill passed by Congress over the president's veto the following day.

—3 April: Signed Foreign Assistance Act of 1948 creating European Recovery Program (ERP) to implement the Marshall Plan for U.S. aid to European recovery. Economic Cooperation Administration established to administer program.

—10 May: Ordered government operation of the railroads by the army to forestall nationwide railroad strike.

—14 May: Recognized new state of Israel.

—3 June: Began "non-political" speaking tour by train to West Coast.

—25 June: Signed Displaced Persons Act authorizing admission into the United States of 205,000 European displaced persons in the following two years.

—26 June: Ordered Berlin airlift, in conjunction with the British, in answer to Russian blockade of the portion of that city occupied by the Western powers. Blockade lasted until 12 May 1949.

—15 July: Nominated Democratic candidate for president on first ballot at Democratic National Convention in Philadelphia, after thirty-five delegates from Alabama and Mississippi had walked out of the convention in protest against strong civil rights plank in the party platform. Senator Alben W. Barkley of Kentucky was chosen vice-presidential candidate.

—15 July: Called Congress into special session on 26 July to act on housing, civil rights, and price controls. Congress adjourned 7 August, having enacted practically no legislation.

—6 September–30 October: Made several extensive campaign trips, traveling through all sections of the country except the South. Calling it a "whistle stop" campaign, he made 275 speeches, centering his attack upon the record of the "do nothing 80th Congress," and traveling about 22,000 miles.

—2 November: Elected to second term as president contrary to the forecasts of newspapers and poll takers, who had almost unanimously predicted his defeat. Popular vote: Truman, 24,105,812; Governor Thomas E. Dewey of New York, the Republican candidate, 21,970,065; Governor J. Strom Thurmond of South Carolina running on the States Rights (Dixiecrat) ticket, 1,169,021; and Henry A. Wallace of New York, the Progressive party candidate, 1,157,172. Electoral vote: Truman, 303; Dewey, 189; Thurmond, 39.

Presidential—Second Term, 1949–53

1949   —5 January: Delivered State of Union message asking for strengthened liberal program characterized as the "Fair Deal."

—20 January: Marshall resigned as secretary of state. Dean Acheson succeeded him on 21 January.

—20 January: Inaugurated for second term. In inaugural address, called for "bold new program" to help underprivileged peoples of the earth (Point IV Program).

—6 June: Signed executive order establishing office of U.S. High Commissioner in Germany as step in replacing army supervision with civilian control in that country.

—15 July: Signed Housing Act establishing a national housing policy and providing for federal aid to slum clearance programs and low-cost housing projects.

—10 August: Signed National Security Act Amendment, establishing a unified Department of Defense.

1949 —24 August: Proclaimed the North Atlantic Pact, which had been signed by twelve nations in Washington on 4 April, to be in effect. Implementation of pact entrusted to North Atlantic Treaty Organization (NATO). On 19 December 1950 Dwight D. Eisenhower was appointed commander of the combined forces, being designated Supreme Allied Commander, Europe.

—23 September: Announced that there was evidence of a Russian atomic explosion.

—6 October: Signed Mutual Defense Assistance Act authorizing appropriation of funds for military assistance to nations signing the North Atlantic Pact.

1950 —31 January: Revealed that he had ordered the Atomic Energy Commission to develop the hydrogen bomb.

—26 June: Ordered U.S. air and sea forces to aid South Korean troops in resisting the Communist forces of North Korea which had invaded South Korea the day before.

—30 June: Announced that he had ordered American ground forces in Japan to Korea and the navy to blockade the Korean coast. The president's Korean policy was backed by the U.N. Security Council. Gen. Douglas MacArthur, the American commander in Japan, was put in charge of all U.N. troops in the area, which included forces from other nations.

—19 July: Sent message to Congress asking for supplemental appropriation to support the Korean police action and for measures to control the country's economy.

—25 August: Ordered seizure of the railroads by the government on 27 August to forestall nationwide strike.

—8 September: Signed Defense Production Act establishing priorities, price and wage stabilization program, and limiting installment buying.

—12 September: Accepted resignation of Louis A. Johnson as secretary of defense. Johnson succeeded by Gen. George C. Marshall on 21 September.

—23 September: Signed the Revenue Act of 1950 increasing corporation and income taxes.

—15 October: Conferred with MacArthur on Wake Island concerning Far Eastern policy.

—1 November: Escaped attempted assassination by two Puerto Rican nationalists.

—6 December: Wrote a personal letter to music critic Paul Hume, assailing him for his "lousy review" of a recital given by daughter Margaret. The president's strong language aroused public controversy, but the majority of mail was in his favor.

—16 December: Proclaimed state of national emergency following entry of Communist China into the Korean conflict on 6 November, after U.N. forces had taken over most of North Korea.

1951   —11 January: Appointed mission headed by John Foster Dulles to go to Japan to confer with MacArthur and Japanese leaders in regard to a Japanese peace treaty. Treaty signed in San Francisco on 8 September by delegates from forty-eight countries, Russia and her satellites refusing to participate.

—26 March: Opened fourth meeting of the foreign ministers of the twenty-one American republics in Constitution Hall, Washington, DC.

—11 April: Relieved MacArthur of all posts as commander of American and U.N. forces in the Far East for making statements critical of the government's military and foreign policies in that area. MacArthur replaced by Lt. Gen. Matthew B. Ridgway.

—15 June: Signed India Emergency Food Aid Act, lending $190 million to India to buy up to two million tons of grain.

—1 August: Proclaimed suspension of tariff reductions for Soviet Russia, People's Republic of China, and other Communist countries.

—10 October: Signed Mutual Security Act authorizing $7,483,400,000 for foreign economic, military, and technical aid and establishing Mutual Security Agency.

—20 October: Nominated Gen. Mark W. Clark to be ambassador to the Vatican. Move was both praised and condemned and Congress failed to act on the appointment. On 13 January 1952 White House announced that at Clark's request his nomination would not be resubmitted.

—24 October: Proclaimed state of war with Germany to be officially at an end as of 19 October.

1952   —2 January: Submitted to Congress plan to reorganize Bureau of Internal Revenue in response to charges of inefficiency and corruption in that agency. Plan, which called for replacing sixty-four politically appointed collectors with twenty-five district commissioners under Civil Service, became effective 15 March after receiving Senate approval.

—5–9 January: Conferred at Washington with Winston Churchill, recently reelected prime minister of Great Britain, and other British and American officials, concerning common problems in Europe and the Middle and Far East.

—27 March: Reestablished residence in the White House after living in Blair House, the official government guest house, since November 1948, while the White House was being rebuilt and renovated.

1952 —29 March: Announced at Jefferson-Jackson Day dinner decision not to run for reelection.

—8 April: Signed executive order directing Secretary of Commerce Charles Sawyer to seize steel mills to prevent strike of steel workers. On 2 June seizure was declared unconstitutional by the Supreme Court in a six to three decision.

—15 April: Signed ratification of peace treaty with Japan and defense treaties with Japan, Australia, New Zealand, and the Philippines.

—29 May: Vetoed joint resolution of Congress confirming state claims to submerged lands below the low water mark (so-called "tidelands" dispute).

—14 June: Laid keel of the U.S.S. *Nautilus*, world's first atomic powered submarine, at Groton, Connecticut.

—2 September–1 November: Made five campaign speaking tours in behalf of Adlai Stevenson, the Democratic party's candidate for president.

—5 November: Invited president-elect Gen. Dwight D. Eisenhower to White House to discuss problems of transition from one administration to the next after Republican victory on 4 November. Meeting between Truman and Eisenhower took place on 18 November.

1953 —20 January: Attended inauguration of President Eisenhower and then left by train for Independence.

Postpresidential—1953–72

1953–55—Worked on his memoirs, the first volume of which, *Year of Decisions*, was published in November 1955. The second volume, *Years of Trial and Hope*, appeared the following year.

1953 —16 November: Addressed a nationwide audience on television to answer charges involving the hiring of Harry Dexter White, an alleged Communist, who was appointed to the International Monetary Fund during Truman's presidency.

1955 —8 May: On his seventy-first birthday, broke ground for the construction of a privately financed Harry S. Truman Library building.

—12 August: Presidential Libraries Act was signed, authorizing the General Services Administration to accept the papers of U.S. presidents, and the land, buildings, and equipment that are offered for a "Presidential archival depository."

1956 —21 April: Attended the marriage of his daughter, Mary Margaret, to E. Clifton Daniel, Jr., well-known newspaperman, in Trinity Episcopal Church, Independence. Grandsons were born in 1957, 1959, 1963, and 1966.

—11 May–3 July: With wife, Bess, toured Europe. Visited historical sites, met with a number of European leaders, including the Winston Churchills, had an audience with Pope Pius XII, and received numerous honors, including an honorary degree from Oxford University on 20 June.

—August: Announced his support of Governor Averell Harriman for the Democratic party's nominee for the presidency, but campaigned subsequently for Adlai Stevenson after the party's national convention selected him instead.

—December: Signed an agreement with the North American Newspaper Alliance to write a series of articles for publication in newspapers around the country. First article appeared in January 1957.

1957 —February: Interviewed by Edward R. Murrow of CBS for a "See It Now" program that was aired one year later.

—5 July: Presided over first meeting of Board of Directors of the Harry S. Truman Institute for National and International Affairs.

—6 July: Participated in the dedication of the Harry S. Truman Library in Independence, Missouri; it was the second presidential library to become part of the National Archives and Records Service.

1958 —June: With wife Bess and the Samuel Rosenmans made second and last trip to Europe in this postpresidential period.

1959 —19 April: Participated in the dedication of his birthplace home in Lamar, Missouri. It had been purchased and restored by the United Auto Workers union, and then accepted by the state as a gift in 1959.

—3 September: Hosted comedian Jack Benny in filming an episode of the Benny TV program in the Truman Library. Telecast on 18 October.

1960 —Published *Mr. Citizen*, a book about his postpresidential experiences.

—20 August: Explained, in a press conference, his decision to support the candidacy of Senator John F. Kennedy who had won the nomination for the presidency at the Democratic party's national convention. Attending the conference also were Senators Henry Jackson and Stuart Symington as well as the nominee himself. Prior to the convention, Truman had publicly endorsed the candidacy of Symington.

—8 October–4 November: Conducted a vigorous campaign speaking tour across the country on behalf of candidate Kennedy.

1961 —20 January: With wife and daughter, was a guest in the White House on inauguration day, their first visit there in eight years.

—9 March: Participated in twentieth anniversary reunion of his wartime Senate investigating committee.

1961 —June: Signed contract with Talent Associates–Paramount, Ltd. for a TV series on the Truman presidency. Rights were purchased later by Screen Gems, Inc., and the first of twenty-six one-half-hour episodes was telecast in November 1964. The series title: *Decision: The Conflicts of Harry S. Truman.*

—10 November: Hosted former President Eisenhower on the latter's first visit to the Truman Library.

—18 November: Joined President Kennedy, former President Eisenhower, and Vice-President Lyndon B. Johnson in attending funeral services in Bonham, Texas for former House Speaker Sam Rayburn.

1962 —10 August: Participated in the dedication of the Herbert Hoover Library in West Branch, Iowa.

1963 —29 May: Large statue of Truman was unveiled in Athens, Greece, commemorating Truman as one of Greece's "greatest benefactors."

—June: An endowed Harry S. Truman Chair in American History was established at Westminster College, Fulton, Missouri.

—26 November: Attended funeral of President Kennedy and met afterward with Eisenhower, effecting, to the press, a final "reconciliation" between these two former political adversaries.

1964 —11–13 March: Attended the funeral of King Paul I in Athens, Greece, as President Johnson's personal representative.

1965 —March: Received award as "The Outstanding Television Personality of the Year" from the American Cinema Editors Association.

—8 May: Became the first former president to address the U.S. Senate while it was in formal session. The Senate honored him on his eightieth birthday.

—25 June: Received from the South Korean ambassador to the United States the "Order of Merit for the National Foundation Joongjang," the republic's highest honor.

—8 July: Brother Vivian died.

—30 July: Participated in ceremony at the Truman Library during which President Johnson signed the Medicare bill, an event that Truman described as a "profound personal experience for me." Mr. and Mrs. Truman received Medicare registration cards numbers one and two in January 1966.

1966 —20 January: Took part in a ceremony at the Truman Library announcing the founding of the Harry S. Truman Center for the Advancement of Peace, to be constructed in Jerusalem.

—4 July: Made his last appearance as a speaker at the eighth annual 4 July celebration on the Truman Library grounds.

—July: As a result of illness, Truman discontinued trips to his office at the Truman Library.

1968 —12 October: Looked on as President Johnson signed a bill, in the Truman home, designating 24 October 1968 as U.N. Day. The president also issued a proclamation noting Truman's part in creating the United Nations organization in 1945.

1969 —21 March: Was visited by President and Mrs. Nixon, after which President Nixon presented to the Truman Library a Steinway piano that had been in the White House during Truman's presidency.

1971 —29 December: With wife Bess, daughter Margaret, and son-in-law E. Clifton Daniel, toured the Truman Library for the last time and viewed the film "For All the People"—a new motion picture designed for the orientation of museum visitors.

1972 —26 December: Died at the age of eighty-eight. His body was interred in the courtyard of the Truman Library on 28 December.

1978 —3 November: The late Mr. Truman's only sister, Mary Jane, died.

1982 —18 October: Mrs. Bess Truman died at the age of ninety-seven. Funeral services were held in the Trinity Episcopal Church in Independence on 21 October, after which her body was interred in the courtyard of the Truman Library.

The Truman Presidential Library: Harry S. Truman's Contribution To the Study of His Presidency

On 18 June 1952 President Harry S. Truman took a break from his busy schedule to deliver a few remarks in the White House Rose Garden to a small group of visiting archivists from all parts of the United States and Canada. In the course of his brief talk, Truman said that he was interested in what the archivists were doing "because the papers of some of our Presidents of the United States, and of the Cabinet officers and of some of our departments, have been scattered from one end of the country to the other." He went on to say that he wanted his own official papers to be properly cared for and kept together in one place "where scholars and archivists can get to them without difficulty." This may have been the first public occasion on which Truman voiced concern over the disposition of his presidential files once he had left office. To his associates, however, it was already clear that he was considering placing his papers in a government institution to be modeled after the Roosevelt Library at Hyde Park, New York, at that time the only federally administered presidential library in the country.

Five short years after Truman's little talk to the archivists, the Harry S. Truman Library became a reality. It was the second presidential library to be administered by the Federal National Archives and Records Service and the first to be created under the recently passed Presidential Libraries Act (1955). Its mission: to preserve the papers, books, and other historical materials relating to former President Truman and to make them available to the people in a place suitable for exhibit and research. Located in Independence, Missouri, Truman's hometown, the new library building included areas devoted to research activities and a museum wing for the public display of the many gifts which Truman received while in the White House.

The library, which had been built with private funds, was formally dedicated and handed over to the federal government for operation on 6 July 1957. Chief Justice Earl Warren, who delivered the principal address, praised Truman for arranging "for the preservation of his papers in such manner that his administration will be one of the 'clearest ages' of history" and predicted that "there will be a sustained use of the Truman papers by future generations of writers, biographers, historians, political scientists and others." Within a few years, those expectations had been fully realized, and by 1984, the centennial of Truman's birth, the library's research facilities had been visited by scholars from almost every state in the Union and from more than forty foreign countries.

The Truman Library is now one of a series of archival institutions—one for each of our recent chief executives beginning with Herbert Hoover—in which the retiring presidents have deposited their White House files along with associated papers and artifacts. Administered by the National Archives and Records Service, each library, while operating along parallel lines, has developed, under the remote and benign supervision of the archivist of the United States, a unique character of its own, reflecting the disparate characters of the presidents they represent. During its early years, the Truman Library was particularly fortunate in that Truman not only had an office in the library building, but for almost the first ten years of its existence, used it on an almost daily basis. During this period, while never interfering or dictating, he was always helpful and cooperative in promoting the development of the library as a research institution and in encouraging the adoption of improvements in its facilities.

In the end Truman's greatest contribution, of course, was his gift of his presidential papers. These papers, which are, as he once noted, ". . . among the most valuable source material of our history," constitute the core of the library's research holdings and are the principal reason for its existence. While they consist principally of Truman's White House files, they also include his senatorial and postpresidential files, as well as smaller quantities of materials relating to his military career, his early business and political careers, and files of his personal correspondence.

Since its opening, and with Truman's encouragement, the library has engaged in an intensive acquisitions program and presently, in addition to the Truman papers, has in its custody more than 400 other manuscript collections representing the papers of individuals who were associated with Truman at some point during his career. The library also has a small quantity of Truman-related federal records in its custody, the largest segment of which consists of the files of various temporary presidential commissions and committees appointed between 1945 and 1952. At present the library has more than 12,600,000 pages of manuscripts, approximately 5,000,000 pages of which consist of Truman's White House files.

Which of the library's many collections a researcher would find most useful would naturally depend on his or her area of concentration. However, there is general agreement among persons who have worked at the library that there are a few collections which almost any Truman scholar would wish to examine. Among the many groups of materials that comprise the Truman papers, by far the richest in the information they contain are probably the so-called President's Secretary's Files (PSF) which were maintained, as the title suggests, by the president's personal secretary in his immediate White House office suite. Included in this series are correspondence with government officials documenting the history of the government during this momentous period, with the emphasis on policy decisions; letters from personal friends of the president; the president's political and speech files; and reports and other documents of a highly sensitive nature prepared by the National Security Council and other security agencies. For this reason the PSF is certainly one of the two or three most significant groups of materials in the library for researchers working in the field of foreign relations.

Other collections which should be of particular interest to diplomatic historians are the papers of Dean Acheson, secretary of state, 1949–52, especially the "Memoranda of Conversations" file in that collection; the papers of Clark Clifford, special counsel to the president, 1946–50, particularly for those interested in the Palestine question; the papers of George Elsey, administrative assistant to the president, who maintained a detailed chronology of the president's activities during the first week of the Korean War; and the papers of Joseph M. Jones, special assistant to the assistant secretary of state for public affairs, who gave the Truman Library the research files he used in the preparation of his book *The Fifteen Weeks* describing the genesis of the Truman Doctrine and the Marshall Plan.

In the domestic area, scholars working in the area of conservation, reclamation, and public power will find the papers of Oscar L. Chapman, secretary of the interior, 1949–53; Dale E. Doty, assistant secretary of the interior, 1950–52; and Joel D. Wolfsohn, who held the same position, 1952–53, to be particularly useful. Economic historians should be interested in the papers of John W. Snyder, secretary of the treasury, 1945–53; the papers of members of Truman's Council of Economic Advisers, including Roy Blough, John D. Clark, and Edwin G. Nourse; and the papers of Walter S. Salant, who served on the council's staff. Students of the budget process will find the papers of Bureau of the Budget directors Frederick J. Lawton, Frank Pace, Harold Smith, and James Webb to be of value.

For those interested in how the White House functioned during the Truman years, the Truman Library has the papers of nearly all of the members of Truman's White House staff. The library also has in its custody the records of seventeen of Truman's presidential commissions and committees. Note should also be made of the Eben Ayers diary, which constitutes a portion of the papers of Eben Ayers. Ayers, who served in the White House as assistant press secretary during much of the Truman administration and in that capacity attended most of Truman's staff meetings, kept a diary in which he recorded the events of the White House day. This unique document is invaluable to historians interested in running down minutiae of the White House story during most of the Truman period. And finally, biographers will particularly be interested in a recently acquired series within the Truman papers collectively entitled: Papers of Harry S. Truman Pertaining to Family, Business and Personal Affairs. This series includes holograph copies of letters from Truman to Mrs. Truman dated from 1910, when their courtship began, until 1959, and from Truman to his daughter Margaret from 1927 until 1955. The series also includes correspondence and other materials relating to Truman's career before he entered the Senate, including his early business and political ventures, and his military service. This series, especially the correspondence files, is particularly valuable for the light it sheds on Truman's inner feelings and facets of his personality which do not always come to the surface in official correspondence files.

These collections are, of course, only a sampling of the library's overall manuscript holdings. They have been listed, and briefly described, only to suggest the richness of the library's research holdings. Anyone wishing information concerning materials in the library relating to a particular subject should write directly to the Harry S. Truman Library, Independence, Missouri 64050.

In addition to its manuscript collections, the Truman Library has an audiovisual collection consisting of approximately 74,000 still pictures, 2,630 disc and tape recordings, and 450 motion pictures. The library also has transcripts of more than 400 oral history interviews conducted by the library staff with Truman's friends and associates. In its oral history program the library has emphasized Truman's presenatorial career, the work of the White House staff during the Truman administration, and U.S. foreign policy during the years 1945 through 1952. The library's collection of printed materials includes more than 44,000 books; 68,000 serials; and nearly 3,000 microfilm copies of printed materials. In adding to its book collection, the library attempts to purchase any new books on the history of the Truman administration or relating to the career of Harry S. Truman so that researchers working at the library can conveniently refer to the works already produced by other Truman scholars.

The Harry S. Truman Library Institute, a nonprofit corporation, was organized in 1957 to foster and assist in the library's growth and development as a national center for study and research. The purposes of the institute are to promote the acquisition of research materials, issue a newsletter, sponsor scholarly conferences, foster publications based on research at the library, and further cooperation of the library with historical and educational institutions. The institute awards several grants each year to persons who are working on the period of the Truman administration or the career of Harry S. Truman to enable them to make use of the resources of the Truman Library. The institute also sponsors a book award which is given every two years for the best book on Harry S. Truman or his presidency published during that period.

Harry Truman, probably the most history-minded of our presidents, believed that the story of his administration would be presented in a fair and objective fashion only if the written record were preserved. "The truth is all I want for history," he wrote in a memo to a member of his staff midway through his second term. "If I appear in a bad light when we have the truth that's just too bad. We must take it." By donating his papers and the Truman Library to the nation, Truman has made it possible for scholars to pass judgment on his administration based on fact not emotion. It is still too early to close the books and make a final judgment on Truman and his administration. However, Truman has done his part by making the evidence fully available. The verdict is now up to history.

Introduction to the Bibliography

That the Truman era (1945–53) established the basic tenor of American foreign affairs for the last half of the twentieth century has been widely acknowledged. That the Truman presidency was also engaged, sometimes rather extensively, with domestic issues which would shape the American scene for several future decades is less well recognized. All in all, those eight event-filled years had an extraordinary influence on the lives of Americans for the next half century.

This bibliographical survey of the Truman years seeks to collect those writings which narrate and analyze these foreign and domestic events. It is hoped that it will also indicate those topics which require additional research and analysis.

Basic Design of Bibliography

To assist researchers in quickly locating desired materials, the bibliography has been arranged by subject themes, beginning with the division of chapters into domestic, foreign, and military topics. Each chapter is, in turn, subdivided by subject themes. The expanded table of contents provides a useful "subject" guide to these themes and should be closely reviewed by researchers. Two indexes, subject and author, have also been included. The subject index is particularly useful for locating those items which contain materials related to several different subject themes.

The bibliography was developed to provide a comprehensive survey of those writings which reflect on the Truman era. That is, it seeks to list and to annotate many, but not all, of the writings which relate to the important events, significant policy decisions, and influential individuals during the years 1945 to 1953. Articles, books, and dissertations make up the vast majority of the items included here; however, those dissertations which have subsequently been published as monographs have been deleted.

No attempt was made to include the multitude of public documents generated by Truman's executive office or related branches of government. Some key documents are cited below; however, the researchers who desire to locate more routine materials should inquire of their library's public documents specialist. Similarly, most foreign language items were excluded as were most ephemeral materials.

The annotations are largely descriptive. They emphasize the basic themes which provide the main focus of each item. They also occasionally include references to individuals who occupied a major office or who played a key role in some significant episode. In addition to a brief narrative, the annotations of books include some indication of whether they contain such scholarly apparatus as a bibliography, index, or notes.

Supplementary Research Tools

All finding aids become dated before they can be published. This bibliography is no exception; however, there are a number of reference works which can be used to supplement and update it. There are several periodical indexes that collect (and often annotate) journal articles dealing with the Truman years. Among these basic indexes are *America: History and Life* (Part A), *Historical Abstracts*, and the American Historical Association's *Recently Published Articles*. Each of these indexes has advantages and disadvantages.

America: History and Life (Part A) is arranged by chronological and subject classifications which include diplomatic, military, and domestic themes. It also furnishes annotated entries which provide comprehensive coverage of journals publishing articles related to American and Canadian history; however, frequently the articles are not listed until eighteen months after publication. *Historical Abstracts* provides wide coverage of foreign-language journals, but distance and the preparation of English-language annotations obviously mean some delay before an article can be listed. Both *America: History and Life* and *Historical Abstracts* have author and subject indexes; the subject indexes are perhaps the most thorough of any similar reference tool. However, those researchers with the time will find that the chronological and subject classifications of these indexes are particularly convenient for browsing. *Recently Published Articles* provides the most current listing of published journal articles, but it does not include annotations. Unfortunately, the usefulness of *Recently Published Articles* is greatly reduced by the lack of subject index or cross-reference system.

There are several other periodical indexes which survey journals for such fields as law, sociology, and political science. Such indexes frequently list articles dealing with the Truman era. While not annotated, *ABC POL SCI* lists the current tables of contents of political science journals and indexes them by author and subject.

Locating newly published books presents a much more difficult problem. No readily available serial publication lists recently printed scholarly books, but *America: History and Life* (Parts B and C) can be useful. Part B (*Index to Book Reviews*) has a title index, which makes it much easier to locate a particular volume. Part C (*American History Bibliography*) is the most useful because it arranges books, dissertations, and articles by chronological stages and subject themes. *Reviews in American History* is a relatively new quarterly journal which provides useful review essays; however, it does not provide an adequate current listing of recently published books on American history.

Information about current dissertations is more readily available. The best known and most frequently consulted listing is the *Dissertation Abstracts International*, which indexes, with lengthy annotations, doctoral dissertations from American, Canadian, and Mexican universities.

Harry S. Truman

Materials which deal with Harry S. Truman's character, family life, early years, and prepresidential and postpresidential political careers provide the major focus of this chapter. However, since separating Truman from his presidency is difficult, and usually arbitrary, the reader should also examine the materials listed in Chapter 2, which emphasize his presidential actions and policies.

Those researchers seeking to understand Truman's character and personality might wish to begin with Jonathan Daniels, *The Man of Independence* (# 1), an authorized biography which has withstood the scrutiny of later scholarship. Various aspects of Truman's personality, including his humor and temperament, are evident in compilations of Truman's writings edited by Robert H. Ferrell: *The Autobiography of Harry S. Truman* (#4), *Off-the-Record: The Private Papers of Harry S. Truman* (#57), and *Dear Bess: The Letters from Harry to Bess Truman, 1910–1959* (#37). See also Monte M. Poen, ed., *Strictly Personal and Confidential: The Letters Harry Truman Never Mailed* (#58), and William Hillman, ed., *Mr. President* (#9).

Additional insight into Truman's role as a family man may be found in a number of books by his daughter, Margaret Truman, *Harry S. Truman* (#18), *Letters From Father: The Truman Family's Personal Correspondence* (#40), and *Souvenir: Margaret Truman's Own Story* (#41).

In his early years, Truman found himself variously employed. One of his endeavors is examined by Richard S. Kirkendall, "Harry S. Truman: A Missouri Farmer in the Golden Age" (#22). Truman's World War I experiences and subsequent National Guard activities are surveyed in Francis B. Kish, "Citizen-Soldier: Harry S. Truman, 1884–1972" (#25), and Benedict K. Zobrist, ed., *Captain Harry* (Kansas City, MO, The Harry S.

Truman Good Neighbor Award Foundation, 1982).

Truman's prepresidential political careers included those of county judge (in Missouri, an administrative position comparable to county commissioner), U.S. senator, and vice-president. Kansas City politics and Truman's involvement in them are examined in Lyle W. Dorsett, *The Pendergast Machine* (#66). As Senator, Truman's first term was inconspicuous; however, in his second term he gained national prominence by chairing a congressional committee charged with investigating national defense expenditures. Donald H. Riddle, *The Truman Committee: A Study in Congressional Responsibility* (#86) reviews the World War II committee's actions and gives Truman high marks. The first nineteen chapters of Harold F. Gosnell, *Truman's Crises: A Political Biography of Harry S. Truman* (#6) are devoted to Truman's prepresidential career.

The 1944 Democratic nomination for vice-president was not without controversy as Franklin D. Roosevelt encouraged James F. Byrnes to seek the nomination. FDR's political power play caused subsequent personal difficulties between Truman and Byrnes. See John W. Partin, "Roosevelt, Byrnes, and the 1944 Vice-Presidential Nomination" (#98), and Robert Messer, *The End of an Alliance: James F. Byrnes, Roosevelt, Truman and the Origins of the Cold War* (#319).

Although Truman was an active former president, his postpresidential years have not been fully examined. However, Truman's *Mr. Citizen* (#17) and Merle Miller, *Plain Speaking: An Oral Biography of Harry S. Truman* (#12) give some insight into Truman's years following the presidency. James Giglio, "Harry S. Truman and the Multifarious Ex-Presidency" (#101) suggests, however, that Truman was too intensely partisan to work with Republican office-holders during those years.

Harry S. Truman in 1899.

Autobiographical and Biographical Materials

Materials relating to Truman as president may be found in Chapter 2, *Truman Presidency*.

0001　Daniels, Jonathan. *The Man of Independence.* Philadelphia: Lippincott, 1950.

In this biography of Truman, Daniels is fascinated by the "everyday" man concept of Truman. Bibliography, index.

0002　Dayton, Eldorous L. *Give 'em Hell Harry: An Informal Biography of the Terrible-Tempered Mr. T.* New York: Devin-Adair, 1956.

Dayton offers a popular biography of Truman. Index.

0003　Eaton, Richard O., and Hart, La Valle. *Meet Harry S. Truman.* Washington, DC: Dumbarton House, 1945.

Truman's biography is presented in a newsprint-style publication. Cover pictures.

0004　Ferrell, Robert H., ed. *The Autobiography of Harry S. Truman.* Boulder, CO: Colorado Associated University Press, 1980.

Ferrell has pieced together handwritten accounts by Truman to fashion this autobiography. Notes, sources, illustrations, index.

0005　Gallu, Samuel. *Give 'Em Hell, Harry: A Play in Two Acts.* New York: Viking, 1975.

"Give 'Em Hell, Harry," was a one-man tour de force for James Whitmore, who played the role of Harry Truman reminiscing about his political career. Illustrations.

0006　Gosnell, Harold F. *Truman's Crises: A Political Biography of Harry S. Truman.* Westport, CT: Greenwood, 1980.

Truman's political career is subjected to analysis; unfortunately it offers little that is new. Notes, biography, index.

0007　Hayman, LeRoy. *Harry S. Truman: A Biography.* New York: Crowell, 1969.

A full-length biography, it concentrates largely on Truman's political activities. Illustrations, bibliography, index.

0008　Hedley, John H. *Harry S. Truman: The "Little" Man from Missouri.* Woodbury, NY: Barron's, 1979.

This is basically a political biography which focuses on Truman's role in international affairs. Chapter 8, "The Verdict of History," is a useful historiographical essay. Appendix, notes, index.

0009　Hillman, William, ed. *Mr. President.* New York: Farrar, Straus and Young, 1952.

This lavishly illustrated volume contains excerpts of Truman's private letters and papers, excerpts from personal diaries, and interviews. Biographical data and pictures of the Truman family are included.

0010　Kornitzer, Bela. *American Fathers and Sons.* New York: Hermitage House, 1952.

This volume has an interesting chapter on Truman, one which he apparently disliked intensely.

0011　Lerner, Max. "Harry S. Truman: A Miniature Portrait." In his *Actions and Passions.* New York: Simon & Schuster, 1949, pp. 219–24.

Lerner sees Truman as the middle-class man whose virtues of honesty, hard work, loyalty, and a sense of detachment from the fighting issues simply aren't sufficient for meeting the critical issues of the day. Index.

0012　Miller, Merle. *Plain Speaking: An Oral Biography of Harry S. Truman.* New York: Berkeley, 1974.

Although well-received by the public, this volume is generally unreliable and must be used with caution.

0013　Parker, Daniel F. "The Political and Social Views of Harry S. Truman." Ph.D. dissertation, University of Pennsylvania, 1951.

Parker believes that "Truman's views on social and political questions greatly broadened as he attained successively higher public positions." He finds Truman's values, however, firmly rooted in a strongly held moral code. Bibliography, notes.

0014　Schauffler, Edward R. *Harry S. Truman: Son of the Soil.* Kansas City, MO: Schauffler, 1947.

This short biography depicts Truman as the common man and covers his life until he assumed the presidency. Illustrations.

0015　Steinberg, Alfred. *The Man From Missouri: The Life and Times of Harry S. Truman.* New York: Putnam's, 1962.

Steinberg, a journalist, covered Truman and his era for various publications. This biography is based upon personal interviews with key individuals of the Truman period; however, questions have been raised about its accuracy. Index.

0016　Truman, Harry S. *Memoirs.* 2 vols. Garden City, NY: Doubleday, 1955–56.

These memoirs emphasize the Truman presidency. Volume 1, *Year of Decisions*, focuses on the United Nations, Potsdam, Hiroshima, and the end of World War II. Volume 2, *Years of Trial and Hope*, recounts such episodes as the Marshall Plan, the Berlin airlift, NATO, and the Korean War. Index.

0017 Truman, Harry S. *Mr. Citizen*. New York: Geis Associates, 1960.

This forthright narrative provides an interesting self-portrait of Truman's life, including the first seven years of retirement.

0018 Truman, Margaret. *Harry S. Truman*. New York: William Morrow, 1973.

The daughter of the president offers her view of her father as a public figure. Her reminiscences are supplemented with excerpts from Truman's letters. Illustrations, index.

0019 Wills, Garry. "I'm Not Wild About Harry." *Esquire* 85 (1976): 90–95.

Recent nostalgia for Truman, the man, draws criticism from Wills. Similar reservations may be found in Barton J. Bernstein's "Wild About Harry—and Not so Wild," *Nation* 217 (16 April 1973): 501–4.

0020 Wolfson, Victor. *The Man Who Cared: A Life of Harry S. Truman*. New York: Farrar, Straus, 1966.

This is a popular account which emphasizes Truman's personality and family, while outlining his political career. Bibliography.

TRUMAN'S FARMING CAREER

0021 Hulston, John K. *An Ozarks Lawyer's Story*. Republic, MO: Western Printing Company, 1976.

This book has an appendix about litigation involving Truman as a farmer, *Gallagher* v. *Chilton et al.* (192 SW 409) and *Truman* v. *Chilton et al.* (197 SW 346). These cases went to the Missouri Supreme Court. Another appendix reflects on Truman's gubernatorial ambitions in 1931.

0022 Kirkendall, Richard S. "Harry S. Truman: A Missouri Farmer in the Golden Age." *Agricultural History* 48 (1974): 467–83.

This account provides a look at Truman's farm years, 1906–16. Additional information may be found in Samuel R. Guard, "From Plowboy to President," *Breeder's Gazette*, June 1945, pp. 5–6, and Bill Renshaw, "President Truman: His Missouri Neighbors Tell of His Farm Years," *The Prairie Farmer*, 12 May 1945, pp. 1ff.

TRUMAN'S MILITARY CAREER (WW I)

0023 Agnews, James B. "Got to Hell . . . but I'll Try." *Field Artillery Journal* 42 (1974): 33–41.

This article employs War Department records to explore the performance of Truman's unit under fire during the Meuse-Argonne drive. The author is not sympathetic to the complaints Truman and National Guard officers raised when their division was severely criticized for poor battle showings. Notes.

0024 Kahana, Yoram. "Captain Harry: The Cussing Doughboy of Battery D." *Mankind* 5 (1977): 36–41.

This popular account focuses on Truman's World War I experiences as a battery commander, and his nostalgia about these military experiences.

0025 Kish, Maj. Francis B. "Citizen-Soldier: Harry S. Truman, 1884–1972." *Military Review* 53 (1973): 30–44.

Truman's military experiences during World War I are reviewed as well as his subsequent relationship with, and attitudes toward, the army. Notes.

0026 Lee, Jay M. *The Artilleryman*. Kansas City, MO: Spencer, 1920.

The authorized and accurate account of Truman's World War I regiment is difficult reading but filled with useful data.

TRUMAN'S WIT AND HUMOR

0027 Aurthur, Robert Alan. "The Wit and Sass of Harry S. Truman." *Esquire* 76 (1971): 62–67ff.

0028 Aurthur, Robert Alan. "Harry Truman Chuckles Dryly." *Esquire* 76 (1971): 136–39ff.

These two essays relate the author's interviews with Truman and, especially, Truman's colorful replies.

0029 Caldwell, George S., comp. *The Wit and Wisdom of Harry S. Truman*. New York: Stein & Day, 1966.

This slim volume offers a collection of Truman anecdotes and photographs.

0030 Goldman, Alex J., ed. *The Truman Wit*. New York: Citadel, 1966.

Collected in this volume are examples of Truman's incisive wit and humor in Congress, as vice-president, and as president. Illustrations.

0031 Goodman, Mark, ed. *Give 'Em Hell, Harry!* New York: Award Books, 1974.

"Give 'em hell, Harry" was the public's reaction to Truman's incisive wit. This volume offers a selection of Truman's repartee.

0032   Settel, T. S., comp. *The Quotable Harry S. Truman*. Anderson, SC: Droke House, 1967.

This compilation of quotations attributed to Truman (1945–64) is arranged by subject; however, citations to many quotations are inadequate for scholary use.

TRUMAN'S SPEECHMAKING

For texts of Truman's speeches, see *Truman's Speeches and Papers*.

0033   Pratt, James W. "A Study of Presidential Crisis Speaking as a Potential Rhetorical Type." Ph.D. dissertation, University of Minnesota, 1971.

Nineteen speeches by Presidents Truman, Eisenhower, Kennedy, and Johnson are defined as "crisis" ones. This study seeks to determine if these speeches share rhetorical characteristics. DAI 32:3466-A.

0034   Rogge, Edward A. "The Speechmaking of Harry S. Truman." Ph.D. dissertation, University of Missouri, 1958.

Although Truman delivered hundreds of addresses as president, none of his presidential speeches aroused extensive acclaim as a great address. As a speaker Truman will probably best be remembered for his hard-hitting campaigning. DAI 19:2189.

0035   Underhill, Robert. *The Truman Persuasions*. Ames, IA: Iowa State University Press, 1981.

Truman was not an eloquent speaker, yet he was extremely successful in his public persuasions. Underhill examines this paradox by looking not only at Truman's addresses but also at the responses they engendered. Notes, index.

TRUMAN FAMILY

0036   Faber, Doris. "Martha Young Truman: Lightfoot Baptist." In her *The Mothers of American Presidents*. New York: New American Library, 1968, pp. 48–62.

This essay focuses on the life of Harry Truman's mother and their relationship until her death on 26 July 1947 at the age of ninety-four. Illustration, notes, index.

0037   Ferrell, Robert H., ed. *Dear Bess: The Letters from Harry to Bess Truman, 1910–1959*. New York: Norton, 1983.

These letters are useful because they expand our insights into Harry Truman's character—the kind of man he was and the kind of man he hoped to be. The bulk of the letters covers the early years from 1910 to 1940. Illustrations, index.

0038   Parks, Lillian Rogers. *My Thirty Years Backstairs at the White House*. New York: Fleet, 1961.

The activities of the Truman family (pp. 275–311) are recalled by the author, who listed Bess Truman as one of her favorite First Ladies.

0039   Robbins, Jhan. *Bess and Harry: An American Love Story*. New York: Putnam's, 1980.

A reporter writes affectionately of Bess and Harry Truman. Illustrations.

0040   Truman, Margaret. *Letters From Father: The Truman Family's Personal Correspondence*. New York: Arbor House, 1981.

Truman started writing to his daughter when she was seventeen years old. Margaret Truman shares her correspondence with her father and with her mother, grandmother, and Mrs. George Wallace in this volume. Illustrations.

0041   Truman, Margaret. *Souvenir: Margaret Truman's Own Story*. New York: McGraw-Hill, 1956.

In this volume the daughter of the president offers her memoirs of her Washington years. Illustrations.

0042   West, J. B. *Upstairs at the White House: My Life with the First Ladies*. New York: Coward, McCann & Geoghegan, 1973.

The Trumans are a featured subject of personal remembrances by the chief usher of the White House (pp. 51–115).

PICTORIAL BIOGRAPHIES

0043   Crane, John d'Murinelly Cirne. *The Pictorial Biography of Harry S. Truman, Thirty-Second President of the United States*. Washington: American Historical Series, 1948.

This small pamphlet offers a brief photo essay of Truman's life to 1948.

0044   Gies, Joseph. *Harry S. Truman: A Pictorial Biography*. Garden City, NY: Doubleday, 1968.

Many photographs illustrate this biography of Truman, which covers his boyhood through his presidency. It focuses more on foreign policy issues than domestic ones. Illustrations, index.

0045   Thomson, David S. *A Pictorial Biography: HST*. New York: Grosset & Dunlap. 1973.

This volume offers a pictorial view of Truman from his early years in Missouri to his retirement.

0046 *The Truman Years: The Words and Times of Harry S. Truman.* Waukesha, WI: *Country Beautiful*, 1976.

This volume, designed by the editors of *Country Beautiful* magazine, includes many photographs and a brief chronology.

CHILDREN'S BIOGRAPHIES OF TRUMAN

0047 Collins, David R. *Harry S. Truman: People's President.* Champaign, IL: Garrard, 1975.

This volume provides brief, but well-written interpretation of Harry S. Truman for young readers.

0048 Faber, Doris. *Harry Truman.* New York: Abelard-Schuman, 1972.

In this biography, Faber describes Truman's childhood, his times in the army, the years he spent in the Senate, and his presidency. Illustrations, index.

0049 Hudson, Wilma J. *Harry S. Truman: Missouri Farm Boy.* Indianapolis: Bobbs-Merrill, 1973.

This is an illustrated book, based upon research.

0050 Martin, Ralph G. *President From Missouri: Harry S. Truman.* New York: Julian Messner, 1964.

Written especially for the young reader, this biography of Truman offers a sympathetic account of his career. Index.

0051 McCandless, Perry, and Foley, William E. *Missouri Then and Now.* Austin, TX: Steck-Vaughn, 1976.

This elementary school textbook on Missouri's history offers a few pages on Missourian Harry Truman. Illustrations, index.

0052 Richards, Kenneth G. *People of Destiny: Harry S. Truman.* Chicago: Children's Press, 1968.

A biography of President Truman prepared for a youthful audience. Illustrations, bibliography, index.

0053 Steinberg, Alfred. *Harry S. Truman.* New York: Putnam's, 1963.

An early popular biography of Harry S. Truman geared to the young adult reader. This slim volume is based primarily on secondary sources.

TRUMAN'S SPEECHES AND PAPERS

0054 Bernstein, Barton J., and Matusow, Allen J., eds. *The Truman Administration: A Documentary History.* New York: Harper & Row, 1966.

Using memos, reports, the *Congressional Record*, and other primary sources, the editors offer firsthand reactions to some of the crucial decisions of the Truman era: the A-bomb decision, inflation, the Fair Deal, the Cold War, China policy, loyalty, and the Korean War. Illustrations, notes, bibliography, index.

0055 Clemens, Cyril, ed. *Truman Speaks.* New York: M. P. Didier, 1946.

Some of Truman's speeches from his first year in the presidency are collected in this volume. These mainly deal with the close of the war, the United Nations, and some postwar domestic issues. Index.

0056 Druks, Herbert, ed. *From Truman through Johnson: A Documentary History.* vol. 1. New York: Robert Speller, 1971.

Through such sources as the *Public Papers of the Presidents*, newspapers, U.S. foreign relations papers, memoirs, and private papers, the Truman presidency is represented. Topics such as the Potsdam Conference, the atomic bomb, Israel, labor, civil rights, the Truman Doctrine, the Marshall Plan, China, and the Korean War are included. Illustrations, index.

0057 Ferrell, Robert H., ed. *Off-the-Record: The Private Papers of Harry S. Truman.* New York: Harper & Row, 1980.

These papers consist of Truman's diary entries, memoranda, and letters covering the period 1947 through 1971. Illustrations, notes, index.

0058 Poen, Monte M., ed. *Strictly Personal and Confidential: The Letters Harry Truman Never Mailed.* Boston: Little, Brown, 1982.

These unmailed letters should assist one in recapturing Truman's mood, or personal feelings, at crucial times. They are important for both a study of policy and personality. Notes, index.

0059 Schnapper, M. B., ed. *The Truman Program: Addresses and Messages.* Washington, DC: Public Affairs Press, 1948.

Included in this volume are those presidential speeches and congressional addresses which spell out Truman's policies and proposals on the major issues, such as international affairs, atomic energy, prices and inflation, business, taxes, agriculture, labor, civil rights, Social Security, and communism.

0060 Sheldon, Ted., ed. *Harry S. Truman: The Man From Missouri.* Kansas City, MO: Hallmark, 1970.

Excerpts from Truman's speeches on such issues as peace, democracy, freedom, human rights, the American way, as well as some Truman witticisms are collected in this volume along with illustrations.

0061 Truman, Harry S. *Freedom and Equality: Addresses.* Edited by David S. Horton. Columbia: University of Missouri Press, 1953.

Three addresses deal with black rights; five are concerned with meeting the threat of internal communism and the Bill of Rights; while the final document focuses on the Immigration and Nationality Act of 1952.

0062 Truman, Harry S. *Public Papers of the Presidents: Harry S. Truman, 1945–1953.* 8 vols. Washington, DC: G.P.O., 1961–66.

These volumes contain most of Truman's public messages, presidential orders, speeches, and statements as president, as well as the full text of press conferences. Appendix, index.

Truman's Political Life: Prepresidential

Chapter 2 contains materials relating to and evaluating Truman's presidency.

THE EARLY YEARS

0063 Blackmore, Charles P. "Joseph B. Shannon, Political Boss and Twentieth Century 'Jeffersonian'." Ph.D. dissertation, Columbia University, 1953.

Shannon was a Democratic factional leader in Kansas City and Jackson County, Missouri for fifty years. He worked with Tom Pendergast on a 50–50 division of patronage spoils. This study is useful for its description of Kansas City's political environment during the 1920s and 1930s. DAI 14:166.

0064 Bradshaw, William L. "The Missouri County Court: A Study of the Organizations and Functions of the County Board of Supervisors in Missouri." *The University of Missouri Studies* 6 (1931): 1–211.

This study is an examination of the Missouri county courts, the administrative bodies charged with county administrative functions in most Missouri counties. At the outset of his political career Harry S. Truman was eastern judge (1923–25) and presiding judge (1927–34) of the Jackson County (Missouri) court.

0065 Clemens, Cyril. *The Man From Missouri: A Biography of Harry S. Truman.* Webster Groves, MO: International Mark Twain Society, 1945.

In this early biography of Truman, Clemens looks at the man shaped by a section of the country "where strong convictions and the willingness to stand by them were common qualities." Bibliography, index.

0066 Dorsett, Lyle W. *The Pendergast Machine.* New York: Oxford University Press, 1968.

Tom Pendergast controlled Democratic party politics in Kansas City where Truman won the senatorial nomination in 1934. Although Pendergast's political machine by that time was monumentally corrupt, Truman emerged unscathed. Notes, bibliography, index.

0067 Grothaus, Larry. "Kansas City Blacks, Harry Truman and the Pendergast Machine." *Missouri Historical Review* 69 ₍1974): 65–82.

During 1922 through 1934, both Truman and black leaders learned how to use the Pendergast machine to advance their own ends. While Truman and the machine were not always correct in dealing with blacks, they had better records than the city's reform groups. Illustrations, notes.

0068 Heed, Thomas J. "Prelude to Whistlestop: Harry S. Truman the Apprentice Campaigner." Ed.D. dissertation, Columbia University, 1975.

This study covers Truman's years of political apprenticeship—his primary and general election campaigns of 1922 and 1924. DAI 36:1722–A.

0069 Mason, Frank [pseud.]. *Truman and the Pendergasts.* Evanston, IL: Regency, 1964.

This account by a Kansas City reporter seeks to provide a fair assessment of the relationship between Truman, Tom Pendergast, and the Pendergast political machine.

0070 McNaughton, Frank, and Hehmeyer, Walter. *This Man Truman.* New York, McGraw-Hill, 1945.

This biography of Harry S. Truman dwells largely on his early years, stopping when he becomes president. Illustrations.

0071 Milligan, Maurice M. *Missouri Waltz: The Inside Story of the Pendergast Machine by the Man Who Smashed It.* New York: Scribner's, 1948.

The federal attorney who prosecuted Tom Pendergast reviews his case and, therein, comments on Truman's relationship with the Kansas City political machine.

0072 Mitchell, Franklin D. "Who is Judge Truman? The Truman for Governor Movement of 1931." *Midcontinent American Studies Journal* 7 (1966): 3–15.

This essay covers a short, abortive campaign Truman started to test the waters for a run in the Democratic primary. When Pendergast finally declared he owed the nod to another former candidate, Truman folded up the campaign. Notes.

0073 Powell, Eugene J. *Tom's Boy Harry*. Jefferson City, MO: Hawthorn, 1948.

Truman's connection with the Pendergast machine is the focus of this volume. Illustrations, appendixes, index.

0074 Reddig, William M. *Tom's Town: Kansas City and the Pendergast Legend*. Philadelphia: Lippincott, 1947.

This account is useful for understanding the political milieu in which Truman moved from judgeship to U.S. senator. Index.

0075 "Truman and the Pendergast Machine." *Midcontinent American Studies Journal* 7 (1966): 3–39.

Brief articles by Franklin D. Mitchell, Lyle W. Dorsett, and Gene Schmidtlein examine this relationship—a relationship that is difficult to define.

THE SENATORIAL YEARS

0076 Blum, John Morton. *V Was for Victory: Politics and American Culture During World War II*. New York: Harcourt Brace Jovanovich, 1976.

Blum covers the fate of small business during World War II, as does Catton, often with more data. This was an issue of major concern to Senator Truman. Notes, index, bibliography.

0077 Catton, Bruce. *The War Lords of Washington*. New York: Harcourt, Brace, 1948.

This volume contains information about the fate of small business in World War II, one of Truman's main concerns.

0078 Crenshaw, James T. "Harry S. Truman: A Study of the Missouri Democratic Senatorial Primary Races of 1934 and 1940." Ph.D. dissertation, George Peabody College for Teachers, 1976.

Senator Truman voted the interests of Missouri's farmers, veterans, labor unions, and blacks, who in turn supported him and returned him to office. DAI 37:5325-A.

0079 Grant, Philip A., Jr. "The Election of Harry S. Truman to the United States Senate." *Missouri Historical Society Bulletin* 36 (1980): 103–9.

Although lacking previous congressional experience, Harry Truman bested two other Democrats in their party's 1934 primary. He carried the general election, by emphasizing his fealty to the New Deal, with 59.9% of the votes.

0080 Helm, William. *Harry Truman: A Political Biography*. New York: Duell, Sloan & Pearce, 1947.

Helm was a newspaper correspondent from Truman's home state, Missouri, and had a warm, friendly relationship with Truman. The book focuses on his tenure as senator. Index.

0081 Leyerzapf, James W. "The Public Life of Lou E. Holland." Ph.D. dissertation, University of Missouri, Columbia, 1972.

A friend of Senator Truman, and from Kansas City, Holland sought in 1940 to organize small firms so they could cooperatively present their bids for defense contracts. In 1942 he became chairman of the Smaller War Plants Corporation; after six months of frustration he was dismissed. DAI 33:5096–A.

0082 Mrozek, Donald J. "Organizing Small Business During World War II: The Experience of the Kansas City Region." *Missouri Historical Review* 71 (1977): 174–92.

Efforts to work through Lou E. Holland's Mid-Central War Resources Board (1940), his Mid-Central Associated Defense Industries (after 1941), and Senator Truman were only modestly successful in competing with Eastern and Western regions. Illustrations, notes.

0083 Schmidtlein, Eugene F. "Truman's First Senatorial Election." *Missouri Historical Review* 57 (1962/63): 128–55.

Truman won a close primary because he was known to county judges, Masons, and veterans' organizations. In the November election he drew heavily from the rural vote. Notes.

0084 Schmidtlein, Eugene F. "Truman the Senator." Ph.D. dissertation, University of Missouri, 1962.

Truman's first term in the Senate was rather inconspicuous. During his second term, however, he came to national attention with his investigation of the defense program. DAI 23:4668.

Truman Committee

0085 Maher, Sister M. Patrick Ellen. "The Role of the Chairman of a Congressional Investigating Committee: A Case Study of the Special Committee of the Senate to Investigate the National Defense Program, 1941–1948." Ph.D. dissertation, St. Louis University, 1962.

Three chairmen are compared: Senators Harry S. Truman, James M. Mead, and Owen Brewster. The success of the committee emanates principally from its chairman, who establishes the objectives of the committee and the means for accomplishing them. DAI 24:4272.

0086 Riddle, Donald H. *The Truman Committee: A Study in Congressional Responsibility*. New Brunswick, NJ: Rutgers University Press, 1964.

The Senate Special Committee to Investigate the National Defense Program, according to Riddle, is an example of a responsible investigating committee. Riddle looks at the members of the committee and printed records of the committee's work. Notes, appendixes, bibliography, index.

0087 Rieman, Guenter. *Patents for Hitler*. New York: Vanguard, 1942.

Truman recommended this book to the public as it was grounded on his committee's investigations and other governmental investigations. It deals with relations between the Nazi government and major U.S. corporations.

0088 Stroud, Virgil C. "Congressional Investigations of the Conduct of War." Ph.D. dissertation, New York University, 1954.

The Truman Committee is examined and compared with four other congressional investigatory committees from the Civil War, the Spanish-American War, and World War I. DAI 15:1432.

0089 Toulmin, Harry A., Jr. *Diary of Democracy: The Senate War Investigating Committee*. New York: R. R. Smith, 1947.

The Truman Senate War Investigating Committee (Special Committee to Investigate the National Defense Program) was formed in 1941 and charged with the full investigation of the operation of the national defense program. This volume covers the work of the committee. Illustrations, index.

0090 Willson, Roger E. "The Truman Committee." Ph.D. dissertation, Harvard University, 1966.

This study of the World War II Truman Committee (Senate Special Committee to Investigate the National Defense Program) draws upon committee files to develop its origins, organization, activities, and accomplishments.

0091 Yang, Matthew Yung-chun. "The Truman Committee." Ph.D. dissertation, Harvard University, 1947.

The author seeks to evaluate the performance of the committee during the period from the standpoint of its organization, procedures, and investigations.

THE VICE-PRESIDENCY

Truman's nomination to the vice-presidency at the 1944 Democratic National Convention estranged him and James F. Byrnes. See Robert Messer, *The End of an Alliance* (#319), and Byrnes, *All in One Lifetime* (#313).

0092 Asbell, Bernard. *When F.D.R. Died*. New York: Holt, Rinehart and Winston, 1961.

Although the main focus of this book is Franklin D. Roosevelt, Truman's brief stint as vice-president and the early days of his administration are recounted. Appendix, index, photographs.

0093 Bateman, Herman E. "The Election of 1944 and Foreign Policy." Ph.D. dissertation, Stanford University, 1953.

The state of Roosevelt's health (and thus the vice-presidency) was a minor issue in the 1944 campaign. DAI 13:543.

0094 Bishop, Jim. *FDR's Last Year: April 1944–April 1945*. New York: Morrow, 1974.

Bishop's account provides good coverage of the events and issues swirling about Vice-President Truman. Index.

0095 Flynn, Edward J. *You're the Boss*. New York: Viking, 1947.

An insider, Flynn tells how a Democratic city "boss" helped switch President Roosevelt's attentions away from Wallace and toward Truman in 1944 preconvention maneuvering.

0096 Kirkendall, Richard S. "Truman's Path To Power." *Social Science* 43 (1968): 67–73.

Truman achieved great power in 1945 because he satisfied the needs of his political party in 1944. The author believes Truman was accepted for the vice-presidency because his pragmatic, gregarious personality enabled him to bridge the gaps in the Democratic party.

0097 McClure, Arthur F., and Costigan, Donna. "The Truman Vice-Presidency: Constructive Apprenticeship or Brief Interlude?" *Missouri Historical Review* 65 (1971): 318–41.

Traditionally, Truman's brief vice-presidency has been viewed as an unspectacular period; however, the authors trace such later programs as the Point 4 program, America's commitment to the United Nations, and NATO to the words and deeds of Vice-President Truman. Notes.

0098 Partin, John W. "Roosevelt, Byrnes, and the 1944 Vice-Presidential Nomination." *Historian* 42 (1979): 85–100.

Franklin D. Roosevelt very consciously played James F. Byrnes and Henry A. Wallace against each other so that Harry S. Truman could be nominated. FDR wanted to enter the campaign with support of his entire party, but he did nothing to repair the schisms that would plague his successor. Notes.

0099 Rovin, Fern R. "Politics and the Presidential Election of 1944." Ph.D. dissertation, Indiana University, 1973.

This account gives some attention to FDR's selection of Truman to be his vice-presidential running mate. DAI 35-350-A.

0100 Tugwell, Rexford Guy. *How They Became President: Thirty-five Ways to the White House.* New York: Simon and Schuster, 1964.

Truman was one of three successors to the presidency by death of the incumbent who went on to win a presidential election on his own. Tugwell examines the events leading up to Truman's nomination as Roosevelt's vice-president more than the election of 1948. Notes, index.

Truman's Political Life: Postpresidential Years

The former president provided some views of his own on the first seven years of retirement in H. S. Truman, *Mr. Citizen* (#17).

0101 Giglio, James. "Harry S. Truman and the Multifarious Ex-Presidency." *Presidential Studies Quarterly* 12 (1982): 239–55.

Truman's postpresidential years are reviewed. His views were shaped by intense partisanship and therefore limited his political effectiveness. Notes.

0102 *Memorial Services in the Congress of the United States and Tributes in Eulogy of Harry S. Truman, Late a President of the United States.* Washington, DC: G.P.O., 1973.

Memorial tributes delivered in the U.S. House of Representatives on 3 January 1973 and in the U.S. Senate on 4 January 1973 in memory of President Harry S. Truman are reprinted here.

0103 Rhodes, Richard. "Harry's Last Hurrah." *Harper's* 240 (January 1970): 48–58.

Truman's postpresidential years are reviewed in this popular account.

0104 Robbins, Charles. *Last of His Kind: An Informal Portrait of Harry S. Truman.* New York: William Morrow, 1979.

This journalist's biography of Truman emphasizes his postpresidential years and is well illustrated by Bradley Smith's photographs. Smith was the photographer Truman selected for his series of "Mr. Citizen" articles, which appeared in *The American Weekly.* Index.

0105 Truman, Harry S. *Truman Speaks.* New York: Columbia University Press, 1960.

In 1959 Truman delivered a series of lectures and discussions at Columbia University. Truman spoke on the presidency, the Constitution, and the menace of demagoguery to democracy.

0106 Williams, Herbert L. "I Was Truman's Ghost." *Presidential Studies Quarterly* 12 (1982): 256–59.

The journalist who helped Truman prepare his memoirs recalls the experience.

Overview of
the Truman Presidency

The Truman presidency, 1945–53, witnessed one of the most turbulent eras in modern American history. In foreign affairs the United States shed its traditional isolationism for a new internationalism (some critics would call it interventionism) and, thus, emerged as the major ideological, political, and military opponent to the Soviet Union in what became known as the Cold War. In domestic affairs, there were the problems of shifting the economy from a war footing to a peacetime basis, the pressure to reduce the power of organized labor, the emerging demand for the end of inequalities based on race—especially from black Americans—and the question of government infringements upon the individual's civil liberties—the "Red Scare."

While each of these issues, along with many others, is treated in detail in the following chapters, the reader who wishes an introduction to these events and issues might consider reading President Truman's two-volume *Memoirs: Year of Decisions* and *Years of Trial and Hope* (#16). Robert H. Ferrell, *Harry S. Truman and the Modern American Presidency* (#117), and Cabell Phillips, *The Truman Presidency: The History of a Triumphant Succession* (#130) are useful and generally favorable one-volume surveys. Robert J. Donovan's two-volume study, *Conflict and Crisis: The Presidency of Harry S. Truman, 1945–1948* (#114) and *Tumultuous Years: The Presidency of Harry S. Truman, 1949–1953* (#115), is the most comprehensive political history of the Truman administration presently available. However, dissenting opinions are not wanting. They may be found in I. F. Stone, *The Truman Era* (#132); Barton J. Bernstein, ed., *Politics and Policies of the Truman Administration* (#109); and Athan Theoharis, ed., *The Truman Presidency: The Origins of the Imperial Presidency and the National Security State* (#133).

Truman's leadership role has been extensively examined by scholars, frequently in comparison with other past chief executives. Among those who have looked favorably upon Truman's performance are Richard E. Neustadt, *Presidential Power: The Politics of Leadership* (#164), and Samuel Rosenman and Dorothy Rosenman, *Presidential Style: Some Giants and a Pygmy in the White House* (#165). An increasingly employed form of evaluating chief executives is an exercise known as "presidential ranking." What began as more or less an academic parlor game has become much more sophisticated. Gary M. Maranell's essay "The Evaluation of Presidents: An Extension of the Schlesinger Polls" (#177) reprints the polls and adds the results of a 1968 poll of American historians. The article by Robert K. Murray and Tim H. Blessing, "The Presidential Performance Study: A Progress Report" (#179) summarizes and analyzes this poll, as well as others. In all of these polls, as well as in other rankings, Truman consistently placed in the "near great" category.

An overview of the administrative features of the Truman administration can be found in Francis H. Heller, ed., *The Truman White House: The Administration of the Presidency, 1945–1953* (#203). Truman's extensive reorganization of the executive branch, generally rated a success, included the creation of the Department of Defense, the Central Intelligence Agency, the Council of Economic Advisers, the National Security Council, as well as the modification and reform of many other departments. William E. Pemberton, *Bureaucratic Politics: Executive Reorganization during the Truman Administration* (#207) examines these activities. Truman's

President Harry S. Truman in 1948. *U.S. Army photo.*

use of his powers as commander-in-chief, sometimes controversially, is extensively studied in Richard F. Haynes, *The Awesome Power: Harry S. Truman as Commander-in-Chief* (#197).

Truman Presidency

Autobiographical and biographical materials relating to Truman, which include much information on his presidency, may be found in Chapter 1. Additional references to Truman's role as president may be found in *Presidential Leadership*, and in Chapter 7, *Truman and Foreign Affairs*.

GENERAL ACCOUNTS

0107   Agar, Herbert. *The Price of Power: America Since 1945*. Chicago: University of Chicago Press, 1957.

Writing from an internationalist point of view, Agar offers a journalistic look at the postwar decade. Index.

0108   Allen, Robert S., and Shannon, William V. *The Truman Merry-go-Round*. New York: Vanguard, 1950.

This contemporary account attempts to sum up and evaluate the Truman presidency. Chapters dealing with Truman appointments, Congress, lobbyists, the Supreme Court, the State Department, and the Pentagon are included. Index.

0109   Bernstein, Barton J., ed. *Politics and Policies of the Truman Administration*. Chicago: Quadrangle, 1970.

These essays take a decidedly critical view of the Truman administration's foreign policy, its policies on internal security, and its civil rights program. Each essay is cited separately under its appropriate subject. Notes, index.

0110   Bernstein, Barton J., ed. *Towards a New Past: Dissenting Essays in American History*. New York: Pantheon, 1968.

Two essays in this collection focus on the Truman administration: Barton J. Bernstein, "America in War and Peace: The Test of Liberalism," (pp. 289–321), discusses the major domestic issues—economic policies, civil rights, civil liberties, and social welfare policies. Christopher Lasch, "The Cultural Cold War:

A Short History of the Congress for Cultural Freedom," (pp. 322–64) looks at the issue of intellectual freedom. Notes.

0111   Cochran, Bert. *Harry Truman and the Crisis Presidency*. New York: Funk & Wagnalls, 1973.

Although this book concentrates mainly on the issues Truman confronted during his presidency, it also offers a brief biography of Truman and his early political activities. Notes, index.

0112   Coffin, Tristram. *Missouri Compromise*. Boston: Little, Brown, 1947.

Coffin offers a popular account of the early years of the Truman presidency.

0113   Dalfiume, Richard M., ed. *American Politics Since 1945*. Chicago: Quadrangle, 1969.

Part 1 of this book offers essays on Truman, Wallace, and party politics in the 1948 election. Short bibliography, index.

0114   Donovan, Robert J. *Conflict and Crisis: The Presidency of Harry S. Truman, 1945–1948*. New York: Norton, 1977.

Donovan examines the Truman presidency from his takeover from Roosevelt through the 1948 election. Photographs, notes, index.

0115   Donovan, Robert J. *Tumultuous Years: The Presidency of Harry S. Truman, 1949–1953*. New York: Norton, 1982.

The glow of Truman's election victory did not last long as foreign policy issues, McCarthyism, and the Korean War came to dominate events. This volume concludes Donovan's examination of the Truman era. Illustrations, notes, bibliography, index.

0116   Edwards, Robert V. *Truman's Inheritance*. Caldwell, ID: Caxton, 1952.

The author argues that the trend under FDR and Truman toward benevolent socialization will, if not checked, lead the United States to deterioration and disintegration. Edwards argues for a minority of the elite to lead the way toward a moral reawakening.

0117   Ferrell, Robert H. *Harry S. Truman and the Modern American Presidency*. Boston: Little, Brown, 1982.

This brief, but friendly survey begins with Truman's early years, moves through his experiences in local and national politics, and concludes with an examination of the Truman role in the early Cold War years. Illustrations, notes, bibliography.

0118   Goldman, Eric F. *The Crucial Decade—And After: America 1945–1960*. New York: Knopf, 1966.

Goldman explores the direction of two critical questions preeminent in the postwar period: Would the United States in its domestic policy continue the "economic and social revolution which had marked the previous decades, and would the United States in its foreign policy keep moving along the path of containment and coexistence?" Index.

0119   Goldman, Eric F. *Rendezvous with Destiny.* New York: Knopf, 1952.

This volume attempts to define the liberalism that culminated in the New Deal and the Fair Deal. Chapters 17 and 18 discuss the Truman administration. Notes, index.

0120   Goulden, Joseph C. *The Best Years, 1945–1950.* New York: Atheneum, 1976.

During the years 1945 through 1950, America was experiencing a general exuberance and a feeling of confidence that this country could solve any postwar problems. Goulden looks at these "best years." Notes, index.

0121   Hamby, Alonzo L. *Beyond the New Deal: Harry S. Truman and American Liberalism.* New York: Columbia University Press, 1973.

Liberals divided over the nature of the Soviet threat and the necessity of the Cold War, and over the scope of the new social programs. Although Hamby favors those who urged reconciliation with Russia and an innovative social program, his volume is an excellent survey of the bitter political contests. Notes, bibliography, index.

0122   Hersey, John. *Aspects of the Presidency: Truman and Ford in Office.* New York: Ticknor & Fields, 1980.

In 1950 Hersey, who was working for the *New Yorker*, requested permission to tag along with Truman to write a series on the president as a human being. This book is based upon those initial *New Yorker* essays.

0123   Hinchey, Mary H. "The Frustration of the New Deal Revival, 1944–1946." Ph.D. dissertation, University of Missouri, 1965.

During the first few months of Truman's tenure, he was surprisingly successful in fulfilling his commitments to Roosevelt's foreign and domestic policies; however, after the war Truman's efforts were frustrated by the conservative coalition, which in 1946 took control of Congress. DAI 26:5398.

0124   Huthmacher, J. Joseph, ed. *The Truman Years: The Reconstruction of Postwar America.* Hinsdale, IL: Dryden, 1973.

These essays, many from books, cover both foreign and domestic affairs, and form a solid survey of the Truman era. Notes, extended bibliography.

0125   Jackson, J. Hampden. *The World in the Postwar Decade, 1945–1955.* Boston: Houghton Mifflin, 1956.

Jackson defines two issues with which the world was preoccupied during the postwar decade: U.S./Soviet rivalry and nationalist independence movements. These issues plus internal developments in the Soviet Union, the United Kingdom, and the United States are discussed. Index.

0126   Johnson, Walter. *1600 Pennsylvania Avenue: Presidents and People Since 1929.* Boston: Little, Brown, 1960.

Truman rates a 160-page treatment in Johnson's balanced survey of presidential leadership from FDR to Eisenhower. Notes, bibliography, index.

0127   Kirkendall, Richard S. "Harry S. Truman." In Morton Borden, ed. *America's Eleven Greatest Presidents.* Chicago: Rand McNally, 1971, pp. 255–88.

Truman promoted significant changes in the role of the United States in the world and in social and economic changes at home. For these achievements, Kirkendall maintains, Truman is entitled to be included as one of our greatest presidents. Bibliography.

0128   Koenig, Louis W., ed. *The Truman Administration: Its Principles and Practice.* New York: New York University Press, 1956.

Koenig characterizes the Truman administration as beginning, proceeding, and ending in an atmosphere of tension produced by the innumerable sources of trouble at home and abroad. Using selective documents, chiefly of the president, he hopes to present an "unbiased" look at the Truman administration. Index.

0129   McNaughton, Frank, and Hehmeyer, Walter. *Harry Truman: President.* New York: Whittlesey House, 1948.

This volume focuses on the time from when Truman assumed the presidency to the end of his first term and assesses his handling of the various international crises and domestic conflicts he faced. Index.

0130   Phillips, Cabell. *The Truman Presidency: The History of a Triumphant Succession.* New York: Macmillan, 1966.

Although written before many of the documents were available, Phillips's account remains a useful, comprehensive study of Truman's administration. It is very sympathetic to Truman. Notes, index.

0131   Rudoni, Dorothy J. "Harry S. Truman: A Study in Presidential Perspective." Ph.D. dissertation, Southern Illinois University, 1968.

This study examines Truman's perception of his responsibility and the social and political experiences which influenced that perception. DAI 29:3657-A.

0132 Stone, Isidor F. *The Truman Era*. New York: Monthly Review Press, 1953.

Stone lacked enthusiasm for and confidence in Truman and his top aides. "Until his election in 1948 transformed a disarming humility into a ludicrous conceit, Mr. Truman was a man without faith in himself, surrounded by men without real faith in American society." This volume collects and reprints Stone's essays on various personalities and issues confronting the Truman administration.

0133 Theoharis, Athan, ed. *The Truman Presidency: The Origins of the Imperial Presidency and the National Security State*. Standfordville, NY: Earl M. Coleman, 1979.

Theoharis finds striking parallels between the Truman and Nixon presidencies, ranging from the use of intelligence agencies, authorization of illegal programs and investigative activities, an interventionist foreign policy based upon the domino theory and initiated unilaterally and secretly by the White House. Presidential documents are used to support this thesis. Index, list of documents.

0134 Theoharis, Athan. "The Truman Presidency: Trial and Error." *Wisconsin Magazine of History* 55 (1971): 49–58.

The author argues that Truman was ineffective in directing legislative reform during his presidency.

0135 Wittner, Lawrence S. *Cold War America: From Hiroshima to Watergate*. New York: Holt, Rinehart and Winston, 1978.

The first four chapters (110 pages) provide a revisionist and essentially critical introduction to domestic and foreign policy issues of the Truman presidency.

0136 Zornow, William F. *America at Mid-Century: The Truman Administration, the Eisenhower Administration*. Cleveland, OH: Allen, 1959.

Zornow presents a brief summary of leading developments in American foreign policy, politics, and domestic legislation during the Truman and Eisenhower administrations. Bibliography, index.

THE WHITE HOUSE

0137 Durbin, Louise. *Inaugural Cavalcade*. New York: Dodd, Mead, 1971.

The contemporary events surrounding the inauguration of each president and the inaugural ceremonies and celebrations are chronicled. Truman's inauguration is discussed on pages 168 through 179. Illustrations, bibliography, index.

0138 Fields, Alonzo. *My 21 Years in the White House*. New York: Coward-McCann, 1961.

Chapters 14 to 18 relate to the Truman years. These personal recollections of the White House's chief butler emphasize the human qualities of the Truman family. Appendixes.

0139 Gustafson, Merlin. "The President's Mail: Is it Worthwhile to Write to the President?" *Presidential Studies Quarterly* 8 (1978): 36–44.

The methods used to screen and process citizen mail received by presidents from Herbert Hoover to Dwight Eisenhower are reviewed. Notes.

0140 Horst, J. F. ter, and Albertazzie, Ralph. *The Flying White House: The Story of Air Force One*. New York: Coward, McCann & Geoghegan, 1979.

Chapter 5 relates the experiences of Truman's official aircraft, *Sacred Cow* and *Independence*. Index.

0141 Kempton, Greta. "Painting the Truman Family." *Missouri Historical Review* 67 (1973): 335–49.

The author recalls the experiences of painting the portraits of President Truman and members of his family. Illustrations.

0142 Klapthor, Margaret Brown. *Official White House China: 1789 to the Present*. Washington, DC: Smithsonian Institution Press, 1975.

Illustrations and discussions of the formal china service of each administration are surveyed. During the Truman administration a porcelain state dinner service was purchased. Illustrations, index.

0143 *Report of the Commission on the Renovation of the Executive Mansion*. Compiled under direction of the commission by Edwin Bateman Morris. Washington, DC, September 1952.

The commission was established by Congress in 1949 to approve plans for reconstruction and modernization of the White House and oversee their implementation. Included is information on the history of the White House, the need for reconstruction, reconstruction operations, and the appearance of the interior and exterior of the building after reconstruction had been completed.

0144 Truman, Margaret. *White House Pets*. New York: David McKay, 1969.

Pets belonging to American presidents and their families from George Washington's horses to Richard Nixon's dogs are discussed.

0145 Woodall, Robert. "The White House." *History Today* [Great Britain] 10 (1960): 695–701.

After a historical survey of the White House, the essay focuses on the renovation which took place under President Truman (1948–52).

POLITICAL SCANDALS

Also see Chapter 1, *Truman's Political Life, The Early Years*, for Truman's relationship to the Kansas City Pendergast machine.

0146 Abels, Jules. *The Truman Scandals*. Chicago: Regnery, 1956.

The Truman administration was rife with tax fraud and influence peddling. The scandals surrounding the Reconstruction Finance Corporation, the Democratic National Committee, the Attorney General's office, the Bureau of Internal Revenue, the Federal Housing Authority, and the men involved, including Robert Hannegan, William Boyle, Jr., Matthew J. Connelly, Donald S. Dawson, Merl Young, and Joseph D. Nunan are examined. Index.

0147 Bolles, Blair. *How to Get Rich in Washington: Rich Man's Division of the Welfare State*. New York: Norton, 1952.

This popular account, based largely upon official reports and documents, reviews charges of fraud and graft at all levels of the federal government during the Truman administration. Index.

0148 Dunar, Andrew J. "All Honorable Men: The Truman Scandals and the Politics of Morality." Ph.D. dissertation, University of Southern California, 1981.

Convinced of the loyalty of close subordinates, Truman refused to recognize corruption, real or alleged, as a significant problem. The corruption issue became a major Republican issue in the 1952 presidential election and influenced the Democratic nominee as well. DAI 42:1282.

0149 Fullington, Michael G. "Presidential Management and Executive Scandal." *Presidential Studies Quarterly* 9 (1979): 192–202.

The author explores some of the reasons for the number of scandals plaguing contemporary American presidents, including Truman. Since the scandals usually involve presidential staff members and advisers rather than the president himself, the incidence of scandal is a function of management technique adopted by the president. Tables, appendix, notes.

0150 Shelton, James H. "The Tax Scandals of the 1950s." Ph.D. dissertation, American University, 1971.

The tax scandals occurred primarily in the Bureau of Internal Revenue but also included criminal conduct by Assistant Attorney General T. Lamar Caudle of the Tax Division of the Department of Justice. Hearings led to the resignations of many members of the two departments and to the reorganization of the Bureau of Internal Revenue. DAI 32:2043–A.

Presidential Leadership

See Chapter 4, *The Economy: Presidential Intervention and Seizures* for Truman's executive actions regarding the railroads and steel mills. Also, many of the accounts listed under the *Truman Presidency* seek to evaluate his leadership qualities.

0151 Barber, James D. *The Presidential Character: Predicting Performance in the White House*. Englewood Cliffs, NJ: Prentice-Hall, 1972.

Chapter 8 provides an interesting attempt to determine what factors influenced Truman as president. Notes, index.

0152 Bass, Harold F., Jr. "Presidential Responsibility for National Party Organization, 1945–1974." Ph.D. dissertation, Vanderbilt University, 1978.

This study focuses on the expanding power of the presidency and the reduced saliency of political parties in American politics by examining the role of the president as party leader. DAI 39:6308–A.

0153 Corwin, Edward S. *The President: Office and Powers, 1787–1957*. 4th rev. ed. New York: New York University Press, 1957.

In this legal history the development and contemporary status of presidential power is analyzed. Notes, table of cases, index.

0154 Dolce, Philip C., and Skau, George H., eds. *Power and the Presidency*. New York: Scribner's, 1976.

Chapter 11, "Harry S. Truman and the Postwar World," pp. 121–30, as well as some later chapters which examine issues related to the growth of presidential power apply to the Truman era. Illustrations, bibliography, index.

0155 Henry, Laurin L. *Presidential Transitions*. Washington: Brookings Institution, 1960.

This book examines the transition process in which a party overturn in the presidency has occurred.

Part 5 looks at the Truman-Eisenhower transition. Notes, index.

0156 Hess, Stephen. *Organizing the Presidency.* Washington, DC: Brookings, 1976.

Chapter 3 examines Truman's administrative structure and habits. Notes, index.

0157 Johnson, Richard T. *Managing the White House: An Intimate Study of the Presidency.* New York: Harper & Row, 1974.

Chapter 3, "Truman's Management by Transgression," reviews his strengths and weaknesses. Notes, index.

0158 Koenig, Louis W. *The Chief Executive.* 3rd ed. New York: Harcourt Brace Jovanovich, 1975.

Koenig advocates a strong presidency, which he believes is readily compatible with democracy. The book is arranged topically, and the Truman presidency is subsumed under various topics, such as nuclear weaponry, the court, labor. Notes, bibliography, index.

0159 Leuchtenburg, William E. "The Legacy of FDR." *Wilson Quarterly* 6 (1982): 77–93.

The author examines the residual impact of Franklin D. Roosevelt's New Deal on three subsequent Democratic presidents: Harry S. Truman, John F. Kennedy, and Lyndon B. Johnson.

0160 Matteodo, Eugene A. "An Analysis of Presidential Roles: Truman Through Nixon." Ph.D. dissertation, Brown University, 1978.

Richard Neustadt, in his *Presidential Power*, suggests that each president has five distinct roles which he must play: party leader, congressional leader, administrative-executive leader, national leader, and foreign leader. This study seeks to apply a quantitative and qualitative analysis of Neustadt's proposal to five presidents. DAI 39:6314-A.

0161 McCoy, Donald R. "Harry S. Truman: Personality, Politics, and Presidency." *Presidential Studies Quarterly* 12 (1982): 216–25.

Truman had a strong sense of his identity as a president and his identity as political leader; his ability to know when to use each was one of the prime reasons for his success. Notes.

0162 McGinnis, Harrill C. "The Presidency and Crisis Decisions: The Application of an Analytical Scheme." Ph.D. dissertation, University of Virginia, 1971.

Eight post-World War II cases are examined, including Truman and the Berlin airlift (1948) and the Steel Plant Seizure (1952), to evaluate the utility of Richard C. Snyder's decision-making model. DAI 32:4683-A.

0163 Neumann, Robert G. "Leadership: Franklin Roosevelt, Truman, Eisenhower, and Today." *Presidential Studies Quarterly* 10 (1980): 10–19.

Since the ability to lead intelligently affects not only America but other countries as well, a criterion of presidential leadership within the U.S. political system should be established. FDR, Truman, Eisenhower, and Carter are tested against a proposed criterion. Notes.

0164 Neustadt, Richard E. *Presidential Power: The Politics of Leadership.* New York: Wiley, 1960.

Neustadt's analysis of the function and authority of the presidency and the politics of executive leadership examines, among other things, Truman's seizure of the steel mills, dismissal of General MacArthur, and pressing of the Marshall Plan. Notes, index.

0165 Rosenman, Samuel, and Rosenman, Dorothy. *Presidential Style: Some Giants and a Pygmy in the White House.* New York: Harper & Row, 1976.

Chapter 4 presents an extended look at those qualities in Truman which the authors consider to contribute to greatness in presidents. Notes, index.

0166 Rossiter, Clinton L. *The American Presidency.* 2d ed. New York: Harcourt, Brace & World, 1960.

This thematic examination of the powers and practices, the personalities and problems of the presidency employs Truman's character and activities (as well as other presidents) to make its points. Appendix, bibliography, index.

0167 Smith, A. Merriman. *A President Is Many Men.* New York: Harper, 1948.

Smith looks at the twentieth century presidency, not from a legalistic, policymaking point of view, but from their everyday impact on the men and women around them. Particular emphasis is on Roosevelt and Truman.

0168 Street, Kenneth W. "Harry S. Truman: His Role as Legislative Leader, 1945–1948." Ph.D. dissertation, University of Texas, 1963.

In analyzing Truman's relations with Congress and his attempts to push through legislation, Street finds that Truman was virtually ineffective from 1945 to 1947. In 1947, with the shift in focus from the domestic scene to the international, and with the enunciation of the Truman Doctrine, Truman assumed a role of leadership as chief legislator.

0169 Tugwell, Rexford Guy. *The Enlargement of the Presidency.* Garden City, NY: Doubleday, 1960.

Tugwell looks at how the role and power of the presidency has enlarged from Washington through Eisenhower. He finds, however, that despite this growing role, the presidency was at an all-time low point during the Truman administration. Notes, index.

0170 von Hoffman, Nicholas. *Make-Believe Presidents: Illusions of Power from McKinley to Carter.* New York: Pantheon, 1978.

How did we arrive at the imperial presidency of Richard Nixon? Von Hoffman traces the "illusional" development of presidential power from McKinley to Carter. Notes, index.

0171 Warren, Sidney. *The President as World Leader.* Philadelphia: Lippincott, 1964.

Chapters 16 to 18 review Truman's role as a "world leader." The focus is basically upon Truman's role as Cold War statesman. Bibliography, notes, index.

0172 Zeidenstein, Harvey G. "Public Images of the President: A Study of Leadership." Ph.D. dissertation, New York University, 1965.

Covering the period from Hoover through Kennedy, Zeidenstein finds that the public has two images of the president: a *preferred image*, which views the president as a man with a minimum of political experience and a high degree of personal appeal, and a *crisis image*, which sees the president as a man experienced in government and willing to use the full authority of his office. DAI 27:3913.

TRUMAN'S PRESIDENTIAL RANKING

0173 Amlund, Curtis A. "President-Ranking: A Criticism." *Midwest Journal of Political Science* 8 (1964): 309–13.

The author argues that systematic, analytical or definable, and comparably measurable factors are lacking for measuring the "greatness" of American presidents.

0174 Bailey, Thomas A. *Presidential Greatness: The Image and the Man From George Washington to the Present.* New York: Appleton-Century, 1966.

While Bailey discussed each president's strengths and weakness, he did not attempt to rank them. Kynerd has interpreted Bailey's evaluation and places Truman twelfth, in the "average" category.

0175 Bailey, Thomas A. *The Pugnacious Presidents.* New York: Free Press, 1980.

How American presidents, from George Washington to Jimmy Carter, have dealt with war or the threat of it is examined. Truman is seen as inaccurately condemned for having started the Cold War, and is chastised for intervention into the Korean conflict. Notes, bibliography, index.

0176 Kynerd, Tom. "An Analysis of Presidential Greatness and 'Presidential Rating'." *Southern Quarterly* 9 (1971): 309–29.

The efforts of scholars to rank presidential greatness is reviewed on the basis of methodology, criteria employed, objectivity, and shortcomings. The A. M. Schlesinger polls (1948, 1962), the T. A. Bailey rating (1968), the Clinton Rossiter rating (1956), and the Eric Sokolsky system (1964) are examined. Notes.

0177 Maranell, Gary M. "The Evaluation of Presidents: An Extension of the Schlesinger Polls." *Journal of American History* 57 (1970): 104–13.

In addition to reprinting both Schlesinger polls (1948 and 1962), the results of a 1968 poll of 571 historians are displayed. Truman ranked fifth in "presidential activeness," sixth in terms of his administration's accomplishments, seventh in "general prestige" and "strength of action," twelfth on "flexibility," and twenty-second on "idealism or practicality." Tables.

0178 Maranell, Gary M., and Doddler, Richard A. "Political Orientation and the Evaluation of Presidential Prestige: A Study of American Historians." *Social Science Quarterly* 51 (1970): 415–21.

A random sample of members of the Organization of American Historians was asked to rate all presidents on seven basic attributes: prestige, strength, activity of approach, degree of idealism, flexibility, significance of work, and the historian's knowledge of the president. Truman ranked within the top ten. Tables, notes.

0179 Murray, Robert K., and Blessing, Tim H. "The Presidential Performance Study: A Progress Report." *Journal of American History* 70 (1983): 535–55.

This is the latest, most thorough examination of the various presidential "ratings." It focuses on the factors taken into consideration by the raters. Tables, notes.

0180 Rossiter, Clinton L. "The Presidents and the Presidency." *American Heritage* 7 (April 1965): 28–33, 94.

Rossiter does not rank-order the presidents; however, his discussion tends to indicate his preference for the order with the "greats" where Truman is listed. This ranking is based on Kynerd's interpretation of Rossiter's preferences.

0181 Schlesinger, Arthur M., Jr. "Rating the Presidents." In his *Paths to the Present.* Boston: Houghton Mifflin, 1964, pp. 104–14.

Schlesinger's 1962 poll of seventy-five historians listed Truman ninth in the "near great" category.

Reprinted from *New York Times Magazine*, 29 July 1962, p. 120.

0182 Schlesinger, Arthur M., Sr. "The U.S. Presidents." *Life* 25 (1948): 65–74.

One of the first comparative assessments of U.S. presidents, it began a minor fad.

0183 Wells, Ronald. "American Presidents as Political and Moral Leaders: A Report on Four Surveys." *Fides et Historia* 11 (1978): 39–53.

Compares the Schlesinger rankings of presidents (1948 and 1962) with a group of British scholars concerned with American Studies and with Christian historians associated with the Conference on Faith and History. The results of the four polls were remarkably similar. Table, notes.

Truman and the Media

See also Chapter 6, *Public Opinion and the Media*, for more general administration relations with the press and radio.

0184 Boaz, John K. "The Presidential Press Conference." Ph.D. dissertation, Wayne State University, 1969.

This study of presidential news conferences, from Theodore Roosevelt to Lyndon Johnson, discusses those of Truman. DAI 32:6580-A.

0185 Cornwell, Elmer E., Jr. *Presidential Leadership of Public Opinion*. Bloomington: Indiana University Press, 1965.

Except for the veto, the only leverage the president has in the law-making process is his ability to muster public opinion. Chapter 7, "The Modern Press Conference: 1933–1952," discusses the Truman presidency. Notes, index.

0186 Cornwell, Elmer E., Jr. "The Presidential Press Conference: A Study of Institutionalization." *Midwest Journal of Political Science* 4 (1960): 370–89.

An extended view of presidential press conferences (1912–60), this essay concentrates on Franklin Roosevelt, Harry Truman, and Dwight Eisenhower. Notes.

0187 Farrar, Ronald. "Harry Truman and the Press: A View From Inside." *Journalism History* 8 (1981): 56–62, 70.

The diaries (1945–53) of Eben A. Ayers, Truman's assistant press secretary, are discussed.

0188 Kerr, Harry P. "The President and the Press." *Western Speech* 27 (1963): 216–21.

The relations which Harry S. Truman, Dwight D. Eisenhower, and John F. Kennedy had with the American press are reviewed here.

0189 Lammers, William W. "Presidential Press-Conference Schedules: Who Hides, and When?" *Political Science Quarterly* 96 (1981): 261–78.

While this essay examines press conferences held by American presidents during 1929 to 1979, it provides a useful backdrop for comparing Truman's relations with the press. Notes.

0190 Locander, Robert. "The Adversary Relationship: A New Look at an Old Idea." *Presidential Studies Quarterly* 9 (1979): 266–74.

This study examines the traditional adversary relationship between presidents and the press, a relationship that is not always critical. It compares these relationships from F. D. Roosevelt to Gerald Ford.

0191 Lorenz, A. L., Jr. "Truman and the Press Conference." *Journalism Quarterly* 43 (1966): 671–79.

This study of the 324 press conferences held by Truman suggests that they were unsuccessful in explaining and interpreting administration policy. They did, however, create an image of Truman as a strong president. Notes.

0192 Merrill, John C. "How *Time* Stereotyped Three U.S. Presidents." *Journalism Quarterly* 42 (1965): 563–70.

The author reviewed ten consecutive issues of *Time* magazine in the Truman, Eisenhower, and Kennedy administrations for various types of bias. *Time* was found to be clearly anti-Truman, for ninety-two examples of bias were found and only one positive.

0193 Murray, Randall L. "Harry S. Truman and Press Opinion, 1945–1953." Ph.D. dissertation, University of Minnesota, 1973.

This study is a critical examination of newspaper opinion of a controversial president in a complex postwar period at a time when professional editorial writers were giving unprecedented attention to their product. DAI 34:7260-A.

0194 Pollard, James E. *The Presidents and the Press: Truman to Johnson*. Washington, DC: Public Affairs Press, 1964.

In this volume of the author's collected essays, Chapters 2 and 3 examine Truman's salty, homespun approach with the press and media. Notes.

0195 Sies, Dennis E. "The Presidency and Television: A Study of Six Administrations." Ph.D. dissertation, University of Cincinnati, 1978.

This study systematically examines the use of television by Presidents Truman through Ford. DAI 39:5704-A.

President as Commander-in-Chief

0196 Cushman, Donald P. "A Comparative Study of President Truman's and President Nixon's Justification for Committing Troops to Combat in Korea and Cambodia." Ph.D. dissertation, University of Wisconsin, 1974.

This study examines the commonalities and differences in Truman's and Nixon's transformations of their reasons for acting into public justifications. DAI 35:7429-A.

0197 Haynes, Richard F. *The Awesome Power: Harry S. Truman as Commander-in-Chief.* Baton Rouge: Louisiana State University Press, 1973.

Haynes provides an extensive account of Truman's decision to use the A-bomb against Japan, and examines his decisions on postwar civilian control of atomic energy, his intervention in Korea, his Cold War leadership, and his dispute with MacArthur. Notes, extensive bibliography, index.

0198 Hoare, Wilbur W., Jr. "Truman." In Ernest May, ed. *The Ultimate Decision: The President as Commander in Chief.* New York: George Braziller, 1960.

Chapter 7 deals with Truman's role. Hoare finds that Truman differed from Roosevelt in that he relied more upon established executive agencies than personal diplomacy. Bibliographic notes, index.

0199 Latzer, Barry. "The Constitutional Authority of the President to Commence Hostilities without a Congressional Declaration of War." Ph.D. dissertation, University of Massachusetts, 1977.

Among the several cases examined is the Korean War. DAI 38:5023-A.

0200 Rossiter, Clinton L. *The Supreme Court and the Commander in Chief.* New York: Cornell University Press, 1951.

This brief, early study recognizes the new, expanded role the United States has begun to play in the world and examines the constitutional authority of the president to (1) conduct martial rule, and (2) wage defensive war. Its focus is on the limitation

rather than extension of presidential power. Notes, tables of cases, index.

0201 Schlesinger, Arthur M., Jr. *The Imperial Presidency.* Boston: Houghton Mifflin, 1973.

This study focuses on the war-making power of the presidency. Chapter 6 deals with Truman's decision to send American troops into the Korean War, without congressional approval. Notes, index.

Executive Office and Cabinet

See also Chapter 3, *Executive Branch*; Chapter 4, *Council of Economic Advisers*; and Chapter 7, *National Security Council*.

0202 Fenno, Richard F., Jr. *The President's Cabinet: An Analysis in the Period from Wilson to Eisenhower.* Cambridge: Harvard University Press, 1959.

The organization of this book is topical and analytical, rather than historical in development. Truman's cabinet is discussed within the framework of its relationship to the president, its strength and weaknesses as an institution, and its relationship to the larger political system. Notes, index.

0203 Heller, Francis H., ed. *The Truman White House: The Administration of the Presidency, 1945–1953.* Lawrence; Regents Press of Kansas, 1980.

This administrative history is based upon a conference sponsored by the Harry S. Truman Library Institute, which was attended by twenty-two persons who had served in Truman's administration. Illustrations, index.

0204 Hobbs, Edward H. *Behind the President: A Study of Executive Office Agencies.* Washington, DC: Public Affairs Press, 1954.

Hobbs's study focuses on the development of the "executive office" and its components since its establishment in 1939. In the process he discusses the Council of Economic Advisers (Chapter 5), the National Security Council (Chapter 7), and the National Security Resources Board (Chapter 6). Notes, index.

0205 Lacy, Alex B., Jr. "The White House Staff Bureaucracy." *Trans-action* 6 (1969): 50–56.

Lacy surveys the evolution of the White House staff and the characteristics of the men who have served on the staff, 1939–67. Truman delegated much work. Illustrations, table, bibliography.

0206 Neustadt, Richard E. "The Presidency and Legislation: The Growth of Central Clearance." *American Political Science Review* 48 (1954): 641–71.

This operations history of the Bureau of the Budget includes (pp. 657–64) an assessment of the Truman years.

0207 Pemberton, William E. *Bureaucratic Politics: Executive Reorganization during the Truman Administration.* Columbia: University of Missouri Press, 1979.

Reorganizing the executive branch of government was one of Truman's most successful domestic reforms. He created such units as the Department of Defense, Central Intelligence Agency, Council of Economic Advisers, National Security Council, and Joint Chiefs of Staff. Notes, bibliography, index.

0208 Peterson, Gale E. "President Harry S. Truman and the Independent Regulatory Commissions, 1945–1952." Ph.D. dissertation, University of Maryland, 1973.

Truman brought increased efficiency to the independent regulatory commissions, but he failed to increase their statutory authority to protect the public against special interests. DAI 34:4165-A.

0209 Roth, Harold H. "The Executive Office of the President: A Study of Its Development with Emphasis on the Period 1939–1953." Ph.D. dissertation, American University, 1959.

This study examines the development of the executive office. Chapter 4 carries the account through the Truman administration, detailing the growth of the White House Office, of institutional facilities for management and counsel, and of new-line development, including the Council of Economic Advisers and various mobilization and security agencies. DAI 19:2130.

0210 Wyszomirski, Margaret J. "Presidential Advisory Circles, 1932–1968." Ph.D. dissertation, Cornell University, 1979.

The purpose of this study is to examine the recruitment of advisers for presidents from Roosevelt to Johnson and to compare them in an effort to discern patterns. DAI 40:5182-A.

Truman and Congress

0211 Amlund, Curtis A. "Executive-Legislative Imbalance: Truman to Kennedy?" *Western Political Quarterly* 18 (1965): 640–45.

This brief essay challenges the view that during the twentieth century the executive branch has had an increasingly preponderant role in decision-making. The author suggests that Truman paid great deference to congressional desires. Notes.

0212 Bailey, Stephen K., and Samuel, Howard D. *Congress at Work.* New York: Holt, 1953.

The process of resolving issues in Congress rather than the debating of the relative merits or demerits of a particular issue is the focus of this book, which discusses the workings of Congress during the Truman administration. Notes, glossary, index.

0213 Brown, William E. "Judicial Review of Congressional Investigative Powers with Special Reference to the Period 1945–1957." Ph.D. dissertation, American University, 1959.

As the number of investigative committees increased after 1945, so did the number of judicial proceedings which came before the federal courts as the result of the indictment of witnesses for contempt of Congress by reason of their refusal to appear when summoned, to be sworn, to testify, to produce subpoenaed documents and records, and other acts. DAI 20:729.

0214 Bullock, Charles S., III. "Freshman Committee Assignments and Reelection in the United States House of Representatives." *American Political Science Review* 66 (1972): 996–1007.

The results of this study of committee assignments to freshman representatives from 1947 to 1967 does not support the hypothesis that committee assignments are paramount for reelection. Tables, notes.

0215 Chamberlain, Hope. *A Minority of Members: Women in the U.S. Congress.* New York: Praeger, 1973.

Among the women surveyed in this volume are the following congresswomen who served during the Truman administration: Congresswomen Bolton, Bosone, Buchanan, Caraway, Church, Douglas, Harden, Kee, Kelly, Lusk, Mankin, Norton, Rogers, St. George, Smith, Thompson, Woodhouse. Index.

0216 Christenson, Reo M. "Presidential Leadership of Congress: Ten Commandments Point the Way." *Presidential Studies Quarterly* 8 (1978): 257–68.

This comparative study, drawing examples from 1932 to 1977, suggests that the application of certain principles can improve a president's effectiveness. Notes.

0217 Hartmann, Susan M. *Truman and the 80th Congress.* Columbia: University of Missouri Press, 1971.

This study examines the foreign and domestic legislation which Truman pressed on the Republican-dominated Eightieth Congress. Congress's failure to pass much of the Fair Deal legislation led Truman to label it a "Do-Nothing Congress" in the campaign of 1948. Footnotes, bibliography, index.

0218 Heubel, Edward J. "Reorganization and Reform of Congressional Investigations, 1945–1955." Ph.D. dissertation, University of Minnesota, 1955.

The Legislative Reorganization Act (1946), as well as other materials, have been surveyed to determine Congress's inclination toward reforming congressional investigating powers. DAI 16:785.

0219 Horn, John S., Jr. "The Cabinet in Congress." Ph.D. dissertation, Stanford University, 1958.

This account is an historical and analytical study of the proposal to admit the president's department heads to congressional proceedings so that they might either freely participate in debate concerning their agencies or submit to interrogation in a question period. The Truman cabinet's views are included. DAI 19:857.

0220 Huitt, Ralph K., and Peabody, Robert L., eds. *Congress: Two Decades of Analysis*. New York: Harper & Row, 1969.

In Part 1 the authors examine the state of congressional research from the mid-40s to the mid-60s. Part 2 is devoted to studies of congressional committees and Congress. Bibliography.

0221 Lester, Robert L. "Developments in Presidential-Congressional Relations: F.D.R.–J.F.K." Ph.D. dissertation, University of Virginia, 1969.

Truman modified the liaison system that had emerged during the Roosevelt administration. The organizational structure and procedures of Truman's approach are examined. DAI 31:438-A.

0222 Marwell, Gerald. "Party, Region and the Dimensions of Conflict in the House of Representatives, 1949–1954." *American Political Science Review* 61 (1967): 380–99.

Several key roll call votes in the House during the Eighty-first and Eighty-second Congresses are subjected to statistical analysis. Civil rights, national security, and domestic legislation are reviewed. Tables.

0223 Mayhew, David R. *Party Loyalty Among Congressmen: The Difference between Democrats and Republicans, 1947–1962*. Cambridge: Harvard University Press, 1966.

This study of political partisanship, well supported by statistical data, focuses on how legislators voted on specific legislation dealing with labor, agricultural, and urban issues. Tables, bibliography, index.

0224 Neustadt, Richard E. "Congress and the Fair Deal: A Legislative Balance Sheet." *Public Policy* 5 (1954): 349–81.

This "balance sheet" provides a useful summary and assessment of Truman's domestic proposals and how they fared with the various Congresses. Notes.

0225 Riddick, F. M. "The Eighty-First Congress: First and Second Sessions." *Western Political Quarterly* 4 (1951): 48–66.

0226 Riddick, F. M. "The Eighty-Second Congress: First and Second Sessions." *Western Political Quarterly* 5 (1952): 94–108, 619–34.

These are useful surveys of the Congress's organization and legislative activities. Notes.

0227 Robinson, James A. "Decision Making in the Committee on Rules." Ph.D. dissertation, Northwestern University, 1957.

Robinson describes the role of the Committee on Rules in arranging and allocating time for the consideration of the legislative program of the House of Representatives and attempts to explain the behavior of the committee in terms of competence, communication and information, and social backgrounds.

0228 Schriftgiesser, Karl. *The Lobbyists: The Art and Business of Influencing Lawmakers*. Boston: Little, Brown, 1951.

In 1946 Congress officially recognized lobbying and, in effect, legalized it by passing the Regulation of Lobby Act as a part of the Legislative Reorganization Act. This account examines the reasons for the act and reviews its fate after 1946. Notes, bibliography, index.

0229 Shipley, George C. "Congress and the Agencies: An Analysis of Legislative Oversight in the United States House of Representatives." Ph.D. dissertation, University of Texas, Austin, 1977.

The 1946 Legislative Reorganization Act, by charging the standing committees of the U.S. House and Senate with the supervision of all federal bureaucracies in their implementation of public policy, signaled an increased concern with committee surveillance and oversight of the executive branch. This study examines the impact of the 1946 act up to revision in 1971. DAI 38:4365-A.

0230 Vogler, David J. "Patterns of One House Dominance in Congressional Conference Committees." *Midwest Journal of Political Science* 14 (1970): 303–20.

This study seeks to determine patterns of relative chamber influence in conference committees in five Congresses between 1945 and 1966. The Senate consistently determined the outcome of these conferences in both Democratic and Republican Congresses. Illustrations, tables, notes.

0231 Wayne, Stephen J. *The Legislative Presidency.* New York: Harper & Row, 1978.

Covering the Truman through Ford period, Wayne examines executive initiative and involvement in the legislative process, from the development of the president's powers to his role in the independent legislative functions. Bibliography, index.

Advisory Commissions and Committees

Most of the various commissions and committees dealt with themes which are discussed below; therefore, compare with table of contents and subject index.

PRESIDENTIAL COMMISSIONS AND COMMITTEES

Truman appointed nineteen ad hoc commissions and committees to study specific problems. The reports, if any, of these groups are listed here; additional materials relating to the topic investigated appear under similar topics listed below.

0232 U.S. Missouri Basin Survey Commission. *Missouri: Land and Water.* Report. Washington, DC: G.P.O., 1953.

This report, complete with maps and detailed charts and tables, examines the water and land problems of the Missouri River basin. Flood control, navigation, federal electric power policies, and many ecological issues are reviewed.

0233 U.S. President's Advisory Commission on Universal Training. [Compton Commission] *A Program for National Security, May 29, 1947.* Report. Washington, DC: G.P.O., 1947.

The Compton report called for universal, male, military service and endorsed extensive U.S. rearmament. It was sharply criticized and the proposal failed.

0234 U.S. President's Advisory Committee on Management Improvement. [Morgan Committee] *Report to the President [by the] President's Advisory Committee on Management.* Washington, DC: G.P.O., December 1952.

Supported by the Bureau of the Budget, this committee worked with most cabinet chiefs and heads of major federal agencies to stimulate better management practices. In this report some general recommendations are offered.

0235 U.S. President's Advisory Committee on the Merchant Marine. [Keller Committee] *Report.* Washington, DC: G.P.O., November 1947.

The committee's report emphasized the need for a modern American merchant fleet and recommended that federal subsidies be provided to build and maintain such a fleet.

0236 U.S. President's Air Policy Commission. [Finletter Commission] *Survival in the Air Age.* A report by the President's Air Policy Commission. Washington, DC: G.P.O., 1948.

The "Finletter Report" foresaw January 1953 as the date the nation might be forced to deal with an atomic attack. To prevent this, the report recommended the United States adopt a "new strategy" emphasizing a seventy-group air force with 700 heavy bombers instead of the fifty-five groups and 580 bombers currently budgeted. Also, the report urged creation of a Department of Civil Aviation under the secretary of commerce. Appendixes.

0237 U.S. President's Airport Commission. [Doolittle Commission] *The Airport and Its Neighbors.* Washington, DC: G.P.O., 1952.

This report stressed the need for additional airports and for the modernizing of those in existence. It looked forward to the new age of commercial aviation.

0238 U.S. President's Commission on the Health Needs of the Nation. [Magnuson Commission] *Building America's Health.* A Report to the President. 5 vols. Washington, DC: G.P.O., 1952–53.

The report examines the current and prospective supply of physicians and other health service personnel, their training facilities, civil defense requirements, availability of medical facilities (hospitals, etc.), and financing of adequate medical care. The report recommended federal support of the training of more personnel and federal grants to provide more hospitals and other medical facilities.

0239 U.S. President's Commission on Higher Education. [Zook Commission] *Higher Education for American Democracy.* A report. Washington, DC: G.P.O., 1947.

This comprehensive report reviews the goals of higher education, the organization and staffing of programs, and the financing of higher education. One of its assumptions is that federal aid would be available to supplement state and local efforts.

0240 U.S. President's Commission on Immigration and Naturalization. [Perlman Commission] *Whom We*

Shall Welcome. A report. Washington, DC: G.P.O., 1953.

This commission was created to address the inadequacies of the Immigration and Nationality Act (1952). The report finds that immigration laws discriminated against people because of their national origins, race, color, or creed and that they reflected a fear of different ideas.

0241 U.S. President's Commission on Internal Security and Individual Rights (1951). [Nimitz Commission] No report.

0242 U.S. President's Commission on Migratory Labor. [Van Hecke Commission] *Migratory Labor in American Agriculture.* A report. Washington, DC: G.P.O., 1951.

Foreign labor importation should be limited and controlled by the Immigration and Naturalization Service. Legislation is needed to make it unlawful to hire aliens who have entered the United States illegally. Migratory farm labor should be provided with housing and a minimum wage.

0243 U.S. President's Committee on Civil Rights. [Wilson Committee] *To Secure These Rights.* The Report of the President's Committee on Civil Rights. Washington, DC: G.P.O., 1947.

This report urged the end of segregation in the armed forces and an end to economic discrimination regarding jobs, wages, and other practices.

0244 U.S. President's Committee on Equality of Treatment and Opportunity in the Armed Services. [Fahy Committee] *Freedom to Serve: Equality of Treatment and Opportunity in the Armed Services.* A report. Washington, DC: G.P.O., 1950.

The Fahy Committee reviewed the implementation of Executive Order 9981 (26 July 1948) by which Truman ordered that all persons in the armed services should be given "equality of treatment and opportunity" without regard to race, color, religion, or national origin.

0245 U.S. President's Committee on Foreign Aid. [Harriman Committee] *European Recovery and American Aid.* A report. 4 parts in 2 vols. Washington, DC: G.P.O., November 1947.

The Harriman report endorsed the European Recovery Program (Marshall Plan) and provided supporting documentation.

0246 U.S. President's Committee on Labor Relations in the Atomic Energy Installations. [Davis Committee] *Report.* Washington, DC: U.S. Atomic Energy Commission, April 1949.

Labor was urged, in the spirit of national security, to relinquish the right to strike atomic energy installations and to agree that neither security rules nor their administration were matters for collective bargaining. The committee recommended that all parties accept arbitration as the final resort in any dispute.

0247 U.S. President's Committee on Religion and Welfare in the Armed Forces. [Weil Committee] *Community Responsibility to Our Peacetime Servicemen and Women.* Washington, DC: G.P.O., 1949.

This is the first of several committee reports issued (1949–51). Basically the committee sought to invite local communities to help base commanders plan wholesome, off-duty activities for service personnel.

0248 U.S. President's Materials Policy Commission. [Paley Commission] *Resources for Freedom.* A report to the president. 5 vols. Washington, DC: G.P.O., 1952.

The basic resources needed to supply American industry in time of war—the so-called "strategic resources"—were studied and various federally sponsored programs were recommended. Involved were electric energy and minerals.

0249 U.S. President's Scientific Research Board. [Steelman Board] *Science and Public Policy.* A report to the president by John R. Steelman. 5 vols. Washington, DC: G.P.O., 1947.

The major thrust of this report was to analyze the federal government's administration of research and development programs (nonmilitary) and to issue recommendations for modernizing government management.

0250 U.S. President's Water Resources Policy Commission. [Cook Commission] *Report.* 3 vols. Washington, DC: G.P.O., 1950–51.

This report recognized that the nation's water supply was limited and that in the future conservation would be a necessity because of increased urban and industrial demands.

HOOVER COMMISSION

0251 Arnold, Peri E. "The First Hoover Commission and the Managerial Presidency." *Journal of Politics* 38 (1978): 46–70.

The first Hoover Commission, with its chairman Herbert Hoover, was the critical, final step in the development of a bipartisan, managerial presidency. Via this commission, Hoover developed into a supporter of managerial vigor in the presidency and helped convince Republican party leadership to accept the organizational and staffing recommendations by which the managerial presidential role was formally implemented.

0252 Evans, Frank B. "Archivists and Record Managers: Variations on a Theme." *American Archivist* 30 (1967): 45–58.

The Hoover Commission recommendations facilitated the development of a formal records management program in the National Archives with the transfer of the National Archives to the new General Services Administration, the Federal Records Act (1950), the establishment of a federal records management staff with a single organizational entity, and the establishment of a series of Federal Records Centers in various regional areas.

0253 Moe, Ronald C. *The Hoover Commissions Revisited.* Boulder, CO: Westview, 1982.

This slim volume provides an analysis of the two Hoover commissions and the impact of their recommendations upon the political structures. Notes, bibliography.

0254 Nash, Bradley D., and Lynde, Cornelius. *A Hook in Leviathan: A Critical Interpretation of the Hoover Commission Report.* New York: Macmillan, 1950.

The authors have condensed the massive Hoover Commission Report to some 225 pages, and in the process have inserted some critical observations of their own. Index.

0255 U.S. Commission on Organization of the Executive Branch of the Government. *The Hoover Commission Report on Organization of the Executive Branch of the Government.* New York: McGraw-Hill, 1949.

Encompassed in these 500-odd pages is the entire report of the Hoover Commission. The last pages list the individuals involved in putting the report together.

L to R: Dean Acheson, President Truman, and George C. Marshall, December 1950.

Administration Personalities: Political, Military, and Diplomatic

Various individuals who played important roles during the Truman era in national politics, diplomacy, and military affairs are grouped together in this chapter. The decision to place references to certain individuals under a subtitle of their name was based on an arbitrary criterion which called for the segregation by individuals if two or more references relating to them were located. It should not be taken to mean that these particular individuals are necessarily more important than those listed under *Others*.

Individuals not listed here may be found grouped together in other chapters. For atomic scientists, see Chapter 9; for union leaders, see Chapter 4; for Supreme Court justices, see Chapter 6; and for individuals caught up in the loyalty investigations, see Chapter 6, *Accusations, Blacklists, and Trials*. The subject index will include references to other individuals listed in this volume but not found in any of these categories.

A somewhat useful dictionary of biographical sketches of individuals who had some relationship to the Truman administration is Eleanora W. Schoenebaum, ed., *Political Profiles: The Truman Years* (#257). This volume also contains a list of the members of Truman's cabinet, the Supreme Court, and the more important regulatory agencies. Patrick Anderson, *The Presidents' Men* (#258) examines the appointment and activities of several members of Truman's White House staff, and Ken Hechler, *Working With Truman: A Personal Memoir of the White House Years* (#288) shows the inner workings of the Truman White House staff from 1949 to 1953.

Brief biographical sketches of members of the House and Senate may be found in the *Biographical Directory of the American Congress, 1774–1971* (#380). Rosters of the various Congresses, including the Seventy-ninth through the Eighty-second, listing all members and some committee assignments are also to be found in this volume.

0256 Garraty, John A., ed. *Encyclopedia of American Biography*. New York: Harper & Row, 1974.

This reference aid contains sketches of over 1,000 individuals, several of whom figured in the activities of the Truman era.

0257 Schoenebaum, Eleanora W., ed. *Political Profiles: The Truman Years*. New York: Facts on File, 1978.

This useful, if eclectic dictionary contains biographical sketches of 435 men and women who "played a significant role in U.S. politics during the late 1940s and early 1950s." It contains a chronology, a list of the members of Truman's cabinet, the Supreme Court, and the more important regulatory agencies. Bibliography, index.

Executive Branch

Included here are the vice-president, cabinet officers, White-House aides, and other ranking officers reporting to the president. Exceptions are the secretaries of state, who are listed under *Diplomats*.

GENERAL

0258 Anderson, Patrick. *The Presidents' Men: White House Assistants of Franklin D. Roosevelt, Harry S.*

Truman, Dwight D. Eisenhower, John F. Kennedy and Lyndon B. Johnson. Garden City, NY: Doubleday, 1968, pp. 87–132.

Truman surrounded himself with men he knew well: political allies, old friends, men who had served on his Senate staff. This chapter examines such appointments as John Steelman, Averell Harriman, Harry Vaughan, Matthew Connelly, Donald Dawson, with particular emphasis on Clark Clifford. Bibliography, index.

0259 Florestano, Patricia S. "The Characteristics of White House Staff Appointees from Truman to Nixon." *Presidential Studies Quarterly* 7 (1977): 184–89.

Truman's staff was found to be well-organized, but lacking in power. Table, notes, bibliography.

0260 Stanley, David T., et al. *Men Who Govern: A Biographical Profile of Federal Political Executives.* Washington, DC: Brookings Institution, 1967.

In response to public attention on the process of selecting presidential appointees, Brookings Institution undertook research on the backgrounds of federal political executives. This study surveys federal appointees from the New Deal through the early years of the Johnson administration. Tables, appendixes, notes, index.

CLINTON P. ANDERSON

0261 Anderson, Clinton P., with Milton Viorst. *Outsider in the Senate: Senator Clinton Anderson's Memoirs.* New York: World, 1970.

Anderson was secretary of agriculture (1945–48) and senator from New Mexico (1949–73). During his tenure as secretary he fought rationing and subsidies policies, which conflicted with those of Chester Bowles, head of the Office of Price Administration. In 1948 he resigned to run for and win a seat in the Senate. Index.

0262 Forsythe, James L. "Clinton P. Anderson: Politician and Businessman as Truman's Secretary of Agriculture." Ph.D. dissertation, University of New Mexico, 1970.

Anderson's goal was abundance in American agriculture and an adequate diet for all Americans. His postwar approach to agricultural problems reflected this orientation. In sum, he helped strengthen the Truman administration domestically and internationally. DAI 31:6496-A.

ALBEN W. BARKLEY

See also Chapter 6, *Election of 1948.*

0263 Barkley, Alben W. *That Reminds Me—.* Garden City, NY: Doubleday, 1954.

Barkley was vice-president during Truman's second term, 1949–53. As a Democratic senator from Kentucky, 1927–49, he endorsed Truman's veto of the Taft-Hartley Act and supported the Truman Doctrine and the Marshall Plan.

0264 Davis, Polly A. *Alben W. Barkley: Senate Majority Leader and Vice President.* New York: Garland, 1979.

A Democrat from Kentucky, Barkley was Senate majority leader (1937–47), minority leader (1947–48), and vice-president (1949–53). He was active in supporting foreign policy legislation such as the Bretton Woods Agreements Act (1945), the British loan (1946), and the Marshall Plan (1947–48). Illustrations, notes, index.

OSCAR L. CHAPMAN

0265 Koppes, Clayton R. "Oscar L. Chapman and McCarthyism." *Colorado Magazine* 56 (1979): 35–44.

Senator Andrew F. Schoeppel (Kansas) attacked the loyalty of Chapman in September 1950. Chapman, a long-time Interior Department administrator and now interior secretary, successfully defended himself before the Senate Committee on Interior and Insular Affairs. Illustrations, notes.

0266 Koppes, Clayton R. "Oscar L. Chapman: A Liberal at the Interior Department, 1933–1953." Ph.D. dissertation, University of Kansas, 1975.

Chapman was undersecretary of interior (1946–49) and secretary (1949–53). In his transition from a New Dealer to a Fair Dealer, he mirrored and contributed to the hardening of American liberalism. As secretary, he moved to an assimilationist position in conservation matters emphasizing development, and he fought to retain federal control of the tidelands oil reserves. DAI 36:1048-A.

CLARK CLIFFORD

0267 Barto, Harold E. "Clark Clifford and the Presidential Election of 1948." Ph.D. dissertation, State University of New Jersey, 1970.

Clifford served as Truman's special counsel from 1946 to 1950 and became the most influential strategist in the administration. Barto focuses on Clifford's role in the 1948 election. DAI 31:5974-A.

0268 Medved, Michael. "Clark Clifford: The Very Special Roman Counsel." In his *The Shadow Presidents: Top Aides in the White House from Lincoln* *to the Present*. New York: Times Books, 1979, pp. 217–34.

This essay seeks to develop the nature and significance of Clifford's influence on Truman's political decisions and actions. Illustrations, notes, index.

0269   Sand, Gregory W. "Clifford and Truman: A Study in Foreign Policy and National Security, 1945–1949." Ph.D. dissertation, St. Louis University, 1972.

The objectives of this study are: (1) to examine the evolution of liberal policy on problems of diplomacy, and (2) to investigate the relationship of domestic economics to issues of foreign policy and national security. Central to this theme is a review of Clifford's role in the Truman administration. DAI 34:5883-A.

JAMES FORRESTAL

See also Chapter 9, *Unification Struggle*.

0270   Albion, Robert C., and Connery, Robert H. *Forrestal and the Navy*. New York: Columbia University Press, 1962.

Chapter 7 has material relating to Forrestal, the navy, and the Truman Committee; while Chapters 8 to 11 focus on Forrestal as secretary of the navy and the unification struggle. Illustrations, appendix, notes, bibliography, index.

0271   Forrestal, James. *The Forrestal Diaries*. Edited by Walter Millis. New York: Viking, 1951.

Forrestal, who served as secretary of the navy, 1944–47, and secretary of defense, 1947–49, left a diary of almost 3,000 pages covering these years. These selections from the diary have been supplemented with references to Forrestal's letters and recorded telephone calls. Index.

0272   Rogow, Arnold A. *James Forrestal: A Study of Personality, Politics, and Policy*. New York: Macmillan, 1963.

Rogow sets out to produce a psychological study of James Forrestal, the first secretary of defense and the highest-ranking American official to have committed suicide. Rogow also explores the question, "Is our fate in the hands of sick men?" Notes, illustrations, index.

JOHN R. STEELMAN

0273   Steelman, John R., and Kreager, H. Dewayne. "The Executive Office as Administrative Coordinator." *Law and Contemporary Problems* 21 (1956): 688–709.

Dr. Steelman was the first to occupy the top White House position of the assistant to the president, a post which he held for nearly seven years under Truman. This essay contains references to his experiences during that time. Notes.

0274   Wagnon, William O., Jr. "John Roy Steelman: Native Son to Presidential Advisor." *Arkansas Historical Quarterly* 27 (1968): 205–25.

This biographical sketch of Steelman emphasizes his role as a presidential assistant to Truman, 1946–53. (See also Patrick Anderson, *The President's Men*.) Notes.

HENRY A. WALLACE

See also Chapter 6, *Election of 1948*.

0275   Blum, John Morton, ed. *The Price of Vision: The Diary of Henry A. Wallace, 1942–1946*. Boston: Houghton Mifflin, 1973.

Wallace, one-time vice-president under FDR, was a constant critic of Truman's Cold War policies. He served as secretary of commerce (1945–46) until Truman called for his resignation. Opposed to Truman's domestic policies (i.e., loyalty oaths) as well as his foreign policy, Wallace was the 1948 presidential candidate of the Progressive Citizens of America. Notes, appendixes, index.

0276   Capalbo, Joseph P. "Looking Backward: The Policies and Positions of Henry Wallace." Ph.D. dissertation, Rutgers University, 1974.

This study focuses on Wallace's opposition to Truman's foreign policy during 1945 to 1948, and seeks to show that his criticisms were valid. DAI 35:6768-A.

0277   Hamby, Alonzo L. "Henry A. Wallace, The Liberals, and Soviet-American Relations." *Review of Politics* 30 (1968): 153–69.

Hamby argues that the liberals left Wallace because he was unable to give them a foreign policy that either met the demands of national security or consistent idealism. This study more than illuminates Wallace's postwar career, it examines liberal thinking about foreign policy in the immediate postwar years. Notes.

0278   Markowitz, Norman D. *The Rise and Fall of the People's Century: Henry A. Wallace and American Liberalism, 1941–1948*. New York: Free Press, 1973.

Markowitz views Wallace as the spokesman of American liberalism who advocated a liberal program for a world New Deal and an American social service state in contrast to the anti-Communist liberalism of postwar America. Illustrations, notes, bibliography, index.

0279 Rosen, Jerold A. "Henry A. Wallace and American Liberal Politics, 1945–1948." *Annals of Iowa* 44 (1978): 462–74.

Wallace was critical of the Truman Doctrine, the Marshall Plan, and especially the notion of containment; however, his opposition to these policies isolated him "from the mainstream of American liberal thought." Thus Wallace's potential political strength was neutralized. Notes.

0280 Schapsmeier, Edward L., and Schapsmeier, Frederick H. *Prophet in Politics: Henry A. Wallace and the War Years, 1940–1965.* Ames: Iowa State University Press, 1970.

The authors examine Wallace's role as vice-president, his plummet from power, and his emergence as the Progressive party's 1948 candidate for the presidency. Notes, illustrations, bibliography, index.

0281 Sirevag, Torbjorn. "The Dilemma of the American Left in the Cold War Years: The Case of Henry A. Wallace." *Norwegian Contributions to American Studies* 4 (1973): 339–421.

This account argues that previous efforts to explain the Wallace phenomenon of 1948 have failed to recognize that he "followed the same road as did the main body of American liberalism in the Cold War Years, only he did so with much less speed. . . ." Notes.

0282 Walker, J. Samuel. *Henry A. Wallace and American Foreign Policy.* Westport, CT: Greenwood, 1976.

This study is a careful assessment of the roots of Wallace's ideas on foreign affairs and the reasons why he refused to join the Cold War consensus. It attempts to explain why his challenges to the Cold War assumptions proved so futile. Notes, index.

0283 Walton, Richard J. *Henry Wallace, Harry Truman, and the Cold War.* New York: Viking, 1976.

Walton argues that, had Wallace been elected, the Korean War might have remained solely a civil war and the American involvement in Indochina would have ceased rather than grown. The book focuses on the 1948 election. Notes, bibliography, index.

0284 Weiler, Richard M. "Statesmanship, Religion, and the General Welfare: The Rhetoric of Henry A. Wallace." Ph.D. dissertation, University of Pittsburgh, 1980.

The focus is on the economic aspects of Wallace's speeches. It is argued that economic concerns are central to Wallace's liberalism, the liberalism of nineteenth century England and America. DAI 41:22.

OTHERS

0285 Bell, James A. "Defense Secretary Louis Johnson." *American Mercury* 70 (June 1950): 643–53.

This brief biographical sketch of Johnson provides as well an interim assessment of his tour as secretary of defense.

0286 Farrar, Ronald T. *Reluctant Servant: The Story of Charles G. Ross.* Columbia: University of Missouri Press, 1969.

Ross was Truman's press secretary while he was in the White House. Notes, bibliography, index.

0287 Hand, Samuel B. "Samuel I. Rosenman: His Public Career." Ph.D. dissertation, Syracuse University, 1960.

Rosenman was one of Roosevelt's most influential advisers. After Roosevelt's death Rosenman tendered his resignation, but Truman insisted that Rosenman complete the assignment upon which he was engaged: a survey of economic conditions in Western Europe and negotiations for international trials of captured Nazi leaders. DAI 22:234.

0288 Hechler, Ken. *Working With Truman: A Personal Memoir of the White House Years.* New York: Putnam's, 1982.

The author was a presidential special assistant who spent most of his time preparing speeches for Truman. Included here is considerable information on Truman's White House staff and its workings. Notes, bibliography, index.

0289 Lapomarda, Vincent A. "Maurice Joseph Tobin, 1901–1953: A Political Profile and an Edition of Selected Public Papers." Ph.D. dissertation, Boston University, 1968.

Tobin was Truman's secretary of labor from 1948 to 1953. He staunchly fought for the rights of the working man and strengthened the Department of Labor. DAI 29:2183-A.

0290 Ritchie, Donald A. *James M. Landis: Dean of the Regulators.* Cambridge: Harvard University Press, 1980.

Landis was chairman of the Civil Aeronautics Board from 1946 to 1947, when Truman chose not to reappoint him. During the Kennedy administration he advised the president on reorganization of federal regulatory agencies. Notes, index.

0291 Sawyer, Charles. *Concerns of a Conservative Democrat.* Carbondale: Southern Illinois University Press, 1968.

Sawyer was secretary of commerce from 1948 to 1953. Throughout his tenure he acted as a liaison between government and big business, attempting to minimize government involvement by promoting voluntary compliance with government policy. Notes, illustrations, index.

0292 Strauss, Lewis L. *Men and Decisions*. Garden City, NY: Doubleday, 1962.

Strauss served on the newly created Atomic Energy Commission (1946–50). He advocated maintaining the U.S. monopoly of atomic technology, and strongly supported the construction of the H-bomb. Illustrations, notes, index.

0293 Winstead, Billy W. "Robert Henry Hinckley: His Public Service Career." Ph.D. dissertation, University of Utah, 1980.

Hinckley was one of the original five members of the Civil Aeronautics Authority, director of the Office of Contract Settlement, and public advisory board member of the Economic Cooperation Administration. He served under both Roosevelt and Truman. DAI 41:1173.

Diplomats

For additional references to U.S. diplomats, see the subject indexes of Richard Dean Burns, ed., *Guide to American Foreign Relations Since 1700* (1983) (#3023).

DEAN ACHESON

0294 Acheson, Dean. *Among Friends: Personal Letters of Dean Acheson*. Edited by David S. McLellan and David C. Acheson. New York: Dodd, Mead, 1980.

This selection of letters, which Acheson wrote to friends, associates, and members of his family, spans the years 1918 to 1971. Index.

0295 Acheson, Dean. " 'Dear Boss': Unpublished Letters From Dean Acheson to Ex-President Harry Truman," *American Heritage* 31 (1980): 44–48.

Acheson, who served as secretary of state under Truman from 1949 to 1953, maintained a lively correspondence with Truman after both men had left office (1953–65).

0296 Acheson, Dean G. *Present at the Creation: My Years in the State Department*. New York: Norton, 1969.

Highly complimentary of Truman, Acheson presents an insider's view of how and why America's Cold War policy (1945–53) emerged as it did. He has few doubts about the decisions he supported. Appendix, notes, index.

0297 Acheson, Dean. *Sketches From Life of Men I Have Known*. New York: Harper, 1959.

Covering the period from the end of World War II to 1953, Acheson presents his impressions of men with whom he had contact during this crucial period. Among them are Ernest Bevin, Robert Schuman, Winston Churchill, Arthur Vandenberg, George C. Marshall, and Konrad Adenauer. Illustrations, index.

0298 LaFeber, Walter. "Kissinger and Acheson: The Secretary of State and the Cold War." *Political Science Quarterly* 92 (1977): 189–97.

Although both men were grounded in nineteenth-century Western diplomacy, their greatest impact might well be their policies toward non-Western revolutionary areas. Both favored order over justice. Notes.

0299 McLellan, David S. *Dean Acheson: The State Department Years*. New York: Dodd, Mead, 1976.

Acheson was undersecretary of state, 1945–47, and secretary of state, 1949–53. Acheson adopted a hard-line approach toward the Soviet Union and extended the containment policy to Asia, championing military and economic aid to the French colonists in Vietnam and advocating intervention in Korea. Notes, illustrations, index.

0300 McLellan, David S. "The 'Operational Code' Approach to the Study of Political Leaders: Dean Acheson's Philosophical and Instrumental Beliefs." *Canadian Journal of Political Science* 4 (1971): 52–75.

Employing a model devised by Alexander L. George, the author examines Acheson's diplomacy while secretary of state, 1949–53. A "striking congruence" is found between personality variables of this key official and his policies. Notes.

0301 "Official Conversations and Meetings with Dean Acheson (1949–1953)." microfilm, 5 rolls. Frederick, MD: University Publications of America, n.d.

These transcripts of Secretary of State Acheson's top-secret meetings with Truman, George Marshall, Winston Churchill, and scores of other leaders related to American policy toward China, Korea, Indochina, Iran, Israel, the Soviet Union, and other areas.

0302 Perlmutter, O. William. "The 'Neo-Realism' of Dean Acheson." *Review of Politics* 26 (1964): 100–123.

The author argues that Acheson in 1945, as undersecretary of state, adopted a concept of the balance of power struggle as the principal element in world affairs, and clearly distinguished between moral and ideological aims and the operating assumptions of power politics. Notes.

0303 Rosenau, James N. "The Senate and Dean Acheson: A Case Study in Legislative Attitudes." Ph.D. dissertation, Princeton University, 1957.

The author employs content analysis to the *Congressional Record* (1949–52) to view legislative attitudes and perceptions. Affairs in the Far East, not Acheson's personal characteristics, brought on senatorial criticism. DAI 18:277.

0304 Smith, Gaddis. *Dean Acheson. American Secretaries of State and Their Diplomacy.* vol. 16. New York: Cooper Square, 1972.

Acheson was chief architect of the Cold War policy. Smith sees Acheson's actions as being rooted in the cyclical theory of international relations and its justification based on the premise that only the United States had the power to maintain world stability. Notes, bibliographic essay, index.

0305 Stupak, Ronald J. "Dean Acheson: The Secretary of State as a Policymaker." Ph.D. dissertation, Ohio State University, 1967.

This study seeks to formulate a model of the role of the secretary of state in foreign policy decision-making by analyzing Acheson's view of the office, his relations within the State Department, and the influences of competing decision-making units and personalities. DAI 28:2317-A.

BERNARD M. BARUCH

See also Chapter 9, *Baruch Plan.*

0306 Baruch, Bernard M. *Baruch: The Public Years.* New York: Holt, Rinehart and Winston, 1960.

Baruch was U.S. representative to the U.N. Atomic Energy Commission and was spokesman of what became known as the Baruch Plan for the international control of atomic energy. Index.

0307 Coit, Margaret L. *Mr. Baruch.* Boston: Houghton Mifflin, 1957.

Baruch presented the U.S. plan for control of atomic energy, the spread of atomic knowledge, and a system for international inspection which became the cornerstone of our atomic policy. Notes, bibliography, index.

0308 Schwarz, Jordan A. *The Spectator: Bernard M. Baruch in Washington, 1917–1965.* Chapel Hill: University of North Carolina Press, 1981.

Baruch's role in launching and "selling" his plan for controlling atomic weapons is told (pp. 490–507). Illustrations, notes, index.

CHARLES E. BOHLEN

0309 Bohlen, Charles E. *The Transformation of American Foreign Policy.* New York: Norton, 1969.

Bohlen, former ambassador to the Soviet Union, the Philippines, and France, maintains that the years 1947 and 1948 provide the basis of what is now our foreign policy and world role. This book is based upon a series of lectures delivered at Columbia University in 1969. Index.

0310 Bohlen, Charles E. *Witness to History, 1929–1969.* New York: Norton, 1973.

Bohlen was adviser to Secretaries of State Byrnes and Marshall during the formation of the containment policy and the Truman Doctrine. Illustrations, index.

CHESTER BOWLES

0311 Bowles, Chester. *Promises to Keep.* New York: Harper & Row, 1971.

Chapters 10 and 11 deal with the decontrol and anti-inflation differences that Bowles had with Truman and other administration officials. Chapters 12 and 13 recount his successful campaign for governor of Connecticut in 1948.

0312 Bowles, Chester. *Ambassador's Report.* New York: Harper, 1954.

.Bowles was director of the Office of Price Administration (1943–46), governor of Connecticut (1949–50), and ambassador to India (1951–52). It is as ambassador that Bowles looks at the U.S. role in South and East Asia. Illustrations, bibliography, index.

JAMES F. BYRNES

0313 Byrnes, James F. *All in One Lifetime.* New York: Harper, 1958.

Former senator, representative, and justice of the Supreme Court, Secretary of State Byrnes (1945–47) had quite an active political life. Index.

0314 Byrnes, James F. *Speaking Frankly.* New York: Harper, 1947.

Secretary of State Byrnes recounts his role in the postwar peace conferences in this early Cold War memoir. Index.

0315 Clements, Kendrick A., ed. *James F. Byrnes and the Origins of the Cold War*. Durham, NC: Carolina Academic Press, 1982.

The four basic essays focus on Byrnes's relations with Truman (by R. L. Messer); Byrnes, the Russians, and the A-bomb (by Gregg Herken); Byrnes and the Paris Conferences (by P. D. Ward); and Byrnes and the division of Germany (by J. Gimbel). Notes, index.

0316 Curry, George W. *James F. Byrnes. The American Secretaries of State and Their Diplomacy*. vol. 14. New York: Cooper Square, 1965, pp. 87–396.

This account was one of the first biographical studies of Byrnes. Notes, bibliographical essay.

0317 Gormly, James L. "Secretary of State James F. Byrnes, An Initial British Evaluation." *South Carolina History Magazine* 79 (1978): 198–205.

Reprinted here is the report of Lord Halifax, British ambassador to the United States, discussing British estimates of competence in 1945 and 1946.

0318 Karl, John F. "Compromise or Confrontation: James F. Byrnes and United States' Policy toward the Soviet Union, 1945–1946." Ph.D. dissertation, University of Toronto (Canada), 1976.

Byrnes was determined to use his political skill for engineering compromise to bring about an agreement with the Soviet Union which would lead to an era of peace. It is only with his departure in January 1947 that the doctrine of containment was accepted as U.S. policy. DAI 39:2528-A.

0319 Messer, Robert L. *The End of an Alliance: James F. Byrnes, Roosevelt, Truman and the Origins of the Cold War*. Chapel Hill: University of North Carolina Press, 1982.

Instead of focusing on international negotiations or basic issues, Messer examines the private, personal ambitions of American political leaders to discover the structuring of Cold War policy. A full examination of Byrnes's and Truman's relationship is included, with material on the 1944 vice-presidential nomination. Notes, bibliography.

0320 Ward, Patricia Dawson. *The Threat of Peace: James F. Byrnes and the Council of Foreign Ministers, 1945–1946*. Kent, OH: Kent State University Press, 1979.

Byrnes served on the Council of Foreign Ministers that was responsible for writing the peace treaties after the war. This volume examines Byrnes's attempt to harmonize the conflicting Soviet and American views at the conferences of the Council of Foreign Ministers. Notes, bibliography, index.

JOHN FOSTER DULLES

0321 Dulles, John Foster. *War or Peace*. New York: Macmillan, 1950.

In this book Dulles first publicly questions the Truman administration's foreign policy, especially the containment doctrine. Index.

0322 Gerson, Louis L. *John Foster Dulles. American Secretaries of State and Their Diplomacy*. vol. 17. New York: Cooper Square, 1967.

Dulles was active during the Truman administration as a delegate to the United Nations, an adviser to the secretary of state at the meetings of the Council of Foreign Ministers, and a negotiator of the Japanese peace treaty (1950–51) and a bilateral U.S.-Japanese mutual security treaty. Notes, bibliographical essay, index.

0323 Hoopes, Townsend. *The Devil and John Foster Dulles*. Boston: Little, Brown, 1973.

During the Truman years Dulles was senator from New York and ambassador to the Japanese Peace Treaty Conference. He was an avid supporter of Truman's policies for containing the Soviet Union. Illustrations, notes, bibliography, index.

0324 Ladenburger, John F. "The Philosophy of International Politics of John Foster Dulles, 1919–1952." Ph.D. dissertation, University of Connecticut, 1969.

Ladenburger traces the evolution of Dulles's philosophy to his acceptance and endorsement of the Truman administration's containment policy. DAI 2469-A.

0325 Yates, Lawrence A. "John Foster Dulles and Bipartisanship, 1944–1952." Ph.D. dissertation, University of Kansas, 1981.

The author believes that what national prestige and distinction Dulles had achieved by 1952 was gained during the Roosevelt and Truman years and that without the assistance of Democratic leaders he could not have acquired his reputation as a Republican expert in the field of foreign policy.

W. AVERELL HARRIMAN

0326 Bland, Larry I. "W. Averell Harriman: Businessman and Diplomat, 1891–1945." Ph.D. dissertation, University of Wisconsin, 1972.

By the time Truman assumed the presidency, Harriman was in the forefront of those senior advisers advocating a "get tough" policy toward the Soviet Union. He believed that U.S. firmness, especially by insisting on Soviet political concessions in exchange for economic aid, would work because the Soviets needed American assistance for reconstruction. DAI 33:2850-A.

0327 Harriman, W. Averell, and Abel, Elie. *Special Envoy to Churchill and Stalin, 1941–1946*. New York: Random House, 1975.

Harriman relates his discussions with Truman and officials of the administration about issues with the Soviet Union. He pressed the argument that the United States must stand firm against Soviet expansionism. Notes, index.

PATRICK J. HURLEY

0328 Buhite, Russell D. *Patrick J. Hurley and American Foreign Policy*. Ithaca: Cornell University Press, 1973.

Hurley was U.S. ambassador to China (1944–45). Unlike some diplomats who believed that Chiang Kai-shek's regime was corrupt and was doomed to fall, Hurley had confidence in Chiang's leadership and advocated U.S. support of Chiang. Hurley became a leading spokesman for the "China lobby." Illustrations, notes, bibliography, index.

0329 DeGroot, Peter T. "Myth and Reality in American Policy Toward China: Patrick J. Hurley's Missions, 1944–1945." Ph.D. dissertation, Kent State University, 1974.

This study focuses on Hurley's view of reality in China. It concludes that he had misread the Chinese political situation and helped perpetuate a myth about what effect the United States might have on China's future. DAI 35:6051-A.

0330 Mulch, Barbara E. Gooden. "A Chinese Puzzle: Patrick J. Hurley and the Foreign Service Officer Controversy." Ph.D. dissertation, University of Kansas, 1972.

Special presidential emissary and later ambassador to China, 1944–45, Hurley found himself in a long-term controversy with Foreign Service officers. Frustrated over his inability to accomplish the major objectives of his mission, Hurley blamed John P. Davies and John S. Service. DAI 33:6283-A.

0331 Smith, Robert T. "Alone in China: Patrick J. Hurley's Attempt to Unify China, 1944–1955." Ph.D. dissertation, University of Oklahoma, 1966.

Hurley was untrained in diplomacy and unprepared to deal with problems peculiar to China. The failure of his mission to unify China led to charges of Communist infiltration of the Foreign Service. DAI 27:1772.

GEORGE F. KENNAN

0332 Coffee, John W. "George Kennan and the Ambiguities of Realism." *South Atlantic Quarterly* 73 (1974): 184–98.

After reviewing Kennan's famous "Mr. X" article in *Foreign Affairs*, Coffee concludes that Kennan did not believe the Soviets offered a military threat to Western Europe in the early postwar years, and that he was highly critical of the militarization of U.S. foreign policy. Coffee does not believe that "realism" is a useful concept in assessing Kennan's thinking. Notes.

0333 Denman, Dorothy I. "The Riddle of Containment as Reflected in the Advice and Dissent of George F. Kennan." Ph.D. dissertation, University of Miami, 1975.

Kennan quickly dissented with the practice of the policy of containment, even though he was closely associated with its development. He did not approve of the Truman Doctrine, and subsequently has criticized every administration from FDR to Lyndon Johnson. DAI 37:3086-A.

0334 Green, James F. "The Political Thought of George F. Kennan: A Study of the Development and Interrelations of American and Soviet Foreign Policies." Ph.D. dissertation, American University, 1972.

Critics fail to examine two assessments which, Kennan explains in *Memoirs, 1925–1950*, are the bases for the formulation of national policy: "First, one's idea of one's own country, its capabilities, and its natural role in the world; the other, the interpretation given to the psychology, the political personality, the intentions, and the likely behavior of an adversary." DAI 34:391-A.

0335 Kennan, George F. *Memoirs, 1925–1963*. 2 vols. Boston: Little, Brown, 1967, 1972.

While these volumes tell much about Kennan and his personality, their essential value here lies in the early Cold War period when he was developing the concept of containment. Appendixes include excerpts from Kennan's famous telegram of 22 February 1946, indexes.

0336 Knight, Jonathan. "George Frost Kennan and The Study of American Foreign Policy: Some Critical Comments." *Western Political Quarterly* 20 (1967): 149–60.

Kennan's writings on international relations and American foreign affairs since 1947 are critically reviewed.

0337 Luttwak, Edward N. "The Strange Case of George F. Kennan." *Commentary* 64 (1977): 30–35.

Luttwak argues that Kennan's writings suggest that he is an isolationist and that his advocacy of the reduction of U.S. military power avoids recognizing the necessity of a global balance of power.

0338 Powers, Richard J. "Kennan Against Himself?: From Containment to Disengagement. A Decade of U.S. Foreign Policy Making as Focused on the Ideas and Concepts of George F. Kennan, 1947–1957." Ph.D. dissertation, Claremont Graduate School and University Center, 1967.

Truman's policy of containment differed from Kennan's enunciation of the policy in its undue reliance upon military defense alliances. This precluded the adoption of disengagement, which was closer in its precepts to the aspirations of Kennan. DAI 28: 602-A.

0339 Wright, C. Ben. "George F. Kennan: Scholar-Diplomat, 1926–1946." Ph.D. dissertation, University of Wisconsin, 1972.

This study is, in effect, an extended critique of Kennan's first volume of his *Memoirs* (1967).

GEORGE C. MARSHALL

See also Chapter 8, *China: Marshall Mission.*

0340 Beal, John R. *Marshall in China.* Garden City, NY: Doubleday, 1970.

Marshall was sent to China in 1946 to negotiate an end to the Chinese civil war and promote a coalition government. Marshall's failure is viewed not so much as a failure of U.S. aid but as a failure on the part of the Kuomintang government. Index.

0341 Ferrell, Robert H. *George C. Marshall. American Secretaries of State and Their Diplomacy.* vol. 15. New York: Cooper Square, 1966.

General Marshall was the first military leader to assume the office of secretary of state, serving in that capacity from 1947 to 1949. During his tenure he reorganized the State Department, was architect of the European Recovery Program, and helped establish the National Security Act of 1947. Because of ill health he resigned his post in 1949. Notes, bibliographic essay, index.

0341a Pogue, Forrest C. *George C. Marshall.* 3 vols. New York: Viking, 1963–73.

While the initial three volumes of Pogue's seminal study of Marshall provide much insight into the general's values, views, and personality, they stop short of the Truman era. However, volume 4, expected momentarily, will focus on Marshall's relationship with Truman. Illustrations, notes, bibliography.

ELEANOR ROOSEVELT

0342 Atwell, Mary Welek. "Notes and Comments: Eleanor Roosevelt and the Cold War Consensus." *Diplomatic History* 3 (1979): 99–113.

Eleanor Roosevelt was ambivalent about the containment consensus which marked American foreign policy after World War Two. She considered the Truman Doctrine unnecessarily provocative, accepted the Marshall Plan, but accorded her full support to the United Nations and its goals of world peace and cooperation. Notes.

0343 Berger, Jason. *A New Deal for the World: Eleanor Roosevelt and American Foreign Policy.* New York: Columbia University Press, 1982.

During the Truman era Mrs. Roosevelt was a delegate to the United Nations where she chaired the Commission on Human Rights. An outspoken critic of repressive policies, she openly deplored Truman's willingness to shore up right-wing, anti-Communist dictatorships; however, she gradually came to support Truman's containment policies. Photographs, notes, bibliography, index.

0344 Lash, Joseph. *Eleanor: The Years Alone.* New York: Norton, 1972.

In this biography commissioned by the Roosevelt family, Lash continues the biography of Mrs. Roosevelt begun in his *Eleanor and Franklin.* After her husband's death, Mrs. Roosevelt continued in public life, serving as a delegate to the United Nations (1946–52) where she was chairman of the Commission on Human Rights. Illustrations, notes, index.

OTHERS

0345 Berle, Adolf A. *Navigating the Rapids, 1918–1971: From the Papers of Adolf A. Berle.* Edited by Beatrice Bishop Berle and Travis B. Jacobs. New York: Harcourt Brace Jovanovich, 1973.

Berle was ambassador to Brazil from 1945 to 1946 and chairman of the New York State Liberal party from 1947 to 1955. This volume contains excerpts from his diaries and papers. Index.

0346 Clayton, Will L. *Selected Papers.* Edited by Frederick J. Dobney. Baltimore: Johns Hopkins University Press, 1971.

As undersecretary of state for economic affairs, 1946–48, Clayton was a major force in the Truman administration's foreign economic policy, recommending that the United States offer Western Europe loans and grants to help rebuild their economies. Notes, index.

0347 Emmerson, John K. *The Japanese Thread: A Life in the U.S. Foreign Service.* New York: Holt, Rinehart and Winston, 1978.

Emmerson was a member of the Foreign Service and was stationed in various places including Japan, Taiwan, and Yenan. He was summoned before the Loyalty Review Board under charges that he had Communist leanings. Illustrations, notes, index.

0348 Fairbank, John K. *Chinabound: A Fifty-Year Memoir.* New York: Harper & Row, 1982.

Chapters 23 to 25 reflect personal experiences and attitudes toward the civil war in China and the impact of McCarthyism in America. Index.

0349 Hughes, H. Stuart. "The Second Year of the Cold War: A Memoir and An Anticipation." *Commentary* 48 (1969): 27–32.

The author, a member of the State Department (1946–48), believes that while the revisionists have made some good points, they have lost the feel and the mood of the 1940s. During these two years, he and others in the department believed that there were several alternative policies available; however, by the end of 1948 policy line had hardened.

0350 Kahn, E. J., Jr. *The China Hands: America's Foreign Service Officers and What Befell Them.* New York: Viking, 1975.

Accused of losing China to communism, the members of the Foreign Service stationed in China were relieved of their positions. What subsequently happened to them is the focus of this book. Such individuals as John S. Service, John Paton Davies, John Carter Vincent, Horace Smith, and Philip D. Sprouse are included. Notes, bibliography, index.

0351 Kallina, Edmund F. "A Conservative Criticism of American Foreign Policy: The Publications and Careers of Louis J. Halle, George F. Kennan, and Charles Burton Marshall, 1950–1968." Ph.D. dissertation, Northwestern University, 1970.

Kallina finds that the thought of Halle, Kennan, and Marshall is an important part of the mid-century revival of Burkean conservatism in America.

0352 Leahy, William D. *I Was There: The Personal Story of the Chief of Staff to Presidents Roosevelt and Truman.* New York: Whittlesey House, 1950.

Leahy was senior military adviser to the president, 1942–49. At the request of Truman, Leahy brought together his notes on the war years, 1941–45, in this volume. Illustrations, index.

0353 May, Gary A. *China Scapegoat: The Diplomatic Ordeal of John Carter Vincent.* Washington, DC: New Republic Books, 1979.

Vincent was head of the Office of Far Eastern Affairs, 1945–47, and was ambassador to Switzerland, 1947–51. After the fall of China in 1949, Vincent was one of the China hands accused by McCarthy

of being a Communist. Despite being cleared by the Tydings Committee, he came under investigation by the Loyalty Review Board and was forced into resigning his post in 1951. Notes, bibliography, illustrations, index.

0354 Mazuzan, George T. *Warren R. Austin at the U.N., 1946–1953.* Kent, OH: Kent State University Press, 1977.

Truman chose Austin, a Republican, as U.S. ambassador to the United Nations in an effort to continue the bipartisan tradition in foreign policy. As spokesman for the administration he was an opponent of the Soviet Union's attempts to use the United Nations as a propaganda forum and was involved in the debates on the Berlin airlift, Palestine, and the Korean War. Notes, bibliographic note, index.

0355 Murphy, Robert D. *Diplomat Among Warriors.* Garden City, NY: Doubleday, 1964.

Chapter 20 deals with membership in the Potsdam delegation, while Chapter 21 focuses on Murphy's role as an adviser to U.S. occupation forces in Germany. Chapter 22 relates his experiences during the Berlin airlift crises. Index.

0356 Noble, Harold J. *Embassy at War.* Seattle: University of Washington Press, 1975.

Noble held several appointments in the Foreign Service. This posthumously published account relates his service as first secretary to the ambassador to Korea, 1949–51. He was a firm advocate of containment in Asia.

0357 Paterson, Thomas G., ed. *Cold War Critics: Alternatives to American Foreign Policy in the Truman Years.* Chicago: Quadrangle, 1971.

These critics include Walter Lippmann, James P. Warburg, Henry A. Wallace, Claude Pepper, Glen H. Taylor, Robert A. Taft, I. F. Stone, and others. Paterson's introductory essay identifies other dissident voices. Notes, index.

0358 Persico, Joseph E. *The Imperial Rockefellers: A Biography of Nelson A. Rockefeller.* New York: Simon & Schuster, 1982.

Rockefeller was assistant secretary of state for Latin American affairs, 1944–45. When Acheson was offered the post of undersecretary, he accepted it pending Rockefeller's ouster. Rockefeller continued to be involved in Latin American affairs. Illustrations, index.

0359 Rawls, Shirley Nelson. "Spruille Braden: A Political Biography." Ph.D. dissertation, University of New Mexico, 1976.

Braden was a blunt, tough, outspoken man, whose charisma and prior achievements made him a logical candidate, in April 1945, to handle U.S. relations with the Argentine revolutionary government.

After four controversial months, Braden was named assistant secretary of state for American Republic Affairs, a post he held from November 1945 until July 1947. His policies and feuds led to chaos in U.S. Latin American policies. DAI 38:4319-A.

0360 Reuter, Paul H., Jr. "William Phillips and the Development of American Foreign Policy, 1933–1947." Ph.D. dissertation, University of Southern Mississippi, 1979. (7919705, September 79).

Phillips closed his career in 1946–47, serving on a twelve-man Anglo-American Committee of Inquiry on Palestine and chairing a conciliation commission concerning a boundary problem in Indochina. DAI 40:1653-A.

0361 Service, John S. *The Amerasia Papers: Some Problems in the History of U.S.-China Relations.* Berkeley: University of California Press, 1971.

This account is a defense of his wartime role in Nationalist China and an argument for the "non-ideological" nature of Mao's foreign policy. Service believes Hurley should be blamed for America's failure to explore the possibilities of accommodation.

Military Officers

Gen. George C. Marshall is listed under *Diplomats* because most studies of his activities during the Truman years have focused on his term as secretary of state and his "China Mission."

OMAR N. BRADLEY

0362 Bradley, Omar N. *A Soldier's Story*. New York: Holt, 1951.

Chapters 22 and 23 deal with the closing months of the war in Europe. Appendix, illustrations.

0363 Bradley, Omar N., and Blair, Clay. *A General's Life: An Autobiography*. New York: Simon & Schuster, 1983.

Part 4 deals with Bradley's years as army chief of staff, while Part 5 focuses on the Korean War years. Illustrations, notes, index.

LUCIUS D. CLAY

0364 Clay, Lucius D. *Decision in Germany*. Garden City, NY: Doubleday, 1950.

General Clay served as deputy military governor of Germany, 1946–47, and as governor of Germany, 1947–49. His book chronicles the four postwar years of Germany's reconstruction and the problems between the United States, France, Britain, and the Soviet Union. Notes, index.

0365 Clay, Lucius D. *The Papers of General Lucius D. Clay: Germany, 1945–1949*. Edited by Jean E. Smith. 2 vols. Bloomington: Indiana University Press, 1974.

These papers, which include private correspondence, official letters, and major documents, cover the years during which General Clay was military governor of the American sectors of occupied Germany. Bibliography, index.

0366 Smith, Jean E. "Selection of a Proconsul for Germany: The Appointment of Gen. Lucius D. Clay, 1945." *Military Affairs* 40 (1976): 123–29.

Civilian, not military leaders selected Clay because he was in tune with the goals and aspirations of wartime Washington. In 1945 Clay was no friend of the Germans, yet he organized and conducted a reasonably even-handed occupation. Notes.

DOUGLAS MacARTHUR

See also Chapter 10, *Truman Dismisses MacArthur*; also Chapter 6, *Election of 1948*.

0367 James, D. Clayton. *The Years of MacArthur*. 2 vols. Boston: Houghton Mifflin, 1970–75.

Volumes 1 and 2 only cover the years through 1945. A third volume, which will include MacArthur's role in the occupation of Japan, the Korean conflict, and his rift with Truman, is forthcoming. Illustrations, notes, index.

0368 MacArthur, Douglas. *Reminiscences*. New York: McGraw-Hill, 1964.

The last two sections of this memoir deal with "The Occupation of Japan, 1945–1950" and "Frustration in Korea, 1950–1951." Illustrations, index.

0369 MacArthur, Douglas. *A Soldier Speaks*. New York: Praeger, 1965.

This volume offers excerpts from the public papers and speeches of Douglas MacArthur. Illustrations.

0370 Manchester, William. *American Caesar: Douglas MacArthur, 1880–1964*. Boston: Little, Brown, 1978.

Manchester characterizes MacArthur as "a great thundering paradox of a man, noble and ignoble, inspiring and outrageous, arrogant and shy, the best of men and the worst of men." In this volume of over 700 pages, Manchester examines the man he claims was the "most gifted man-at-arms this nation has produced." Notes, illustrations, bibliography, index.

0371 Quinn, Carolyn S. "The Speaking of Douglas MacArthur in 1951 and 1952." Ph.D. dissertation, Southern Illinois University, 1971.

General MacArthur was dismissed from his Far East command on 11 April 1951, and in the ensuing fifteen months he spoke in many cities across the United States. This study examines his concept of the U.S. role as a world power and his techniques of apologies used in his address before Congress. DAI 32:4749.

0372 Whitney, Courtney. *MacArthur: His Rendezvous with History.* New York: Knopf, 1956.

Whitney served with MacArthur. His account of MacArthur spans the period from when MacArthur took command of the Philippine forces in 1941 through his return home after his ouster in 1951. Index.

0373 Willoughby, Charles Andrew, and Chamberlain, John. *MacArthur, 1941–1951.* New York: McGraw-Hill, 1954.

Willoughby, as a member of the operations section under MacArthur, was editor-in-chief of the operational history of MacArthur's campaigns and Chamberlain was a journalist. In this book, the authors analyze the political, strategic, and economic factors that influenced MacArthur's major decisions, 1941–51. Illustrations, index.

OTHERS

0374 Alberts, Robert C. "Profile of a Soldier: Matthew B. Ridgway." *American Heritage* 27 (1976): 4–7, 73–82.

In August of 1945 Ridgway went to the Far East to assume command of all airborne operations planned for the invasion of Japan. Sent to Korea in 1950, he replaced MacArthur in April 1951. Illustrations, notes.

0375 Ambrose, Stephen E. *Eisenhower: Soldier, General of the Army, President-Elect, 1890–1952.* New York: Simon & Schuster, 1983.

This substantive, recent biography has considerable material on the Truman years. Pages 433 to 572 take Ike from chief of staff to Columbia University to NATO and the 1952 election. Illustrations, notes, index.

0376 Bauer, Boyd H. "General Claire Lee Chennault and China, 1937–1958: A Study of Chennault,

His Relationship with China, and Selected Sino-American Relations." Ph.D. dissertation, American University, 1973.

After World War II, Chennault and Whiting Willauer founded CAT (airline) which proved as profitable as it had been important in its initial UNRRA-CNRRA emergency relief missions, 1945–47. After 1948, CAT's activities could be categorized as a part of the fight against communism. Chennault remained a strong supporter of Chiang Kai-shek. DAI 35:550-A.

0377 Clark, Mark W. *From the Danube to the Yalu.* New York: Harper, 1954.

General Clark was U.S. high commissioner for Austria and commander in chief, U.N. Command, in Korea. In this volume he recounts his experiences and his impressions of dealing with the Communists. Illustrations, index.

0378 Smith, Robert L. "The Influence of U.S.A.F. Chief of Staff General Hoyt S. Vandenberg on United States National Security Policy." Ph.D. dissertation, American University, 1965.

Vandenberg was instrumental in changing the U.S. concept of balanced military forces. The role of the air force was enhanced, its strategic atomic bomber forces received first claim on the defense dollar, and U.S. air power became a formidable instrument of national security. DAI 26:1151.

0379 Wolk, Herman S. "The Men Who Made the Air Force." *Air University Review* 23 (1972): 9–23.

Wolk reviews the creation of the air force as an independent service in 1946, emphasizes the roles of Generals Henry H. Arnold, Carl A. Spaatz, Ira C. Eaker, Hoyt S. Vandenberg, Lewis Norstad, and Curtis LeMay, and discusses USAF's Cold War role, 1946–48. Illustrations, notes.

Congressional and Political Leaders

For materials on state and local political officials, see Chapter 6, *State and Local Politics.*

0380 *Biographical Directory of the American Congress, 1774–1971.* Washington, DC: G.P.O., 1971.

Brief biographical sketches of each member of the House and Senate of the Seventy-ninth through Eighty-second Congress (3 January 1945 to 3 January 1953) can be found there. Two other sources contain useful information on many senators and representatives: John T. Salter, ed., *Public Men In and Out of Office* (Chapel Hill, 1946), and John Gunther, *Inside U.S.A.* (New York, 1947).

THEODORE G. BILBO

0381 Ethridge, Richard C. "The Fall of the Man: The United States Senate's Probe of Theodore G. Bilbo in December 1946, and Its Aftermath." *Journal of Mississippi History* 38 (1976): 241–62.

In January 1947 the Senate declined to seat Bilbo, who died in August, after two Senate committees investigated charges that he had profited illegally from war contractors and that he illegally prevented blacks from voting. Notes.

0382 Smith, Charles P. "Theodore G. Bilbo's Senatorial Career: The Final Years, 1941–1947." Ph.D. dissertation, University of Southern Mississippi, 1983.

Bilbo's increased militance in opposition to equal rights for blacks, and two U.S. Senate investigations into his financial activities, form the core of this account. DAI 44:1551-A.

THOMAS E. DEWEY

See also Chapter 6, *Election of 1948*.

0383 Beyer, Barry K. "Thomas E. Dewey, 1937–1947: A Study in Political Leadership." Ph.D. dissertation, University of Rochester, 1962.

Beyer finds Dewey a dynamic, progressive leader, extremely concerned about the welfare of society as a whole and yet an ardent champion of individualism, local government, and responsible public administration. He finds him more interested in public policy than in political power for its own sake. DAI 24:713.

0384 Smith, Richard N. *Thomas E. Dewey and His Times*. New York: Simon & Schuster, 1982.

Chapters 14 and 15 deal with the election of 1948. Smith gives the best account of Dewey's campaign. Notes, bibliography, index.

TOM CONNALLY

0385 Connally, Tom. *My Name is Tom Connally; As Told to Alfred Steinberg*. New York: Crowell, 1954.

Connally was Democratic senator from Texas from 1929 to 1953. Although he opposed the Truman administration's stand on domestic issues, he was a loyal supporter of Truman's foreign policies. Index.

0386 Matheny, David L. "A Comparison of Selected Foreign Policy Speeches of Senator Tom Connally." Ph.D. dissertation, University of Oklahoma, 1965.

Connally was regarded as the chief administration spokesman in the Senate, the originator of a working bipartisan foreign policy, and the chief American troubleshooter in postwar international conferences. He was charged, along with Secretary of State Dean Acheson and President Truman, with formulating a foreign policy that saved Europe at the expense of losing Asia. DAI 26:4119.

J. WILLIAM FULBRIGHT

0387 Coffin, Tristram. *Senator Fulbright: Portrait of a Public Philosopher*. New York: Dutton, 1966.

A Democratic senator from Arkansas (1945–75), Fulbright was first critical of Truman's foreign policy. When the Soviet Union rejected an American plan for the internationalization of atomic weapons, he supported the Truman Doctrine, full funding of the Marshall Plan, and the establishment of the North Atlantic Treaty (NATO). Illustrations, bibliography, index.

0388 Johnson, Hayes, and Gwertzmann, Bernard M. *Fulbright: The Dissenter*. Garden City, NY: Doubleday, 1968.

Fulbright's criticism of Truman's foreign policy is recounted here. While his vote on civil rights issues reflected his Southern background, Fulbright was an outspoken critic of Senator McCarthy. Illustrations, notes, appendix, bibliographic essay, index.

HERBERT HOOVER

See also Chapter 2, *Hoover Commission*.

0389 Hoover, Herbert. *Addresses on the Open Road, 1945–1948*. New York: Van Nostrand, 1949.

0390 Hoover, Herbert. *Addresses on the Open Road, 1948–1950*. Stanford, CA: Stanford University Press, 1951.

0391 Hoover, Herbert. *Addresses on the Open Road, 1950–1955*. Stanford, CA: Stanford University Press, 1955.

These speeches were directed at foreign and domestic policy issues and were generally critical of the Truman administration. Many of the speeches addressed specific issues, such as the need for government reorganization and a return to traditional isolationism—"fortress America." Index.

0392 Mrozek, Donald J. "Progressive Dissenter: Herbert Hoover's Opposition to Truman's Overseas Military Policy." *Annals of Iowa* 43 (1976): 275–91.

Hoover broke in late 1950 with the Truman administration over the policy of creating a large permanent American military force overseas. Notes.

0393 Rogers, Benjamin. " 'Dear Mr. President': The Hoover-Truman Correspondence." *Palimpsest* 55 (1974): 152–58.

Former President Herbert Hoover was much interested in solutions to famines and food shortages around the world. Included here is the correspondence between Hoover and Truman regarding the World Famine Mission (1945–48).

0394 Wilson, Joan Hoff. *Herbert Hoover: Forgotten Progressive*. Boston: Little, Brown, 1975.

Chapter 7, "The Quaker Out of Tune with the World," discusses Hoover's postwar activities in food relief and his critical view of the administration's foreign policy. Bibliographic essay, index.

ESTES KEFAUVER

See also Chapter 6, *Kefauver Committee*.

0395 Fontenay, Charles L. *Estes Kefauver: A Biography*. Knoxville: University of Tennessee Press, 1981.

A political biography of a Senate "outsider" during the late 1940s and 1950s; it is useful for understanding the man and his decisions. Illustrations, notes, bibliography, index.

0396 Gorman, Joseph B. *Kefauver: A Political Biography*. New York: Oxford University Press, 1971.

Kefauver was the representative from Tennessee (1939–49) and senator (1949–63). With the exception of certain civil rights issues Kefauver had a liberal voting record. As chairman of the Senate Crime Investigating Committee (1950–51), he gained national attention. Illustrations, notes, index. See also, Jack Anderson and Fred Blumenthal, *The Kefauver Story* (New York, 1956).

0397 Graham, Hugh D. "Kefauver: A Political Biography." *Tennessee Historical Quarterly* 30 (1971): 413–18.

Graham reviews Joseph Gorman's *Kefauver: A Political Biography* (1971), and examines the enigmatic personality of Estes Kefauver. He concludes

that the senator's primary legislative thrust was the public interest.

0398 McFadyen, Richard E. "Estes Kefauver and the Tradition of Southern Progressivism." *Tennessee Historical Quarterly* 37 (1978): 430–43.

Kefauver's work on the Senate Subcommittee on Antitrust and Monopoly provides considerable insight into his views. His investigation of the pharmaceutical industry brought him to the forefront of the modern consumer movement. Notes.

WILLIAM E. JENNER

0399 Poder, Michael P. "The Senatorial Career of William E. Jenner." Ph.D. dissertation, University of Notre Dame, 1976.

Jenner was a Republican senator from Indiana (1947–59) during which he opposed the Marshall Plan, NATO, the United Nations, and foreign aid, but advocated an aggressive Asian policy, supporting the "unleashing" of Chiang Kai-shek and General MacArthur's Korean strategy. Jenner was also a close friend and supporter of McCarthy and became a prominent Red-hunter. DAI 37:3859-A.

0400 Ross, Rodney J. "Senator William E. Jenner: A Study in Cold War Isolationism." Ph.D. dissertation, Pennsylvania State University, 1973.

A Republican senator from Indiana, Jenner was oriented toward a right-wing viewpoint which was combined with a basic isolationism. DAI 35:1604-A.

LYNDON B. JOHNSON

0401 Caro, Robert A. *The Years of Lyndon Johnson*. Vol. 1: *The Path to Power*. New York: Knopf, 1982.

Although this unflattering volume only covers the years up to 1941, it certainly delineates many of Johnson's character traits and his political connections which would be important during the Truman years. Notes, bibliography, index.

0402 Dugger, Ronnie. *The Politician: The Life and Times of Lyndon Johnson*. New York: Norton, 1982.

This critical biography of Johnson sheds light on his senatorial activities, including those during the Truman years. Notes, bibliography, index.

0403 Evans, Rowland, and Novak, Robert. *Lyndon B. Johnson: The Exercise of Power*. New York: New American Library, 1966.

Johnson was first a representative (1937–49) and then senator (1949–61) during the Truman administration. During his tenure he became increasingly conservative, opposing civil rights legislation, and voting to override Truman's veto of the Taft-Hartley bill. He was also an outspoken advocate of higher defense expenditures. Notes, index.

0404   Miller, Merle. *Lyndon: An Oral Biography*. New York: Putnam's, 1980.

During the Truman era, Johnson was Democratic senator from Texas and assistant majority leader, 1951–53. A staunch supporter of the containment policy, Johnson moved increasingly toward the right in domestic issues, such as civil rights and labor. Notes, bibliography, index.

WILLIAM LANGER

0405   Smith, Glenn H. "Senator William Langer: A Study in Isolationism." Ph.D. dissertation, University of Iowa, 1968.

From the outset of his senatorial career in 1940, Langer was an isolationist. The Republican senator from North Dakota (1941–59) opposed lend-lease, military conscription, the United Nations, collective security arrangements, and especially foreign aid programs, preferring to help the economically deprived at home rather than abroad. DAI 29:1854.

0406   Wilkins, Robert P. "Senator William Langer and National Priorities: An Agrarian Radical's View of American Foreign Policy, 1945–1952." *North Dakota Quarterly* 42 (1974): 42–59.

Langer consistently attacked Truman's foreign policy, especially the exaggerating of the Soviet challenge and the necessary employment of U.S. foreign aid programs. Notes.

VITO MARCANTONIO

0407   Kaner, Norman. "Towards a Minority of One: Vito Marcantonio and American Foreign Policy." Ph.D. dissertation, Rutgers University, 1968.

Marcantonio was congressman from East Harlem from 1934 to 1950. An opponent of Truman's containment policy, he denounced the administration's attempts to bolster Chiang Kai-shek's and Syngman Rhee's regimes. He was the sole dissenter in the vote to send troops to Korea. DAI 29:3952-A.

0408   LaGumina, Salvatore J. *Vito Marcantonio: The People's Politician*. Dubuque, IA: Kendall/Hunt, 1969.

This political biography has two chapters (7 and 8) which deal with the Truman era. Marcantonio was a radical congressman who staunchly supported civil liberties (and opposed the House Un-American Activities Committee), defended American Communists in Congress, and tried to bring Puerto Rican issues to the attention of the administration. Notes, index.

0409   Schaffer, Alan L. "Caucus in a Phone Booth: The Congressional Career of Vito Marcantonio, 1934–1950." Ph.D. dissertation, University of Virginia, 1962.

Marcantonio was a leftist congressman from East Harlem, New York. He voted against the Taft-Hartley Act, against the elimination of price and rent controls, against all anti-Communist legislation, against the Marshall Plan, the Truman Doctrine, NATO, and American intervention in Korea. DAI: 23:3339.

PATRICK A. McCARRAN

0410   Ostrander, Gilman M. *Nevada: The Great Rotten Borough, 1859–1964*. New York: Knopf, 1966.

Senator Patrick A. McCarran, as chairman of the Judiciary Committee (1948–51), opposed many Truman administration policy proposals. See pp. 188–96. Notes.

0411   Pittman, Von Vernon, Jr. "Senator Patrick A. McCarran and the Politics of Containment." Ph.D. dissertation, University of Georgia, 1979.

McCarran (D-NV) become one of the most outspoken critics of the Truman administration's leadership in the realms of foreign and defense policies. He fought against the entry of European displaced persons into this country; he accused the administration of "losing" China; and he supported U.S. relations with Spain. DAI 40:5981-A.

0412   Steinberg, Alfred. "McCarran: Lone Wolf of the Senate." *Harper's* 201 (November 1950): 89–95.

This is a brief biographical sketch which focuses mostly on McCarran's early life.

JOSEPH R. McCARTHY

See also Chapter 6, *Internal Security and Civil Liberties*.

0413   Bayley, Edwin R. *Joe McCarthy and the Press*. Madison: University of Wisconsin Press, 1981.

Senator McCarthy's relationship with the press is explored. Such questions as whether the press helped to create McCarthy or to destroy him are examined. Notes, bibliography, index.

0414   Buckley, William F., Jr., and Bozell, L. Brent. *McCarthy and His Enemies: The Record and Its Meaning*. Chicago: Regnery, 1954.

The authors condemn the liberals for their predictable opposition to McCarthy and then proceed to demonstrate their own right-wing "knee-jerk" response. While the authors have some (a few) qualms about McCarthy's tactics, they applaud his motives and objectives. Appendix, notes, index.

0415 Cook, Fred J. *The Nightmare Decade: The Life and Times of Senator Joe McCarthy*. New York: Random House, 1971.

Cook puts McCarthy in perspective by arguing that McCarthy was more a product of his times than an instigator of attitudes. Bibliography, index.

0416 Deaver, Jean F. "A Study of Senator Joseph R. McCarthy and 'McCarthyism' as Influences upon the New Media and the Evolution of Reportorial Method." Ph.D. dissertation, University of Texas, Austin, 1969.

McCarthy proved the ability of a demagogue to exploit the traditional "objective" press coverage. He confirmed and accelerated the trend toward interpretative news reporting, and this interpretative reporting has become more responsible. DAI 30: 2957-A.

0417 Griffith, Robert. *The Politics of Fear: Joseph R. McCarthy and the Senate*. Lexington: University Press of Kentucky, 1970.

McCarthy's rise to preeminence, Griffith argues, was a result of the dynamics of party politics. He also finds probable cause in America's deep-rooted fear of radicalism and in the atmosphere created by the Cold War. Notes, bibliographic essay, index.

0418 O'Brien, Michael. *McCarthy and McCarthyism in Wisconsin*. Columbia: University of Missouri Press, 1980.

This account includes biographical material on McCarthy, but has as its focal point his political career, 1946–57. Notes, bibliographical essay, index.

0419 Oshinsky, David M. *A Conspiracy So Immense: The World of Joe McCarthy*. New York: Free Press, 1983.

McCarthy is treated even-handedly in this well-written, well-researched biography. It may be read in conjunction with Reeves's biography with profit. Notes, bibliography, index.

0420 Reeves, Thomas C. *The Life and Times of Joe McCarthy*. Briarcliff Manor, NY: Stein & Day, 1981.

This is a thorough and balanced biography of McCarthy. Chapters 7 to 17 are related to the Truman years. Illustrations, notes, bibliography, index.

0421 Reeves, Thomas C. "Tail Gunner Joe: Joseph R. McCarthy and the Marine Corps." *Wisconsin Magazine of History* 62 (1979): 300–313.

Reeves concludes that McCarthy "served the corps and his country ably and with distinction. He

risked his life on several occasions and not entirely for the later political dividend." McCarthy did not enter the corps as a buck private but as a first lieutenant, and did not sustain any wounds in actual combat.

0422 Rovere, Richard. *Senator Joe McCarthy*. Cleveland: World, 1959.

An early account by a skilled journalist, this biography has been influential in shaping historical attitudes toward McCarthy.

RICHARD M. NIXON

0423 Brodie, Fawn M. *Richard Nixon: The Shaping of His Character*. New York: Norton, 1981.

During the Truman administration, Nixon was a member of the House of Representatives (1947–50) and Senate (1950–53). He gained national recognition for his strong anti-Communist stance. Brodie seeks to explain the factors which shaped his political life. Notes, bibliography, index.

0424 Mazo, Earl. *Richard Nixon: A Political and Personal Portrait*. New York: Harper, 1959.

Nixon became a national figure when, as a member of the House Un-American Activities Committee, he pushed the investigation of Alger Hiss. Index.

0425 Nixon, Richard M. *RN: The Memoirs of Richard Nixon*. New York: Warner, 1979.

There are somewhat more than 100 pages which retell Nixon's election to Congress in 1946, his activities on the House Un-American Activities Committee, and his selection as Eisenhower's vice-presidential running mate in 1952. Illustrations, index.

0426 Nixon, Richard M. *Six Crises*. Garden City, NY: Doubleday, 1962.

Among the six crises about which Nixon writes are the Hiss case, which propelled him to national prominence, and the controversy surrounding a "political fund," which he had been accused of using for personal expenses.

SAM RAYBURN

0427 Hairgrove, Kenneth. "Sam Rayburn: Congressional Leader, 1940–1952." Ph.D. dissertation, Texas Tech University, 1974

Rayburn was Speaker of the House from 1940 until his death in 1961, except for the Eightieth Congress. He endorsed most of Truman's foreign policy initiatives, while his support of domestic issues was mixed. DAI 35:2172-A.

0428 Little, Dwayne L. "The Political Leadership of Speaker Sam Rayburn, 1940–1961." Ph.D. dissertation, University of Cincinnati, 1970.

Little finds that Rayburn possessed a unique moderate style, which was founded on personal rather than institutional strength, and had as its objective the reconciling of the disparate Democratic coalition into an effective governing majority. DAI 31: 3476-A.

0429 Steinberg, Alfred. *Sam Rayburn*. New York: Hawthorn Books, 1975.

As Speaker of the House during most of Truman's tenure, Rayburn championed most of Truman's legislative programs and generally supported his foreign policy. Notes, illustrations, bibliography, index.

ADLAI E. STEVENSON

0430 Johnson, Walter, ed. *The Papers of Adlai E. Stevenson*. Vol. 3: *Governor of Illinois, 1949–1953*. Boston: Little, Brown, 1973.

These papers cover the year 1952 (pp. 489–579) as Stevenson moved from reluctant candidate to Democratic nominee for president. Included in this volume is an essay "Korea in Perspective" published as the lead article in *Foreign Affairs* (April 1952). Index.

0431 Martin, John Bartlow. *Adlai Stevenson of Illinois*. Garden City, NY: Doubleday, 1977.

From 1945 to 1948 Stevenson was very active in the United Nations. He was governor of Illinios (1948–52) and was the Democratic presidential candidate in 1952 and 1956. Notes, illustrations, index.

ROBERT A. TAFT

0432 Armstrong, John P. "The Enigma of Senator Taft and American Foreign Policy." *Review of Politics* 17 (1955): 206–31.

Armstrong argues that Taft from the beginning of his Senate career in the 1930s could only judge a foreign policy proposal on the basis of its domestic effects. Consequently, Taft was unable to offer a coherent alternative to the Democratic foreign policy of the 1940s and 1950s.

0433 DeJohn, Samuel, Jr. "Robert A. Taft, Economic Conservatism, and Opposition to United States

Foreign Policy, 1944–1951." Ph.D. dissertation, University of Southern California, 1976.

Taft exercised a direction over party congressional affairs which no other Republican enjoyed, with the exception of Arthur H. Vandenberg, the ranking Republican on the Senate Foreign Relations Committee. DAI 37:7268-A.

0434 Isaacson, Pauline H. "Robert Alphonso Taft: An Assessment of a Persuader." Ph.D. dissertation, University of Minnesota, 1957.

Although the study covers several of Senator Taft's political campaigns, it focuses on the one of 1950. DAI 18:1900.

0435 Matthews, Geoffrey. "Robert A. Taft, the Constitution and American Foreign Policy, 1939–1953." *Journal of Contemporary History* [Great Britain] 17 (1982): 507–22.

Taft opposed American entry into World War II, NATO, and the sending of troops to Korea, not out of isolationism, but as a staunch opponent to the expansion of presidential power. Notes.

0436 McManua, Thomas R. "A Study of Robert A. Taft's Speeches on Social Welfare Issues." Ph.D. dissertation, Ohio State University, 1960.

Senator Taft first opposed and later sponsored legislation on public housing, federal aid to education, and medical care. DAI 21:2406.

0437 McMenamin, Michael. "Anticommunist? Yes. Cold Warrior? No." *Reason* 11 (1979): 34–40.

Robert A. Taft's political career and foreign policy ideals are reviewed with emphasis on the senator's reluctance to become involved in foreign entanglements, his abhorrence of imperialism, and his passion for personal liberty.

0438 Patterson, James T. *Mr. Republican: A Biography of Robert A. Taft*. Boston: Houghton Mifflin, 1972.

Taft led Republican opposition to many of the Truman administration's programs, especially the domestic ones. Chapter 23 of this exceptional biography examines the Taft-Hartley Act. Illustrations, notes, bibliographical note, index.

0439 Ricks, John A., III. "'Mr. Integrity' and McCarthyism: Senator Robert A. Taft and Senator Joseph R. McCarthy." Ph.D. dissertation, University of North Carolina, Chapel Hill, 1974.

Before 1950, Taft had held and deserved the title of "Mr. Integrity" for his impeccable morality; however, when he began to eye the presidency, he adopted anticommunism as an issue. He refused to attack McCarthy because of his own political ambitions and for party harmony. DAI 36:493-A.

0440 Taft, Robert A. *A Foreign Policy for Americans*. Garden City, NY: Doubleday, 1951.

Taft was Republican senator from Ohio, 1939–53. A quite vocal critic of Truman's foreign policy, Taft offers his own views on what our foreign policy should be. While recognizing the Communist threat, he nonetheless was opposed to Greek-Turkish aid, the Marshall Plan, and the North Atlantic Treaty.

0441 Van Dyke, Vernon, and Lane, Edward. "Senator Taft and American Security." *Journal of Politics* 14 (1952): 177–202.

This is an effort to analyze Senator Robert A. Taft's views toward foreign and military policies from the 1930s to 1952. Notes.

0442 White, William S. *The Taft Story*. New York: Harper, 1954.

A staunch conservative, Taft denounced the Nuremberg trials as violating the fundamental principle of American law, while his stands on civil rights reflected the importance he placed on the freedom of the individual. Labor was a particular target, and he was chief architect of the Taft-Hartley Act. Illustrations, index.

STROM THURMOND

See also Chapter 6, *Election of 1948; Dixiecrats.*

0443 Banks, James G. "Strom Thurmond and the Revolt against Modernity." Ph.D. dissertation, Kent State University, 1970.

Since his decision to bolt the Democratic party and run as the Dixiecrat presidential candidate in 1948, Thurmond has been an outspoken critic of all civil rights legislation and liberal policies in general. This study recounts the political life of Thurmond and attempts to make some estimate of his historical significance. DAI 32:348-A.

0444 Lachicotte, Alberta. *Rebel Senator: Strom Thurmond of South Carolina*. New York: Devin-Adair, 1966.

During Truman's tenure Thurmond was governor of South Carolina (1947–51). Opposed to the civil rights platform of the Democratic party in the 1948 election, Thurmond became the presidential candidate of the "Dixiecrats." Illustrations.

ARTHUR H. VANDENBERG

0445 Anderson, Joel E., Jr. "The 'Operational Code' Belief System of Senator Arthur H. Vandenberg: An Application of the George Construct." Ph.D. dissertation, University of Michigan, 1974.

Using nonquantitative methods of analysis, this study employs a revised version of Alexander George's construct to study Vandenberg's senatorial career. DAI 35:3085-A.

0446 Barber, James D., ed. *Political Leadership in American Government*. Boston: Little, Brown, 1964.

Dean Acheson comments on Senator Arthur H. Vandenberg's role as a Republican party leader on foreign policy issues (pp. 74–83).

0447 Eldersveld, A. Martin. "A Review and Thematic Analysis of Arthur H. Vandenberg's Senate Addresses on Foreign Policy." Ph.D. dissertation, University of Michigan, 1960.

This study examines thirty-two major foreign policy speeches by Vandenberg (1934–49); eighteen were delivered prior to World War II, the remaining fourteen during the postwar period. DAI 21:2404.

0448 Gazell, James A. "Arthur Vandenberg, Internationalism, and the United Nations." *Political Science Quarterly* 88 (1973): 375–94.

Vandenberg shifted his position from isolationism to that of a leading spokesman for the United Nations. This slow transformation is examined in detail. Notes.

0449 Gregg, Richard G. "A Rhetorical Re-Examination of Arthur Vandenberg's 'Dramatic Conversion', January 10, 1945." *Quarterly Journal of Speech* 61 (1975): 154–68.

An outspoken, prewar isolationist, Senator Vandenberg is believed to have announced his conversion to internationalism in an effort to persuade Roosevelt to clarify his foreign policy. During the Truman years, Vandenberg would become a champion of bipartisanship in foreign affairs. Notes.

0450 Hudson, Daryl J. "Vandenberg Reconsidered: Senate Resolution 239 and American Foreign Policy." *Diplomatic History* 1 (1977): 46–63.

This essay argues that Vandenberg was a major influence in the determination of American foreign policy during the Truman administration. This is evident in the drafting of the Vandenberg Resolution. Notes.

0451 Patterson, J. W. "Arthur Vandenberg's Rhetorical Strategy in Advancing Bipartisan Foreign Policy." *Quarterly Journal of Speech* 56 (1970): 284–95.

Senator Arthur H. Vandenberg employed a rhetorical strategy (1943–49) in an effort to force Roosevelt and Truman to share decision-making powers in foreign policy matters.

0452 Patterson, J. W. "A Study of the Changing Views in Selected Foreign Policy Speeches of Senator Arthur H. Vandenberg, 1937–1949." Ph.D. dissertation, University of Oklahoma, 1961.

While Vandenberg changed the means by which he felt the United States should pursue its policy objectives, his fundamental views on those objectives remained constant: (1) national security, (2) maximum sovereignty for the United States, (3) peace and justice, and (4) an appropriate check and balance between the executive and congressional branches of the federal government. DAI 22:943.

0453 Vandenberg, Arthur H., Jr., ed. *The Private Papers of Senator Vandenberg*. Boston: Houghton Mifflin, 1952.

Edited by his son, this collection of the senator's personal papers covers the decade 1941 to 1951 and includes such topics as Yalta, MacArthur, the atom bomb, the Marshall Plan, and the 1948 election. Notes, index.

0454 Yang, Ryh-hsiuh. "The Role of Chairman Arthur H. Vandenberg of the Senate Foreign Relations Committee in the 80th Congress, 1947–1948." Ph.D. dissertation, New School for Social Research, 1966.

Vandenberg was instrumental in forging a bipartisan foreign policy. He played a decisive role as one of the architects of crucial policies, such as the Truman Doctrine, the Marshall Plan, and the Vandenberg Resolution. DAI 28:757-A.

KENNETH S. WHERRY

0455 Dalstrom, Harl A. "Kenneth S. Wherry." Ph.D. dissertation, University of Nebraska, 1965.

Wherry was Republican senator from Nebraska. He was an opponent of most Fair Deal legislation and of Truman's foreign policy. An isolationist, he believed that only through the maintenance of a strong nuclear deterrent could the United States find security. 27:1750.

0456 Stromer, Marvin E. *The Making of a Political Leader: Kenneth S. Wherry and the United States Senate*. Lincoln: University of Nebraska Press, 1969.

Wherry was senator from Nebraska (1943–51) and Republican floor leader (1949–51). He opposed most of the domestic and foreign policies of the Truman administration. Notes, illustrations, appendixes, bibliography, index.

OTHERS

0457 Bloom, Sol. *Autobiography of Sol Bloom*. New York: Putnam, 1948.

Bloom was chairman of the Foreign Affairs Committee from 1939 to 1947. He served as a delegate to the Rio Conference of 1947 and was a representative to the United Nations. Index.

0458 Celler, Emanuel. *You Never Leave Brooklyn*. New York: John Day, 1953.

Celler was the Democratic representative from New York from 1923 to 1973. During the Truman administration he was chairman of the Judiciary Committee and a vocal critic of the postwar anti-Communist crusade. Index.

0459 Chenoweth, Richard R. "Francis Case: A Political Biography." Ph.D. dissertation, University of Nebraska, Lincoln, 1977.

Case was a Republican senator from South Dakota (1937–62) and reflected a political conservatism. He viewed communism as the "enemy" of all that was good in America and believed that the Soviet Union directed the "enemy" in the United States; hence, he argued that Communist infiltration must be uprooted and the Soviet Union must be curbed by American military strength. He is also remembered for the Case Labor Bill (1946) which called for the use of federal power to curb unions. DAI 38:1596-A.

0460 Douglas, Paul H. *In The Fullness of Time: The Memoirs of Paul H. Douglas*. New York: Harcourt Brace Jovanovich, 1971.

Douglas was a Democratic senator from Illinois (1949–67). As a liberal he worked for repeal or modification of the Taft-Hartley Act, toward providing good housing, and toward fighting "pork barrel" projects. A vigorous foe of Communist expansion, Douglas was a consistent support of Truman's foreign policy. Illustrations, index.

0461 Fausold, Martin L. *James W. Wadsworth, Jr.: The Gentleman from New York*. Syracuse, NY: Syracuse University Press, 1975.

Always interested in defense programs, Wadsworth (R-NY) initiated and served as vice-chairman of the House's committee to study postwar military planning—which prepared the way for the Unification Act of 1947. While he supported the Truman administration's foreign policies program, he disagreed with most of its domestic proposals.

0462 Felsenthal, Edward. "Kenneth Douglas McKellar: The Rich Uncle of the T.V.A." *West Tennessee Historical Society Papers* 20 (1966): 108–22.

Senator McKellar, because he opposed certain features of the TVA program, gave the impression that he was an enemy of the project. A closer look finds that McKellar was instrumental in the development and passage of the bill, and lobbied for continued appropriations, 1933–53. Notes.

0463 Goodno, Floyd R. "Walter H. Judd: Spokesman for China in the United States House of Representatives." Ph.D. dissertation, Oklahoma State University, 1970.

Goodno seeks to explain why Judd gained the title of China expert, to ascertain his role in formulating a revised attitude toward racial restrictions, to assess his role in formulating the doctrines of the new isolationists, and to judge his influence in the early months of the Eisenhower administration. DAI 31:5299-A.

0464 Griffith, Winthrop. *Humphrey: A Candid Biography.* New York: William Morrow, 1965.

Humphrey was Democratic senator from Minnesota during the Truman administration. Initially quite liberal, he drifted toward the center in 1950, advocating a strong loyalty-security program and defending the postponement of Fair Deal legislation. Also see Robert Sherrill and Harry Ernst, *The Drugstore Liberal* (New York, 1968). Illustrations, index.

0465 Henderson, Cary S. "Congressman John Taber of Auburn: Politics and Federal Appropriations, 1923–1962." Ph.D. dissertation, Duke University, 1964.

Taber, as a member of the Deficiencies Subcommittee of the House Appropriations Committee, held an influential role over foreign aid requests. With a long record of negative votes against the Truman administration, he used his position to reduce appropriations, sometimes very unrealistically. DAI 25:1174.

0466 Huthmacher, J. Joseph. *Senator Robert F. Wagner and the Rise of Urban Liberalism.* New York: Atheneum, 1968.

In the immediate postwar years (1945–49), Wagner sided with the consumers and workers against the farmer-businessman bloc. The latter wanted inflationary conditions (immediate ending of all controls) while Wagner fought for controls (extension of the OPA) he thought necessary for an orderly and equitable conversion. He resigned in poor health after the passage of the Taft-Hartley Act. Bibliography, index.

0467 Hyman, Sidney. *The Lives of William Benton.* Chicago: University of Chicago Press, 1969.

Benton served as assistant secretary of state for public affairs (1945–47) and senator (D-CT) from 1949 to 1953. An opponent of McCarthy, he was defeated for reelection in 1952. Index.

0468 Kemper, Donald J. *Decade of Fear: Senator Hennings and Civil Liberties.* Columbia: University of Missouri Press, 1965.

In the turbulent decade of the 1950s, Thomas C. Hennings (D-MO) was a leading opponent of Senator McCarthy and a proponent of civil liberties. This work focuses on Hennings's contribution to the cause of civil liberties. Notes, bibliography, index.

0469 Kirwin, Harry W. *The Inevitable Success: Herbert R. O'Conor.* Westminster, MD: Newman Press, 1962.

O'Conor was Democratic senator from Maryland (1947–53). He served on the subcommittee to investigate the affairs of the Institute of Pacific Relations and was a member of Kefauver's Senate Crime Committee. Notes, illustrations, index.

0470 Leary, William M., Jr. "Smith of New Jersey: a Biography of H. Alexander Smith, United States Senator from New Jersey, 1944–1959." Ph.D. dissertation, Princeton University, 1966.

Smith, an influential Republican member of the Foreign Relations Committee, was a strong internationalist. He supported the United Nations, promoted postwar economic cooperative measures, and urged bipartisanship in foreign relations. DAI 27:2119.

0471 Leslie, Jacques. "H. R. Gross: The Conscience of Uncle Sucker." *Washington Monthly* 3 (1971): 36–44.

The Iowa Republican representative was known for his one-man crusades (1948–71) against what he found to be irresponsible government spending.

0472 Levine, Erwin L. *Theodore Francis Green: The Washington Years, 1937–1960.* Providence: Brown University Press, 1971.

Green was senator from Rhode Island (1937–60). He was a staunch advocate of labor, attacking the Taft-Hartley Act, and an avowed internationalist. Notes, index.

0473 Loth, David. *A Long Way Forward: The Biography of Congresswoman Frances P. Bolton.* New York: Longmans, Green, 1957.

Frances Bolton was Republican congresswoman from Ohio (1940–69). Although an ardent defender of women's rights and even an advocate of the conscription of women, she was a staunch conservative on other issues, such as Taft-Hartley, and a strong anti-Communist. Index.

0474 MacNeil, Neil. *Dirksen: Portrait of a Public Man.* New York: World, 1970.

Dirksen was Republican representative from Illinois, 1933–48, and senator, 1951–69. During the Truman administration he backed much Fair Deal legislation but voted for the Taft-Hartley Act. As senator he increasingly attacked Truman's foreign policy. Illustrations, index.

0475 Maddox, Robert F. *The Senatorial Career of Harley Martin Kilgore.* New York: Garland, 1981.

Chapter 5 discusses Kilgore's work on the Truman Committee, which studied the wartime industrial mobilization, while Chapter 6 deals with reconversion issues. Chapter 7 emphasizes Kilgore's interest in creating a National Science Foundation. The close relations of Kilgore and Truman are highlighted. Notes, bibliography, index.

0476　Martin, Joe. *My Fifty Years in Politics; As Told to Robert J. Donovan.* New York: McGraw-Hill, 1960.

Martin was Republican representative from Massachusetts (1925–67) and Speaker of the House (1947–49). He opposed most of Truman's domestic policy, and clashed with Truman's Korean policies. Index.

0477　Morgan, Anne Hodges. *Robert S. Kerr: The Senate Years.* Norman: University of Oklahoma Press, 1977.

Kerr was Democratic senator from Oklahoma (1948–63). A leading champion of the oil and gas industry, Kerr gained an appointment to the Finance Committee where he waged a vigorous defense of tax breaks to the oil industry. Notes, illustrations, bibliography, index.

0478　Nevins, Allan. *Herbert H. Lehman and His Era.* New York: Scribner, 1963.

Lehman had been governor of New York and was senator from New York (1949–57). He backed most of Truman's Fair Deal policies, was an outspoken critic of McCarthy, and fought for liberalized immigration policies. Illustrations, notes, index.

0479　Nurse, Ronald J. "America Must Not Sleep: The Development of John F. Kennedy's Foreign Policy Attitudes, 1947–1960." Ph.D. dissertation, Michigan State University 1971.

John F. Kennedy's attitudes toward foreign policy during his years in Congress are examined. The author finds change and continuity, as well as an early Cold War state of mind. DAI 32:5159-A.

0480　Paul, Justus F. *Senator Hugh Butler and Nebraska Republicanism.* Lincoln: Nebraska State Historical Society, 1976.

Butler was senator from Nebraska (1941–54). Throughout his tenure he was a member of the Republican "Old Guard," defending farm and cattle interests, denouncing internationalism and foreign aid, and opposing all manifestations of the New Deal and Fair Deal. Notes, bibliographical essay, index.

0481　Peterson, F. Ross. *Prophet Without Honor: Glen Taylor and the Fight for American Liberalism.* Lexington: University of Kentucky Press, 1974.

A freshman senator from Idaho, Taylor broke with Truman over the administration's postwar foreign policy. He ran as the vice-presidential candidate with Henry Wallace in the 1948 election. Footnotes, bibliographical essay, index.

0482　Schapsmeier, Edward L., and Schapsmeier, Frederick H. "Scott W. Lucas of Havana: His Rise and Fall as Majority Leader in the United States Senate." *Journal of the Illinois State Historical Society* 70 (1977): 302–20.

Elected Democratic Senate whip in 1946, Lucas supported Truman's 1948 renomination. After the 1948 victory, Lucas became Senate majority leader until he lost his seat to Everett Dirksen in 1950. Lucas was a supporter of Fair Deal legislation and Truman's foreign policies. Illustrations, notes.

0483　Scheele, Henry Z. *Charlie Halleck: A Political Biography.* New York: Exposition, 1966.

Halleck was Republican representative from Indiana (1935–69), and majority leader (1947–49). He was a vigorous foe of organized labor, criticized U.S. entry into the Korean War, and opposed Truman's dismissal of MacArthur. Notes, appendixes, index.

0484　Shadegg, Stephen C. *Clare Boothe Luce.* New York: Simon & Schuster, 1970.

Luce, a journalist, was a Republican representative from Connecticut (1943–47). An ardent internationalist, she criticized Truman's foreign policy and held Truman responsible for Chiang's defeat and the fall of China to the Communists. Illustrations, index.

0485　Smith, A. Robert. *Tiger in the Senate: The Biography of Wayne Morse.* Garden City, NY: Doubleday, 1962.

Morse was Republican senator from Oregon (1945–52). He allied himself with the internationalist wing of the Republican party in foreign affairs, while on domestic issues he favored the views of organized labor. An outspoken critic of McCarthy, he joined five other Republicans in signing Margaret Chase Smith's "Declaration of Conscience." Illustrations.

0486　Smith, Margaret Chase. *Declaration of Conscience.* Garden City, NY: Doubleday, 1972.

Smith was Republican representative from Maine (1940–48) and senator (1949–73). In 1950 she and five other Republicans made their "Declaration of Conscience" protesting the tactics of McCarthy and accusing their colleagues of aiding and abetting such behavior. Appendixes, index.

0487　Stoesen, Alexander R. "The Senatorial Career of Claude D. Pepper." Ph.D. dissertation, University of North Carolina, 1965.

Pepper was Democratic senator from Florida from 1936 to 1950. A militant liberal, he sought a higher minimum wage, opposed the Taft-Hartley Act, and proposed a federal health insurance plan. Initially opposed to the Truman Doctrine, he eventually accepted the realities of the Cold War and gave U.S. policy his support. DAI 26:3918.

0488 Taylor, John R. "Homer E. Capehart: United States Senator, 1944–1962." Ph.D. dissertation, Ball State University, 1977.

A Republican senator, Capehart is studied here as a "cold warrior." Chapter 3 examines Capehart's career during the Truman administration. DAI 38:1607-A.

0489 Voorhis, Jerry. *Confessions of a Congressman*. Garden City, NY: Doubleday, 1947.

Chapter 22 relates events at the close of World War II, while Chapter 23 recounts how Voorhis lost an election contest in 1946 with Richard M. Nixon.

0490 Wilkinson, J. Harvie, III. *Harry Byrd and the Changing Face of Virginia Politics, 1945–66*. Charlottesville: University Press of Virginia, 1968.

Byrd was Democratic senator from Virginia (1933–65). During the Truman era, Byrd actively attempted to obstruct the president's Fair Deal program and was a leader in efforts to block civil rights legislation. Notes, appendixes, bibliography, index.

4

Domestic Affairs: Agriculture, Business, the Economy, Labor, and Veterans

Domestic matters, largely economic in nature, occupied a great deal of national attention during the immediate postwar years and required a considerable amount of Truman's time. These issues involved reconversion, agriculture, energy, housing, labor, and general fiscal and economic problems. The retrospective views of a number of former Truman administration officials, who played active roles in developing policy, are contained in Francis H. Heller, ed., *Economics in the Truman Administration* (#491).

The most current studies dealing with economic conversion, from wartime to peacetime production, and decontrol of wages and prices are generally in the form of dissertations. However, Herman M. Somers, *Presidential Agency: The Office of War Mobilization and Reconversion* (#498), and Joel Seidman, *American Labor from Defense to Reconversion* (#503) introduce many of the basic issues. Clinton P. Anderson, *Outsider in the Senate: Senator Clinton Anderson's Memoirs* (#261) reviews his tenure as secretary of agriculture, 1945–48, and relates his conflicts with Chester Bowles of the Office of Price Administration over rationing and subsidies. For Bowles's position, see Chapters 10 and 11 of his *Promises to Keep: My Years in Public Life, 1941– 1969* (#311).

Agricultural policies often were contentious. Allen J. Matusow, *Farm Policies and Politics in the Truman Years* (#523), and Reo M. Christenson, *The Brannan Plan: Farm Politics and Policy* (#533) reveal the issues and factions involved in agricultural politics. Barton J. Bernstein's essay, "Clash of Interests: The Postwar Battle Between the Office of Price Administration and the Department of Agriculture" (#531), focuses on farm politics and reconversion. Conservation issues also arose and are related in Elmo Richardson, *Dams, Parks and Politics: Resource Development and Preservation in the Truman-Eisenhower Era* (#558).

Although energy issues did not take on a crisis status during the Truman years, many of the future problems were identified. Chapters 1 and 2 of Craufurd D. Goodwin, ed., *Energy Policy in Perspective: Today's Problems, Yesterday's Solutions* (#580) argues that the Truman administration recognized the need for a coherent national energy policy but failed to develop one. Lucius J. Barker, "The Supreme Court as Policy Maker: The Tidelands Oil Controversy" (#586) reviews the struggle between Truman and Congress over federal ownership of the off-shore oil.

A critical housing shortage existed at the end of World War II, a shortage that was exacerbated by the demands of returning veterans for houses. Richard O. Davies, *Housing Reform During the Truman Administration* (#600) is a survey of reforms and policy failures. Barton J. Bernstein, "Reluctance and Resistance: Wilson Wyatt and Veterans' Housing in the Truman Administration" (#599) reveals the crippling effect that bureaucratic competition had on efforts to obtain low-cost veterans' housing.

President Truman's Council of Economic Advisers, July 1949. L to R: Charles S. Murphy; David E. Bell; Leon H. Keyserling, vice chairman; Robert C. Turner; Edwin G. Nourse, chairman; and John D. Clark. *US Government photo*.

Surprisingly few published scholarly studies have probed the successes and failures of World War II veterans' programs. Davis R. B. Ross, *Preparing for Ulysses: Politics and Veterans During World War II* (#842) examines the legislative origins of most veterans' programs which came into existence during the early Truman years. Keith W. Olson, *The G. I. Bill, the Veterans and the Colleges* (#847) reviews the provisions for higher education.

The passage of the Employment Act of 1946 was one indication that the nation's leaders recognized the mounting importance of the federal government in the shaping of the nation's economy. This act created the President's Council of Economic Advisers to assist the executive branch in its assessment of the potential effects of its economic programs. E. Ray Canterbery, *The President's Council of Economic Advisers* (#661), and Edward S. Flash, Jr., *Economic Advice and Presidential Leadership* (#662) evaluate the council's activities and, generally, hold that Truman did not fully exploit its potential.

The Truman administration's fiscal policies are examined by Lester Chandler, *Inflation in the United States, 1940–1948* (#711), and Seymour E. Harris, *The Economics of Mobilization and Inflation* (#714). An overview of federal policies may be found in A. E. Holmans, *United States Fiscal Policy, 1945–1959* (#688) which provides considerable data on the Truman years.

The Employment Act of 1946 was a compromise of the full employment idea. Stephen K. Bailey, *Congress Makes a Law: The Story Behind the Employment Act of 1946* (#735) traces the development of the act, while Arthur F. McClure, *The Truman Administration and the Problems of Postwar Labor, 1945–1948* (#727) deals with labor's demands. The Taft-Hartley Act (1947), which considerably revised the Wagner Act, is examined by R. Alton Lee, *Truman and Taft-Hartley: A Question of Mandate* (#746).

Truman's most dramatic personal intervention into domestic economic matters was his 1952 seizure of the steel mills. Maeva Marcus, *Truman and the Steel Seizure Case: The Limits of Presidential Power* (#653) reviews the legal aspects of his actions, including the Supreme Court's ruling against Truman. John L. Blackman, Jr., *Presidential Seizures in Labor Disputes* (#649) places Truman's actions in historical perspective by examining seventy-one instances of presidential seizure—eleven of which occurred during the Truman administration.

0491 Heller, Francis H., ed. *Economics in the Truman Administration*. Lawrence: Regents Press of Kansas, 1981.

These useful essays and comments came from a conference (1979) which brought together a number

of individuals who had played an active role in developing economic policy during the Truman years. Bibliography, index.

Reconversion and Decontrol

0492 Alexander, Thomas G. "Utah's Small Arms Ammunition Plant During World War II." *Pacific Historical Review* 34 (1965): 185–96.

The economic effects (1941–48) of a $19 million plant constructed by the federal government and eventually sold at a fraction of cost is examined. Notes.

0493 Ballard, Jack S. "The Shock of Peace: Military and Economic Demobilization After World War II." Ph.D. dissertation, University of California, Los Angeles, 1974.

Complex military and economic problems faced the United States after World War II. Despite the Truman administration's uneven and at times hesitant handling of the major economic challenges, the nation moved through the immediate postwar months reasonably well. DAI 35:2163-A.

0494 Cady, Darrel. "The Truman Administration's Reconversion Policies, 1945–1947." Ph.D. dissertation, University of Kansas, 1974.

Truman introduced a political economy of abundance which offered a solution to the underconsumption that had plagued the economy for two decades. To match the nation's ability to mass produce, his reconversion policies encouraged the development of an equivalent capacity among Americans to mass consume. DAI 35:6049-A.

0495 Chandler, Lester V., and Wallace, Donald H., eds. *Economic Mobilization and Stabilization*. New York: Holt, 1951.

Drawing on the experience of the United States in World War II, the essays cover such topics as use of manpower, facilities, and materials; war finance and stabilization; price and wage controls; and rationing. Bibliography, index.

0496 Committee on Public Administration Cases. *The Reconversion Controversy*. Washington, DC: The Committee, 1950.

Prior to the conclusion of World War II problems of reconversion began to intrude. This study by

Jack Peltason discusses those issues and the evolution of policy. Chronology, appendix.

0497 Shepard, David H. "Reconversion, 1939–1946: Images, Plans, Realities." Ph.D. dissertation, University of Wisconsin, Madison, 1981.

Shepard looks at the various efforts geared toward postwar planning, which culminated in the Employment Act of 1946 whereby governmental action in the economy was no longer rejected but was embraced as inevitable and even desirable. DAI 42:3724.

0498 Somers, Herman M. *Presidential Agency: The Office of War Mobilization and Reconversion*. Cambridge: Harvard University Press, 1950.

This volume is arranged topically, rather than chronologically, therefore materials dealing with the Truman years are scattered throughout. The role of Dr. John Steelman is discussed on pages 95ff, while Chapter 6 contains material dealing with industrial reconversion. Footnotes, index.

0499 U.S. Office of Contract Settlement. *A History of War Contract Terminations and Settlements*. Washington, DC: July 1947.

This pamphlet provides an excellent summary of the problems and costs associated with terminating wartime contracts. Tables, bibliography.

ECONOMIC DECONTROL

0500 Bartels, Andrew H. "The Politics of Price Control: The Office of Price Administration and the Dilemmas of Economic Stabilization, 1940–1946." Ph.D. dissertation, Johns Hopkins University, 1980.

Bartels examines how interest group demands, institutional imperatives, and ideologies shaped and reshaped price controls in the 1940s. Attention is paid to Truman's lifting of controls in 1946 and the ensuing inflation. DAI 41:768.

0501 Bernstein, Barton J. "The Removal of War Production Controls on Business, 1944–1946." *Business History Review* 39 (1965): 243–60.

Truman is criticized for not actively supporting Chester Bowles's efforts to maintain sufficient government economic controls to achieve an "orderly reconversion, aid small business, protect consumers, and restrain inflation." Notes.

0502 Bernstein, Barton J. "The Truman Administration and Its Reconversion Wage Policy." *Labor History* 6 (1965): 214–31.

Conflict among administrative councils and inexperienced executive leadership, together with competing pressures from labor and management

resulted in the Truman administration losing support of the latter two groups and heightened inflation. Notes.

0503 Seidman, Joel. *American Labor from Defense to Reconversion*. Chicago: University of Chicago Press, 1953.

The last four chapters deal with the Truman administration's efforts to further reconversion. Notes, index.

0504 Wright, Peter M. "Wyoming and the O.P.A.: The Postwar Politics of Decontrol." *Annuals of Wyoming* 51 (1980): 25–33.

Wyoming Senator Joseph C. O'Mahoney sponsored the Truman administration's plan to establish cooperation among labor, management, and consumers to control postwar inflation. Illustrations, notes.

WAR SURPLUS PROPERTY

0505 Cain, Louis, and Neumann, George. "Planning for Peace: The Surplus Property Act of 1944." *Journal of Economic History* 41 (1981): 129–37.

The Surplus Property Act (1944) established social objectives for the disposal of war surplus: (1) small businesses were to benefit, and (2) concentration was to be reduced. Notes, comments.

0506 Farmer, James H. "Saga of the Civil Forts: The Era of the W.A.A. and the 'Years of Plenty', 1946–1947." *American Aviation Historical Society Journal* 22 (1977): 292–302.

Surplus B-17 Flying Fortress bombers were stored by the War Assets Administration and offered for sale to civilians; eventually most were scrapped.

0507 Steinmeyer, George W. "Disposition of Surplus War Property: An Administrative History, 1944–1949." Ph.D. dissertation, University of Oklahoma, 1969.

The Surplus War Property Administration (1944) was supplemented later that year by the Surplus Property Board. This study focuses on various aspects of its operation. DAI 30:3414-A.

Agriculture and the Environment

See also Chapter 3, *Clinton P. Anderson*.

0508 Block, William J. *The Separation of the Farm Bureau and the Extension Service: Political Issue in* *a Federal System.* Urbana: University of Illinois Press, 1960.

This analytical survey focuses on the often highly partisan struggle between federal bureaucracies, agricultural colleges, and farm groups from 1939 to 1956 when the separation was mandated. Bibliography, index.

0509 Bowers, Douglas E. "The Research and Marketing Act of 1946 and Its Effects on Agricultural Marketing Research." *Agricultural History* 56 (1982): 249–63.

An expanded program of marketing research by the Department of Agriculture resulted from this act; however, the act was never funded at anticipated levels. It never narrowed the spread between wholesale and retail prices. Notes.

0510 Chin, Sean Bun. "Exhaustible Resources and Technological Change in United States Agriculture, 1940–1969." Ph.D. dissertation, University of Missouri, 1973.

This statistical study seeks to determine the effect of seven variables on aggregate farm output from 1940 to 1969. DAI 35:63-A.

0511 Cochrane, Willard W., and Ryan, Mary E. *American Farm Policy, 1948–1973.* Minneapolis: University of Minnesota Press, 1976.

This study is arranged topically. The numerous charts, however, provide annual statistics valuable for the Truman years and useful for comparison. Charts, notes, index.

0512 Dobson, Gordon J. "The Use of Intergovernmental Agreements in the Marketing of Agricultural Commodities, with Particular Reference to the International Wheat Agreement of 1949." Ph.D. dissertation, Ohio State University, 1953.

A significant aspect of the Wheat Agreement was the manner in which it was able to be dovetailed in with domestic farm programs. DAI 19:1585.

0513 Forsythe, James L. "World Cotton Technology Since World War II." *Agricultural History* 54 (1980), 208–22.

At the end of World War II, the United States developed programs to dispose of surplus cotton to Germany and Japan, for humanitarian reasons and to promote American export markets. Cotton fiber technology developed to compete with synthetics. Notes.

0514 Hadwiger, Don F. "Farm Organizations and United States Foreign Trade Policy, 1946–1955." Ph.D. dissertation, State University of Iowa, 1956.

The national farm organizations were more interested in finding foreign markets than in preventing imports. They favored freer trade and initiated and developed into law proposals for promoting commodity exports. DAI 16:1935.

0515 McGovern, George, ed. *Agricultural Thought in the Twentieth Century.* Indianapolis: Bobbs-Merrill, 1967.

Part 4 includes the Truman era, focusing on such issues as collective bargaining, payment programs, surpluses, and migratory labor issues. Index.

0516 Raid, Howard D. "Analysis of the Operation of the Federal Crop Insurance Wheat Program in Ten Selected Ohio Counties, 1946–1952." Ph.D. dissertation, Ohio State University, 1953.

Because of large cotton losses, Congress closed the national program in 1948 but immediately inaugurated one on a limited experimental basis. This study reviews the history of crop insurance and the federal government's efforts to provide effective coverage of damages. DAI 20:2064.

0517 Rau, Allan. *Agricultural Policy and Trade Liberalization in the United States, 1934–1956: A Study of Conflicting Policies.* Genève: E. Droz, 1957.

Between 1949 and 1951 the United States exported more than one-third of its wheat, cotton, and rice production, and approximately one-quarter of its soybeans, tobacco, rye, grains, sorghum, etc. Appendix, bibliography.

0518 U.S. Commission on Civil Rights. *Equal Opportunity in Farm Programs: An Appraisal of Services Rendered by Agencies of the United States Department of Agriculture; a Report.* Washington, DC: G.P.O., 1965.

This report is useful for background information and statistics, but its emphasis is on the 1960s. There are statistical comparisons between 1950 and 1960. Bibliography, tables.

0519 Wilcox, Walter W. *Farmers in the Second World War.* Ames: Iowa State University Press, 1947.

Together with Bela Gold's *Wartime Economic Planning in Agriculture* (New York, 1944), this study provides a dated but still useful background to postwar food and agricultural policies.

0520 Wilson, Theodore A., and McKinzie, Richard D. "The Food Crusade of 1947." *Prologue* 3 (1971): 136–52.

In 1947 the Truman administration tried, unsuccessfully, to persuade the American people to accept voluntary food rationing to meet a potentially grave European food crisis. Notes, illustrations.

FARM POLICIES AND POLITICS

See also Chapter 6, *Election of 1948.*

0521 Kirkendall, Richard S. *Social Scientists and Farm Politics in the Age of Roosevelt.* Columbia: University of Missouri Press, 1966.

Although the thrust of this book deals with agricultural planning during the Roosevelt administration, some attention is directed to the early Truman years. Notes, bibliography, index.

0522 Livermore, Charles H. "James G. Patton: Nineteenth-Century Populist, Twentieth-Century Organizer, Twenty-First Century Visionary." Ph.D. dissertation, University of Denver, 1976.

During the Truman years Patton (president of the National Farmers' Union) spoke out for an equalitarian society, as defined in terms of the family farmer, and for greater economic democracy. DAI 37: 1173-A.

0523 Matusow, Allen J. *Farm Policies and Politics in the Truman Years.* Cambridge: Harvard University Press, 1967.

During the Truman administration farm policies played a critical role in both domestic and foreign affairs. Truman was faced with resolving the problems of surplus as well as famine. Notes, index.

0524 McCune, Wesley. "Farmers in Politics." *Annals of the American Academy of Political and Social Science* 319 (1958): 41–51.

McCune surveys the farm vote (1948–56) and assesses the impact which this vote had on policy-making. He also examines the political positions of various farm organizations.

0525 Peterson, William H. *The Great Farm Problem.* Chicago: Regnery, 1959.

This general account puts the Agricultural Act of 1948 and the Brannan Plan in historical perspective (see pp. 120–28). In this same vein are Ezra Taft Benson's *Freedom to Farm* (New York, 1960) (see Chapters 11 and 12); and Troy J. Cauley's *Agriculture in an Industrial Economy: The Agrarian Crisis* (New York, 1956).

0526 Ryan, Thomas G. "Farm Prices and the Farm Vote in 1948." *Agricultural History*, 54 (1980): 387–401.

Ryan demonstrates that, contrary to usual analysis, most farm prices were rising or stable in 1948. Thus the farmer's support for Truman (and the Democratic party) followed the historical trend of supporting incumbents when farm prices are high. Tables, notes.

0527 Saloutos, Theodore. "Agricultural Organizations and Farm Policy in the South After World War II." *Agricultural History* 53 (1979): 377–404.

In the South the membership of the American Farm Bureau Federation outstripped the older National Farmers' Union and the Grange during 1946 to 1976, as it took more conservative positions on issues. Notes.

0528 Schapsmeier, Edward L., and Schapsmeier, Frederick H. "Farm Policy from FDR to Eisenhower: Southern Democrats and the Politics of Agriculture." *Agricultural History* 53 (1979): 352–71.

Southern agriculture has defied Roosevelt, Truman, and Eisenhower on the substance of farm programs, but favored federal intervention in keeping prices high. Notes, comments.

0529 Waters, Jerry B. "The Conflicts in Agricultural Policy Making." Ph.D. dissertation, Michigan State University, 1965.

Preservation of the family farm has been the overarching goal of agricultural policy. Price supports and production controls have fallen far short of their promise, yet these policies remain immune to significant alteration. DAI 27:810.

COMMODITY AND PRICE CONTROLS

0530 Benedict, Murray R., and Stine, Oscar C. *The Agricultural Commodity Programs: Two Decades of Experience.* New York: Twentieth Century Fund, 1956.

Federal legislation aimed at improving farm prices was largely tied to specific farm commodities. This study examines policy and prices of specific commodities (1934–54). It is also a supplementary companion volume to Benedict's *Can We Solve the Farm Problem?* (1955). Extensive tables, index.

0531 Bernstein, Barton J. "Clash of Interests: The Postwar Battle Between the Office of Price Administration and the Department of Agriculture." *Agricultural History* 41 (1967): 45–57.

The major issues between the Office of Price Administration and the Department of Agriculture after World War II were the elimination of subsidies on agricultural products and the termination of price controls on food. Agriculture Secretary Clinton Anderson pressed for the prompt elimination of both; Truman vacillated but was forced to end both in 1946. Notes.

0532 Bernstein, Barton J. "The Postwar Famine and Price Controls, 1946." *Agricultural History* 38 (1964): 235–40.

When the administration reluctantly raised the price of corn and wheat on 8 May 1946, grain that had been set aside for livestock was marketed, making it possible for the United States to meet export commitments; however, the food prices at home went up. Notes.

0533 Christenson, Reo M. *The Brannan Plan: Farm Politics and Policy.* Ann Arbor: University of Michigan Press, 1959.

In 1949 Secretary of Agriculture Charles F. Brannan presented a comprehensive agricultural program to a joint session of Congress. The plan touched off a vigorous political controversy. Notes, index.

0534   Hall, Tom G. "The Aiken Bill, Price Supports and the Wheat Farmer in 1948." *North Dakota History* 39 (1972): 13–22, 47.

The Aiken Bill called for a new parity formula and a flexible price support system on key agricultural commodities. This measure drew unusual bipartisan congressional support, especially from the farm belt. Illustrations, tables, charts, notes.

0535   Williams, Oliver P. "The Commodity Credit Corporation and the 1948 Presidential Election." *Midwest Journal of Political Science* 1 (1957): 111–24.

Truman's attack on the Republican-dominated Eightieth Congress's modification of the Commodity Credit Corporation does not show that all parties contributed to the making of a confusing issue. Notes.

FARM LABOR

0536   Becnel, Thomas A. "With Benefit of Clergy: Catholic Church Support for the National Agricultural Workers Union in Louisiana, 1948–1958." Ph.D. dissertation, Louisiana State University and A & M College, 1973.

In 1952 Archbishop Joseph Francis Rummel and his prolabor priests offered union organizers more assistance than they had ever received from a church group, whereupon the NAWU made Louisiana the center of its operations. DAI 34:3283-A.

0537   Lyon, Richard M. "The Legal Status of American and Mexican Migratory Farm-Labor: An Analysis of U.S. Farm-Labor Legislation, Policy and Administration." Ph.D. dissertation, Cornell University, 1954.

This study examines the nature of federal migrant labor policies, especially policies toward foreign labor. The legislative history of Public Law 78 (Eighty-second Congress) is detailed, especially the postwar debate over farm-labor policy. DAI 14:995.

Bracero Program

0538   Coalson, George O. "The Development of the Migratory Farm Labor System in Texas, 1900–1954." Ph.D. dissertation, University of Oklahoma, 1955.

After World War II, Mexican nationals occupied a substantial place in Texas agricultural labor, particularly in South Texas. These contract laborers (*braceros*) and illegal aliens depressed wages resulting in Texas-Mexicans working largely in the northern sugar beet fields. DAI 16:108.

0539   Craig, Richard B. *The Bracero Program: Interest Groups and Foreign Policy.* Austin: University of Texas Press, 1971.

The political and interest groups which developed and sustained the twenty-two-year Mexican Contract Workers Program are examined. The Mexican government had as much interest as did the United States in maintaining this program. Notes, bibliography, index.

0540   Gilmore, N. Ray, and Gilmore, Gladys W. "The Bracero in California." *Pacific Historical Review* 32 (1963): 265–82.

The evolution of the *bracero* (temporary Mexican agricultural worker) system in California from World War I to the end of 1963 is traced in this essay. The authors examine the political and economic issues involved. Notes.

0541   Hawley, Ellis W. "The Politics of the Mexican Labor Issue, 1950–1965." *Agricultural History* 60 (1966): 157–76.

Most of this essay focuses on the post-Truman years; however, pages 158–59 summarize the issues of immediate postwar years, while the footnotes contain valuable references to documents. Notes.

0542   Kirstein, Peter N. "Agribusiness, Labor, and the Wetbacks: Truman's Commission on Migratory Labor." *Historian* 40 (1978): 650–67.

The author relates the various themes examined by Truman's commission as it investigated social, economic, health, and education conditions among migratory workers, as well as the special problems of the *bracero* program. Notes.

0543   Kirstein, Peter N. "American Railroads and the Bracero Program, 1943–1946." *Journal of Mexican American History* 5 (1975): 57–90.

Legal problems and personal experiences confronting Mexican workers are examined. Notes.

0544   Kirstein, Peter N. *Anglo Over Bracero: A History of the Mexican Worker in the United States from Roosevelt to Nixon.* San Francisco: R & E Research Associates, 1977.

In 1947 the "disharmonious diplomatic venture" was terminated by Public Law 40, setting the stage for the 1948 *braceros* agreement. The Truman years are well covered. Notes, bibliography.

0545   Kiser, George C., and Kiser, Martha Woody, eds. *Mexican Workers in the United States: Historical and Political Perspectives.* Albuquerque: University of New Mexico Press, 1979.

Part III, "The Second Bracero Era (1942–1964)," provides an introduction to the issue. Truman's letter to Mexican President Miguel Aleman, and Aleman's response, are reprinted (pp. 157–58). Bibliography, documents, index.

0546 Scruggs, Otey M. "Texas and the Bracero Program, 1942–1947." *Pacific Historical Review* 32 (1963): 251–64.

Scruggs traces the development of American-Mexican relations during the *bracero* program. He describes the discrimination these temporary Mexican agricultural workers encountered and the efforts undertaken to counteract it. Notes.

0547 Tomasek, Robert D. "The Political and Economic Implications of Mexican Labor in the United States under the Non Quota System, Contract Labor Program, and Wetback Movement." Ph.D. dissertation, University of Michigan, 1958.

Although this account is basically a historical survey of the problem (1900–1955), it does contain (Chapters 4 and 5) material relating to the Truman years. DAI 19:862.

0548 Number not used.

LAND USE: RECLAMATION AND RECREATION

See also D. F. Paulsen's *Natural Resources in the Government Process: A Bibliography Selected and Annotated* (#3015).

0549 Ferrell, John R. "Water Resources Development in the Arkansas Valley: A History of Public Policy to 1950." Ph.D. dissertation, University of Oklahoma, 1968.

This account focuses on the policymaking process for the development of the Arkansas River during 1940 to 1950. Public policy was, unfortunately, heavily influenced by "pork barrel" politics. DAI 29:1182-A.

0550 Hardin, Charles M. *The Politics of Agriculture: Soil Conservation and the Struggle for Power in Rural America.* Glencoe, IL: Free Press, 1952.

This volume provides a vast array of data relating to soil conservation and agricultural politics. Notes, index.

0551 Hoover, Roy O. "Public Law 273 Comes to Shelton: Implementation of the Sustained-Yield Forest Management Act of 1944." *Journal of Forest History* 22 (1978): 86–101.

After extended negotiations, the Forest Service and Simpson Logging Company of Shelton, Washington, in 1946, put into practice the Forest Management Act. Widely heralded as a success, it remains today the only arrangement of its kind. Illustrations, map, notes.

0552 Hurt, R. Douglas. "Return of the Dust Bowl: The Filthy Fifties." *Journal of the West* 18 (1979): 85–93.

By the late 1940s the newly plowed areas again began to show the effects of wind erosion. While the wind damaged large portions of the farmland (1950 to 1957), the farmers fought back with emergency tillage and reseeding.

0553 Juda, Lawrence. "The Development of American Policy on the Continental Shelf." Ph.D. dissertation, Columbia University, 1973.

One aspect of U.S. policy reviewed here is the 1945 Truman Proclamation and the domestic forces that shaped it. DAI 34:2738-A.

0554 Kathka, David A. "The Bureau of Reclamation in the Truman Administration: Personnel, Politics, and Policy." Ph.D. dissertation, University of Missouri, 1976.

The Bureau of Reclamation in the Truman years practiced political and economic conservation. It opposed changes that might have led to more scientific management and was unwilling to concede that underdeveloped resources had intrinsic value. DAI 38:975-A.

0555 Koppes, Clayton R. "Public Water, Private Land: Origins of the Acreage Limitation Controversy, 1933–1953." *Pacific Historical Review* 47 (1978): 607–36.

The acreage limitations of the Newlands Reclamation Act of 1902 had been neglected until the New Deal. It was not enforced during the Truman administration when there was greater interest in commercial agriculture and economic growth. Notes.

0556 McCloskey, Michael. "Wilderness Movement at the Crossroads, 1945–1970." *Pacific Historical Review* 41 (1972): 346–61.

Summarized here is the status of the movement for wilderness legislation during the Truman years. Notes.

0557 Richardson, Elmo. *BLM's Billion Dollar Checkerboard: Managing the O & C Lands.* Washington, DC: G.P.O., 1980.

Included in this broadly gauged work is reference to the Truman era reorganization of the General Land Office as the Bureau of Land Management. Notes, bibliography.

0558 Richardson, Elmo. *Dams, Parks, and Politics: Resource Development and Preservation in the Truman-Eisenhower Era.* Lexington: University Press of Kentucky, 1973.

Truman inherited a New Deal commitment to resource development and preservation, yet the postwar world clamored for unencumbered economic development. The first five chapters discuss Truman's approach to this problem. Notes, index.

0559   Scheele, Paul E. "Resource Development Politics in the Missouri Basin: Federal Power, Navigation, and Reservoir Operation Policies, 1944–1968." Ph.D. dissertation, University of Nebraska, 1969.

Authorization of the Missouri Basin Development Program is treated in Chapter 2. The impact of the Truman administration is covered in Chapter 3. DAI 30:3069-A.

0560   Warne, William E. *The Bureau of Reclamation.* New York: Praeger, 1973.

Scattered throughout this topically organized volume are references to policies established and action taken during the Truman years. Appendix, bibliography, index.

ENVIRONMENTAL ISSUES

0561   Allison, Oscar H. "Raymond R. Tucker: The Smoke Elimination Years, 1934–1950." Ph.D. dissertation, St. Louis University, 1978.

Tucker was one of the pioneers in the struggle against urban smog. He began in St. Louis where he became known as a specialist in preventing air pollution, especially that which came from burning of soft coal. DAI 39:1779-A.

0562   Flannery, James J. "Water Pollution Control: Development of State and National Policy." Ph.D. dissertation, University of Wisconsin, 1956.

This study contains a good deal of background material relating to the political dimensions of the problem. It also deals with the Federal Water Pollution Control Act (1948), which enlarged the federal role but circumscribed federal enforcement activities. DAI 16:2499.

0563   Whitaker, Adelynne Hiller. "A History of Federal Pesticide Regulations in the United States to 1947." Ph.D. dissertation, Emory University, 1974.

The Federal Insecticide, Fungicide, and Rodenticide Act (1947) revised the 1910 insecticide act. None of the public controversy, which later developed, existed in 1947. DAI 35:1032-A.

Business, Energy, Housing, Trade, and Transportation

0564   Eckes, Alfred E., Jr. *The United States and the Global Struggle for Minerals.* Austin: University of Texas Press, 1979.

It is the author's contention that the contest for control of vital minerals in Africa and Southeast Asia, which influenced U.S. foreign policy in the post-war era, began in the Truman years. Notes, appendixes, bibliography, index.

0565   Jensen, James R. "The 'New Conservatism' of *Fortune* Magazine (1930–1952)." Ph.D. dissertation, State University of Iowa, 1956.

In the postwar period, *Fortune* became complacent about reform and seemed to feel that now the business community, because of a moral regeneration, is using its power in a socially beneficial manner. DAI 16:1166.

0566   Nicholls, William H. "Industrial-Urban Development and Agricultural Adjustments, Tennessee Valley and Piedmont, 1939–1954." *Journal of Political Economy* 68 (1960): 135–49.

This study compares industrialization, urbanization, and agriculture in Georgia's upper East Tennessee Valley to the Piedmont of South Carolina.

0567   Schnabel, Morton. "An Oligopoly Model of the Cigarette Industry." *Southern Economic Journal* 38 (1972): 325–35.

The author examines the oligopoly case in which assumed properties of consumer preference had a strong bearing on the qualitative nature of the sales functions of firms and, consequently, upon firms' conjectural independence, 1949–63.

0568   Wells, Lloyd M. "The Defense of 'Big Business,' 1933–1953: A Study in the Development of an Ideology." Ph.D. dissertation, Princeton University, 1955.

This study is concerned with the ideological reactions of leading businessmen to the political currents of the New Deal-Fair Deal period and is based on a broad sample of business literature. DAI 15:2278.

0569   Zelinsky, Wilbur. "Has American Industry Been Decentralized? Evidence For the 1939–1954 Period." *Economic Geography* 38 (1962): 251–69.

The expansion of U.S. industries has brought about locational diffusions to subindustrial areas, 1939–54.

Steel Industry

See also *Presidential Intervention and Seizures*, regarding the 1952 seizure episode.

0570   Adams, Walter, and Dirlam, Joel B. "Big Steel, Invention, and Innovation." *Quarterly Journal of Economics* 80 (1966): 167–89.

Engineers at the big steel mills were unaware of the Austrian breakthrough in the oxygen steelmaking process in 1951. A small firm introduced the process in the United States, but the large firms failed to carry out a genuine modernization program in the 1950s.

0571 Alexandersson, Gunnar. "Changes in the Locational Patterns of the Anglo-American Steel Industry, 1948–1959." *Economic Geography* 37 (1961): 95–114.

Differences in economic growth rates of existing steel centers and plants, during 1948 to 1959, created changes in locational patterns.

0572 Braff, Allan J. "Wage and Price Decisions in the Basic Steel Industry (1945–1956)." Ph.D. dissertation, University of Wisconsin, 1959.

The ability of the steel industry to shift the burden of a wage increase by increasing prices appears to be the crucial factor in determining the ultimate size of the wage bargain. DAI 20:918.

0573 Broude, Henry W. *Steel Decisions and the National Economy.* New Haven: Yale University Press, 1963.

A controversy developed within the steel industry immediately after the war: Was the industry expanding its capacity sufficient to accommodate the needs of a growing, full-employment economy? Tables, notes, bibliography, index.

0574 Hogan, William T. *Economic History of the Iron and Steel Industry in the United States.* Lexington, MA: Lexington Books, 1971.

Volume 4 of this history of the iron and steel industry covers 1946 to 1971 and discusses such postwar issues as changes in raw materials, technological improvements, labor relations, and corporate reorganization. Illustrations, notes.

0575 Schroeder, Gertrude G. *The Growth of the Major Steel Companies, 1900–1950.* Baltimore: Johns Hopkins University Press, 1953.

Organized topically, this volume does provide useful statistical data on the years 1945–50. Tables, notes, bibliography, index.

FEDERAL TRADE COMMISSION

0576 Parkany, John. "Federal Trade Commission Enforcement of the Robinson-Patman Act, 1946–1952." Ph.D. dissertation, Columbia University, 1955.

The encroachment of newer methods of distribution of goods led in 1936 to the enactment of the Robinson-Patman Amendment to the Clayton Act. The purpose of this amendment was to eliminate the alleged "unfair" competitive advantages of chain stores while maintaining the advantages of mass distribution. DAI 15:1184.

0577 Samonte, Aberlardo G. "Development of Administrative Adjudication in the Federal Trade Commission Since 1946." Ph.D. dissertation, Princeton University, 1959.

Adjudication has played an increasing role in FTC cases. This study analyzes the basic features and growth of the adjudicatory process in the Federal Trade Commission. DAI 22:907.

ENERGY

0578 DeLuna, P. R. "Bureaucratic Opposition as a Factor in Truman's Failure to Achieve a Columbia Valley Authority." *Canadian Historical Association History Papers* (1975): 231–56.

Liberal supporters of Truman wanted low-cost federal electricity for the public while private power companies wanted to control its distribution. The liberals lost. Notes.

0579 DeLuna, Phyllis R. "Public versus Private Power during the Truman Administration: A Study in Fair Deal Liberalism." Ph.D. dissertation, University of Alberta, 1974.

Truman and his secretaries of interior espoused public power policies consistent with American liberalism. However, Truman, often for political reasons, did not consistently work to realize liberal power aims and the record shows more failures than successes.

0580 Goodwin, C. D., and Garber, W. J. "Energy, 1945–1980: Setting the Stage." *Wilson Quarterly* 5 (1981): 54–69.

Chapters 1 to 3 of *Energy Policy in Perspective: Today's Problems, Yesterday's Solutions* (1981) are adapted here. The authors conclude that the Truman administration failed to develop a coherent energy policy.

0581 Goodwin, Craufurd D., ed. *Energy Policy in Perspective: Today's Problems, Yesterday's Solutions.* Washington, DC: Brookings Institution, 1981.

Truman's attempt to deal with the energy problem is discussed in Chapters 1 and 2. Notes, appendixes, index.

0582 Hamilton, William R. "The President's Materials Policy Commission (Paley Commission): A History and Analytical Inquiry Into Policy Formulation by a Presidential Commission." Ph.D. dissertation, University of Maryland, 1962.

Hamilton examines the methods used by the commission to arrive at its conclusions regarding electric energy, government organization for resource administration, and minerals tax incentive policies. He discovers that the facts which they found were seldom true in the sense that they led to universally accepted policy recommendations. DAI 24:1678.

0583 Waltrip, John R. "Public Power during the Truman Administration." Ph.D. dissertation, University of Missouri, 1965.

The Truman era saw the most extensive development of federal power in U.S. history. Public power was a significant campaign issue in the West in the 1948 election. DAI 27:1773.

0584 White, Irvin L. "Energy Policy-Making: Limitations of a Conceptual Model." *Bulletin of the Atomic Scientists* 27 (1971): 20–26.

This study examines the growth of the gas, electric, nuclear, and solar energy industries between 1947 and 1971.

Oil and Natural Gas

See also Chapter 8, *Saudi Arabia*.

0585 Barker, Lucius J. "Offshore Oil Politics: A Study in Public Policy Making." Ph.D. dissertation, University of Illinois, 1954.

Although the offshore oil controversy had begun more than fifteen years before, it was not until the decision in *United States* v. *California* (1947) that the issue came to the fore. This account examines the issue from World War II to 1953. DAI 15:145.

0586 Barker, Lucius J. "The Supreme Court as Policy Maker: The Tidelands Oil Controversy." *Journal of Politics* 24 (1962): 350–66.

Truman vetoed a law by Congress which would have given control of the tidelands to the states, while the court, in 1947 and 1950 decisions, held that offshore lands belonged to the federal government. Notes.

0587 Bartley, Ernest R. *The Tidelands Oil Controversy: A Legal and Historical Analysis.* Austin: University of Texas Press, 1950.

In 1947 the Supreme Court held that the federal government rather than the state was the owner of the three-mile marginal belt along California's coast. This volume examines the case's history and legal background. Notes, table of cases, index.

0588 Fehd, Carolyn S. "Productivity in the Petroleum Pipelines Industry." *Monthly Labor Review* 94 (1971): 46–48.

This study finds that increased output per manhour, growing numbers of refineries, improved pipelines, and new uses for petroleum products contributed to the uninterrupted productivity increase in the petroleum pipeline industry, 1947–68.

0589 Harris, Joseph P. "The Senatorial Rejection of Leland Olds." *American Political Science Review* 45 (1951): 674–92.

In 1949 Truman nominated Olds for a third term as a member of the Federal Power Commission. Olds was opposed because he supported effective public regulation of utilities.

0590 Kaufman, Burton I. "Oil and Antitrust: The Oil Cartel Case and the Cold War." *Business History Review* 51 (1977): 35–56.

The Truman administration initiated antitrust prosecution of the five largest American oil companies in 1952, seeking to force divestment of their integrated corporations. Subsequently government policy shifted. Notes.

0591 Krammer, Arnold. "Technology Transfer As War Booty: The U.S. Technical Oil Mission to Europe, 1945." *Technology and Culture* 22 (1981): 68–103.

In 1945 a team of two dozen petroleum experts followed the American army into Germany and gathered and shipped home some 175 tons of technical documents from forty-nine German plants. However, as cheap Middle Eastern oil began to flow into America, the German processes were forgotten. Illustrations, notes.

0592 Lovejoy, Wallace F. "The Regulation of Natural Gas and Its Economic Background." Ph.D. dissertation, University of Wisconsin, 1956.

This study examines the production and utilization problems associated with the development of the postwar pipelines. Two major attempts to amend the Natural Gas Act to exempt gas producers from regulations (including the Kerr-Rizley Bills of 1949–50) are discussed to give some insight into the arguments used by both sides in the controversy.

0593 Marcus, Kenneth K. "The National Government and the Natural Gas Industry, 1946–56: A Study in the Making of a National Policy." Ph.D. dissertation, University of Illinois, 1962.

In the postwar period, the natural gas industry sought deregulation. Although they met with some success in Congress, they suffered vetoes by Truman and Eisenhower and the judiciary. DAI 23:682.

0594 Nash, Gerald D. *United States Oil Policy, 1890–1964.* Pittsburgh: University of Pittsburgh Press, 1968.

Nash looks at the oil industry against the broader theme of the developing consensus concerning cooperation between government and industry. Chapters 9 and 10 discuss the Truman administration. Notes, appendix, bibliographical essay, index.

0595 Pack, Lindsey E. "The Political Aspects of the Texas Tidelands Controversy." Ph.D. dissertation, Texas A & M University, 1979.

Texas wanted to believe that Truman recognized their claim to the tidelands. Even though Truman carried Texas in 1948, the state sued his administration to keep control of these riches. DAI 40:6394-A.

0596 Vietor, Richard H. K. "The Synthetic Liquid Fuels Program: Energy Politics in the Truman Era." *Business History Review* 54 (1980): 1–34.

The Truman administration inherited a wartime program to develop synthetic fuels which would achieve energy self-sufficiency. After the war, the program came under increasing attack from the petroleum industry which saw its own vested interests threatened by the government activity.

HOUSING

See also Chapter 6, *Civil Rights*, for rulings on restrictive covenants.

0597 Alberts, William W. "Business Cycles, Residential Construction, and the Mortgage Market." *Journal of Political Economy* 70 (1962): 263–81.

This essay analyzes the relationship between business cycles, housing construction, and mortgages from 1946 to 1960.

0598 Berg, Irving. "Racial Discrimination in Housing: A Study in Quest for Governmental Access by Minority Interest Groups, 1945–1962." Ph.D. dissertation, University of Florida, 1967.

This study deals with the efforts made by blacks and their civil rights allies to curb effectively discrimination in governmental housing policies. Their failure is attributed to the inability of civil rights groups to gain firm and constant access within the governmental system. DAI 29:295-A.

0599 Bernstein, Barton J. "Reluctance and Resistance: Wilson Wyatt and Veterans' Housing in the Truman Administration." *Register of the Kentucky Historical Society* 65 (1967): 47–66.

The failure of the Veterans Emergency Housing Program, in the face of a severe postwar housing shortage, is an example of the failure of the early Truman administration. Head of VEHP, Wyatt wanted 2.7 million low-cost housing units under construction within two years; however, competing bureaucracies thwarted his efforts. Notes.

0600 Davies, Richard O. *Housing Reform During the Truman Administration*. Columbia: University of Missouri Press, 1966.

Because of the critical postwar housing shortage, housing policy played an important role in Fair Deal politics. This book analyzes the reforms and failures of the Truman administration. Notes, bibliography, index.

0601 Dreier, Peter. "The Politics of Rent Control." *Working Papers for a New Society* 6 (1979): 55–63.

After a short review of the background of rent control in the United States since 1942, Dreier describes current urban efforts to continue the practice.

0602 Ginsberg, Benjamin. "*Berman* v. *Parker*: Congress, the Court, and the Public Purpose." *Polity* 4 (1971): 48–75.

The essay examines the effects of the congressional acts of 1945 and 1949 and the Supreme Court's decision in 1954 related to housing in southwestern Washington, D.C. Ginsberg criticizes both the Congress and the courts for not including a sufficiently detailed standard to prevent the law from being misused.

0603 Hudson, Anne Mooney. "Urban Redevelopment in American Cities, 1950–1965." Ph.D. dissertation, University of Michigan, 1973.

The study examines differential participation by 458 cities of 25,000 or more population in the federal program of redevelopment assistance from its beginning until 30 June 1965. DAI 35:583-A.

0604 Straus, Nathan. *Two-thirds of a Nation: A Housing Program*. New York: Knopf, 1952.

Most facets of Truman's commitment to providing a good home for every American family are examined. Tables, index.

0605 Williams, Randall, and Dent, Hilda. "Billion Dollar Shell Game." *Southern Exposure* 8 (1980): 86–91.

In 1946 the Jim Walter Company began manufacturing shell homes, to be completed by the purchaser. In 1980 it was the nation's largest builder of single-family homes. Illustrations.

Public Housing

0606 Barnes, William R. "The Origins of Urban Renewal: The Public Housing Controversy and the Emergence of a Redevelopment Program in the District of Columbia, 1942–1949." Ph.D. dissertation, Syracuse University, 1977.

The District of Columbia Redevelopment Act (1946) was used by advocates of urban renewal to test congressional sentiments. The District controversy foreshadowed and helped to shape the national debate that resulted in the Housing Act of 1949. DAI 39:1053-A.

0607 Brown, Charles C. "Robert A. Taft, Champion of Public Housing and National Aid to Schools." *Cincinnati Historical Society Bulletin* 26 (1968): 219–53.

The essay finds Taft the "virtual leader of Senate Republicans on most domestic issues from 1946 to 1953," and especially supportive of programs in housing and education. Illustrations, notes.

0608 Davies, Richard O. "'Mr. Republican' Turns 'Socialist': Robert A. Taft and Public Housing." *Ohio History* 73 (1964): 135–43.

Taft developed the Taft-Ellender-Wagner public housing bill because he was convinced of its necessity. However, prior to the election of 1948, Taft voted against his own bill because of the split between conservative and liberal Republicans. Notes.

TRADE AND TARIFFS

0609 Barrie, Robert W. "Congress and the Executive: The Making of U.S. Foreign Trade Policy." Ph.D. dissertation, University of Minnesota, 1968.

This study attempts to identify major factors affecting the course of decisions in U.S. foreign trade policy as they relate to congressional-executive relations. DAI 29:3645-A.

0610 Grether, Ewald T. "Consistency in Public Economic Policy with Respect to Private Unregulated Industries." *American Economic Review* 53 (1963): 26–37.

The impact of economic and foreign trade policies on economic sectors regulated by market mechanisms (1930–62) is evaluated.

0611 Hinshaw, Randall. "Implications of the Shift in the U.S. Balance of Payments." *American Economic Review* 49 (1959): 274–83.

An economic upsurge during 1947 to 1949 resulting from a reversal in the U.S. balance of payments brought about an improvement in foreign monetary reserves from 1949 to 1959.

0612 Krause, Lawrence B. "United States Imports and the Tariffs." *American Economic Review* 49 (1959): 542–51.

This survey and analysis of import-export movements and tariff levels during 1949 to 1956 leads to the conclusion that tariff reductions do not lead to significant increases in the volume of imports.

0613 Leary, Thomas J. "An Economic Analysis of the Tariff and Other Measures of the United States for Aiding Industries Essential to National Defense." Ph.D. dissertation, Ohio State University, 1955.

The Defense Production Act (1950) charged the federal government to construct and maintain a mobilization base. Various government measures, such as a rapid tax amortization program, stockpiling, and the import policy, were instituted. The impact of this upon the American economy is analyzed. DAI 16:674.

0614 Truman, Harry S. *The Free World and Free Trade*. Dallas: Southern Methodist University Press, 1963.

This is taken from the typescript of an address former President Truman delivered in 1957 along with a postscript from 1963. Truman opposes high tariffs and favors the expansion of international trade.

0615 Weiss, Leonard W. "Import Price Control in the United States, 1940–1953." Ph.D. dissertation, Columbia University, 1954.

This study is concerned with import policy for a general emergency price control program. DAI 15:202.

TRANSPORTATION

0616 Banks, Larry H. "The Debate Surrounding Direct Maritime Subsidies to the American Merchant Marine, 1936–1960." Ph.D. dissertation, Case Western Reserve University, 1975.

For almost a decade following World War II government policy toward the Merchant Marine was one of drift and vacillation. DAI 36:5489-A.

0617 Dearing, Charles I., and Owen, Wilfred. *National Transportation Policy*. Washington, DC: Brookings Institution, 1949.

Although organized topically, this volume contains data on the early Truman years in text and charts. The study was undertaken for the Hoover Commission to define the federal role; its recommendations included creating a cabinet position for transportation. Appendix, notes, index.

0618 Mabee, Carleton. *The Seaway Story*. New York: Macmillan, 1961.

Mabee relates the story of the St. Lawrence Seaway, the inception of the idea, the struggle to build it, and its effects. Notes, illustrations, index.

0619 Nupp, Byron LeRoy. "Transportation Policy Formation in the Federal Government, 1948–1960: A Test of an Administrative Theory." Ph.D. dissertation, American University, 1965.

In 1948 the Hoover Commission recommended that transportation policy should be the responsibility of the secretary of commerce. Four problems which emerged (1948–60) under this system are examined. Nupp concludes that cabinet officer responsibility, by itself, proved unworkable. DAI 26:1759.

0620 Smerk, George. "Rail Passage Service in the Northeast Corridor, 1947–63." *Quarterly Review of Economics and Business* 7 (1967): 5–20.

Smerk traces changes in passenger traffic and service in the railroads between Washington, DC and New York City, and assesses reasons for the decrease in traffic.

Automobiles and Highways

0621 Carroll, Philip M. "Highway Needs and their Public Financing in the Postwar Period." Ph.D. dissertation, University of Illinois, 1955.

At the end of World War II the nation's highway system was not only badly in need of repair but much of it was functionally obsolete. In 1950 the dollar cost of correcting these deficiencies was put at $41 billion. DAI 15:739.

0622 Fisher, Franklin M.; Griliches, Zvi; and Kaysen, Carl. "The Costs of Automobile Model Changes Since 1949." *Journal of Political Economy* 70 (1962): 433–51.

Costs incurred from consumer suggestions for model changes, 1949–62, are reviewed.

0623 Nevins, Allan, and Hill, Frank E. *Ford: Decline and Rebirth, 1933–1962.* New York: Scribner, 1962.

In this the third volume on the history of the Ford Company, the postwar issues with the United Auto Workers Union and the company's recuperation are discussed. Illustrations, notes, index.

0624 Rose, Mark H. "Express Highway Politics, 1939–1956." Ph.D. dissertation, Ohio State University, 1973.

This account covers the relative lack of federal support and interest in expanding the interstate system, begun in 1944, during the Truman years. Not until 1956 did Congress commit itself to completing the job. DAI 34:5075-A.

0625 Sloan, Alfred P., Jr. *My Years with General Motors.* Garden City, NY: Doubleday, 1964.

Sloan was president (1923–37) and chairman (1937–1944) of General Motors. He devotes a chapter to "Personnel and Labor Relations," and discusses the United Auto Workers strike of 1945–46 and the Taft-Hartley Act. Illustrations, index.

0626 Trainor, Linda L. "The Great American Dream Car." *American History Illustrated* 15 (1980): 18–21.

Preston T. Tucker built fifty-one of his innovative and popular Tucker automobiles in 1948 before federal indictments closed his operations; later he was acquitted on all counts.

Airlines and Aviation

See also Chapter 2, *Presidential Commissions and Committees.*

0627 Alvord, Ben M. "A Study of the Financing of the U.S. Trunk Airlines, 1946–55." Ph.D. dissertation, University of Illinois, 1960.

The phenomenon of poor or mediocre financial success in a period of rapid expansion is of public concern. One reason for this is that the airline industry is subject to a higher degree of business risk than is typical for public utilities. DAI 21:1411.

0628 Handerson, Harold B. "The Air Coordination Committee (ACC): Interagency Coordination in Federal Aviation Matters, 1945–1960." Ph.D. dissertation, American University, 1971.

This study deals with aviation policy in particular and the use of an interagency group established by executive order of the president. DAI 32:2168-A.

0629 Kahn, Mark L. "Regulatory Agencies and Industrial Relations: The Airline Case." *American Economic Review* 42 (1952): 686–98.

Essentially a study of the role of the Civil Aeronautics Board, this account focuses on the post-1945 years and examines air safety, routes, subsidies, and strikes. Notes.

0630 Kuter, Laurence S. "Truman's Secret Management of the Airlines." *Aerospace Historian* 24 (1977): 181–83.

This is a personal account of Truman's appointment of General Kuter as chairman of the Civil Aeronautics Board (1948). Congress refused to confirm the appointment because it did not want a military man in a civil position.

0631 Miller, John A. "Air Diplomacy: The Chicago Civil Aviation Conference of 1944 in Anglo-American Wartime and Post-War Planning." Ph.D. dissertation, Yale University, 1971.

Low-cost mass air transportation overseas was unknown before the war. This study traces the growth of U.S. civil aviation policy from the interwar years through 1944. DAI 32:1449-A.

0632 Whitnah, Donald R. *Safer Skyways: Federal Control of Aviation, 1926–1966.* Ames: Iowa State University Press, 1966.

Whitnah examines the activities of the Federal Aviation Agency and Civil Aeronautics Board. Chapters 11 and 12 focus on the postwar period and the problems of expansion. Illustrations, notes, bibliography, index.

0633 Williams, Nicholas M. "Globemaster: The Douglas C-74." *American Aviation History Society Journal* 25 (1980): 82–106.

The history of the design and performance of the Douglas C-74 Globemaster from 1942 to 1972, including its air force flights from 1945 to 1955, is reviewed.

The Economy

0634 Bernstein, Marver H. *Regulating Business by Independent Commission.* Princeton: Princeton University Press, 1955.

Although essentially a history of economic regulation, the chapter on "The Politics of Adjudication" discusses the Administrative Procedure Act of 1946. Notes, index.

0635 Collins, Robert M. "American Corporatism: The Committee for Economic Development, 1942–1964." *Historian* 44 (1982): 151–73.

The Committee for Economic Development is examined for its influence on national macroeconomic policy to trace the development of American corporatism. The committee contributed economic thought, personnel, and special relationships. Notes.

0636 Collins, Robert M. *The Business Responses to Keynes, 1929–1964.* New York: Columbia University Press, 1981.

Chapters 4 and 5 deal with World War II and the early Truman years and focus on the efforts of three business organizations—the Chamber of Commerce of the United States, the National Association of Manufacturers, and the Committee for Economic Development—to forge a new, post-Depression political economy. Notes, bibliography, index.

0637 Fredlund, John R. "Keynesian Ideas as Reflected in the Domestic Fiscal and Monetary Policies of the United States, 1945–1953." Ph.D. dissertation, American University, 1956.

Fredlund analyzes the degree to which the doctrines and policies of John Maynard Keynes have influenced U.S. economic policy in the postwar period to 1953. DAI 17:1248.

0638 Hansen, Alvin H. *Postwar American Economy: Performance and Problems.* New York: Norton, 1964.

This is essentially a statistical study of the American economy, 1945–63. Tables, index.

0639 Harrison, William B. "Annals of a Crusade: Wright Patman and the Federal Reserve System." *American Journal of Economy and Sociology* 40 (1981): 317–20.

As a congressman from Texas (1929–76), Patman endorsed Populist-style legislation aimed at farmers, small businessmen, and consumers. To make this legislation viable, he wanted to hold the Federal Reserve System more accountable to Congress. Notes.

0640 Jones, Endsley T. "The House of Representatives and Keynesian Economics, 1945–1964." Ph.D. dissertation, Georgetown University, 1967.

This study attempts to identify the factors influencing congressmen's voting behavior on Keynesian policies. Two factors stand out: Democratic party membership and urbanism. DAI 28:3235-A.

0641 Lane, Robert E. *The Regulation of Businessmen: Social Conditions of Government Economic Control.* New Haven: Yale University Press, 1954.

Lane focuses on the social and personal aspects of regulation not reached by more orthodox investigation by dealing with business ideologies and the roles businessmen assume. Notes, bibliography, index.

0642 Lee, R. Alton. "The Truman-80th Congress Struggle Over Tax Policy." *Historian* 33 (1970): 68–82.

Truman became the first president in American history to veto tax reduction bills; he did it twice, in 1947 and again in 1948. Lee traces the events and debates, and concludes that Truman read public opinion better than did congressional leaders. Notes.

0643 McQuaid, Kim. "The Business Advisory Council of the Department of Commerce, 1933–1961: A Study of Corporate/Government Relations." *Research in Economic History* (1976): 171–97.

Relationships with the federal government were stormy from the outset; however, there is no evidence to suggest that the council really ran the country, or even served as a focus for a unified corporate ideal. Notes.

0644 Steiner, George A. *Government's Role in Economic Life.* New York: McGraw-Hill, 1953.

Steiner examines such topics as the impact of pressure groups, the national security crisis of the 1940s, the causes of expanding federal controls, and the constitutional economic powers of government. Notes, bibliography, index.

0645 Vatter, Harold G. *The U.S. Economy in the 1950's: An Economic History.* New York: Norton, 1963.

Although it covers only the last years of the Truman administration, this study contains a considerable amount of materials on the immediate postwar years. This is especially true of the tables and charts. Footnotes, index.

0646 Wagnon, William O., Jr. "The Politics of Economic Growth: The Truman Administration and the 1949 Recession." Ph.D. dissertation, University of Missouri, 1970.

To counter the recession, the administration emphasized a policy of business and government cooperation to maintain an ever-expanding economy.

By encouraging economic growth, the Fair Deal developed a new type of government intervention in the economy. DAI 31:2327-A.

Soviet-American Comparisons

0647 Kaplan, Norman M., and Wainstein, Eleanor S. "A Comparison of Soviet and American Retail Prices in 1950." *Journal of Political Economy* 64 (1956): 470–91.

U.S. and U.S.S.R. retail prices on several commodities for 1950 are compared and related to exchange rates and relative wages.

0648 Pesek, Boris P. "Soviet and American Inventory-Output Ratios Once Again." *American Economic Review* 49 (1959): 1030–32.

After comparing the performance of Soviet, Czechoslovakian, and American economies as indicated by retailing (1930–57), the author concludes that the U.S. economy was substantially superior to the two socialist economies.

PRESIDENTIAL INTERVENTION AND SEIZURES

0649 Blackman, John L., Jr. *Presidential Seizure in Labor Disputes.* Cambridge: Harvard University Press, 1967.

Of the seventy-one instances of presidential seizure in labor disputes chronicled in this study, eleven occurred during the Truman administration. Appendixes, notes, index.

0650 Cimini, Michael. "Government Intervention in Railroad Disputes." *Monthly Labor Review* 94 (1971): 27–34.

This study summarizes federal government intervention in railroad disputes under the auspices of the Railway Labor Act through the National Mediation Board, 1950–71.

0651 DiBacco, Thomas V. "'Draft the Strikers (1946) and Seize the Mills (1952)': The Business Reaction." *Duquesne Review* 13 (1968): 63–75.

While the business press was not particularly upset with Truman's 1946 proposal to draft railroad strikers, it became quite excited by the alleged presidential trampling of the Constitution when he seized the steel mills in 1952. Notes.

0652 Hah, Chong-do, and Lindquist, Robert M. "The 1952 Steel Seizure Revisited: A Systematic Study in Presidential Decision Making." *Administrative Science Quarterly* 20 (1975): 587–605.

By using Truman's 1952 seizure of the steel mills as a case study, the authors develop a coherent framework for analyzing presidential decision making. Notes.

0653 Marcus, Maeva. *Truman and the Steel Seizure Case: The Limits of Presidential Power.* New York: Columbia University Press, 1977.

Truman's seizure of the steel industry under the Taft-Hartley Act to avert a strike raised fundamental questions about the role of the president and the nature of presidential power. The court held against Truman. Notes, bibliography, index.

0654 McConnell, Grant. *The Steel Seizure of 1952.* Inter-University Case Program, Case Series No. 52. University: University of Alabama Press, 1960.

Six months of negotiations between the steel industry, labor, and the federal government failed and President Truman on 8 April 1952 announced that he was ordering the seizure of the mills because of national security. This pamphlet provides a useful review of the entire episode.

0655 Randall, Clarence B. *Over My Shoulder: A Reminiscence.* Boston: Little, Brown, 1956.

Randall relates his experiences as the first steel and coal consultant for the Marshall Plan (1948) in Chapter 13. As chief executive of Inland Steel Company, he became the industry's chief spokesman in opposition to Truman's seizure of the mills (1952). See Chapter 15.

0656 Schaefer, Arthur M. "Presidential Intervention in Labor Disputes During the Truman Administration: A History and Analysis of Experience." Ph.D. dissertation, University of Pennsylvania, 1967.

Truman intervened in the coal and railroad disputes, intervened under the Taft-Hartley emergency procedures, and intervened during the Korean War. All of these episodes are examined. DAI 25-A.

0657 Smith, J. Malcolm, and Cotter, Cornelius P. *Powers of the President During Crises.* Washington, DC: Public Affairs Press, 1960.

Truman especially came under criticism for his seizure of the steel industry in 1952 when the court refused to uphold his right to do so under the emergency powers policy.

0658 Stebbins, Phillip E. "Truman and the Seizure of Steel: A Failure in Communication." *Historian* 34 (1971): 1–21.

Truman's failure to win judicial and public support for his 1952 seizure of the steel mills is attributed largely to the administration's failure to rebut steel propaganda and to inform the public of the serious impact the steel strike was having on American commitments in Korea. Notes.

0659 Westin, Alan F., ed. *The Anatomy of a Constitutional Law Case: Youngstown Sheet and Tube*

Co. v. Sawyer; The Steel Seizure Decision. New York: Macmillan, 1958.

This study is essentially a collection of political and legal documents relating to the steel seizure case. Included is Truman's "seizure" speech, Clarence Randall's objection, congressional debates, court transcripts, and judicial opinions. Footnotes.

COUNCIL OF ECONOMIC ADVISERS

See also *Employment Act (1946).*

0660 Brady, Patrick G. "Toward Security: Postwar Economic and Social Planning in the Executive Office, 1939–1946." Ph.D. dissertation, Rutgers University, 1975.

Liberals sought a postwar program for full employment, economic stabilization, and a rising standard of living. They looked to three executive office agencies, the National Resources Planning Board, the Bureau of the Budget, and the Council of Economic Advisers, to plan and coordinate federal programs. DAI 36:3067-A.

0661 Canterbery, E. Ray. *The President's Council of Economic Advisers: A Study of Its Functions and Its Influence on the Chief Executive's Decisions.* New York: Exposition Press, 1961.

The President's Council of Economic Advisers was created by the Employment Act of 1946, which recognized the growing importance of the federal government's role in the U.S. economy. Truman, often indifferent to the complexities of economics, did not put the council to its best use. Notes, bibliography.

0662 Flash, Edward S., Jr. *Economic Advice and Presidential Leadership: The Council of Economic Advisers.* New York: Columbia University Press, 1965.

The Council of Economic Advisers was established as an advisory council to the president. Chapters 1 to 3 focus on the Truman administration. Notes, bibliography, index.

0663 Gross, Bertram M., and Lewis, John P. "The President's Economic Staff during the Truman Administration." *American Political Science Review* 48 (1954): 114–30.

This account is basically the view of two insiders—Gross was executive secretary of the Council of Economic Advisers, while Lewis was a council staff member.

0664 Naveh, David. "The Political Role of the Professional in the Formation of National Policy: The Case of the President's Council of Economic Advisers." Ph.D. dissertation, University of Connecticut, 1978.

The creation of the Council of Economic Advisers transformed the science of economics into a policymaking tool. This is an account of its founding and an assessment of its first three decades of activity. DAI 39:6942-A.

0665 Naveh, David. "The Political Role of Academic Advisers: The Case of the U.S. President's Council of Economic Advisers, 1946–1976." *Presidential Studies Quarterly* 11 (1981): 492–510.

Since its creation in 1946, the highly informal council has tended to add to presidential power and legitimacy. Tables, notes, bibliography.

0666 Norton, Hugh S. *The Employment Act and the Council of Economic Advisers, 1946–1976.* Columbia: University of South Carolina Press, 1977.

Chapter 4 provides a useful introduction to the establishment of the council in 1946 and the impact of Truman economics. Appendix, tables, bibliography, notes, index.

0667 Nourse, Edwin G., and Gross, Bertram M. "The Role of the Council of Economic Advisers." *American Political Science Review* 42 (1948), 283–95.

Both authors were officials of the council and present here an early insider's assessment of its activities.

0668 Salant, Walter S. "Some Intellectual Contributions of the Truman Council of Economic Advisers to Policy-Making." *History of Political Economy* 5 (1973): 36–49.

Truman's Council of Economic Advisers, chaired by Leon Keyserling, carried out an educational program which resulted in (1) the replacement of a "cyclical model" of the economy by a "growth model"; (2) the setting of quantitative targets for the economy; (3) use of the theories of fiscal drag and full-employment budget; (4) recognition of the need for greater flexibility in taxation; and (5) replacement of the notion of unemployment as a structural problem. Notes.

0669 Silverman, Corrine. *Presidential Economic Advisers.* University: University of Alabama Press, 1959.

A useful pamphlet, it relates the establishment of the Council of Economic Advisers and the personalities and philosophies of its first three members: Edwin G. Nourse, chairman; Leon H. Keyserling, vice-chairman; and John D. Clark.

0670 "Stabilizing the Economy: The Employment Act of 1946 in Operation: A Symposium." *American Economic Review* 40:2 (1950), 144–90.

These critical essays review the activities of the Council of Economic Advisers.

0671 Turner, Robert C. "Problems of Forecasting for Economic Stabilization." *American Economic Review* 45 (1955): 329–40.

The forecasts of the Council of Economic Advisers are examined, and their impact on the general economy is assessed.

ANTIMONOPOLY ACTIVITIES

0672 Asch, Peter. "Public Merger Policy and the Meaning of Competition." *Quarterly Review of Economics and Business* 6 (1966): 53–64.

Section 7 of the Clayton Act, as amended in 1950, prohibits any corporate merger whose effect may be "substantially to lessen competition or to tend to create a monopoly." This essay reviews the Supreme Court's definition of "competition" in a number of merger cases. Notes.

0673 Branyan, Robert. "Anti-Monopoly Activities During the Truman Administration." Ph.D. dissertation, University of Oklahoma, 1961.

Although antimonopoly activities under Truman were not great, several advances were made, notably in strengthening small businesses. This study traces these developments, as well as the innovations under the Truman administration. DAI 22:1137.

0674 Dewey, Donald. *Monopoly in Economics and Law*. Chicago: Rand McNally, 1959.

This book is arranged topically. For a discussion of monopoly legislation during the Truman administration, it is necessary to pinpoint the material in the index of cases. Has good description of the Supreme Court's Alcoa Case (1945). Notes, indexes.

0675 Kitch, Edmund W. "The Yellow Cab Antitrust Case." *Journal of Law and Economics* 15 (1972): 327–36.

The Supreme Court's Yellow Cab opinion (1949) has been considered the major effort by the court to rule on vertical acquisitions. In various decisions affecting Yellow Cab (1947–49), it was held that veteran operators had been removed "not by restrictive licensing laws but by competition." Notes.

0676 Lewis-Beck, Michael S. "Maintaining Economic Competition: The Causes and Consequences of Antitrust." *Journal of Politics* 41 (1979): 169–91.

This review of major antitrust legislation examines, among other acts, the Celler-Kefauver Antimerger Act (1950). Notes.

FEDERAL BUDGET

0677 Abbot, Charles C. *The Federal Debt: Structure and Impact*. New York: Twentieth Century Fund, 1953.

This volume provides a useful examination of the growth and service of the federal debt during the Truman years. Tables, index.

0678 Berman, Larry. *The Office of Management and Budget and the Presidency, 1921–1979*. Princeton: Princeton University Press, 1979.

Truman's interaction with the Bureau of the Budget is discussed in Chapter 2, "The Development of an Institutional Bureau of the Budget, 1939–1952." Appendixes, notes, bibliography, index.

0679 Critchlow, Donald T. "The Political Control of the Economy: Deficit Spending as a Political Belief, 1932–1952." *Public History* 3 (1981): 5–22.

The relationship of economic policy formation to electoral politics is examined by reviewing political attitudes toward deficit spending. During 1945 to 1952, the Republicans accepted much of the New Deal but did not endorse the "New Economists." Notes.

0680 Piccillo, Peter E. "The Role of the Budget Bureau in Truman's Domestic Legislative Program: An Examination of Atomic Energy Control, Military Unification, Housing, and Civil Rights." Ph.D. dissertation, State University of New York, Binghamton, 1974.

The Bureau of the Budget was a central repository of information and expertise in 1945. Its director, Harold Smith, became a much-valued adviser to Truman. DAI 35:1602-A.

0681 Ramsey, John W. "The Director of the Bureau of the Budget as a Presidential Aide, 1921–1952: With Emphasis on the Truman Years." Ph.D. dissertation, University of Missouri, 1967.

The director of the Bureau of the Budget is potentially an extremely important aide to the president because he scrutinizes virtually every program of the national government. DAI 28:4283-A.

0682 Teigen, Robert L. "Trends and Cycles in Composition of the Federal Budget, 1947–78." *Policy Studies Journal* 9 (1980): 11–19.

Teigen identifies trend, cyclical, and price-indexing phenomena and concludes that there is little evidence of structural change during this period.

FISCAL POLICIES

0683 Brown, E. Cary. "Federal Fiscal Policy in the Postwar Period." In Ralph E. Freeman, ed., *Postwar*

Economic Trends in the United States. New York: Harper, 1960, pp. 139–88.

This essay examines the recession of 1949 and the impact of the Korean War on fiscal policy, as well as the Eisenhower recessions. Notes.

0684 Carson, Robert B. "Changes in Federal Fiscal Policy and Public Attitudes Since the Employment Act of 1946." *Social Studies* 58 (1967): 308–14.

Carson argues that the Employment Act of 1946 signaled the acceptance of the Keynesian school of economics by American economists. The act brought about greater federal authority over the American economy. Notes.

0685 Collins, Robert M. "Business Responses to Keynesian Economics, 1929–1964: An Analysis of the Process by Which the Modern American Political Economy Was Defined." Ph.D. dissertation, Johns Hopkins University, 1975.

This study examines the responses of three major American business organizations—the Chamber of Commerce, the Committee for Economic Development, and the National Association of Manufacturers—to the enlargement of the federal government's economic role. Business influence was significant in shaping the Employment Act of 1946 and for reducing government investment in social projects. DAI 39:3081-A.

0686 Fels, Rendigs. "The U.S. Downturn of 1948." *American Economic Review* 55 (1965): 1059–76.

The author employs an economic model to explain the 1948–49 recession.

0687 Freeman, Ralph E., ed. *Postwar Economic Trends in the United States.* New York: Harper, 1960.

Within these essays there is considerable data on monetary, trade, income and corporate policies during the Truman years. Charts, graphs, notes, index.

0688 Holmans, A. E. *United States Fiscal Policy, 1945–1959.* New York: Oxford University Press, 1961.

In the postwar period the United States refused to use antideflationary measures to combat unemployment. Yet despite this, the United States managed to avoid a slump. Notes, tables, bibliography, index.

0689 Hyman, Sidney. *Marriner S. Eccles.* Stanford: Stanford University Graduate School of Business, 1976.

Eccles served on the board of governors of the Federal Reserve System (1934–51), and as chairman until eased out by Truman in 1948. An anti-inflationist and advocate of a balanced budget in times of plenty, Eccles was frequently at odds with Truman's secretary of the treasury, John W. Snyder. Appendixes, notes, index.

0690 McKinnon, Ronald I. "Dollar Stabilization and American Monetary Policy." *American Economic Review* 70 (1980): 382–86.

Industrial and nonindustrial economics make different demands on the dollar. This analysis covers 1945 to 1978. Notes.

0691 Olson, John M. C., Jr. "An Analysis of Fiscal Policy during the Truman Administration (1945–1953)." Ph.D. dissertation, University of Southern California, 1966.

The Truman administration did not achieve the economic goals of the Employment Act of 1946. Although near full employment was achieved, production did not provide the levels of aggregate supply, the purchasing power of the dollar declined, and inflation was great. DAI 27:3205.

0692 Stein, Herbert. "The Evolving International Monetary System and Domestic Economic Policy." *American Economic Review* 55 (1965): 200–207.

Stein describes the evolution of the international monetary system during 1944 to 1965 and reviews its impact on U.S. economic policy.

0693 Stein, Herbert. *The Fiscal Revolution in America.* Chicago: University of Chicago Press, 1969.

Chapters 9 and 10 examine the Truman administration's contribution to fiscal policy, discussing the Employment Act of 1946, tax cuts, and the relationship between the Federal Reserve and the Treasury. Notes, index.

Income Data

0694 Fulmer, John L. "State Per Capita Income Differentials: 1940 and 1950." *Southern Economic Journal* 22 (1955): 32–47.

Employing census data, the author tested four factors with state per capita incomes, comparing regression coefficients for 1940 and 1951. All factors changed from 1940 to 1950, toward less agriculture, greater percentage of population employed, relatively fewer blacks, and a higher level of education.

0695 Gwartney, James. "Changes in the Nonwhite/White Income Ratio—1939–1967." *American Economic Review* 60 (1970): 872–83.

The nonwhite/white income ratio is a guide to determining reductions in discrimination against nonwhites. This study reveals that education, more than all other factors, is responsible for the improved economic conditions of many nonwhites. Table, notes.

0696 Lydall, Harold, and Lansing, John B. "A Comparison of the Distribution of Personal Income and Wealth in the United States and Great Britain." *American Economic Review* 49 (1959): 43–67.

This study compares income distribution, ownership, and type of capital in the two countries for

1950 to 1954, and concludes that the distributions were similar, with the United States having relatively more low-income spending units.

0697 McGee, Leroy R., and Goodman, Seymour S. "Postwar Cyclical Fluctuations in Income and Employment: Southeast and United States." *Southern Economics Journal* 31 (1965): 298–313.

This study examines the relatively cyclical stability of the Southeast (1945–61) in terms of the comparatively stabilizing or destabilizing nature of industrial composition. Few differences were found.

0698 Palmer, Ransord W. "Equality, Incentives, and Economic Policy." *American Economic Review* 70 (1980): 123–27.

In analyzing the problem of future reduction of income inequality between blacks and whites (1947–77), the solutions must be found in incentives to both human and physical capital investments. Tables, notes.

0699 Sorkin, Alan L. "Occupational Earnings and Education." *Monthly Labor Review* 91 (1968): 6–9.

This study examines census data (1940, 1950, and 1960) and concludes that during the wartime years (1940s) there was little correlation between earnings and education. However, in the 1950s a greater correlation grows between education and earnings. Tables, graphs, and notes.

Consumer Credit

0700 Brandt, Harry. "U.S. Monetary and Credit Policies Between the End of World War II and the Outbreak of the Korean War, with Special Emphasis on Quantitative Credit Controls." Ph.D. dissertation, Columbia University, 1954.

Monetary management was unimpressive since it was predominantly influenced by debt considerations rather than changing economic and business conditions. Also examined here are credit controls during 1946 to 1948 and the recession of 1949. DAI 14:1954.

0701 Brehm, Carl T., Jr. "An Evaluation of the Voluntary Credit Restraint Program of 1951–1952." Ph.D. dissertation, Indiana University, 1958.

This program was an attempt to control the level and direction of lending through the voluntary cooperation of financial institutions. There is some question whether commercial bankers cooperated. DAI 19:2257.

0702 Curtis, Clayton C. "Institutional Lenders in a Local Residential Mortgage Market, Los Angeles County, 1946–1951." Ph.D. dissertation, Indiana University, 1959.

This study investigated the county's housing market, including changes in population and families, income payments, and prices. DAI 20:1218.

0703 Kaczor, Ralph S. "Consumer Credit Controls and Their Economic Effects, 1941–1952." Ph.D. dissertation, Syracuse University, 1954.

On 1 November 1947 regulation of consumer credit was discontinued. From 20 September 1948 to 30 June 1949 it was reinstated to combat inflationary forces. From 12 October 1950 to 16 September 1952 regulations were established to control housing credits. DAI 14:2218.

0704 Sim, Herbert E. "The Internal Financing of Corporations in the United States, 1946–1954." Ph.D. dissertation, Syracuse University, 1958.

This study seeks to discover to what extent U.S. corporations depended upon internal or external funds for expansion. DAI 20:551.

0705 Wolozin, Harold. "The Control of Consumer Credit from 1941–1949." Ph.D. dissertation, Columbia University, 1955.

The enactment of Regulation W in 1941 marked the beginning of a decade of control of consumer credit by the board of governors of the Federal Reserve System. DAI 15:1749.

Inflation and Controls
See also *Wage Stabilization (Korean War)*.

0706 Auerbach, Carl A. "Presidential Administration of Prices and Wages." *George Washington Law Review* 35 (1966): 191–201.

The approaches of Presidents Truman, Eisenhower, Kennedy, and Johnson in combating the problems of unemployment and price instability are reviewed. Special emphasis is placed on presidential price-wage policies and intervention in private wage and price decision making. Notes.

0707 Bernstein, Barton J. "Charting a Course Between Inflation and Depression: Secretary of the Treasury Fred Vinson and the Truman Administration's Tax Bill." *Register of the Kentucky Historical Society* 66 (1968): 53–64.

Vinson and, reluctantly, Truman accepted the notion of a tax cut and a resulting unbalanced budget in 1945 as a means of avoiding either inflation or depression during the immediate postwar years. Notes.

0708 Bernstein, Barton J. "The Truman Administration and the Politics of Inflation." Ph.D. dissertation, Harvard University, 1963.

No abstract available.

0709 Bhatia, Rattan J. "Profits and the Rate of Change of Money Earnings in the United States, 1935–1959." *Economica* [Great Britain] 29 (1962): 255–62.

The implications of this study are that so-called cost-inflation has been generated by profit-push rather than wage-push in the United States, and that the period since World War II has witnessed general demand-pull inflation.

0710 Bronfenbrenner, Martin, and Holzman, Franklyn D. "Survey of Inflation Theory." *American Economic Review* 53 (1963): 593–661.

This is a bibliographical review of the main theoretical developments since 1945 regarding the causes and characteristics of inflation.

0711 Chandler, Lester. *Inflation in the United States, 1940–1948*. New York: Harper, 1951.

From the outbreak of war in 1939 to 1948, inflation escalated. Chandler suggests the course of inflation, its causes, and its curtailment. Bibliography, index.

0712 Goldberg, Benjamin. "Price Control During the Korean Emergency: The Petroleum Industry in the U.S.A." Ph.D. dissertation, American University, 1957.

When the Korean conflict broke out, the nation was not prepared to deal with the inflationary forces, a failure which was compounded by a tardiness in applying direct government controls. DAI 17:1001.

0713 Goodwin, Craufurd D., ed. *Exhortation and Controls: The Search for a Wage-Price Policy, 1945–1971*. Washington, DC: Brookings Institution, 1975.

To curb inflation, Truman instituted a complex system of controls. Chapter 1 discusses the Truman administration. Notes, bibliography, appendixes, index.

0714 Harris, Seymour E. *The Economics of Mobilization and Inflation*. New York: Norton, 1951.

Harris was a consultant to the president's Council of Economic Advisers. He examines the problems of mobilization and inflation during 1950 and 1951. Notes, bibliography, index.

0715 Herren, Robert S. "Wage-Price Policy During the Truman Administration: A Postwar Problem and the Search for Its Solution." Ph.D. dissertation, Duke University, 1974.

This study traces the evolution of executive decision making about wage-price policy during the Truman administration, particularly how economic analysis influenced policy formation. DAI 36: 1698-A.

0716 Zimmerman, Joseph F. "The Inflation of 1950–1955." Ph.D. dissertation, Syracuse University, 1954.

The outbreak of the Korean War precipitated a sharp inflation in the United States, especially during the first nine months following American intervention in 1950. DAI 15:203.

Labor and Veterans

The bibliography by G. S. Stroud and G. S. Donahue, *Labor History in the United States* (#3022), may be of value.

0717 Bernstein, Barton J. "The Truman Administration and the Steel Strike of 1946." *Journal of American History* 52 (1966): 791–803.

The Truman administration was the victim of the politics of inflation, factor disputes, and mediocre advisers. To demonstrate this conclusion, the author focuses on the steel strike of 1946. Notes.

0718 Cabe, John C., Jr. "Govermental Intervention in Labor Disputes from 1945–1952." Ph.D. dissertation, University of Illinois, 1952.

This analysis includes the nonstatutory boards established by the president, beginning in 1946; the boards of inquiry (Taft-Hartley Act, 1947); the Atomic Energy Labor Relations Panel; and the Railroad Emergency boards. DAI 13:23.

0719 Ebanks, Walter W. "Government Employment and Post-World War II Economic Fluctuations: A Study of Stabilizing Effects of Government Employment." Ph.D. dissertation, New York University, 1973.

The central purpose of this statistical analysis is to determine whether government employment had a stabilizing or destabilizing effect on total employment. DAI 34:7439-A.

0720 Gallaway, Lowell E. "Labor Mobility, Resource Allocation, and Structural Unemployment." *American Economic Review* 53 (1963): 694–716.

This study of unemployment rates in eight sectors of the American economy and on eight occupational levels (1948–60) shows no significant historical changes in pattern. Notes.

0721 Heidenreich, Charles W. "An Analysis of Administrative Authority as Exercised by the National Labor Relations Board." Ph.D. dissertation, University of Minnesota, 1968.

This study examines the discretionary authority of the National Labor Relations Board and the discrepancies which are contained within the 1935 act and the 1947 act. DAI 29:3650-A.

0722 Holen, Arlene S. "Effects of Professional Licensing Arrangements on Interstate Labor Mobility and Resource Allocation." *Journal of Political Economy* 73 (1965): 492–98.

This essay demonstrates that while professional (lawyer, doctor, dentist) licensing aims at protecting the public, it also restricts freedom of entry and provides the basis for occupation monopolies. The author focuses on 1949 to arrive at these conclusions.

0723 Hughes, Jonathan. "The Great Strike at Nushagak Station, 1951: Institutional Gridlock." *Journal of Economic History* 41 (1982): 1–20.

The Bering Sea fishermen's union strike against the Bristol Bay salmon packers signaled the end of traditional labor-management relations. These events (1951–52) provide a microcosm of a larger evolution in American industry. Notes.

0724 Lammie, Wayne D. "Unemployment in the Truman Administration: Political, Economic and Social Aspects." Ph.D. dissertation, Ohio State University, 1973.

This study examines the historical development of unemployment and unemployment insurance during the Truman administration. DAI 34:705-A.

0725 Lipsitz, George. *Class and Culture in Cold War America: "A Rainbow at Midnight."* New York: Praeger, 1981.

The major focus of this volume is on the struggle of union workers to achieve higher wages and better working conditions during and at the end of World War II. Notes, appendix, bibliography, index.

0726 Mann, Seymour T. "Policy Formation in the Executive Branch: The Taft-Hartley Experience." *Western Political Quarterly* 13 (1960): 597–608.

The concerns and policies of the National Labor Relations Board, Department of Labor, and Bureau of the Budget during 1946 and 1947 with the anticipated labor legislation of the Eightieth Congress are examined.

0727 McClure, Arthur F. *The Truman Administration and the Problems of Postwar Labor, 1945–1948.* Rutherford: Fairleigh Dickinson University Press, 1969.

During the postwar period, labor problems posed some of the most pressing domestic issues facing Truman. Despite their differences, Truman received great support from organized labor in the 1948 election. Illustrations, bibliography, index.

0728 Parsley, C. J. "Labor Union Effects on Wage Gains: A Survey of Recent Literature." *Journal of Economic Literature* 18 (1980): 1–31.

This essay examines recent writings on the union-nonunion wage differential in the United States and Great Britain from the 1920s to the 1970s.

0729 Penington, Ralph A. "The National Labor Relations Board: Three Decades of Operations." Ph.D. dissertation, Purdue University, 1968.

This study focuses on an analysis of the board's workload and the flow of labor cases through the board process. Decisional aspects of the cases are not examined. DAI 29:2406-A.

0730 Rones, Philip L. "The Retirement Decision: A Question of Opportunity?" *Monthly Labor Review* 103 (1980): 14–17.

This essay examines retirement trends in America, 1950–59.

0731 Seligman, Ben B. "Automation and the State." *Commentary* 37 (1964): 49–54.

The research director of the Retail Clerks International Association reviews the years 1944 to 1964 and concludes that new technology has led to increasing unemployment for those who need jobs the most: the young and the unskilled.

0732 Sussna, Edward. "Public Policy Toward Labor-Management Relations in Local Public Utilities in Selected States, 1947–1952." Ph.D. dissertation, University of Illinois, 1954.

In 1947 seven states (Florida, Indiana, Missouri, Nebraska, New Jersey, Pennsylvania, and Wisconsin) passed laws which restricted public utility employees from the right to strike. DAI 14:1949.

0733 Warne, Colston E., ed. *Yearbook of American Labor.* Vol. 2: *Labor in Postwar America.* New York: Remsen, 1949.

These essays cover such topics as decontrol of wages and prices, industrial relations, labor conditions, Social Security, NLRB, Employment Act of 1946, and collective bargaining during 1945 to 1948. Roster of postwar labor unions, footnotes, index.

0734 Wolkinson, Benjamin W., and Barton, David. "Arbitration and the Rights of Mentally Handicapped Workers." *Monthly Labor Review* 103 (1980): 41–47.

This essay reviews the rights and protections of mentally disabled workers from 1947 to 1978.

EMPLOYMENT ACT (1946)

0735 Bailey, Stephen K. *Congress Makes a Law: The Story Behind the Employment Act of 1946.* New York: Columbia University Press, 1950.

The Employment Act of 1946 is a compromise of the full employment principle. This volume traces the development of that act. Notes, appendixes, bibliography, index.

0736 Bailey, Stephen K. "Political Elements in Full Employment Policy." *American Economic Review: Papers and Proceedings* 45 (1955): 341–50.

While this essay covers a broad era, it does examine the impact of the Employment Act of 1946 and compares it with previous organizational changes and subsequent reforms.

0737 Colm, Gerhard, ed. *The Employment Act; Past and Future: A Tenth Anniversary Symposium.* Washington, DC: National Planning Association, 1956.

This volume consists of statements and evaluations by government officials and academics who are commenting on the scope and achievements of the 1946 Employment Act.

0738 Fisher, Louis. "Developing Fiscal Responsibility." *Proceeding of the Academy of Political Science* 34 (1981): 62–75.

This study examines the budgetary process of Congress by comparing three episodes: the Budget and Accounting Act (1921), the Employment Act (1946), and the Congressional Budget and Impoundment Control Act (1974). Notes.

0739 Ginsburg, Helen. "Full Employment as a Policy Issue." *Policy Studies Journal* 8 (1979): 359–68.

This study describes the federal legislative debate on full employment since the Full Employment Bill of 1946 and traces the unemployment pattern.

0740 Lansdowne, Jerry W. "An Appraisal of a National Policy: The Employment Act of 1946." Ph.D. dissertation, University of Arizona, 1968.

The Employment Act prescribed that the federal government provide for maximum employment and purchasing power while maintaining a free enterprise economy. The Joint Economic Committee of Congress was responsible for the appraisal of economic performance. DAI 29:1257-A.

0741 Mitchell, Howard E. "The Employment Act of 1946 and the Economic Role of Government: Trends in Economic Thinking and Prescription." Ph.D. dissertation, University of Washington, 1958.

With the introduction of the concept of "growth" in the January 1948 *Economic Report*, emphasis shifted away from "preventing unemployment" to "assuring" maximum employment by achieving and maintaining a rate of growth adequate to absorb the entire U.S. labor force. DAI 19:694.

0742 Nourse, Edwin G. "Early Flowering of the Employment Act." *Virginia Quarterly Review* 43 (1967): 233–47.

The first twenty-one years (1946–67) of the Employment Act of 1946, which created the Joint Economic Committee of Congress and the Council of Economic Advisers, are examined.

0743 Nourse, Edwin G. *Economics in the Public Service: Administrative Aspects of the Employment Act.* New York: Harcourt, Brace, 1953.

Nourse, chairman of the Council of Economic Advisers, offers his personal interpretation of the Employment Act and discusses the role of the council. Appendixes, index.

0744 Rogers, Joe O. "The Impact of Economic Theory on Public Policy: The Case of Technological Change and Employment Policy." Ph.D. dissertation, Duke University, 1978.

This study, which covers 1930 to 1962, selects the Employment Act of 1946 as one of three pieces of legislation for examination. DAI 39:7459-A.

TAFT-HARTLEY ACT (1947)

0745 Kovarsky, Irving. "A Social and Legal Analysis of the Secondary Boycott in Labor Disputes." Ph.D. dissertation, State University of Iowa, 1956.

This study examines the impact of the Taft-Hartley Act on the use of secondary boycotts, an issue that became blurred with the 1947 legislation. DAI 16-678.

0746 Lee, R. Alton. *Truman and Taft-Hartley: A Question of Mandate.* Lexington: University of Kentucky Press, 1966.

Lee finds a basic dichotomy between the legislative and executive branches: Congress tends to be dominated by members who reflect the interests of the business and agricultural segments of society, whereas the president tends to represent the interests of the urban laborer. Lee discusses the Taft-Hartley act within this context. Notes, bibliographical essay, index.

0747 Levitan, Sar A. "Labor Under the Taft-Hartley Act." *Current History* 37 (1959): 160–64.

This survey of the major provisions of the Labor Management Relations Act (1947) focuses on internal affairs, finance reporting, collective bargaining, communist affiliation, and strikes during 1947 to 1959.

0748 Luck, Thomas J. "Effects of the Taft-Hartley Act on Labor Agreements, 1947–1952." *Southern Economic Journal* 20 (1953): 145–55.

The unions appeared to have gained in the development of union security provisions since the passage of the act. Notes.

0749 Mayer, Erwin S. "Union Attitudes Toward the Taft-Hartley Act, 1947–1954." Ph.D. dissertation, University of Washington, 1956.

Unions were concerned with specific problems of operation under the act relating to union security, problems of adaptation to the act, the administrative machinery and its functioning, and restrictions on strikes and on picketing. DAI 16:2045.

0750 Millis, Harry A., and Brown, Emily Clark. *From the Wagner Act to Taft-Hartley: A Study of National Labor Policy and Labor Relations.* Chicago: University of Chicago Press, 1950.

This volume contains a lengthy contemporary account of the Labor-Management Relations Act (1947) from inception to 1949; additionally, the initial chapters on the Wagner Act (1935) provide an introduction to postwar labor legislation. Notes, bibliography, index.

0751 Pomper, Gerald. "Labor and Congress: The Repeal of Taft-Hartley." *Labor History* 2 (1961): 323–43.

After labor's victory in the 1948 election, efforts were made in the Eighty-first Congress to repeal the Taft-Hartley Act. Labor contributed to the failure to achieve significant modifications because of its disunity and unwillingness to compromise. Notes.

0752 Pomper, Gerald M. "Organized Labor in Politics: The Campaign to Revise the Taft-Hartley Act." Ph.D. dissertation, Princeton University, 1959.

This study focuses on the activities of the American Federation of Labor and Congress of Industrial Organizations, 1947–54. DAI 20:2366.

0753 Rehmus, Charles M. "Government and Critical Labor-Management Disputes." Ph.D. dissertation, Stanford University, 1958.

This account details the nature of the dispute and the operation of the machinery established by the Taft-Hartley Act (1947) on thirteen occasions from 1947 to 1956. The author focuses his analysis on the "national security" provisions of the Taft-Hartley Act. DAI 19:349.

0754 Reilly, Gerard D. "The Legislative History of the Taft-Hartley Act." *George Washington Law Review* 29 (1960): 285–300.

A brief history of the act is provided here; it is useful for an introduction to the issues.

0755 Richardson, James R. "The Taft-Hartley Act: Punishment or Progress?" *Kentucky Law Journal* 42 (1953): 27–52.

An early assessment of the act, this essay reviews the attitudes of both labor and management toward possible revision. Notes.

0756 Rives, Stanley G. "Dialectic and Rhetoric in Congress: A Study of Congressional Consideration of the Labor Management Relations Act of 1947." Ph.D. dissertation, Northwestern University, 1963.

This study looks at the relationship between the hearings and the congressional debate on the Taft-Hartley Act. The debates revealed that data acquired in the hearings were used extensively. DAI 24:3883.

0757 Schlichter, Sumner H. "Revision of the Taft-Hartley Act." *Quarterly Journal of Economics* 67 (1953): 149–80.

The author argues that the act is an improvement over the Wagner Act because it strikes a balance between employer, individual worker, neutrals, and the general public. Notes.

0758 Schlichter, Sumner H. "The Taft-Hartley Act." *Quarterly Journal of Economics* 63 (1949): 1–31.

Written under the assumption that the Taft-Hartley Act would soon be replaced, the author seeks to determine its merits and defects. Notes.

0759 "The Taft-Hartley Act After Ten Years: A Symposium." *Industrial and Labor Relations Review* 11 (1958): 327–412.

The act remained virtually unchanged after ten years. These essays examine the calls for reform of the act and the experiences under it.

0760 Taylor, Zachary, Jr. "The Secondary Boycott and the Taft-Hartley Act, 1947–1954." Ph.D. dissertation, University of Illinois, 1957.

The Taft-Hartley Act appears to provide a workable atmosphere for collective bargaining. The act restricting unilateral union restraints facilitates a free market and technological advance. DAI 18:431.

0761 Templeton, Ronald K. "The Campaign of the American Federation of Labor and the Congress of Industrial Organizations to Prevent the Passage of the Labor Management Relations Act of 1947." Ph.D. dissertation, Ball State University, 1967.

Labor launched an aggressive campaign to defeat congressional passage of the Taft-Hartley Act; however, the tide had been running against them since 1938. DAI 28:3793-A.

0762 Toner, Jerome L. "Union Shop under Taft-Hartley." *Southern Economic Journal* 20 (1954): 258–73.

A union shop contract, made by an employer and a union, was permitted by the Taft-Hartley Act. Its evolution under the act is developed. Notes.

0763 Young, James E. "Unfair Labor Practices under the Labor-Management Relations Act, 1947–1957: A Study of N.L.R.B. Cases Pertaining to the Unfair Labor Practices of Unions under Section 8(b) of the Act." Ph.D. dissertation, Ohio State University, 1959.

This study focuses on the development of policy under Section 8(b) by examining the decisions and orders of the National Labor Relations Board and court decisions. DAI 20:3977.

WAGE STABILIZATION (KOREAN WAR)

See also *Inflation and Controls.*

0764 Henning, Dale A. "Wage Stabilization Policies and Problems, 1950–1953." Ph.D. dissertation, University of Illinois, 1954.

This study examines the wage control program established to control economic disturbances during the Korean War. DAI 14:1955.

0765 Stein, Bruno. "Labor Participation in Stabilization Agencies: The Korean War Period as a Case Study." Ph.D. dissertation, New York University, 1959.

The relationship between organized labor and the government in the establishment and operation of an economic stabilization program, 1950–53, is reviewed. Labor's aims were more or less achieved. DAI 27:115-A.

0766 Stein, Bruno. "Wage Stabilization in the Korean War Period: The Role of the Subsidiary Wage Boards." *Labor History* 4 (1963): 161–77.

Generally wage problems were heard by fourteen Regional Wage Stabilization Boards. Special boards were set up for the railways and airline unions and for the construction industry. A Review and Appeals Committee heard appeals and reviewed wage increases.

0767 Stieber, Jack. "Labor's Walkout From the Korean War Wage Stabilization Board." *Labor History* 21 (1980): 239–60.

Organized labor walked out of participation in the Wage Stabilization Board on 16 February 1951, resulting in making the WSB more concerned with labor issues than had the union representatives remained. Notes.

UNION ACTIVITIES

0768 Barbash, Jack. *Unions and Telephones: The Story of the Communications Workers of America.* New York: Harper, 1952.

The Communications Workers of America (CWA) is one of the youngest unions, not forming until 1947. Barbash discusses its origins and its struggle for survival. Index.

0769 Beck, E. M. "Labor Unionism and Racial Income Inequality: A Time Series Analysis of the Post-World War II Period." *American Journal of Sociology* 85 (1980): 791–814.

Beck finds that labor union activity in the United States during 1947 to 1974 has increased between-race inequality in family income and reduced within-race inequality.

0770 Bell, Daniel. "The Subversion of Collective Bargaining." *Commentary* 29 (1960): 185–97.

Using the steel industry (1947–57) as an example, Bell concludes that collective bargaining has resulted in securing a marketplace position for large corporations.

0771 Brooks, Thomas R. *Picket Lines and Bargaining Tables: Organized Labor Comes of Age, 1935–1955.* New York: Grosset & Dunlap, 1968.

In the immediate postwar years, strikes in the auto, steel, and coal industries consolidated union power. The merger of the AFL and the CIO is traced in this book. Illustrations, index.

0772 Calkins, Fay. *The CIO and the Democratic Party.* Chicago: University of Chicago Press, 1952.

Through five case studies of union-party relationships, Calkins seeks to uncover the relationships between the CIO and the Democratic party in the 1950 local, state, and congressional elections. Illustrations, bibliography.

0773 Carey, James B. "Organized Labor in Politics." *Annals of the American Academy of Political and Social Science* (1958): 52–62.

Carey surveys the presence of organized labor groups in national politics during the 1940s and 1950s and focuses on its effects in public policy formation.

0774 Chamberlain, Neil W., et al., eds. *A Decade of Industrial Relations Research, 1946–1956.* New York: Industrial Relations Research Associates, 1958.

Essays in this volume cover such topics as union government and union leadership, collective bargaining, wage determination, economic effects of unionism, employee benefit plans, and the labor movement abroad. Notes.

0775 Dulles, Foster Rhea. *Labor in America.* 3rd ed. New York: Crowell, 1966.

This broad survey of America's labor movement provides a fine perspective from which to view the policies of the Truman administration. Bibliography, index.

0776 El-Messidi, Kathyanne Groehn. "Sure Principles Midst Uncertainties: The Story of the 1948 GM-UAW Contract." Ph.D. dissertation, University of Oklahoma, 1976.

In May 1948 the richest corporation and largest union in the United States agreed to a contract which initiated three history-making principles: (1) wage escalation according to the Consumer Price Index increases or decreases; (2) automatic yearly wage increases according to historical annual manufacturing worker productivity, between 2 and 3 percent; and (3) longer term contracts. DAI 37:3126-A.

0777 Foster, James C. *The Union Politic: The CIO Political Action Committee.* Columbia: University of Missouri Press, 1975.

The Political Action Committee of the CIO (1943) coordinated the organization's political efforts. This volume details some of the crucial issues of the 1940s. Notes, bibliography, index.

0778 Goldberg, Arthur J. *AFL-CIO Labor United.* New York: McGraw-Hill, 1956.

Goldberg was general counsel of the CIO. He recounts the events leading to the 1955 merger of the AFL-CIO. Appendixes, index.

0779 Greenstone, J. David. *Labor in American Politics.* New York: Knopf, 1969.

Greenstone finds that the American labor movement, however much it appeals to economic interests in recruiting its members, has increasingly come to act in national politics less as an economic interest group than as an integral part of the Democratic party. Notes, bibliography, index.

0780 Hardisky, David L. "The Rochester General Strike of 1946." Ph.D. dissertation, University of Rochester, 1983.

On 16 May 1946 Louis B. Cartwright, city manager in Rochester, New York, fired 489 Department of Public Works employees to prevent the spread of unions into the public sector. Even though forced to reinstate these workers, he succeeded in destroying the DPW workers' local. DAI 44:1549-A.

0781 Jensen, Vernon H. *Strife on the Waterfront: The Port of New York Since 1945.* Ithaca, NY: Cornell University Press, 1974.

The longshoremen's strike (1945) marked the beginning of new labor relations in the longshoring industry. Notes, bibliography, index.

0782 Lichtenstein, Nelson. "Auto Worker Militancy and the Structure of Factory Life, 1937–1955." *Journal of American History* 67 (1980): 335–53.

This study found the United Automobile Workers of America centralizing its power after World War II in order to curb the power of the semiskilled workers and the locals. Notes.

0783 Matles, James, and Higgins, James. *Them & Us: Struggles of a Rank & File Union.* Englewood Cliffs, NJ: Prentice-Hall, 1975.

The general secretary of the United Electrical, Radio and Machine Workers union provides a selected history. Chapters 11 to 14 deal with the impact of the Cold War, McCarthyism, Hubert Humphrey, and the 1948 election. Index.

0784 Nagle, Richard W. "Collective Bargaining in Basic Steel and the Federal Government, 1945–1960." Ph.D. dissertation, Pennsylvania State University, 1978.

United Steelworkers of America, federal government, and steel industry negotiations were essentially three-way activities. While the Truman administration became greatly involved, the Eisenhower administration maintained a posture of noninvolvement. DAI 39:1062-A.

0785 Pierson, Frank C. "The Economic Influence of Big Unions." *Annals of the American Academy of Political and Social Sciences* (1961): 96–107.

After reviewing Big Labor's influence (1947–59), Pierson assigns the greatest influence to automobile, coal, construction, railroad, steel, and trucking unions.

0786 Roukis, George S. "American Labor and the Conservative Republicans, 1946–1948: A Study in Economic and Political Conflict." Ph.D. dissertation, New York University, 1973.

Although organized labor rejected the Taft-Hartley Act, and trained their heaviest rhetoric on it, they were equally disappointed in the taxing and housing features of Republican legislation. DAI 34:5076-A.

0787 Schatz, Ronald W. "American Electrical Workers: Work, Struggles, Aspirations, 1930–1950." Ph.D. dissertation, University of Pittsburgh, 1977.

The union leaders who emerged in the 1940s were relatively young, predominantly semiskilled, unconcerned with ideology, and outspokenly hostile to management. DAI 38:5669-A.

0788 Seaton, Douglas P. "The Catholic Church and the Congress of Industrial Organizations: The Case of the Association of Catholic Trade Unionists, 1937–1950." Ph.D. dissertation, Rutgers University, 1975.

The Association of Catholic Trade Unionists enjoyed the official support of the Church and was the largest Catholic organization active in the labor movement. Its conservative mood stood against communism and socialism in the labor movement. DAI 36:6869-A.

0789 Skeels, Jack M. "The Development of Political Stability within the United Auto Workers Union." Ph.D. dissertation, University of Wisconsin, 1957.

This study examines Walter Reuther's rise to the UAW presidency following the 1945–46 General Motors strike. DAI 17:2868.

0790 Sweeney, Vincent D. *The United Steelworkers of America: Twenty Years Later, 1936–1956.* Pittsburgh: United Steelworkers, 1956.

Chapters 10 to 16 of this self-advertisement relate to the steel union in the Truman years. Among the issues emphasized here are "cleaning out the communists" and fighting for pensions. Illustrations, tables.

0791 Taft, Philip. *The A.F. of L. from the Death of Gompers to the Merger.* New York: Harper, 1959.

Such topics as postwar economic and political programs, foreign policy, and black workers are examined in this history of the AFL from the 1920s to its merger with the CIO in 1955. Notes, index.

0792 Troy, Lee. "The Growth of Union Membership in the South, 1939–1953." *Southern Economic Journal* 24 (1958): 407–20.

The relative growth of unions in the South (1939–53) was greater than for the nation, but measured by the increase in the nonfarm employees organized, the South lagged behind the national average. Notes.

0793 Zeiger, Robert H. "Memory Speaks: Observations on Personal History and Working Class Structure." *Maryland History* 8 (1977): 1–12.

The author comments on the social history available in four labor publications. Each of the studies additionally sheds light on the United Auto Workers. Notes.

Benefits Programs

0794 Hardbeck, George W. "Union-Management Health and Welfare Programs since 1945." Ph.D. dissertation, University of Illinois, 1958.

Relying on the Senate hearings on "Health and Welfare Plans" and on case studies of specific health and welfare plans, the author proceeds to ask questions relating to the needs of workers and management. DAI 19:973.

0795 Munts, Raymond. *Bargaining for Health: Labor Unions, Health Insurance, and Medical Care.* Madison: University of Wisconsin Press, 1967.

This account contains much material on the Truman years. However, since it is arranged topically, the researcher will have to examine each chapter. Notes, index.

0796 Somers, Norman, and Schwartz, Louis. "Pension and Welfare Plans: Gratuities or Compensation?" *Industrial and Labor Relations Review* 4 (1950): 79–89.

In 1949 the Supreme Court upheld the National Labor Relations Board's decision requiring the Inland Steel Company to bargain collectively with the United Steelworkers for a pension plan. A month later, the courts upheld an NLRB order requiring the W.W. Cross Company to bargain collectively concerning a health insurance plan. Notes.

UNION LEADERS

Many of the accounts listed in *Union Activities* contain material on these and other labor leaders.

0797 Fink, Gary M., ed. *Biographical Dictionary of American Labor Leaders.* Westport, CT: Greenwood, 1964.

This volume provides a useful guide to some 500 selected men and women, many of whom played a significant role in the labor movement during the Truman years.

0798 Madison, Charles A. *American Labor Leaders: Personalities and Forces in the Labor Movement.* New York: Ungar, 1962.

The chapters provide biographical information on such labor leaders as John L. Lewis, William Green, David Dubinsky, Philip Murray, Sidney Hillman, Walter Reuther, and Harry Bridges.

Walter Reuther

0799 Barnard, John W. *Walter Reuther and the Rise of the Auto Workers.* Boston: Little, Brown, 1983.

Reuther's role in organizing the United Auto Workers union is examined. Chapters 6 to 8 focus on the Truman years. Illustrations, notes, bibliography, index.

0800 Bernstein, Barton J. "Walter Reuther and the General Motors Strike of 1945–1946." *Michigan History* 49 (1965): 260–77.

Reuther pressed the strike for ideological and practical reasons: (1) he sought a pay raise without price compensation, and (2) he hoped the strike would help him gain the UAW presidency. Notes.

0801 Cormier, Frank, and Eaton, William. *Reuther.* Englewood Cliffs, NJ: Prentice-Hall, 1970.

During the postwar period, Reuther emerged as one of labor's most aggressive and imaginative leaders. Photographs, notes, bibliography, index.

0802 Reuther, Victor. *The Brothers Reuther and the Story of the U.A.W.: A Memoir.* Boston: Houghton Mifflin, 1976.

This account contains material relating to the issues of Communists in unions and McCarthyism during the Truman era. Appendix, index.

0803 Slack, Walter H. "Walter Reuther: A Study of Ideas." Ph.D. dissertation, State University of Iowa, 1965.

This study examines Reuther's views on a variety of subjects, including unemployment, automation, administered prices, economic planning, collective bargaining, the Kohler strike, the farm problem, poverty, and civil rights. DAI 26:2849.

John L. Lewis

0804 Dubovsky, Melvyn, and Van Tine, Warren. *John L. Lewis: A Biography.* New York: Quadrangle/New York Times Book Co., 1977.

This is the best biographical treatment of the coal miners union chief. Chapters 19 and 20 deal with Lewis's confrontations with the Truman administration. Notes, bibliographical sketch, index.

0805 Shurbet, Joanna Healey. "John L. Lewis: The Truman Years." Ph.D. dissertation, Texas Tech University, 1975.

Truman's control over the problems of reconversion was threatened by Lewis's United Mine Workers whom he led in 1946 to a prolonged and costly strike. DAI 36:6902-A.

Harry Bridges

0806 Schwartz, Harvey. "Harry Bridges and the Scholars: Looking at History's Verdict." *California History* 59 (1980): 66–79.

While the government tried to deport him, Bridges approved of Communist unionists, opposed American entry in the Korean War, and supported Henry Wallace in 1948. Scholars have varied widely in their assessments.

0807 Larrowe, Charles P. *Harry Bridges: The Rise and Fall of Radical Labor in the United States.* New York: Lawrence Hill, 1972.

President of the International Longshoremen's and Warehousemen's Union (1937–77), Bridges denounced Truman's foreign policy and endorsed Soviet aims. Because of this outspoken position, the ILWU was ousted from the CIO in 1950. Index.

Others

0808 Dubinsky, David, and Raskin, A. H. *David Dubinsky: A Life with Labor.* New York: Simon & Schuster, 1977.

Dubinsky was president of the International Ladies Garment Workers Union and a founder of Americans for Democratic Action. Illustrations, index.

0809 Goulden, Joseph C. *Meany.* New York: Atheneum, 1972.

George Meany was secretary-treasurer of the AFL during the Truman era. Although he fought the administration over labor issues, he firmly supported Truman's foreign policy and anticommunism. Notes, index.

0810 Josephson, Matthew. *Sidney Hillman: Statesman of American Labor.* Garden City, NY: Doubleday, 1952.

The last chapter deals with Hillman's activities at the close of World War II and during the early Truman years. Notes, index.

0811 McDonald, David J. *Union Man.* New York: Dutton, 1969.

McDonald was elected president of the United Steelworkers of America in 1953 but had been involved with the union for many years. This is as much a study of the steelworkers union as it is an autobiography of McDonald. Illustrations, index.

0812 Tate, Juanita Diffay. "Philip Murray as a Labor Leader." Ph.D. dissertation, New York University, 1962.

Murray was vice-president of the United Mine Workers union, and later president of the CIO. DAI 27:3595.

0813 Whittemore, L. H. *The Man Who Ran the Subways: The Story of Mike Quill.* New York: Holt, Rinehart and Winston, 1968.

As president of the Transport Workers Union (1935–66), Quill vigorously attacked the Truman administration and supported Wallace in 1948. He was a central figure in the CIO-Communist controversy. Illustrations, bibliography, index.

LABOR AND COMMUNISM

For labor's views on the Cold War, see Chapter 7, *Labor and Foreign Affairs;* also see Chapter 6, *Internal Security and Civil Liberties.*

0814 Andrew, William D. "Factionalism and Anticommunism: Ford Local 600." *Labor History* 20 (1979): 227–55.

Although the House Un-American Activities Committee hearings (1952) provided a rationale for the United Auto Workers to create an administratorship of Local 600, its factionalism and anti-Reuther activities were also important elements in the decision. Notes.

0815 Cochran, Bert. *Labor and Communism: The Conflict That Shaped American Unions.* Princeton: Princeton University Press, 1977.

This volume looks at the Communist issue, particularly in regard to the CIO and several important industrial unions. Photographs, notes, index.

0816 Emspak, Frank. "The Break-up of the Congress of Industrial Organizations (CIO), 1945–1950." Ph.D. dissertation, University of Wisconsin, 1972.

The CIO expelled almost a million members in 1949 as a result of a prolonged struggle between conservative and liberal factions, according to the author. Between 1945 and 1949 the CIO changed from a progressive antiwar force to an anti-Communist, status-quo-oriented organization. DAI 32:6886-A.

0817 Huntley, Horace. "Iron Ore Miners and Mine Mill in Alabama, 1933–1952." Ph.D. dissertation, University of Pittsburgh, 1977.

As a case study, Mine Mill is used here to balance the unfair portrayal of the allegedly Communist-dominated and inspired unions affiliated with the CIO. The loss of the union deeply affected black workers. DAI 38:3657-A.

0818 Johnson, Ronald W. "Organized Labor's Postwar Red Scare: The UE in St. Louis." *North Dakota Quarterly* 48 (1980): 28–39.

Liberal and right-wing individuals within the Congress of Industrial Organizations led antiradical attacks on District 8 of the United Electrical, Radio and Machine Workers of America (UE) during the late 1940s.

0819 Kampelman, Max M. *The Communist Party vs. the C.I.O.: A Study in Power Politics.* New York: Praeger, 1957.

Kampelman discusses Communist infiltration and its subsequent purge from the CIO, 1936–55. Notes, appendix, bibliography, index.

0820 Keeran, Roger R. "Everything For Victory: Communist Influence in the Auto Industry During World War II." *Science and Society* 43 (1979): 1–28.

Even with waning power after 1943, Communists remained influential among black workers and were by no means a negligible force in the United Automobile Workers in the immediate postwar period. Notes.

0821 Oshinsky, David M. "Labor's Cold War: The CIO and the Communists." In Robert Griffith and Athan Theoharis, eds. *The Specter: Original Essays on the Cold War and the Origins of McCarthyism.* New York: New Viewpoints, 1974, pp. 116–50.

The CIO moved to its anti-Communist position for a number of reasons, most of which are presented here. Notes.

0822 Oshinsky, David M. *Senator Joseph McCarthy and the American Labor Movement.* Columbia: University of Missouri Press, 1976.

When McCarthy discovered the Communist issue in 1950, he alarmed organized labor, especially the CIO. In the 1952 campaign labor almost defeated McCarthy in a Republican year.

0823 Prickett, James R. "Communists and the Communist Issue in the American Labor Movement, 1920–1960." Ph.D. dissertation, University of California, Los Angeles, 1975.

Chapters 5 and 6 cover the struggle between Communists and anti-Communists in the National Maritime and the United Electrical unions in the postwar years. Chapter 7 explores the Communist controversy in the national CIO. DAI 36:5499-A.

0824 Prickett, James R. "Some Aspects of the Communist Controversy in the CIO." *Science and Society* 33 (1969): 299–321.

Foreign policy issues appear to the author to be the major reason for the expulsion in 1946 and 1947 of several CIO unions. Notes.

0825 Saposs, David J. *Communism in American Unions.* New York: McGraw-Hill, 1959.

The postdepression eagerness for social reform plus international events which made Russia our ally created an atmosphere that promoted Communist activities. Saposs looks at Communist infiltration of unions and the unions' efforts to combat it. Notes, index.

MINORITY AND WOMEN WORKERS

For Mexican-American farm workers, see *Bracero Program*.

Fair Employment Practice Committee

0826 Bailey, Robert J. "Theodore G. Bilbo and the Fair Employment Practices Controversy: A Southern Senator's Reactions to a Changing World." *Journal of Mississippi History* 42 (180): 27–42.

Senator Dennis Chavez (New Mexico) sought to establish a permanent Fair Employment Practice Committee in 1945. Senator Bilbo (Mississippi) launched a campaign including a twenty-four-day filibuster which led to the bill's defeat.

0827 Kesselman, Louis. *The Social Politics of FEPC: A Study in Reform Pressure Movements.* Chapel Hill: University of North Carolina Press, 1948.

This is an account of the National Council for a Permanent FEPC (1943–45). Notes, bibliography, index.

0828 Reed, Merl E. "FEPC and the Federal Agencies in the South." *Journal of Negro History* 65 (180): 43–56.

Employment discrimination on the basis of race was a way of life in the South. Consequently, efforts of the Fair Employment Practice Committee on behalf of nondiscrimination were revolutionary even during the emergency of World War II.

0829 Ruchames, Louis. *Race, Jobs & Politics: The Story of FEPC.* New York: Columbia University Press, 1953.

Chapter 13 focuses on the unhappy efforts to achieve a permanent Fair Employment Practice Committee from 1945 to 1950. Notes, index.

Minority Workers

0830 Dickerson, Dennis C. "Black Steelworkers in

Western Pennsylvania, 1915–1950." Ph.D. dissertation, Washington University, 1978.

The United Steelworkers failed to push vigorously for racial equality in the mills. In 1950 black steelworkers were, as in 1915, disproportionately represented in lower paying, unskilled, and semiskilled jobs. DAI 39:6902-A.

0831 Gilman, Harry J. "Economic Discrimination and Unemployment." *American Economic Review* 55 (1965): 1077–96.

Unemployment rates for whites and minorities are analyzed for 1940 to 1961.

0832 Reich, Michael. "The Persistence of Racial Inequality in Urban Areas and Industries, 1950–1970." *American Economic Review* 70 (180): 128–31.

Aside from gains in the South for black males, the decline in equality, nationally, results from blacks moving between economic sectors. Notes.

0833 Smith, Alonzo N. "Black Employment in the Los Angeles Area, 1938–1948." Ph.D. dissertation, University of California, Los Angeles, 1978.

From 1945 to 1948 some of the wartime gains were preserved, but many were lost. There was far more public commitment to the idea of racial equality as black workers had risen in the ranks of organized labor, yet many of the new postwar industrial activities hired only whites. DAI 39:6285-A.

Women Workers

0834 Decter, Midge. "Women At Work." *Commentary* 31 (1961): 243–50.

Women's role in the labor force (1946–60) is reviewed from statistics dealing with occupation, wages, and union clout of women workers.

0835 Gabin, Nancy. "Women Workers and the UAW in the Post-World War II Period, 1945–54." *Labor History* 21 (1980): 5–30.

Women were discriminated against not only by management but by local appeals committees and the International Executive Board of the Automobile Workers. These bodies systematically upheld agreements prohibiting the employment of married women, providing unequal hiring and wage rates on similar jobs, and disallowing women's seniority rights. Notes.

0836 Peter, Esther. "Working Women." *Daedalus* 93 (1974): 671–99.

This essay provides statistics on employment, salary, and occupation of working women, 1940–62.

0837 Suelzle, Marijean. "Women in Labor." *Trans-Action* 8 (1970): 50–58.

This survey (1930–70) of the changing profile of American working women finds that declining birth, marriage, and death rates have allowed more women

to enter the working class at all levels, but primarily in low-paying jobs.

VETERANS

0838 Bodenger, Robert G. "Soldier's Bonuses: A History of Veterans' Benefits in the United States, 1776–1967." Ph.D. dissertation, Pennsylvania State University, 1971.

This study relates how the post-World War II "G.I. Bill of Rights" compares with other veterans' bonuses. DAI 32:6328-A.

0839 Cole, Garold. "Home from the Wars: the Popular Press Views the Veteran Problem, 1944–1948." *North Dakota Quarterly* 46 (1978): 41–61.

The press displayed considerable concern with the psychological readjustment of World War II veterans, as well as with G.I. benefits and the economy. Notes.

0840 Little, Roger D., and Fredland, J. Eric. "Veteran Status, Earnings, and Race: Some Long Term Results." *Armed Forces and Society* 5 (1979): 244–60.

Veterans' wages twenty years after their service suggest that military service exerted a positive influence on the 1966 earnings of all racial groups, but that blacks and other minorities profited most. Tables, notes.

0841 Pearson, Alec P., Jr. "Olin E. Teague and the Veterans' Administration." Ph.D. dissertation, Texas A & M University, 1977.

While the congressman prevented veterans' "raids" on the treasury, he did fight to maintain medical and loan programs. During the Truman years, he led an investigation of the Servicemen's Readjustment Act (G.I. Bill) in the early 1950s and discovered staggering abuses in the program. Later his Korean G.I. Bill provided for a sounder program. DAI 38:2306-A.

0842 Ross, Davis R. B. *Preparing for Ulysses: Politics and Veterans During World War II*. New York: Columbia University Press, 1969.

Ross examines the legislative origins of veterans' programs during the war years. His account is an essential introduction for the Truman years. Footnotes, extensive bibliography, index.

Education Programs

0843 Bloom, Samuel B. "The Servicemen's Readjustment Act of 1944: A Case Study of Federal Aid to Higher Education, 1944–1954." Ph.D. dissertation, University of California, Berkeley, 1963.

Veterans were able to attend denominational schools, which thus constitutes federal aid to religious schools. This study explores the arguments that have been advanced for and against federal aid to education in light of this experience. DAI 24:5509.

0844   Dooher, Philip M. "Higher Education and the Veteran: An Historical Study of Change in a Select Number of Massachusetts' Colleges and Universities, 1944–1949." Ph.D. dissertation, Boston College, 1980.

Massachusetts's colleges and universities prepared for veterans by establishing new programs and services. New directions were established in admissions, academic policy, and credit for service-connected programs. DAI 41:549-A.

0845   Fleming, George M. "Historical Survey of the Educational Benefits Provided Veterans of World War II by the Servicemen's Readjustment Act of 1944." Ed.D. dissertation, University of Houston, 1957.

The study emphasizes the administrative problems and abuses encountered in applying the G.I. Bill. DAI 17:2578.

0846   Nam, Charles B. "Impact of the 'GI Bills' on the Educational Level of the Male Population." *Social Forces* 43 (1964): 26–32.

The rising trend in formal education before the war would have continued even without the G.I. bills; therefore, the G.I. bills were essentially responses to the growing demands for formal education.

0847   Olson, Keith W. "The G.I. Bill and Higher Education: A Success and Surprise." *American Quarterly* 25 (1973): 596–610.

Veterans interpreted the bill as a bonus, not an antidepression measure, and successfully pursued higher education in unexpected numbers. Higher education was little affected, however, by these competent students. Notes.

0848   Olson, Keith W. *The G.I. Bill, the Veterans and the Colleges*. Lexington: University Press of Kentucky, 1974.

Using the University of Wisconsin for a case study, Olson examines the higher education provisions of the World War II G.I. Bill, the veterans who used them, and the colleges at which the veterans studied. Notes, bibliographical essay, index.

0849   O'Shea, John A., Jr. "The Veterans' Cost-of-Instruction Program (VCIP): Its Genesis, Problems, and Successes." Ed.D. dissertation, George Washington University, 1978.

Included in the wide-ranging study is a review of World War II and Korean War veterans' programs in education. DAI 39:2092-A.

0850   Scott, Herbert H. "A Survey of the Institutional On-Farm Training Program in Oklahoma (1946–1950)." Ph.D. dissertation, Washington University, 1954.

While general provisions were made for veteran rehabilitation, there were no provisions applicable to training in farm operations. This study examines the development of specific programs and legislation for veteran training, including the disabled, under the "Institutional On-Farm Training Program." DAI 14:1591.

0851   Warriner, David R. "The Veterans of World War II at Indiana University, 1944–1951." Ph.D. dissertation, Indiana University, 1978.

Veterans caught colleges and universities unprepared for the enrollment, which at Indiana University doubled in 1945. The changes brought on by the new students signaled a new era for higher education. DAI 39:1066-A.

President Truman greets representatives of the motion picture industry, October 8, 1951: Elizabeth Taylor, Adolph Zukor, President Truman, Mrs. Randolph Scott, Joyce O'Hara, Debbie Reynolds, Louise Albritton, Arthur Mayer, Arthur Arthur, Julian Brylanski, Virginia Kellogg, and Randolph Scott. *Reproduced courtesy of UPI/Bettmann Archives.*

Domestic Affairs: The Arts, Culture, Health and Welfare, and Science and Technology

The Truman years were somber ones in many respects, but in the popular arts there was the emergence of a mass culture that drew vitality from the new medium of television and from the spread of the inexpensive, paperback book. New technology and general affluence propelled this trend. Writers took up the theme, and some important books dealt with the resultant problems of "conformity" and the role of the individual in a society of mass culture. David Riesman, et al., *The Lonely Crowd: A Study of the Changing American Character* (#964) is perhaps the classic study of this period regarding the shaping of American social and cultural values.

Trends in poetry, drama, and literature during the postwar era are summarized in Robert E. Spiller, et al., *Literary History of the United States* (#881), chapter 82, pages 1392–1410. Frank A. Ninkovich, "A New Criticism and Cold War America" (#893) examines the controversial decision to award the Bollingen Prize in Poetry (1949) to Ezra Pound, who had been indicted for treason during World War II and confined to a mental hospital.

Films were perhaps more reflective of the issues affecting American society. Michael J. Yavenditti, "Atomic Scientists and Hollywood: *The Beginning or the End*" (#906), June Sochen, "*Mildred Pierce* and Women in Film" (#902), and Thomas R. Cripps, "The Death of Rastus: Negroes in American Films Since 1945" (#899) focus on three such issues. The emerging Cold War also found its way into the movies, as shown by Leslie K. Adler, "The Politics of Culture: Hollywood and the Cold War" (#907).

Efforts at reforming educational practices continued during the Truman years. The biggest hurdle to the providing of federal aid to local schools was the religious (Church vs. State) issue. The legal ramifications are explored in Philip Gleason, "Blurring the Line of Separation: Education, Civil Religion, and Teaching About Religion" (#980); while Seymour P. Lachman, "The Cardinal, the Congressman, and the First Lady" (#983) focuses on the political aspects of the issue. W. Johnson and F. J. Colligan, *The Fulbright Program: A History* (#971) reviews the origins (1946) of this international scholarly exchange program. Minority admission (Catholics and Jews) to colleges is explored in Marcia G. Synnott, *The Half-Opened Door: Discrimination and Admissions at Harvard, Yale, and Princeton, 1900–1970* (#997).

Several compulsory national health insurance programs were proposed during the years immediately after World War II. Truman's support of one such program is discussed in Monte M. Poen, *Harry S. Truman versus the Medical Lobby: The Genesis of Medicare* (#939). The American Medical Association's position on compulsory health insurance and several other Fair Deal proposals may be found in Chapters 15 through 17 of James G. Burrow, *AMA: Voice of American Medicine* (#932). The passage of the National Mental Health Act of 1946, and the subsequent creation of a National Institute of Mental Health in 1949, is reviewed by Jeanne L. Brand, "The National Mental Health Act of 1946: A Retrospective" (#929).

The origins of the National Science Foundation (1950) are traced by Robert F. Maddox, "The Politics of World War II Science: Senator Harley M. Kilgore and the Legislative Origins of the National Science Foundation" (#1042); while Kenneth M. Jones, "The Endless Frontier" (#1041), examines the efforts of

Vannevar Bush, especially in 1945, toward the same end. The activities of the atomic scientists are discussed in Chapter 9. During these same years there was considerable activity toward the development of the modern computer. Herman H. Goldstine, *The Computer from Pascal to von Neumann* (#1036) provides a good introduction from the non-scientist; for the Truman era, see Part Three.

Arts and Music

0852 Buettner, William S. "American Art Theory, 1940–1960." Ph.D. dissertation, Northwestern University, 1973.

While the central focus is on the Abstract Expressionist movement, the account also treats the formation of the Abstract Expressionist aesthetic and the consequences which that set of ideas had for subsequent American art. DAI: 34:5830-A.

0853 Haymes, Howard J. "The Relationship of Selected Nonfictional Popular and Scholarly Literature about Women in the Post World War II Period (1946–1962) to the Ideas of Noted Writers of the American Women's Liberation Movement (1963–1970)." Ph.D. dissertation, New York University, 1974.

This study sought to uncover the relationship between the women's liberation movement and the popular and scholarly conceptions of women in the preceding postwar years. DAI 35:1009-A.

0854 Mathews, Jane DeHart. "Art and Politics in Cold War America." *American Historical Review* 81 (1976): 762–87.

Public patronage of the arts during the 1940s and 1950s is examined. Ironically, federal support of cultural exchange programs came under attack by certain congressional anti-Communists as containing subversive items. Notes.

0855 Root, Robert, and Root, Christine V. "Magazines in the United States: Dying or Thriving?" *Journalism Quarterly* 41 (1964): 15–22.

These statistics indicate that between 1938 and 1963 circulations of many magazines grew faster than the rate of population increase. The "leisure" magazines grew most rapidly.

ARCHITECTURE

0856 Brown, Sharon. "Jefferson National Expansion Memorial: The 1947–1948 Competition." *Gateway Heritage* 1 (1980): 40–48.

The landmark Jefferson National Expansion Memorial at St. Louis, Missouri finally found an acceptable design in the 1947–48 competition. The arch design of Eero Saarinen won first place. Illustrations, notes.

0857 Evanoff, Alexander. "Frank Lloyd Wright: Organic Form and Individuality." *Michigan Quarterly Review* 5 (1966): 181–90.

By focusing on the writings of Wright from 1949 to 1958, the author seeks to determine Wright's concepts of architecture.

0858 Schulze, Franz. "The New Chicago Architecture." *Art in America* 56 (1968): 60–71.

Since World War II, Chicago has led all American cities in the quantity and quality of its new architecture (1945–68). The new era was begun by Ludwig Mies van der Rohe, beginning with his Illinois Institute of Technology campus (1940s and 1950s) and his high-rise glass and steel apartments at 860 North Lake Shore Drive (1952).

DRAMA

0859 Bigsby, C. W. E. "Drama As Cultural Sign: American Dramatic Criticism, 1945–1978." *American Quarterly* 30 (1978): 331–57.

American drama has never been taken very seriously by either critics or the public; dramatic criticism hardly existed at all before 1945. Notes.

0860 Stein, Roger B. "'The Glass Menagerie' Revisited: Catastrophe Without Violence." *Western Humanities Review* 18 (1964): 141–53.

Stein finds this 1945 play arranges images, without the violence characteristic of Tennessee Williams, while presenting three themes: (1) the personal tragedy of the characters; (2) the failure of the American dream; and (3) the abandonment of man by his God.

0861 Watts, John G. "Economics of the Broadway Legitimate Theatre, 1948–1958." Ph.D. dissertation, Columbia University, 1969.

The impact of movies upon the legitimate theater is reviewed, along with the problems of the theater's supply of actors, its real estate, and the marketing of tickets. DAI 30:1297-A.

0862 Wilmeth, Don B. "The Margo Jones Theatre." *Southern Speech Journal* 32 (1967): 188–95.

Led by Jones, Dallas, Texas began a movement (1947–59) to decentralize the American theater. Notes.

LITERATURE

A useful overview and bibliography may be found in R. E. Spiller, et al., eds. *Literary History of the United States* (#881).

0863 Auerbach, Doris N. "The Reception of German Literature in America as Exemplified by the *New York Times*, 1945–1970." Ph.D. dissertation, New York University, 1974.

The overwhelming concern expressed by reviewers of the *New York Times Book Review*, 1945–63, was the reemergence of fascism. DAI 35:1084-A.

0864 Baker, Donald G. "Political Values in Popular Fiction: 1919–1959." Ph.D. dissertation, Syracuse University, 1961.

A racial transformation in the attitudes toward the American dream has occurred since World War II. Instead of a belief in the innate goodness of man and a faith in his abilities, man is viewed as innately corrupt, unable to govern himself, and disillusioned with life. DAI 23:679.

0865 Belfrage, Cedric, and Aronson, James. *Something to Guard: The Stormy Life of the National Guardian, 1948–1967.* New York: Columbia University Press, 1978.

The founders of the antiestablishment newsweekly, the *National Guardian*, recall their efforts on behalf of radical causes during the Truman years and after. Index.

0866 Bellios, John G., II. "The Open Road: A Study in the Origins of the Beat Generation, 1944–1955." Ph.D. dissertation, University of North Carolina, Chapel Hill, 1977.

The beat generation began in 1944 when three aspiring writers, Jack Kerouac, Allen Ginsberg, and William Burroughs, met in New York City. It concluded eleven years later in San Francisco with Ginsberg's first public reading of his seminal poem, "Howl." DAI 39:424-A.

0867 Cagle, Charles. "*The Catcher in the Rye* Revisited." *Midwest Quarterly* 4 (1963): 343–51.

J. D. Salinger published *Catcher in the Rye* in 1951; here are reviewed the critical interpretations published since that time.

0868 Camara, George C. "War and the Literary Extremist: The American War Novel, 1945–1970." Ph.D. dissertation, University of Massachusetts, 1973.

This study focuses on the fiction of John Hawkes, Joseph Heller, and Kurt Vonnegut.

0869 Cobb, Nina Kressner. "Alienation and Expatriation: Afro-American Writers in Paris After World War II." Ph.D. dissertation, City University of New York, 1975.

After World War II, a new generation of American expatriates went to Paris in search of freedom. This new wave—predominantly black—included Richard Wright, Chester Himes, and James Baldwin. DAI 36:1736-A.

0870 Cowley, Malcolm. "Remembering Allen Tate." *Georgia Review* 34 (1980): 7–10.

Tate was a member of the southern Agrarians and as such helped to create the southern literary renaissance of the 1930s and 1940s. He also was active in the New Criticism of the 1950s.

0871 Dawson, Hugh J. "America and the West at Mid-Century: An Unpublished Santayana Essay on the Philosophy of Enrico Castelli." *Journal on the History of Philosophy* 17 (1979): 449–54.

Reprinted here is George Santayana's projected but never published 1948 preface to Enrico Castelli's *Il Tempo Esuarito* and *Introduzione ad una Fenomenologia della Nostra Epoca*. Santayana's essay "is important for what it tells of Santayana's views of the crisis of the West and of American culture following the two great wars."

0872 Dickstein, Morris. "The Black Aesthetic in White America." *Partisan Review* 38 (1971/72): 376–95.

The author reviews the literary works of James Baldwin, Richard Wright, and other black authors and concludes that they produced new myths and modes of consciousness rather than literature. He questions Ralph Ellison's argument that blacks must master the forms and crafts of fiction, since the revolutionary imperative of personal and racial identity has a higher priority.

0873 Lewis, Clifford L. "William Faulkner: The Artist As Historian." *Midcontinent American Studies Journal* 10 (1969): 36–48.

Faulkner's novel, *Intruder in the Dust* (1948), emphasizes the social conflict between black and white by dramatizing segregational practices and in so doing anticipates the lifting of black demands for civil rights to a national level. Notes.

0874 Lieber, Todd M. "Ralph Ellison and the Metaphor of Invisibility in Black Literary Tradition." *American Quarterly* 24 (1972): 86–100.

The author traces the metaphor of "invisibility" in the works of Claude McKay, Richard Wright, Paul L. Dunbar, James W. Johnson, and Charles Chesnut to its culmination in Ellison's *Invisible Man* (1952). Notes.

0875 Linick, Anthony. "A History of the American Literary *Avant-Garde* Since World War II." Ph.D.

dissertation, University of California, Los Angeles, 1965.

The chief organs of the postwar avant-garde were the little magazines and small presses. The writers' chief preoccupations were with the concepts of God, love, beauty, and freedom thwarted by the American environment. DAI 25:7226.

0876 Marsden, Michael T. "The Taming of Civilization in the Western Fiction of Wayne D. Overholser." *Kansas Quarterly* 10 (1978): 105–11.

In tracing the western fiction of Overholser, 1949–76, Marsden assesses it in terms of its main themes: law on the frontier, the nature of civilization on the frontier, and images of western womanhood.

0877 Radford, Frederick. "The Journey Towards Castration: Interracial Sexual Stereotypes in Ellison's 'Invisible Man'." *Journal of American Studies* [Great Britain] 4 (1971): 227–31.

The sexual incidents in Ralph Ellison's novel, *Invisible Man* (1952), are analyzed. Ellison sought to explain black-white conflicts on the basis of Freud's interpretations of human sexual taboos and desires. Notes.

0878 Raymer, John D. "Nelson Algren and Simone de Beauvoir: The End of Their Affair at Miller, Indiana." *Old Northwest* 5 (1979/80): 401–7.

The love affair between Algren and Beauvoir, during which he introduced her to postwar life in America's Midwest, including Chicago's skid row, lasted from 1947 to 1951. Beauvoir recreated the affair in three of her later works—*The Mandarin, America Day by Day*, and "American Rendezvous." Notes.

0879 Roth, David S. "The Strongest Link: A Study of the Family in the Fiction of Three Major Jewish-American Novelists, 1945–1970." Ph.D. dissertation, Kent State University, 1974.

This study examines the fiction of Philip Roth, Bernard Malamud, and Saul Bellow in an attempt to discover shared values and common perspectives. DAI 35:6157-A.

0880 Smock, Susan Wanless. "*Lost in the Stars* and *Cry, The Beloved Country*: A Thematic Comparison." *North Dakota Quarterly* 48 (1980): 53–59.

The theme of racial brotherhood in Alan Paton's South African novel, *Cry, the Beloved Country* (1948), and Maxwell Anderson's musical drama, *Lost in the Stars* (1949), are compared.

0881 Spiller, Robert E., et al., eds. *Literary History of the United States*. 3 vols., 4th ed. New York: Macmillan, 1974.

Chapter 82 (pp. 1392–1410) summarizes the trends in poetry, drama, and literature during the Truman years. These editors argue that World War II marks the end of an era, and that 1945 to the mid-1950s was a rather somber, quiet period. Volumes 2 and 3 are extensive bibliographies.

0882 Wall, Richard J., and Craycraft, Carl L. "A Checklist of Works of Truman Capote." *New York Public Library Bulletin* 71 (1967): 165–72.

This checklist includes scholarly accounts as well as popular magazine and newspaper items (1947–66) concerning Capote and his works.

0883 Walser, Richard. "On Faulkner's Putting Wolfe First." *South Atlantic Quarterly* 78 (1979): 172–81.

In a 1947 summer workshop at Oxford, Mississippi, William Faulkner ranked contemporary American authors in order of their importance. This ranking stirred considerable controversy. Notes.

0884 Whitfield, Stephen J. "Dwight MacDonald's 'Politics' Magazine, 1944–1949." *Journalism History* 3 (1976): 86–88, 96.

MacDonald's capacity to attract scholarly writers and to develop serious discussion of political issues is reviewed.

MUSIC

0885 Anderson, Bruce, et al. "Hit Record Trends, 1940–1977." *Journal of Communication* 30 (1980): 31–43.

628 records on *Billboard*'s popularity chart are examined, including data on manufacturer, song type, artist type, and lyric content.

0886 Atwell, Cynthia M. "Harry S. Truman and His Presidential Administration as an Influence on Music in the United States, 1945–1952." D.M.A. dissertation, University of Missouri, Kansas City, 1979.

The author argues that Truman, while in the White House, had a personal influence on music. DAI 40:5353-A.

0887 Garofalo, Reebee, and Chapple, Steve. "The Pre-History of Rock and Roll." *Radical America* 14 (1980): 61–71.

The collapse of the big bands after World War II, the scramble by record companies for new markets including rhythm and blues (formerly "race music"), the development of new recording technology (tapes and hi-fi) by the late 1940s, and the local disc jockey made possible the ascent of rock and roll by 1955.

0888 Reuss, Richard A. "American Folksongs and Left-Wing Politics, 1935–56." *Journal of the Folklore Institute* 12 (1975): 89–111.

Accusations of Communist party and leftist ideological influence in the lyrics of American folk songs (1935–56), including the works of Woody Guthrie, are examined.

0889 Rumble, John W. "Fred Rose and the Development of the Nashville Music Industry, 1942–1954." Ph.D. dissertation, Vanderbilt University, 1980.

Rose was a central figure in the growth of the music industry in Nashville, Tennessee during the years 1942 to 1954. During this period the South's folk music grew into a national music industry. DAI 41:1190.

POETRY

0890 Corrigan, Robert A. "Ezra Pound and the Bollingen Prize Controversy." *Midcontinent American Studies Journal* 8 (1967): 43–57.

The initial attack on the award to Pound focused on the poet's pro-Fascist activities during World War II; but soon it shifted from Pound to the New Poetry, T. S. Eliot, and the Higher Criticism. Bibliography, notes.

0891 Holder, Alan. "Prisoner Ezra Pound." *Virginia Quarterly Review* 44 (1968): 337–41.

Reviewed here are three books about the final unhappy phase of Pound's career which began with his detention in an American military prison at Pisa in 1945. Brought to the United States to face treason charges, he was found insane and sent to St. Elizabeth's Hospital where he remained until 1958. The books—*The Case of Ezra Pound* by Charles Norman (1968), *Ezra Pound: A Close-up* by Michael Reck (1968), and *The Caged Panther: Ezra Pound at Saint Elizabeth's* by Harry M. Meacham (1968)—complement each other.

0892 Mazzaro, Jerome. "Robert Lowell and the Kavanaugh Collapse." *University of Windsor Review* 5 (1969): 1–24.

The author finds Lowell's 1951 poem "The Mills of the Kavanaughs" beset with numerous faults and shortcomings. He finds that Lowell has pulled together many psychological possibilities which could have been meaningful, but that the work remains vague and without focus.

0893 Ninkovich, Frank A. "A New Criticism and Cold War America." *Southern Quarterly* 20 (1981): 1–24.

The Library of Congress awarded the Bollingen Prize in Poetry in 1949 to Ezra Pound who had been indicted for treason (during World War II) and confined to a mental hospital. Critics failed to deny him the award and the New Critics emerged victorious. Notes.

Entertainment Media

0894 DiFazio, John S. "A Content Analysis to Determine the Presence of Selected American Values Found in Comic Books during Two Time Periods, 1946–1950, 1966–1970." Ph.D. dissertation, University of Iowa, 1973.

The purpose of this study was to investigate the premise that comic books contain value-influencing material which might affect youthful readers. DAI 34:5578-A.

0895 Shadoian, Jack. "Yuh Got Pecos! Doggone Belle, Yuh're As Good As Two Men!" *Journal of Popular Culture* 12 (1979): 721–36.

The late 1940s and early 1950s saw a brief flurry of western female comic book heroines. All of these tough, well-proportioned models of female competence were eliminated with the coming of the Comics Code. Illustrations.

0896 Smith, Rodney D. "A Study of the International Political Events and Commentary in Selected American Comic Strips from 1940–1970." Ph.D. dissertation, Ball State University, 1980.

Smith analyzes five strips: "Li'l Abner," "Little Orphan Annie," "Smilin' Jack," "Terry and the Pirates," and "Pogo." He finds that the cartoonists used their medium to support the United States in its international activities. DAI 41:4144.

0897 Smithsonian Institution. *Images of An Era: The American Poster, 1945–1975.* Washington, DC: Smithsonian Institution, 1975.

Included in this collection are a dozen posters relating to themes of the Truman years. Bibliography.

MOVIES

See also Chapter 6, *Entertainment Industry Blacklist.*

0898 Atkins, Irene Kahn. "*Seeds of Destiny:* A Case History." *Film & History* 11 (1981): 25–33.

The 1945 documentary film, *Seeds of Destiny,* sponsored by the United Nations Relief and Rehabilitation Administration showed the horrors of war and the need to alleviate the devastating effects of war on children. It was produced by an American, won the Academy Award for Best Documentary in 1947, and raised more than $200 million in donations.

0899 Cripps, Thomas R. "The Death of Rastus: Negroes in American Films Since 1945." *Phylon* 28 (1967): 267–75.

Throughout the 1930s and 1940s only racial comics such as Rochester crept into American films, while from 1945 to 1954 films depicted blacks as social problems. Not until the 1960s did blacks begin to be seen as fully articulated characters. Notes.

0900 Fishbein, Leslie. "*The Snake Pit* (1948): The Sexist Nature of Sanity." *American Quarterly* 31 (1979): 641–65.

The 1948 movie *The Snake Pit* equates the heroine's mental health with domesticity, while the book by Mary Jane Ward stressed the social problems of overcrowding and inhumane conditions in mental hospitals. Illustrations, notes.

0901 Shain, Russell E. "Effect of Pentagon Influence on War Movies, 1948–1970." *Journalism Quarterly* 49 (1972): 641–47.

Shain provides a statistical review of the financial support given to Hollywood producers by the Pentagon and suggests its influence on the war film industry.

0902 Sochen, June. "*Mildred Pierce* and Women in Film." *American Quarterly* 30 (1978): 3–20.

The author discusses the interpretation of women's roles in *Mildred Pierce* (1945) and compares this with subsequent films.

0903 Stratford, Philip. "Evelyn Waugh and *The Loved One*." *Encounter* [Great Britain] 51 (1978): 46–51.

Waugh's 1947 trip to Hollywood and his satirical book *The Loved One* (1948), as well as the film that came from it, are discussed.

0904 Suid, Lawrence. "*The Sands of Iwo Jima*, The United States Marines, and the Screen Image of John Wayne." *Film and History* 8 (1978): 25–32.

The making of *The Sands of Iwo Jima* (1949) is discussed, along with the haggling of the Marine adviser, John Wayne, and the producer.

0905 Telotte, J. P. "Self and Society: Vincente Minnelli and Musical Formula." *Journal of Popular Film and Television* 9 (1982): 181–93.

The musical as directed by Minnelli for Metro-Goldwyn-Mayer studio during the 1940s and 1950s— *The Pirate, Meet Me in St. Louis, An American in Paris,* and *Ziegfeld Follies*—is seen as exemplifying the movie musical genre which combines an affirmation of society and the necessity of self-expression.

0906 Yavenditti, Michael J. "Atomic Scientists and Hollywood: *The Beginning or the End* (1947)." *Film and History* 8 (1978): 73–88.

This essay discusses the scientists' involvement with making this film which portrayed favorably the Manhattan Project, capitalized on post-Hiroshima curiosity about things atomic, and strengthened public support for the building and employment of atomic bombs against Japan. Notes.

Cold War in Movies

0907 Adler, Leslie K. "The Politics of Culture: Hollywood and the Cold War." In R. Griffith and A. Theoharis, eds. *The Specter: Original Essays on the Cold War and the Origins of McCarthyism.* New York: New Viewpoints, 1974, pp. 240–60.

Adler suggests that "Hollywood's particular contribution after 1947 was to capture and interpret in a contemporary setting the negative images created by decades of antiradical, anti-Communist agitation and feeling." Notes.

0908 Pauly, Thomas H. "The Cold War Western." *Western Humanities Review* 33 (1979): 256–73.

The major western films (1946–52) reflect the tensions and uncertainties of the early Cold War years, according to this analysis.

0909 Sayre, Nora. *Running Time: Films of the Cold War.* New York: Dial, 1982.

Finding almost no Communist propaganda in pre-Cold War films, Sayre discovers much anti-Communist propaganda in films of the 1950s. Illustrations, bibliography, index.

0910 Shain, Russell E. "Cold War Films, 1948–1962: An Annotated Bibliography." *Journal of Popular Film* 3 (1974): 365–72.

Listed here are forty-eight films which purport some relationship, either direct or indirect, to Cold War politics and anticommunism.

0911 Shain, Russell E. "Hollywood's Cold War." *Journal of Popular Film* 3 (1974): 334–50.

This brief essay reviews some trends in Hollywood's response to Cold War politics, 1948–62. Illustrations, notes.

0912 Skinner, James M. "Cliché and Convention in Hollywood's Cold War Anti-Communist Films." *North Dakota Quarterly* 46 (1978): 35–40.

Films promoted anticommunism (1947–52) in part because of the filmmaker's political beliefs and in part because of the scrutiny of the House Committee on Un-American Activities.

RADIO AND TELEVISION

See also Chapter 6, *Entertainment Industry Blacklist.*

0913 Barnouw, Erik. *The Golden Web: A History of Broadcasting in the United States.* Vol. 2: *1933–1953.* New York: Oxford University Press, 1968.

The role of the Federal Communications Commission in regulating the broadcasting corporations during the Truman years is covered, pp. 216–303. Chronology, bibliography, index.

0914 Beck, Joe. "Pioneering in Television in the Twin Cities." *Minnesota History* 46 (1979): 274–85.

Beck relates his personal experiences in getting television started in Minneapolis-St. Paul during the last half of the 1940s. Illustrations, notes.

0915 Fuller, Daniel J., and Ruddy, T. Michael. "Myths in Progress: Harry Truman and *Meeting at Potsdam*." *American Studies* [Lawrence, KS] 18 (1977): 99–106.

This television movie skirts the major issues of the Potsdam Conference and focuses on personalities; thus, the accuracy of the portrayal is highly questionable. Notes.

0916 Kagan, Norman. "Amos 'n Andy: Twenty Years Late, Or Two Decades Early?" *Journal of Popular Culture* 6 (1972): 71–75.

Civil rights groups and the National Association for the Advancement of Colored People opposed the "Amos 'n Andy" television program (1951–52) because it perpetuated stereotypes of blacks. The author suggests, however, that it was "frighteningly accurate as a comic satire."

0917 Levin, Harvey J. "Economic Effects of Broadcast Licensing." *Journal of Political Economy* 72 (1964): 151–62.

The Federal Communications Commission's license allocation policy (1939–60) is found to have had positive effects on the sales and profitability of television stations.

0918 Long, Stewart L. "A Fourth Television Network and Diversity: Some Historical Evidence." *Journalism Quarterly* 56 (1979): 341–45.

This article compares the television programming diversity by the American Broadcasting Company, the National Broadcasting Company, the Columbia Broadcasting System, and the DuMont network from 1948 to 1954. After DuMont folded, "special appeal" programming declined. Tables, notes.

0919 Mall, Richard M. "Some Aspects of Political Broadcast Policies of Radio and Television Stations in the United States." Ph.D. dissertation, Ohio State University, 1953.

A study of the policies of radio and television stations in the United States in regard to political broadcasting.

0920 MacDonald, J. Fred. "Radio's Black Heritage: *Destination Freedom*, 1948–1950." *Phylon* 39 (1978): 66–73.

The history of *Destination Freedom*, a radio program which explored the achievements of eminent blacks, is examined. The program emphasized women's rights, the need to fight for emancipation, and black social and political positions. Notes.

0921 Moore, Barbara. "The Cisco Kid and Friends: The Syndication of Television Series From 1948 to 1952." *Journal of Popular Film and Television* 8 (1980): 26–33.

Syndicated television shows were produced during 1948 to 1952 to fill the programming hours of television stations not affiliated with a network. This essay focuses on the people involved and the technical development and marketing of such series as *The Cisco Kid, Sports Album*, and many others.

0922 Pusateri, C. Joseph. "Radio Broadcasters and the Challenge of Television: A New Orleans Case." *Business History Review* 54 (1980): 303–29.

During 1947 and 1948 the conservative management of radio station WWL debated the costs and risks of starting a television station. This study shows the assessment of economic risks in a technologically innovative society. Table, notes.

0923 Rollins, Peter C. "Victory At Sea: Cold War Epic." *Journal of Popular Culture* 6 (1972): 463–82.

The *Victory at Sea* television series, first shown in 1952, portrays the Cold War mentality of the post-World War II era in that it emphasizes America's role in preserving freedom versus totalitarian dictators' evil plans. The implications of emphasizing power are ignored. Notes.

0924 Tullos, Allen, and Waid, Candace. "Clifford Durr: The FCC Years, 1941–48." *Southern Exposure* 2 (1975): 14–22.

Durr served on the Federal Communications Commission under Roosevelt and Truman. Discussed here are some of the issues he confronted, including the freedom of speech issue.

0925 Wertheim, Arthur F. " 'The Bad Boy of Radio': Henry Morgan and Censorship." *Journal of Popular Culture* 12 (1978): 347–52.

Henry Morgan's urbane wit gained him a small but loyal following within the radio listening audience during the 1940s. However, his insistence on lambasting his commercial sponsors, radio station management, and middle-class society made him the bane of industry censors.

Health and Welfare Issues

See also Chapter 4, *Benefits Programs*, for organized labor's efforts to obtain health benefits.

HEALTH AND MEDICAL ISSUES

0926 Aronson, Bernard. "Black Lung: Tragedy of Appalachia." *New South* 26 (1971): 49–62.

Health problems in the Appalachia coal mines are studied, focusing on coal worker's pneumonconiosis, a lung disease, 1950–71.

0927 Bedworth, David A. "An Analysis of Selected Presidential Advisory Commissions on Health-Related Problems, 1948–1973." Ph.D. dissertation, University of Illinois, Urbana, 1976.

The basic positions and trends established by Truman's commissions continued to influence the commissions of four subsequent administrations. DAI 37:140-A.

0928 Berkowitz, Edward D. "Rehabilitation: The Federal Government's Response to Disability, 1935–1954." Ph.D. dissertation, Northwestern University, 1976.

After World War II, physicians attempted to introduce medical rehabilitation into federal disability programs, but failed. DAI 37:4550-A.

0929 Brand, Jeanne L. "The National Mental Health Act of 1946: A Retrospective." *Bulletin of the History of Medicine* 39 (1965): 231–45.

The circumstances leading up to the passage of the National Mental Health Act (1946) and to the creation of a National Institute of Mental Health (1949) are examined. A substantial increase in funds for research resulted from these two actions. Notes.

0930 Brown, D. Clayton. "Health of Farm Children in the South, 1900–1950." *Agricultural History* 53 (1979): 170–87.

Although data before the 1930s is incomplete and inaccurate, the farm child of the South had relatively poorer health with accompanying low school achievement and high mortality. By 1950 the worst conditions had disappeared. Tables, notes.

0931 Bud, R. F. "Strategy in American Cancer Research After World War II." *Social Studies of Science* [Great Britain] 8 (1978): 425–59.

Discussed here is the influence of industrial research approaches on the activities of the Sloan Kettering Institute, New York City, and the Institute for Cancer Research, Philadelphia, during 1945 to 1950.

0932 Burrow, James G. *AMA: Voice of American Medicine.* Baltimore: Johns Hopkins Press, 1963.

This is a critical examination of the American Medical Association. Chapters 15 to 17 deal with the Truman years, focusing especially on the treatment of veterans and Fair Deal proposals, including the compulsory health insurance issue. Footnotes, appendix, bibliographical essay, index.

0933 Conrad, James H. "Health Services of the United States Children's Bureau, 1935–1953." Ph.D. dissertation, Ohio State University, 1974.

After World War II, federally funded maternal and child health programs continued to expand and develop. Federal grants to state health and crippled children agencies resulted in significant scientific discoveries. DAI 35:5291-A.

0934 Cote, Joseph A. "Clarence Hamilton Poe: Crusading Editor, 1881–1964." Ph.D. dissertation, University of Georgia, 1976.

Truman appointed Poe to the President's Commission on the Health Needs of the Nation, and the International Development Advisory Board, a committee to study the underdeveloped nations of the world. DAI 37:5297-A.

0935 Rothstein, Joan L. "The Government of the United States and the Young Child: A Study of Federal Child Care Legislation Between 1935–1971." Ph.D. dissertation, University of Maryland, 1979.

Ninety-seven pieces of legislation are examined in this study, including the major pieces of the Truman administration. DAI 40:4215-A.

0936 Ward, Patricia Spain. "Antibiotics and International Relations At the Close of World War II." In John Parascandola, ed. *The History of Antibiotics: A Symposium.* Madison, WI: American Institute of the History of Pharmacy, 1980, pp. 101–12.

The Hugh Cabot Memorial Fund was organized in the United States in 1946 to raise money to provide the Soviet Union with a penicillium plant and laboratory for studying the medical uses of molds. The on-coming Cold War forced the fund's demise in the late 1940s.

National Health Insurance

0937 Bachman, George W., and Meriam, Lewis. *The Issue of Compulsory Health Insurance.* Washington, DC: Brookings Institution, 1948.

This study was prepared to aid legislators in reviewing the several compulsory health insurance measures then currently being considered. The study also contains a substantial amount of data relating to the state of American health (and sickness). Tables, index.

0938 Ewing, Oscar R. *The Nation's Health: A Ten Year Program.* Washington, DC: G.P.O., 1948.

The recommendation of this report by the federal security administrator to President Truman was for a program of "prepaid Government health insurance." The study focuses on those Americans who could not afford adequate medical treatment and on the inadequacies of the existing system of health delivery.

0939 Poen, Monte M. *Harry S. Truman versus the Medical Lobby: The Genesis of Medicare.* Columbia: University of Missouri Press, 1979.

Throughout his term of office Truman had promoted enactment of a national compulsory health insurance program only to have his efforts defeated by congressional committees and by the powerful American Medical Association lobby. Notes, bibliography, index.

WELFARE AND SAFETY ISSUES

0940 Bauman, John F. "The Scope of the Poverty Program." *Current History* 61 (1971): 284–89, ff.

Federal programs dealing with poverty among blacks in rural areas during 1930s to 1971 are discussed. Included are New Deal programs and the Aid to Families of Dependent Children program.

0941 Berkowitz, Edward. "Growth of the U.S. Social Welfare System in the Post-World War II Era: The UMW Rehabilitation, and the Federal Government." *Research in Economic History* (1980): 233–47.

That government social welfare expenditures tripled between 1945 and 1956 contradicts the views of political historians that these years were marked by conservatism and inactivity. In 1946 the federal government helped create the United Mine Workers of America's Welfare and Retirement Fund and continued to support the vocational rehabilitation program.

0942 Bradley, John P. "Party Platforms and Party Performance: Social Security, 1920–1960." Ph.D. dissertation, University of Washington, 1962.

Party platforms and what actually occurred in Social Security legislation were closely related. Although platforms sometimes revealed the alternative positions of the two parties, there was a converging tendency once a program was established. 23:4405.

0943 Kress, Guenther; Koehler, Gustav; and Springer, Fred J. "Policy Drift: An Evaluation of the California Business Enterprise Program." *Policy Studies Journal* 8 (1980): 1101–8.

The administrative and conceptual differences of the California Business Enterprise Program—a federally sponsored, state-administered program which employs blind people in food service facilities since 1945—are examined.

0944 Krueger, Thomas A. *And Promises to Keep: The Southern Conference for Human Welfare, 1938–1948.* Nashville: Vanderbilt University Press, 1967.

Chapters 6 to 8 provide information on the organization's struggle against segregation, the CIO's efforts to organize southern labor in 1946, and the election of 1948. Notes, bibliography, index.

0945 Lee, R. Alton. "Federal Assistance in Depressed Areas in the Postwar Recessions." *Western Economic Journal* 2 (1963): 1–23.

The Truman administration provided aid to depressed areas as temporary relief measures, a practice followed until 1960. This approach neglected the permanent nature of the problem. Notes.

0946 Levitan, Sar A., and Marwick, David. "The Mounting and Insurmountable Welfare Problem." *Current History* 61 (1971): 261–65.

The influence of the Social Security Act (1935) is emphasized in this discussion of federal aid to poor families, 1935–71.

0947 Oh, John C. "The Presidency and Public Welfare Policy." *Presidential Studies Quarterly* 8 (1978): 377–90.

Various elements of presidential effectiveness are studied in the context of Roosevelt's Aid to Dependent Children (ADC), Truman's Aid to Families with Dependent Children (AFDC), the Kennedy-Johnson War on Poverty and "self-help" services strategy, and Nixon's Family Assistance Plan (FAP). Tables, notes.

0948 Olson, Thomas L. "Unfinished Business: American Social Workers in Pursuit of Reform, Community, and World Peace, 1939–1950." Ph.D. dissertation, University of Minnesota, 1972.

Social workers were among the early critics of Cold War militarism. They had no more success in aiding postwar domestic reform. By 1950 respect for expertise and "areas of competence" led social workers to speak only on the narrowest of issues rather than as a critic and conscience of society. DAI 33:2301-A.

0949 Phee, Catherine A. "The Centralia Mine Disaster of 1947." Ph.D. dissertation, St. Louis University, 1971.

On 25 March 1947, in Centralia, Illinois, an explosion ripped through Mine No. 5 of the Centralia Coal Company killing 111 men. Public outcry sparked five investigations but had little effect on improving safety conditions in the mines. DAI 32:4535-A.

0950 Vinyard, Dale. "White House Conferences and the Aged." *Social Service Review* 53 (1979): 655–71.

This survey of the history and function of the White House meetings focuses on the 1950 National Conference on Aging, and the 1961 and 1971 White House Conferences.

Immigration

See also Chapter 7, *Refugees and Displaced Persons*, and Chapter 4, *Bracero Program*, for illegal immigration issues.

0951 Dimmitt, Marius A., Sr. "The Enactment of the McCarran-Walter Act of 1952." Ph.D. dissertation, University of Kansas, 1970.

The Immigration and Nationality Act (1952), or McCarran-Walter Act, codified existing policy, reaffirmed the national origins quota system, and introduced other restrictive clauses. DAI 31:5980-A.

0952 Divine, Robert A. *American Immigration Policy, 1924–1952*. New Haven: Yale University Press, 1957.

Postwar immigration issues and the decisive McCarran Act are covered in the last two chapters of this book. Notes, appendixes, bibliography, index.

0953 Hess, Gary R. "The 'Hindu' in America: Immigration and Naturalization Policies in India, 1917–1946." *Pacific Historical Review* 38 (1969): 59–79.

Truman personally supported legislation which ended Indian exclusion and provided for a modest immigration quota. Notes.

0954 Jaffe, Erwin A. "Passage of the McCarran-Walter Act: The Reiteration of American Immigration Policy." Ph.D. dissertation, Rutgers University, 1962.

Congress's decision to pass the McCarran-Walter Act was due to a complex of factors: the Cold War crisis, the persistence of hostility toward newcomers, the strategic location of restrictionists in Congress and the executive branch. DAI 23:680.

0955 Narayanan, R. "Indian Immigration and the India League of America." *Indian Journal of American Studies* [India] 2 (1972): 1–30.

The wartime circumstances leading to the passage of an amendment to the Nationality Act of 1946 and the role played by the East Indian community are examined. Notes.

0956 Power, Jonathan. "The Great Debate on Illegal Immigration: Europe and the USA Compared." *Journal of International Affairs* 33 (1979): 239–48.

Power compares European and U.S. attempts to control illegal immigration from 1947 to 1978.

0957 Strange, Steven L. "Private Consensual Sexual Conduct and the 'Good Moral Character' Requirement of the Immigration and Nationality Act."

Columbia Journal of Transnational Law 14 (1975): 357–81.

The relationship between law, morality, and private sexual conduct in the McCarran-Walter Immigration Act (1952) is examined and compared with immigration and naturalization policy, 1952 through the 1970s. Notes.

Society and Culture

0958 Brooks, John N. *The Great Leap: The Past Twenty-Five Years in America*. New York: Harper & Row, 1966.

The years 1939 to 1964 are reviewed from a social-economic viewpoint in this interesting survey. Sources, index.

0959 Kinsey, Alfred C. *Sexual Behavior in the Human Male*. Philadelphia: Saunders, 1948.

Sensational at publication, this book pioneered research in an area which heretofore had been considered taboo. Tables, notes.

0960 McGiffert, Michael. "Selected Writings on American National Character." *American Quarterly* 15 (1963): 271–88.

This essay provides a useful collection of the principal writings since 1940 made by social scientists and cultural historians on the subject of the American character.

0961 Mills, C. Wright. *White Collar: The American Middle Classes*. New York: Oxford University Press, 1951.

One of several works during this period which employed a sociological approach to examine the changes taking place in American society. Notes, index.

0962 Modell, John. "Normative Aspects of American Marriage Timing Since World War II." *Journal of Family History* 5 (1980): 210–34.

Survey research data and colorful vignettes from popular fiction are employed to study changes in attitudes, beliefs, and values of marriage during 1939 to 1974. Tables, notes, appendix.

0963 Porter, Jack N. "The Jewish Intellectual." *Midstream* 25 (1979): 18–25.

Porter examines Jews within the American intellectual elite from 1945 to 1978 and discusses their divisions and intergroup conflicts as well as their broader impact on modern American ideas.

0964 Riesman, David, et al. *The Lonely Crowd: A Study of the Changing American Character.* New Haven: Yale University Press, 1950.

This classic study focused public, as well as academic, attention on how one's values were being shaped in the American society of the late 1940s. Notes, index.

0965 Schroeder, E. H. "A Bellyful of Coffee: The Truckdrivin' Man As Folk Hero." *Journal of Popular Culture* 2 (1969): 679–86.

This essay examines the truck driver in fiction and popular culture during the 1930s to 1960s.

0966 Tucker, Charles W. "A Comparative Analysis of Subjective Social Class, 1945–1963." *Social Forces* 46 (1968): 508–14.

This essay compares a study made in 1945 with one conducted in 1963. By comparing such variables as subjective social class, occupations, education, and age, the author concludes that there was a reduction in the use of "working-class" labels from 1945 to 1963. Tables, notes.

EDUCATION

See also, Chapter 4, *Veterans: Education Programs*, and Chapter 6, *Civil Rights: Desegregation of Schools.*

0967 Benson, Warren S. "A History of the National Association of Christian Schools During the Period of 1946–1972." Ph.D. dissertation, Loyola University of Chicago, 1975.

The National Association of Christian Schools began in 1947. This study examines the organization's theological and educational bases of administrative leadership and clarifies its educational philosophy. DAI 36:158-A.

0968 Brown, Richard J. "Public Criticism of Secondary School History Teaching, 1930 through 1950." Ph.D. dissertation, State University of Iowa, 1955.

Books and periodicals with nationwide circulation were examined. The most persistent criticisms of history teaching appeared in publications affiliated with national patriotic organizations. DAI 15:2057.

0969 Cordasco, Frank M., and Covello, Leonard. "Studies of Puerto Rican Children in American Schools: A Preliminary Bibliography." *Journal of Human Relations* 16 (1968): 264–85.

Published here is an unannotated bibliography of Puerto Rican children and their experiences in American mainland schools since 1945. It includes published and unpublished sources.

0970 Cowhig, James D., and Beale, Calvin L. "Vocational-Agriculture Enrollment and Farm Employment Opportunities." *Southwestern Social Science Quarterly* 47 (1967): 413–23.

This essay considers the effects of new, accelerated education programs and analyzes the supply and demand for agricultural labor, financial aid programs for training for farm occupations, and the vocational agricultural program, 1950–60. Tables, notes.

0971 Johnson, Walter, and Colligan, Francis J. *The Fulbright Program: A History.* Chicago: University of Chicago Press, 1965.

The Fulbright Program, which involved international education and scholarly interchange with other countries, was established by Public Law 584 (1946). Chapters 1 to 6 examine the program's origins and criticisms. Notes, bibliographical essay, index.

0972 Oshiro, Yoshinobu. "Historical Development of the Department of Defense Schools with Emphasis on Japan, Far East-Pacific Area, 1946–1973." Ph.D. dissertation, Utah State University, 1974.

This dissertation compiles and lists the available literature and relative data, 1946–73, about the Department of Defense overseas schools in the Far East and especially Japan. DAI 36:110-A.

0973 Reeves, Thomas C. "The Fund for the Republic 1951–1957: An Unusual Chapter in the History of American Philanthropy." Ph.D. dissertation, University of California, Santa Barbara, 1966.

The Fund for the Republic engaged in the study and public education of civil liberties and civil rights. It was a valuable and responsible instrument for easing some of the least flattering fears and tensions of postwar America. DAI 28:1378-A.

0974 St. Jacques, Ernest H. "A History of the Guidance-Personnel Movement in the United States from 1946 to 1961." Ph.D. dissertation, George Peabody College for Teachers, 1963.

During the postwar period the guidance-personnel movement really got under way, with federal government assistance in counseling and guidance services to veterans, providing occupational information and statistical data for counselors, sponsoring conferences, and making recommendations. DAI 25:441.

0975 Veillette, Peter D. "State and Local Efforts to Finance Schools Since 1945." *Current History* 62 (1972): 293–97.

This study examines how property taxes and sales taxes are used to finance teachers' salaries and school expenditures.

0976 Weaver, Samuel H. "The Truman Administration and Federal Aid to Education." Ph.D. dissertation, American University, 1972.

The Truman administration was the first in the United States to make general aid to education one of its principal domestic goals. Despite the lack of concrete achievements the administration did attract interest and support. DAI 33:2311-A.

Church and Schools Issue

0977 Boggs, Timothy J. "An Analysis of the Opinions in the United States Supreme Court Decisions on Religion and Education from 1948–1972." Ph.D. dissertation, University of Colorado, 1973.

Of the ten cases examined here, *McCollum* (1948) and *Zorach* (1952) took place during the Truman years. DAI 34:3931-A.

0978 Carroll, William A. "The Constitution, the Supreme Court, and Religion." *American Political Science Review*, 61 (1967): 657–74.

The author has analyzed five important cases, including *Everson* v. *Board of Education* (1947) and *McCollum* v. *Board of Education* (1948), decided by the Supreme Court which relate to the religion clauses of the Constitution. Notes.

0979 Citron, Henry. "The Study of the Arguments of Interest Groups Which Opposed Federal Aid to Education From 1949–1965." Ph.D. dissertation, New York University, 1977.

The Catholic Church and black groups played major roles in stimulating the controversy as they pressed for federal aid. This study traces their opponents as they appeared in or before the House of Representatives during these years. DAI 38:2298-A.

0980 Gleason, Philip. "Blurring the Line of Separation: Education, Civil Religion, and Teaching About Religion." *Journal of Church and State* 19 (1977): 517–38.

Arguing that the distinction between "teaching about" and "teaching" is not as clear as some believe, the author examines three major cases on Church-State relations and education: *Everson* (1947), *McCollum* (1948), and *Zorach* (1952). Notes.

0981 Grant, Philip A. "Catholic Congressmen, Cardinal Spellman, Eleanor Roosevelt, and the 1949–1950 Federal Aid to Education Controversy." *Records of the American Catholic Historical Society of Philadelphia* 90 (1979): 3–14.

A comprehensive federal aid to education bill failed in 1950 because it had become a divisive issue when support for parochial schools was raised. Francis Cardinal Spellman and Eleanor Roosevelt engaged in unfortunate polemics rather than leadership, while Catholic congressmen avoided the issue. Notes.

0982 Kizer, George A. "Federal Aid to Education, 1945–1963." *History of Education Quarterly* 10 (1970): 84–102.

The Church-State issue prevented much support for federal aid to public education during the Truman years. See pages 84–90.

0983 Lachman, Seymour P. "The Cardinal, the Congressman, and the First Lady." *Journal of Church and State* 7 (1965): 35–66.

This essay focused on the Thomas-Taft bill and the Barden bill which failed in the Eighty-first Congress. Catholics opposed the Barden bill because it prohibited use of public funds for social services to students of nonpublic schools. This brought Eleanor Roosevelt and Francis Cardinal Spellman into the debate. Congressman John F. Kennedy also played an important role in negotiations over the bill. Notes.

0984 Moynihan, Daniel Patrick. "What Do You Do When The Supreme Court Is Wrong?" *Public Interest* (1979): 3–24.

Treats two examples in detail: *Everson* v. *Board of Education* (1947), which prohibits state aid to nonpublic schools, and *Gannett* v. *DePasqual* (1979), which denies the public an independent constitutional right of access to pretrial judicial proceedings. The *Everson* decision has been undone by a "hierarchy of responses."

0985 Smith, Gilbert E., III. "The Limits of Reform: Politics and Federal Aid to Education, 1937–1950." Ph.D. dissertation, Columbia University, 1975.

From 1945 to 1950 education proposals continued to move closer to success, but racial and religious issues still posed a constant threat. The author argues that intransigent leadership in the National Education Association also contributed to the defeat. DAI 36:3075-A.

Colleges and Universities

0986 Baker, Carlos. "The Expanding Universe at Old Nassau." *Horizon* 2 (1959): 22–27, 118–19.

Princeton, New Jersey, formerly a little-known academic retreat, has grown between 1945 and 1958, to become a center of higher education, research, and educational testing.

0987 Bloomgarden, Lawrence. "Our Changing Elite Colleges." *Commentary* 29 (1960): 1950–54.

This essay examines social status attached to elite higher education institutions, increased competition for entrance, and standards set for entrance, 1945–60.

0988 Bullough, Robert V., Jr. "General Education: Bode and the Harvard Report." *Journal of General Education* 33 (1981): 102–12.

Boyd H. Bode's criticism of the 1945 report, *General Education in a Free Society: Report of the Harvard Committee*, is examined. Bode argued that the key issues, such as the determination of what is worth knowing and what is meant by knowing, were lost in the report. Notes.

0989 Donnelly, J. B. "The Vision of Scholarship: Johns Hopkins After the War." *Maryland History Magazine* 73 (1978): 137–62.

This account recalls the unique combination of refugee professors and returning veterans at Johns Hopkins University in the late 1940s and relates how Hopkins became "a school for grinding" scholarship. Notes.

0990 Harris, Robert L., Jr. "Segregation and Scholarship: The American Council of Learned Societies' Committee on Negro Studies, 1941–1950." *Journal of Black Studies* 12 (1982): 315–31.

The committee drew up a roster of scholars in black studies, microfilmed black newspapers printed before 1900, and published a guide to materials on blacks in the National Archives. It failed to deal with the problems of discrimination against black scholars. Bibliography.

0991 Kerr, Clark. "The Frantic Race to Remain Contemporary." *Daedalus* 93 (1964): 1051–70.

Kerr discusses four areas of readjustment confronting American universities (1945–64): growth; shifting academic emphasis; involvement in the life of society; and response to the new federal involvement.

0992 Newman, Frank J. "The Era of Expertise: The Growth, The Spread and Ultimately the Decline of the National Commitment to the Concept of the Highly Trained Expert: 1945 to 1970." Ph.D. dissertation, Stanford University, 1981.

The expanding role of science following World War II created a need for experts which spread to all aspects of society. This study traces the causes, development, and limits of this movement as well as its collapse during the 1970s due to an oversupply of Ph.D.s and other experts and to the public's disillusionment with the consequences. DAI 42:3722.

0993 Partridge, Elinore H. "A. Ray Olpin and the Post-War Emergency at the University of Utah." *Utah Historical Quarterly* 48 (1980): 195–206.

When returning veterans doubled the university's enrollment, President Olpin found help from the federal government. Adjacent Fort Douglas provided veteran housing and later classrooms, while nearly a half-million dollars worth of equipment and furniture was obtained (as surplus) for the cost of transportation. Illustrations, notes.

0994 Snavely, Guy E. "Methodism and American University." *Methodist History* (1963): 18–24.

In 1948 the Methodist General Conference created a "Commission to Study Educational Responsibilities in Washington, D.C." Ultimately, this resulted in support for American University by the Methodist Church.

0995 Steahr, Thomas E., and Schmid, Calvin F. "College Student Migration in the United States." *Journal of Higher Education* 43 (1972): 441–63.

The migration of students from state to state in search of colleges and universities is examined for 1938 to 1968.

0996 Synnott, Marcia G. "The Admission and Assimilation of Minority Students at Harvard, Yale and Princeton, 1900–1970." *History of Education Quarterly* 19 (1979): 285–304.

These universities, from their beginnings, restricted the admittance of Jews and other minorities; however, after World War II—especially when veterans under the G.I. Bill flooded admissions offices—ethnic prejudice came under condemnation. Notes.

0997 Synnott, Marcia G. *The Half-Opened Door: Discrimination and Admissions at Harvard, Yale, and Princeton, 1900–1970*. Westport, CT: Greenwood, 1979.

The impact of World War II, together with the G.I. bill of rights, succeeded in removing discriminating quotas which affected minority students (Catholics and Jews) seeking to enter the "Big Three." Tables, notes, bibliography, index.

Education and the Cold War

See also Chapter 6, *Internal Security and Civil Liberties*, for additional data.

0998 Gietschier, Steven P. "The 1951 Speaker's Rule At Ohio State." *Ohio History* 87 (1978): 294–309.

The appearance of Harold O. Rugg at the Bode Conference on Education (1951) resulted in a rule which required the Ohio State University president to approve any speaker. This rule was in line with OSU's emphasis on the practical arts, and reflected the prevailing Cold War mentality of the OSU Board of Trustees. Illustration, notes.

0999 Marden, David L. "The Cold War and American Education." Ph.D. dissertation, University of Kansas, 1976.

As one step toward understanding the nature of America's Cold War culture, this study examines the interaction between the Cold War and American education from 1945 to 1953. DAI 37:548-A.

1000 Mass, Deanna R. "The Image of Academic Freedom Conveyed By Selected Scholarly Journals of the McCarthy Era." 2 vols. Ph.D. dissertation, Columbia University, 1979.

This study develops quantitative and qualitative analyses of a selected number of scholarly journals in an effort to determine their concern with academic freedom and their anti-McCarthy sentiments. DAI 40:5560-A.

1001   Schrecker, Ellen. "Academic Freedom and the Cold War." *Antioch Review* 38 (1980): 313–27.

Pre-Cold War events in 1940 and 1941 as well as events during the 1950s are discussed. U.S. colleges and universities, contrary to popular belief, had anti-Communist policies and denied jobs to or purged faculty members who were, or would not deny being, Communist party members.

RELIGION

See N. R. Burr's *A Critical Bibliography of Religion in America* (#3012) for possible references; also see *Church and Schools Issue*.

1002   Abramowicz, Alfred L. "The Catholic League For Religious Assistance to Poland." *Polish American Studies* 20 (1963): 28–33.

From 1943 to 1959 the league contributed some $4.5 million to the Church and needs of Poland.

1003   Arndt, Karl J. R. "Missouri and the Bad Boll, 1948." *Concordia Historical Institute Quarterly* 52 (1979): 2–31.

American and German synodic leaders of the Lutheran Church held discussions at the Bad Boll Conferences, 1948, with the intention of repairing torn church affiliations and providing a positive note in the gloom of post-World War II Germany.

1004   Gustafson, Merlin. "Church, State, and the Cold War, 1945–1952." *Journal of Church and State* 8 (1966): 49–63.

"Peace through strength" summarized the Truman years. In this examination of the military aspects of Church-State relations, the author argues that the overall influence of the State was to encourage the nationalization of religion. Notes.

1005   Gustafson, Merlin. "Religion and Politics in the Truman Administration." *Rocky Mountain Social Science Journal* 3 (1966): 125–34.

A "consensus religion" with a religious posture that agreed with the National Council of Churches and the Roman Catholic Church existed throughout the Truman administration. On Church-State issues the presidency reflected a broad theological consensus. Notes.

1006   Gustafson, Merlin. "The Religion of a President." *Journal of Church and State* 10 (1968): 379–87.

A Baptist, Truman did not find his roles as political leader and religious person contradictory. His religious ideology was social Gospel-oriented, but in foreign policy he believed that America had a mission to spread Christian values. Notes.

1007   Harvey, Charles E. "Congregationalism On Trial, 1949–1950: An Account of the Cadman Case." *Journal of Church and State* 12 (1970): 255–72.

The Congregational Christian churches voted to merge with the Evangelical and Reformed Church in 1949. An antimerger group sued, claiming all assets of denominational organizations were joint property of the congregations; they lost an appeal in New York courts. Notes.

1008   Hastings, Philip K., and Hoge, Dean R. "Religious Change Among College Students Over Two Decades." *Social Forces* 49 (1970): 16–27.

Identical questionnaires were administered to identical samples of Williams College undergraduates in 1948 and 1967, and the 1948 nonveterans were compared with the 1967 sample. The students in 1948 held more to traditional religious commitments.

1009   Kim, Richard C. C. "Jehovah's Witnesses and the Supreme Court. An Examination of the Cases Brought Before the United States Supreme Court Involving the Rights Claimed by Jehovah's Witnesses, From 1938 to 1960." Ph.D. dissertation, University of Oklahoma, 1963.

The Jehovah's Witnesses played an important role in compelling the court to define, clarify, and amplify the meaning of the constitutional provisions affecting freedom of speech, assembly, press, and especially freedom of religion as protected by the First Amendment. DAI 24:371.

1010   Millican, Charles N. "Church Financing by Financial Institutions in the United States, 1946–1952." Ph.D. dissertation, University of Florida, 1954.

The church building boom after World War II is reviewed with regard to its financing. Insurance companies and banks were surveyed to determine what criteria they applied to loan requests. DAI 16:2339.

1011   Morris, Clovis G. "He Changed Things: The Life and Thought of J. Frank Norris." Ph.D. dissertation, Texas Tech University, 1973.

As pastor of the First Baptist Church, Fort Worth, Texas for over forty years, Norris became widely known especially as a fundamentalist leader. His papers include extensive correspondence (1927–52) with such political leaders as Truman, Senator

Tom Connally, and Speaker Sam Rayburn. DAI 34:1831-A.

1012　Schmidt, William J. "Samuel McCrea Cavert: American Bridge to the German Church, 1945–1946." *Journal of Presbyterian History* 51 (1973): 3–23.

American Presbyterian Samuel Cavert, as a member of the Provisional Council of the World Council of Churches, was instrumental in the reintegration of postwar German churches into the world church movement.

Churches and Race

1013　Kemper, Donald J. "Catholic Integration in St. Louis, 1935–1947." *Missouri Historical Review* 73 (1978): 1–22.

In 1947 the archbishop of St. Louis, Joseph E. Ritter, ordered the admission of black children to local parochial schools thus bringing an end to one phase of the desegregation struggle. Illustrations, notes.

1014　Mounger, Dwyn M. "Racial Attitudes in the Presbyterian Church in the United States, 1944–1955." *Journal of Presbyterian History* 48 (1970): 36–68.

Racial attitudes were drawn from two denominational journals, the conservative *Southern Presbyterian Journal* and the reform-minded *Presbyterian Outlook*. The reformers, stressing the social Gospel, grew stronger as the decade progressed. Notes.

1015　Reimers, David M. "Protestant Churches and the Negro: A Study of Several Major Protestant Denominations and the Negro from World War One to 1954." Ph.D. dissertation, University of Wisconsin, 1961.

During the 1940s churches became increasingly critical of their own practices regarding blacks. They criticized segregation and discrimination and called for a truly interracial Christian church. DAI 22:849.

SPORTS

1016　Bishop, Elva, and Fulton, Katherine. "Shooting Stars: The Heyday of Industrial Women's Basketball." *Southern Exposure* 7 (1979): 50–56.

The Hanes Hosiery women's basketball team of Winston-Salem, North Carolina dominated women's industrial basketball during the late 1940s and early 1950s.

1017　Gwartney, James, and Haworth, Charles. "Employer Costs and Discrimination: The Case of Baseball." *Journal of Political Economy* 82 (1974): 873–81.

Using economic theory, an examination of major baseball teams which desegregated during 1947 to 1959 shows that they gained a competitive advantage over the other teams.

1018　"Jackie Robinson: A Man For All Seasons." *Crisis* 79 (1972): 345–49, 355.

This essay discusses Jackie Robinson and recounts his breaking of the color barrier in baseball in 1947.

1019　Jennison, Christopher. *Wait 'Til Next Year: The Yankees, Dodgers, and Giants, 1947–1957*. New York: Norton, 1974.

This popular sports book focuses on Jackie Robinson, the 1948 Cleveland Indians, Mickey Mantle, and other baseball stars in the Truman era. Illustrations, appendix.

1020　Robinson, Jackie, as told to Alfred Duckett. *I Never Had It Made*. New York: Putnam's, 1972.

Robinson's "memoir" focuses on his breaking the "color barrier" in professional baseball.

1021　Stern, Robert N. "The Development of an Interorganizational Control Network: The Case of Intercollegiate Athletics." *Administrative Science Quarterly* 24 (1979): 242–66.

The historical transformation of the network of organizations participating in the National Collegiate Athletic Association, 1906–52, is examined.

1022　Washburn, Pat. "New York Newspapers and Robinson's First Season." *Journalism Quarterly* 58 (1981): 640–44.

The author finds that New York newspapers covered Robinson's rookie season without bias; however, they did not report Robinson's harassment by other teams. Notes.

1023　Weaver, Bill L. "The Black Press and the Assault on Professional Baseball's 'Color Line,' October, 1945–April, 1947." *Phylon* 40 (1979): 303–17.

Using newspapers, this essay focuses on the black press's response to Branch Rickey's signing of Jack Roosevelt "Jackie" Robinson and assigning him to the minor league Montreal Royals in 1945 and moving him to the Brooklyn Dodgers in 1947.

Science and Technology

See also Chapter 9, *Atomic Scientists and Policy*.

1024　Dupree, A. Hunter. "The Structure of the Government-University Partnership After World

War II." *Bulletin of the History of Medicine* 39 (1965): 245–51.

This essay focuses on the questions historians must ask to illuminate the various dimensions of the active partnership that developed between the federal government and the universities. This relationship extended beyond health research to scientific research generally.

1025   Fox, Judith. "Immanuel Velikovsky and the Scientific Method." *Synthesis* 5 (1980): 45–57.

Fox suggests that the scientific community overreacted in their vehement opposition to Velikovsky's *Worlds in Collision* (1950) and his theories, and that in the history of science that incident stands out as an example of "the social pathology of science." Notes.

1026   Hewlett, R. G. "A Pilot Study of Contemporary Scientific History." *Isis* 53 (1962): 31–38.

Hewlett discusses the methodology used to write the history of the Atomic Energy Commission's Experimental Breeder Reactor No. 1, 1945–53.

1027   Jones, Kenneth M. "Science, Scientists, and Americans: Images of Science and the Formation of Federal Science Policy, 1945–1950." Ph.D. dissertation, Cornell University, 1975.

The U.S. government laid the foundations for its present support of science during World War II and the immediate postwar years. The author seeks to evaluate the intellectual climate in which science policy was made by employing newspapers and public opinion polls. DAI 36:3070-A.

1028   Keezer, Dexter M. "The Outlook for Expenditures on Research and Development During the Next Decade." *American Economic Review* 50 (1960): 355–69.

In seeking to project a trend, this essay examines the published estimates of research and development expenditures since 1945.

1029   Lasby, Clarence G. *Project Paperclip: German Scientists and the Cold War.* New York: Atheneum, 1971.

Between May 1945 and December 1952 the United States imported 642 alien specialists under several programs known collectively as "Project Paperclip." In part this was an effort to exploit Nazi Germany's scientific accomplishments and in part it was an effort to deny the Soviet Union the services of these highly trained specialists. Notes, bibliography, index.

1030   Lasby, Clarence G. "Project Paperclip: German Scientists Come To America." *Virginia Quarterly Review* 42 (1966): 366–77.

Over opposition from the public and the State Department, the military services imported and employed German scientists after World War II. The most publicized result of this long-range program was the development of rocket launchers and satellites.

1031   Marshak, Robert E. "The Rochester Conferences: The Rise of International Cooperation in High Energy Physics." *Bulletin of the Atomic Scientists* 26 (1970): 92–98.

Nuclear scientists have shared information at the International Rochester Conferences since 1950, although the Cold War has threatened to interfere with the conferences.

1032   Napier, Peggy. "Charles E. Yeager: Supersonic Flight Pioneer." *West Virginia History* 40 (1979): 293–303.

Yeager was the first man to fly faster than sound, on 14 October 1947 in the SX-1 aircraft.

1033   Price, Don K. *Government and Science: Their Dynamic Relation in American Democracy.* New York: New York University Press, 1954.

The roots of the military-scientific complex which began during the Truman years are described.

1034   Wells, William G., Jr. "Science Advice and the Presidency, 1933–1976." D.B.A. dissertation, George Washington University, 1978.

The general objective of this study is to provide a comprehensive account of how science advice has been provided to and used by each president from Franklin D. Roosevelt to Gerald R. Ford. DAI 39:1832-A.

1035   Wiener, Norbert. *Cybernetics: Or Control and Communication in the Animal and the Machine.* Cambridge: MIT Press, 1948.

Wiener coined the term *cybernetics* to help define the mathematical analysis of the flow of information among electronic, mechanical, and biological systems. Notes, index.

DEVELOPMENT OF COMPUTERS

1036   Goldstine, Herman H. *The Computer from Pascal to von Neumann.* Princeton, NJ: Princeton University Press, 1972.

Part Three focuses on the post-1945 development of the computer. Illustrations, notes, appendix, index.

1037   Huskey, Harry D. "The National Bureau of Standards Western Automatic Computer (SWAC)." *Annals of the History of Computing* 2 (1980): 111–21.

The status of automatic computing in 1948 and 1949 is presented along with some details of SWAC design. Illustrations, tables, bibliography.

1038 Stern, Nancy Fortgang. "From ENIAC to UNIVAC: A Case Study in the History of Technology." Ph.D. dissertation, State University of New York, Stony Brook, 1978.

This study attempts to provide a relatively unbiased account of the Eckert-Mauchly computer organization from 1943 to 1951. Controversial issues addressed include those relating to John von Neumann and the stored-program concept, the ENIAC's claim to uniqueness, the BINAC's performance record, and the failure of large corporations to develop commercial computers in the 1940s. DAI 39:3107-A.

1039 Stern, Nancy. "John William Mauchly, 1907–1980." *Annals of the History of Computing* 2 (1980): 100–103.

As consultant for the Electronic Numerical Integrator and Computer project during 1943 to 1946, physicist John Mauchly developed the concept of the vacuum tube computer to solve the ballistics problems of the military. He developed and marketed the Universal Automatic Computer (UNIVAC). Notes, bibliography.

1040 Tomash, Erwin, and Cohen, Arnold A. "The Birth of an Era: Engineering Research Associates, Inc., 1946–1955." *Annals of the History of Computing* 1 (1979): 83–97.

This is an account of the early years of a pioneering computer company which was formed in 1946, at St. Paul, Minnesota with navy encouragement. This company merged into Remington Rand, Inc. in 1952, and became the basis of the UNIVAC division of Sperry Rand Corporation.

NATIONAL SCIENCE FOUNDATION

See Chapter 3, *Congressional and Political Leaders*, for a biography of Senator Harley M. Kilgore.

1041 Jones, Kenneth M. "The Endless Frontier." *Prologue* 8 (1976): 35–46.

Efforts to establish a federally funded National Science Foundation in 1945, especially those of Vannevar Bush, are examined. The question of academic freedom versus national security demands was raised. Notes.

1042 Maddox, Robert F. "The Politics of World War II Science: Senator Harley M. Kilgore and the Legislative Origins of the National Science Foundation." *West Virginia History* 41 (1979): 20–39.

Kilgore (D-WV) found in 1942 the wartime administrative machinery for science and technology to be confusing. He introduced legislation which ultimately led to the creation of the NSF which Truman signed into law in 1950. Opponents of the bill included Vannevar Bush and Alexander Smith.

1043 McCune, Robert P. "Origins and Development of the National Science Foundation and Its Division of Social Sciences, 1945–1961." Ph.D. dissertation, Ball State University, 1971.

The National Science Foundation grew out of the wartime Office of Scientific Research and Development. McCune traces this development and the reasons for the government assuming a major role in basic scientific research. DAI 32:1448-A.

1044 Schaffter, Dorothy. *The National Science Foundation*. New York: Praeger, 1969.

While the focus of this volume is the contemporary scene, its initial pages relate to the foundation's origins during the Truman years. Notes, index.

1045 Sherwood, Morgan. "Federal Policy For Basic Research: Presidential Staff and the National Science Foundation, 1950–1956." *Journal of American History* 55 (1968): 599–615.

This essay examines the early problems of the National Science Foundation and the background to Executive Order 10521 (1954). Notes.

6

Domestic Affairs:
Civil Rights, Internal Security
and Civil Liberties,
Politics and Public Opinion,
and the Supreme Court

Almost every major issue, domestic as well as foreign, had an effect on public opinion and, consequently, on the politics of the Truman years. The civil rights movement, then in its infancy, and the fear of Communist espionage kindled by the House Un-American Activities Committee and Senator Joseph McCarthy, generated widespread feelings of prejudice and alarm. These feelings were reflected in the balloting of 1948 and 1952. Additionally, civil rights and civil liberties issues were heavily involved in the judicial process and eventually reached the Supreme Court.

The pressures building to force improved conditions for minorities are reviewed in Donald R. McCoy and Richard T. Ruetten, *Quest and Response: Minority Rights and the Truman Administration* (#1062). Specific civil rights issues which thrust themselves forward when American minorities, especially blacks, sought to end segregation and discrimination, have been discussed in a number of books and essays listed below. Three issues which figured prominently during the Truman era are treated in Clement E. Vose, *Caucasians Only: The Supreme Court, the NAACP, and the Restrictive Covenant Case* (#1068), Richard M. Dalfiume, *Desegregation of the Armed Forces: Fighting on Two Fronts, 1939–1953* (#1103), and H. C. Hudgins, Jr., *The Warren Court and the Public Schools* (#1118).

The issue of civil liberties arose when some Americans found their loyalty called into question by congressional investigating bodies and by so-called patriotic organizations. These citizens often felt that they had been tried in the media and found guilty without an opportunity to present their side of the story. Senator Joseph McCarthy was a relative latecomer to the movement in the Truman period. Earlier, the House Un-American Activities Committee raised the specter of Communist infiltration into the entertainment industry, the clergy, government, labor unions, the military, and the schools. Those who felt that Communist agents were penetrating all aspects of American society and government generally accepted the views of such writers as James Burnham, *The Web of Subversion: Underground Network in the U.S. Government* (#1327), and Ralph DeToledano, *The Greatest Plot in History* (#1332). Those who condemned the loyalty probe as far too excessive and counterproductive, include Cedric Belfrage, *The American Inquisition, 1945–1960* (#1323), and David Caute, *The Great Fear: The Anti-Communist Purge Under Truman and Eisenhower* (#1328).

Writers now have the opportunity for a less passionate, retrospective view of this contentious period, but often their findings are still conditioned by political loyalties. Alan D. Harper, *The Politics of Loyalty: The White House and the Communist Issue,*

November 3, 1948: "Dewey Defeats Truman" according to the *Chicago Daily Tribune. Reproduced courtesy of the St. Louis* Globe-Democrat.

1946–1952 (#1335), and Earl Latham, *The Communist Controversy in Washington: From the New Deal to McCarthy* (#1338) provide useful introductions to the issues. Bert Cochran, *Labor and Communism: The Conflict That Shaped American Unions* (#815) reviews the factionalism which arose within the unions especially in the CIO. A few writers, such as Athan Theoharis, *Seeds of Repression: Harry S. Truman and the Origins of McCarthyism* (#1351), argue that President Truman did not do all that he should have to support civil liberties; indeed, by focusing on foreign affairs, he stimulated the loyalty investigations.

While the House Un-American Activities Committee has had its supporters and detractors, a new study of its role during this period would be a worthy undertaking. Until the Federal Bureau of Investigation's files are fully opened, K. O'Reilly, *Hoover and the Un-Americans: The FBI, HUAC, and the Red Menace* (#1387) provides a probing view of the FBI's activities. Investigation of espionage activities descended into local politics as well. Walter Gellhorn, ed., *The States and Subversion* (#1462) is a useful, though contemporary, introduction to such activities in several states.

Politics became high drama during the 1948 election. The search for the reasons for Truman's "upset" victory over Thomas E. Dewey has spawned scores of accounts. A good survey of the issues may be found in Irwin Ross, *The Loneliest Campaign: The Truman Victory of 1948* (#1250), and R. Shogan, "1948 Election" (#1251). The role of Henry A. Wallace and the Progressives also has been widely studied, thus Allen Yarnell, *Democrats and Progressives: The 1948 Presidential Election as a Test of Postwar Liberalism* (#1275) should only be considered introductory. The South's response to Truman's increased support of civil rights is examined in R. A. Garson, "The Alienation of the South: A Crisis for Harry S. Truman and the Democratic Party, 1945–1948" (#1265), and Harvard Sitkoff, "Harry Truman and the Election of 1948: The Coming of Age of Civil Rights in American Politics" (#1253).

The Supreme Court's decisions and views, especially as they related to loyalty investigations, have come in for considerable criticism. Indeed, Truman has been given low marks for his appointments to the highest court. An introduction to the activities of the court during the Truman era may be found in Chapters 8 and 9 of P. L. Murphy, *The Constitution in Crisis Times, 1918–1969* (#1499). Numerous studies relating to individual justices have been included below.

Organized crime was investigated during the Truman years by the Kefauver Committee. Estes Kefauver, *Crime in America* (#1502) condenses material from the hearings, while William H. Moore,

The Kefauver Committee and the Politics of Crime, 1950–1952 (#1503) seeks to put this episode of the Truman years in perspective.

Civil Rights

1046 Abrams, Charles. *Forbidden Neighbors: A Study of Prejudice in Housing.* New York: Harper, 1955.

Organized by topical themes, this account traces racial discrimination in housing from 1935 to 1950. Notes, index.

1047 Berman, William C. *The Politics of Civil Rights in the Truman Administration.* Columbus: Ohio State University Press, 1970.

This book looks at the origins of the civil rights movement and its impact on the Democratic party, and assesses its contribution to black rights. Notes, bibliography, index.

1048 Bernstein, Barton J. "The Ambiguous Legacy: The Truman Administration and Civil Rights." In Barton J. Bernstein, ed. *Politics and Policies of the Truman Administration.* Chicago: Quadrangle, 1970, pp. 269–314.

This essay takes issue with the thesis that Truman made any extensive contributions to the extension of civil rights to black Americans. Notes.

1049 Bernstein, Barton J. "The Truman Administration and Minority Rights: A Review Essay." *Journal of Ethnic Studies* 1 (1973): 66–77.

The author reviews *Quest and Response: Minority Rights and the Truman Administration* (1973) by Donald R. McCoy and Richard T. Ruetten. He is interested in determining what was behind Truman's middle-of-the-road policies. Notes.

1050 Bernstein, Barton J. "Truman on the Home Front." *Civil Liberties Review* 5 (1978): 50–57.

This review of Robert J. Donovan's *Conflict and Crisis: The Presidency of Harry S. Truman* (1977) focuses on civil rights issues.

1051 Billington, Monroe. "Civil Rights, President Truman and the South." *Journal of Negro History* 58 (1973): 127–39.

Truman's public positions on civil rights are detailed, together with the mail and press responses they generated from Southerners. Notes.

1052 Carr, Robert K. *Federal Protection of Civil Rights: Quest for a Sword.* Ithaca, NY: Cornell University Press, 1947.

Carr examines the work of the Civil Rights Section in the Department of Justice from its inception until 1945. Appendixes, tables of statutes and cases, index.

1053 Greenberg, Jack. *Race Relations and American Law.* New York: Columbia University Press, 1959.

This volume provides a solid, useful topical survey of the legal aspects of race relations, beginning before the Truman era and continuing into the late 1950s. Appendix, table of cases, bibliography, notes, index.

1054 Henry, David R. "Decision-Making in the Truman Administration." Ph.D. dissertation, Indiana University, 1976.

The analysis is centered on Truman's civil rights policies: Truman's leadership, the administration's early efforts to establish a civil rights stance, and the methods eventually adopted to promote civil rights progress. DAI 37:4699-A.

1055 Johnson, Dennis W. "Friend of the Court: The United States Department of Justice as *Amicus Curiae* in Civil Rights Cases Before the Supreme Court." Ph.D. dissertation, Duke University, 1972.

Until 1947 the U.S. Department of Justice did not participate in any Supreme Court disputes concerning state racial discrimination. Since then department policy has been reversed and the Department of Justice has appeared *amicus curiae* (friend of the court) in every major civil rights case in which it was not a direct party. DAI 33:6982-A.

1056 Johnson, Oakley C. "New Orleans Story." *Centennial Review* 12 (1968): 194–219.

The author has written of his experiences (1947–51) as a professor of English at Dillard University in New Orleans. He sought to register voters (unsuccessfully) for the Wallace campaign in 1948 and was active in the Louisiana branch of the Civil Rights Congress. He was finally released because he was politically conspicuous as a white professor at a black college.

1057 Juhnke, William E., Jr. "Creating a New Charter of Freedom: The Organization and Operation of the President's Committee on Civil Rights, 1946–1948." Ph.D. dissertation, University of Kansas, 1974.

This study illuminates the origins of the civil rights movement, sheds light on the functioning of a presidential committee, and examines the final report—*To Secure These Rights* (1948). DAI 36: 1046-A.

1058 Kellogg, Peter J. "The Americans for Democratic Action and Civil Rights in 1948: Conscience in Politics or Politics in Conscience?" *Midwest Quarterly* 20 (1978): 49–63.

The issue of civil rights was significant in American politics in 1948. This study examines the motives of members of ADA in the 1940s and the impact of this group on the issue.

1059 Marr, Carmel C. "New York's Human Rights Court." *Crisis* 78 (1971): 48–52.

In 1945 the state of New York became the first to create a Fair Employment Practice Committee (later known as the State Division of Human Rights). The six-member appeal board handled cases at the appellate level in employment, housing, and public accommodations discrimination.

1060 Martin, John F. *Civil Rights and the Crisis of Liberalism: The Democratic Party, 1945–1975.* Boulder: Westview Press, 1979.

Truman was the first Democratic president to formulate a civil rights program. Chapter 6 looks at Truman's Fair Deal legislation and his endeavor to make "active government and civil rights articles of the liberal faith." Notes, index.

1061 McCoy, Donald R., and Ruetten, Richard T. "The Civil Rights Movement, 1940–1954." *Midwest Quarterly* 11 (1969): 11–36.

A useful survey, this essay emphasizes Truman's activities on behalf of civil rights.

1062 McCoy, Donald R., and Ruetten, Richard T. *Quest and Response: Minority Rights and the Truman Administration.* Lawrence: University Press of Kansas, 1973.

The authors maintain that between 1945 and 1953 the quest for minority rights underwent a drastic change in patterns of thought and behavior which set the stage for further minority gains. Even so, there were significant advances during the Truman administration. Notes, bibliography, index.

1063 Mendelson, Wallace. *Discrimination: Based on the Report of the United States Commission on Civil Rights.* Englewood Cliffs, NJ: Prentice-Hall, 1962.

Although the U.S. Commission on Civil Rights was not created until 1957 and its report did not come out until 1961, this summary discusses some actions of the Truman administration. Notes.

1064 Morgan, Ruth. *The President and Civil Rights: Policy-Making by Executive Order.* New York: St. Martin's, 1970.

The civil rights policies of five modern presidents—F. D. Roosevelt to L. B. Johnson—are compared. Truman's efforts come in for considerable discussion. Notes, bibliography, index.

1065 Vaughan, Philip H. "The City and the American Creed: A Liberal Awakening During the Early Truman Period, 1946–48." *Phylon* 34 (1973): 51–62.

Urban problems and blacks are discussed for the Truman years.

1066 Vaughan, Philip H. "President Truman's Committee on Civil Rights: The Urban Implications." *Missouri Historical Review* 66 (1972): 413–30.

The committee's proposals were designed to bring prompt improvement in black living conditions in the city, through desegregation of facilities and the removal of restrictive covenants. Illustrations, notes.

1067 Vaughan, Philip H. "Urban Aspects of Civil Rights and the Early Truman Administration, 1946–1948." Ph.D. dissertation, University of Oklahoma, 1971.

The impact of deplorable urban conditions on blacks provided the impetus for an emerging civil rights movement and pointed the way toward new and imaginative programs for urban reform. Together, these forces influenced the Truman administration's civil rights program. DAI 32:3897-A.

1068 Vose, Clement E. *Caucasians Only: The Supreme Court, the NAACP, and the Restrictive Covenant Case.* Berkeley: University of California Press, 1959.

In 1948 the Supreme Court ruled that restrictive housing (real estate) covenants were not enforceable, and in 1953 it ruled that damages could not be collected from individuals' violating a restrictive covenant. Notes, index.

CIVIL RIGHTS LEADERS AND ORGANIZATIONS

1069 Anderson, Jervis. *A. Philip Randolph.* New York: Harcourt Brace Jovanovich, 1972.

Randolph, president of the Brotherhood of Sleeping Car Porters and a prominent black leader, led the campaign for the Fair Employment Practice Committee and against segregation in the armed forces. Notes, index.

1070 Broderick, Francis L. *W.E.B. DuBois: Negro Leader in Time of Crisis.* Stanford, CA: Stanford University Press, 1959.

Chapter 8 develops DuBois's role in the NAACP from 1944 to 1952, when he became sympathetic to the Soviet Union's policies and critical of U.S. policies toward colonialism. Bibliographical note, notes, index.

1071 Gill, Robert L. "Legacy of a Civil Rights Lawyer." *Journal of Human Relations* 12 (1964): 60–72.

Recounted here are the achievements of George L. Vaughn, a black who was a pioneer St. Louis civil rights lawyer. Most important was Vaughn's fight against restrictive covenants, a struggle which climaxed in his argument before the U.S. Supreme Court in the case of *Shelley v. Kraemer* (1948).

1072 Gillete, Michael L. "The Rise of the NAACP in Texas." *Southwestern Historical Quarterly* 81 (1978): 393–416.

Revived in Texas in the late 1930s, the group began challenging the exclusion of blacks from juries and Democratic primaries. By the late 1940s there were 104 branches and 30,000 members. Illustrations, notes.

1073 Hazel, David W. "The National Association for the Advancement of Colored People and the National Legislative Process, 1940–1954." Ph.D. dissertation, University of Michigan, 1957.

The NAACP's legislative program focused on such objectives as antilynching, antipoll tax, and Fair Employment Practice Committee legislation, and on such general objectives as equalization of education, housing, and treatment in the armed forces. The author reviews its successes and tactics. DAI 18:1478.

1074 Meier, August, and Rudwick, Elliott. *CORE: A Study in the Civil Rights Movement, 1942–1968.* New York: Oxford University Press, 1973.

The Congress of Racial Equality (CORE) was formed in 1942 by individuals committed to applying Gandhian techniques of nonviolent direct action to resolving racial conflicts. Notes, index.

1075 Moore, Jesse M., Jr. "The Urban League and the Black Revolution, 1941–1961: Its Philosophy and Its Policies." Ph.D. dissertation, Pennsylvania State University, 1971.

Although the Urban League has been in the midst of civil rights activities and its programs have been designed to alleviate discrimination against blacks, its approach has differed from other civil rights organizations. DAI 32:2612-A.

1076 Parris, Guichard, and Brooks, Lester. *Blacks in the City: A History of the National Urban League.* Boston: Little, Brown, 1971.

The National League on Urban Conditions among Negroes, forerunner of the National Urban League, was formed in 1911. Housing, employment, and civil rights were its focus of activity during the Truman administration. Notes, index.

1077 Record, Wilson. *Race and Radicalism: The NAACP and the Communist Party in Conflict.* Ithaca, NY: Cornell University Press, 1964.

The Communist party's general inability to attract black support is examined. Chapters 4 and 5 focus on World War II and the Truman era. Notes, index.

1078 Streater, John B., Jr. "The National Negro Congress, 1936–1947." Ph.D. dissertation, University of Cincinnati, 1981.

This study covers the founding of the NNC as a Popular Front organization during the 1930s through its increasingly leftist leanings in the 1940s to its merger with the young left-oriented Civil Rights Congress in 1947. DAI 42:2252.

1079 Strickland, Arvarh E. *History of the Chicago Urban League*. Urbana: University of Illinois Press, 1966.

In the postwar period, the league became increasingly militant. This antagonized many of the agency's white supporters, and they forced a complete reorganization of the league in 1956.

1080 White, Walter. *A Man Called White: Autobiography of Walter White*. New York: Viking, 1948.

The last chapters of this personal account of a longtime leader of the NAACP relate to the Truman years.

1081 Zangrando, Robert L. *The NAACP Crusade Against Lynching, 1909–1950*. Philadelphia: Temple University Press, 1980.

The final two chapters of this well-documented study deal with the Truman years and the efforts of the Truman administration to develop a civil rights program. Notes, bibliography, index.

MINORITIES: BLACKS

See also Chapter 5, *Churches and Race*; Chapter 4, *Fair Employment Practice Committee* and *Minority Workers*. E. W. Miller and M. L. Fisher's *The Negro in America: A Bibliography* (#3014) may be useful.

1082 Banks, Melvin J. "The Pursuit of Equality: The Movement for First Class Citizenship Among Negroes in Texas, 1920–1950." Ph.D. dissertation, Syracuse University, 1962.

In the 1940s the Texas Council of Negro Organizations was created, and under its leadership launched suits attacking inequalities and the doctrine of separate but equal, which became a national issue in the 1950s. DAI 24:365.

1083 Bartley, Numan V., Jr. *The Rise of Massive Resistance: Race and Politics in the South During the 1950's*. Baton Rouge: Louisiana State University Press, 1969.

This study describes the rise of massive resistance to public school desegregation in the South during the 1950s. Truman's civil rights programs and a series of U.S. Supreme Court decisions struck at institutionalized white supremacy.

1084 Eagles, Charles W. "Prudent Rebel: Jonathan Daniels and Race Relations." Ph.D. dissertation, University of North Carolina, Chapel Hill, 1978.

This study covers Daniels's editorials in the Raleigh (NC) *News and Observer* (1930s–1950s). Combining paternalism, democratic idealism, and economic pragmatism, Daniels sought to achieve racial justice for blacks within the segregated South. He supported Truman in the election of 1948. DAI 39:4444-A.

1085 Feinman, Saul. "Trends in Racial Self-Image of Black Children: Psychological Consequences of Social Movement." *Journal of Negro Education* 48 (1979): 488–99.

Four comparable studies of black children, conducted in 1947, 1966, 1968, and 1970, are used to measure changes in racial self-image correlated with phases of the civil rights movement. Table, notes.

1086 Gilpin, Patrick J. "Charles S. Johnson: Scholar and Educator." *Negro History Bulletin* 39 (1976): 544–48.

Johnson became the first black president of Fisk University in 1947. Illustrations, notes.

1087 Grafton, Carl. "James E. Folsom and Civil Liberties in Alabama." *Alabama Review* 32 (1979): 3–27.

A two-time governor of Alabama, 1947–50 and 1955–58, Folsom consistently advocated a gradual extension of civil liberties to blacks and women. Interviews, notes.

1088 Jirran, Raymond J. "Cleveland and the Negro Following World War II." Ph.D. dissertation, Kent State University, 1972.

This study examines the cultural dimensions of black life in Cleveland after 1945. DAI 34:249-A.

1089 Johnson, James W. "The Associated Negro Press: A Medium of International News and Information, 1919–1967." Ph.D. dissertation, University of Missouri, 1975.

ANP publicized the struggles of colonialized peoples in Africa (1945–56). It helped to increase the awareness of Afro-Americans about the relationship between racism and colonialism. DAI 37:5980-A.

1090 Johnson, Oakley C. "One Year in the Deep South: A Documentary of Seventeen Years Earlier." *Journal of Human Relations* 12 (1964): 34–49.

A white schoolteacher's experiences (1946–47) at Talladega College, school for blacks in Alabama.

1091 Katz, Maude White, ed. "Learning From History: The Ingram Case of the 1940's." *Freedomways* 19 (1979): 82–86.

W. E. B. DuBois submitted a petition in 1949 to the United States requesting its intercession on behalf of a black Georgian, Rosa L. Ingram, who was serving (with two of her sons) a life sentence for the 1947 death of her neighbor who, after severely beating her, was clubbed by her sixteen-year-old son. The petition is reprinted here.

1092 Landis, Kenesaw M. *National Committee on Segregation in the Nation's Capitol. Segregation in Washington: A Report, November, 1948.* Chicago: 1948.

One-quarter of the population of the nation's capitol was segregated by color. The report examines discrimination in housing, health care, employment, and access to public and private services. Illustrations, notes.

1093 Meier, August, and Rudwick, Elliott. "The First Freedom Ride." *Phylon* 30 (1969): 213–22.

The Journey of Reconciliation of 1947, in which black and white bus riders tested Southern compliance with Supreme Court rulings banning segregation of interstate transport, served as a model for the more famous Freedom Ride of 1961.

1094 O'Kelly, Charlotte G. "Black Newspapers and the Black Protest Movement, 1946–1972." *Phylon* 41 (1980): 313–24.

The greatest attention was given to the National Association for the Advancement of Colored People and the Urban League in the four major regional newspapers reviewed here. The black press was found to be overwhelmingly integrationist and nonviolent. Tables, notes.

1095 Peterson, F. Ross. "Glen H. Taylor and the Bilbo Case." *Phylon* 31 (1970): 344–50.

Idaho Senator Glen Taylor sought to have the Senate (1946–47) refuse to seat Theodore G. Bilbo of Mississippi because of his racist demagoguery. Taylor was unsuccessful.

1096 Potenziani, David D. "Striking Back: Richard B. Russell and Racial Relocation." *Georgia History* 65 (1981): 263–77.

The Georgia senator, a white supremacist, responded to agitation for civil rights legislation in 1948 by introducing a bill which would provide funds for the relocation of Southern blacks in the North and Northern whites in the South. Notes.

1097 Saunders, Charles. "Assessing Race Relations Research." *Black Scholar* 1 (1970): 17–25.

This study points out that although black self-concepts and white attitudes toward blacks have been assessed, black attitudes toward whites have seldom been studied, 1938–70.

1098 Saxe, Janet Cheatham. "Malik El Shabazz: A Survey of His Interpreters." *Black Scholar* 1 (1970): 51–55.

The life of Malcolm X, Malik E. Shabazz, is briefly sketched and his beliefs and his critics are critiqued, 1946–68.

1099 Stafford, Walter W. "Dilemmas of Civil Rights Groups in Developing Urban Strategies and Changes in American Federalism, 1933–1970." *Phylon* 37 (1976): 59–72.

The interaction of black civil rights groups is chronicled as they reviewed urban development and established viable relationships with local and federal governments.

1100 Vaughan, Philip H. "The Truman Administration's Fair Deal for Black America." *Missouri Historical Review* 70 (1976): 291–305.

In his 1949 Fair Deal Truman insisted on a meaningful civil rights program. Although his administration actually accomplished little reform, it did begin the process of making Congress more aware of black demands. Notes.

1101 Young, Virginia Heyer. "Family and Childhood in a Southern Negro Community." *American Anthropologist* 72 (1970): 269–88.

This study suggests that child-rearing patterns in Southern black families lead to a behavior pattern which results from indigenous culture rather than from deprivation, 1949–59. Notes.

Desegregation of Armed Forces

1102 Billington, Monroe. "Freedom to Serve: The President's Committee on Equality of Treatment and Opportunity in the Armed Services, 1949–1950." *Journal of Negro History* 51 (1966): 262–74.

The Fahy Committee was charged with examining the rules, procedures, and practices of the armed services toward minorities to determine how these might be altered to encourage equality of treatment and opportunity. Notes.

1103 Dalfiume, Richard M. *Desegregation of the Armed Forces: Fighting on Two Fronts, 1939–1953.* Columbia: University of Missouri Press, 1969.

Truman ordered the desegregation of the armed forces in 1948. This was the first major step in federal civil rights involvement. Bibliography, index.

1104 Dalfiume, Richard M. "The Fahy Committee and Desegregation of the Armed Forces." *Historian* 31 (1968): 1–20.

This account suggests political reasons why Truman issued an executive order ending segregation in the armed services. It reviews the Fahy Committee established by the president to supervise its implementation. The committee had several disagreements with the army before integration occurred. Notes.

1105 Foner, Jack D. *Blacks and the Military in American History: A New Perspective*. New York: Praeger, 1974.

Chapters 7 and 8 deal with black servicemen and World War II, and Truman's desegregation of the armed services. Bibliography, index.

1106 Gropman, Alan L. *The Air Force Integrates, 1945–1964*. Washington, DC: Office of Air Force History, 1978.

The air force confronted a black office mutiny in April 1945, and one massive and several minor race incidents in 1946 and 1947. The latter episodes were blamed on Communist influences, while overlooking other factors such as overcrowded living conditions and segregation. Illustrations, notes, bibliography, index.

1107 Hachey, Thomas. "Walter White and the American Negro Soldier in World War II: A Diplomatic Dilemma for Britain." *Phylon* 39 (1978): 241–49.

In 1944 Walter F. White, executive secretary of the NAACP, traveled to Britain to investigate race discrimination in the American army. White's trip was an important contribution to the process which led to Truman's desegregation of the armed forces in 1948. Notes.

1108 Johnson, Campbell C. *Special Groups*. 2 vols. Washington, DC: Selective Service System, 1953.

Regulations affecting minorities serving in the armed forces, through World War II, are examined. Recommendations for improvements were included in the Selective Service Act of 1949. Appendix, index.

1109 MacGregor, Morris J., Jr. *Integration of the Armed Forces, 1940–1965*. Washington, DC: Center for Military History, U.S. Army, 1981.

Truman's decision to integrate the armed forces by executive order is detailed in Chapters 12 and 13. Also the recommendations of the Fahy Committee are reviewed in Chapter 14. Illustrations, notes, bibliography, index.

1110 McGuire, Phillip. "Black Civilian Aides and the Problems of Racism and Segregation in the United States Armed Forces, 1940–1950." Ph.D. dissertation, Howard University, 1975.

Judge William H. Hastie, Truman K. Gibson, Jr., Colonel Marcus H. Ray, and James C. Evans were civilian aides to the secretary of war (1940–50)

with instructions to assist formulating policies which would ensure equality of treatment. DAI 37:4568-A.

1111 Mrozek, Donald J. "The *Croatan* Incident: The U.S. Navy and the Problem of Racial Discrimination After World War II." *Military Affairs* 44 (1980): 187–91.

The removal of 123 black enlisted men, scheduled to return home, from the *USS Croatan* at Le Havre, France, led to protests from black communities. The navy decided that the army was to blame and argued that it did not discriminate. Notes.

1112 Nelson, Dennis D. *The Integration of the Negro into the U.S. Navy*. New York: Farrar, Strauss & Young, 1951.

This semiofficial account deals with the navy's efforts to respond to the Fahy Committee's report and to achieve integration in the navy from World War II to 1951. Appendix, tables.

1113 Nichols, Lee. *Breakthrough on the Color Front*. New York: Random House, 1954.

Nichols has written a popular account, based on considerable research, of the integration of blacks into the armed forces during and immediately after World War II. Bibliography, index.

1114 Paszek, Lawrence J. "Negroes and the Air Force, 1939–1949." *Military Affairs* 31 (1967): 1–9.

The air force's efforts to retain segregated units are examined. Notes.

1115 Sitkoff, Harvard. "Racial Militancy and Interracial Violence in the Second World War." *Journal of American History* 58 (1971): 661–81.

This account of the violence visited upon black men and women, many of which were in the armed forces, provides a useful background to Truman's efforts to achieve civil rights legislation—especially his elimination of segregation in the armed services. Notes.

1116 Stillman, Richard J., II. *Integration of the Negro in the United States Armed Forces*. New York: Praeger, 1968.

This is an analytical study of the impact of World War II politics and actions, as well as Truman's 1949 decision, upon the integration of blacks in the armed services. Tables, notes, bibliography.

Desegregation of Schools

1117 Berman, Daniel M. *It Is So Ordered: The Supreme Court Rules on School Segregation*. New York: Norton, 1966.

The background of *Brown* v. *Board of Education*, including the legal activities during the Truman years, is reviewed here. Appendix, index.

1118 Hudgins, H. C., Jr. *The Warren Court and the Public Schools.* Danville, IL: Interstate Printers, 1970.

Several cases decided during the Truman years helped to create the precedents which led to the Warren Court's decisions. Notes, table of cases, bibliography, index.

1119 Kluger, Richard. *Simple Justice: The History of Brown v. Board of Education and Black America's Struggle for Equality.* New York: Knopf, 1976.

Much of the legal argument relating to this eventful decision was presented during the Truman years. This is developed in Chapters 11 to 22. Notes, index to cases, index.

1120 Schwartz, Ruth E. "A Descriptive Analysis of Oral Argument Before the United States Supreme Court in the School Segregation Cases, 1952–1953." Ph.D. dissertation, University of Southern California, 1966.

The focus of this study is the process of oral advocacy, the substance and language of the arguments advanced, and the questions, answers, and comments by the justices and counsel. DAI 27:3975.

1121 Southern, David W. "An American Dilemma: Gunnar Myrdal and the Civil Rights Cases, 1944–1954." *Journal of the History of Sociology* 3 (1981): 81–107.

The author examines the use of Gunnar Myrdal's massive indictment of segregation in the United States, *An American Dilemma* (1944), in civil rights cases.

1122 Tussman, Joseph, ed. *The Supreme Court on Racial Discrimination.* New York: Oxford University Press, 1963.

This casebook reprints extracts from nearly a dozen decisions handed down during the Truman years relating to restrictive covenants, economic discrimination, educational segregation, and discrimination regarding jury service.

1123 Vandever, Elizabeth J. "*Brown v. Board of Education of Topeka:* Anatomy of a Decision." Ph.D. dissertation, University of Kansas, 1971.

This study focuses on trial court records, the oral arguments before the Supreme Court in 1952 and 1953, and related legal history involving racial segregation. Much of this data reflects affairs and conditions during the Truman years. DAI 32:5724-A.

Politics and Black Voters

See also *Political Affairs.*

1124 Bailey, Harry A., Jr., ed. *Negro Politics in America.* Columbus: Merrill, 1967.

Several essays explore the significance of the black vote in the 1948 presidential election. Oscar Glantz maintains that the black vote in placing California, Illinois, and Ohio was indispensable to the Democrats. Tables, index.

1125 Danigelis, Nicholas L. "Race and Political Activity in the United States, 1948–1968: A Trend Analysis." Ph.D. dissertation, Indiana University, 1973.

This study describes and attempts to explain the reasons behind variation in the amount of legitimate political activity among black Americans between 1948 and 1968. DAI 34:6777-A.

1126 Fenton, John R., and Vines, Kenneth N. "Negro Registration in Louisiana." *American Political Science Review* 51 (1957): 704–13.

The single greatest determining factor in effecting the percentage of blacks registered to vote was religious affiliation in localized areas, 1944–56. Notes.

1127 Lawson, Steven F. *Black Ballots: Voting Rights in the South, 1944–1969.* New York: Columbia University Press, 1976.

Despite the Fifteenth Amendment, blacks in the South remained disenfranchised in the immediate postwar period. Lawson studies the process by which blacks gained the right to vote. Notes, bibliography, index.

1128 Moon, Henry L. *Balance of Power: The Negro Vote.* Garden City, NY: Doubleday, 1949.

Writing before the 1948 election, Moon maintained that the black vote would have a significant impact on the election's outcome. Party politics and the issue of civil rights are explored. Appendixes, index.

1129 Moon, Henry L. "The Southern Scene." *Phylon* 16 (1955): 351–58.

Following a 1944 Supreme Court ruling on the illegality of "white primaries," blacks increasingly participated in the political process despite Southern state legislatures' efforts to disenfranchise them, 1944–54.

1130 Scott, William B. "Judge J. Waties Waring: Advocate of 'Another' South." *South Atlantic Quarterly* 77 (1978): 320–34.

A federal judge and native South Carolinian, Waring was responsible for the court's finding in 1947 that the white Democratic party primary was unconstitutional. Scott believes that Waring only anticipated the rejection of segregation by an increasingly large number of Southern whites after World War II. Notes.

MINORITIES: NATIVE AMERICANS

1131 Fixico, Donald L. "Termination and Relocation: Federal Indian Policy in the 1950s." Ph.D. dissertation, University of Oklahoma, 1980.

Congress (1945–63) abrogated federal recognition of Indian groups and responsibilities to Native Americans and initiated a program of termination and relocation. Fixico presents points of view of the government, non-Indians and the Indian. DAI 41:2475.

1132 Hasse, Larry J. "Termination and Assimilation: Federal Indian Policy, 1943–1961." Ph.D. dissertation, Washington State University, 1974.

This study concentrates on the period of reaction to Indian Commissioner John Collier's "Indian New Deal," 1943 to 1950. DAI 35:365-A.

1133 Heizer, Robert F., and Kroeber, Alfred L. "For Sale: California at 47 Cents an Acre." *Journal of California Anthropology* 3:2 (1976), 38–65.

The statements of various individuals made at the hearings before the Indian Claims Commission, 1946, are reprinted here. This effort was to regain some Indian lands in California for Native Americans.

1134 Koppes, Clayton R. "From New Deal to Termination: Liberalism and Indian Policy, 1933–1953." *Pacific Historical Review* 46 (1977): 543–66.

The Truman administration allowed Indian policy to be refocused on assimilation, in keeping with the Fair Deal's own emphasis on economic prosperity and individual competition and on individual civil rights and freedom from group identity. Notes.

1135 LeDuc, Thomas. "The Work of the Indian Claims Commission under the Act of 1946." *Pacific Historical Review* 26 (1957): 1–16.

This study examines the land claims settlements made under the Indian Claims Act of 1946 and assesses precedents set and decisions made. Notes.

1136 Lurie, Nancy O. "The Indian Claims Commission Act." Amer. Acad. of Political and Social Sciences *Annals* (Autumn 1957): 56–70.

The act, passed on 13 August 1946, was to give Indians ten years in which to present their claims against the U.S. government.

MINORITIES: WOMEN

See also Chapter 4, *Women Workers.*

1137 Bouraoui, H. A. "La Femme Révoltée: A Contrastive Cultural Study." *Journal of Popular Culture* 2 (1969): 593–614.

Feminine attitudes of discontent and revolt against sex roles and discrimination in French and American society, represented by Simone de Beauvoir and Betty Friedan, respectively, are used to investigate and compare cultural attitudes toward women, 1945–69.

1138 Brown, Carol. "Sexism and the Russell Sage Foundation." *Feminist Studies* 1 (1972): 25–44.

The Sage Foundation, a major social research organization, was founded by a woman and at first emphasized women; however, in its financial crisis of 1947, a major reorganization resulted in a modification of goals and a change in the proportion and status of women personnel. Notes.

1139 George, Elsie L. "The Women Appointees of the Roosevelt and Truman Administrations: A Study of Their Impact and Effectiveness." Ph.D. dissertation, American University, 1972.

This study examines the work of several women appointed to middle rank positions within the federal government during the Roosevelt and Truman administrations. These women include Mary W. Dewson, Hilda W. Smith, Mrs. Marion Banister, and Frieda B. Hennock (appointed by Truman to the Federal Trade Commission). DAI 33:2284-A.

1140 St. John, Jacqueline D. "Sex Role Stereotyping in Early Broadcast History: The Career of Mary Margaret McBride." *Frontiers* 3 (1978): 31–38.

This essay examines the myth of women's "natural" inferiority as radio and television broadcasters by focusing on McBride's career during 1934 to 1954.

MINORITIES: MEXICAN-AMERICANS AND OTHERS

See also Chapter 4, *Farm Labor: Bracero Program.*

1141 Allsup, Vernon C. "The American G.I. Forum: A History of a Mexican American Organization." Ph.D. dissertation, University of Texas, Austin, 1976.

In 1948 many ex-servicemen of Mexican descent formed a pressure group in Corpus Christi, Texas. After initial success, the founder, Dr. Hector Perez Garcia, guided the organization into action on all areas of Mexican-American life and the organization spread to twenty-eight states (1948 to the 1960s). DAI 37:5295-A.

1142 Broom, Leonard, and Riemer, Ruth. *Removal and Return: The Socio-Economic Effects of the War* *on Japanese-Americans*. Berkeley: University of California Press, 1949.

This early account contains a great deal of statistical data bearing on the economic costs of internment to Japanese-Americans. Tables, bibliography, appendix, notes.

1143 Busey, James L. "Domination and the Vote in a Southwestern Border Community: The 1950 Primary Campaign in El Paso, Texas." Ph.D. dissertation, Ohio State University, 1952.

This "case study" examines the problems of Mexican-Americans in the immediate postwar years. Hispanics, while a majority in population, were a minority of the voting population; consequently, their needs were ignored. DAI 18:1836.

1144 Kashima, Tetsuden. "Japanese American Internees Return, 1945 to 1955: Readjustment and Social Amnesia." *Phylon* 41 (1980): 107–15.

Understanding the model minority image of Japanese-Americans must begin with the crisis of readjustment after 1945. Notes.

1145 McWilliams, Carey. *A Mask for Privilege: Anti-Semitism in America*. Boston: Little, Brown, 1948.

While this volume contains only a little information relating directly to the Truman years, it is most useful as an introduction to the problem of anti-semitism. Notes, index.

1146 McWilliams, Carey. *North from Mexico: The Spanish-Speaking People of the United States*. Philadelphia: Lippincott, 1949.

Chapter 25 discusses World War II; but the book's essential value here is its background to the Truman era. Notes, index.

1147 Neuber, Frank William. "The Radical of the Right: A Case Study of W. H. Harold and His Northwest League for Christian Americanism." Ph.D. dissertation, University of Oregon, 1958.

Harold and his league aimed to expose a Jewish-Negro-Communist international plot to subvert America. Neuber looks at anti-Semitic political agitation when applied to an individual agitator, W. H. Harold.

1148 Vecoli, Rudolph J. "The Coming of Age of Italian Americans, 1945–1954." *Ethnicity* 5 (1978): 119–47.

About two-thirds of America's Italian immigrants arrived between 1900 and 1920. Most had little education or skills. However, the 1970 census shows that the second generation had achieved a level of education approaching the national average. Notes, figures.

Political Affairs

See also Chapter 2, *Truman Presidency*.

NATIONAL POLITICS

1149 Coulter, Philip, and Gordon, Glen. "Urbanization and Party Competition: Critique and Research of Theoretical Work." *Western Political Quarterly* 21 (1968): 274–88.

The theoretical work and research done by political theorists in relations between urbanization and political party competition (1946–58) is reviewed.

1150 Ficken, Robert E. "The Democratic Party and Domestic Politics During World War II." Ph.D. dissertation, University of Washington, 1973.

The study stresses the decayed state of the Democratic party in the final years of FDR's presidency. The G.O.P. sweep of the 1946 by-elections and Dewey's near-victory in 1948 were previewed by the wartime elections. DAI 34:5056-A.

1151 Garson, Robert A. *The Democratic Party and the Politics of Sectionalism, 1941–1948*. Baton Rouge: Louisiana State University Press, 1974.

During the 1940s Southern Democrats became increasingly dissatisfied with the Democratic party, causing it to become a sectional party by 1948. Notes, bibliography, index.

1152 Gertzog, Irwin N. "The Role of the President in the Midterm Congressional Election." Ph.D. dissertation, University of North Carolina, 1965.

The midterm campaign activities of presidents from Wilson to Kennedy are examined. Presidents give more attention to Senate than House candidates and candidates from their own states. DAI 26:4048.

1153 Hasting, Ann C. "Intraparty Struggle: Harry S. Truman, 1945–1948." Ph.D. dissertation, St. Louis University, 1972.

Truman inherited a Democratic party in disarray. This account focuses on the potential competitors he could have had for the nomination in 1948. DAI 33:1108-A.

1154 Ladd, Everett C., Jr., and Hadley, Charles D. *Transformations of the American Party System: Political Coalitions from the New Deal to the 1970s*. 2d ed. New York: Norton, 1978.

Chapter 2 focuses on the transformation of the Democratic party during the Truman years. Notes, illustrations, index.

1155 Lubell, Samuel. *The Future of American Politics*. New York: Harper, 1952.

Truman's astonishing 1948 victory was the beginning of a new political era. The trends giving rise to this realignment include urban "minorities," a new middle class, economic revolution in the South, America's international role, organized labor, changing farm policies, and the impact of the Cold War. Index.

1156 Madison, Charles A. *Leaders and Liberals in 20th Century America*. New York: Ungar, 1961.

The chapters "Hugo L. Black: New Deal Justice," pp. 363–411, and "Harry S. Truman: The New Deal in Eclipse," pp. 463–73, are useful. Bibliography, index.

1157 Martin, Glenn R. "Conservatism and Liberalism in the American Congress: A Selected Study of Congressional Voting Ratings, 1947–1972." Ph.D. dissertation, Ball State University, 1973.

Congress experienced four ideological epicycles during 1947 to 1972. Following a 1947–49 conservative reactionism, a 1949–58 liberalizing moderation set in. DAI 34:5066-A.

1158 Mayer, George. *The Republican Party, 1854–1966*. New York: Oxford University Press, 1967.

Mayer's summary of Republican party activities during the Truman years (pp. 466–95) emphasizes the elections of 1946, 1948, and 1952. Notes, index.

1159 McGinnis, Patrick E. "Republican Party Resurgence in Congress, 1936–1946." Ph.D. dissertation, Tulane University, 1967.

In 1946 Republicans won control of both the Senate and House for the first time since 1930. Their resurgence was in part a product of diverse economic and social forces, but it was a temporary gain. DAI 28:3612-A.

1160 Parmet, Herbert S. *The Democrats: The Years After FDR*. New York: Macmillan, 1976.

Parmet looks at the forces comprising the Democratic party in the post-Roosevelt era. Part 1 focuses on the Truman era. Notes, illustrations, bibliography, index.

1161 Reinhard, David W. *The Republican Right Since 1945*. Lexington: University of Kentucky Press, 1983.

This account focuses on the political fortunes of the Republican party's right wing since the death of F. D. Roosevelt.

1162 Sherrill, Robert. *Gothic Politics in the Deep South: Star of the New Confederacy*. New York: Grossman, 1968.

In the 1960s the South lost the battle of civil rights. Sherrill looks at the postwar Southern politicians and the major issues that led to the South's defeat. Index.

1163 Stinnett, Ronald F. *Democrats, Dinners, and Dollars: A History of the Democratic Party, Its Dinners, Its Rituals*. Ames: Iowa State University Press, 1967.

One of the political rituals of the Democratic party is its Jefferson-Jackson Day dinners. Truman used these yearly dinners as appeals to the party to support his proposed programs. Notes, illustrations, index.

1164 Tuttle, Daniel W., Jr. "National Political Convention Delegates, 1944–1952: Their Characteristics, Qualifications, and Opinions." Ph.D. dissertation, University of Minnesota, 1964.

A survey of delegates reveals that: (1) socioeconomic characteristics of delegates differed significantly from the population; (2) delegates included most identifiable social, economic, ethnic, and religious groups; and (3) Republicans and Democrats were similar in terms of characteristics. DAI 25:2018.

1165 Tyler, Robert L. "The American Veterans Committee: Out of a Hot War and Into the Cold." *American Quarterly* 18 (1966): 419–36.

The American Veterans Committee began in 1944 as a liberal coalition of young World War II veterans; but dissension and decline occurred when Soviet-American relations cooled and Wallace sought the presidency in 1948. Notes.

POLITICAL IDEOLOGIES

See also *Internal Security and Civil Liberties*, for the interaction of the ideologies.

1166 Gillam, Richard D. "C. Wright Mills, 1916–1948: An Intellectual Biography." Ph.D. dissertation, Stanford University, 1972.

This study is an intellectual and, in part, a personal biography of the late sociologist, Charles Wright Mills, up to the publication of his first book, *The New Men of Power: America's Labor Leaders* (1948). The major theme of this study is the nature of Mills's contribution to what the author calls the "new radicalism" in America. DAI 39:406-A.

1167 Hero, Alfred O., Jr. "Liberalism-Conservatism Revisited: Foreign vs. Domestic Federal Policies,

1937–1967." *Public Opinion Quarterly* 33 (1969): 399–408.

Hero examines "linkages of American attitudes toward major foreign policy issues since the late 1930s with self-perceptions as liberal or conservatives and with policy preferences on critical national domestic issues of the day." Notes.

Conservatism

See especially *McCarthyism and Opponents.*

1168 Diggins, John P. *Up From Communism: Conservative Odysseys in American Intellectual History.* New York: Harper & Row, 1975.

Part 2 of this volume covers such topics as McCarthyism and the Cold War in light of leading social critics, such as Eastman, Dos Passos, Herberg, and Burnham. Photographs, notes, index.

1169 Lora, Ronald. "A View From the Right: Conservative Intellectuals, the Cold War, and McCarthy." In R. Griffith and A. Theoharis, eds. *The Specter: Original Essays on the Cold War and the Origins of McCarthyism.* New York: New Viewpoints, 1974, pp. 40–70.

Although "McCarthyism" was much more than "simply conservatism on parade," it did owe "its political potency to those conservative intellectuals who supplied ideological support and rationalization for the political right." Notes.

1170 Nash, George. *The Conservative Intellectual Movement in America Since 1945.* New York: Basic Books, 1976.

Conservatism, Nash maintains, was no "closet philosophy" after World War II, but was a decidedly activist force, whose objective was not simply to understand the world but to change it, restore it, and preserve it. Notes, bibliographical essay, index.

1171 Toy, Eckard V., Jr. "Ideology and Conflict in American Ultra-conservatism, 1945–1960." Ph.D. dissertation, University of Oregon, 1965.

This study examines the roots of ultraconservative ideology, illustrates some of the ideological differences among ultraconservatives, and indicates some of the reasons why many ultraconservatives joined the John Birch Society. DAI 26:4616.

Liberalism

1172 Brock, Clifton. *Americans for Democratic Action: Its Role in National Politics.* Washington, DC: Public Affairs Press, 1962.

The ADA, formed in 1947, was a left-of-center group that had as one of its major goals the nomination and election of liberal candidates, regardless of their political party affiliation.

1173 Engelhardt, Carroll. "Man in the Middle: Arthur M. Schlesinger, Jr., and Postwar American Liberalism." *South Atlantic Quarterly* 80 (1981): 119–38.

Schlesinger emerges as a representative centrist liberal in this essay which articulates the basic assumptions and major themes of his thought. Notes.

1174 Epstein, Marc J. "The Third Force: Liberal Ideology in a Revolutionary Age, 1945–1950." Ph.D. dissertation, University of North Carolina, 1971.

By focusing on two groups that appear to be the most articulate and representative of the liberal-left in immediate postwar years, Americans for Democratic Action and the 1948 Progressive party, this study seeks to analyze their programs, policies, and outlook. DAI 32:2597-A.

1175 Hamby, Alonzo. "The Liberals, Truman, and FDR as Symbol and Myth." *Journal of American History* 56 (1970): 859–67.

After FDR's death, liberals formed the Americans for Democratic Action and the Political Action Committee, criticized Truman's foreign policy for destroying Big Three unity, blasted his "crony" administration, and searched in 1948 for alternative candidates. Notes.

1176 Hamby, Alonzo L. "The Vital Center, the Fair Deal, and the Quest for a Liberal Political Economy." *American Historical Review* 77 (1972): 653–78.

The forces which restructured American liberalism to meet the pressures of the Cold War are discussed here. Truman's Fair Deal is seen as not far from Schlesinger's *Vital Center.* Notes.

1177 McAuliffe, Mary Sperling. *Crisis on the Left: Cold War Politics and American Liberals, 1947–1954.* Amherst: University of Massachusetts Press, 1978.

The old left was destroyed by the growing tensions between the United States and the Soviet Union and the emergence of anti-Communist tactics at home, leaving in its wake a new liberalism to deal with Cold War politics and policies. Notes, bibliographical essay, index.

1178 Merkley, Paul. *Reinhold Niebuhr: A Political Account.* Montreal: McGill-Queen's University Press, 1975.

Niebuhr was the political philosopher *par excellence* of the liberal intellectuals of the 1940s and 1950s. Arthur Schlesinger, Jr., George F. Kennan, and Hubert Humphrey have left testimonials to his influence. This volume discovers the source of Niebuhr's political behavior in his dogmatic Christianity rather than pragmatism. Notes, index, and bibliography of Niebuhr's writings.

1179 Nuechterlein, James A. "Arthur M. Schlesinger, Jr., and the Discontents of Postwar American Liberalism." *Review of Politics* 39 (1977): 3–40.

This essay focuses on Schlesinger's views in the late 1940s (*The Vital Center*) and in the 1960s (with John F. Kennedy and George McGovern). Notes.

1180   Pierce, Robert. "Liberals and the Cold War: Union for Democratic Action and Americans for Democratic Action, 1940–1959." Ph.D. dissertation, University of Wisconsin, Madison, 1979.

Although the ADA strongly supported containment, it was disappointed Truman did not listen to liberal advice. The ADA helped destroy the popular front in 1948 by use of innuendo, character assassination, and guilt-by-association. DAI 40:3494-A.

1181   Rosenof, Theodore. "The American Democratic Left Looks at the British Labour Government, 1945–1951." *Historian* 38 (1975): 98–119.

American reformist liberals such as Will Herberg, Paul H. Douglas, David C. Williams, A. M. Schlesinger, Jr., and Norman Thomas regarded the 1945 Labour party victory in Great Britain as instructive. Notes.

1182   Schlesinger, Arthur M., Jr. *The Vital Center: The Politics of Freedom*. Boston: Houghton Mifflin, 1962.

Written during and after the bitter presidential campaign of 1948 (and initially published in 1949), Schlesinger justifies the actions and beliefs of those liberals who had adopted a more conservative bent. He also seeks to draw a sharp distinction between liberal thought and Communist doctrine. New introduction, notes, index.

1183   Shaw, Lonel E., Jr. "The Political Theory of Reinhold Niebuhr." Ph.D. dissertation, University of North Carolina, Chapel Hill, 1971.

This is a systematic study and evaluation of the "complete" political theory of Reinhold Niebuhr. DAI 32:2764-A.

1184   Wright, Palmer W. "The 'New Liberalism' of the Fifties: Reinhold Niebuhr, David Riesman, Lionel Trilling, and the American Intellectual." Ph.D. dissertation, University of Michigan, 1966.

The "New Liberals" emerged in the late 1940s, embracing an "end-of-ideology" reaction against political extremes and an "end-of-innocence" reaction against the alienated political postures of many intellectuals and against totalitarian definitions of the self. DAI 28:275-A.

Communism/Socialism

See also Chapter 4, *Labor and Communism*.

1185   Fleischman, Harry. *Norman Thomas: A Biography, 1884–1968*. New York: Norton, 1964.

Thomas was the Socialist party's candidate for president from 1928 to 1948. Although he opposed the hysterical brand of anticommunism, he agreed that Communists should be expelled from places of responsibility. Bibliography, index.

1186   Johnpoll, Bernard K. *Pacifist's Progress: Norman Thomas and the Decline of American Socialism*. Chicago: Quadrangle Books, 1970.

Rather than being a biography of Socialist party leader Norman Thomas, Johnpoll focuses on Thomas as a political leader and analyzes his role in the disintegration of American socialism. Notes, index.

1187   Saposs, David J. *Communism in American Politics*. Washington, DC: Public Affairs Press, 1960.

The author's purpose in preparing this book, which focuses on the 1940s and 1950s, was to realert Americans to "understand why and how a Communist minority could become subversively powerful in our political life." Notes.

1188   Shannon, David A. *The Decline of American Communism: A History of the Communist Party of the United States Since 1945*. Chatham, NJ: Chatham Bookseller, 1971.

Party upheavals, from the ejection of Earl Browder from leadership in 1945 to the Russian intervention in Hungary in 1956, form the focus of this survey. Notes, index.

1189   Starobin, Joseph R. *American Communism in Crises, 1943–1957*. Cambridge: Harvard University Press, 1972.

The author traces the decline of the party from the struggle for leadership between Earl Browder and William Z. Foster, the 1948 Wallace campaign, the Right-Left contest within the CIO, and the relationship of the party to Moscow. Notes, bibliography, index.

STATE AND LOCAL POLITICS

1190   Barnard, William D. *Dixiecrats and Democrats: Alabama Politics, 1942–1950*. University: University of Alabama Press, 1974.

Alabama politics was subject to intraparty strife during the 1940s. The story of the clashes between rival factions of the Democratic party is explored in this volume. Notes, appendix, bibliography, index.

1191   Bartley, Numan V., and Graham, Hugh B. *Southern Politics and the Second Reconstruction*. Baltimore: Johns Hopkins University Press, 1975.

In the postwar era the South's previously solid democratic alliance underwent a restructuring. Did the South join the two-party political system? Illustrations, bibliography, index.

1192 Blevin, William L., Jr. "The Georgia Gubernatorial Primary of 1946." *Georgia Historical Quarterly* 50 (1966): 36–53.

Eugene Talmadge won the nomination although he lost in popular votes, because of his racist appeal to rural voters and the operation of the county unit system. Notes.

1193 Carter, Robert F. "Pressure from the Left: The American Labor Party, 1936–1954." Ph.D. dissertation, Syracuse University, 1965.

This New York State party tended to be more a pressure group than a genuine political party. In the 1948 election it became the New York State arm of the Wallace Progressive party. DAI 26:3275.

1194 Cosman, Bernard. "Republicanism in the Metropolitan South." Ph.D. dissertation, University of Alabama, 1960.

Cosman finds that although a grass roots Republican party (1920–58) is still a long way off, the important base for such a party lies in the cities and their prosperous neighborhoods. DAI 21:2859.

1195 Crawley, William B., Jr. "The Governorship of William M. Tuck, 1946–1950: Virginia Politics in the 'Golden Age' of the Byrd Organization." Ph.D. dissertation, University of Virginia, 1974.

While Tuck sought to keep Truman off the ballot in Virginia in 1948, he failed to keep Truman from carrying the state. DAI 35:2892-A.

1196 Ethridge, Richard C. "Mississippi's Role in the Dixiecrat Movement." Ph.D. dissertation, Mississippi State University, 1971.

National Dixiecrat campaign headquarters was located in Jackson, Mississippi. Although unable to capture the vote throughout the South, they significantly weakened the hold of the Democratic party in 1948, thus providing the impetus for party realignment toward the Republican party. DAI 32:1435-A.

1197 Fenton, John. *Politics in the Border States: A Study of the Patterns of Political Organization, and Political Change, Common to the Border States—Maryland, West Virginia, Kentucky and Missouri.* New Orleans: Hauser, 1957.

Information on border-state politics during the Truman years is available here. Footnotes, bibliography, index.

1198 Gardner, James B. "Political Leadership in a Period of Transition: Frank G. Clement, Albert Gore, Estes Kefauver, and Tennessee Politics, 1948–1957." Ph.D. dissertation, Vanderbilt University, 1978.

These leaders represent the return of the two-party structure to Tennessee politics and the emergence of these Tennesseans as national figures. DAI 39:3771-A.

1199 Grayson, A. G. "North Carolina and Harry Truman, 1944–1948." *Journal of American Studies* [Great Britain] 9 (1975): 283–300.

North Carolinians at first supported Truman's positions on civil rights, labor, and other issues; however, he gradually lost support to conservative factions. Notes.

1200 Grove, Stephen B. "The Decline of the Republican Machine in Philadelphia, 1936–52." Ph.D. dissertation, University of Pennsylvania, 1976.

In the 1947 mayoral election the Democratic nominee and Americans for Democratic Action activist, Richardson Dilworth, conducted a campaign of streetcorner rallies and attacks on the integrity of Republican leaders. Although this effort lost, the Philadelphia "machine" was badly damaged and soon declined. DAI 37:4559-A.

1201 Haney, Richard C. "A History of the Democratic Party in Wisconsin Since World War II." Ph.D. dissertation, University of Wisconsin, 1970.

Prior to the war, Wisconsin politics was controlled by "progressive" and "stalworth" factions of the Republican party, but following WWII the Democratic party rose to majority-party strength. The decline of the Wisconsin Progressive party, the rise of McCarthy, and the ambitions of a group of young Roosevelt followers contributed to this change. DAI 31:1191-A.

1202 Hansen, Gerald E. "The Conservative Movement in Utah after World War II." Ph.D. dissertation, University of Missouri, 1962.

Immediately after WWII, cleavage between the two parties was great, but by 1960 Republicans were moving left toward the center while liberal Democrats moved right toward center. DAI 23:4732.

1203 Haynes, John E. "Liberals, Communists, and the Popular Front in Minnesota: The Struggle to Control the Political Direction of the Labor Movement and Organized Liberalism, 1936–1950." Ph.D. dissertation, University of Minnesota, 1978.

In 1946 the Popular Front with the Communist party abandoned its accommodationist policies, outmaneuvered the forces under Hubert Humphrey, and took control of the Democratic-Farmer-Labor party. In 1948 Humphrey forces regained control of the DFL. However, this study indicates that the struggle with the Communist party in Minnesota had little to do with Cold War issues of the "Red Scare." DAI 39:1059-A.

1204 Henriques, Peter R. "The Byrd Organization Crushes a Liberal Challenge, 1950–1953." *Virginia Magazine of History and Biography* 87 (1979):3–29.

Although later some liberal positions would receive popular favor, during these years the conservative, states' rights, and limited federal government advocates banded together to support Harry F. Byrd, Sr. Illustrations, tables, notes.

1205 Henriques, Peter R. "John S. Battle and Virginia Politics, 1948–1953." Ph.D. dissertation, University of Virginia, 1971.

The career of Governor Battle (1950–54) is used to concentrate on an analysis of Senator Harry F. Byrd, Sr.'s political organization. Byrd's efforts to deny Truman a place on Virginia's ballot for the 1948 election severely split the organization, allowing Battle to win. DAI 32:4527-A.

1206 Jeffries, John W. "Testing the Roosevelt Coalition: Connecticut Society and Politics, 1940–1946." Ph.D. dissertation, Yale University, 1973.

Republicans overwhelmed Democrats in the 1946 by-election; however, Truman almost succeeded in carrying the state in 1948. DAI 34:703-A.

1207 Key, V. O., Jr. *Southern Politics in State and Nation.* New York: Knopf, 1949.

Southern politics in the twentieth century are surveyed, with pages 329 to 344 devoted to the Dixiecrat revolt of 1948. Notes, tables, index.

1208 Kinsella, Dorothy C. "Southern Apologists: A Liberal Image." Ph.D. dissertation, St. Louis University, 1971.

This study, concentrating on the years 1938 through 1954, investigated the image and vision of three Southern journalists—Hodding Carter, Gerald Johnson, and Ralph McGill. DAI 33:1114-A.

1209 Lester, James E., Jr. "Sidney Sanders McMath and the Southern Reform Tradition: An Administrative and Political Study of Arkansas' Thirty-Ninth Governor." Ph.D. dissertation, Washington State University, 1975.

McMath began his public career in 1946 and became governor (1949–53) with the support of reform-minded war veterans. DAI 36:5496-A.

1210 Miller, William D. *Mr. Crump of Memphis.* Baton Rouge: Louisiana State University Press, 1964.

Crump was Democratic party chairman of Memphis, 1922–54. He supported the Dixiecrat candidate in 1948. Notes, illustrations, bibliographical essay, index.

1211 Ori, Kan. "Basic Ideas in Federal-State Relations: The Indiana 'Revolt' of 1951." Ph.D. dissertation, Indiana University, 1961.

The Hoosier rebellion of 1951 was a statutory protest against increasing federal assimilation of state functions via federal aid. DAI 22:3252.

1212 Orkin, Saul. "New Jersey Democratic Party Politics, 1949–1953: The Downfall of State Boss Frank Hague." Ph.D. dissertation, Columbia University, 1971.

After almost three decades as the leader of the state Democratic party, Hague was toppled by a group of county leaders, his former lieutenants and allies. DAI 36:3115-A.

1213 Pritchard, Robert L. "Southern Politics and the Truman Administration: Georgia as a Test Case." Ph.D. dissertation, University of California, Los Angeles, 1970.

Georgians in Congress formed a major element in the Southern Democrats' opposition to many of Truman's policies. This opposition was mainly toward his domestic programs, especially in the area of civil rights. DAI 31:1735-A.

1214 Reinhard, David W. "The Republican Right: Leadership, Policies, and Intra-Party Politics, 1945–1965." Ph.D. dissertation, Pennsylvania State University, 1981.

This study investigates the general doctrine of the Republican Right and its response to major postwar domestic and foreign policy issues, as well as intraparty political battles in 1948, 1952, and 1964. DAI 42:1764.

1215 Rosenberg, Bernard. "New York Politics and the Liberal Party." *Commentary* 37 (1964): 69–75.

The history (1944–64), record, and influence of the Liberal party on state, national, and New York City politics is reviewed.

1216 Scott, George W. "Arthur B. Langlie: Republican Governor in a Democratic Age." Ph.D. dissertation, University of Washington, 1971.

Langlie won a second term (first term 1940–44) as governor in 1948 in time to inherit highway, welfare, and education needs and a fiscal crisis. He sought, unsuccessfully, to broaden the tax base in order to deal with state needs. DAI 32:2619-A.

1217 Sims, George E. " 'The Little Man's Big Friend' James E. Folsom in Alabama Politics, 1946–1958." Ph.D. dissertation, Emory University, 1981.

Because of his inexperience and lack of preparation, a political stalemate developed between the governor and the traditional legislative leaders, allowing for the success of the States' Rights party in Alabama during the 1948 presidential election. DAI 32:3276.

1218 Soapes, Thomas F. "Republican Leadership and the New Deal Coalition: Missouri Republican

Politics, 1947–1952." Ph.D. dissertation, University of Missouri, Columbia, 1973.

After the fall of the Pendergast machine, the Republican party was able to achieve some successes, especially in the elections of 1946. In 1948 the Democratic party regained control. DAI 35:1031-A.

1219 Sosna, Morton P. "In Search of the Silent South: White Southern Racial Liberalism, 1920–1950." Ph.D. dissertation, University of Wisconsin, 1972.

Among the significant individual white Southern liberals were University of North Carolina sociologist Howard W. Odum, *Richmond Times-Dispatch* editor Virginius Dabney, and Georgia writer Lillian Smith. DAI 33:6853-A.

1220 Sweeney, James R. "Byrd and Anti-Byrd: The Struggle for Political Supremacy in Virginia, 1945–1954." Ph.D. dissertation, University of Notre Dame, 1973.

The state and national elections are analyzed as to internal Democratic opponents and Republican challengers. DAI 34:2536-A.

1221 Ungs, Thomas D. "The Republican Party in Iowa, 1946–1956." Ph.D. dissertation, State University of Iowa, 1957.

The Republican party in Iowa actually is made up of two competing groups: (1) an urban-based progressive wing; and (2) a rural conservative wing which opposes progressive ideas. DAI 17:3078.

1222 Weaver, John D. *Warren: The Man, the Court, the Era*. Boston: Little, Brown, 1967.

Governor of California (1943–53) and Republican vice-presidential candidate for 1948, Warren opposed loyalty oaths and criticized parts of the Taft-Hartley Act. Notes, table of cases, index.

1223 White, G. Edward. *Earl Warren: A Public Life*. New York: Oxford University Press, 1982.

Chapter 4 briefly surveys Warren's years as governor of California, 1943–53. Notes, index.

1224 Yarnell, Allen. "Pension Politics in Washington State, 1948." *Pacific Northwest Quarterly* 61 (1970): 147–55.

In 1947 the Washington State legislature undid most of the previous efforts to achieve a meaningful old-age pension program. The attempt of the Pension Union to reverse these changes became immersed in the "Red Scare" when the state's Un-American Activities committee charged that the union was infiltrated by "subversive elements." Notes.

ELECTIONS

1225 Berelson, Bernard R.; Layarsfeld, Paul F.; and McPhee, William N. *Voting: A Study of Opinion Formation in a Presidential Campaign*. Chicago: University of Chicago Press, 1954.

While the chapters are arranged topically, information on the 1948 and 1952 elections is included. Tables, index.

1226 Boylan, James. *The New Deal Coalition and the Election of 1946*. New York: Garland, 1981.

An extensive study of the voting trends of the 1946 by-election, it forecast the problems that Truman would face in 1948. This useful study has a fine bibliography. Index.

1227 Cummings, Milton C., Jr. *Congressmen and the Electorate: Elections for the U.S. House and the President, 1920–1964*. New York: Free Press, 1966.

Cummings examines the interrelationship between the vote for president and the vote for congressmen in presidential election years. Notes, tables, index.

1228 Key, V. O., Jr. *The Responsible Electorate: Rationality in Presidential Voting, 1936–1960*. Cambridge: Harvard University Press, 1966.

Key finds that the American voter votes more in accordance with relevant questions of public policy, governmental performance, and executive personality than with party alignment. Notes, tables, index.

1229 Nie, Norman H., et al. *The Changing American Voter*. Cambridge: Harvard University Press, 1979.

Using fifteen national surveys (1939–74), the changing patterns of the American voter are analyzed. Some attention is paid to the 1948 election. Notes, illustrations, appendixes, index.

1230 Press, Charles. "Voting Statistics and Presidential Coattails." *American Political Science Review* 52 (1958): 1041–50.

This study identifies in-district competition, presidential candidate popularity, and candidate seniority as major influences on motivation in voting behavior, 1940–56.

1231 Rhyne, Edwin H. "Political Parties and Decision-making in Three Southern Counties." *American Political Science Review* 52 (1958): 1091–1107.

A survey of voting statistics, 1940–52, in three Southern counties (given fictitious names) indicates that the electoral process may not necessarily contribute to democratic practices in decision-making. Tables, notes.

1232 Roseboom, Eugene H., and Eckes, Alfred E., Jr. *A History of Presidential Elections from George Washington to Jimmy Carter*. New York: Macmillan, 1979.

Each presidential election and the developments in each administration that influenced the work of party conventions and campaigns are surveyed. Notes, bibliography, index.

1233 Zikmund, Joseph, II. "Suburban Voting in Presidential Elections, 1948–1964." *Midwest Journal of Political Science* 12 (1968): 239–58.

This study of presidential elections focuses on 198 suburban communities distributed among four major eastern and midwestern metropolitan areas. They confirmed a slight Democratic shift in suburban voting. Appendix, tables, notes.

Election of 1948

See Chapter 3, *Thomas E. Dewey.*

1234 Abels, Jules. *Out of the Jaws of Victory.* New York: Holt, 1959.

Truman's surprising victory over Dewey in the 1948 presidential election is the focus of this book. Bibliography, index, illustrations.

1235 Barber, James D. *The Pulse of Politics: Electing Presidents in the Media Age.* New York: Norton, 1980.

Chapter 4 discusses Truman's surprising victory in the 1948 presidential election. Notes, bibliography.

1236 Blanchard, Robert; Meyer, Richard; and Morley, Blaine. *Presidential Elections, 1948–1960.* Research Monograph No. 4. Salt Lake City: Institute of Government, University of Utah, 1961.

Chapter 1 focuses on the 1948 election. This brief (pp. 7–13) account summarizes campaign charges, summarizes preelection predictions, and contains maps which show the 1948 vote by counties and states. Footnotes, maps, appendix, bibliography.

1237 Borowski, Harry R. "A Narrow Victory: The Berlin Blockade and the American Military Response." *Air University Review* 32 (1981): 18–30.

The author believes that Truman's decision to rely upon an airlift to keep food and supplies flowing into Berlin, instead of employing military force to reduce the Soviet blockade, was the key to his narrow election victory in 1948.

1238 Brembeck, Cole S. "The Persuasive Speaking of Truman and Dewey in the 1948 Presidential Campaign." Ph.D. dissertation, University of Wisconsin, 1951.

This is a study of speechmaking by the Democratic and Republican candidates during the 1948 presidential campaign.

1239 Chrisman, James R. "The Rhetoric of the Presidential Campaign of 1948. A Content Analysis of Selected Addresses of Harry S. Truman and Thomas E. Dewey." Ph.D. dissertation, Oklahoma State University, 1974.

This study examines forty speeches by Truman and twenty-three speeches by Dewey to determine the differences in their rhetoric during the presidential campaign of 1948. DAI 36:7587-A.

1240 Davies, Richard O. "Whistle-Stopping Through Ohio." *Ohio History* 71 (1962): 113–23.

The rail route which Truman took through Ohio is depicted. An effort is made to assess the success of Truman's campaigning in Ohio. Illustrations, notes.

1241 Divine, Robert A. *Foreign Policy and U.S. Presidential Elections, 1940–1948.* 2 vols. New York: New Viewpoints, 1974.

Since World War II foreign policy issues played a large role in the electoral process. Chapters 5 to 7 discuss the 1948 election. Notes, bibliography, index.

1242 Divine, Robert A. "The Cold War and the Election of 1948." *Journal of American History* 59 (1972): 90–110.

Divine argues that Truman's tough stands on foreign policy issues—Berlin crisis, Czech crisis, and Marshall Plan—were important in his reelection. Notes.

1243 Forsythe, James L. "Postmortem on the Election of 1948: An Evaluation of Cong. Clifford R. Hope's Views." *Kansas Historical Quarterly* 38 (1972): 338–59.

Hope blames party leaders for not defending the Agricultural Act of 1948, for misunderstanding the Commodity Credit Corporation Charter Act, and for not assisting Republican candidates in the farm belt. Notes.

1244 Kirkendall, Richard S. "The Election of 1948." in A. M. Schlesinger, Jr., and F. Israel, eds. *History of American Presidential Elections.* New York: Chelsea House, 1971, 4:3099–3214.

The introductory essay, collected documents, and table of election results provide a useful overview of the 1948 presidential election.

1245 Lee, R. Alton. "The Turnip Session of the Do-Nothing Congress: Presidential Campaign Strategy." *Southwestern Social Science Quarterly* 44 (1963): 256–67.

This essay argues that Truman's hard-hitting attack upon the Eightieth Congress was the key to his reelection. It cast the president in an underdog role.

1246 McGrath, James H. *The Power of the People.* New York: Messner, 1948.

Senator McGrath (D-RI) was chairman of the Democratic National Committee. This volume was to be a handbook for the 1948 election, with a sketch of Truman and political issues. Illustrations.

1247 Michigan University. Survey Research Center. *A Study of the Presidential Vote, November, 1948: A National Survey*. Ann Arbor: Survey Research Center, Institute for Social Research, University of Michigan, April 1949.

This mimeograph pamphlet (120 pages) contains an extraordinary amount of information about how and why people voted the way they did in 1948. Tables.

1248 Mosteller, Frederick, et al. *The Pre-election Polls of 1948: Report to the Committee on Analysis of Pre-election Polls and Forecasts*. New York: Social Science Research Council, 1949.

The study concluded that errors in sampling and interviewing and in failure to assess voting behavior of undecided voters and shifts in voting intentions near the end of the campaign were at fault. Tables, appendixes, index.

1249 Redding, John M. *Inside the Democratic Party*. Indianapolis: Bobbs-Merrill, 1958.

Redding was director of publicity for the Democratic National Committee. He recounts the events preceding and following the 1948 election. Index.

1250 Ross, Irwin. *The Loneliest Campaign: The Truman Victory of 1948*. New York: New American Library, 1968.

Ross finds that Truman had essentially the same basis of support as did Roosevelt. Notes, index.

1251 Shogan, Robert. "1948 Election." *American Heritage* 19 (1968): 22–31.

Shogan examines Truman's campaign strategy, which emphasized labor and farm support. Truman traveled 31,600 miles by train to make 356 formal speeches and 300 extemporaneous talks.

1252 Silber, Irwin. *Songs Americans Voted By: With the Words and Music that Won and Lost Elections and Influenced the Democratic Process*. Harrisburg, PA: Stackpole, 1971.

Campaign songs were diminishing (because of radio) by the end of World War II; consequently, there were few songs identified with the campaign of 1948. "I'm Just Wild About Harry" appeared with updated lyrics, and "Date in '48" was written for a confident Dewey. Wallace had the most original works as Pete Seeger and Woody Guthrie each prepared songs. See pages 281–86. Bibliography, indexes.

1253 Sitkoff, Harvard. "Harry Truman and the Election of 1948: The Coming of Age of Civil Rights in American Politics." *Journal of Southern History* 37 (1971): 597–616.

Civil rights became part of the political agenda in 1948. If Truman was a reluctant champion, he nevertheless aided in the education of Americans about "the righteousness of the crusade for equality." Notes.

1254 Stacy, Bill W. "The Campaign Speaking of Harry S. Truman in the 1948 Presidential Election." Ph.D. dissertation, Southern Illinois University, 1968.

Truman's campaign succeeded because of his personality and his appeal to the common man. He focused on domestic issues, particularly consumer-related issues. DAI 29:2826-A.

1255 Wallace, Harold. "The Campaign of 1948." Ph.D. dissertation, Indiana University, 1970.

Wallace looks at the Republican and Democratic national conventions and the nomination process. He also analyzes the two parties' campaigns. DAI 31:3487-A.

1256 Wallace, Lew. "The Truman-Dewey Upset." *American History Illustrated* 11 (1976): 20–30.

Truman's election upset of Thomas Dewey in the 1948 presidential election is recounted.

Alben Barkley

See Chapter 3, *Alben W. Barkley*, for more data.

1257 Claussen, E. Neal. "Alben Barkley's Rhetorical Victory in 1948." *Southern Speech Communications Journal* 45 (1979): 79–92.

Claussen reviews the political episodes and rhetorical milieu which led to the nomination of Senator Barkley for the vice-presidency at the 1948 Democratic National Convention.

1258 Mofield, William R. "The Speaking Role of Alben Barkley in the Campaign of 1948." Ph.D. dissertation, Southern Illinois University, 1964.

Barkley was the keynote speaker for the 1948 Democratic National Convention and gained the vice-presidential nomination. He waged an active campaign, speaking in thirty states and giving up to fifteen talks daily. DAI 25:5447.

1259 Wallace, Lew. "Alben Barkley and the Democratic Convention in 1948." *Filson Club Historical Quarterly* 55 (1981): 231–52.

This narrative reviews the events at the 1948 Democratic convention, while touching rather briefly on Barkley's nomination as vice-president. Notes.

Douglas MacArthur

1260 Mattern, Carolyn J. "The Man on the Dark Horse: The Presidential Campaign for General Douglas MacArthur, 1944 and 1948." Ph.D. dissertation, University of Wisconsin, Madison, 1976.

At two crucial times during this century (the Bonus March and the Korean War) Americans suspected that General MacArthur harbored political ambitions. DAI 37:3856-A.

1261 Schonberger, Howard B. "The General and the Presidency: Douglas MacArthur and the Election of 1948." *Wisconsin Magazine of History* 57 (1974): 201–19.

MacArthur wanted the 1948 Republican presidential nomination; however, his defeat in the Wisconsin primary doomed his hopes. Notes.

Dixiecrats

See Chapter 3, *Strom Thurmond*, for more data.

1262 Ader, Emile B. "Why the Dixiecrats Failed." *Journal of Politics* 15 (1953): 356–69.

The Dixiecrat strategy failed because it could not control the "solid South's" 127 electoral votes necessary to block the election of Truman or Dewey, and throw the presidential selection into the House of Representatives. Notes.

1263 Ashley, Frank W. "Selected Southern Liberal Editors and the States' Rights Movement of 1948." Ph.D. dissertation, University of South Carolina, 1959.

This study is concerned with the impact of Jonathan Daniels of the Raleigh *News and Observer*, North Carolina; Virginius Dabney of the *Richmond Times-Dispatch*, Virginia; and Ralph McGill of the *Atlanta Constitution*, Georgia, upon the fortunes of the 1948 States' Rights Movement. DAI 20:2243.

1264 Chesteen, Richard D. " 'Mississippi Is Gone Home': A Study of the 1948 Mississippi States' Rights Bolt." *Journal of Mississippi History* 32 (1970): 43–59.

Mississippi Democrats left the national convention in July 1948 over the civil rights issue and created the Jeffersonian States' Rights party. Notes.

1265 Garson, Robert A. "The Alienation of the South: A Crisis for Harry S. Truman and the Democratic Party, 1945–1948." *Missouri Historical Review* 64 (1970): 448–71.

Truman's Fair Deal which emphasized housing, federal aid to education, Social Security, minimum wages, and other similar objectives upset the Southerners. But Truman's appointment of a civil rights committee and publication of its report, "To Secure These Rights," convinced the South that Truman's renomination would be a rejection of the South's traditional role in the party. Notes.

1266 Grant, Philip A., Jr. "The 1948 Presidential Election in Virginia: Augury of the Trend Toward Republicanism." *Presidential Studies Quarterly* 8 (1978): 319–28.

As the civil rights issue split Democrats, Dewey threatened to carry the state. Thus Truman's unimpressive victory is seen as a precursor to future Republican presidential wins. Tables, notes.

1267 McLaurin, Ann Mathison. "The Role of the Dixiecrats in the 1948 Election." Ph.D. dissertation, University of Oklahoma, 1972.

Truman's civil rights proposals caused Southern Democrats to break with the party and form the Dixiecrats in 1948. DAI 33:681-A.

1268 Ness, Gary C. "The States' Rights Democratic Movement of 1948." Ph.D. dissertation, Duke University, 1972.

The States' Rights Democratic Movement, through both shrewdness and guile, nearly achieved their most publicized political goal of depriving Truman of the election in 1948. DAI 33:5100-A.

Progressives

See Chapter 3, *Henry A. Wallace,* for more data.

1269 Lader, Lawrence. "The Wallace Campaign of 1948." *American Heritage* 28 (1976): 42–51.

This assessment focuses on the reasons for Wallace's failure to mobilize support for his presidential bid. Illustrations.

1270 MacDougall, Curtis D. *Gideon's Army*. 3 vols. New York: Marzani & Munsell, 1965.

MacDougall examines the issues prompting the development of a third party (volume 1), the decisions and organization of the Progressive party (volume 2), and the 1948 campaign and vote (volume 3). Index.

1271 Peterson, Frank R. "Protest Songs for Peace and Freedom: People's Songs and the 1948 Progressives." *Rocky Mountain Social Science Journal* 9 (1972): 1–10.

Henry Wallace became the hero of the songs because of his attack on Truman's foreign policy. The song topics, authors, and lyrics are discussed, as well as some analysis of the election results. Notes.

1272 Schmidt, Karl M. *Henry A. Wallace: Quixotic Crusade 1948*. Syracuse, NY: Syracuse University Press, 1960.

Schmidt examines the background, the leaders, the organization, the campaign, and finally the disintegration of Wallace's Progressive party. Notes, bibliography, index.

1273 Wise, James W. *Meet Henry Wallace*. New York: Boni & Gaer, 1948.

Wise likens Wallace to Roosevelt in this campaign biography of Wallace and the Wallace program. Illustrations.

1274 Yarnell, Allen. "The Democratic Party's Response to the Progressive Party in 1948." *Research Studies* 39 (1971): 20–33.

The Progressive party's policy stand actually aided Truman for it allowed the president to take a hard line on communism and attack Republican party dealings. Notes.

1275 Yarnell, Allen. *Democrats and Progressives: The 1948 Presidential Election as a Test of Postwar Liberalism.* Berkeley: University of California Press, 1974.

The Progressives made it easier for the Truman forces to take tough stands on foreign policy issues, thus aiding the Democrats in their 1948 election. Notes, bibliography, index.

1276 Yarnell, Allen. "Liberals in Action: The ADA, Henry Wallace, and the 1948 Election." *Research Studies* 40 (1972): 260–73.

The Americans for Democratic Action engaged in red-baiting tactics to discredit Henry A. Wallace and the Progressive party in order to secure for themselves leadership of the American liberal community. Notes.

Election of 1952

1277 Biles, Roger. "Jacob J. Arvey, Kingmaker: The Nomination of Adlai E. Stevenson in 1952." *Chicago History* 8 (1979): 130–43.

This essay briefly traces Arvey's political career from 1932 and focuses on his successful efforts to obtain the Democratic presidential nomination for Illinois Governor Adlai Stevenson.

1278 Bone, Hugh A., ed. "The 1952 Elections in the Eleven Western States." *Western Political Quarterly* 6 (1953): 93–138.

The impact of the election at congressional and state levels is reviewed.

1279 Epstein, Joseph. "Adlai Stevenson in Retrospect." *Commentary* 46 (1968): 71–83.

Stevenson gained a reputation for indecision during the nominating process. His other characteristics were humility, urbanity, and decency.

1280 Fried, Richard M. "Fighting Words Never Delivered: Proposed Draft of Senator Kefauver's Acceptance Speech." *Tennessee Historical Quarterly* 29 (1970): 176–83.

Estes Kefauver sought the Democratic nomination in 1952. Richard Borwick prepared an acceptance speech, a draft of which was circulated among campaign lieutenants. A draft is reproduced here. Notes.

1281 Johnson, Walter. *How We Drafted Adlai Stevenson.* New York: Knopf, 1955.

This is a personal account by an influential member of the "Draft Stevenson Committee," an informal citizens' group which played some role in the Democratic party's selection of Stevenson as its nominee in 1952. Index.

1282 Merrill, Irving R. "Campaign Expenditures and Their Control: A Study of Expenditures for Television Time in the 1952 Federal Election." Ph.D. dissertation, University of Illinois, 1954.

Section 315 of the Federal Communications Act as Amended, which becomes operative for political broadcasts in only those cases where the legally qualified candidates appear in person on their own behalf, is investigated. DAI 15:115.

1283 Parmet, Herbert S. *Eisenhower and the American Crusades.* New York: Macmillan, 1972.

The first part of the book discusses the motivation behind Eisenhower's decision to run for president. Illustrations, notes, bibliography, index.

1284 Ryan, Halford R. "A Rhetorical Analysis of General Eisenhower's Public Speaking from 1945–1951." Ph.D. dissertation, University of Illinois, Urbana-Champaign, 1972.

During this period Eisenhower delivered 169 speeches on the general theme of peace. He apparently wished to assure his audiences that he would be a competent and trustworthy president. DAI 33:5871-A.

1285 Sievers, Rodney M. "Adlai E. Stevenson: An Intellectual Portrait." Ph.D. dissertation, University of Virginia, 1971.

Adlai Stevenson (1900–1965) was a thoughtful observer of the American political system, international relations, and the historical process itself. While he worked to organize support for the United Nations in 1945–46 and always defended it, he also became a cold warrior. DAI 32:4541.

1286 Stevenson, Adlai E. *Major Campaign Speeches, 1952.* New York: Random House, 1953.

Some fifty of Stevenson's speeches (out of more than 250) are reprinted here.

Public Opinion and the Media

See also Chapter 2, *Truman and the Media.*

1287 Chester, Edward W. *Radio, Television and American Politics.* New York: Sheed & Ward, 1969.

The role of the media in presidential elections as well as the use of the media by candidates, government agencies, and public figures are examined. Bibliography, index.

1288 Epstein, Laurily. "Components of Presidential Voting in Selected American Cities, 1872–1968." Ph.D. dissertation, Washington University, 1974.

This study examines participation and partisanship in presidential voting in twenty-two American cities from 1872 to 1968. DAI 36:509-A.

1289 Fenton, John M. *In Your Opinion . . . The Managing Editor of the Gallup Poll Looks at Polls, Politics and the People from 1945–1965*. Boston: Little, Brown, 1960.

Truman's popularity, his handling of the issues, as well as popular opinion on such subjects as hemlines are analyzed.

1290 Gallup, George H. *The Gallup Poll: Public Opinion, 1935–1971*. 3 vols. New York: Random House, 1972.

The results of public polls dealing with domestic and foreign issues are listed. Volume 1 covers 1935 to 1948, while Volume 2 covers 1949 to 1958.

1291 McIntyre, Jerilyn S. "The Hutchins Commission's Search for a Moral Framework." *Journalism History* 6 (1979): 54–57, 63.

The Hutchins Commission on Freedom of the Press (1944–46) criticized the performance of the American press and debated whether the press should be self or government regulated.

1292 Mueller, John E. "Presidential Popularity From Truman to Johnson." *American Political Science Review* 64 (1970): 18–34.

Presidential popularity generally declined some 5 percent per year. Major international events usually raise popularity as the public "rallies 'round the flag." The Korean War, however, cost Truman some eighteen points. Economic slumps hurt, but economic booms do not affect popularity. Tables, notes.

1293 Mullaly, Donald P. "Broadcasting and Social Change." *Quarterly Journal of Speech* 56 (1970): 40–44.

Mullaly finds that the fairness doctrine has allowed more varied views to be expressed on radio and television from 1929 to 1970.

1294 Rogers, Lindsay. *The Pollsters: Public Opinion, Politics and Democratic Leadership*. New York: Knopf, 1949.

Truman's 1948 election shocked pollsters who had predicted an overwhelming Dewey win. Rogers looks at the pollsters' methods and the nature of public opinion. Notes, index.

1295 Roper, Elmo. *You and Your Leaders: Their Actions and Your Reactions, 1936–1956*. New York: Morrow, 1957.

This collection of Roper polls focuses upon how Americans responded to the actions of such men as Thomas E. Dewey, Harry S. Truman, Douglas MacArthur, George C. Marshall, Adlai E. Stevenson, and Dwight D. Eisenhower. Polls and graphs, index.

1296 Rosenfield, L. W. "A Case Study in Speech Criticism: The Nixon-Truman Analog." *Speech Monographs* 35 (1968): 435–50.

This study involves a critical comparison of Richard Nixon's "Checkers" speech (12 September 1952) and Harry Truman's "Harry Dexter White" speech (16 November 1953). Both speeches are seen as mass media apologies, and both appeared to vindicate their authors. Notes.

1297 Sigelman, Lee. "Presidential Popularity and Presidential Elections." *Public Opinion Quarterly* 43 (1979): 532–34.

This article reviews presidential popularity in seven elections, 1940–76, by employing the Gallup Poll.

1298 Smith, Tom W. "America's Most Important Problem: A Trend Analysis, 1946–1976." *Public Opinion Quarterly* 44 (1980): 164–80.

Both long-term and short-term changes in public concern are charted. The problem profiles of major sociodemographic groups are analyzed and changes in the problem concerns of these groups are also followed across time.

COLUMNISTS, PUBLISHERS, AND REPORTERS

1299 Abell, Tyler, ed. *The Drew Pearson Diaries, 1949–1959*. New York: Holt, Rinehart and Winston, 1974.

The first 240 pages cover the Truman years from 1949 to 1952. Pearson was a persistent critic of Truman whom he considered inadequate for the job of president.

1300 Alsop, Joseph, and Alsop, Stewart. *The Reporter's Trade*. New York: Reynal, 1958.

Admittedly politically conservative reporters, the Alsops relate their opinions on Truman and the issues of the Truman administration. Index.

1301 Baillie, Hugh. *High Tension: The Recollections of Hugh Baillie*. New York: Harper, 1959.

Baillie, a reporter for the United Press for forty years, was a leading proponent of worldwide freedom of news disseminating. He covered many of the leading foreign events during the Truman era. Photographs, index.

1302 Becker, Stephen. *Marshall Field III: A Biography.* New York: Simon & Schuster, 1964.

As publisher of the *Chicago Daily Sun*, Field was critical of Truman's foreign policies and had little confidence in Truman's ability to carry through the New Deal. Nonetheless, he endorsed Truman's reelection in 1948. Notes, photographs, index.

1303 Frey, Richard C., Jr. "John T. Flynn and the United States in Crisis, 1928–1950." Ph.D. dissertation, University of Oregon, 1969.

Flynn was a journalist, economist, and radio commentator who became disillusioned with the New Deal. He became active in noninterventionist organizations. DAI 31:1188-A.

1304 Krock, Arthur. *Memoirs: Sixty Years on the Firing Line.* New York: Funk & Wagnalls, 1968.

Chapter 12 deals with domestic and foreign issues confronted by the Truman administration. Krock reprints, as an appendix, the Clark M. Clifford Report of September 1946, which many critics see as setting a hawkish tone for the containment policy. Appendix, index.

1305 McWilliams, Carey. *The Education of Carey McWilliams.* New York: Simon & Schuster, 1978.

McWilliams was editor of *The Nation* during the turbulent years of the Cold War and McCarthyism. Topics such as the Hollywood Ten, the Wallace movement, the cultural Cold War, and McCarthyism are discussed. Notes, bibliography, index.

1306 Pilat, Oliver. *Drew Pearson: An Unauthorized Biography.* New York: Harper's Magazine Press, 1973.

Drew Pearson was one of the most influential and prolific journalists, writing eight syndicated columns a week in addition to articles, books, and a newsletter. Chapters 11 to 13 discuss his activities during the Truman era. Illustrations, index.

1307 Steel, Ronald. *Walter Lippmann and the American Century.* Boston: Little, Brown, 1980.

Never a Truman admirer, Lippmann became so disgruntled that he blamed Truman's reelection for everything that went wrong after—McCarthyism, the rearmament of Germany, and the Korean War. See Chapters 33 to 36.

1308 Strout, Richard L. *TRB: Views and Perspectives on the Presidency.* New York: Macmillan, 1979.

Strout began writing the TRB column in *The New Republic* in 1943. In this volume are reprints of this column with his views on the presidency from Roosevelt through Carter. Index.

1309 Sulzberger, Cyrus L. *A Long Row of Candles: Memoirs and Diaries, 1934–1954.* New York: Macmillan, 1969.

Most of these memos, letters, and diary entries by a renowned reporter relate to foreign affairs; they cover the Truman years (Chapters 16–18). Index.

1310 Swanberg, W. A. *Luce and His Empire.* New York: Scribner's, 1972.

Chapters 20 to 25 deal with Luce's political ambitions and points of view (strident anticommunism). This account presents some insight into the editorial policies of *Time* and *Life* during the Truman years. Illustrations, index.

1311 Trohan, Walter. *Political Animals: Memoirs of a Sentimental Cynic.* Garden City, NY: Doubleday, 1975.

Trohan wrote critically of the Truman administration, yet liked the president as an individual. Pages 203 to 263 are devoted to his views of Truman and the 1948 election.

1312 Williams, Herbert L. "Truman and the Press (April 12, 1945–January 20, 1953)." Ph.D. dissertation, University of Missouri, 1954.

This dissertation studies the nature of the relations of President Harry S. Truman with the press. It includes an analysis of these relations in the light of Truman's utterances regarding the press.

Internal Security and Civil Liberties

See also *Civil Rights*, for issues related to civil liberties.

1313 Crandell, William F. "A Party Divided Against Itself: Anticommunism and the Transformation of the Republican Right, 1945–1956." Ph.D. dissertation, Ohio State University, 1983.

After Dewey's defeat in 1948, the only issue which could unite the GOP was the "softness" of the Democratic administration toward communism. While this charge was perceived in 1950 and 1952 as increasing GOP votes, it was Eisenhower—not McCarthyism—that united the party and drew new voters. DAI 44:1179-A.

1314 Cushman, Robert E. *Civil Liberties in the United States: A Guide to Current Problems and*

Experience. Ithaca, NY: Cornell University Press, 1956.

This volume seeks: (1) to indicate the status of each civil liberty case in 1945; (2) to summarize the principal subsequent developments; and (3) to indicate in each case the current or unsolved problems. Bibliographies, table of cases, index.

1315 Longaker, Richard P. *The Presidency and Individual Liberties*. Ithaca, NY: Cornell University Press, 1961.

The presidency was forced into the field of civil and political rights by the Cold War. Longaker finds the president in a crucial role in protecting or ignoring individual liberties. Notes, index.

1316 O'Neill, William L. *A Better World: The Great Schism: Stalinism and the American Intellectuals*. New York: Simon & Schuster, 1982.

This book is "about the struggle among non-Communist leftists and liberals over American relations with the Soviet Union from 1939 through the 1950s." There are brief discussions of most of the episodes of the post-World War II "Red Scare." Notes, index.

1317 Roche, John P. *The Quest for the Dream: The Development of Civil Rights and Human Relations in Modern America*. New York: Macmillan, 1963.

Roche disagrees that McCarthyism symbolized a new low in a progressive decline of American liberty. Looking at the past five decades, he finds that civil liberties have grown markedly. Notes, index.

1318 Westin, Alan F., and Hayden, Trudy. "Presidents and Civil Liberties from FDR to Ford: A Rating by 64 Experts." *Civil Liberties Review* 3 (1976): 9–35.

The experts offer their opinions of the impact that various presidents, including Truman, have had on civil liberties.

INTERNAL SECURITY

See also Chapter 3, for Senators *William E. Jenner, Joseph R. McCarthy*, and others involved in the second Red Scare; and Chapter 5, *Education and the Cold War*.

1319 Bailey, Percival R. "The Case of the National Lawyers Guild, 1939–1958." In Athan Theoharis, ed. *Beyond the Hiss Case: The FBI, Congress and the Cold War*. Philadelphia: Temple University Press, 1982, pp. 129–75.

This essay focuses upon the FBI's efforts, especially during the Truman era, to brand the Guild a subversive organization. Notes.

1320 Bailey, Percival R. "Progressive Lawyers: A History of the National Lawyers Guild, 1936–1958." Ph.D. dissertation, State University of New Jersey, New Brunswick, 1979.

Most of the lawyers representing radicals during the 1947–57 Red Scare were members of the National Lawyers Guild, as were several strategists of Henry Wallace's 1948 Progressive presidential campaign. In 1949 the NLG charged the FBI with political surveillance, wiretapping, and other illegal activities. DAI 40:416-A.

1321 Barth, Alan. *Government by Investigation*. New York: Viking, 1955.

This volume seeks to put congressional investigating powers in historical perspective. It also criticizes the House Un-American Activities Committee for its "legislative" trials during the Truman years. Notes, index.

1322 Barth, Alan. *The Loyalty of Free Men*. New York: Viking, 1951.

At the time of the Red Scare, Barth argued that "tolerance of diversity is imperative, because without it life would lose its savor." Also, he examines the role of the congressional investigating committee, the FBI, and the U.S. Communist party. Index.

1323 Belfrage, Cedric. *The American Inquisition, 1945–1960*. Indianapolis: Bobbs-Merrill, 1973.

Belfrage characterizes this period as an attempt to brainwash Americans. This volume chronicles this era from the victims' viewpoint. Index.

1324 Biddle, Francis. *The Fear of Freedom*. Garden City, NY: Doubleday, 1952.

Former U.S. Attorney General Biddle (1941–45) discusses "the contemporary obsession of anxiety and fear in the United States" as well as its historical background. He is especially critical of the impact of the 1945–51 Red Scare on federal institutions. Notes.

1325 Blanchard, Margaret A. "Americans First, Newspapermen Second? The Conflict Between Patriotism and Freedom of the Press during the Cold War, 1946–1952." Ph.D. dissertation, University of North Carolina, Chapel Hill, 1981.

The press joined the national euphoria of triumph at the conclusion of the war and fell prey to the fear of communism characterizing the Cold War years. DAI 42:5218.

1326 Brown, Ralph S., Jr. *Loyalty and Security: Employment Tests in the United States*. New Haven: Yale University Press, 1958.

This detailed study has much on events of 1945 to 1953. Of particular importance is the author's examination of the impact of government loyalty tests on employment of individuals in federal offices. Footnotes, appendixes, notes.

1327 Burnham, James. *The Web of Subversion.* New York: John Day, 1954.

This is a contemporary account which seeks to justify the search for subversive agents among American government officials, teachers, ministers, and other important elites.

1328 Caute, David. *The Great Fear: The Anti-Communist Purge Under Truman and Eisenhower.* New York: Simon & Schuster, 1978.

Sections dealing with anti-Communist purges include congressional investigations, the purge of the civil service, the Communist party, unions, education, and show business. Appendixes, notes, bibliography, index. Sidney Hook takes issue with most of Caute's assumptions and contentions. See *Encounter* (Great Britain) 52 (1979): 56–64.

1329 Chase, Harold W. "Controlling Subversive Activities: An Analysis of the Efforts of the National Government to Control Indigenous Communists, 1933–1952." Ph.D. dissertation, Princeton University, 1954.

Most of the controls were aimed at preventing a revolution that never could have taken place; yet much was ignored which could have safeguarded the nation from possible sabotage and espionage. Also these controls abridged important civil liberties. DAI 14:1785.

1330 Clark, Wayne A. "An Analysis of the Relationship Between Anti-Communism and Segregationist Thought in the Deep South, 1948–1964." Ph.D. dissertation, University of North Carolina, Chapel Hill, 1976.

Beginning with the 1948 States' Rights party, the white elite systematically opposed communism and civil rights. DAI 37:5297-A.

1331 Crosby, Donald F. "The Politics of Religion: American Catholics and the Anti-Communist Impulse." In R. Griffith and A. Theoharis, eds. *The Specter: Original Essays on the Cold War and the Origins of McCarthyism.* New York: New Viewpoints, 1974, pp. 18–39.

Crosby's evidence suggests that "Catholic spokesmen, both conservative and liberal, played an important role in injecting the Communist issue into American politics." Notes.

1332 DeToledano, Ralph. *The Greatest Plot in History.* New York: Duell, Sloan, & Pearce, 1963.

This account purports to trace Soviet agents' efforts to obtain nuclear secrets. Although it begins before and continues beyond the Truman years, this volume does summarize the charges of nuclear espionage made during 1945 to 1953. Index.

1333 Diamond, Sigmund. "On the Road to Camelot." *Labor History* 21 (1980): 279–90.

Reprinted here are the 1 March 1947 questions of Congressman John F. Kennedy to (among others) Robert Buse, president of the United Automobile Workers of America, Local 248. Diamond suggests that Kennedy tried to link the 1945–47 Allis-Chalmers strike in Wisconsin to the Communist party. Notes.

1334 Gates, John. *The Story of an American Communist.* New York: Nelson, 1958.

Gates joined the U.S. Communist party at the age of seventeen and stayed until he was forty-four, when he left the party in 1958. This is an account of the growth of the party and its subsequent decline—from the point of view of the former editor-in-chief of the *Daily Worker.* Index.

1335 Harper, Alan D. *The Politics of Loyalty: The White House and the Communist Issue, 1946–1952.* Westport, CT: Greenwood, 1969.

Truman was caught in the dilemma of balancing the essential claims of liberty with the legitimate requirements of security. Notes, bibliography, appendixes, index.

1336 Irons, Peter H. "American Business and the Origins of McCarthyism: The Cold War Crusade of the United States Chamber of Commerce." In R. Griffith and A. Theoharis, eds. *The Specter: Original Essays on the Cold War and the Origins of McCarthyism.* New York: New Viewpoints, 1974, pp. 72–88.

Irons sees McCarthyism as an outgrowth of the business community's hostility, not only to Soviet foreign policy, but to domestic labor unions and the social programs of the New Deal. Notes.

1337 Johnsen, Julia E., ed. *Should the Communist Party Be Outlawed?* New York: Wilson, 1949.

Presented here is a wide range of contemporary views on the issue, followed by an extensive bibliography.

1338 Latham, Earl. *The Communist Controversy in Washington: From the New Deal to McCarthy.* Cambridge: Harvard University Press, 1966.

The author concludes that evidence seems to indicate that there was a Communist "problem" in government in the 1940s, but that the evidence does not warrant the conclusion that these functionaries had any substantial influence. Appendix, footnotes, index.

1339 Lens, Sidney. *The Futile Crusade: Anti-Communism as American Credo.* Chicago: Quadrangle, 1964.

Chapters 2 and 3 seek to explain the Red Scare in the context of the development of the Cold War.

Subsequent chapters also contain material on this issue during the Truman years but are arranged topically. Notes, index.

1340 Markowitz, Norman. "A View from the Left: From the Popular Front to Cold War Liberalism." In R. Griffith and A. Theoharis, eds. *The Specter: Original Essays on the Cold War and the Origins of McCarthyism*. New York: New Viewpoints, 1974, pp. 90–114.

Anti-Communist liberals who usually opposed McCarthyite methods frequently "acted in ways that compromised the defense of traditional civil liberties." Notes.

1341 Marlowe, Lon D., III. "The Roots of McCarthyism: The House of Representatives and Internal Security Legislation, 1945–1950." Ph.D. dissertation, University of Georgia, 1981.

This study tests two theories on the origins of McCarthyism: that McCarthyism is a product of partisan conflicts and that McCarthyites held strong isolationist views. Looking at the Seventy-ninth through Eighty-first Congresses' votes on anti-Communist measures, Marlowe finds a correlation between isolationism and McCarthyism. DAI 42:2263-A.

1342 McWilliams, Carey. *Witch Hunt: The Revival of Heresy*. Boston: Little, Brown, 1950.

This is a highly critical account of the agents of the Red Scare and their tactics during the late 1940s. Index.

1343 Nagy, Alex. "Federal Censorship of Communist Political Propaganda and the First Amendment, 1941–1961." Ph.D. dissertation, University of Wisconsin, 1973.

U.S. government efforts to suppress Communist political propaganda from abroad are reviewed. The policies of the Truman years are summarized. DAI 35:490-A.

1344 O'Reilly, Kenneth. "Liberal Values, the Cold War, and American Intellectuals: The Trauma of the Alger Hiss Case, 1950–1978." In Athan Theoharis, ed. *Beyond the Hiss Case: The FBI, Congress and the Cold War*. Philadelphia: Temple University Press, 1982, pp. 309–40.

Using the Hiss case as "a litmus test" of Cold War liberals' views of the frequent conflict between civil liberties and anticommunism, O'Reilly finds that "with few exceptions, anti-Communist liberals have failed to reassess their earlier role in legitimating the indiscriminate anti-radicalism. . . ." Notes.

1345 Pomerantz, Charlotte, ed. *A Quarter-Century of Un-Americana*. New York: Marzani & Munsell, 1963.

This collection of quotes and cartoons provides a critical view of the Red Scare years.

1346 Spector, Bert A. " 'Wasn't that a Time?' Pete Seeger and the Anti-Communist Crusade, 1940–1968." Ph.D. dissertation, University of Missouri, Columbia, 1977.

Seeger, folksinger and political activist, was a frequent target of the anti-Communist crusade. During the postwar years, the anti-Communist consensus managed to isolate Seeger. DAI 42:4122-A.

1347 Theoharis, Athan. "Attorney General Tom Clark, Internal Security, and the Truman Administration." *New University Thought* 6 (1968): 16–22.

Clark's views of radicalism and dissent are criticized, and his impact on internal security issues is examined. Notes.

1348 Theoharis, Athan, ed. *Beyond the Hiss Case: The FBI, Congress and the Cold War*. Philadelphia: Temple University Press, 1982.

The essays in this volume seek to examine the FBI's, Congress's, HUAC's, and conservative reporters' abuse of power. Specific essays are cited under appropriate topics. Notes, index.

1349 Theoharis, Athan G. "McCarthyism: A Broader Perspective." *Maryland History* 12 (1981): 1–7.

Scholars are urged to avoid the simplistic labeling that is prevalent among students of the Cold War. This historiographic survey argues that recently declassified documents point to McCarthyism rooted in institutions of the executive branch. Notes.

1350 Theoharis, Athan. "The Rhetoric of Politics: Foreign Policy, Internal Security, and Domestic Politics in the Truman Era, 1945–1950." In Barton J. Bernstein, ed. *Politics and Policies of the Truman Administration*. Chicago: Quadrangle, 1970, pp. 196–268.

Theoharis argues that the administration failed to define the limits of American power (and thereby public expectations) or the specific nature of the Communist threat. Notes.

1351 Theoharis, Athan. *Seeds of Repression: Harry S. Truman and the Origins of McCarthyism*. Chicago: Quadrangle, 1971.

Theoharis argues that, as regards Cold War politics, McCarthy and the Truman administration "differ not so much over ends as over means and emphasis." Where the senator emphasized internal subversion, the administration focused on external affairs. Bibliography, index.

1352 Theoharis, Athan, and Griffith, Robert, eds. *The Specter: Original Essays on the Cold War and the Origins of McCarthyism*. New York: New Viewpoints, 1974.

The editors suggest that McCarthy may have been the least important aspect of "McCarthyism."

"He was the product of America's Cold War politics, not its progenitor; and his success can be fully appreciated only by reference to the issues he symbolized." Notes, index.

1353 Weyl, Nathaniel. *The Battle Against Disloyalty*. New York: Crowell, 1951.

This contemporary account supports the search for Communists in the federal government. While the early chapters go back to the American Revolution to find disloyalty, Chapters 14 to 20 deal with the Truman years. Notes, index.

Truman's Loyalty Program
1354 Bontecou, Eleanor. *The Federal Loyalty-Security Program*. Ithaca, NY: Cornell University Press, 1953.

An attorney, Bontecou was particularly well prepared to deal with the technical legal issues involved in the postwar loyalty-security program which began with Truman's Loyalty Order of 1947. Appendix, notes, index.

1355 Clubb, O. Edmund. *The Witness and I*. New York: Columbia University Press, 1974.

Clubb was one of the Foreign Service diplomats in China who came under investigation. This account is of his own personal experience. Bibliography, index.

1356 Gelhorn, Walter. *Security, Loyalty and Science*. Ithaca, NY: Cornell University Press, 1950.

An early attempt to delineate the issues, this account has value today as a contemporary view of the loyalty question. Notes, index.

1357 Shattuck, Henry L. "The Loyalty Review Board of the U.S. Civil Service Commission, 1947–1953." *Massachusetts Historical Society Proceedings* 78 (1966): 63–80.

The author's service on the board, established by Truman, is described. Although the board dealt with several controversial cases, the board did forestall the clamor for wholesale purges and more drastic action by Congress. Notes.

1358 Theoharis, Athan. "The Escalation of the Loyalty Program." In Barton J. Bernstein, ed. *Politics and Policies of the Truman Administration*. Chicago: Quadrangle, 1970, pp. 242–68.

This is a useful summary arguing that initially Truman sought to balance the requirements of the program with safeguards on individual liberties. In the end he failed, and liberties were sacrificed to "national security." Notes.

1359 Thompson, Francis H. *The Frustration of Politics: Truman, Congress, and the Loyalty Issue,*

1945–1953. Rutherford, NJ: Fairleigh Dickinson University Press, 1979.

Truman's March 1947 executive order calling for a far-reaching loyalty probe of all government officials drew criticism from all political groups. This account reexamines the revisionist critique of Truman's action. Appendixes, bibliography, notes, index.

Internal Security Act (1950)
1360 Allen, Charles R., Jr. *Concentration Camps U.S.A.* Philadelphia: Robin's Distributing Co., 1969.

This pamphlet investigates the existence of installations established under terms of the 1950 McCarran Act to serve as so-called detention camps if an "internal security emergency" were declared.

1361 "Campaign to Repeal the Emergency Detention Act." *Amerasia Journal* 2 (1974): 71–111.

The Internal Security Act (1950) allowed the attorney general to place persons in detention camps, six of which were established during 1952 to 1957. In 1971, following rumors that black Americans were to be detained in the camps, a campaign was begun to have the act repealed. The detention section was repealed in 1971.

1362 Cotter, Cornelius P., and Smith, Malcolm. "An American Paradox: The Emergency Detention Act of 1950." *Journal of Politics* 19 (1957): 20–33.

The provisions, legal questions, and political aspects of the Internal Security Bill of 1950 are examined, with special emphasis on the establishment of detention centers.

1363 Lee, R. Alton. " 'New Dealers, Fair Dealers, Misdealers, and Hiss Dealers': Karl Mundt and the Internal Security Act of 1950." *South Dakota History* 10 (1980): 277–90.

Senator Karl Mundt (1900–1974) of South Dakota contributed more to the enactment of the Internal Security Act (1950), popularly called the McCarran Act, than has been credited to him. Mundt called for the registration of Communists in 1947, and suggested a Subversive Activities Control Board in 1949. Illustrations, notes.

1364 Longaker, Richard. "Emergency Detention: The Generation Gap, 1950–1971." *Western Political Quarterly* 27 (1974): 395–408.

Title II, The Emergency Detention Act, of the McCarran Internal Security Act (1950), permitted the incarceration of Communist and political saboteurs in detention camps.

1365 Tanner, William R., and Griffith, Robert. "Legislative Politics and 'McCarthyism': The Internal Security Act of 1950." In R. Griffith and A. Theoharis, eds. *The Specter: Original Essays on the*

Cold War and the Origins of McCarthyism. New York: New Viewpoint, 1974, pp. 174–88.

The Internal Security Act of 1950 tightened existing espionage and sabotage laws. Moreover, the act's two most controversial sections required all Communist organizations and individual members of "communist action" organizations to register with the attorney general, and authorized—in time of national emergency—the preventive detention of suspected subversives. Notes.

1366 Tanner, William R. "The Passage of the Internal Security Act of 1950." Ph.D. dissertation, University of Kansas, 1971.

The Internal Security Act was a lengthy and complex legislative effort passed over Truman's veto on 23 September 1950. The act purported to control domestic Communist activity. DAI 32:5723–A.

American Civil Liberties Union

1367 Lamson, Peggy. *Roger Baldwin: Founder of the American Civil Liberties Union.* Boston: Houghton Mifflin, 1976.

Baldwin was director of the American Civil Liberties Union (1920–50). During the Truman era, the ACLU opposed loyalty oaths for government employees, objected to Communists being refused entry into the United States, and criticized the McCarran Act. Illustrations, index.

1368 McAuliffe, Mary S. "The Politics of Civil Liberties: The American Civil Liberties Union During the McCarthy Years." In R. Griffith and A. Theoharis, eds. *The Specter: Original Essays on the Cold War and the Origins of McCarthyism.* New York: New Viewpoints, 1974, pp. 152–70.

This essay illustrates the kinds of compromises liberals felt they were compelled to make and finds that the ACLU wavered in its defense of freedom and contributed to the mounting national hysteria. Notes.

HOUSE UN-AMERICAN ACTIVITIES COMMITTEE

1369 Andrews, Bert. *Washington Witch Hunt.* New York: Random House, 1948.

This critical account by a prominent journalist raises questions about the contemporary activities of the FBI and the Un-American Activities Committee.

1370 Beck, Carl. *Contempt of Congress: A Study of the Prosecutions Initiated by the Committee on Un-American Activities, 1945–1957.* New Orleans: Hauser, 1959.

This is an analysis of the legal dimension of the Congress's contempt citations. It deals with the

cases topically: freedom of speech, Fifth Amendment, etc. Appendixes, table of cases, notes, bibliography, index.

1371 Buckley, William F., Jr., ed. *The Committee and Its Critics: A Calm Review of the House Committee on Un-American Activities.* New York: Putnam's, 1962.

The contributors were, for the most part, editors of, or contributors to, the *National Review* and constitute a rather strident defense of the committee. Chapter 10 provides a valuable list of committee publications and reports. Index.

1372 Carlson, Lewis H. "J. Parnell Thomas and the House Committee on Un-American Activities, 1938–1948." Ph.D. dissertation, Michigan State University, 1967.

Thomas was an influential and active member of the committee, becoming its chairman in 1947. Under his direction, the committee investigated Communist inroads into organized labor, higher education, government agencies, atomic energy, and the movie industry. 28:1756–A.

1373 Carr, Robert K. *The House Committee on Un-American Activities, 1945–1950.* Ithaca, NY: Cornell University Press, 1952.

This is a critical, contemporary account of the committee's action arranged by Congresses with additional chapters focusing on personnel, committee planning, and press treatment. Appendix, index.

1374 Goodman, Walter. *The Committee: The Extraordinary Career of the House Committee on Un-American Activities.* New York: Farrar, Straus and Giroux, 1968.

Goodman, an avowed liberal, examines the committee from its inception in 1938 through 1967. Illustrations, notes, bibliography, index.

1375 Kahn, Albert E. *Treason in Congress: The Record of the Un-American Activities Committee.* New York: Progressive Citizens of America, 1948(?).

This highly critical pamphlet is a sample of the anticommittee literature which appeared at the time.

1376 Potter, Charles E. *Days of Shame.* New York: Coward-McCann, 1965.

Potter (R-MI) served on the House Un-American Activities Committee and, subsequently as senator, sat on McCarthy's Senate Government Operations Committee. Eventually, he voted for McCarthy's censure in 1954. Illustrations, index.

1377 Preston, William, Jr. "The 1940's: The Way We Really Were." *Civil Liberties Review* 2 (1975): 4–38.

Preston reviews public opinion and governmental attitudes toward civil liberties during the 1940s; his criticism focuses on the House Un-American Activities Committee.

1378 Schneier, Edward B. "The Politics of Anti-Communism: A Study of the House Committee on Un-American Activities and Its Role in the Political Process." Ph.D. dissertation, Claremont Graduate School and University Center, 1964.

The committee has tended to play a role normally ascribed to pressure groups. It has tended to act as an advocate rather than an arbiter, as prosecutor rather than judge, and as a forum for the fulminations of reactionaries rather than as an investigator of political conflicts. DAI 28:4234–A.

1379 Simmons, Jerold L. "Operation Abolition: The Campaign to Abolish the House Un-American Activities Committee, 1938–1965." Ph.D. dissertation, University of Minnesota, 1971.

Three distinct campaigns were launched with the objective of abolishing HUAC. The second of these came after the famous Hollywood hearings of October 1947. DAI 32:6353–A.

1380 Worth, Stephen W. "The Congressional Investigating Committee as an Instrument of Subversive Control: An Analysis of the Nature of the Committee, its Procedures, and its Scope of Inquiry." Ph.D. dissertation, University of Washington, 1957.

Worth analyzes several committees of Congress, including the House Un-American Activities Committee, the Permanent Subcommittee on Investigations of the Senate Committee on Government Operations, the Internal Security Committee of the Senate Judiciary Committee, and the select committee to investigate tax-exempt foundations for the House of Representatives.

Government Witnesses

1381 Bentley, Elizabeth. *Out of Bondage: The Story of Elizabeth Bentley*. New York: Devin-Adair, 1951.

Bentley was a regular government witness before HUAC and court trials. This is her memoir of life as a "red" agent and repentant citizen.

1382 Budenz, Louis F. *This is My Story*. Dublin, Ireland: Browne & Nolan, 1947.

The former managing editor of the *Daily Worker,* the organ of the U.S. Communist party, renounced the party and adopted Catholicism in 1946. His "confessions" fed the Red Scare. Index.

1383 Josephson, Harold. "Ex-Communists in Crossfire: A Cold War Debate." *Historian* 44 (1981): 69–84.

The author believes that historical emphasis upon the politics of McCarthyism has obscured the contemporary debate over the role of the ex-Communists. Conservatives and liberals used the testimony of a massive evil conspiracy for their own ends. Notes.

1384 Matusow, Harvey. *False Witness*. New York: Cameron & Kahn, 1955.

Matusow began testifying against Communists and their activities in 1950. In this account he describes how he became a paid government informant and how "information" was invented. Index.

1385 Packer, Herbert L. *Ex-Communist Witnesses: Four Studies in Fact Finding*. Stanford, CA: Stanford University Press, 1962.

Packer reviews the testimony of Whittaker Chambers, Louis Budenz, Elizabeth Bentley, and John Lautner. Appendixes, index.

FBI

1386 Diamond, Sigmund. "The Arrangement: The FBI and Harvard University in the McCarthy Period." In Athan Theoharis, ed. *Beyond the Hiss Case: The FBI, Congress, and the Cold War*. Philadelphia: Temple University Press, 1982, pp. 341–71.

During the late 1940s and early 1950s, the FBI and many universities had secret arrangements to share information about the activities and views of various staff members. Notes.

1387 O'Reilly, Kenneth. *Hoover and the Un-Americans: The FBI, HUAC, and the Red Menace*. Philadelphia: Temple University Press, 1983.

J. Edgar Hoover and the Federal Bureau of Investigation, especially the assistant directors, played important roles in the Red Scare. This book describes the FBI's linkage with HUAC in the evolution of the anti-Communist impulse after World War II. Notes, bibliography, index.

1388 Overstreet, Harry, and Overstreet, Bonaro. *The FBI in our Open Society*. New York: Norton, 1969.

Chapters 11 to 13 deal with the Truman years. Unfortunately a thorough, reasonably objective account of the FBI does not exist. Index.

1389 Theoharis, Athan G. "FBI Surveillance During the Cold War Years: A Constitutional Crisis." *Public Historian* 3 (1981): 4–14.

While focusing on the Cold War years, the surveillance of supposed dissident political activities from 1940 to 1980 by the Federal Bureau of Investigation is discussed. Notes.

1390 Theoharis, Athan. "The Truman Administration and the Decline of Civil Liberties: The FBI's

Success in Securing Authorization for a Preventive Detention Program." *Journal of American History* 64 (1978): 1010–30.

The FBI's preventive detention program demonstrates either the lack of effective executive control or a disregard for the restrictions of the Internal Security Act (1950). Notes.

1391 Ungar, Sanford J. *The FBI*. Boston: Little, Brown, 1975.

Chapter 5, " 'Applicant Work' and Civil Investigations," discusses the loyalty investigations into the State Department and other loyalty-security programs during the Truman era. Glossary, bibliography, index.

1392 Waltzer, Kenneth. "The FBI, Congressman Vito Marcantonio, and the American Labor Party." In Athan Theoharis, ed. *Beyond the Hiss Case: The FBI, Congress, and the Cold War*. Philadelphia: Temple University Press, 1982, pp. 176–214.

While the American Labor party came under investigation in the late 1930s, these activities increased during the early Cold War years. Notes.

ACCUSATIONS, BLACKLISTS, AND TRIALS

See also *House Un-American Activities Committee*, and *Government Witnesses*.

1393 Kempton, Murray. *Part of Our Time: Some Ruins and Monuments of the Thirties*. New York: Simon & Schuster, 1955.

Kempton writes of the backgrounds of many of the figures who became prominent during the Red Scare, such as Hiss, Chambers, Lee Pressman, Elizabeth Bentley, and others. These essays provide an excellent background for the 1940s and 1950s.

1394 Kutler, Stanley I. *The American Inquisition: Justice and Injustice in the Cold War*. New York: Hill & Wang, 1982.

Provocative case studies deal with "Tokyo Rose," John William Powell, Owen Lattimore, Harry Bridges, and the defense lawyers at the "Foley Square" trial. Chapter 7 additionally suggests that Senator Patrick McCarran's anti-Communist activities were far more intimidating than McCarthy's. Notes, index.

1395 Lattimore, Owen. *Ordeal by Slander*. New York: Little, Brown, 1950.

Lattimore defends himself in this volume. His statement is also an indictment of an era when Americans were "tried" in the media and in congressional committees for their political affiliations.

1396 Rees, David. *Harry Dexter White: A Study in Paradox*. New York: Coward, McCann & Geoghegan, 1973.

White was assistant secretary of the treasury (1945–46) and American executive director of the International Monetary Fund (1946–47). In 1948 he was accused of being a Russian spy. Shortly thereafter he died of a heart attack, but the controversy continued, his guilt or innocence never really being affirmed. Notes, bibliography, index.

1397 Reuben, William A. *The Atom Spy Hoax*. New York: Action Books, 1955.

The premise that "atomic spies"—such as Alfred Dean Slack and the Rosenbergs—infested the United States and conveyed much information to Russia comes under a slashing criticism. Notes, appendix, index.

Entertainment Industry Blacklist

See also Chapter 5, *Cold War in Movies*.

1398 Bentley, Eric. *Are You Now or Have You Ever Been: The Investigation of Show Business by the Un-American Activities Committee, 1947–1958*. New York: Harper & Row, 1972.

This volume is an edited version of the committee's hearings.

1399 Cailteaux, Karen S. (Byers). "The Political Blacklist in the Broadcast Industry: The Decade of the 1950s." Ph.D. dissertation, Ohio State University, 1972.

This historical study of the political blacklist era focuses on: (1) sources and origins of blacklists; (2) types of pressure tactics used; (3) response of the industry employers to the pressure to blacklist; (4) mechanisms of clearance for the accused; (5) some complaints filed with the FCC; and (6) some of the impact of blacklist upon individuals. DAI 33: 4563–A.

1400 Ceplair, Larry, and Englund, Steven. *The Inquisition in Hollywood: Politics in the Film Community, 1930–1960*. Garden City, NY: Doubleday, 1980.

This reasoned account seeks to reexamine the impact of "industry" Communists and the House Un-American Activities Committee on Hollywood films and politics. The Truman-era "black-lists" are explained in historical and political perspective. Appendix, notes, bibliography, index.

1401 Cogley, John. *Report on Blacklisting II: Radio-Television*. New York: Fund for the Republic, 1956.

This study examines the process of blacklisting TV and radio entertainers and the impact upon its victims. Index.

1402 Fagan, Myron C. *Documentation of the Red Stars in Hollywood.* Hollywood, CA: Cinema Educational Guild, 1950.

In this "classic" bit of hysteria, Fagan lists the names of those stars whom he finds to be associated with Communist-front organizations.

1403 Gill, Glenda E. "Careerist and Casualty: The Rise and Fall of Canada Lee." *Freedomways* 21 (1981): 15–27.

Black actor Canada Lee (d. 1952), born Leonard Lionel Cornelius Canegata, was active in American theater, 1934–46, and in films, 1944–52; however, probes by the House Un-American Activities Committee and the Federal Bureau of Investigation destroyed his career.

1404 Glazer, Nathan. "An Answer to Lillian Hellman." *Commentary* 61 (1976): 36–39.

Hellman's account of her 1952 appearance before the House Un-American Activities Committee, recounted in her *Scoundrel Time* (1976), is criticized.

1405 Hellman, Lillian. *An Unfinished Woman.* Boston: Little, Brown, 1969.

Hellman, a successful playwright and prominent member of the left-wing intelligentsia, opposed the Truman administration's Cold War policies. She refused to testify before the House Un-American Activities Committee and although not prosecuted, she was blacklisted by the movie industry. Illustrations.

1406 Hellman, Lillian. *Scoundrel Time.* Boston: Little, Brown, 1976.

While Hellman writes of her involvement with the House Un-American Activities Committee, Garry Will's extended introduction is useful in recreating the anti-Communist fever of the late 1940s and early 1950s.

1407 Hook, Sidney. "Lillian Hellman's *Scoundrel Time.*" *Encounter* [Great Britain] 48 (1977): 82–91.

This review of Hellman's *Scoundrel Time* (1976) deals with her experiences and observations of civil rights abuses during the McCarthy era (1951–53).

1408 Howe, Irving. "Lillian Hellman and the McCarthy Years." *Dissent* 23 (1976): 378–82.

This essay critiques Hellman's book *Scoundrel Time* (1976) and Garry Will's introduction.

1409 Kanfer, Stefan. *A Journal of the Plague Years.* New York: Atheneum, 1973.

This account, principally of cinema and broadcasting, covers the political blacklisting of entertainers in the late 1940s and 1950s. Bibliography, index.

1410 Miller, Merle. *The Judges and the Judged.* Garden City, NY: Doubleday, 1952.

Miller was commissioned by the American Civil Liberties Union to investigate the radio-television blacklisting. He shows how a very small group came to wield considerable power.

1411 Nizer, Louis. *The Jury Returns.* Garden City, NY: Doubleday, 1966.

Nizer has an extended chapter (pp. 225–438) on John Henry Faulk's case against those who blacklisted him and prevented him from working in radio and television.

1412 Schwartz, Nancy Lynn. *The Hollywood Writers War.* New York: Knopf, 1982.

This account of the screen writers guild brings the struggle up to 1946.

1413 Suber, Howard. "The Anti-Communist Blacklist in the Motion Picture Industry." Ph.D. dissertation, University of California, Los Angeles, 1968.

This historical narrative traces the growth and development of the motion picture blacklist which stemmed from the HUAC investigations. At least 214 persons can be established as having been blacklisted, the majority of whom were writers. DAI 29:4131–A.

1414 Suber, Howard. "Politics and Popular Culture: Hollywood at Bay, 1933–1953." *American Jewish History* 68 (1979): 517–34.

Suber finds that long-term labor union and political conflicts in the film industry contributed significantly to the Second Red Scare of 1947 and its resultant "Hollywood Ten" and blacklist.

1415 Vaughn, Robert. *Only Victims: A Study of Show Business Blacklisting.* New York: Putnam's, 1972.

This account examines the influence of the House Un-American Activities Committee on the American theater, 1938–58. The author has limited his coverage to the "living" theater, that is, excluding movies, radio, and television. Bibliography, index, notes.

1416 Wertheim, Larry M. "Nedrick Young, et al. *v.* MPAA, et al.: The Fight Against the Hollywood Blacklist." *Southern California Quarterly* 57 (1975): 383–418.

The efforts to obtain an official judgment against the motion picture industry for blacklisting actors, writers, and producers are traced in this article. Over 200 artists were affected; however, the campaign to recover damages through the legal process was characterized by a lack of collective support. Notes.

The "Hollywood Ten"

1417   Bessie, Alvah. *Inquisition in Eden*. New York: Macmillan, 1965.

A prominent member of the Hollywood Ten, Bessie recounts his experiences at congressional hearings, court trials, and on the blacklist. Index.

1418   Biberman, Herbert. *Salt of the Earth: The Story of a Film*. Boston: Beacon, 1965.

One of the "Hollywood Ten," Biberman set out to make a movie, *Salt of the Earth,* in 1951. This is the story of the difficulties he encountered when those who had been blacklisted sought to form their own movie company. Appendix, illustrations.

1419   Biskind, Peter. "The Past Is Prologue: The Blacklist In Hollywood." *Radical America* 15 (1981): 59–65.

This commentary uses Victor Navasky's *Naming Names* (1980) and other recent materials on the House Un-American Activities Committee and the Hollywood Ten blacklist to argue that the policy of having good dissenters turn in bad ones was the same with handling Vietnam protesters. Illustrations.

1420   Cogley, John. *Report on Blacklisting: I: Movies*. New York: Fund for the Republic, 1956.

This highly critical account has chapters on the 1947 hearings, the issue of communism in Hollywood, the role of the American Legion, and an assessment of film content related to communism. Index.

1421   Cook, Bruce. *Dalton Trumbo*. New York: Scribner's, 1977.

Trumbo, a screenwriter, refused to answer House Un-American Activities Committee questions. As a result, he and nine others were charged with contempt of court. The Hollywood Ten, as they became known, were fired from their jobs and blacklisted in the industry. Photographs, bibliography, index.

1422   Kahn, Gordon. *Hollywood on Trial: The Story of the Ten Who Were Indicted*. New York: Boni & Gaer, 1948.

This account is a contemporary public statement by the ten indicted men.

1423   Navasky, Victor S. *Naming Names*. New York: Viking, 1980.

Those called before the House Un-American Activities Committee were given the choice of "naming names" or being in contempt. It is Navasky's premise that most of these "name-namers" would have preferred not to collaborate with the committee. Notes, index.

1424   Trumbo, Dalton. *The Time of the Toad: A Study of Inquisition in America and Two Related Pamphlets*. New York: Harper & Row, 1972.

This small volume is a collection of essays written by Trumbo over the years. "The Time of the Toad" first appeared in 1949; "The Devil in the Book" in 1956; and "Honor Bright and All That Jazz" in 1965. Trumbo was one of the Hollywood Ten and on the blacklist for years.

The "Foley Square" Trial

1425   Belknap, Michael R. *Cold War Political Justice: The Smith Act, the Communist Party, and American Civil Liberties*. Westport, CT: Greenwood, 1977.

The author has focused on the Smith Act prosecutions, especially the leadership of the U.S. Communist party at the infamous "Foley Square" trial. He has also followed the legal appeals. It is his conclusion that American justice is not always blind; indeed, that during the early years of the Cold War its treatment of American radicals constituted political injustice. Bibliographical essay, notes, index.

1426   O'Brien, Kevin J. "*Dennis v. U.S.*: The Cold War, the Communist Conspiracy and the F.B.I." Ph.D. dissertation, Cornell University, 1979.

While public prosecution of Communist party leaders (1948–51) produced a compelling human drama and important legal doctrine, the prosecution's historical significance is closely tied to the development of the FBI's secret and unaccountable domestic intelligence activities. DAI 40:3492–A.

1427   Steinberg, Peter L. "The Great 'Red Menace': U.S. Prosecution of American Communists, 1947–1951." Ph.D. dissertation, New York University, 1979.

The policies of both the Truman administration and the American Communist party during these years encouraged the growth of "McCarthyism." Each sought to deter the development of political repression, but succeeded only in quickening its pace. DAI 40:2844–A.

Hiss-Chambers Case

1428   Andrews, Bert, and Andrews, Peter. *A Tragedy of History: A Journalist's Confidential Role in the Hiss-Chambers Case*. Washington, DC: Luce, 1962.

Bert Andrews was Washington bureau chief of the *New York Herald Tribune* and covered the Hiss-Chambers case. His son has completed the manuscript. Chronology, appendix, index.

1429   Brodie, Fawn M. "I Think Hiss Is Lying." *American Heritage* 32 (1981): 4–21.

Richard Nixon's role in the trial and conviction (for perjury) of Alger Hiss is retraced; also the similarities between the character of Hiss and Nixon are noted. Notes.

1430   Chambers, Whittaker. *Witness*. New York: Random House, 1952.

Alger Hiss's accuser states his case. Indeed, this extremely well-written book has convinced many readers that Chambers was telling the truth. Index.

1431   Cook, Fred J. *The Unfinished Story of Alger Hiss*. New York: William Morrow, 1958.

Sympathetic to Hiss, this account provides a useful survey of events and charges. Index.

1432   Cooke, Alistair. *A Generation On Trial: U.S.A. v. Alger Hiss*. New York: Knopf, 1951.

This is an extremely readable account of Hiss's two trials by a sympathetic viewer. The Hiss case became, for that generation and perhaps subsequent ones, a political symbol. Chronology, index.

1433   DeToledano, Ralph, and Lasky, Victor. *Seeds of Treason: The True Story of the Hiss-Chambers Tragedy*. New York: Funk & Wagnalls, 1950.

This contemporary account is highly critical of Hiss and supportive of Chambers. Notes.

1434   Hiss, Alger. *In the Court of Public Opinion*. New York: Knopf, 1957.

Hiss tells his side of the case, denying the charges and refuting the evidence used against him. Appendix, index.

1435   Hook, Sidney. "An Autobiographical Fragment: The Strange Case of Whittaker Chambers." *Encounter* [Great Britain] 46 (1976): 78–89.

Chambers's role as the key witness in the 1949 trial which convicted Alger Hiss is recounted.

1436   Jeffreys-Jones, Rhodri. "Review Essay: Weinstein on Hiss." *Journal of American Studies* [Great Britain] 13 (1979): 115–26.

This essay was prompted by Allen Weinstein's *Perjury: The Hiss-Chambers Case* (1978), which argues that Hiss perjured himself (for which he was sentenced to five years imprisonment). While the book incorporates new materials, it has not stilled Hiss's partisans. Notes.

1437   Levin, David. "In the Court of Historical Criticism: Alger Hiss's Narrative." *Virginia Quarterly Review* 52 (1976): 41–78.

The author compares Hiss's *In the Court of Public Opinion* (1957), Whittaker Chambers's *Witness* (1952), and Richard M. Nixon's *Six Crises* (1962). It is his conclusion that Hiss was innocent.

1438   Levin, David. "Perjury, History, and Unreliable Witnesses." *Virginia Quarterly Review* 54 (1978): 725–32.

Allen Weinstein's *Perjury: The Hiss-Chambers Case* prompted this review essay which challenges Weinstein's objectivity.

1439   Marbury, William L. "The Hiss-Chambers Libel Suit." *Maryland Historical Magazine* 76 (1981): 70–92.

The author was counsel for and lifelong friend of Alger Hiss. Here he reviews the background and facts of the filing of Hiss's libel suit against Chambers on 27 September 1948.

1440   Navasky, Victor. "Weinstein, Hiss, and the Transformation of Historical Ambiguity into Cold War Verity." In Athan Theoharis, ed. *Beyond the Hiss Case: The FBI, Congress and the Cold War*. Philadelphia: Temple University Press, 1982, pp. 215–308.

This is an extended, critical examination of Weinstein's *Perjury* which seeks to deal with the ideological biases every commentator brings to such an episode. Where Weinstein finds Hiss guilty, Navasky reserves his opinion. Chronology of Hiss-Chambers case, notes.

1441   Seth, Ronald. *The Sleeping Truth: The Hiss-Chambers Affair Reappraised*. New York: Hart, 1968.

This account is an indictment of Chambers and a defense of Hiss. Footnotes, index.

1442   Smith, John C. *Alger Hiss: The True Story*. New York: Holt, Rinehart and Winston, 1976.

It is Smith's verdict that Hiss was innocent. Notes, illustrations, bibliography, index.

1443   Van Dusen, George. "The Continuing Hiss: Whittaker Chambers, Alger Hiss and *National Review* Conservatism." *Cithara* 11 (1971): 67–89.

Among conservatives, Alger Hiss came to be the symbol of all that was wrong with New Deal-Fair Deal domestic and foreign policies. The point of view expressed by the *National Review,* however, goes deeper—it is almost religious. Notes.

1444   Weinstein, Allen. "The Alger Hiss Case Revisited." *American Scholar* 41 (1972): 121–32.

Several questions and problems in reexamining the Hiss case were discussed. Partisan views have hardened into myths.

1445   Weinstein, Allen. *Perjury: The Hiss-Chambers Case*. New York: Knopf, 1978.

Reappraising the case in the aftermath of Watergate, Weinstein offers new evidence which he believes points to the fact that Hiss stole the documents and that Chambers told the truth about their relationship. Notes, bibliography, index.

1446   Younger, Irving. "Was Alger Hiss Guilty?" *Commentary* 60 (1975): 23–27.

The issues involved in the Hiss case of the late 1940s and early 1950s are reviewed.

The Rosenbergs

1447 Anders, Roger M. "The Rosenberg Case Revisited: The Greenglass Testimony and the Protection of Atomic Secrets." *American Historical Review* 83 (1978): 388–400.

Anders examines the Atomic Energy Commission's efforts to resolve the problems posed by Greenglass's testimony and concludes that Greenglass tried to tell the truth about the technology of the atomic bomb. Notes.

1448 Bickel, Alexander M. "[Book Review] *The Rosenberg Affair: Invitation to an Inquest,* By Walter and Miriam Schneir." *Commentary* 41 (1966): 69–76.

This book (Doubleday, 1965) builds an uncompromising argument for the innocence of the Rosenbergs. The reviewer concludes it fails to be convincing; however, he does call the whole affair "an unforgivable disgrace to the American administration of justice."

1449 Goldstein, Alvin H. *Unquiet Death of Julius and Ethel Rosenberg.* New York: Lawrence Hill, 1975.

Public television commissioned Goldstein to prepare a documentary on the Rosenberg case. This is an account of his impressions, based on conversations with some 200 persons. Exceptional photos.

1450 Marker, Jeffrey. "The Jewish Community and the Case of Julius and Ethel Rosenberg." *Maryland History* 3 (1972): 104–21.

This survey of the reactions of American Jews to the arrest and trial of the Rosenbergs concludes that most Jews either acquiesced in the general anti-Communist hysteria of the time or else avoided the entire issue for fear of seeing Jews used as scapegoats once again. Notes.

1451 Meeropol, Robert, and Meeropol, Michael. *We Are Your Sons: The Legacy of Julius and Ethel Rosenberg.* Boston: Houghton, 1975.

While much of this book is beyond the Truman years, the early chapters do contain letters written by the Rosenbergs while in jail and on trial. Appendix, notes, index.

1452 Nizer, Louis. *The Implosion Conspiracy.* Garden City, NY: Doubleday, 1973.

Nizer reviews the Rosenberg trial and, as a skilled attorney, concludes that there was enough evidence to convict them. He does, however, believe that the sentence was unduly harsh. Appendix.

1453 Parrish, Michael E. "Cold War Justice: The Supreme Court and the Rosenbergs." *American Historical Review* 82 (1977): 805–42.

This reinterpretation of the Rosenberg case focuses upon the many efforts to secure a new trial through appeals to the Supreme Court. The personal conflicts among members of the court are examined. Notes.

1454 Pilat, Oliver. *The Atom Spies.* New York: Putnam, 1952.

This is an early account of the Rosenbergs and their dealings with the courts. Index.

1455 Price, Frank J. "The Rosenberg Case in Four Selected French and Italian Daily Newspapers." Ph.D. dissertation, State University of Iowa, 1956.

Two of the four newspapers were the official Communist party organs, *l'Humanité* of Paris and *l'Unità* of Milan, while the other two were *Le Monde* of Paris and the *Corriere della Sera* of Milan. The coverage was on the whole critical of the U.S. government's case. DAI 16:746.

1456 Radosh, Ronald, and Milton, Joyce. *The Rosenberg File: A Search for the Truth.* New York: Holt, Rinehart and Winston, 1983.

This review of the case finds Julius guilty of spy activities, but believes that Ethel was badly treated by federal authorities. Few characters fare well in this tragedy, certainly not the Communist party, the United States, the FBI, the Justice Department, or the Supreme Court. Notes, bibliography, index.

1457 Root, Jonathan. *The Betrayers: The Rosenbergs—A Reappraisal of an American Crisis.* New York: Coward-McCann, 1964.

The author, after reexamining the case, concludes that "as to the guilt of the Rosenbergs, there is no reasonable doubt now surviving." Index.

1458 Schneir, Walter, and Schneir, Miriam. *Invitation to an Inquest: A New Look at the Rosenberg-Sobell Case.* Garden City, NY: Doubleday, 1983. Rev. ed.

The authors sift through the "evidence" presented at the Rosenbergs' trial and introduce some new data. Notes, illustrations, index.

1459 Sobell, Morton. *On Doing Time.* New York: Scribner's, 1974.

Sobell was convicted along with Julius and Ethel Rosenberg; they were executed on 19 June 1953, while he was sentenced to thirty years imprisonment. He was released on 14 January 1969. This memoir is his account of his role in the conviction of the Rosenbergs and his years in jail.

LOCAL GOVERNMENTS AND THE RED SCARE

See also Chapter 5, *Education and the Cold War.*

1460 Carleton, Don E. "A Crisis of Rapid Change: The Red Scare in Houston, 1945–1955." Ph.D. dissertation, University of Houston, 1978.

Houston, Texas experienced a Red Scare (1948–55) with pluralistic causative sources that was influenced by international and national events, nourished by an atmosphere of unease caused by rapid urban change, encouraged and sustained by community elites, and given credibility by leftist activities. DAI 40:1024–A.

1461 Chamberlain, Lawrence H. *Loyalty and Legislative Action: A Survey of Activity by the New York State Legislature, 1919–1949.* Ithaca, NY: Cornell University Press, 1951.

Chapter 5 surveys the development of the Feinberg Law (1949) which aimed to "eliminate subversive persons from the public school system." Appendix, notes, index.

1462 Gelhorn, Walter, ed. *The States and Subversion.* Ithaca, NY: Cornell University Press, 1952.

These essays include: Chapter 1, "California: Regulations and Investigation of Subversive Activities"; Chapter 2, "Illinois: The Broyles Commission"; Chapter 3, "Maryland: The Ober Anti-Communist Law"; Chapter 4, "Michigan: State and Local Attack on Subversion"; Chapter 5, "New York: A Generation of Legislative Alarm"; and Chapter 6, "Washington: The Canwell Committee." Appendixes (state statutes relating to subversive activity), index.

1463 Holmes, Thomas M. "The Specter of Communism in Hawaii, 1947–1953." Ph.D. dissertation, University of Hawaii, 1975.

In Hawaii there were some features of the era's Red Scare which were unique to the area: (1) the strategic location of the islands; (2) the issue of statehood; (3) the nature of Hawaii's plantation economy and labor force; and (4) the emergence of the International Longshoremen's and Warehousemen's Union as a major island force. DAI 36:6264–A.

1464 Johnson, Ronald W. "The Communist Issue in Missouri, 1946–1956." Ph.D. dissertation, University of Missouri, Columbia, 1973.

During the decade following World War II, contemporary events and underlying anxieties provoked by the Communist issue led to Red Scare activity in Missouri. DAI 35:1014–A.

1465 Johnson, Ronald W. "The Korean War Red Scare in Missouri." *Red River Valley Historical Review* 4 (1979): 72–86.

Missourians responded to the war by forming groups such as the Crusade for Freedom and enacted anti-Communist city ordinances.

1466 Rogow, Arnold A. "The Loyalty Oath Issue in Iowa, 1951." *American Political Science Review* 55 (1961): 861–69.

A measure introduced in Iowa's General Assembly to require employees in courts, schools, and government agencies to swear to loyalty oaths failed to pass because of the overemotionalism of A. L. Douds, and the general political, social, and economic homogeneity. Notes.

1467 Selcraig, James T. "The Red Scare in the Midwest, 1945 to 1955: A State and Local Study." Ph.D. dissertation, University of Illinois, Urbana-Champaign, 1981.

This comparative study of Wisconsin, Illinois, Indiana, Ohio, and Michigan considers the Red Scare with such issues as state politics, city elections and government, schools and libraries, voluntary organizations, and universities. DAI 42:2824.

1468 Sorenson, Dale R. "The Anticommunist Consensus in Indiana, 1945–1958." Ph.D. dissertation, Indiana University, 1980.

Sorenson rejects the thesis that the virulent anticommunism of the 1950s was due to the action of the elites or conversely that McCarthyism was a revolt against the elites. He finds that intolerant attitudes toward Communists penetrated all levels of Indiana society. DAI 41:1191–A.

California

1469 Barrett, Edward L., Jr. *The Tenney Committee: Legislative Investigation of Subversive Activities in California.* Ithaca, NY: Cornell University Press, 1951.

This is a useful, if dated, account of California's version of the Red Scare. The report looks at the broad-brush effect of the Tenney Committee's activities and actions. Appendixes, index.

1470 Brazil, Burton R. "Loyalty Oaths in California: Theoretical Background and Implications." Ph.D. dissertation, Stanford University, 1954.

The history of loyalty oaths is examined, along with immediate events leading up to the Levering loyalty oath being grafted onto the California Constitution in 1952. DAI 14:1784.

1471 Long, Edward R. "Loyalty Oaths in California, 1947–1952: The Politics of Anti-Communism." Ph.D. dissertation, University of California, San Diego, 1981.

The adoption of loyalty measures by state and local government was made possible by the dissolution of left-liberal coalitions, which could have resisted the anti-Communist movement. DAI 42:1762–A.

1472 Scobie, Ingrid W. "Jack B. Tenney: Molder of Anti-Communism Legislation in California, 1940–1949." Ph.D. dissertation, University of Wisconsin, 1970.

In 1941 the California legislature established the first committee to investigate activities, and state Senator Tenney became chairman (1941–49). Tenney introduced most of the state's anti-Communist legislation. DAI 34:6575–A.

Washington

1473 Baldasty, Gerald J., and Winfield, Betty H. "Institutional Paralysis in the Press: The Cold War in Washington State." *Journalism Quarterly* 58 (1981): 273–78.

This study reviews the press coverage of Washington State's Committee on Un-American Activities and its investigation of Communist influence at the University of Washington during the 1940s. Notes.

1474 Countryman, Vern. *Un-American Activities in the State of Washington: The Work of the Canwell Committee*. Ithaca, NY: Cornell University Press, 1951.

In 1947 the Washington State legislature created a committee to investigate "un-American activities." This committee functioned for two years, held two public meetings, and made its report to the legislature in 1949. Notes, index.

1475 Rader, Melvin. *False Witness*. Seattle: University of Washington Press, 1969.

The author was a professor of philosophy at the University of Washington in 1948 and 1949 when he was accused before the state legislature's Committee on Un-American Activities of Communist membership and activities. This account contains information on the operation of the state committee and on governmental use of professional witnesses.

1476 Sanders, Jane. *Cold War on the Campus: Academic Freedom at the University of Washington, 1946–64*. Seattle: University of Washington Press, 1979.

The University of Washington's troubled years with the "loyalty" issue are examined. Chronology, illustrations, appendix, notes, bibliography, index.

McCARTHYISM AND OPPONENTS

See also Chapter 3, *Joseph McCarthy*, for additional materials.

1477 Colie, Stuart E. " 'McCarthyism' and Some European Images of America: A Study of British and French Quality Papers, 1947–1954." Ph.D. dissertation, Princeton University, 1963.

The papers analyzed include the *New Statesman, Economist, Spectator, Times, Le Monde,* and *Figaro*. Generally unfavorable attitudes and assumptions were reinforced while favorable assumptions were weakened. DAI 24:2970.

1478 Crosby, Donald F. *God, Church, and Flag: Senator Joseph R. McCarthy and the Catholic Church, 1950–1957*. Chapel Hill: University of North Carolina Press, 1978.

This account examines the limits and intensity of Senator McCarthy's Catholic support and describes how the argument over McCarthyism forced Catholics to interact with the rest of the American community. Notes, bibliography, index.

1479 Davis, Elmer H. *But We Were Born Free*. New York: Bobbs-Merrill, 1954.

Davis was an outspoken critic of McCarthy's tactics.

1480 DeSantis, Vincent P. "American Catholics and McCarthyism." *Catholic Historical Review* 51 (1965): 1–20.

An examination of Catholic newspapers and periodicals, including letters written to their editors, from 1950 to 1954 found Catholics were divided as much as other Americans in their opinion of McCarthy. The majority of those Catholics publicly expressing an opinion, however, supported McCarthy. Notes.

1481 Fried, Richard M. "Electoral Politics and McCarthyism: The 1950 Campaign." In R. Griffith and A. Theoharis, eds. *The Specter: Original Essays on the Cold War and the Origins of McCarthyism*. New York: New Viewpoints, 1974, pp. 190–222.

This essay examines the often overexaggerated influence of McCarthy (but not anticommunism) in the congressional elections of 1950. Notes.

1482 Fried, Richard M. *Men Against McCarthy*. New York: Columbia University Press, 1976.

Fried views McCarthyism as a partisan weapon used by Republicans and looks at the Democratic response to McCarthyism from the Tydings Committee through the 1952 election. Notes, bibliography, index.

1483 Griffith, Robert. "The Political Context of McCarthyism." *Review of Politics* 33 (1971): 24–35.

Senator Joseph McCarthy rose to power because he was supported by those who used the issue of communism as a stepping-stone to power. An analysis of the McCarran Internal Security Act (1950) and the Communist Control Act (1954) demonstrates that the Communist issue had strength quite apart from the Wisconsin senator. Notes.

1484 Keiser, Kenneth R. "McCarthyism and Anti-Subversion in American Politics." Ph.D. dissertation, University of North Carolina, Chapel Hill, 1971.

Three elements of American politics—the Cold War and Korean conflict, the Republican party, and the Lockean political culture—together provided the primary causes behind the events during the McCarthy period. DAI 32:7056–A.

1485 Peterson, Arthur L. "McCarthyism: Its Ideology and Foundation." Ph.D. dissertation, University of Minnesota, 1962.

The foundations of McCarthyism can be found in the American political environment, the socio-psychological milieu of mid-century America, and the support given the movement by certain leadership elements. DAI 25:1306.

1486 Reeves, Thomas C. "McCarthyism: Interpretations since Hofstadter." *Wisconsin Magazine of History* 60 (1976): 42–54.

Reeves carefully surveys the literature, scholarly and journalistic, which relates to McCarthy and his influence. Notes.

1487 Vinz, Warren L. "A Comparison Between Elements of Protestant Fundamentalism and McCarthyism." Ph.D. dissertation, University of Utah, 1968.

There is evidence of mutual interest between Protestant fundamentalism and McCarthyism. Both attacked the same targets, used similar methods, appealed to similar constituencies, and had common leadership. DAI 29:2200–A.

Administrative and Legal

See H. K. Becker and G. T. Felkenes, *Law Enforcement: A Selected Bibliography* (#3011) for possible references to the Truman years.

ADMINISTRATION OF TERRITORIES

1488 Cravens, Raymond L. "The Constitutional and Political Status of the Non-Contiguous Areas of the United States." Ph.D. dissertation, University of Kentucky, 1958.

This study analyzes the following postwar developments: the institution of reports to the United Nations on these areas; the passage of an organic act for Guam (1950); the transfer of American Samoa

from the navy to the Interior Department (1952); the innovation of the Commonwealth status for Puerto Rico; the passage of a revised organic act for the Virgin Islands (1954); and the annual attempts by Alaska and Hawaii to obtain statehood. DAI 24:2106.

1489 Griffith, Richard R. "From Island Colony to Strategic Territory: The Development of American Administration on the Island of Guam, 1898–1950." Ph.D. dissertation, University of Denver, 1978.

This study covers the period of U.S. naval administration of Guam and ends with its transfer from the navy to the Interior Department in 1950, from military to civilian control. DAI 39:3757–A.

1490 Lynch, David M. "United States Policy Toward Micronesia, 1945–1972." Ph.D. dissertation, West Virginia University, 1973.

This study examines the perceived military-strategic considerations which shaped U.S. policy. DAI 34:4366–A.

1491 Paul, Justus F. "The Power of Seniority: Senator Hugh Butler and Statehood for Hawaii." *Hawaiian Journal of History* 9 (1975): 140–47.

Butler, as chairman of the Committee on Public Lands, sought to prevent passage of statehood bills for Hawaii and Alaska mainly because of the danger of Communist domination. Robert Taft persuaded him to change his position in 1953.

1492 Runde, William H. "Trusteeship During and After World War II." Ph.D. dissertation, University of Missouri, Columbia, 1975.

This study examines how the United States obtained the trusteeship, including diplomatic negotiations and internal debates. DAI 36:4683–A.

Puerto Rico
1493 Baver, Sherrie Lynn. "Policy-Making For Industrialization in Puerto Rico, 1947–1976." Ph.D. dissertation, Columbia University, 1979.

This study begins in 1947, when the island legislature, under the leadership of Luis Munoz Marin, adopted an industrial incentives program—100% tax exemption—to attract private mainland U.S. capital to Puerto Rico. DAI 40:5999–A.

1494 Bhana, Surendra. *The United States and the Development of the Puerto Rican Status Question, 1936–1968.* Lawrence: University Press of Kansas, 1975.

The Truman administration's role in Puerto Rico's struggle for political autonomy is discussed. It was during Truman's term of office that Puerto Rico evolved from territorial to Commonwealth status. Notes, bibliography, index.

1495 Gaudet, Joseph A. "The First 1000 Days of the Governorship of Luis Munoz Marin in Puerto

Rico, 1949–1952." Ph.D. dissertation, St. John's University, 1971.

Puerto Rico made a major gain in self-government with the Elective Governor Act (1947). Munoz Marin became governor on 2 January 1949 and immediately began to seek additional powers of local autonomy, such as a constitution for Puerto Rico. In 1952 Puerto Rico gained its constitution and became a Commonwealth. DAI 32:2600–A.

LEGAL

1496 Belz, Herman. "Changing Conceptions of Constitutionalism in the Years of World War II and the Cold War." *Journal of American History* 59 (1972): 640–69.

The impact of the Cold War on the U.S. Constitution is discussed, especially its influence upon domestic legislation. The struggles of the immediate postwar years focused on civil rights and liberties. Notes.

1497 Fabiano, G. J. "An Analysis and Interpretation of the Use of Presidential Authority to Order United States Armed Forces into Military Action and to Quell Domestic Disturbances." Ph.D. dissertation, New York University, 1962.

In most instances, employment of the armed forces (1790–1960) was used to enforce federal statutes, to quell race riots, to maintain peace during labor strikes, and to protect U.S. property and enforce court orders. DAI 23:1060.

1498 Morgan, Ruth L. Prouse. "The Presidential Executive Order as an Instrument for Policy-Making." Ph.D. dissertation, Louisiana State University, 1966.

Eight consecutive orders under three presidents are analyzed. The presidents used executive orders to establish significant domestic policies about civil rights. DAI 27:1415.

1499 Murphy, Paul L. *The Constitution in Crisis Times, 1918–1969.* New York: Harper & Row, 1972.

Two chapters apply to the Truman era: Chapter 8, "The Fair Deal and Judicial Pragmatism, 1946–50," discusses labor, civil liberties, and civil rights; Chapter 9, "The Korean Crisis and the Cold War Constitution," discusses the president's power to commit troops, seizure of the steel industry, the McCarran Act, civil rights, and civil liberties. Notes, bibliography, index.

Kefauver Committee

See also Chapter 3, *Estes Kefauver*, for additional information.

1500 Arnold, Truman. *Fair Fights and Foul: A Dissenting Lawyer's Life.* New York: Harcourt, Brace & World, 1965.

Chapter 20 discusses the Kefauver Committee, while Chapter 21 finds Arnold as attorney for Owen Lattimore.

1501 Hawkins, Gordon. "God and the Mafia." *Public Interest* (1969): 24–51.

The author questions whether there is sufficient evidence to prove the existence of a complex, well-organized national criminal syndicate. Estes Kefauver's *Crime In America* makes such a claim but fails to produce the evidence to support it.

1502 Kefauver, Estes. *Crime in America.* Garden City, NY: Doubleday, 1951.

Kefauver was chairman of the Senate Crime Investigating Committee which held hearings from 10 May 1950 to 1 May 1951. This volume condenses these hearings under specific themes, episodes, and individuals.

1503 Moore, William H. *The Kefauver Committee and the Politics of Crime, 1950–1952.* Columbia: University of Missouri Press, 1974.

The Kefauver Crime Committee viewed crime in the United States as conspiratorial. This volume is a study of the background pressures and considerations that shaped the committee's conclusions. Notes, bibliography, index.

1504 Moore, William H. "Was Estes Kefauver 'Blackmailed' During the Chicago Crime Hearings? A Historian's Perspective." *Public Historian* 4 (1982): 4–28.

Reviewed here is Seymour Hersh and Jeff Gerth's questionable 1976 account in the *New York Times,* which claimed Chicago labor lawyer Sidney R. Korshak and others blackmailed Senator Kefauver in 1950 in an effort to end the investigation.

Twenty-second Amendment

1505 Davis, Paul B. "The Results and Implications of the Enactment of the Twenty-Second Amendment." *Presidential Studies Quarterly* 9 (1979): 289–303.

The Twenty-second Amendment limits a president's term to two and was passed during Truman's administration (1950). This study reviews the implications of the amendment and presents the views of Presidents Truman through Carter on it.

1506 Zucker, Frederick D. "The Adoption of the Twenty-Second Amendment." Ph.D. dissertation, Pennsylvania State University, 1958.

The Twenty-second Amendment, limiting the tenure of the president to two elected terms, or a maximum of ten years should a vice-president succeed to the presidency, became part of the Constitution on 27 February 1951. It represented a victory for Republicans. DAI 19:3002.

SUPREME COURT

1507 Ball, Howard. "Careless Justice: The United States Supreme Court's Shopping Center Opinions, 1946–1976." *Polity* 11 (1978): 200–228.

With the examination of cases involving the right of free speech on private property, the author concludes that in addition to impersonal forces and correction of prior error, majority consensus on the bench was sensitive to the instability aroused by the direct overturn of precedents. Notes.

1508 Benson, Paul R., Jr. *The Supreme Court and the Commerce Clause, 1937–1970.* New York: Dunellen, 1970.

Court decisions (1942) gave Congress virtual authority over the national economy. Federal and state power over commerce, including employment and civil rights, during the Truman administration are surveyed. Notes, table of cases, bibliography.

1509 Berg, Larry L. "The Supreme Court and Congress: Conflict and Interaction, 1947–1968." Ph.D. dissertation, University of California, Santa Barbara, 1972.

This study analyzes a single aspect of relations between Congress and the Supreme Court—that of congressional voting behavior on two types of court-related legislation. The bills included those designed to curb the powers of the court and those aimed at its decisions. DAI 33:2437–A.

1510 Brenner, Saul. "Fluidity on the United States Supreme Court: A Reexamination." *American Journal of Political Science* 24 (1980): 526–35.

Reviewing the court during the period Harold Burton served as a justice (1945–58), the study found that 88 percent of the time the justices voted the same way on the original vote to determine merit and on the final vote.

1511 Ferguson, Edward, III. "State Bill of Rights, 1945–1955." Ph.D. dissertation, University of Illinois, 1960.

This study examines the existing differences in interpretation of the national Bill of Rights by state and federal courts. DAI 21:3506.

1512 Keele, Robert L. "The Supreme Court, Totalitarianism, and the National Security of Democratic America, 1941–1960." Ph.D. dissertation, Emory University, 1960.

On no occasion did the court manifest any inclination to curb the powers of the government on vital questions of security. The court sustained wartime invasions of property rights and investigations into subversion and legislation designed to cope with the threat of Communist infiltration. DAI 22:620.

1513 Kremm, Walter P. "Justice Holmes on Constitutionality and Evidence of His Influence Upon the Vinson Court, 1946–1949." Ph.D. dissertation, University of North Carolina, 1961.

The opinions of the justices of the Vinson court are examined in light of how closely they followed Holmes's opinions on matters of the existence of a constitutional issue, the presence of civil liberties or economic questions, and interpretations of both state and federal legislation. DAI 22:3721.

1514 McLaughlan, William P. "Research Note: Ideology and Conflict in Supreme Court Opinion Assignment, 1946–1962." *Western Political Quarterly* 25 (1972): 16–27.

The assignments of Chief Justices Vinson and Warren and Justices Black and Frankfurter are reviewed to see if assignment patterns existed and if they were related to individual ideologies. Tables, notes.

1515 Morgner, Fred. "Ultraconservative Response to Supreme Court Judicial Behavior: A Study in Political Alienation, 1935–1965." Ph.D. dissertation, University of Minnesota, 1970.

In 1937 the traditionally conservative court embarked upon a revolutionary reversal of priorities, embracing issues related to equality for minority groups, freedom of expression and association, and procedural safeguards of due process. This study traces the response of ultraconservatives to the court's behavior. DAI 32:363–A.

1516 Pritchett, C. Herman. *The Roosevelt Court: A Study in Judicial Politics and Values, 1937–1947.* New York: Quadrangle, 1948.

The topical chapters in this book focus on such themes as economic regulation, civil liberties, crime, and labor. As such it provides a fine background for understanding the court during the Truman years. Table of cases, index, notes.

1517 Schubert, Glendon A. *The Judicial Mind: The Attitudes and Ideologies of Supreme Court Justices, 1946–1963.* Evanston: Northwestern University Press, 1965.

This theoretical examination of ideological components employs statistical analysis rather than historical narrative to examine what stimuli affected Supreme Court justices. Footnotes, tables, index.

1518 Stern, Arthur. "The Influence of the Clear and Present Danger Formula on Constitutional Law." Ph.D. dissertation, University of Arizona, 1968.

The clear and present danger formula was applied in the Dennis case to curb First Amendment rights of Communists. This study discusses the origins of the formula and its application. DAI 29:656–A.

1519 Ulmer, S. Sidney. "Social Background as an Indicator to the Votes of Supreme Court Justices in Criminal Cases, 1947–1956 Terms." *American Journal of Political Science* 17 (1974): 622–30.

Author doubts that even an intimate knowledge of the social backgrounds of justices will permit precise prediction of decisions. Table, notes.

1520 Winkle, John W., III. "Judicial Statesmanship: Protagonists for Habeas Corpus Reform, 1948–73." Ph.D. dissertation, Duke University, 1974.

The intimacy between courts and politics is a recurrent theme of recent research in public law. This study examines a little-explored dimension of that relationship, namely, the actual participation by judges in the legislative process. DAI 35:5494–A.

SUPREME COURT JUSTICES

1521 Alfange, Dean, Jr. "The Role of the Supreme Court in the Protection of Freedom of Expression in the United States." Ph.D. dissertation, Cornell University, 1967.

Two conflicting doctrines dominated the court in First Amendment rights: the doctrine of constitutional absolutism associated with Justice Black and the doctrine of self-restraint associated with Justice Frankfurter. DAI 28:265–A.

1522 Atkinson, David N., and Neuman, Dale A. "Toward a Cost Theory of Judicial Alignments: The Case of the Truman Bloc." *Midwest Journal of Political Science* 11 (1969): 271–83.

Using the papers of Burton and Minton, the authors seek to develop a theory which "holds that voting behavior on the Supreme Court may be dependent on certain 'costs' which can be operationalized according to an index based on the size of voting coalitions within the Court." Notes, tables.

1523 Meek, Roy L. "Justices Douglas and Black: Political Liberalism and Judicial Activism." Ph.D. dissertation, University of Oregon, 1964.

The two justices share a basically similar orientation; however, Douglas more consistently supported the claims of individual freedom and political rights, while Black more often supports claims for public welfare and individual security. DAI 25:3086.

1524 Mendelson, Wallace. *Justices Black and Frankfurter: Conflict in the Court.* Chicago: University of Chicago Press, 1961.

Black and Frankfurter represent two differing traditions in American jurisprudence: activism versus judicial restraint. Mendelson examines the role of the court through these two justices. Notes, table of cases, index.

Hugo L. Black

1525 Berman, Daniel M. "The Political Philosophy of Hugo L. Black." Ph.D. dissertation, Rutgers University, 1957.

Black's view was that there is never any necessity to weigh the individual's interest in free expression against society's interest in security, for it is society which has the real stake in freedom. He was firm in his opposition to all the internal repressions of the Cold War years. DAI 17:2664.

1526 Beth, Loren P. "Mr. Justice Black and the First Amendment: Comments on the Dilemma of Constitutional Interpretation." *Journal of Politics* 41 (1979): 1105–24.

Black sought to define substantive due process within the limits set by the first eight amendments, to prevent judges from substituting their own policy preferences for those of the legislative or executive branch. Notes.

1527 Dunne, Gerald T. *Hugo Black and the Judicial Revolution.* New York: Simon & Schuster, 1977.

Black was an associate justice (1937–71). During the Truman era he voted to overturn the restrictions and penalties imposed on Communists and was a critic of loyalty oaths. Illustrations, notes, bibliography, index.

1528 Frank, John P. *Mr. Justice Black: The Man and His Opinions.* New York: Knopf, 1949.

Frank provides a brief biographical sketch and a collection of the opinions of Justice Black from his first ten years on the court. Index.

1529 Magee, James J. "Mr. Justice Black and the First Amendment: The Development and Dilemmas of an Absolutist." Ph.D. dissertation, University of Virginia, 1975.

The focus of this study is on Justice Black's absolutist construction of the First Amendment and his conception of free speech. DAI 36: 4735–A.

1530 Mauney, Connie P. "Mr. Justice Black and First Amendment Freedoms: A Study in Constitutional Interpretation." Ph.D. dissertation, University of Tennessee, 1975.

Justice Black promoted the ideal that the First Amendment was the keystone and foundation of free government. DAI 36:5516–A.

1531 Mendelson, Wallace. "Hugo Black and Judicial Discretion." *Political Science Quarterly* 85 (1970): 17–39.

Black chose to ignore judicial discretion, preferring to rely on vague absolutes. The author examines the seeming inconsistencies in Black's efforts to apply these absolutes. Notes.

1532 Strickland, Stephen P., ed. *Hugo Black and the Supreme Court*. Indianapolis: Bobbs-Merrill, 1967.

During the Truman era Black was a leading proponent on the court for civil liberties and civil rights. The essays focus on these and such topics as taxation and antitrust legislation. Notes, table of cases, index.

1533 Williams, Charlotte. *Hugo L. Black: A Study in the Judicial Process*. Baltimore: Johns Hopkins University Press, 1950.

This dated but useful survey examines Black's decisions from 1937 to 1949. Notes, index.

Harold H. Burton
1534 Atkinson, David N. "American Constitutionalism Under Stress: Mr. Justice Burton's Response to National Security Issues." *Houston Law Review* 9 (1971): 271–88.

The Vinson court generally, and Justice Burton specifically, sustained security precautions which, in retrospect, appear excessive. Notes.

1535 Kirkendall, Richard. "Harold Burton." In Leon Friedman and Fred L. Israel, eds. *The Justices of the U.S. Supreme Court, 1789–1969*. New York: Chelsea House, 1969, 4:2617–36.

As one of Truman's appointments, serving on the court from 1945 to 1958, Burton followed a policy of judicial restraint and supported the government in individual rights cases. Among the cases discussed are *Henderson* v. *United States* and *Beilan* v. *Board of Public Education*. Notes, index.

1536 Marquardt, Ronald G. "The Judicial Justice: Mr. Justice Burton and the Supreme Court." Ph.D. dissertation, University of Missouri, Columbia, 1973.

This account evaluates Harold H. Burton's contribution to the U.S. Supreme Court and suggests he contributed more than critics have given him credit for. DAI 34:7298–A.

Tom C. Clark
1537 Dorin, Dennis D. "Mr. Justice Clark and State Criminal Justice, 1949–1967." Ph.D. dissertation, University of Virginia, 1974.

Dorin examines the impact of Clark's "conceptualization of his role" upon his participation in the Supreme Court's formulation of policies in the field of state criminal justice. DAI 34:7832–A.

1538 Kirkendall, Richard. "Tom C. Clark." In L. Friedman and F. L. Israel, eds. *The Justices of the*

United States Supreme Court, 1789–1969. New York: Chelsea House, 1969, 4:2665–77.

Clark (1949–67) chose to emphasize the power of the government to safeguard the national security; consequently, "he brought the fears of the Cold War to the Supreme Court and helped to translate them into the law of the land." Bibliography.

1539 Warnock, Alvin T. "Associate Justice Tom C. Clark: Advocate of Judicial Reform." Ph.D. dissertation, University of Georgia, 1972.

This study focuses on Clark's interest in judicial reform, especially the elimination of court congestion. DAI 33:5260–A.

William O. Douglas
1540 Countryman, Vern. *The Judicial Record of Justice William O. Douglas*. Cambridge: Harvard University Press, 1974.

Douglas is best known as a leading proponent of civil liberties, frequently dissenting from the majority opinion in anti-Communist cases. Notes, table of cases, index.

1541 Douglas, William O. *The Court Years: The Autobiography of William O. Douglas*. New York: Random House, 1980.

Douglas, an associate justice of the Supreme Court (1939–75), was a staunch proponent of individual rights. Illustrations, list of cases, index.

1542 Frank, John P. "William O. Douglas." In Leon Friedman and Fred L. Israel, eds. *The Justices of the U.S. Supreme Court, 1789–1969*. New York: Chelsea House, 1969, 4:244–90.

Douglas was the court's foremost proponent of individual liberty and freedom of speech. Index, selected bibliography.

1543 Kennedy, Harry L., Jr. "Justice William O. Douglas on Freedom of the Press." Ph.D. dissertation, Ohio University, 1980.

Kennedy traces the development of the attitudes of Douglas toward freedom of the press as expressed in his Supreme Court opinions from 1939 to 1975. DAI 41:2265–A.

1544 "Mr. Justice William O. Douglas." *Columbia Law Review* 74 (1974): 341–411.

Douglas's positions and views on a wide range of topics are reviewed in this memorial issue. Notes.

1545 Pollock, Paul K. "Judicial Libertarianism and Judicial Responsibilities: The Case of Justice William O. Douglas." Ph.D. dissertation, Cornell University, 1968.

Pollock concludes that Douglas's judicial philosophy was deficient because it represented a denial of the three types of responsibility a judge must assume: personal, democratic, and institutional responsibility. DAI 29:4073–A.

Felix Frankfurter

1546 Baker, Liva. *Felix Frankfurter*. New York: Coward-McCann, 1969.

An associate justice during the Truman era, Frankfurter advocated judicial restraint and accepted much government action that infringed on civil liberties. Illustrations, notes, index.

1547 Kurland, Philip B. *Mr. Justice Frankfurter and the Constitution*. Chicago: University of Chicago Press, 1971.

Kurland offers excerpts from the justice's opinions on the court and the Constitution. The selections are arranged topically. Notes, index.

1548 McWilliams, Wilson C. "The Constitutional Doctrine of Mr. Justice Frankfurter." *Political Science Quarterly* 38 (1963): 92–98.

McWilliams believes that Frankfurter attempted to impose a constitutional doctrine quite alien to the American system, and that this imposition led to a serious contradiction in Frankfurter's own views. Notes.

1549 Mendelson, Wallace, ed. *Felix Frankfurter: The Judge*. New York: Reynal, 1964.

The essays examine Frankfurter's views on basic legal issues, such as labor and the law, administrative law, personal freedom, and federalism. Notes.

1550 Mendelson, Wallace, ed. *Felix Frankfurter: A Tribute*. New York: Reynal, 1964.

These essays constitute a tribute to the man, to his work as a justice of the Supreme Court, and to his influence on a generation. Notes.

1551 Phillips, Harlan B., ed. *Felix Frankfurter Reminisces*. New York: Reynal, 1960.

Frankfurter recorded his views and opinions concerning various topics in detailed conversations with the editor.

1552 Sacks, Albert M. "Felix Frankfurter." In Leon Friedman and Fred L. Israel, eds. *The Justices of the U.S. Supreme Court, 1789–1969*. New York: Chelsea House, 1969, 2401–43.

Frankfurter, associate justice (1939–62), was the court's foremost proponent of judicial restraint, which led him to accept much government infringement of civil liberties. Selected bibliography.

1553 Thomas, Helen S. *Felix Frankfurter: Scholar on the Bench*. Baltimore: Johns Hopkins University Press, 1960.

Thomas seeks to assess the techniques of legal interpretation by examining the decisions of Justice Frankfurter. Notes, index.

Robert H. Jackson

1554 Desmond, Charles S., et al. *Mr. Justice Jackson: Four Lectures in His Honor*. New York: Columbia University Press, 1969.

These essays focus on Jackson's views on individual rights, his influence on federal-state relations, and his contributions during the Nuremberg Trials. Notes.

1555 Gerhart, Eugene C. *America's Advocate: Robert H. Jackson*. New York: Bobbs-Merrill, 1958.

Jackson, an associate justice (1941–54) and U.S. chief of counsel at the Nuremberg War Crimes Trials, was considered to be somewhat right of center. Notes, illustrations, bibliography, index.

1556 Kurland, Philip B. "Robert H. Jackson." In Leon Friedman and Fred L. Israel, eds. *The Justices of the U.S. Supreme Court, 1789–1969*. New York: Chelsea House, 1969, 4:2543–90.

Jackson served on the court from 1941 to 1954 and was U.S. chief of counsel at the Nuremberg War Crimes Trials. Cases discussed include *Youngstown Sheet & Tube Co.* v. *Sawyer,* and *West Virginia State Board of Education* v. *Barnette*. Notes, index.

1557 Steamer, Robert J. "The Constitutional Doctrines of Mr. Justice Robert H. Jackson." Ph.D. dissertation, Cornell University, 1954.

Justice Jackson's overall judicial philosophy manifests primarily a concern for orderly government. The author finds him a zealous guardian of individual rights and a careful trustee of governmental power. DAI 14:2113.

Sherman H. Minton

1558 Atkinson, David N. "Justice Sherman Minton and the Balance of Liberty." *Indiana Law Journal* 50 (1974): 34–59.

Mixed reactions have followed Minton's voting on civil liberties issues. In most instances, if there were a clash between an individual and the government, he came down on the government's side. Notes.

1559 Atkinson, David N. "Mr. Justice Minton and the Supreme Court, 1949–1956." Ph.D. dissertation, University of Iowa, 1969.

Minton's term is closely examined to assess his performance and his voting patterns. DAI 30: 3031–A.

1560 Braden, George D. "Mr. Justice Minton and the Truman Bloc." *Indiana Law Journal* 26 (1951): 153–68.

The article assesses Justice Minton's first year on the Supreme Court, paying particular attention to the voting patterns of other Truman appointees. Notes.

1561 Hull, Elizabeth A. "Sherman Minton and the Cold War Court." Ph.D. dissertation, New School for Social Research, 1977.

Minton served as the court's "politician." By his encouragement of collective enterprises, and by his willingness to mediate, he contributed to the institution's stability. DAI 38:3699–A.

1562 Kirkendall, Richard. "Sherman Minton." In L. Friedman and F. L. Israel, eds. *The Justices of the United States Supreme Court, 1789–1969.* New York: Chelsea House, 1969, pp. 2699–2709.

Minton (1949–56) had been a militant New Dealer in the 1930s, but on the court he emerged as one of its most conservative members. He was not an outstanding justice. Bibliography.

Frank Murphy

1563 Frank, John P. "Frank Murphy." In L. Friedman and F. L. Israel, eds. *The Justices of the United States Supreme Court, 1789–1969.* New York: Chelsea House, 1969, pp. 2493–2506.

Murphy (1940–49) was the most consistent advocate of kindness, tolerance, and humanity on the bench. He voted against the procedures of the war crimes trials, opposed Truman's handling of the coal strike, and rejected the broadening of the right to search. He was in the minority in each case. Bibliography.

1564 Howard, J. Woodford, Jr. *Mr. Justice Murphy: A Political Biography.* Princeton, NJ: Princeton University Press, 1968.

Murphy, an associate justice (1940–49), emerged as the foremost civil libertarian on the bench during the postwar years. Illustrations, notes, index.

Stanley Reed

1565 O'Brien, F. William. *Justice Reed and the First Amendment: The Religion Clauses.* Washington, DC: Georgetown University Press, 1958.

Reed served on the court (1938–57) and adopted a center position on most issues but favored a narrow interpretation of the First Amendment clause barring the establishment of religion. Notes, bibliography, index.

1566 Pritchett, C. Herman. "Stanley Reed." In Leon Friedman and Fred L. Israel, eds. *The Justices of the United States Supreme Court, 1789–1969.* New York: Chelsea House, 1969, 2373–98.

Reed, an associate justice (1938–57), had one of the poorest records of support for civil liberties.

Wiley Rutledge

1567 Harper, Fowler V. *Justice Rutledge and the Bright Constellation.* Indianapolis: Bobbs-Merrill, 1965.

Rutledge, an associate justice (1943–49), was one of the foremost defenders of civil liberties. Illustrations, notes, appendix, index.

1568 Israel, Fred L. "Wiley Rutledge." In Leon Friedman and Fred L. Israel, eds. *The Justices of the U.S. Supreme Court, 1789–1969.* New York: Chelsea House, 1969, 4:2593–2613.

Rutledge served on the court (1943–49) and was one of the court's foremost defenders of civil liberties. Among the cases discussed is *Thomas* v. *Collins.* Notes, index.

Fred M. Vinson

1569 Bolner, James J. "Mr. Chief Justice Vinson: His Politics and His Constitutional Law." Ph.D. dissertation, University of Virginia, 1962.

Vinson made significant contributions in two areas: the narrow construction given constitutional guarantees concerning freedom of communication and association; and the broad construction given to Fourteenth Amendment rights, particularly in the area of racial equality. DAI 23:2970.

1570 Bolner, James. "Mr. Chief Justice Vinson and the Communist Controversy: A Reassessment." *Register of the Kentucky Historical Society* 66 (1968): 378–91.

Critics have charged that Vinson subverted the civil liberties work of Justices Holmes and Brandeis, but Bolner believes that they have failed to weigh fairly his literary shortcomings and failed to consider the weight of his arguments. Notes.

1571 Bolner, James. "Mr. Chief Justice Fred M. Vinson and Racial Discrimination." *Register of the Kentucky Historical Society* 64 (1966): 29–43.

The impact of Vinson on the constitutional problems of racial discrimination is examined. The author finds that Vinson acted with good sense and paved the way for the 1954 school desegregation cases. Notes.

1572 Grant, Philip A., Jr. "Press Reaction to the Appointment of Fred M. Vinson as Chief Justice of the United States." *Register of the Kentucky Historical Society* 75 (1977): 304–13.

Most of the press opinion summarized here on Vinson's appointment on 6 June 1946 was favorable, although some, notably the *New York Times* and *Chicago Tribune,* expressed some reservations. Notes.

1573 Kirkendall, Richard. "Fred M. Vinson." In L. Friedman and F. L. Israel, eds. *The Justices of the United States Supreme Court, 1789–1969.* New York: Chelsea House, 1969, pp. 2639–49.

Truman appointed Fred M. Vinson chief justice (1946–53). Vinson believed that the federal government required greater power to resolve the problems which confronted the nation, and his court usually granted these powers. Bibliography.

1574 Pritchett, C. Herman. *Civil Liberties and the Vinson Court*. Chicago: University of Chicago Press, 1954.

This book is especially valuable for its quantitative analysis. Tables. One of Vinson's most outspoken critics, Fred Rodell, discusses the chief justice in *Nine Men: A Political History of the Supreme Court from 1790 to 1955* (New York, 1955).

Foreign Affairs: Ending World War II and the Beginning of the Cold War

Truman's presidency witnessed the end of American isolationism as World War II and the Cold War permanently altered America's traditional role in global affairs. The administration's foreign policy debates and decisions, as well as its actions and reactions to events, gave shape and substance to America's Cold War posture. This chapter, together with Chapter 8, collects much of the literature dealing with American foreign affairs during the years from 1945 to 1953.

A basic bibliographical resource which supplements this volume is Richard Dean Burns, ed., *Guide to American Foreign Relations Since 1700* (#3023); it includes many additional items relating both to the ending of World War II and to the unfolding of the Cold War. A contemporary narrative, still very useful today, which chronicles issues and events during the Truman years is the Council on Foreign Relations' *United States in World Affairs* (#1576). The U.S. Senate's Committee on Foreign Relations collected and published *A Decade of American Foreign Policy: Basic Documents, 1941–49* (#1575) which provides ready access to many postwar treaties and policy statements.

Truman's role in ending World War II is related in Herbert Feis's traditionalist *Churchill, Roosevelt, Stalin: The War They Waged and the Peace They Sought* (#1706), and in Gabriel Kolko's revisionist *The World and United States Foreign Policy, 1943–1945* (#1709). Decisions made during the Yalta Conference by President Roosevelt, as detailed in Diane S. Clemens, *Yalta* (#1715), had a significant impact on Truman's initial efforts to formulate a policy toward the Soviet Union. Truman's attendance at the Potsdam Conference is reviewed in Herbert Feis, *Between*

War and Peace: The Potsdam Conference (#1724), and in Eduard M. Mark, " 'Today Has Been a Historical One': Harry S. Truman's Diary of the Potsdam Conference" (#1730).

Controversy still swirls around Truman's sanction of the use of atomic bombs against Japan. The basic issues considered in the decision to use the bombs are developed in Barton J. Bernstein, ed., *The Atomic Bomb: The Crucial Issues* (#1742); while the effects of the explosions are detailed in *Hiroshima and Nagasaki: The Physical, Medical, and Social Effects of the Atomic Bombings* (#1749).

Attempts to place the responsibility for starting the Cold War have prompted a vast outpouring of books and articles; unfortunately, too, many of these accounts reflect the ideological biases of their authors more than they illuminate how and why the Soviet-American conflict arose. No attempt has been made here to list all of the studies relating to the origins of the Cold War; however, historiographical and bibliographical information about these various "schools of interpretation" may be found in the footnotes of John L. Gaddis, "The Emerging Post-Revisionist Synthesis on the Origins of the Cold War" (#1796), and in the initial chapter of Geir Lundestad, *The American Non-Policy Towards Eastern Europe* (#2641). Additional information may be secured in Chapter 11, The Cold War, which lists other review essays.

A representative sampling of different interpretations on the origins of the Cold War may be found in James V. Compton, ed., *America and the Origins of the Cold War* (#1790). Other useful introductory accounts, employing varying interpretations, include John L. Gaddis, *The United States and the*

Prime Minister Churchill, President Truman, and Marshal Stalin at Potsdam, July 1945. *US Navy photo*.

Origins of the Cold War, 1941–1947 (#1797), Thomas G. Paterson, *Soviet-American Confrontation: Postwar Reconstruction and the Origins of the Cold War* (#1822), and Daniel Yergin, *Shattered Peace: The Origins of the Cold War and the National Security State* (#1831).

Many of the specific episodes of the early Cold War years are listed in Chapter 8 under the countries involved; for example, the Greek civil war and American aid to that country are listed under Greece, and the Berlin blockade is listed under Germany. The more thematic episodes are included here; for example, John Gimbel, *The Origins of the Marshall Plan* (#1894), and A. K. Henrikson, "The Creation of the North Atlantic Alliance, 1948–1952" (#1915) are useful introductions to the Marshall Plan and NATO.

Other works which introduce significant topics include Thomas M. Campbell, *Masquerade Peace: America's UN Policy, 1944–1945* (#1990). Alfred E. Eckes, Jr., *A Search for Solvency: Bretton Woods and the International Monetary System, 1941–1971* (#1936), and R. N. Gardner, *Sterling-Dollar Diplomacy* (#1938) provide introductions to international economic issues.

Foreign Affairs: General

See especially R. D. Burns, ed. *Guide to American Foreign Relations Since 1700* (#3023) for more references to issues in U.S. foreign affairs during the Truman years.

1574a U.S. Department of State. *Foreign Relations of the United States*. Washington, DC: G.P.O., 1861–.

Volumes for the years 1945–52—most of which have been published—contain correspondence, notes, memoranda, documents, etc., produced during one calendar year. Each volume relates to a specific geographical area or topical theme. This is an exceptionally valuable source of basic data dealing with U.S. foreign affairs. The researcher should be aware that many documents, still classified, have been excluded.

1575 U.S. Senate. Committee on Foreign Relations. *A Decade of American Foreign Policy: Basic Documents, 1941–49*. Senate Doc. 123. 81st Cong., 1st sess., 1950.

This is an exceptionally useful collection of addresses, treaties, agreements, and other documents. It is organized topically. Index.

1576 *The United States in World Affairs, 1931–*. New York: Simon & Schuster, 1932–.

The volumes for 1945 through 1953 provide an indispensable annual survey of events in American foreign affairs and provide a solid introduction for beginning researchers. Each volume has a chronology and bibliography.

GENERAL ACCOUNTS

1577 Beal, Richard S. "Systems Analysis of International Crises: Event Analysis of Nine Pre-Crisis Threat Situations, 1948–1962." Ph.D. dissertation, University of Southern California, 1977.

Two of nine precrises tested here include the Berlin blockade (1948) and the outbreak of the Korean War (1950). DAI 38:1634-A.

1578 Beugel, Ernst H. van der. "From Marshall Aid to Atlantic Partnership." *Atlantic Community Quarterly* 41 (1966): 5–16.

The concluding chapter of van der Beugel's book, *From Marshall Aid to Atlantic Partnership* (New York: American Elsevier, 1966) is reprinted here. It presents a European view of the Truman administration's emerging Cold War policies.

1579 Gamble, John K., Jr. "Multilateral Treaties: Patterns and Trends from 1945–1965." Ph.D. dissertation, University of Washington, 1971.

This study provides a comprehensive view of global multilateral treatymaking. Some 524 such treaties came into force from 1945 to 1965, and for each 158 characteristics were chosen. DAI 32:4682-A.

1580 Gilbert, Amy M. *Executive Agreements and Treaties, 1946–1973: Framework of the Foreign Policy of the Period*. Endicott, NY: Thomas-Newell, 1973.

Executive agreements have outstripped treaties as the dominant mode of foreign policy. Gilbert examines these agreements and attempts to show how they shaped the foreign policy. Notes, bibliography, index.

1581 Morris, Richard B., ed. *Great Presidential Decisions: State Papers that Changed the Course of History*. Philadelphia: Lippincott, 1960.

Chapter 32, "The Decision to Contain Soviet Expansion: Truman Enunciates a New Doctrine," and Chapter 33, "The Decision to Resist the Communist Invasion of Korea: Truman's Announcement that the United States Would Aid the Korean Republic," pertain to the Truman administration. A discussion of the issue and the text of the president's address is included.

1582 Ninkovich, Frank. "The Currents of Cultural Diplomacy: Art and the State Department, 1938–1947." *Diplomatic History* 1 (1977): 215–37.

After World War Two, the State Department purchased examples of modern art from several galleries and exhibited them around the world. This display of avant-garde forms caused considerable congressional protest. Notes.

1583 Ninkovich, Frank A. *The Diplomacy of Ideas: U.S. Foreign Policy and Cultural Relations, 1938–1950.* Cambridge: Cambridge University Press, 1981.

While the State Department's programs in cultural relations have been minor relative to other programs, the author finds that the "study of the cultural programs can illuminate suggestively some of the connections between foreign policy ideas and their social underpinnings." Notes, bibliography, index.

1584 Quade, Quentin L. "A Second Dimension of Leadership: The Truman Administration in Foreign Policy." Ph.D. dissertation, University of Notre Dame, 1965.

Analyzed here are the Truman administration's efforts to gather congressional and public support for two of its most significant proposals of the foreign policy field: the Greek-Turkish Aid Program of 1947 and the European Recovery Act of 1948.

1585 Rosenberg, Jerry P. "Berlin and Israel, 1948: Foreign Policy Decision-Making during the Truman Administration." Ph.D. dissertation, University of Illinois, Urbana, 1977.

The findings of this study support the hypothesis that a decision-maker's belief is the crucial variable in the decision-making process. DAI 38: 6301-A.

1586 Rostow, Walt W. *The United States in the World Arena.* New York: Harper, 1960.

Rostow looks at such issues as: "How has the nature and evolution of our life at home affected the nation's military and foreign policy performance, notably over the past quarter-century. . . ." Index.

1587 Secrest, Donald E. "American Policy Toward Neutralism During the Truman and Eisenhower Administrations." Ph.D. dissertation, University of Michigan, 1967.

Executive policy toward neutralism was never cordial during the period examined; however, American policymakers were tolerant of the nonaligned position of the neutralist states. DAI 28:5129-A.

1588 Smith, H. Lafollette. "The Reconciliation of Energy and Objectives: A Study of Three Cases in American Foreign Policy." Ph.D. dissertation, Emory University, 1958.

"National interest" as used in the analysis of international relations is studied by examining the Berlin blockade (1948) and the Korean crisis (1950). DAI 19:2643.

1589 Stebbins, Phillip E. "A History of the Role of the United States Supreme Court in Foreign Policy." Ph.D. dissertation, Ohio State University, 1966.

The court has been reluctant to pass upon questions involving American foreign policy; however, the court has justified the expansion of the executive power over the legislative. DAI 27:2125.

1590 Welles, Sumner. *Seven Decisions that Shaped History.* New York: Harper, 1951.

Welles briefly criticizes Truman's early foreign policies (see Chapter 8). Index.

1591 Welles, Sumner. *Where Are We Heading?* New York: Harper, 1946.

Former State Department official Sumner Welles offers his analysis and policy recommendations for the immediate postwar years. Index.

1592 White, Donald W. " 'The American Century': The History of an Idea, 1941–1971." Ph.D. dissertation, New York University, 1979.

Proclaimed in the 1940s, the "American Century" was widely used by both liberals and conservatives to explain the uses of national power. Misrepresentations of the American Century reflected the bias of an ethnocentric view of the world. DAI 40:5984-A.

1593 Williams, William Appleman. *Empire as a Way of Life: An Essay on the Causes and Character of America's Present Predicament Along With a Few Thoughts About an Alternative.* New York: Oxford University Press, 1980.

U.S. postwar policy was not merely to check the Soviets, but to foster a fundamental change in the nature of their system.

1594 Williams, William Appleman. *The Tragedy of American Diplomacy.* 2d rev. ed. New York: Dell, 1972.

Williams finds the origins of the Cold War (pp. 224–75) in America's desire to develop and control new markets around the world. He argues that Truman was "an enthusiastic and militant advocate of America's supremacy in the world" and that Truman believed that the Soviets could be forced to accept the American postwar proposals without recourse to war. Notes.

TRUMAN AND FOREIGN AFFAIRS

See also Chapter 1, *Autobiographical and Biographical Materials*, and Chapter 2, *Truman Presidency*, for much more on this theme.

1595 Bullard, Anthony R. "Harry S. Truman and the Separation of Powers in Foreign Affairs." Ph.D. dissertation, Columbia University, 1972.

Truman's views of his constitutional powers were integrated within the separation of powers doctrine. He felt he should jealously guard executive powers from any legislative encroachment. DAI 34:388-A.

1596 Clifford, J. Garry. "President Truman and Peter the Great's Will." *Diplomatic History* 4 (1980): 371–85.

Clifford suggests that Truman's attempts to use history's lessons may have led him to accept the validity of the forged political will of Peter the Great which purported to contain a blueprint for Russian domination of the world. Notes.

1597 Druks, Herbert. "Dealing With the Russians: The Truman Experience." *East Europe* 20 (1971): 2–8.

Described here is how Truman put aside the isolationist tradition and stood up to Soviet aggression in Central Europe, Asia, and the Middle East, thereby saving the peace.

1598 Heim, Keith M. "Hope Without Power: Truman and the Russians." Ph.D. dissertation, University of North Carolina, Chapel Hill, 1973.

Heim examines Truman's search for advice on how to deal with the Soviets from "hard-liners" like Harriman to more even-handed advisers. When Truman left Potsdam, however, he was convinced that cooperation with the Russians was impossible. DAI 35:366-A.

1599 Heinrichs, Waldo. "Roosevelt and Truman: The Presidential Perspective." In Dorothy Borg and Waldo Heinrichs, eds. *Uncertain Years: Chinese-American Relations, 1947–1950.* New York: Columbia University Press, 1980, pp. 3–12.

This essay discusses Roosevelt's postwar plans, Truman's early Cold War policies, assistance to Chiang Kai-shek, and the Marshall mission.

1600 Hensley, Carl W. "Harry S. Truman: Fundamental Americanism in Foreign Policy Speechmaking, 1945–1946." *Southern Speech Communication* 40 (1975): 180–90.

Truman built his foreign policy on the traditional American dream. This policy, as revealed in his early speeches, is vital to understanding the rhetoric of the Cold War years. Notes.

1601 Hoffecker, Carol E. "President Truman's Explanation of His Foreign Policy to the American People." Ph.D. dissertation, Harvard University, 1967.

This study examines President Truman's role as the principal spokesman for his administration's foreign policy.

1602 Miscamble, Wilson D. "The Evolution of an Internationalist: Harry S. Truman and American Foreign Policy." *Australian Journal of Politics and History* [Australia] 23 (1977): 268–83.

Truman's foreign policy ideas are traced to his experiences in World War I, to his reading of military history, and to his middle political career, 1935–45. The views he espoused as president evolved from the previous decade. Notes.

1603 O'Connor, Raymond G. "Truman: New Powers in Foreign Policy." *Australian Journal of Politics and History* 25 (1979): 319–26.

Truman added greatly to the authority of the presidency in international affairs. Essentially, this new role developed as the roles of nuclear weapons, military forces, alliances, and intelligence operations expanded. Notes.

1604 Robinson, Edgar E., et al. *Powers of the President in Foreign Affairs, 1945–1965.* San Francisco: The Commonwealth Club of California, 1966.

Chapter 2, "Harry S. Truman: New Dimensions of Power," by Raymond G. O'Connor analyzes the Truman presidency. Notes, bibliography, index.

1605 Rosenberg, J. Philip. "The Belief System of Harry S. Truman and Its Effect on Foreign Policy Decisionmaking during his Administration." *Presidential Studies Quarterly* 12 (1982): 226–38.

By focusing on the recognition of Israel and the Berlin blockade, Rosenberg studies Truman's belief system and its impact on policy. Tables, notes.

1606 Schmidt, Terry P. "An Image Analysis of International Politics: Harry S. Truman and the Soviet Union, 1945–1947." Ph.D. dissertation, University of Denver, 1977.

The author focuses on Truman to discover whether his personal views were antagonistic toward the Soviet Union, or whether Stalin's actions prompted the Truman Doctrine. DAI 38:1639-A.

1607 Siegel, Howard B. "Strengths and Limitations of Informal Resources for Presidential Influence on Foreign Policy Legislation: The Truman Years." Ph.D. dissertation, Brown University, 1978.

Using the Marshall Plan and Universal Military Training as case studies, the author seeks to examine the utility of informal resources in assisting a president in developing and implementing foreign policy legislation. DAI 39:6320-A.

1608 Sorenson, Dale. "The Language of a Cold Warrior: A Content Analysis of Harry Truman's Public Statements." *Social Science History* 3 (1979): 171–86.

Content analysis reveals little change in the rhetoric of Truman's public statements concerning the Soviet Union and domestic communism during 1945 through 1950. This finding questions the revisionist theory that Truman's rhetoric played a major role in increasing the Red Scare. Graphs, notes.

DIPLOMATS AND PRESIDENTIAL ADVISERS

See also Chapter 3, *Diplomats*, for additional references to specific individuals.

1609   Clamporcero, Alan F. "The State-War-Navy Coordinating Committee and the Beginning of the Cold War." Ph.D. dissertation, State University of New York, Albany, 1980.

East Asian issues played as significant a role in the postwar conflicts as did Eastern Europe. The author believes that the SWNCC dominated foreign policymaking and that it severely handicapped Secretary of State Byrnes's efforts. DAI 41:4828.

1610   Conway, John S. "Myron C. Taylor's Mission to the Vatican, 1940–1950." *Church History* 44 (1975): 85–99.

Taylor was the personal representative of Roosevelt and Truman to Pope Pius XII. Since Congress refused to establish a formal mission at the Vatican, his task was to provide a link between the papacy and Washington. Notes.

1611   Conway, Maurice B. "The Intellectual Origins of the Cold War." Ph.D. dissertation, University of California, Santa Barbara, 1974.

This study examines the social, intellectual, and historical origins of some fifty important American foreign policymakers who served under Roosevelt and Truman (1933–45). The author focuses on the views of the Soviet Union held by these individuals. DAI 36:6239-A.

1612   DeSantis, Hugh. "Conflicting Images of the USSR: American Career Diplomats and the Balkans, 1944–1946." *Political Science Quarterly* 94 (1979): 475–94.

The period 1944 to 1946 was a watershed during which American Foreign Service officers began to overcome their negative views of the U.S.S.R. based on previous Soviet behavior. Their new-found admiration for the U.S.S.R.'s war efforts (1944–45) reversed itself, however, with the Soviets' rude behavior in the Balkans at the war's end. Notes.

1613   DeSantis, Hugh. *The Diplomacy of Silence: The American Foreign Service, the Soviet Union and the Cold War, 1933–1947.* Chicago: University of Chicago Press, 1980.

This volume defines the different images of the Soviet Union held by American Foreign Service officers: ideological cooperation; ideological confrontation; or realistic cooperation. Notes, bibliography, index.

1614   Donovan, John C. *The Cold Warriors: A Policy-Making Elite.* Lexington, MA: Heath, 1974.

This synthesis of printed memoirs and analytical studies focuses on the impact of the atomic bomb on the Soviets in 1945, the emergence of the containment doctrine, and the development of NSC-68. Notes, index.

1615   Gardner, Lloyd C. *Architects of Illusion: Men and Ideas in American Foreign Policy, 1941–1949.* Chicago: Quadrangle, 1970.

U.S. actions during the war, such as the decision to rely upon the "bomb," were major influences in the Cold War that developed. This book examines the influences on key American policymakers as the Cold War began and developed to 1949. Notes, bibliographical essay, index.

1616   Handelman, James M. "The Secretary of State's Images of the World Arena: The Influence of Personality and Situational Factors." Ph.D. dissertation, University of Michigan, 1973.

This study consists of a content analysis of the public statements of U.S. secretaries of state (1946–70) to determine their view of world politics. DAI 34:1997-A.

1617   Harrington, Daniel F. "Kennan, Bohlen, and the Riga Axioms." *Diplomatic History* 2 (1978): 423–37.

This review essay of D. H. Yergin's *Shattered Peace* (1977) questions the author's assertion that George F. Kennan and Charles E. Bohlen were responsible for the hard-liners' triumph within the State Department. Neither Kennan nor Bohlen enjoyed much influence after 1950, and neither subscribed to the hard-liners' extreme positions. Notes.

1618   Lairson, Thomas D. "Decision-making in Groups: Social Paradigms and Postwar American Foreign Policy." Ph.D. dissertation, University of Kentucky, 1980.

Using eight cases in postwar American foreign policy, drawn from 1944 to 1947 and 1961 to 1965, Lairson examines the way decision-makers interact and communicate and its relationship to how well a foreign policy paradigm is being formulated and institutionalized. DAI 41:795.

1619   Newcomer, James B. "Acheson, Dulles, and Rusk: Information, Coherence, and Organization in the Department of State." Ph.D. dissertation, Stanford University, 1976.

While under Acheson the system worked reasonably well, the new changes brought on by Dulles introduced an incoherence in information and organization that exists today. DAI 36:8276-A.

1620 Miscamble, Wilson D. "George F. Kennan: The Policy Planning Staff and American Foreign Policy, 1947–1950." Ph.D. dissertation, University of Notre Dame, 1980.

This study focuses on the U.S. response to Soviet antagonism by examining the major elements of U.S. policy: the Marshall Plan, the North Atlantic Treaty, the division of Germany, and the development of the hydrogen bomb. DAI 41:370-A.

1621 Poole, Walter S. "From Conciliation to Containment: The Joint Chiefs of Staff and the Coming of the Cold War, 1945–1946." *Military Affairs* 42 (1978): 12–16.

The Joint Chiefs completely changed their view of the Soviet Union between 1944 and 1946, from a role of mediating Anglo-Russian disputes to the stopping of Soviet aggression. Notes.

1622 Pratt, James W. "Leadership Relations in United States Foreign Policy-Making: Case Studies, 1947–1950." Ph.D. dissertation, Columbia University, 1963.

This study focuses on the behavior of leaders in the executive and legislative branches in formulating foreign policy: the Greek-Turkish assistance program (1947), the post-UNRRA relief program (1947), the interim aid program (1947), Marshall Plan (1948), MDAP (1949), and NATO (1949). DAI 25:1307.

1623 Ruddy, T. Michael. "Realist versus Realist: Bohlen, Kennan and the Inception of the Cold War." *Midwest Quarterly* 17 (1976): 122–41.

While the two men held similar views, Kennan "was a theorist and a pessimist" and Bohlen "was an optimist and a man of action." The author believes that Bohlen's influence was the more enduring. Bibliography, notes.

1624 Yurechko, John J. "From Containment to Counteroffensive: Soviet Vulnerabilities and American Foreign Policy Planning, 1946–1953." Ph.D. dissertation, University of California, Berkeley, 1980.

George Kennan formulated two basic assumptions about the Soviet Union—that the Soviet Union was expansionist and that it was vulnerable. Yurechko concentrates on the conduct of the Soviet-American confrontation. DAI 41:3687-A.

NATIONAL SECURITY COUNCIL

1625 Falk, Stanley L. "The National Security Council Under Truman, Eisenhower, and Kennedy." *Political Science Quarterly* 79 (1964): 403–34.

Truman appeared to limit the role of the NSC in policy-forming and integration, while tailoring it to his preference for a strong executive. Notes.

1626 Fischer, John. "Mr. Truman's Politburo." *Harpers* 202 (June 1951): 29–36.

The author surveys the procedures and problems of Truman's National Security Council.

1627 Johnson, Robert H. "The National Security Council: The Relevance of Its Past To Its Future." *Orbis* 13 (1969): 709–35.

This review focuses on how Presidents Truman to Nixon have used the NSC and concludes that the council conforms to the desires of the president in power. Notes.

1628 May, Ernest R. "The Development of Political-Military Consultation in the United States." *Political Science Quarterly* 70 (1955): 161–80.

May's essay traces the development of consultation techniques from 1896 to Truman's establishment of the National Security Council. Notes.

1629 Reichart, John F. "National Security Advice to the President: A Comparative Case Study Analysis of the Structural Variable in Decision-Making." Ph.D. dissertation, Ohio State University, 1979.

Good advice is seen as advice formulated in the presence of seven process criteria. Twenty-two decisions were examined from the administrations of Truman, Eisenhower, Kennedy, Johnson, and Nixon. DAI 40:2253-A.

1630 Sander, Alfred D. "Truman and the National Security Council, 1945–1947." *Journal of American History* 59 (1972): 369–88.

Truman saw the council as a possible encroachment on his powers and as giving undue military weight in decision-making. After the establishment of the NSC in 1947, Truman attended few meetings until the Korean War. Notes.

NSC-68

The text of NSC-68 may be found in *Foreign Relations of the United States: 1951*, 1:237–92; *Naval War College Review* 27 (1975): 51–108; and T. H. Etzold and J. L. Gaddis, *Containment; Documents on American Policy and Strategy*, 1945–1950 (#1853).

1631 Block, Fred. "Economic Instability and Military Strength: The Paradoxes of the 1950 Rearmament Decision." *Politics and Society* 10 (1980): 35–58.

This analysis of the militarization of American foreign policy focuses on National Security Council document #68. NSC-68 supposedly argued that the creation of an international capitalist economic order could be met by increased defense spending. Notes.

1632 Hammond, Paul Y. "NSC-68: Prologue to Rearmament." In Warner Schilling, Paul Hammond, and Glenn Snyder. *Strategy, Politics and Defense Budgets*. New York: Columbia University Press, 1962, pp. 267–378.

Hammond's essay was the first attempt to examine this document. It remains a useful introductory account but must be supplemented with more recent accounts.

1633 Postbrief, Sam. "Departure from Incrementalism in U.S. Strategic Planning: The Origins of NSC-68." *Naval War College Review* 33 (1980): 34–57.

Using recently declassified documents and other materials, the essay reexamines the Truman administration's national security planning apparatus. Notes.

1634 Siracusa, Joseph M. "NSC 68: A Reappraisal." *Naval War College Review* 33 (1980): 4–14.

This review of the Truman administration's decisions on foreign policy suggests that the 1948 Berlin blockade triggered the decisions summarized in NSC-68 rather than the Korean conflict. Notes.

1635 Wells, Samuel F., Jr. "Sounding the Tocsin: NSC 68 and the Soviet Threat." *International Security* 4 (1979): 116–58.

The assumptions behind NSC-68 are examined in this thorough review. John Lewis Gaddis and Paul Nitze respond in ibid., 4 (1980): 164–76. Notes.

CONGRESS AND FOREIGN AFFAIRS

See also Chapter 3, *Congressional and Political Leaders*, for additional information.

1636 Andrew, Jean D. "The Effect of Senate Foreign Relations Committee Membership in Terms of Support of Foreign Policy, 1946–1966." Ph.D. dissertation, University of Connecticut, 1968.

When taken as a whole for the entire period, no significant change was observed; however, between 1946 and 1956 there was a committee effect, reflecting a measure of bipartisanship. DAI 29:2762-A.

1637 Farnsworth, David N. *The Senate Committee on Foreign Relations*. Urbana: University of Illinois Press, 1961.

This study covers the role of the Senate Committee on Foreign Relations from 1947 to 1956. Notes, bibliography, index.

1638 Graham, Charles J. "Republican Foreign Policy, 1939–1952." Ph.D. dissertation, University of Illinois, 1955.

This account examines the shift in Republican party foreign policy from isolationism to internationalism. Bipartisanship, as practiced by Senator Arthur Vandenberg, is also dealt with. DAI 16:368.

1639 Grimmett, Richard F. "The Politics of Containment: The President, the Senate, and American Foreign Policy, 1947–1956." Ph.D. dissertation, Kent State University, 1973.

This study focuses on the political interaction between the Senate and Presidents Truman and Eisenhower to illustrate the impact of domestic politics on foreign policy. DAI 34:4153-A.

1640 Jewell, Malcolm E. "The Role of Political Parties in the Formation of Foreign Policy in the Senate, 1947–1956." Ph.D. dissertation, Pennsylvania State University, 1958.

The president who can increase senatorial support for his foreign policy through bipartisan consultation, private appeals, and public statements is an important influence on voting in the Senate. DAI 19:1432.

1641 Johnson, Loch, and McCormick, James M. "Foreign Policy by Executive Fiat." *Foreign Policy* (1977): 117–38.

Legislation (1946–77) drafted to enhance congressional involvement with respect to treaties and executive powers in foreign affairs is reviewed.

1642 Ogul, Morris S. "Reforming Executive-Legislative Relations in the Conduct of American Foreign Policy: The Executive-Legislative Council as a Proposed Solution." Ph.D. dissertation, University of Michigan, 1958.

This study attempts to evaluate the idea of an executive-legislative council as a proposal to reform the conduct of American foreign policy. DAI 19:860.

1643 Robinson, James A. *Congress and Foreign Policy-Making: A Study in Legislative Influence and Initiative*. rev. ed. Homewood, IL: Dorsey, 1967.

Robinson sees Congress as legitimizing or amending recommendations (1933–61) made by the executive. Notes, bibliography, index.

1644 Rosenau, James N. "The Senate and Dean Acheson: A Case Study in Legislative Attitudes." Ph.D. dissertation, Princeton University, 1957.

Rosenau rejects the premise that members of Congress are necessarily hostile to the secretary of state by analyzing the *Congressional Record* for attitudes toward Acheson (1949–52). DAI 18:277.

1645 Rourke, John T. "Congress and the Cold War: Congressional Influences on the Foreign Policy Process." Ph.D. dissertation, University of Connecticut, 1975.

This study focuses on congressional efforts (1945–48) to influence the executive branch. DAI 35:7987-A.

1646 Sellen, Albert R. "Congressional Opinion of Soviet-American Relations, 1945–1950." Ph.D. dissertation, University of Chicago, 1954.

Sellen investigates the opinions of U.S. senators and representatives toward Soviet-American relations individually, by groups, and collectively as a legislative body.

1647 Vardys, Vytas S. "Select Committees of Congress in Foreign Relations: A Case Study in Legislative Process." Ph.D. dissertation, University of Wisconsin, 1958.

Three select committees were chosen for this study, two of them in the Truman years—the Select Committee on Foreign Aid (Eightieth Congress), and the Select Committee to Conduct an Investigation of . . . the Katyn Forest Massacre (Eighty-second Congress). DAI 18:2192.

1648 Westerfield, H. Bradford. *Foreign Policy and Party Politics; Pearl Harbor to Korea.* New Haven: Yale University Press, 1955.

Foreign policy is less subject to partisanship because policy needs to appear consistent, must be flexible, and requires that the United States appears united. Notes, bibliography, index.

Bipartisanship

1649 Berger, Henry W. "Bipartisanship, Senator Taft, and the Truman Administration." *Political Science Quarterly* 90 (1975): 221–37.

The notion of "bipartisanship" in foreign policy emerged after World War II. Taft refused to acknowledge that his disagreements with certain of the Truman administration's foreign policies constituted a violation of the spirit of bipartisanship.

1650 Kepley, David R. "Challenges to Bipartisanship: Senate Republicans and American Foreign Policy, 1948–1952." Ph.D. dissertation, University of Maryland, 1979.

In 1949 and 1950 bipartisanship received a series of jolts that weakened it—the defeat of Thomas Dewey (1948) for "me tooism" and the fall of China. In 1952, infused with McCarthyism, the forces headed by Senator Robert A. Taft attacked the administration's East Asian policies. DAI 40:6393-A.

1651 Padgett, Edward R. "The Role of the Minority Party in Bipartisan Foreign Policy Formulation in the United States, 1945–1955." Ph.D. dissertation, University of Maryland, 1957.

Bipartisanship resulted in a centrist coalition, but many critics feel that this creates a sense of harmony at the expense of full debate of major issues.

Others believe that it created a national foreign policy. DAI 18:638.

1652 Silverman, Sheldon A. "At the Water's Edge: Arthur Vandenberg and the Foundation of American Bipartisan Foreign Policy." Ph.D. dissertation, University of California, Los Angeles, 1967.

Bipartisanship developed during the war, centering around plans for a U.N. organization and around challenges to Russian domination of Eastern Europe. This study concentrates on the role of Vandenberg during the war. DAI 28:2189-A.

Congressional Opposition

1653 Atwell, Mary W. "Congressional Opponents of Early Cold War Legislation." Ph.D. dissertation, St. Louis University, 1973.

Although Truman's major Cold War programs passed Congress by large margins, approximately one-third of the members of each house opposed them. The opponents remained outside the Cold War consensus for philosophical rather than partisan reasons. DAI 35:2888-A.

1654 Bryniarski, Joan L. "Against the Tide: Senate Opposition to the Internationalist Foreign Policy of Presidents Franklin D. Roosevelt and Harry S. Truman, 1943–1959." Ph.D. dissertation, University of Maryland, 1972.

The majority of the dissenting senators were Middle Western Republicans who represented rural citizens that believed a foreign policy involving economic and military aid to Western Europe brought them no direct benefit. DAI 34:241-A.

1655 Philipose, Thomas. "The 'Loyal Opposition': Republican Leaders and Foreign Policy, 1943–1946." Ph.D. dissertation, University of Denver, 1972.

American foreign policy went through a revolutionary transformation during these years as the policy of noninvolvement abroad was abandoned and the principle of collective security, envisioned in American U.N. membership, was accepted. A prominent feature of this transformation was the support of Republican leaders. DAI 33:3552-A.

PUBLIC OPINION AND FOREIGN AFFAIRS

See also Chapter 6, *Political Affairs*, for additional references.

1656 Cutler, Neal E. "Generational Succession As a Source of Foreign Policy Attitudes: A Cohort Analysis of American Opinion, 1946–1966." *Journal of Peace Research* [Norway] 7 (1970): 33–48.

In general the data support the image of older generations of the Truman years being somewhat isolationist, while the more recent generations support broader engagement with the outside world. This essay is probably more useful for the statistically inclined.

1657 Lefever, Ernest W. *Ethics and United States Foreign Policy*. New York: Meridian, 1957.

Lefever attempts to assess the role of Judeo-Christian values in the development of American foreign policy. Bibliography.

1658 Melosi, Martin V. *The Shadow of Pearl Harbor: Political Controversy over the Surprise Attack, 1941–1946*. College Station: Texas A & M University Press, 1977.

The controversy existed over responsibility for America's military defeat at Pearl Harbor (1941–46). Truman became caught up in it when Congress decided in mid-1946 to hold a public investigation. Notes, bibliography, index.

1659 Paterson, Thomas G. "Presidential Foreign Policy, Public Opinion, and Congress: The Truman Years." *Diplomatic History* 3 (1979): 1–18.

Paterson argues that, as Congress and public opinion were malleable, Truman successfully freed himself on several occasions from political and constitutional restraints to carry on with his foreign policy preferences. Notes.

1660 Poole, Walter S. "The Quest for a Republican Foreign Policy, 1941–1951." Ph.D. dissertation, University of Pennsylvania, 1968.

Three quite different policy alternatives appeared: Taft's policy of the free hand, Vandenberg's bipartisanship, and Dulles's policy of boldness. This study also examines the revisionists' critiques of Republican policies. DAI 29:2192.

1661 Roark, James L. "American Black Leaders: The Response To Colonialism and the Cold War, 1943–1953." *African Historical Studies* 4 (1971): 253–70.

The failure of the United Nations to support colonial independence led to strong panracial and anticolonial sentiment among American blacks. In 1947, however, most black leaders began to support rather than criticize such programs as the Marshall Plan and NATO. Notes.

1662 Roberds, Elmo. "The South and the United States Foreign Policy, 1933–1952." Ph.D. dissertation, University of Chicago, 1954.

Roberds examines the role played by the South in the formulation of American foreign policy (1933–52).

1663 Robinson, Donald L. "Editorials of American Purpose: A Content Analysis of Selected Newspaper Editorials Concerning International Relations." Ph.D. dissertation, American University, 1963.

Following the war, editorials focused on Western Europe, shifting to Asia in the 1950s. Key words (1945–62) were the Cold War, Communist world, and *isms*. DAI 24:3406.

1664 Rothbard, Murray N. "The Foreign Policy of the Old Right." *Journal of Libertarian Studies* 2 (1978): 85–96.

The "Old Right" (a group of conservatives originally united by their dissatisfaction with New Deal domestic and foreign policies) steadfastly opposed intervention in World War II and Korea (1930s–52).

Anticommunism and Cold War

1665 Adler, Leslie K. "The Red Image: American Attitudes Toward Communism in the Cold War Era." Ph.D. dissertation, University of California, Berkeley, 1970.

During the postwar era, the "red image" provided Americans with an antitotalitarian, non-Communist definition of themselves, and a means of avoiding the anxiety bred by rapid technological and social change. DAI 31:5309-A.

1666 Adler, Leslie K., and Paterson, Thomas G. "Red Fascism: The Merger of Nazi Germany and Soviet Russia in the American Image of Totalitarianism, 1930s–1950s." *American Historical Review* 75 (1970): 1046–64.

During the 1930s, many Americans focused on the similarities between Nazi Germany and Soviet Russia, an analogy which reappeared in the late 1940s and 1950s. The analogy suggested that Russia, like Germany, would employ its military prowess to sweep over Europe. Notes.

1667 Beck, Kent M. "American Liberalism and the Cold War Consensus: Policies and Policymakers of the Moderate Democratic Left, 1945–1953." Ph.D. dissertation, University of California, Irvine, 1976.

For most liberals, supporting the administration's foreign policy (1947–50) meant backing the Marshall Plan, to restore a democratic, economically viable Atlantic community. The Korean War altered this approach. DAI 38:4321-A.

1668 Boe, Jonathan E. "American Business: The Response to the Soviet Union, 1933–1947." Ph.D. dissertation, Stanford University, 1979.

In the postwar years, while liberal and moderate businessmen supported the government's anti-Communist initiatives abroad, conservatives resisted because they felt too much government spending would weaken the free enterprise system. DAI 40:5154-A.

1669 Hamilton, Mary A. "A Progressive Publisher and the Cold War: J. W. Gitt and *The Gazette and Daily*, York, Pennsylvania, 1946–1956." Ph.D. dissertation, Michigan State University, 1980.

Gitt's paper supported the presidential candidacy of Henry Wallace and opposed red-baiting hysteria. Hamilton finds that the publisher was an influential activist. DAI 41:4870.

1670 Irons, Peter H. "America's Cold War Crusade: Domestic Politics and Foreign Policy, 1942–1948." Ph.D. dissertation, Boston University, 1973.

This account focuses on the domestic roots of the Cold War by studying (1) the business community; (2) organized labor; (3) the Catholic Church; (4) major right-wing groups; and (5) East European ethnic groups. DAI 33:6842-A.

1671 Kirby, Linda K. "Communism, the Discovery of Totalitarianism, and the Cold War: *Partisan Review*, 1934–1948." Ph.D. dissertation, University of Colorado, 1974.

This study examines the ideas of the editors of *Partisan Review* as they moved from communism, through a perception of totalitarianism, to a Cold War perspective. DAI 35:7840-A.

1672 LaFeber, Walter. "American Policy-Makers, Public Opinion, and the Outbreak of the Cold War, 1945–50." In Yonosuke Nagai and Akira Iriye, eds. *The Origins of the Cold War in Asia.* New York: Columbia University Press, 1977, pp. 43–65.

In the early phase of the Cold War, Truman, along with a small number of advisers, controlled foreign policy; yet by 1947 he managed to create a domestic consensus that made possible the militarization and Asianization of American Cold War policy. Notes.

1673 Leigh, Michael. *Mobilizing Consent: Public Opinion and American Foreign Policy, 1937–1947.* Westport, CT: Greenwood, 1976.

Chapter 5 analyzes the Truman Doctrine: Was it a classic example of the manipulation of the public? Notes, bibliography, index.

1674 Lillehaugen, Nels M. "Survey of American Policy in the Cold War, 1945–1950: As Reflected by the North Dakota Press." Ph.D. dissertation, University of Idaho, 1971.

Although isolationist in the 1930s, most North Dakota editors strongly endorsed the United Nations immediately after World War II. Gradually, however, these editors endorsed the Truman administration's view of the Cold War, including NATO. DAI 32:5691-A.

1675 Preston, Edmund R. "Prelude to Cold War: American Reactions to the Growth of Soviet Power, 1944–1945." Ph.D. dissertation, University of Virginia, 1979.

As the Soviet Union achieved an unprecedented power through its victory over Germany and resulting control of Eastern Europe, the American public's view of the Soviets shifted from optimistic admiration to a puzzled mood of growing resentment and mistrust. DAI 40:5157-A.

1676 Quester, George H. "Origins of the Cold War: Some Clues from Public Opinion." *Political Science Quarterly* 93 (1978/79): 657–63.

Quester argues that American opinion saw the Cold War as emerging only slowly and gradually. Notes.

1677 Reinig, Ronald S. "America Looking Outward: American Cold War Attitudes During the Crucial Years, 1945–1947, as Reflected in the American Magazine Medium." Ph.D. dissertation, Syracuse University, 1974.

This study helps to complement the personal memoirs, government documents, first-hand accounts, and historical interpretations of a crucial period in American diplomatic relations. DAI 36:492-A.

1678 Richman, Alvin. "The Changing American Image of the Soviet Union." Ph.D. dissertation, University of Pennsylvania, 1968.

This study examines changes in American public opinion toward the Soviet Union from 1940 to 1965, using public opinion polls. DAI 29:3660-A.

1679 Small, Melvin. "When did the Cold War Begin? A Test of an Alternative Indicator of Public Opinion." *Historical Methods Newsletter* 8 (1975): 61–73.

The Cold War began in early 1946, but as late as December 1946 a considerable portion of the American public did not realize that it existed.

1680 Sylwester, Harold. "American Public Reaction to Communist Expansion: From Yalta to NATO." Ph.D. dissertation, University of Kansas, 1969.

Examined here are the changes in public opinion from Soviet-American friendship to opposition to Soviet expansion. DAI 31:2859-A.

1681 Underhill, William R. "Public Address: Its Role in the Cold War, 1945–1951." Ph.D. dissertation, Northwestern University, 1955.

This study covers three periods: (1) January 1945 to March 1947 found six American speakers reluctant to discuss existing international tensions; (2) 12 March 1947 to 31 July 1949 found six speakers challenging Soviet actions and proposing new programs; and (3) December 1950 to February 1951 found six speakers engaged in the so-called "Great Debate." DAI 15:1932.

Isolationism

1682 Campbell, Thomas M. "The Resurgence of Isolationism At the End of World War II." *West Georgia College Studies in the Social Sciences* 13 (1974): 41–56.

The American people's faith in the United Nations and their attitudes toward isolationism (1945–50) are examined. Notes.

1683 Carpenter, Ted G. "The Dissenters: American Isolationists and Foreign Policy, 1945–1954." Ph.D. dissertation, University of Texas, Austin, 1980.

Carpenter finds that a persistent isolationist minority provided significant opposition to the Truman Doctrine, the Marshall Plan, and NATO. DAI 41:4810.

1684 Doenecke, Justus D. *Not to the Swift: The Old Isolationists in the Cold War Era.* Lewisburg, PA: Bucknell University Press, 1979.

While many isolationists changed their views after Pearl Harbor, the "old" isolationists continued to oppose America's global activity. These businessmen, scholars, and publicists frequently served as a mainstay of the Republican party. Notes, bibliography, index.

1685 Dyer, George E. "Military Isolationism in the United States, 1939–1966: A Comparative Study of Isolationism and Isolationists." Ph.D. dissertation, Texas Technological College, 1967.

Most of the isolationism prior to involvement in Vietnam was conservatively oriented, while the opposition to Vietnam involvement has come from the Left. DAI 28:3725-A.

1686 Goldman, Steven C. "The Conservative Critique of Containment: An Isolationist Alternative to Cold War Diplomacy." Ph.D. dissertation, Johns Hopkins University, 1974.

Postwar isolationists hoped to insulate the United States from overseas problems, yet they wanted to contain communism; they opposed the extension of government authority, yet their patriotic instincts forced them to support national leadership. Anticommunism triumphed over isolationism. DAI 38: 1007-A.

1687 Graebner, Norman A. *The New Isolationism: A Study in Politics and Foreign Policy Since 1950.* New York: Ronald, 1956.

This book is a study of the impact of isolationist attitudes. Before 1952, pressure from the new isolationists led to serious modifications of Truman's policy and made negotiations increasingly difficult. Notes, index.

1688 Griffith, Robert. "Old Progressives and the Cold War." *Journal of American History* 66 (1979): 334–47.

The few old progressives in office during the Truman administration disapproved of nearly every aspect of its foreign policy. They opposed the efforts to deploy American military and economic power around the world. Notes.

1689 Grimmett, Richard F. "Who Were the Senate Isolationists?" *Pacific Historical Review* 42 (1973): 479–98.

This study makes a statistical examination of the 1947–56 Senate roll-call votes on key foreign policy issues. The results suggest a more reliable method of determining who were isolationists. Tables, notes.

Pressure Groups

1690 Gerson, Louis L. *The Hyphenate in Recent American Politics and Diplomacy.* Lawrence: University of Kansas Press, 1964.

Hyphenated Americans (1890–1956) are those immigrants and their descendants who link their American nationality with that of their ancestral land. These groups have an impact on American foreign policy. Appendix, notes, index.

1691 Karcz, Valerian. "The Polish American Congress, 1944–1959." *Polish American Studies* 16 (1959): 89–94.

The author claims this stridently anti-Communist organization represented seven million Polish-Americans. The congress was organized to support the principles of American democracy here and abroad.

1692 Lall, Betty Goetz. "The Foreign Policy Program of the League of Women Voters of the United States: Methods of Influencing Government Action, Effects on Public Opinion and Evaluation of Results." Ph.D. dissertation, University of Minnesota, 1964.

Lall finds that while the league (1920–55) thought of itself as a leader of public opinion in foreign policy, it seldom adopted positions ahead of the executive branch. Eventually the league shifted to community education. DAI 27:3916.

1693 Osmer, Harold. "United States Religious Press Response to the Containment Policy During the Period of the Korean War." Ph.D. dissertation, New York University, 1970.

Osmer finds that two major characteristics of the religious press emerged: a sustained concern with the containment policy, and a wide diversity of reaction toward it. DAI 31:2318-A.

1694 Pienkos, Donald E. "The Polish American Congress: An Appraisal." *Polish American Studies* 36 (1979): 5–43.

The PAC was launched in 1948 to put pressure on Roosevelt to rescue Poland from communism; however, later its mission shifted to promotion of Polish-American interests.

1695 Sanders, Jerry W. "Peddlers of Crisis: The Committee on the Present Danger and the Legitimation of Containment Militarism in the Korean War and Post-Vietnam Periods." Ph.D. dissertation, University of California, Berkeley, 1980.

The Committee on the Present Danger had two major resurgences—in 1950 and in 1976. Sanders argues that both periods were marked by protracted interelite conflict over foreign policy. DAI 41:3291.

1696 Sparks, Donald T. "The Influence of Official Protestant Church Groups on the Formulation and Conduct of American Foreign Policy, 1940–1950." Ph.D. dissertation, University of Chicago, 1954.

This analysis of the influence of Protestant denominational organizations finds that the high moral focus maintained by American foreign policymakers during this period was the result of the active influence of church groups.

1697 Whiteford, Daniel F. "The American Legion and American Foreign Policy, 1950 to 1963." Ph.D. dissertation, University of Maryland, 1967.

The legion believed that communism was the world's major problem. It supported the United Nations and NATO and the Rio Pact and was quite outspoken on what it deemed threats to internal security. DAI 28:3589-A.

LABOR AND FOREIGN AFFAIRS

See also Chapter 4, *Labor and Communism*, for additional references.

1698 Berger, Henry W. "Union Diplomacy: American Labor's Foreign Policy in Latin America, 1932–1955." Ph.D. dissertation, University of Wisconsin, 1966.

Although concerned about competition from cheap labor and goods, American labor with the aid of the U.S. government launched a militant offensive to spread American union ideas and power throughout Latin America in the postwar period. DAI 28: 3101-A.

1699 Carwell, Joseph. "The International Role of American Labor." Ph.D. dissertation, Columbia University, 1956.

The CIO and AFL played important roles in the labor politics of many countries (1945–55). American labor after 1949 sought to encourage the growth of unions in underdeveloped areas, often in connection with the aspirations of the nationalist movement in colonial countries. DAI 16:2056.

1700 Godson, Roy. "The AFL Foreign Policy Making Process from the End of World War II to the Merger." *Labor History* 16 (1975): 325–37.

The AFL's foreign policy was made independently of the U.S. government, contrary to traditional interpretations. The most important body was the Free Trade Union Committee, composed of Matthew Woll, David Dubinsky, George Meany, and William Green, which was largely autonomous in foreign policy. Notes.

1701 Godson, Roy. "American Labor's Continuing Involvement in World Affairs." *Orbis* 19 (1975): 93–116.

The AFL-CIO's involvement in U.S. economic and foreign policy and international trade programs (1930s–1970s) is reviewed.

1702 Godson, Roy. *American Labor and European Politics: The AFL as a Transnational Force.* New York: Crane, Russak, 1976.

Both American and European trade unions played a major role in emerging Cold War politics during the late 1940s and early 1950s. This account focuses on how and why the AFL became involved in European affairs, especially France. Notes, appendix, bibliography, index.

1703 Lenburg, LeRoy J. "The CIO and American Foreign Policy, 1935–1955." Ph.D. dissertation, Pennsylvania State University, 1973.

The CIO left wing exerted influence until it was purged from the organization (1949–50). Dissatisfaction with Truman's Cold War policies drove the left into Wallace's camp during the 1948 campaign. DAI 34:5065-A.

1704 Radosh, Ronald. *American Labor and United States Foreign Policy.* New York: Random House, 1969.

During the post-World War II period, labor essentially followed a reactionary program, which, rather than supporting forces of social change in Europe, Latin America, and Asia, sided with the administration's anti-Communist policies. Notes, index.

1705 Weiler, Peter. "The United States, International Labor, and the Cold War: The Breakup of the World Federation of Trade Unions." *Diplomatic History* 5 (1981): 1–22.

Western unionists charged that their Soviet counterparts brought on the 1949 breakup by trying to turn the organization into a tool of Soviet foreign policy. Actually, it was the U.S. government and the American Federation of Labor who caused the collapse. Notes.

Ending World War II

See J. E. O'Neill and R. W. Krauskopf, *World War II: An Account of Its Documents* (#3037) for possible references.

1706 Feis, Herbert. *Churchill, Roosevelt, Stalin: The War They Waged and the Peace They Sought.* Princeton, NJ: Princeton University Press, 1957.

When Truman assumed the presidency he also stepped into the wartime coalition with Churchill and Stalin. The last few chapters deal with Truman's role in the conduct of the war against Germany and the arrangement of the peace in Europe. Notes, index.

1707 Foy, David A. " 'For You the War Is Over': The Treatment and Life of United States Army and Army Air Corps Personnel Interned in POW Camps in Germany, 1942–1945." Ph.D. dissertation, University of Arkansas, 1981.

Germany attempted to follow the Geneva Convention, and compared with American POWs in Japan, those in Germany were fortunate. Yet compared with German POWs interned in the United States, American POWs in Germany were treated poorly. DAI 42:2811.

1708 James, D. Clayton. "MacArthur's Lapses From an Envelopment Strategy in 1945." *Parameters* 10 (1980): 26–32.

This essay challenges the traditional views of MacArthur's strategy in the Southwest Pacific in 1945. Notes.

1709 Kolko, Gabriel. *The Politics of War: The World and United States Foreign Policy, 1943–1945.* New York: Random House, 1969.

Aside from the desire to defeat the Axis, the United States had an elaborate set of economic and political goals in World War II. These included restricting the Left, containing the influence of the Soviet Union, and reducing the role of Great Britain. Notes, index.

1710 Spidle, Jake W., Jr. "Axis Prisoners of War in the United States, 1942–1946: A Bibliographical Essay." *Military Affairs* 39 (1975): 61–66.

In 1945, camps scattered across the United States confined over 425,000 prisoners of war. The bibliographical essay suggests many sources of investigation and includes a state-by-state listing of the larger base and branch camps. Notes.

WARTIME CONFERENCES

1711 Hoska, Lukas E., Jr. "Summit Diplomacy During World War II: The Conferences at Tehran, Yalta and Potsdam." Ph.D. dissertation, University of Maryland, 1966.

A shift in the emphasis of discussions occurred between Tehran and Potsdam, as the United States reversed its drift toward isolationism, a defensive big navy, and intense nationalism, and assumed a position of world leadership. DAI 27:3100.

1712 Neumann, William L. *After Victory: Churchill, Roosevelt, Stalin and the Making of the Peace.* New York: Harper & Row, 1967.

Neumann views the failure of the "Big Three" to create a viable peace as less an indictment of their personal qualities than as the product of the international and national systems. Bibliographical essay, index.

1713 Wheeler-Bennett, John W., and Nicholls, Anthony. *The Semblance of Peace: The Political Settlement After the Second World War.* New York: Norton, 1972.

This extensive account by a leading British historian focuses on the peacemaking efforts at the end of World War II. The Potsdam Conference, surrender of Germany and Japan, trial of war criminals, the origins of the United Nations, the Japanese peace treaty, and other conferences are examined. Maps, illustrations, appendix, documents, chronology, bibliography, notes, index.

Yalta Conference

See Chapter 3, *Diplomats: James F. Byrnes*, for his role in interpreting the Yalta agreements to Truman.

1714 Buhite, Russell D. "Patrick J. Hurley and the Yalta Far Eastern Agreement." *Pacific Historical Review* 37 (1968): 343–53.

As the idea that the agreement was "evil and conspiratorial" gained currency, Hurley sought to alter his relationship to it. Notes.

1715 Clemens, Diane Shaver. *Yalta.* New York: Oxford University Press, 1970.

While the account focuses on the eight days of the conference, Chapter 8 deals with the impact of the decisions on the Truman administration. Notes, appendix, bibliography, index.

1716 Fenno, Richard F., Jr., ed. *The Yalta Conference*. 2d ed. Boston: Heath, 1972.

These edited selections present many differing interpretations of what was intended at Yalta, what happened, and what repercussions occurred. Bibliography.

1717 Snell, John L., et al. *The Meaning of Yalta: Big Three Diplomacy and the New Balance of Power*. Baton Rouge: Louisiana State University Press, 1956.

This early examination of the Yalta Conference and agreements concludes (Chapter 6) with a retrospective view which examines the impact on the Truman years. Notes, appendix, index.

1718 Theoharis, Athan. "James F. Byrnes: Unwitting Yalta Myth-Maker." *Political Science Quarterly* 81 (1966): 581–92.

The Truman administration's failure to publish the Yalta agreements upon Japan's surrender created the notion of secret agreements and provided its domestic enemies with political opportunities. Notes.

1719 Theoharis, Athan. "The Origins of the Cold War: A Revisionist Interpretation." *Peace and Change* 4 (1976): 3–11.

Roosevelt's vagueness at the Yalta Conference is held to be a source of the Cold War during the Truman administration (1945–47). Notes.

1720 Theoharis, Athan. "The Republican Party and Yalta: Partisan Exploitations of the Polish American Concern Over the Conference, 1945–1960." *Polish American Studies* 28 (1971): 5–19.

The author examines the unsuccessful techniques and means employed by the Republican party to cut into traditionally Democratic Polish-American voting districts. Notes.

1721 Theoharis, Athan G. "Roosevelt and Truman on Yalta: The Origins of the Cold War." *Political Science Quarterly* 87 (1972): 210–41.

The author closely reviews the Truman administration's commitment to the Yalta Conference agreement. If the United States were not responsible for the Cold War, it "was more responsible for the way in which the cold war developed" as there was an opportunity for détente after Yalta but this was ignored by the Truman administration. Notes.

1722 Theoharis, Athan G. *The Yalta Myths: An Issue in U.S. Politics, 1945–1955*. Columbia: University of Missouri Press, 1970.

After 1949, anti-Communist zeal shifted from criticism of domestic reforms to foreign policy issues,

with conservative critics charging that Yalta had created the Cold War. Notes, appendixes, bibliography, index.

1723 U.S. Department of State. *Foreign Relations of the United States: World War II Conference Series. The Conference at Malta and Yalta, 1945*. Washington, DC: G.P.O., 1955.

The documents printed here, from State Department files and from other agencies, provide an invaluable record of the issues discussed. Index.

Potsdam Conference

1724 Feis, Herbert. *Between War and Peace: The Potsdam Conference*. Princeton, NJ: Princeton University Press, 1960.

This account continues the author's *Churchill-Roosevelt-Stalin*. Feis employed official records then not available to other historians; consequently its views should be compared with more recent accounts. Notes, supplementing notes, index.

1725 Feis, Herbert. "The Secret That Traveled to Potsdam." *Foreign Affairs* 38 (1960): 300–317.

Using still classified papers, Feis reviews the effect that the secret knowledge of the successful test of the atomic bomb had on American and British diplomacy at the Potsdam Conference.

1726 Ferrell, Robert H., ed. "Truman At Potsdam." *American Heritage* 31 (1980): 36–47.

Reprinted here are portions of Truman's diary of his trip to the Potsdam Conference at Berlin in 1945. Compare with E. Mark, below; however, texts vary.

1727 Hogan, W. C., and Hogan, Phyllis J. "Soviet Faith: A Case Study of Poland." *U.S. Naval Institute Proceedings* 80 (1954): 869–81.

If Truman had known the facts concerning the Katyn massacre, he would have taken an even harder line at Potsdam. The authors argue that a report carried by an American officer released from German captivity never reached Roosevelt or Truman.

1728 Lord Strang. "Prelude to Potsdam: Reflections On War and Foreign Policy." *International Affairs* [Great Britain] 46 (1970): 441–54.

Divergent allied postwar interests and objectives affected events leading up to the Potsdam negotiations. If Britain and America were to prevail over Russia, they had to use the threat of war—a threat that was extremely undesirable at home. Notes.

1729 Maddox, Robert J. "Harry S. Truman's Early Months in the White House." *American History Illustrated* 7 (1972): 12–22.

This brief account reviews the issues confronting Truman at the Potsdam Conference.

1730 Mark, Eduard. " 'Today Has Been a Historical One': Harry S. Truman's Diary of the Potsdam Conference." *Diplomatic History* 4 (1980): 317–26.

Reprinted here is the hitherto-unpublished diary kept by Truman while at the Potsdam Conference in 1945. Notes. See R. H. Ferrell, above.

1731 Mee, Charles L., Jr. *Meeting at Potsdam.* New York: Evans, 1975.

Mee finds Potsdam as the point where allied harmony collapsed, but he apportions responsibility evenly. Illustrations, notes on sources, appendix, index.

1732 Nagorski, Zygmunt. "The Potsdam Conference: Two Viewpoints." *Polish Review* 6 (1961): 108–16.

The author reviews Herbert Feis, *Between War and Peace: The Potsdam Conference*, and Alfons Klafkowski, *The Potsdam Agreement of August 2, 1945: Legal Cases for the Liquidation of the Polish-German War of 1939–1945* (in Polish).

1733 U.S. Department of State. *Foreign Relations of the United States: World War II Conference Series. The Conference of Berlin (Potsdam).* Washington, DC: G.P.O., 1960.

The documents printed here, from State Department and other agencies' files, provide an invaluable record of the issues discussed. Index.

SURRENDER NEGOTIATIONS

1734 Boyle, James M. "The XXI Bomber Command: Primary Factor in the Defeat of Japan." Ph.D. dissertation, St. Louis University, 1964.

Boyle maintains that the reason Japan surrendered prior to an invasion of the homeland was airpower in general and the B-29 bomber in particular. DAI 25:4668.

1735 Butow, Robert J. C. *Japan's Decision to Surrender.* Stanford, CA: Stanford University Press, 1954.

This account recreates the behind-the-scenes activities of those Japanese leaders who produced Japan's decision to accept the Potsdam ultimatum in August 1945. Footnotes, bibliography, index.

1736 Feis, Herbert. *The Atomic Bomb and the End of World War II.* Princeton, NJ: Princeton University Press, 1966.

This book, originally published as *Japan Subdued: The Atomic Bomb and the End of the War in the Pacific* (1961), complements his *Between War and Peace: The Potsdam Conference.* Severe criticism of the initial edition, especially that portion which

dealt with the decision to drop the A-bomb, led to substantial revisions. Notes, bibliography, index.

1737 Pacific War Research Society, comp. *Japan's Longest Day.* Tokyo: Kodansha, 1968.

Japanese scholars emphasize oral histories to reconstruct a detailed account of Japan's surrender. Illustrations, list of participants.

1738 Smith, Bradley F., and Agarossi, Elena. *Operation Sunrise: The Secret Surrender.* New York: Basic Books, 1979.

The secret 1945 Anglo-American-German negotiations for the surrender of Axis troops in Italy would influence affairs in the Truman period. It revealed the stresses and suspicions in the victorious Allied coalition, and it enhanced the reputation of Allen Dulles. Notes, bibliography.

1739 Stein, Harold. "The Rationale of Japanese Surrender." *World Politics* 15 (1962/63): 138–50.

This extended essay uses Herbert Feis, *Japan Subdued: The Atomic Bomb and the End of the War in the Pacific* (1961) to review the plans for securing the Japanese surrender decided upon in the spring of 1945.

DECISION TO USE A-BOMBS

1740 Baker, Paul R., ed. *The Atomic Bomb: The Great Decision.* New York: Holt, Rinehart and Winston, 1968.

These selections provide a variety of viewpoints regarding the various issues gathered around the dropping of the A-bomb. Chronology, bibliography.

1741 Batchelder, Robert C. *The Irreversible Decision, 1939–1950.* New York: Macmillan, 1961.

Batchelder's useful account reviews the decisions to make and drop the A-bomb in moral and ethical terms. Notes, index.

1742 Bernstein, Barton J., ed. *The Atomic Bomb: The Crucial Issues.* Boston: Little, Brown, 1976.

These essays focus on questions related to the decision to drop the atomic bomb. Was the bomb needed to end the Pacific war? What role did "atomic diplomacy" play? What is the moral significance of Hiroshima? Notes, bibliography.

1743 Bernstein, Barton J. "The Atomic Bomb and American Foreign Policy, 1941–1945: An Historiographical Controversy." *Peace and Change* 2 (1974): 1–16.

This essay examines in depth the basic questions raised by the use of atomic bombs to end the

Pacific war. The exponents of various points of view are identified. Notes.

1744 Bernstein, Barton J. *Hiroshima and Nagasaki Reconsidered: The Atomic Bombings of Japan and the Origins of the Cold War, 1941–1945.* Morristown, NJ: General Learning, 1975.

This twenty-six-page essay reviews many of the arguments concerning whether the atomic bomb needed to have been dropped on Japanese cities to end the war promptly. Notes, bibliography.

1745 Bernstein, Barton J. "The Perils and Politics of Surrender: Ending the War with Japan and Avoiding the Third Atomic Bomb." *Pacific Historical Review* 46 (1977): 1–27.

America's ambiguous response to Japan's 10 August 1945 offer to surrender strengthened the Japanese militarists and nearly prolonged the war. Truman and Byrnes considered the use of a third bomb, but Secretary of War Stimson and Admiral Leahy urged acceptance of Japan's offer. Notes.

1746 Bernstein, Barton J. "Roosevelt, Truman, and the Atomic Bomb: A Reinterpretation." *Political Science Quarterly* 90 (1975): 23–69.

Roosevelt's decision to treat the atomic bomb as a legitimate weapon and to exclude the Soviets from the atomic partnership paved the way for Truman's decision to use the bomb on Japanese targets and to practice postwar atomic diplomacy. Notes.

1747 Bernstein, Barton J. "Shatter of Worlds: Hiroshima and Nagasaki." *Bulletin of the Atomic Scientists* 31 (1975): 12–22.

American policymakers had few reservations about using the atomic bombs to force Japan's surrender and to intimidate the Soviets. Notes.

1748 Giovannitti, Len, and Freed, Fred. *The Decision to Drop the Bomb.* New York: Coward-McCann, 1965.

The authors find that "the decision was made because a decision not to use it could *not* be justified." If not used, Congress and the public would want to know why two billion dollars had been spent on developing the weapons; if an invasion of Japan took place relatives of American casualties would ask whether these lives could have been saved. Appendix, bibliography, index.

1749 *Hiroshima and Nagasaki: The Physical, Medical, and Social Effects of the Atomic Bombings.* Trans. by Eisei Ishikawa and D. L. Swain. New York: Basic Books, 1981.

Japanese officials and scholars have painstakingly collected an impressive amount of data relating to the two attacks. Their account, including extensive statistics, is the most comprehensive in print. Illustrations, tables, charts, extensive bibliography, index.

1750 Lamont, Lansing. *Day of Trinity.* New York: Atheneum, 1965.

The birth of the atomic bomb, including the initial explosion in July 1945 which opened the nuclear age, is reviewed. Index.

1751 Loebs, Bruce D. "Nagasaki: The Decision and the Mistake." *Rendezvous* 7 (1972): 53–69.

This account reviews the decision to drop an A-bomb on Nagasaki and pays particular attention to the roles of Truman, General Leslie Groves, and Emperor Hirohito.

1752 McElroy, William G., Jr. "The Hiroshima Decision: Its Political, Legal, and Moral Dimensions." Ph.D. dissertation, New York University, 1977.

No abstract available.

1753 Nicholson, Jack B. "The Atomic Bomb and Hiroshima: Historical Impact and Teaching Unit." Ph.D. dissertation, Illinois State University, 1980.

This study focuses on the decision to drop an atomic bomb on Hiroshima, the reaction of the people of Hiroshima to the devastation which occurred, and the construction, teaching, and evaluation of a teaching unit. DAI 41:2248.

1754 Schoenberger, Walter S. *Decision of Destiny.* Athens: Ohio University Press, 1969.

The factors which entered into the complex decision to use the atomic bombs in 1945 are examined in this account. Notes, bibliography, index.

1755 Sherwin, Martin J. "The Atomic Bomb and the Origins of the Cold War: U.S. Atomic Energy Policy and Diplomacy, 1941–45." *American Historical Review* 78 (1973): 945–68.

As early as 1943 Roosevelt began to recognize the diplomatic value of the bomb. The assumption that the bomb could be used to secure postwar diplomatic advantages carried over into the Truman administration. Notes.

1756 Sherwin, Martin J. *A World Destroyed: The Atomic Bomb and the Grand Alliance.* New York: Knopf, 1975.

Sherwin examines the views and proposals of scientists, military men, and political leaders as they faced the enormous challenge of building and finally using the most destructive weapon yet created. Appendixes, footnotes, bibliographical essay, index.

1757 Sigal, Leon V. "Bureaucratic Politics and Tactical Use of Committees: The Interim Committee and the Decision to Drop the Atomic Bomb." *Polity* 10 (1978): 326–64.

This is an extensive study of the decision to drop the bomb, which focuses on bureaucratic actions. Notes.

1758 Snowman, Daniel. "President Truman's Decision to Drop the First Atomic Bomb." *Political Studies* [Great Britain] 14 (1966): 365–73.

The political process which led to Truman's decision to drop the Hiroshima bomb is examined.

1759 Yavendetti, Michael J. "The American People and the Use of the Atomic Bombs on Japan, the 1940s." *Historian* 36 (1974): 224–47.

The American public's immediate response to the dropping of the atomic bombs was favorable because it was argued that they had ended the war. The moral aspects of the issue were developed by a small minority of the critics. Notes.

1760 Yavendetti, Michael J. "American Reactions to the Use of Atomic Bombs on Japan, 1945–1957." Ph.D. dissertation, University of California, Berkeley, 1970.

Yavendetti finds that the use of the atomic bomb on Japan aroused only limited debate in the United States. DAI 31:3490-A.

1761 Yavendetti, Michael J. "John Hersey and the American Conscience: The Reception of 'Hiroshima'." *Pacific Historical Review* 43 (1974): 24–49.

Hersey's *Hiroshima* (1946) focuses on the larger implications of the atomic bombings for the American conscience; it did succeed in activating the consciences of some Americans. Notes.

Atomic Scientists Protest

See also Chapter 9, *Atomic Scientists and Policy*.

1762 Frisch, David H. "Scientists and the Decision to Bomb Japan." *Bulletin of the Atomic Scientists* 26 (1970): 107–15.

This essay reviews the decision to drop the atomic bombs on Hiroshima and Nagasaki and discusses alternative targets and demonstrations which were considered.

1763 Steiner, Arthur. "Baptism of the Atomic Scientists." *Bulletin of the Atomic Scientists* 31 (1975): 21–28.

The author follows the development of the Franck Report, prepared by a committee of atomic scientists chaired by James Franck, and argues that it never received "the careful consideration it required." Notes.

1764 Villa, Brian L. "A Confusion of Signals: James Franck, the Chicago Scientists and Early Efforts to Stop the Bomb." *Bulletin of the Atomic Scientists* 31 (1975): 36–42.

The author compares two contradictory reports submitted by Franck: his April 1945 memorandum for Henry A. Wallace; and the Franck Committee Report of 11 June 1945. Apparently, the latter did not supersede the former at the War Department. Notes.

Atomic Diplomacy Thesis

See also Chapter 3, for *James F. Byrnes*, and Chapter 9, *Atomic Weapons and Strategy*.

1765 Alperovitz, Gar. *Atomic Diplomacy: Hiroshima and Potsdam; The Use of the Atomic Bomb and the American Confrontation with Soviet Power.* New York: Simon & Schuster, 1965.

It is Alperovitz's much-criticized thesis that "shortly after taking office Truman launched a powerful foreign policy initiative aimed at reducing or eliminating Soviet influence from Europe" and that Truman believed that the A-bomb would allow the United States to dictate its terms. Notes, bibliography.

1766 Boller, Paul F., Jr. "Hiroshima and the American Left, August 1945." *International Social Science Review* 57 (1982): 13–28.

While many leftists today insist that the United States dropped the atomic bombs primarily to impress the Soviets, a review of American leftists at the time indicates that the groups friendliest to Stalin were among the stoutest supporters of the bombings.

1767 Hammond, Thomas T. "Did the United States Use Atomic Diplomacy Against Russia in 1945?" In Peter J. Potichny and Jane P. Shapiro, eds. *From Cold War to Détente.* New York: Praeger, 1976, pp. 26–56.

Alperovitz's *Atomic Diplomacy* (1973) "simply does not stand up under careful analysis. Its main theses are either implausible, exaggerated, or unsupported by the evidence." Also see Robert James Maddox, "Atomic Diplomacy: A Study in Creative Writing." *Journal of American History* 59 (1973): 925–34. Notes.

1768 Paterson, Thomas G. "Potsdam, the Atomic Bomb, and the Cold War. A Discussion With James F. Byrnes." *Pacific Historical Review* 41 (1972): 225–30.

The document provides insights on Soviet-American diplomacy at the Potsdam Conference and includes information about the relationship between the dropping of the atomic bomb and Russian participation in the Pacific war. Notes.

DEMOBILIZATION

1769 Lee, R. Alton. "The Army 'Mutiny' of 1946." *Journal of American History* 53 (1966): 555–71.

In 1946 there were massive demonstrations by servicemen in Manila, Paris, Frankfurt, and other U.S. bases protesting the alleged slowness in demobilization and in bringing the veterans home. Notes.

1770 Sharp, Bert M. " 'Bring the Boys Home': Demobilization of the United States Armed Forces After World War II." Ph.D. dissertation, Michigan State University, 1976.

This study focuses on the emotional and chaotic experience of discharging American servicemen at the close of World War II. The peril to our national security was not as great with rapid demobilization as feared at the time, as the Soviets had problems with their rapid demobilization. DAI 38:1605-A.

1771 Sparrow, John C. *History of Personnel Demobilization in the United States Army.* Washington, DC: Department of the Army, July 1952.

This account contains a wealth of information about the demobilization of American forces at the end of World War II. Appendix, glossary, bibliographical note, chronology, charts, tables, illustrations.

REFUGEES AND DISPLACED PERSONS

See also Chapter 5, *Immigration.*

1772 Baskauskas, Liucija. "Planned Incorporation of Refugees: The Baltic Clause." *International Migration* [Netherlands] 14 (1976): 219–28.

This essay examines the relocation of Lithuanian refugees in Los Angeles as a result of the post-World War II Displaced Persons Act (1948).

1773 Bethell, Nicholas. *The Last Secret: The Delivery to Stalin of over Two Million Russians by Britain and the United States.* New York: Basic Books, 1974.

The basic problems of diplomacy and law which led to the return of Russians who fell into British and American hands are examined. Some of the Russians were captured in German uniform, some were exiles, and some were refugees. Illustrations, notes, index.

1774 Buhite, Russell D. "Soviet-American Relations and Repatriation of Prisoners of War, 1945." *Historian* 35 (1973): 384–97.

Thousands of Americans taken prisoner during World War II fell into Soviet hands as their armies advanced into Manchuria, Eastern Europe, and Germany. Negotiations for their return found the Soviets seeking to exchange the prisoners for U.S. recognition of the newly established Communist government in Poland. Notes.

1775 Dinnerstein, Leonard. *America and the Survivors of the Holocaust.* New York: Columbia University Press, 1982.

Dinnerstein analyzes the displaced persons issue during the postwar era and the role played by the United States in attempting to solve it. Particular attention is focused on Jewish displaced persons and attempts by American Jewry to influence U.S. treatment of them. Notes, appendixes, bibliography, index.

1776 Dinnerstein, Leonard. "Anti-Semitism in the Eightieth Congress: The Displaced Persons Act of 1948." *Capital Studies* 6 (1978): 11–26.

The Displaced Persons Act (1948) was enacted to aid homeless victims of World War II. The author holds that it discriminated against Jews in favor of ethnic Germans who fled Eastern Europe.

1777 Dinnerstein, Leonard. "The U.S. Army and the Jews: Policies Toward the Displaced Persons After World War II." *American Jewish History* 68 (1979): 353–66.

The U.S. army adequately met the challenge of caring for millions of displaced persons; unfortunately, it often showed little awareness of the particular difficulties of Jewish DPs. Notes.

1778 Elliott, Mark R. "The Repatriation Issue in Soviet-American Relations, 1944–1947." Ph.D. dissertation, University of Kentucky, 1974.

At Yalta in February 1945, the United States agreed to return Soviet POWs and forced laborers formerly held by the Germans, in exchange for American ex-POWs (23,000) stranded in Eastern Europe. The United States returned over two million Soviet POWs and civilians, many by force, in order to ensure the return of our servicemen. DAI 36:1719-A.

1779 Elliott, Mark. "The United States and Forced Repatriation of Soviet Citizens, 1944–47." *Political Science Quarterly* 88 (1973): 253–75.

The West agreed to the Soviet Union's demand that all of its citizens be returned, whether they wished to go or not. Notes.

1780 Epstein, Julius. *Operation Keelhaul: The Story of Forced Repatriation from 1944 to the Present.* Old Greenwich, CT: Devin-Adair, 1973.

The plight of millions of Russian refugees who were forcibly returned to the Soviet Union is reviewed, along with the American and British decisions which allowed this to happen. Illustrations, appendix, notes, bibliography, index.

1781 Gottlieb, Amy Zahl. "Refugee Immigration: The Truman Directive." *Prologue* 13 (1981): 5–17.

Truman's directive of 22 December 1945, a forerunner of the Displaced Persons Act, provided visas for some 35,000 special immigrants from Europe to the United States. Illustrations, notes.

1782 Lorimer, M. Madeline. "America's Response to Europe's Displaced Persons, 1948–1952: A Preliminary Report." Ph.D. dissertation, St. Louis University, 1964.

Although the Truman administration favored emergency immigration legislation, public opinion was restrictionist. The first Displaced Persons Act was passed in 1948; by 3 June 1952, some 392,547 persons had been admitted under the act. DAI 25:4672.

1783 Lowenstein, Sharon R. "A New Deal for Refugees: The Promise and Reality of Oswego, 1944–1945." Ph.D. dissertation, University of Kansas, 1983.

Some 1,000 predominantly Jewish victims of Nazism spent eighteen months (1944–46) at a refugee camp at Fort Ontario in Oswego, New York. Their hopes and disappointments, along with their eventual immigrant status, are discussed. DAI 44:1180-A.

1784 Schwartz, Leo W. *The Redeemers: A Saga of the Years 1945–1952*. New York: Farrar, Straus and Young, 1953.

The redeemers were displaced Jews who in 1945 remained in the German camps, where they sought to reestablish their lives until they could proceed to Israel or other countries. Notes, index.

1785 Willson, John P. "Carlton J. H. Hayes, Spain, and the Refugee Crisis, 1943–45." *American Jewish Historical Quarterly* 62 (1972): 99–100.

Hayes, the wartime U.S. ambassador to Spain, sought to expedite relief efforts for Jewish refugees moving through Spain. He was frequently in conflict with the U.S. War Refugee Board. Notes.

1786 de Zayas, Alfred M. *Nemesis at Potsdam: The Anglo-Americans and the Expulsion of the Germans*. rev. ed. London: Routledge & Kegan Paul, 1979.

Germans east of the Oder-Neisse line were forcibly removed from their traditional lands and villages. Britain and America are blamed for failing to ensure that post-World War II population transfers would be humanely conducted. Illustrations, notes, appendix, bibliography, index.

Beginning of the Cold War

See also R. D. Burns, *Guide To American Foreign Relations Since 1700* (#3023), especially Chapter 24; and Chapter 11, *The Cold War*, for additional references.

1787 Bernstein, Barton J. "American Foreign Policy and the Origins of the Cold War." In Barton J. Bernstein, ed. *Politics and Policies of the Truman Administration*. Chicago: Quadrangle, 1970, pp. 15–77.

This revisionist essay has as its underlying assumption that "by overextending policy and power and refusing to accept Soviet interests, American policymakers contributed to the Cold War." Bernstein believes that initially "Russian policies were reasonably cautious and conservative, and that there was at least a basis for accommodation." Notes.

1788 Carr, Albert Z. *Truman, Stalin and Peace*. Garden City, NY: Doubleday, 1950.

Four issues provide the focus in this volume: (1) the causes of the Soviet-American dispute; (2) Truman's efforts to keep Western Europe in the democratic camp; (3) the struggle for China; and (4) the revival of Germany.

1789 Clayton, James L. "The Fiscal Cost of the Cold War to the United States: The First 25 Years, 1947–1971." *Western Political Quarterly* 25 (1972): 375–95.

Clayton argues that the Cold War absorbed 42 percent of all money spent by the federal government at the expense of consumer durables, capital investment, and welfare expenditures. Tables, notes.

1790 Compton, James V., ed. *America and the Origins of the Cold War*. Boston: Houghton Mifflin, 1972.

While these edited materials were designed for classroom use, they do offer many differing views regarding the Cold War's origins. Bibliography.

1791 Cragan, John F. "The Cold War Rhetorical Vision, 1946–1972." Ph.D. dissertation, University of Minnesota, 1972.

This study seeks to: (1) determine the rhetorical origins of the Cold War; (2) describe the original Cold War rhetorical vision; and (3) examine the meanings, emotions, and motives of the Cold War rhetoric. DAI 33:5865-A.

1792 Doenecke, Justus D. "Lawrence Dennis: Revisionist of the Cold War." *Wisconsin Magazine of History* 55 (1972): 275–86.

Dennis wrote bitter attacks on the Truman administration's Cold War policies during the late 1940s and early 1950s.

1793 Druks, Herbert. *Harry S. Truman and the Russians, 1945–1953*. New York: Robert Speller & Sons, 1966.

Truman's decision to take a "tough" stand toward the Soviet Union receives a strong, rarely qualified endorsement. Notes, bibliography, index.

1794 Feis, Herbert. *From Trust to Terror: The Onset of the Cold War, 1945–1950*. New York: Norton, 1970.

In 1945 hopes for a sustained peace were high, but by 1949, with the explosion of a Russian atomic bomb, the fall of China, and the dissension in the United Nations, Soviet-American relations were characterized by distrust and mutual terror. Notes, illustrations, index, bibliography.

1795 Fleming, D. F. *The Cold War and Its Origins, 1917–1960*. 2 vols. Garden City, NY: Doubleday, 1961.

Fleming traces the origins of the Cold War from November 1917 and the U.S. reaction to the beginnings of the communization of the heart of Eurasia. Notes, index.

1796 Gaddis, John Lewis. "The Emerging Post-Revisionist Synthesis on the Origins of the Cold War." *Diplomatic History* 7 (1983): 171–90.

This essay provides a useful examination of the essential issues raised by the revisionist and suggests that the debates between revisionist and orthodox historians have led to a new consensus which draws from both schools. Extensive notes. Responses to Gaddis's arguments follow, *ibid*, pp. 191–204.

1797 Gaddis, John Lewis. *The United States and the Origins of the Cold War, 1941–1947*. New York: Columbia University Press, 1972.

This prize-winning study analyzes the forces—domestic, bureaucratic, and personalities—and the perceptions which affected American policymakers. The policymakers actually worked within a much narrower range of alternatives than revisionist historians have allowed. Extensive bibliography, index.

1798 Gardner, Lloyd C. "The Cold War in the Truman Era." *Foreign Service Journal* 50 (1973): 13–16.

The entire issue deals with the theme of revisionism and the Cold War, while this essay focuses on revisionist interpretations of the Truman period.

1799 Gardner, Lloyd C.; Schlesinger, Arthur, Jr.; and Morgenthau, Hans J. *The Origins of the Cold War*. Waltham, MA: Ginn, 1970.

While Schlesinger included his *Foreign Affairs* (October 1967) essay, Gardner and Morgenthau prepared essays for this volume. Each contributor then criticized his colleagues' interpretations.

1800 Gray, Robert C. "The Social Construction of the Cold War: Image and Process in Soviet-American Relations, 1941–1947." Ph.D. dissertation, University of Texas, Austin, 1975.

American and Soviet images are described: Roosevelt during the Grand Alliance; Truman upon succeeding to the presidency; Henry A. Wallace and James Forrestal provide alternative American definitions; and Stalin's images are then described. DAI 36:3106-A.

1801 Halle, Louis J. *The Cold War as History*. New York: Harper & Row, 1968.

Halle believes that the best foreign policy is one that avoids power vacuums and ideological generalizations and animosities. The first half of the book focuses on the Truman administration's efforts to deal with the Cold War. Bibliography, index.

1802 Hammond, Thomas T., ed. *Witnesses to the Origins of the Cold War*. Seattle: University of Washington Press, 1982.

These essays expand the debate over the origins of the Cold War by focusing on American and Soviet policies and behavior in Eastern Europe during 1945 to 1947. The essays are the recollections of authors who were among the first Americans to arrive in Eastern Europe. Notes, index.

1803 Herz, Martin F. *Beginnings of the Cold War*. New York: McGraw-Hill, 1966.

Herz draws on documentary materials to trace the background and sequence of events that disrupted the cooperation between wartime allies. Notes, bibliography, index.

1804 Hoffman, Paul G. *Peace Can Be Won*. New York: Doubleday, 1951.

In this pamphlet, Hoffman urges that America focus on the political, economic, and psychological aspects of the Cold War, especially in the Third World. Index.

1805 Kolko, Gabriel, and Kolko, Joyce. *The Limits of Power: The World and United States Foreign Policy, 1945–1954*. New York: Harper & Row, 1972.

This revisionist account is highly critical of the Truman administration's foreign policy: "The United States' ultimate objective at the end of World War II was both to sustain and to reform world capitalism." Notes, index.

1806 LaFeber, Walter. *America, Russia, and the Cold War, 1945–1975*. 3rd ed. New York: Wiley, 1976.

The first 100 pages of this survey provide an overview of issues and episodes affecting American foreign relations during Truman's presidency. Bibliographical essay, index.

1807 LaFeber, Walter, ed. *The Origins of the Cold War, 1941–1947: A Historical Problem with Interpretations and Documents*. New York: Wiley, 1971.

The collection of forty-three extracts and documents provides an introduction to basic issues.

1808 Lerche, Charles O., Jr. *The Cold War and After*. Englewood Cliffs, NJ: Prentice-Hall, 1965.

The Cold War is a result of a political process rooted in the international system itself; moreover, it is a distinct, closed historical era from 1945 to 1962. Bibliography, index.

1809 Levine, Alan J. "Some Revisionist Theses on the Cold War, 1943–1946: A Study of a Modern Mythology." *Continuity* (1980): 75–97.

Questioned here are such arguments that the United States and Britain alienated the Soviet Union because they did not launch an early "second front" in Europe, or that their failure to agree on a German policy dissipated the Allies' postwar united front, or that the Anglo-American policies forced the Soviets to establish Communist regimes in Eastern Europe.

1810 Lindsley, Arthur W. "The Cold War: Origins, Techniques and Problems." Ph.D. dissertation, New York University, 1960.

Lindsley defines the Cold War as a nonmilitary war of aggression waged unilaterally by the Soviet Union on behalf of international communism. He finds its origins in the political developments of the postwar period. DAI 27:1096.

1811 Lynd, Staughton. "How the Cold War Began." *Commentary* 30 (1960): 379–89.

Lynd takes a critical view of the Truman administration's policies as a contributing factor to the origins of the Cold War (1941–47).

1812 Maddox, Robert J. *The New Left and the Origins of the Cold War*. Princeton, NJ: Princeton University Press, 1973.

This critique of revisionists' research techniques caused quite a furor, but its central theme—the proper use of sources—is one that all historians must seriously contemplate. Index (See Warren Kimball's critical review in *American Historical Review* 79 (1974): 1119–36.)

1813 Maier, Charles S. "Revisionism and the Interpretation of Cold War Origins." *Perspectives in American History* 4 (1970): 313–47.

This essay is a careful analysis of the Cold War revisionist positions and is sensitive to their differing interpretations; however, it is also critical of their inconsistencies and other deficiencies. Notes.

1814 Mark, Eduard M. "The Intepretation of Soviet Foreign Policy in the United States, 1928–1947." Ph.D. dissertation, University of Connecticut, 1978.

Two questions are paramount: (1) Why during the Second World War did so many Americans believe in the prospects of a postwar *modus vivendi* with the Soviets? and (2) Why did this optimistic mood yield to the fears of the Cold War? DAI 39:6918-A.

1815 McNeill, William H. *America, Britain, and Russia: Their Cooperation and Their Conflict, 1941–1946*. London: Oxford University Press, 1953.

Although this account was written before government records were available, it is still very readable and insightful. Notes, index.

1816 Melanson, Richard A. "Revisionism Subdued? Robert James Maddox and the Origins of the Cold War." *Political Science Review* 7 (Fall 1977): 229–71.

This extended review examines, rather unsympathetically, Maddox's charges that revisionists made improper use of their sources. Notes.

1817 Messer, Robert L. "Paths Not Taken: The United States Department of State and Alternatives to Containment, 1945–1946." *Diplomatic History* 1 (1977): 297–319.

During the winter of 1945–46, the State Department discussed numerous alternatives of a general policy toward the U.S.S.R. before George Kennan's "long telegram" from Moscow carried the day. Notes.

1818 Miscamble, William D. "Anthony Eden and the Truman-Molotov Conversation of April, 1945." *Diplomatic History* 2 (1978): 167–80.

The Truman-Molotov conversation of 23 April 1945 did not indicate a reversal of America's wartime policy of cooperation. Its focus was on the refusal of Soviet Foreign Minister V. M. Molotov to agree to an acceptable settlement of the Polish question. Notes.

1819 Parks, Jimmy D. "Culture, Conflict and Coexistence: American-Soviet Cultural Relations, 1917–1958." Ph.D. dissertation, University of Oklahoma, 1980.

Parks surveys the trend of American-Soviet cultural relations, from its ease during the prerecognition period, its dwindling during the thirties, its resurgence during World War II, to its sharp decline in the postwar period. DAI 41:3234.

1820 Paterson, Thomas G., ed. *The Origins of the Cold War*. 2d ed. Lexington, MA: Heath, 1974.

These edited selections usefully review a wide range of viewpoints, personalities, and issues. Maps, cartoons, chronology, extensive bibliographical essay.

1821 Paterson, Thomas G. *On Every Front: The Making of the Cold War*. New York: Norton, 1979.

Paterson does a fine job of synthesizing the voluminous historical literature and divergent schools of historical interpretation relating to the origins of the Cold War, 1944–50. Notes, extensive bibliographical essay.

1822 Paterson, Thomas G. *Soviet-American Confrontation: Postwar Reconstruction and the Origins of the Cold War*. Baltimore: Johns Hopkins University Press, 1973.

This account of the late 1940s focuses on the economic issues. The author's interweaving political ideas, domestic politics, and personalities, however, provide a broad base from which he criticizes the Truman administration's foreign policy. Notes, bibliography, index.

1823 Reitzel, William; Kaplan, Morton A.; and Coblenz, Constance G. *United States Foreign Policy, 1945–1955*. Washington, DC: Brookings Institution, 1956.

This volume analyzes official purposes and actions of U.S. foreign policy and relations. Attention is focused on the general pattern of U.S. policy. Notes, bibliography, index.

1824 Richardson, J. L. "Cold War Revisionism: A Critique." *World Politics* 24 (1972): 579–612.

The works of Gabriel Kolko, Gar Alperovitz, and David Horowitz are found to possess a narrow, bipolar image. Notes.

1825 Rose, Lisle A. *After Yalta*. New York: Scribner's, 1973.

Rose seeks to rebut revisionist charges that the Truman administration (1945–48) "pursued an aggressive policy aimed at world economic and military hegemony." Notes, bibliography, index.

1826 Rose, Lisle A. *Dubious Victory: The United States and the End of World War II*. Kent, OH: Kent State University Press, 1973.

This study is offered as a corrective to Cold War revisionism which emphasizes the economic interpretation of events (1945–46). Footnotes, index.

1827 Schlesinger, Arthur, Jr. "Origins of the Cold War." *Foreign Affairs* 46 (1967): 22–52.

This lengthy essay reflects the orthodox point of view that fears, needs, ideology, and misinterpretation before and during World War II led to the Cold War.

1828 Thompson, Kenneth W. *Cold War Theories*. Vol. 1: *World Polarization, 1944–1953*. Baton Rouge: Louisiana State University, 1981.

Thompson examines how various writers, especially historians, have viewed the origin and conduct of the Cold War. He divides these historians between two schools: orthodox and revisionist. Footnotes, index.

1829 Ulam, Adam B. *The Rivals: America and Russia Since World War II*. New York: Viking, 1971.

This analytical essay by a specialist in Soviet affairs provides a critical introduction to the policies and actions of both sides. Ulam's *Expansion and Coexistence: The History of Soviet Foreign Policy, 1917–1967* (1968) is useful for those students wishing to dig deeper into Soviet foreign affairs. Index.

1830 Williams, William Appleman. "Demystifying Cold War Orthodoxy." *Science and Society* 39 (1975): 346–51.

A revisionist historian concludes that the confrontation with the Soviet Union would have been different under Roosevelt from what it was under Truman. However, he is convinced that the economic demands of both were a major cause of the Cold War.

1831 Yergin, Daniel. *Shattered Peace: The Origins of the Cold War and the National Security State*. Boston: Houghton Mifflin, 1977.

The Truman administration in 1946–47 abandoned negotiation for confrontation and led the world into the most intense years of the Cold War. This well-written book finds a fundamental dichotomy in how the Truman administration viewed the Soviet Union. Notes, bibliography, index.

Soviet Policies

1832 Eudin, Xenia J. "Moscow's Views of American Imperialism." *Russian Review* 13 (1954): 276–84.

In spite of the temporary cooperation between the Communist and non-Communist camps, Soviet ideology remained unchanged. Compared here is the Soviet attitude toward the Marshall Plan and the proposed federation of Europe to the Soviet interpretation of the Dawes Plan and another thirty-year-old Pan-European union. Notes.

1833 Harbutt, Fraser. "American Challenge, Soviet Response: The Beginning of the Cold War, February–May 1946." *Political Science Quarterly* 96 (1981/82): 623–39.

Until the end of 1945, the Soviets perceived Britain to be their main adversary. In February 1946 Truman began collaborating with the British against the Soviets, as well as challenging Soviet positions in Eastern Europe and Iran. By May both the Americans and Soviets recognized each other as major adversaries. Notes.

1834 Mastny, Vojtech. *Russia's Road to the Cold War*. New York: Columbia University Press, 1979.

Drawing upon available Soviet and East European sources, Mastny reconstructs Stalin's wartime diplomacy and lays major blame for the Cold War upon the opportunism of the Soviet dictator in the face of Western vacillation. Notes, bibliography, index.

1835 McCagg, William O., Jr. "Soviet Politics at the Start of the Cold War: The Soviet Party Revival

Reassessed." In Peter J. Potichnyj and Jane P. Shapiro, eds. *From Cold War to Détente*. New York: Praeger, 1976, pp. 57–77.

This study suggests that Soviet leadership itself was not united at the onset of the Cold War, and that a reinterpretation is needed of the sudden escalation of Soviet war aims during the early months of 1945. Perhaps Soviet internal politics influenced its foreign policy. Notes.

1836 Shulman, Marshall D. *Stalin's Foreign Policy Reappraised*. Cambridge: Harvard University Press, 1963.

This account focuses on the shaping of Soviet foreign policy from the end of the Berlin Blockade in 1949 to the Nineteenth Congress of the Communist party of the U.S.S.R. in October 1952. Bibliography, notes, index.

1837 Sivachev, Nikolai V., and Yakoviev, Nikolai N. *Russia and the United States*. Translated by Olga A. Titelbaum. Chicago: University of Chicago Press, 1979.

Two Soviet historians review Russian-American relations from 1776 to the present. Chapter 6 deals with their view of the role of Truman in the origins of the Cold War. Notes, index.

1838 Taubman, William. *Stalin's American Policy: From Entente to Détente in Cold War*. New York: Norton, 1982.

Taubman focuses on Stalin's conception of the United States, the policies he devised for dealing with the United States, and the threats and opportunities the United States posed. Notes, index.

1839 Trout, Ben T. "Soviet Policy-making and Cold War: Domestic and Foreign Policy Relationships, 1945–1947." Ph.D. dissertation, Indiana University, 1972.

This study is designed to: (1) examine the relationship of foreign and domestic policy; (2) develop and utilize an analytic framework which views the development of Soviet postwar policy; and (3) explore Soviet policy in terms of its foreign-domestic relationship. DAI 33:4514-A.

UNITED STATES-SOVIET UNION: SPECIAL ISSUES

Many issues arose affecting U.S.-Soviet affairs. Chapter 8 contains references to such issues as recognition of the Polish government, the Berlin blockade, the civil war in Greece, and the Korean unification dispute; while other issues are listed immediately below.

Conferences and Negotiations

See Chapter 3, *Diplomats*, especially *Dean Acheson* and *James F. Byrnes*.

1840 Dunn, Keith A. "A Conflict of World Views: The U.S., the Soviet Union, and Peace with Hitler's Former Allies." Ph.D. dissertation, University of Missouri, Columbia, 1973.

Preconceived ideas and assumptions about their long-run and immediate requirements defined Washington's and Moscow's behavior in the postwar negotiations and limited viable alternatives. DAI 35:1001-A.

1841 Jarvis, Bertrand F. "The Role of the Small Powers in the Development of the Western Bloc at the 1946 Paris Peace Conference: A Study into the Origins of the Cold War." Ph.D. dissertation, University of Alabama, 1973.

The draft peace treaties for Italy, Hungary, Bulgaria, Romania, and Finland were discussed at the 1946 Paris Conference. This study seeks to determine when and how a Western bloc was formed. DAI 34:2517-A.

1842 Walker, J. Samuel. " 'No More Cold War': American Foreign Policy and the 1948 Soviet Peace Offensive." *Diplomatic History* 5 (1981): 75–91.

Twice in May 1948 the Soviet Union offered to discuss points in dispute with the United States, only to have the Americans reject the initiatives out of hand. It was not likely that much could have been resolved, given the mutual distrust and misperceptions, yet the American refusal was self-righteously rigid. Notes.

Economic Issues

1843 Brewer, John C. "Lend-Lease: Foreign Policy Weapons in Politics and Diplomacy, 1941–1945." Ph.D. dissertation, University of Texas, Austin, 1974.

The final chapter deals with the Truman administration's decisions in 1945 to terminate abruptly lend-lease aid—which probably hurt Britain more than the Soviet Union. DAI 35:5286-A.

1844 Herring, George C., Jr. *Aid to Russia, 1941–1946: Strategy, Diplomacy, the Origins of the Cold War*. New York: Columbia University Press, 1973.

This study reveals that U.S. policymakers were keenly aware of the potential political value of economic assistance to the U.S.S.R. and that they vigorously debated the tactics that should be employed. Unfortunately, the Truman administration's use of this diplomatic weapon was without success, even intensifying the Cold War. Appendix, notes, bibliography, index.

1845 Herring, George C., Jr. "Lend-Lease to Russia and the Origins of the Cold War, 1944–1945." *Journal of American History* 56 (1969): 93–114.

The Truman administration's abrupt reduction of lend-lease aid to Russia in May 1945 was not an attempt to coerce the Soviets but to carry out the law's requirements. Notes.

1846 Linz, Susan J. "Economic Origins of the Cold War? An Examination of the Carryover Costs of World War II to the Soviet People." Ph.D. dissertation, University of Illinois, Urbana-Champaign, 1980.

The actual allocation of the carry-over costs of World War II might have changed with different postwar economic policies. Linz examines lend-lease and U.N. relief and rehabilitation assistance, the proposed special U.S. loan, and the Marshall Plan. DAI 41:4790.

1847 Martel, Leon C. *Lend-Lease, Loans, and the Coming of the Cold War: A Study of the Implementation of Foreign Policy.* Boulder, CO: Westview, 1979.

This study focuses on Truman's order cutting back lend-lease to the U.S.S.R. after Germany's defeat, the abrupt termination of it after Japan's surrender, and the delayed response to two Soviet requests (1945) for long-term credits. Notes, bibliography, index.

1848 Paterson, Thomas G. "The Abortive Loan to Russia and the Origins of the Cold War, 1943–1946." *Journal of American History* 56 (1969): 70–92.

From 1944 to 1946 the United States sought to employ the possibility of a postwar reconstruction loan to the Soviet Union as a bargaining lever which could be employed to influence U.S.-Soviet negotiations. Notes.

U.S. Propaganda

1849 Collins, Larry D. "The Free Europe Committee: An American Weapon of the Cold War." Ph.D. dissertation, Carleton University (Canada), 1974.

FEC was an instrument of the Central Intelligence Agency (1948–71) and a major foreign policy instrument. The two principal subdivisions of the FEC were Radio Free Europe and the Crusade for Freedom. DAI 35:6785-A.

1850 Holt, Robert R. "The Munich Operation of Radio Free Europe." Ph.D. dissertation, Princeton University, 1957.

Radio Free Europe was established in 1949 to broadcast to five Soviet Eastern European satellites. The author emphasizes the "private" organizational structure—not until the 1960s was it known that the Central Intelligence Agency funded much of the operation. DAI 18:274.

1851 Ludden, Howard R. "The International Information Program of the United States: State Department Years, 1945–1953." Ph.D. dissertation, Princeton University, 1966.

Between 1945 and 1953 the State Department took over the conduct of international information activities. This study examines the operation of its programs and the violent criticisms toward it, particularly by McCarthy, which helped terminate State Department conduct of the program. DAI 28:753-A.

1852 Pirsein, Robert W. "The Voice of America: A History of the International Broadcasting Activities of the United States Government, 1940–1952." Ph.D. dissertation, Northwestern University, 1970.

In this history of the Voice of America, Pirsein looks at the major trends, agencies, pressures, events, and personalities surrounding the VOA. DAI 31: 3686-A.

CONTAINMENT POLICIES AND PROGRAMS

See also Chapter 3, *Diplomats*, especially *George F. Kennan.*

1853 Etzold, Thomas H., and Gaddis, John Lewis, eds. *Containment: Documents on American Policy and Strategy, 1945–1950.* New York: Columbia University Press, 1978.

The editors selected recently declassified documents believed "to illustrate the first systematic attempt by the United States in peacetime to integrate political and military considerations in national security planning." These fifty-two documents, including NSC-68, are grouped around geographical and topical themes. Introductions, index.

1854 Gaddis, John Lewis. "Containment: A Reassessment." *Foreign Affairs* 55 (1977): 873–87.

Gaddis seeks to define just what Kennan *meant* by containment by comparing Kennan's famous "long telegram" and his *Memoirs*. Eduard Mark replies, *ibid.* 56 (1978): 430–41. Notes.

1855 Gaddis, John Lewis. *Strategies of Containment: A Critical Appraisal of Postwar American National Security Policy.* New York: Oxford University Press, 1982.

Gaddis traces the evolution of containment from its roots in Franklin Roosevelt's wartime diplomacy to the Carter presidency. In the process he develops Kennan's strategy of containment, explains how the Truman administration actually implemented containment, and analyzes the significance of NSC-68 and the Korean War. Appendix, notes, bibliography, index.

1856 Gati, Charles, ed. *Caging the Bear: Containment and the Cold War.* New York: Bobbs-Merrill, 1974.

These essays include George Kennan's "Mr. 'X' " essay as well as his later reflections. Gati reprints his critique "What Containment Meant," *Foreign Policy* (1972), and criticizes the Truman Doctrine. And William Zimmerman speculates about what might have happened even if the United States had responded in a less hostile manner toward the Soviet Union. Footnotes, index.

1857 Gati, Charles. "What Containment Meant." *Foreign Policy* (1972): 22–40.

Gati analyzes George F. Kennan's 1947 "Mr. 'X' " essay in *Foreign Affairs*.

1858 Graebner, Norman A. "Global Containment: The Truman Years." *Current History* 57 (1969): 77–83, 115–16.

The containment policy was prejudiced by political instability along the Asian periphery of Russia and China, and by the notion of monolithic communism.

1859 Harbutt, Fraser J. "The Fulton Speech and the Iran Crisis of 1946: A Turning Point in American Foreign Policy." Ph.D. dissertation, University of California, Berkeley, 1976.

The appeal of Churchill's proposal that his forthcoming Fulton speech be used to urge a full Anglo-American military alliance is placed against the blooming Cold War. It was calculated that the threatened marriage of American power and British interests would alarm Stalin. DAI 37:6011-A.

1860 Koenig, Louis W. "The Truman Doctrine and NATO." *Current History* 57 (1969): 18–23, 53.

The author believes that the Truman administration's swift and resolute actions—the Truman Doctrine, containment policy, and the North Atlantic Treaty (1949)—deterred a Soviet invasion of Western Europe and halted the advance of the Iron Curtain.

1861 Landa, Ronald D. "The Triumph and Tragedy of American Containment: When the Lines of the Cold War Were Drawn in Europe, 1947–48." Ph.D. dissertation, Georgetown University, 1971.

The Soviets were restrained not only by their own internal weaknesses, but by the extent of the U.S. commitment to Western Europe. Thus the scare tactics by which Truman won congressional and public support led to a polarized world. DAI 32: 2034-A.

1862 Lippmann, Walter. *The Cold War: A Study in U.S. Foreign Policy.* New York: Harper & Row, 1947.

In this rebuttal to George F. Kennan's "Mr. 'X' " essay in *Foreign Affairs* (July 1947), Lippmann challenges the basic Kennan assumptions, especially the "containment" notion.

1863 McLellan, David S. "Who Fathered Containment? A Discussion." *International Studies Quarterly* 17 (1973): 205–26.

America's Cold War policy of containing the Soviet Union developed as a result of the State Department's experience in dealing with aggressive Soviet behavior in Turkey and Iran during 1945–46. Notes.

1864 Puhek, Ronald E. "The Rationale of American Foreign Policy: Containment." Ph.D. dissertation, University of Nebraska, 1967.

The containment rationale introduced grave policy inconsistencies and gradually helped to lead America to a kind of international behavior which, while pursuing international stability, risked the most serious kind of instability—war. DAI 28:756-A.

1865 Ryan, Henry B. "A New Look at Churchill's 'Iron Curtain' Speech." *Historical Journal* 22 (1979): 895-920.

Churchill's Fulton, Missouri speech of 5 March 1946 is discussed in detail, including Truman's role in encouraging the former prime minister. Notes.

1866 Wright, C. Ben. "Mr. 'X' and Containment." *Slavic Review* 35 (1976): 1–31.

This essay examines what Wright believes to be contradictions in Kennan's writings concerning Soviet expansionism and his containment policy. Kennan replies, *ibid.*, pp. 32–36.

1867 "X" [George F. Kennan]. "The Sources of Soviet Conduct." *Foreign Affairs* 25 (1947): 566–82.

In this controversial essay, Kennan seeks to analyze the Soviets' approach to foreign policy. The ideas contained here, and in his earlier "long telegram," were and have been perceived to be those underlying the Truman administration's policies.

Truman Doctrine

See also Chapter 8, *Greece, Iran,* and *Turkey,* for additional references.

1868 Buckley, Gary J. "The Truman Doctrine and Public Opinion: An Application of a Conceptual Framework of James N. Rosenau." Ph.D. dissertation, University of Denver, 1973.

This study was designed to examine the impact of American public opinion—both mass and elite—on foreign policy issues. DAI 34:7854-A.

1869 Freeland, Richard M. *The Truman Doctrine and the Origins of McCarthyism: Foreign Policy, Domestic Politics, and Internal Security, 1946–1948.* New York: Knopf, 1972.

Freeland argues that the emotional and political forces and patterns of belief that provided the postwar anti-Communist hysteria were a result of the Truman administration's program for economic recovery in Europe. Notes, bibliography, index.

1870 Gaddis, John Lewis. "Reconsiderations: Was the Truman Doctrine a Real Turning Point?" *Foreign Affairs* 52 (1974): 386–402.

In spite of Truman's pronouncements, his administration had neither the intention nor the capability of policing the world. Until the Korean conflict, one must be careful to distinguish between the language of the Truman Doctrine and the actual policies of the administration. Notes.

1871 Heinlein, David L. "The Truman Doctrine: A Chief Executive in Search of the Presidency." Ph.D. dissertation, Johns Hopkins University, 1975.

This study traces the Truman administration's increasing sensitivity to Soviet behavior and apparent intentions and defines the difficulties of reorienting American priorities toward postwar realities. DAI 39:3123-A.

1872 Iselin, John J. "The Truman Doctrine: A Study in the Relationship Between Crisis and Foreign Policy-Making." Ph.D. dissertation, Harvard University, 1964.

This is a detailed examination of the making of the Truman Doctrine which signaled the dawn of U.S. maturity in postwar foreign affairs.

1873 Jefferson, Charles J. "Bureaucracy, Diplomacy and the Origins of the Cold War." Ph.D. dissertation, Claremont Graduate School, 1975.

This study employs an "organization process" approach to the analysis of the decision-making underlying the Truman Doctrine—the focal event. DAI 36:3107-A.

1874 Jones, Joseph M. *The Fifteen Weeks (February 21–June 5, 1947).* New York: Viking, 1955.

During these fifteen weeks, with the commitment of aid to Greece and Turkey, U.S. foreign policy was dramatically transformed. Notes, index, appendix.

1875 Kernell, Samuel. "The Truman Doctrine Speech: A Case Study of the Dynamics of Presidential Opinion Leadership." *Social Science History* 1 (1976): 20–44.

Using available data, the author suggests that the speech was less than a dynamic force in consolidating American opinion. Subsequent events, not the speech, created a militant anticommunism. Tables, notes.

1876 Kousoulas, D. George. "The Success of the Truman Doctrine Was Not Accidental." *Military Affairs* 29 (1965): 88–92.

The author believes that the success of the Truman Doctrine, as seen in Greece, resulted from

an understanding of the political nature of guerrilla warfare and a wise choice of ground and weapons. Notes.

1877 Lehman, Ronald F. "Vandenberg, Taft, and Truman: Principle and Politics in the Announcement of the Truman Doctrine." Ph.D. dissertation, Claremont Graduate School, 1975.

The Truman Doctrine must be understood in the light of the efforts of Truman to advance both his foreign and domestic policies, and to ensure his own reelection. DAI 36:1774-A.

1878 Lun, Ngoh Geok. "Truman and Containment: The Rationale and Application of the Truman Doctrine." *Journal of the Historical Society* [Singapore] (1978): 63–68.

Lun discusses the transformation of U.S. foreign policy from one of isolationism and total warfare to a strategy of "containment" and "cold war" in opposition to Soviet expansionism.

1879 McFadyen, Barbara Dwyer. "The Truman Doctrine: Its Origins and Evolution." Ph.D. dissertation, University of Colorado, 1965.

The Truman Doctrine was enunciated as an emergency measure to aid Greece and Turkey. Belatedly, the administration explained that the doctrine would be applied to other countries. DAI 26:6831.

1880 Paone, Rocco M. "Military Aid to Turkey, 1947–1950." *Military Review* 50 (1970): 74–79.

The U.S. State Department created a military, economic, and naval survey team, headed by Maj. Gen. Lunford E. Oliver, to review Turkey's needs and to make recommendations on what form aid should take. Illustrated.

1881 Ryan, Henry G., Jr. "The American Intellectual Tradition Reflected in the Truman Doctrine." *American Scholar* 42 (1973): 294–307.

The process of formulating and drafting the Truman Doctrine is examined at length.

1882 Selton, Robert W. "The Cradle of U.S. Cold War Strategy." *Military Review* 46 (1966): 47–55.

Colonel Selton finds the cradle of U.S. strategy for the first twenty years of the Cold War in Greece (1946–49). He describes the contributions of the U.S. army group in Greece in helping the Greek national army defeat the Communist guerrillas.

1883 Weiner, Bernard. "The Truman Doctrine: Background and Presentation." Ph.D. dissertation, Claremont Graduate School, 1967.

Truman had not prepared Congress for the new role he expected America to play and thus placed his request for aid to Greece and Turkey in the context of a great emergency in order to gain congressional approval. DAI 28:4235-A.

1884 Wittner, Lawrence S. "The Truman Doctrine and the Defense of Freedom." *Diplomatic History* 4 (1980): 161–87.

The Truman Doctrine justified American aid to Greece as a defense of freedom and individual liberties. In Greece itself, however, American policy supported severe curbs on free institutions; consequently the Truman Doctrine acted more to repress than to protect freedom. Notes.

1885 Xydis, Stephen G. "The Truman Doctrine in Perspective." *Balkan Studies* [Greece] 8 (1967): 239–62.

On 12 March 1947 Truman requested Congress to provide $400 million in military and economic aid to Greece and Turkey. Xydis reviews the event leading to the request, and compares the Monroe Doctrine (1823) to the Truman Doctrine (1947). Notes.

Marshall Plan

See also Chapter 3, *George C. Marshall*.

1886 Arkes, Hadley. *Bureaucracy, the Marshall Plan, and the National Interest*. Princeton, NJ: Princeton University Press, 1972.

Arkes is mainly interested in identifying the "national interest." The Marshall Plan had the unique characteristics of conforming to the national interest which could be supported by both liberals and conservatives. Notes, appendixes, bibliography, index.

1887 Bailey, Thomas A. *The Marshall Plan Summer: An Eyewitness Report on Europe and the Russians in 1947*. Stanford, CA: Hoover Institution Press, 1977.

Bailey was commissioned by the U.S. National War College to tour Europe in the summer of 1947 prior to teaching at that institution in the fall. This book is "a diary—a primary source." Bibliography, index.

1888 Beugel, E. H. van der. *From Marshall Aid to Atlantic Partnership*. New York: Elsevier, 1966.

Van der Beugel, director-general and minister of foreign affairs of the Netherlands, was intimately involved with the operation of the Marshall Plan. He discusses the U.S. and European partnership. Notes, bibliography, index.

1889 Conley, Manuel A. "Merci, America." *American Heritage* 32 (1981): 94–97.

In 1947 a French railroad worker suggested that France show its appreciation to the United States for wartime and postwar aid. In February 1949 a ship loaded with boxcars carrying a gift for America arrived in Weehawken, New Jersey. Illustrations.

1890 Cromwell, William C. "The Marshall Non-Plan, Congress and the Soviet Union." *Western Political Quarterly* 32 (1979): 422–43.

While U.S. policymakers hoped the Russians would find the Marshall aid proposal unacceptable, the administration declined to pose stringent conditions for Soviet participation. The subsequent interplay of British, French, and Soviet diplomacy accomplished the exclusion of the Russians. Notes.

1891 Edelstein, Alex S. "The Marshall Plan Information Program in Western Europe as an Instrument of United States Foreign Policy, 1948–1952." Ph.D. dissertation, University of Minnesota, 1958.

The Marshall Plan information program proceeded in three stages: (1) an initial period of press agentry; (2) next a period of closer support for economic objectives, and (3) the merging of the Economic Cooperation Administration (ECA) into defense-supported activities. DAI 19:2598.

1892 Ehrlich, Larry G. "Ambassador in the Yard." *Southern Speech Communication* 38 (1972): 1–12.

Secretary of State George C. Marshall's speech at Harvard University calling for a program of economic assistance for postwar Europe—the Marshall Plan—is found to have made effective use of academic rhetoric.

1893 Ellis, Howard S. *The Economics of Freedom: The Progress and Future of Aid to Europe*. New York: Harper, 1950.

The United States inaugurated the Marshall Plan believing that an economically secure Europe would aid in achieving a politically and militarily secure Europe. This is a contemporary account by the Council on Foreign Relations. Notes, tables, index.

1894 Gimbel, John. *The Origins of the Marshall Plan*. Stanford: Stanford University Press, 1976.

Gimbel's thesis is that "the Marshall Plan originated as a crash program to dovetail German economic recovery with a general European economic recovery program in order to make German economic recovery politically acceptable in Europe and in the United States." Bibliographical note, notes, index.

1895 Gordon, Lincoln. "ERP in Operation." *Harvard Business Review* 27 (1949): 129–50.

An official of the agency in 1948, Gordon presents his assessment of the European Recovery Program's early accomplishments.

1896 Hartmann, Susan M. *The Marshall Plan*. Columbus, OH: Merrill, 1968.

This is a brief (seventy pages) narrative sketch of the development of the Marshall Plan.

1897 Hitchens, Harold L. "Influences On the Congressional Decision To Pass the Marshall Plan." *Western Political Quarterly* 21 (1968): 51–68.

Many individuals played major roles in the congressional debate including Truman, Marshall,

Henry L. Stimson, Dean Acheson, and Senators Robert A. Taft and J. William Fulbright in order to gain passage of the program. Table, notes.

1898 Hogan, Michael J. "The Search for a 'Creative Peace': The United States, European Unity, and the Origins of the Marshall Plan." *Diplomatic History* 6 (1982): 267–85.

The idea of European economic integration to achieve long-term stability—though not new—exerted considerable influence on Americans who ultimately shaped the Marshall Plan. Notes.

1899 Jackson, Scott. "Prologue To the Marshall Plan: The Origins of the American Commitment For a European Recovery Program." *Journal of American History* 65 (1979): 1043–68.

Europe's economic distress, Britain's economic and financial woes, Europe's balance of trade and dollar problems, and the threat of Communist expansion combined in 1947 to stimulate Marshall's speech of 5 June 1947.

1900 Johnson, James H. "The Marshall Plan: A Case Study in American Foreign Policy Formulation and Implementation." Ph.D. dissertation, University of Oklahoma, 1966.

This study focuses on the deterioration of American-Soviet relations, domestic political developments, and the effect of the Truman Doctrine in the development of the Marshall Plan. DAI 27:1095.

1901 Kindleberger, Charles P. "The Marshall Plan and the Cold War." *International Journal* 23 (1968): 369–81.

The author, a marginal participant in the events of 1945–48, believes the plan succeeded in "stabilizing political life in Western Europe and in halting the advance of Communist parties and Soviet influence." Notes.

1902 Mallalieu, William C. "The Origins of the Marshall Plan: A Study in Policy Formation and National Leadership." *Political Science Quarterly* 73 (1958): 481–504.

This early, but still useful account reviews the role of American and European leaders to explain how and why the Marshall Plan took the shape that it did. Notes.

1903 Miscamble, Wilson D. "George F. Kennan, The Policy Planning Staff and the Origins of the Marshall Plan." *Mid-America* 62 (1980): 75–89.

In April 1947 Marshall instructed Kennan and the new Policy Planning Staff to explore postwar European economic problems and to formulate proposals for American aid. Notes.

1904 Paterson, Thomas G. "The Quest for Peace and Prosperity: International Trade, Communism, and the Marshall Plan." In Barton J. Bernstein, ed. *Politics and Policies of the Truman Administration.* Chicago: Quadrangle, 1970, pp. 78–112.

In his examination of America's international economic policies under the Truman administration, Paterson questioned whether the Marshall Plan was the best approach. Notes.

1905 Pentony, DeVere E. "The Marshall Plan: Declared Objectives and Apparent Results." Ph.D. dissertation, State University of Iowa, 1956.

The United States promoted Western Europe's political and economic strength in the hope that U.S. military security would be enhanced by gaining powerful allies, but also that the American economy would be more secure. DAI 16:1717.

1906 Pittman, Von V., Jr. " 'Gideon's Army' and the Marshall Plan: An Example of Consensus." *Research Studies* 43 (1975): 189–92.

Socialist Norman Thomas and conservative Republican Senator Vandenberg exchanged letters (1947–48) which reveal a broad consensus on issues such as the Marshall Plan. This consensus, reflective of the American public, thwarted Wallace's attempt to challenge the Truman administration's foreign policy.

1907 Price, Harry B. *The Marshall Plan and Its Meaning.* Ithaca, NY: Cornell University Press, 1955.

This contemporary, semiofficial history is useful in the information it provides and in the contemporary tone it carries. It is a classic early Cold War document. Illustrations, notes, index.

1908 Quade, Quentin. "The Truman Administration and the Separation of Powers: The Case of the Marshall Plan." *Review of Politics* 27 (1965): 58–77.

The Truman administration's efforts to obtain congressional approval of the Marshall Plan marked the beginning of the modern partnership in the realm of foreign affairs. Notes.

1909 Wilson, Theodore A. *The Marshall Plan, 1947–1951.* Headline Series, no. 236. New York: Foreign Policy Association, 1977.

Wilson's useful survey ties together domestic and foreign aspects of the decision to establish the Marshall Plan, and he reviews the impacts of its implementation.

1910 Winham, Gilbert R. "An Analysis of Foreign Aid Decision-Making: The Case of the Marshall Plan." Ph.D. dissertation, University of North Carolina, Chapel Hill, 1968.

This study examines the motivations underlying the development of the Marshall Plan (May 1947–April 1948). The major concern was for the economic plight of Europe; only later did the Communist threat become a significant factor. DAI 29:2335-A.

1911 Winks, Robin, ed. *The Marshall Plan and the American Economy*. Boston: Holt, 1960.

Collected in this pamphlet are various documents, public comments, and official statements regarding the launching of the plan and its public acceptance. Notes.

1912 Woods, Elsworth P. "The Marshall Plan: A Study in Legislation." Ph.D. dissertation, University of Iowa, 1949.

This analysis of the legislative process regarding the Marshall Plan contends that in congressional discussion of the proposed European Recovery Program the issue of communism tended to obscure the issue of economic recovery.

North Atlantic Treaty Organization

1913 Bills, Scott L. "Cold War Rimlands: The United States, NATO, and the Politics of Colonialism, 1945–1949." Ph.D. dissertation, Kent State University, 1981.

There was no U.S. program of unconditional support for the self-determination of colonial peoples, and strains within the Euro-American system over colonial issues would not be risked. NATO institutionalized the Cold War ethos and affirmed the European priority. DAI 42:4905-A.

1914 Gordon, Morton. "American Opposition to the ERP and the North Atlantic Treaty: A Study of Anti-Administration Opinion." Ph.D. dissertation, University of Chicago, 1953.

The opposition to the European Recovery Program and the North Atlantic Treaty, as set forth primarily in congressional hearings and newspaper editorials, is analyzed.

1915 Henrikson, Alan K. "The Creation of the North Atlantic Alliance, 1948–1952." *Naval War College Review* 33 (1980): 4–39.

This essay examines the founding of NATO: the treaty, the organizational structure, and the military forces—what conditions required and fostered NATO and why what resulted, rather than something else, did result. Notes.

1916 Ireland, Timothy P. *Creating the Entangling Alliance: The Origins of the North Atlantic Treaty Organization*. Westport, CT: Greenwood, 1981.

Ireland develops the role of the "European initiative" in overcoming the initial reluctance of the Truman administration (1946–50) toward discarding 150 years of isolationism. Notes, bibliography, index.

1917 Ismay, Lionel [Lord Hastings]. *NATO: The First Five Years, 1949–1954*. Paris: NATO, 1955.

This detailed official study chronicles the historical development of NATO and provides some insight into its internal workings.

1918 Kaplan, Lawrence S. *A Community of Interests: NATO and the Military Assistance Program, 1948–1951*. Washington, DC: Office of the Secretary of Defense, Historical Office, 1980.

This closely written account seeks to clarify the objectives and activities of various American governmental bureaucracies as plans for foreign aid and military assistance were developed. Tables and charts, notes, bibliographical notes, appendixes, index.

1919 Kaplan, Lawrence S. "The Korean War and U.S. Foreign Relations: The Case of NATO." In F. H. Heller, *The Korean War: A 25-Year Perspective*. Lawrence: Regents Press of Kansas, 1977, pp. 36–78.

Kaplan points out how the Korean War was instrumental in transforming NATO from largely a paper organization into an effective military force with a substantial American military contribution. Notes and comments.

1920 Kaplan, Lawrence S. "Toward the Brussels Pact." *Prologue* 12 (1980): 73–86.

The division of Germany, widespread disunity, and the Czech crisis of February 1948 led to the signing of the collective defense treaty at Brussels on 17 March 1948. The United States had clearly signaled its readiness to abandon its traditional isolationism and to provide aid. Notes.

1921 Kaplan, Lawrence S. "The United States and the Atlantic Alliance: The First Generation." In John Braeman, Robert H. Bremmer, and David Broday, eds. *Twentieth-Century American Foreign Policy*. Columbus: Ohio State University Press, 1971, pp. 294–342.

The acceptance of NATO by the U.S. Senate assured the success of the Mutual Defense Assistance Act of 1949, and the beginnings of massive shipments of military supplies to the Allies under Article 3. Footnotes.

1922 Kaplan, Lawrence S. "The United States and the Origins of NATO, 1946–1949." *Review of Politics* 31 (1969): 210–22.

Kaplan suggests that one significant aspect of World War II and the postwar years was the rediscovery of Europe and its importance to the well-being of the United States. Consequently, there was little public opposition to U.S. membership in NATO. Notes.

1923 Newman, Parley W., Jr. "The Origins of the North Atlantic Treaty: A Study in Organization and Politics." Ph.D. dissertation, Columbia University, 1977.

This study reconstructs the political process which led the Truman administration in early 1948 to open negotiations with Western European nations and Canada on a North Atlantic security pact. DAI 38:3038-A.

1924 Osgood, Robert E. *NATO: The Entangling Alliance.* Chicago: University of Chicago Press, 1962.

Chapters 1 to 4 deal with the establishment and early functioning of NATO during the Truman years. Notes, index.

1925 Petersen, Nikolaj. "Who Pulled Whom and How Much? Britain, the United States and the Making of the North Atlantic Treaty." *Millennium* [Great Britain] 11 (1982): 93–114.

NATO developed out of repeated suggestions and responses between the Americans and British during the first six months of 1948. Notes.

1926 Reid, Escott. *Time of Fear and Hope: The Making of the North Atlantic Treaty, 1947–1949.* Toronto: McClelland & Stewart, 1981.

This account is a full examination of the origins and formulation of the North Atlantic Treaty Organization (NATO), which concludes that the U.S. entry into NATO was a revolutionary change in American foreign policy. Notes, index.

1927 Smith, E. Timothy. "The Fear of Subversion: The United States and the Inclusion of Italy in the North Atlantic Treaty." *Diplomatic History* 7 (1983): 139–55.

The United States pressed for the inclusion of Italy in NATO. This account reviews the negotiations and provides insight into Italian-American relations. Notes.

1928 Szent-Miklosy, Istvan. "Development of American Thinking on an Atlantic Community, 1945–1962." Ph.D. dissertation, Columbia University, 1962.

While the concept of an Atlantic Community resulted in the pooling of strength in the face of common enemies, the Atlantic Community concept has grown to encompass cultural and economic ideas. DAI 24:4775.

1929 Truitt, Wesley B. "The Troops of Europe Decision: The Process, Politics, and Diplomacy of a Strategic Commitment." Ph.D. dissertation, Columbia University, 1968.

This study investigates the political and diplomatic factors involved in the American decision to send troops to Europe (1950–51), establish SHAPE,

appoint Eisenhower commander, and rearm West Germany. DAI 32:3402-A.

1930 Vaern, Grethe. "The United States, Norway, and the Atlantic Pact, 1948–1949." *Scandinavian Studies* 50 (1978): 150–76.

Norway's entry into NATO is reviewed. Notes.

INTERNATIONAL ECONOMICS

See also Chapter 4, *Trade and Tariffs*, for additional references.

Trade and Overseas Investment

1931 Brewer, William C., Jr. "The Proposal for Investment Guarantees by an International Agency." *American Journal of International Law* 58 (1964): 62–87.

Proposals advanced through the World Bank between 1947 and 1961 to establish international investment guarantee agencies to secure private foreign investments against political risks are discussed.

1932 Burnham, Jeffrey B. "The Overseas Private Investment Guaranty Program: From the Marshall Plan to the Overseas Private Investment Corporation." Ph.D. dissertation, Claremont Graduate School, 1978.

U.S. policy since 1948 has been to encourage and assist social and economic development of the less-developed countries. The Overseas Private Investment Guaranty Program was the primary instrument to encourage private American investment; its evolution, from originating as part of the Marshall Plan, is traced. DAI 38:6919-A.

1933 Cahn, Linda A. "National Power and International Regimes: United States Commodity Policies, 1930–1980." Ph.D. dissertation, Stanford University, 1981.

This study investigates the relationship between changes in state power and policy strategies in the context of international markets. DAI 41:4828.

1934 Carlisle, Rodney. "The American Century Implemented: Stettinius and the Liberian Flag of Convenience." *Business History Review* 54 (1980): 175–91.

The Liberian Maritime Code, which now registers a major portion of the world's shipping, resulted from private activities of former Secretary of State Edward R. Stettinius, Jr. (1947–49). He hoped to stimulate new development in Liberia through the infusion of U.S. capital and expertise. Notes.

1935 Chu, Gail Yanagihara. "The Relationship Between U.S. Foreign Direct Investments and U.S.

Treaties and Agreements, 1946–1966." Ph.D. dissertation, University of Washington, 1973.

This study questions if a discernible relationship exists between U.S. foreign direct investment earnings and capital outflows, and the number of bilateral economic-related treaties signed by the United States (1946–66). DAI 34:4486-A.

1936 Eckes, Alfred E., Jr. *A Search for Solvency: Bretton Woods and the International Monetary System, 1941–1971.* Austin: University of Texas Press, 1975.

This volume concentrates on American planning for the postwar monetary order, emphasizing the efforts of Treasury policymakers, particularly Morgenthau and Harry Dexter White, to formulate and effect the Bretton Woods system. Notes, bibliography, index.

1937 Folts, David W. "The Role of the President and Congress in the Formulation of United States Economic Policy Towards the Soviet Union, 1947–1968." Ph.D. dissertation, University of Notre Dame, 1971.

This study examines the impact of the division of powers between the president and Congress on the development of U.S. economic policy toward the Soviet Union. DAI 32:4075-A.

1938 Gardner, Richard N. *Sterling-Dollar Diplomacy.* Expanded ed. New York: McGraw-Hill, 1969.

In the interaction of public opinion and economic relations between the United States and Britain, such institutions as the Bretton Woods organizations, the Anglo-American Loan Agreement, the International Trade Organization, and the General Agreement on Tariffs and Trade are discussed. Illustrations, notes, bibliography, index.

1939 Green, Philip E. "Conflict Over Trade Ideologies During the Early Cold War: A Study of American Foreign Economic Policy." Ph.D. dissertation, Duke University, 1978.

In an effort to expand American postwar trade, the Department of State devised a world multilateral trade system to replace the restrictive and bilateral measures of the 1930s. During 1944 to 1947 the Soviet Union did not accept Washington's trade concepts. DAI 39:7468-A.

1940 Kuznets, Simon. "Quantitative Aspects of the Economic Growth of Nations." *Economic Development and Cultural Change* 2 (1963): 1–80.

Income distribution is reviewed for Europe, Great Britain, the Near East, Latin America, and the United States, 1945–63.

1941 Lehman, Ernest D. "Attitudes of Selected Business Groups toward American Foreign Economic

Policy, 1945–1955." Ph.D. dissertation, University of Chicago, 1961/62.

Policies of the Committee for Economic Development and the National Association of Manufacturers are reviewed as they related to American foreign policy. Neither the NAM nor the CED were willing to sacrifice domestic tranquility to innovation in international economic relations.

1942 Maier, Charles S. "The Politics of Productivity: Foundations of American International Economic Policy After World War II." *International Organization* 31 (1977): 607–33.

Although American policymakers had an opportunity to shape the international economic order immediately after World War II, U.S. representatives vacillated between political and economic objectives. Notes.

1943 Murans, Francis. "Reciprocal Trade Agreements Program, 1945–1955." Ph.D. dissertation, Michigan State University, 1957.

The Reciprocal Trade Agreements Act (1945) increased the power of the chief executive to expand the U.S. trading markets. Subsequently, Congress passed a restrictive Trade Agreements Act (1948). DAI: 20:1203.

1944 Oliver, Robert W. *International Economic Cooperation and the World Bank.* London: Macmillan, 1975.

American plans for the International Bank for Reconstruction and Development, as envisioned by Harry Dexter White, are reviewed. The Bretton Woods Agreements (1945) established the bank. Notes, bibliography, index.

1945 Parks, Wallace J. *United States Administration of Its International Economic Affairs.* Baltimore: Johns Hopkins University Press, 1951.

This account comprises a broad survey of most of the significant international activities during the Truman years. Its thrust is essentially thematic, focusing on the operations of such agencies as the Civil Aeronautics Board, Department of Agriculture, Department of Interior, Treasury Department, etc. Notes, index.

1946 Pollard, Robert A. "Economic Security and the Origins of the Cold War: The Strategic Ends of U.S. Foreign Economic Policy, 1945–1950." Ph.D. dissertation, University of North Carolina, 1983.

The United States opposed all forms of economic nationalism, Left or Right, and moved as vigorously against commercial discrimination by Britain as by Russia. The Truman administration largely achieved its mission of an integrated world economy that served the collective security of the Western democracies. DAI 44:1181-A.

1947 Saxberg, Borje O. "United States Governmental Investment Guarantee Program for Private Foreign Direct Investments, Development and Application, 1946–1954." Ph.D. dissertation, University of Illinois, 1958.

A system of federal government investment guarantees was provided in the Economic Cooperation Act of 1948 and renewed in subsequent foreign assistance legislation. Investors utilized $48.6 million in guarantees (1945–54). Available guarantee authority was $200 million; in comparison, U.S. postwar private foreign direct investment averaged some $1.2 billion annually. Since large international corporations, rather than small businesses, claimed the guarantees, it indicated that the investment guarantees did not promote new investment. DAI 19:978.

1948 Schwartz, Robert J. "Obstacles to the United States Private Foreign Investments, 1946–1953." Ph.D. dissertation, American University, 1957.

Obstacles take the form of two major classifications, language and government, which of the latter there were found four factors: (1) nationalism and socialistic philosophies; (2) opposition of domestic interests; (3) unsatisfactory past experiences; and (4) fundamental disequilibrium in balance-of-payments. DAI 18:873.

1949 Stocking, Thomas E. "The Political Objectives of American Foreign Trade Policy, 1948–1973." Ph.D. dissertation, University of Minnesota, 1977.

This study seeks to describe how trade is used to accomplish political objectives; to determine how foreign policy objectives have influenced foreign trade policymaking; and to draw conclusions about the effectiveness of foreign trade as an instrument of foreign policy. DAI 38:6301-A.

Foreign Aid Programs
Also see, *UNRRA*.

1950 Aghassi, Marjorie E. "Little Legislatures: Four Committees and the Foreign Aid Program, 1947–1964." Ph.D. dissertation, Columbia University, 1967.

This study examines foreign aid decision-making in the House Appropriations and Foreign Affairs Committees and the Senate Foreign Relations and Appropriations Committees. The committees voted constituents' views and amended programs in response to interest groups. DAI 28:1861-A.

1951 Atwell, Mary W. "A Conservative Response to the Cold War: Senator James P. Kem and Foreign Aid." *Capitol Studies* 4 (1976): 53–66.

Kem's was a dissenting voice in the U.S. Senate (1945–50) when the Truman administration sent in foreign aid bills. Notes.

1952 Barber, Willard F. "Foreign Assistance Program: Some Basic Data." *Military Review* 45 (1965): 45–55.

Barber provides a chronological review of American foreign assistance agencies and their administrators (1941–64).

1953 Brown, David S. "The Public Advisory Board in the Federal Government: An Administrative Analysis of Several Boards with Particular Attention to the Public Advisory Board of the Economic Cooperation Administration and the Mutual Security Program." Ph.D. dissertation, Syracuse University, 1955.

Of twelve public advisory boards selected for this study, the Public Advisory Board of the Economic Cooperation Administration (later the Mutual Security Program) was examined closely. DAI 16:371.

1954 Brown, George Thompson, Jr. "Foreign Policy Legitimation: The Case of American Foreign Aid, 1947–1971." Ph.D. dissertation, University of Virginia, 1971.

Foreign policy legitimation is defined as the means by which foreign policy decision-makers attempt to achieve domestic acceptance of their policy objectives and the instruments for implementing those objectives. DAI 32:4690-A.

1955 Brown, William A., Jr., and Opie, Redvers. *American Foreign Assistance.* Washington, DC: Brookings Institution, 1953.

This study details U.S. foreign assistance during and after World War II. Bibliography, index.

1956 Chasteen, Robert J. "American Foreign Aid and Public Opinion, 1945–1952." Ph.D. dissertation, University of North Carolina, 1958.

Two major factors governing American foreign policy appear in foreign aid programs: (1) the primary reliance on anti-Sovietism to secure domestic and foreign support; (2) the movement to interventionism with emphasis on rearmament. DAI 19:2072.

1957 Hunt, Bonita L. "Bipartisanship: A Case Study of the Foreign Assistance Program, 1947–1956." Ph.D. dissertation, University of Texas, 1958.

This study covers eight cases, including the Truman Doctrine, the Marshall Plan, NATO, the Mutual Defense Assistance Act (1949), the Point Four Program, and the Mutual Security Act (1951). DAI 19:2383.

1958 Kutger, Joseph P. "The Military Assistance Program: Symphysis of the United States Foreign and

Military Policies." Ph.D. dissertation, University of Colorado, 1961.

Although nominally the Military Assistance Program is a component of U.S. military policy, it is not truly integrated into that policy, and the United States fails to reap the full advantage of the military aid programs. DAI 22:3254.

1959 Mangan, Mary. "The Congressional Image of Aid to the Underdeveloped Countries (1949–1959), As Revealed in the Congressional Hearings and Debates." Ph.D. dissertation, Yale University, 1964.

Because aid programs were never considered permanent by the majority of congressmen, no agreed foreign aid philosophy evolved. DAI 25:4242.

1960 McHale, James M. "The New Deal and the Origins of Public Lending for Foreign Economic Development, 1933–1945." Ph.D. dissertation, University of Wisconsin, 1970.

McHale finds that postwar programs of foreign aid emerged from the New Deal's approach to foreign lending. DAI 31:2851-A.

1961 O'Leary, Michael K. *Politics of American Foreign Aid.* New York: Atherton, 1967.

Although organized topically, there is scattered material which relates to the Truman years—especially on the Marshall Plan. Tables, notes, bibliography, index.

1962 Pach, Chester J., Jr. "Arming the Free World: The Origins of the United States Military Assistance Program, 1945–1949." Ph.D. dissertation, Northwestern University, 1981.

It was not until the Truman Doctrine that the United States embarked upon a comprehensive military assistance program, yet even then planning suffered from confusion and uncertainty. DAI 42:2264.

1963 Rieselbach, Leroy N. "The Demography of the Congressional Vote on Foreign Aid, 1939–1958." *American Political Science Review* 58 (1964): 577–88.

One of the Congresses singled out for quantitative analysis is the Eightieth (1947–48). Three variables are examined: personal, political, and constituency.

1964 Simpson, James R. "The Origins of United States' Academic Interest in Foreign Economic Development." *Economic Development and Cultural Change* 24 (1976): 633–44.

The role of the academic community is examined regarding the formation of economic development programs and foreign aid for developing nations (1940s–1950s). Notes.

1965 Smith, Gaddis. "What We Got for What We Gave: The American Experience with Foreign Aid." *American Heritage* 29:3 (1978): 64–71.

Smith points to 1947 as the beginning of foreign aid projects in the Truman administration; he finds that the setbacks in China and Korea and the Russian explosion of an atomic bomb in 1949–50 led to an almost complete militarization of foreign aid. Illustrations.

1966 Stamey, Roderick A., Jr. "The Origin of the United States Military Assistance Program." Ph.D. dissertation, University of North Carolina, Chapel Hill, 1972.

The central concern of the study is the development of the U.S. military assistance program, from its genesis in the wartime military aid program to Latin America until its institutionalization in the Mutual Security Program of 1951. DAI 33:4514-A.

1967 Stewart, Edward C. "American Advisors Overseas." *Military Review* 45 (1965): 3–9.

This account discusses the employment of American advisers, 1945–65, in foreign countries, especially Western Europe and Southeast Asia.

1968 U.S. Department of State. Office of Public Affairs. *Land Reform: A World Challenge; with Related Papers.* Publ. 4445. Economic Cooperation Series, 29.

This eighty-page pamphlet provides a useful survey of the land reform issues as perceived by the State Department in the early 1950s. U.S. policy is stated. Appendix.

1969 Wood, C. Tyler. "Problems of Foreign Aid Viewed From the Inside." *American Economic Review* 49 (1959): 203–15.

Philosophical misunderstanding plagued American foreign aid programs (1950–58) because it was assumed that the United States could quickly exert economic influence leading to political stability and democratization.

Point Four Assistance

1970 Atwood, Rollin S. "The United States Point Four Program: A Bilateral Approach." *Annals of the American Academy of Political and Social Sciences* (1959): 33–39.

The article examines the development of bilateral technical cooperation programs through the International Cooperation Administration of the Overseas Mission (1939–58).

1971 Baldwin, David A. *Economic Development and American Foreign Policy.* Chicago: University of Chicago Press, 1966.

This study contains over 100 pages devoted to the development and functioning of the Point Four Program (1949–53). Tables, notes, bibliography, index.

1972 Bose, Tarun C. "The Point Four Programme: A Critical Study." *International Studies* [India] 7 (1965): 66–97.

The motives, objectives, and accomplishments of Truman's Point Four Program—to make technical and scientific information available to underdeveloped areas—are surveyed. The author applauds the initial phase (1949–53) but criticizes later years. Notes.

1973 Engel, Salo. "Point Four and Codification." *American Journal of International Law* 53 (1959): 889–92.

This essay describes codification of law undertaken under the auspices of the Point Four Program in Liberia, Panama, Turkey, and Thailand (1952–58).

1974 Freidell, Theodore P. "Truman's Point Four: Legislative Enactment and Development in Latin America." Ph.D. dissertation, University of Missouri, Kansas City, 1965.

Truman's Point Four Program called for a U.S. policy to combat communism through long-range economic development based on technical cooperation. The program did overcome congressional opposition toward helping underdeveloped countries. DAI 28:590-A.

1975 Grant, James P. "Perspectives on Development Aid: World War II to Today and Beyond." *American Academy of Political and Social Sciences* (1979): 1–12.

Beginning with Truman's Point Four Program, Grant traces the growth and directions of American developmental aid.

1976 Hardin, William H. "John Kee and the Point Four Compromise." *West Virginia History* 41 (1979): 40–58.

This study describes Kee's role as chairman of the House Foreign Affairs Committee in guiding the Point Four Program past Republican opposition.

1977 Hummon, John P. "Protestants and Point Four: The Churches' Response to U.S. Programs of Aid to the Underdeveloped Countries." Ph.D. dissertation, University of Michigan, 1958.

Protestant spokesmen argued that long-range developmental assistance should be free of any political and military "strings" and that the United States should make greater use of multilateral channels for distribution of its economic and technical assistance. DAI 19:1431.

1978 Kaufman, Frank L. "United States Developmental Foreign Aid: An Examination of the Needs of Under-Developed Nations as Represented in the Statements of the Policy-Makers." Ph.D. dissertation, George Washington University, 1969.

This study examines the viewpoints of high-level policymakers (1949–66) on which needs of underdeveloped nations foreign aid programs should attempt to satisfy and whether these needs are related to the U.S. interests. DAI 29:4083-A.

1979 Paterson, Thomas G. "Foreign Aid Under Wraps: The Point Four Program." *Wisconsin Magazine of History* 56 (1972/73): 119–26.

Paterson argues that the Point Four Program was settled upon when it became clear that it could no longer assume that developing nations would automatically side with the West in the Cold War. Notes.

1980 Rulon, Philip R. "Henry Garland Bennett: The Father of the 'Great Adventure' in University Contracts Abroad." *Red River History Review* 2 (1975): 255–72.

Bennett was the first administrator of the Technical Cooperation Administration.

1981 Salamon, Benjamin. "Point Four: A Study in Political Motivation and Administrative Techniques." Ph.D. dissertation, London School of Economics, 1957.

Examined are the motives behind the Point Four Program, the passage of Point Four legislation, and administration of that program by the Technical Cooperation Administration (1950–52).

Private Agencies

1982 Cazier, Stanford O. "CARE: A Study of Cooperative Voluntary Relief." Ph.D. dissertation, University of Wisconsin, 1964.

CARE was created in 1945 by twenty-two private welfare agencies as an emergency vehicle through which Americans could aid relatives and friends in war-torn Europe. Its activities spread to include Asia and South America and grew to include distribution of surplus agricultural commodities. DAI 24:4158.

1983 Curti, Merle. *American Philanthropy Abroad: A History*. New Brunswick: Rutgers University Press, 1963.

In this history of nonofficial efforts to help peoples abroad, several chapters are devoted to American philanthropy during the Truman era. Notes, bibliography, index.

1984 Sullivan, Robert R. "The Politics of Altruism: The American Church-State Conflict in the Food-For-Peace Program." *Journal of Church and State* 11 (1969): 47–61.

Since the Agricultural Act of 1949, a partnership has existed between the federal government and voluntary agencies to distribute surplus food abroad. A Church-State conflict arose between two of the four private agencies: the Catholic Relief Services sought to increase its government allotment, while the

Lutheran World Relief resisted expansion in order to stress self-reliance and individual initiative among Third World peoples. Notes.

1985 Sullivan, Robert R. "The Politics of Altruism: A Study of the Partnership Between the United States Government and American Voluntary Relief Agencies for the Donation Abroad of Surplus Agricultural Commodities, 1949–1967." Ph.D. dissertation, Johns Hopkins University, 1968.

From the government's point of view, the primary interests served are those of American agriculture through disposal of surplus farm products. The primary interests served by the voluntary agencies are those of suffering humanity abroad. DAI 29: 1942-A.

INTERNATIONAL ORGANIZATIONS

See also Chapter 3, *Diplomats*, for Warren Austin.

1986 Bantell, John F. "The Origins of the World Government Movement: The Dublin Conference and After." *Research Studies* 42 (1974): 20–35.

The American concern with an international security organization resulted in a conference held at Dublin, New Hampshire on 11 October 1945. The Dublin Conference, the emerging Declaration of the Dublin Conference, and the decline of interest in the face of the emerging Cold War are discussed.

1987 Bantell, John F. "Perpetual Peace Through World Law: The United World Federalists and the Movement for Limited World Government, 1945–1951." Ph.D. dissertation, University of Connecticut, 1980.

The world government movement (UWF) conducted a lobbying and educational campaign (1945–51) to convince the American people and their leaders that the United States should take the lead in transforming the United Nations into a genuine world government. DAI 40:6412-A.

1988 Barros, James. "Pearson or Lie: The Politics of the Secretary-General's Selection, 1946." *Canadian Journal of Political Science* 10 (1977): 65–92.

The motives and methods of the United States, Britain, and Russia are examined as they reflected on the selection of the United Nations' first secretary-general. Notes.

1989 Brindley, Thomas A. "American Goals in the Educational Policy of UNESCO, 1946–1964." Ph.D. dissertation, University of Michigan, 1968.

The U.S. efforts to shape the structure and organization, its concern with ideological questions, and its direct advocacy of major programs in education, science, and culture are examined. DAI 30: 484-A.

1990 Campbell, Thomas M. *Masquerade Peace: America's UN Policy, 1944–1945*. Tallahassee: Florida State University Press, 1973.

The conflicting dreams and aspirations of American leaders for a democratic and economically open world led tragically to the Cold War. Notes, bibliography, index.

1991 Cefkin, John L. "A Study of the United States National Commission for UNESCO." Ph.D. dissertation, Columbia University, 1954.

The U.S. national commission (1946–52) consisted of 100 persons: sixty representing national organizations, fifteen representing state and local governments, fifteen selected at large, and ten representing the federal government. The commission was concerned with education, science, and culture. DAI 14:2114.

1992 Cohen, Benjamin V. "The Impact of the United Nations on United States Foreign Policy." *International Organization* 5 (1951): 274–81.

U.S. policies (1945–51) toward former colonies and other non-Western nations are reviewed by a former State Department counselor. Notes.

1993 Divine, Robert A. *Second Chance: The Triumph of Internationalism in America During World War II*. New York: Atheneum, 1967.

The last chapter brings Truman into the picture; however, the earlier chapters are useful in understanding American hopes, expectations, and programs at the San Francisco Conference. Bibliographical essay, notes, index.

1994 Eilers, John A. "Origins of the Cold War: The Founding of the United Nations." Ph.D. dissertation, University of Iowa, 1972.

The author concludes that the Cold War had begun even before the establishment of the United Nations in the early summer of 1945. The United States believed at San Francisco that the United Nations must further the American view of the world. DAI 33:6996-A.

1995 Epstein, Mathew H. "A Study of the Editorial Opinions of the New York City Newspapers Toward the League of Nations and the United Nations During the First Year of Life, 1919–1920 and 1945–1946." Ph.D. dissertation, New York University, 1954.

This study reveals the expanded interest in international affairs by 1945–46. DAI 14:816.

1996 Finger, Seymour M. *Your Man in the U.N.: People, Politics, and Bureaucracy in the Making of Foreign Policy.* New York: New York University Press, 1980.

It is Finger's thesis that the individual chosen by the president to represent the United States at the United Nations is a key figure in American foreign policy. Chapter 3 covers Stettinius and Austin, Truman appointees. Notes, index.

1997 Gross, Franz B. "The U.S. National Interest and the UN." *Orbis* 7 (1963): 367–85.

The author reviews U.S. policies (1945–63) while noting the various dilemmas and shifts in goals. Notes.

1998 Mann, Peggy. *Ralph Bunche: U.N. Peacemaker.* New York: Coward, McCann & Geoghegan, 1975.

Bunche's background and his efforts on behalf of the United Nations (from Dumbarton Oaks to his death in 1971) are surveyed. Illustrations, bibliography, index.

1999 Mazuzan, George T. "America's U.N. Commitment, 1945–1953." *Historian* 40 (1978): 309–30.

The account reviews U.S. policy at the United Nations by viewing the work of Warren Austin. See Mazuzan's biography of Austin in Chapter 3. Notes.

2000 Michalak, Stanley J., Jr. "The Senate and the United Nations: A Study of Changing Perceptions About the Utilities and Limitations of the United Nations as an Instrument of Peace and Security and its Role in American National Security Policy." Ph.D. dissertation, Princeton University, 1967.

This study reconstructs the Senate's image of international politics during crisis periods, among them the debate over ratification of the United Nations, the Vandenberg Resolution, and the Korean War. DAI 28:3246-A.

2001 Morales-Yordan, Jorge. "The United States and Non-Self Governing Areas: A Study of the Relationship of the United States and the United Nations under Chapter XI of the Charter." Ph.D. dissertation, American University, 1958.

This study examines the policies of the United States regarding non-self-governing territories (1944–57). Basically, this involves Third World peoples and the colonial powers, a combination which has put severe pressure on American policy. DAI 19:3005.

2002 Raith, Charles A. "The Anti-UN Coalition Before the Senate Foreign Relations and the House Foreign Relations Committees During the Years, 1945–1955." Ph.D. dissertation, University of Pennsylvania, 1962.

Those groups most frequently opposing the United Nations were the National Economic Council, the American Coalition, the Christian Nationalist Crusade, the National Sojourners, the Daughters of the American Revolution, the Veterans of Foreign Wars, and the American Legion, all organizations on the extreme right. DAI 23:1407.

2003 Riggs, Robert E. "Overselling the U.N. Charter: Fact and Myth." *International Organization* 14 (1960): 277–90.

The author concludes that the United Nations was not oversold to the American people, and suggests that the myth may have had its basis in the personal disappointments of the people whose hopes for a better world were frustrated by the Cold War. Notes.

2004 Riggs, Robert E. *Politics in the United Nations: A Study of United States Influence in the General Assembly.* Illinois Studies in the Social Sciences, Vol. 41. Urbana: University of Illinois Press, 1958.

American influence in the first nine sessions of the U.N. General Assembly "has varied from session to session, apparently reaching a peak in 1950, and declining markedly in 1953 and 1954." Tables, bibliography, index.

2005 Smith, Jesse R. "Role of the United States in Building the United Nations Organization, 1944–1945." Ph.D. dissertation, University of Utah, 1973.

American leaders went all out to "sell" the United Nations to the American public, but they avoided many of the procedural mistakes of the past. DAI 34:4172-A.

2006 Wooley, Wesley T., Jr. "The Quest for Permanent Peace: American Supranationalism, 1945–1947." *Historian* 35 (1972): 18–31.

This review finds that the individuals and organizations rejected isolationism and collective security in favor of a reformed, cooperative world order. Notes.

Collective and Regional Security

2007 Bradshaw, James S. "Senator Arthur H. Vandenberg and Article 51 of the United Nations Charter." *Mid-America* 57 (1975): 145–56.

Vandenberg was responsible for the acceptance of Article 51, which restated a nation's inherent right to self-defense. The author believes that this point of view has prevailed in America's postwar foreign policy. Notes.

2008 Briggs, Philip J. "Senator Vandenberg, Bipartisanship and the Origins of United Nations' Article 51." *Mid-America* 60 (1978): 163–69.

Arthur H. Vandenberg was an American delegate to the San Francisco Conference where the U.N. Charter was drafted. He, Nelson A. Rockefeller, and Harold Stassen were responsible for Article 51 which allowed regional commitments to self-defense organizations. Notes.

2009 Frolick, David A. "The Law and Practice of Collective Security in Contemporary International Relations." Ph.D. dissertation, American University, 1971.

This study evaluates the impact of the use of military force under Article 51 of the U.N. Charter and the major multilateral collective security agreements on the law of collective self-defense. Among the cases examined are NATO and the United Nations in Korea. DAI 32:5319-A.

2010 Stromberg, Roland N. *Collective Security and American Foreign Policy: From the League of Nations to NATO*. New York: Praeger, 1963.

Stromberg discusses the inception, growth, and decline of the idea of collective security, finding that the concept of collective security is relatively utopian and that the modern democratic mind has turned toward a more realistic politik. Notes, index.

2011 Tillapaugh, J. "Closed Hemisphere and Open World? The Dispute over Regional Security at the U.N. Conference, 1945." *Diplomatic History* 2 (1978): 24–42.

The dispute over regional security was not an attempt by the United States to control the Western Hemisphere; rather it resulted as Latin American nations forced the issue. Notes.

UNRRA

2012 George, James H., Jr. "United States Postwar Relief Planning: the First Phase, 1940–1943." Ph.D. dissertation, University of Wisconsin, 1970.

George's focus is on the formation of the United Nations Relief and Rehabilitation Administration (UNRRA) and the inter-Allies discussions and revisions that ensued. DAI 31:2305-A.

2013 Gustafson, Milton O. "Congress and Foreign Aid: The First Phase, UNRRA, 1943–1947." Ph.D. dissertation, University of Nebraska, 1966.

UNRRA operated during and after the war, mainly supported by U.S. funds. Congress became increasingly critical of UNRRA and in 1947 refused new appropriations. UNRRA ran out of money and had to terminate its activities. DAI 27:1755.

2014 Schiller, Herbert I. "The United States Congress and the American Financial Contribution to the United Nations Relief and Rehabilitation Administration." Ph.D. dissertation, New York University, 1960.

From its inception, Congress was an unenthusiastic supporter of UNRRA (1943–47) and was increasingly reluctant to be held responsible for its financial upkeep. DAI 21:3292.

2015 UNRRA: *The History of the United Nations Relief and Rehabilitation Administration*. 3 vols. New York: Columbia University Press, 1950.

This contemporary and official history of UNRRA provides an administrative and operational history from 1943 to 1948. It is important for understanding UNRRA activities. Maps, graphs, charts, tables, chronology, index (vol. 2), and documents (vol. 3).

Human Rights Convention

See Chapter 3, *Diplomats*, for *Eleanor Roosevelt*.

2016 Formicola, Jo Renee. "The American Catholic Church and Its Role in the Formulation of United States Human Rights Foreign Policy 1945–1978." Ph.D. dissertation, Drew University, 1981.

During the early Cold War years, the Church was complacent about human rights and was more concerned with how to respond to communism. DAI 42:1296.

2017 Funston, James A. "The Definition of an International Bill of Human Rights." Ph.D. dissertation, Indiana University, 1955.

This study, based principally on the debates in the Commission on Human Rights and the General Assembly (1945–53), describes the main issues which arose during the drafting of the international Bill of Human Rights. DAI 15:1434.

2018 Grammatico, Angelina C. "The United Nations and the Development of Human Rights." Ph.D. dissertation, New York University, 1957.

The Commission on Human Rights sought to translate the Declaration of Human Rights (1948) into the Covenant on Economic, Social, and Cultural Rights. The U.S. Senate refused to ratify the covenant on the grounds it might supersede the U.S. Constitution on such issues as working conditions, wages, housing, education, etc. DAI 18:2193.

2019 Kendrick, Frank J. "The United States and the International Protection of Human Rights." *North Dakota Quarterly* 36 (1968): 29–45.

In tracing U.S. policies toward human rights (1941–68), the author finds that from 1941 to 1953 the United States was the leading advocate of international protection and sought treaties to achieve this end. Notes.

2020 Pratt, Virginia A. "The Influence of Domestic Controversy on American Participation in the United Nations Commission on Human Rights, 1945–1953." Ph.D. dissertation, University of Minnesota, 1971.

American enthusiasm and leadership in the U.N. Commission on Human Rights culminated in the Universal Declaration of Human Rights in 1948. Yet efforts to translate the declaration into a legal covenant resulted in the United States announcing in 1953 it did not intend to sign any international covenants on human rights. DAI 32:6349-A.

2021 Whiteman, Marjorie M. "Mrs. Franklin D. Roosevelt and the Human Rights Commission." *American Journal of International Law* 62 (1968): 918–21.

The qualities of character, persistence, and wisdom that enabled Mrs. Roosevelt, as chairman, to lead the commission (1947–51) to the drafting of the Declaration of Human Rights are reviewed.

Genocide Convention

2022 Korey, William. "America's Shame: The Unratified Genocide Treaty." *Midstream* 27 (1981): 7–13.

The author traces the history of the Genocide Treaty passed by the U.N. General Assembly in 1948 and explains why the treaty has remained unratified by the U.S. Senate for thirty-two years.

2023 Korey, William. "What Hope for the Genocide Convention?" *Vista* 8 (1972): 43–45, 51.

The U.N. role in investigating possible cases of genocide (1948–72) is discussed along with the reasons the United States has failed to ratify the convention.

2024 McFarland, Richard F. "The United States and the United Nations Convention on the Prevention and Punishment of the Crime of Genocide." Ph.D. dissertation, American University, 1971.

The U.S. Senate refused to ratify the U.N. Convention on Genocide when it was submitted for approval in 1949 and resubmitted in 1970. The two sets of hearings are compared as are the responses of the Truman administration. DAI 32:5322-A.

General George C. Marshall inspects Communist Chinese troops during his mission to China. L to R: Mao Zedong, Zhou Enlai, General Marshall, unidentified Chinese officer, and General Chu Teh.

8

Foreign Affairs: Bilateral Relations

One legacy of World War II was the end of America's political isolationism and its increased bilateral involvement around the globe. While the reasons for this expanded involvement vary from nation to nation, they generally centered on strategic or economic factors. Whereas previous U.S. involvement in foreign areas had largely taken the form of private commercial enterprise, the Truman administration often felt compelled to supplement private activities with government programs for economic and military assistance. While the general nature of these economic activities is discussed in Chapter 7, "International Economics," the political relationships with specific nations are dealt with in this chapter. Additional references may be found in Richard Dean Burns, *Guide to American Foreign Relations Since 1700* (#3023).

The Truman administration demonstrated little interest in African affairs; on the other hand, it found itself increasingly involved with Australia and New Zealand. The extension of this World War II relationship to the ANZUS Pact of 1951 is reviewed by Joseph M. Siracusa and Glen St. J. Barclay, "Australia, the United States, and the Cold War, 1945–51" (#2038). At the same time American corporations greatly expanded their investments in Canada, the implication of which is explored by R. S. Bothwell and J. R. English, "Canadian Trade Policy in the Age of American Dominance and British Decline, 1945–1947" (#2043).

East Asian and Southeast Asian affairs also commanded much of the Truman administration's attention as Cold War issues came to influence American policy considerations. An introduction to these policies may be found in Russell D. Buhite, *Soviet-American Relations in Asia, 1945–1954* (#2055), and Akira Iriye, *The Cold War in Asia: A Historical*

Introduction (#2062). Sino-American relations are surveyed in Dorothy Borg and Waldo Heinrichs, eds., *Uncertain Years: Chinese-American Relations, 1947–1950* (#2069), and Tang Tsou, *America's Failure in China, 1941–50* (#2100). American policies during the Chinese civil war are discussed by John F. Melby, *The Mandate of Heaven: Record of a Civil War, 1945–1949* (#2112), and S. I. Levine, "A New Look at American Mediation in the Chinese Civil War: The Marshall Mission" (#2117). N. B. Tucker, *Patterns in the Dust: Chinese-American Relations and the Recognition Controversy, 1949–1950* (#2151) examines the political implications of American recognition of the new Communist Chinese government.

The Truman administration's policies and aspirations in Korea have been widely explored. William W. Stueck, Jr., *The Road to Confrontation: American Policy Toward China and Korea, 1947–1950* (#2238), Frank Baldwin, ed., *Without Parallel: The American-Korean Relationship Since 1945* (#2217) argue that American anticommunism and security concerns provided the foundations for the Truman administration's interest in Korea. Bruce Cumings, *The Origins of the Korean War: Liberation and the Emergence of Separate Regimes, 1945–1947* (#2223) suggests that American policymakers overlooked significant cultural factors in that country. Chapter 10 deals with the Korean War.

American occupation policies in Japan have also come in for considerable scrutiny. J. C. Perry, *Beneath the Eagle's Wings: Americans in Occupied Japan* (#2182), and J. W. Dower, "Occupied Japan as History and Occupation History as Politics" (#2166) introduce the reader to issues and interpretations. Japanese war crimes are reviewed by Philip R. Piccigallo, *The Japanese on Trial: Allied War Crimes Operations in the East, 1945–1951* (#2197);

American-Japanese efforts to write a peace treaty are examined by Frederick S. Dunn, *Peacemaking and the Settlement with Japan* (#2204).

Indonesia's struggle to achieve independence, with American assistance, is reviewed in Robert J. McMahon, *Colonialism and Cold War: The United States and the Struggle for Indonesian Independence, 1945–1949* (#2272). G. C. Herring, "The Truman Administration and the Restoration of French Sovereignty in Indochina" (#2292) examines America's involvement in the early days of the first Indochina War. American politics and hopes in South Asia are summarized by Gary R. Hess, *America Encounters India, 1941–1947* (#2315).

Latin American issues were largely ignored during the Truman years. R. R. Trask, "The Impact of the Cold War on United States-Latin American Relations, 1945-1949" (#2344) provides a useful summary of the issues. America's objections to the Peron government are detailed in C. A. MacDonald, "The Politics of Intervention: The United States and Argentina, 1941–1946" (#2354).

Expanding American interests in the Middle East found the Cold War to be only one of several problems it confronted there. Bruce R. Kuniholm, *The Origins of the Cold War in the Near East: Great Power Conflict and Diplomacy in Iran, Turkey, and Greece* (#2372) identifies the initial Soviet-American confrontations. Arab-Israeli issues pressed themselves to the forefront during the Truman years, as can be seen in E. M. Wilson, *Decision on Palestine: How the U.S. Came to Recognize Israel* (#2417), and Zvi Ganin, *Truman, American Jewry and Israel, 1945–1948* (#2409). Michael B. Stoff, *Oil, War and American Security: The Search for a National Policy on Foreign Oil, 1941–1947* (#2441) emphasizes that petroleum requirements also raised serious considerations.

While Chapter 7, "Containment Policies and Programs," relates to America's concerns with Western Europe, this chapter provides much supplementary material relating to specific Cold War issues. For example, Geir Lundestad, *America, Scandinavia, and the Cold War, 1945–1949* (#2471), and Lawrence S. Wittner, *American Intervention in Greece, 1945–1949* (#2603) look at American policies in different regions. Issues affecting British and French relations with the United States are discussed by Donald C. McKay, *The United States and France* (#2486), and Terry H. Anderson, *The United States, Great Britain, and the Cold War, 1944–1947* (#2574).

Questions relating to Germany required considerable attention from the Truman administration. U.S. occupation policies are reviewed by J. H. Backer, *Priming the German Economy: American Occupation Policies, 1945–1948* (#2511), and John Gimbel, *The American Occupation of Germany: Politics and the Military, 1945–1949* (#2520). War crimes trials are examined by Bradley F. Smith, *Reaching Judgment at Nuremberg* (#2552); while Soviet-American differences are the subject of W. P. Davison, *The Berlin Blockade: A Study in Cold War Politics* (#2556).

Africa

2025　American Assembly. *The United States and Africa.* New York: Columbia University Press, 1958.

This volume is a summary of a three-day conference which discussed postwar American policy toward Africa. Tables, maps, index.

2026　Baum, Edward. "The United States, Self-Government and Africa: An Examination of the Nature of the American Policy on Self-Determination with Reference to Africa in the Postwar Era." Ph.D. dissertation, University of California, Los Angeles, 1964.

After the war, the United States found itself caught between the European nations seeking to maintain their empires and the colonial peoples demanding self-determination. The Cold War focused American attention on rebuilding Europe in order to protect its national security. DAI 25:5367.

2027　Emerson, Rupert. *Africa and the United States' Policy.* Englewood Cliffs, NJ: Prentice-Hall, 1967.

American policy toward Africa, from Truman to Johnson, is summarized in this volume. There was little concern with Africa during the Truman years. Notes, index.

2028　Isaacman, Allan, and Davis, Jennifer. "United States Policy toward Mozambique since 1945: 'The Defense of Colonialism and Regional Stability'." *Africa Today* 25 (1978): 29–55.

The United States desired stability and anti-communism; therefore, Mozambique has been considered in a global context and not as an independent entity. Notes.

2029　Miller, Jean-Donald. "The United States and Colonial Sub-Saharan Africa, 1939–1945." Ph.D. dissertation, University of Connecticut, 1981.

During the war, colonial Africa occupied a central place in Allied strategy, and America refrained from supporting nationalism in Africa. With the emerging tensions between the United States and the Soviet Union at the close of the war, Washington viewed as inappropriate African decolonization. DAI 42:822.

2030 Solomon, Mark. "Black Critics of Colonialism and the Cold War." In Thomas G. Paterson, ed. *Cold War Critics: Alternatives to American Foreign Policy in the Truman Years.* Chicago: Quadrangle, 1971, pp. 205–39.

Solomon argues that "by the end of World War II, black American intellectuals were united in believing that the battle against white racism in their own country could not be won without a larger international battle against colonial imperialism in Africa." Notes.

2031 Zingg, Paul J. "The Cold War in North Africa: American Foreign Policy and Postwar Muslim Nationalism, 1945–1962." *Historian* 39 (1976): 40–61.

U.S. foreign policy saw Morocco, Algeria, and Tunisia in terms of the East-West conflict, frequently blinding it to rising Third World nationalism. Notes.

SOUTH AFRICA

2032 Lake, Anthony. "Caution and Concern: The Making of American Policy toward South Africa, 1946–1971." Ph.D. dissertation, Princeton University, 1974.

Chapter 2 covers U.S. policymaking toward South Africa during the Truman years. DAI 35: 6222-A.

2033 Martin, Patrick H. "American Views on South Africa, 1948–1972." Ph.D. dissertation, Louisiana State University and Agricultural and Mechanical College, 1974.

This study contains early American criticism of the Nationalist party's apartheid policies. DAI 35:2906-A.

Australia, New Zealand, and Canada

AUSTRALIA/NEW ZEALAND

2034 Bell, Roger. "Australian-American Discord: Negotiations for Post-War Bases and Security Arrangements in the Pacific, 1944–1946." *Australian Outlook* 27 (1973): 12–23.

Australia was interested in a regional security pact but was opposed to the U.S. proposals for unilateral use of Manus Island and general U.S. expansion into the South Pacific region. Notes.

2035 Bell, Roger. "Australian-American Relations and Reciprocal Wartime Economic Assistance, 1941–46: An Ambivalent Association." *Australian Economic Historical Review* 16 (1976): 23–49.

Each nation attempted to exploit the wartime economic arrangement for national economic and trade benefits after the war. Notes.

2036 Collins, Hugh H. "Assuming Primacy: The Australian-American Alliance, 1950–1968." Ph.D. dissertation, Harvard University, 1979.

No abstract available.

2037 Dedman, John J. "Encounter Over Manus." *Australian Outlook* 20 (1966): 135–53.

American-Australian negotiations over the Manus Island naval base in the Admiralty Islands during 1946 to 1948 are reviewed. The former Australian minister of defense (1946–49) refutes charges that "Australia has virtually thrown the Americans out of Manus Island." Notes.

2038 Siracusa, Joseph M., and Barclay, Glen St. John. "Australia, the United States, and the Cold War, 1945–51: From V-J Day to ANZUS." *Diplomatic History* 5 (1981): 39–52.

U.S.-Australian relations entered a new phase after World War II, stimulated by Australia's desire for a formal military alliance and the U.S. unwillingness to enter into such a rigid arrangement. The Korean War changed the U.S. mind, and the result was the ANZUS Pact of 1951. Notes.

2039 Walter, Austin F. "Australia's Relations with the United States, 1941–1949." Ph.D. dissertation, University of Michigan, 1954.

The Labor party controlled the Australian government during this period, and Dr. Herbert V. Evatt was minister for external affairs. World War II signaled a new Australian interest in stronger ties with the United States. DAI 14:1247.

2040 Watt, Alan. "The Anzus Treaty: Past, Present and Future." *Australian Outlook* 24 (1970): 17–36.

The former permanent head of the Australian External Affairs Department recalls, at some length, the early efforts which led to the Anzus Treaty. Notes.

CANADA

See also Chapter 7, *North Atlantic Treaty Organization.*

2041 Aronsen, Lawrence R. "The Northern Frontier: United States Trade and Investment in Canada, 1945–1953." Ph.D. dissertation, University of Toronto, 1980.

Aronsen finds that investment in Canada during this period was particularly favorable. In the immediate postwar period, the U.S. government often had difficulty persuading businessmen to invest abroad, while Canada posed few problems regarding economic expansion. DAI 42:342.

2042 Augus, Henry F. *Canada and the Far East, 1940–1953*. Toronto: University of Toronto Press, 1953.

In this early account of the problems of the U.S.-Canadian alliance, the author focuses on the Korean War. Notes, index.

2043 Bothwell, Robert S., and English, John R. "Canadian Trade Policy in the Age of American Dominance and British Decline, 1945–1947." *Canadian Review of American Studies* 8 (1977): 52–65.

The authors believe that Canadian trade policy after World War II swung between a desire for multilateral agreements to resigned acceptance of American or British market preference. Notes.

2044 Harrington, Daniel F. "As Others Saw Us: A Canadian View of U.S. Policy Toward the Soviet Union, 1947." *Diplomatic History* 7 (1983): 239–44.

Hume Wright and Ambassador H. Hume Wrong of the Canadian embassy in Washington, DC prepared a critical review of U.S. foreign policy toward the Soviet Union on 4 December 1947. An edited version of this document is reprinted here. Notes.

2045 Holmes, John W. *The Shaping of Peace: Canada and the Search for World Order, 1943–1957*. Toronto: University of Toronto Press, 1979.

This volume, while it deals generally with Canada's foreign policy, does have material on the Truman years. Notes, bibliography, index.

2046 Jockel, Joseph T. "The United States and Canadian Efforts at Continental Air Defense, 1945–1957." Ph.D. dissertation, Johns Hopkins University, 1978.

This study examines the extent to which the relationship between the U.S. and Canadian air defense systems (1945–57) was affected by activities of the military establishments of the two countries. DAI 39:5709-A.

2047 Miller, E. H. "Canada's Role in the Origin of NATO." In G. N. Grob, ed. *Statesmen and Statescraft of the Modern West*. Barre, MA: Barre Publishers, 1967, pp. 251–90.

This dated analysis shows that Canada played a significant role in the founding and development of NATO. Notes.

2048 Page, Donald M., and Muton, Donald. "Canadian Images of the Cold War, 1946–47." *International Journal* 33 (1977): 577–604.

Official perceptions of Canadian officials of their Soviet and American counterparts are discussed, especially the assessments of Soviet intentions and U.S. responses. Notes.

2049 Pearson, Lester B. *Mike: The Memoirs of the Right Honourable Lester B. Pearson*. 3 vols. Edited by John A. Munro and Alex I. Inglis. Ontario: University of Toronto Press, 1972–73.

The last portion of volume 1 (pp. 239ff) and the early portion of volume 2 deal with Pearson's role as Canadian ambassador to Washington and his position as secretary of state for external affairs during the Truman years. This personal account touches on many aspects of U.S. foreign policy and relations with Canada. Index.

2050 Talarico, Joseph F. "A Study of the Postwar Pattern of Commerce and Finance between the United States and Canada, 1946–1953." Ph.D. dissertation, Rutgers University, 1958.

Attention is focused on the traditional U.S. surpluses on current account transactions with Canada and the methods of their redress. The most striking feature of this relationship, according to the author, has been the growth in economic interdependence. The movement of tremendous sums of U.S. investment money to Canada, beginning in 1950, is noted. DAI 19:243.

East Asia

2051 Allen, Louis. *The End of the War in Asia*. London: Hart-Davis, MacGibbon, 1976.

Allen discusses the impact of the surrender of the Japanese forces overseas and the political changes it brought in its wake. Notes, bibliography, index.

2052 Beloff, Max. *Soviet Policy in the Far East, 1944–1951*. London: Oxford University Press, 1953.

This dated study still provides a useful introduction to Soviet policy during these years. Appendix, footnotes, index.

2053 Blum, Robert M. *Drawing the Line: The Origins of the American Containment Policy in East Asia*. New York: Norton, 1982.

U.S. policy in China and Southeast Asia (1945–50) is the focal point of this account. Blum examines the impact of the Chinese Communist victory upon American policies in Southeast Asia. Notes, bibliography, index.

2054 Buhite, Russell D. " 'Major Interests': American Policy toward China, Taiwan, and Korea, 1945–1950." *Pacific Historical Review* 47 (1978): 425–51.

The author finds that American policymakers placed East Asian interests in a middle category between vital and peripheral, that is, as "major interests." These policymakers were concerned that no single power dominate Asia. Notes.

2055 Buhite, Russell D. *Soviet-American Relations in Asia, 1945–1954.* Norman: University of Oklahoma Press, 1981.

Buhite takes issue with revisionist historians who argue that policymakers misjudged Soviet intentions, thereby fomenting the Cold War; instead, American officials correctly read Soviet intentions but did not always form sound judgments on where or how to restrain Soviet expansion. Notes, bibliography, index.

2056 Chang, Yu Nan. "American Security Problems in the Far East, 1950–1952." Ph.D. dissertation, University of Washington, 1954.

This account focuses on the "Communist political plot" in the Far East as represented by the various national Communist movements, and on the U.S. efforts to strengthen the local government with military and economic aid. DAI 14:2114.

2057 Cohen, Warren I., ed. *New Frontiers in American East Asian Relations: Essays Presented to Dorothy Borg.* New York: Columbia University Press, 1983.

These essays examine recent writings on both sides of the Pacific regarding U.S.-East Asian relations, including the first comprehensive survey of American-Korean relations. Notes, index.

2058 Collier, Joseph M. "Editorial Reaction of Certain Catholic Periodicals to United States Department of State Policy in the Far East, 1950." Ph.D. dissertation, University of Kansas, 1969.

A comparison of editorials and public opinion polls indicates either widespread public apathy toward the threat of internal subversion or ignorance of Far Eastern problems. DAI 30:2924-A.

2059 Daoust, George A., Jr. "The Role of Air Power in U.S. Foreign Policy in the Far East, 1945–1958." Ph.D. dissertation, Georgetown University, 1967.

In each of three crises—Korea (1950–53), Indochina (1954), and Taiwan (1958)—U.S. actions were precipitated on the deterrent mission of strategic air power. DAI 28:3243-A.

2060 Foltos, Lester J. "The Bulwark of Freedom: American Security Policy for East Asia, 1945–1950." Ph.D. dissertation, University of Illinois, Urbana-Champaign, 1980.

This study examines the shifts in American policy from Roosevelt's plan to establish Western political, social, and economic values throughout the Far East through Truman's efforts to implement the Yalta agreement despite the deterioration of Soviet-American relations to the drastic shift in policy to containment. DAI 41:2734-A.

2061 Gaddis, John Lewis. "The Strategic Perspective: The Rise and Fall of the 'Defensive Perimeter' Concept, 1947–1951." In D. Borg and W. Heinrichs, eds. *Uncertain Years: Chinese-American Relations, 1947–1950.* New York: Columbia University Press, 1980, pp. 61–118.

Gaddis focused on the strategic dimension— war plans and capabilities, strategic estimates, and military influence on foreign policy—of America's East Asian policy. Notes.

2062 Iriye, Akira. *The Cold War in Asia: A Historical Introduction.* Englewood Cliffs, NJ: Prentice-Hall, 1974.

Iriye's focus is on the 1940s, a decade that was of crucial importance in shaping the subsequent history of Asia and America's place in it. Notes, bibliography, index.

2063 Iriye, Akira. "Was There a Cold War in Asia?" In John Chay, ed. *The Problems and Prospects of American-East Asian Relations.* Boulder, CO: Westview, 1977, pp. 3–24.

While the United States tended to view Asian developments in a Cold War perspective, it did not formulate a Cold War strategy until late 1949 and early 1950. The Soviets' A-bomb test and Mao's victory in China led to a new strategy. Notes.

2064 Latourette, Kenneth S. *The American Record in the Far East, 1945–1951.* New York: Macmillan, 1954.

Latourette traces U.S. involvement in the Far East, its effect on American public opinion and on party politics, and its overall impact on U.S. policy in general. Index.

2065 Nagai, Yonosuke, and Iriye, Akira, eds. *The Origins of the Cold War in Asia.* New York: Columbia University Press, 1977.

These essays, by leading scholars, focus on a number of important topics, such as American public opinion, Japanese-American relations, and the origins of the Korean War. Notes, index.

2066 Rose, Lisle A. *Roots of a Tragedy: The United States and the Struggle for Asia, 1945–1954.* Westport, CT: Greenwood, 1976.

Rose seeks to explain why U.S. responses to turbulent events in East and Southeast Asia were so inappropriate. He rejects the revisionist emphasis on economic motives and offers more traditional ones. Notes, bibliography, index.

2067 Stueck, William W., Jr. *The Road to Confrontation: American Policy Toward China and Korea, 1947–1950*. Chapel Hill: University of North Carolina Press, 1981.

Stueck argues that fear about American credibility played a major role in U.S. China policy and was central in America's policy toward Korea. Notes, bibliography, index.

CHINA

Robert Dallek's historiographic essay (#2075) offers a useful introduction to various interpretations.

2068 Baron, Michael L. "Tug of War: The Battle Over American Policy Toward China, 1946–1949." Ph.D. dissertation, Columbia University, 1980.

While American officials considered China policy in the context of the global Cold War against the Soviet Union, military and State Department leaders did not share assumptions about the nature of the problems or the alternatives. Military leaders favored military and economic aid to the Nationalists while the State Department favored only limited ties to Chiang, excluding military components. Further, Truman is viewed as an activist who based decisions on personal proclivities. DAI 41:793.

2069 Borg, Dorothy, and Heinrichs, Waldo, eds. *Uncertain Years: Chinese-American Relations, 1947–1950*. New York: Columbia University Press, 1980.

This outstanding set of essays, with comments, reviews most aspects of U.S.-Chinese (Nationalist and Communist) policies during these three critical years. Michael L. Baron prepared a chronology of events for these years which is exceptionally useful. Notes, index.

2070 Byers, Gertrude C. "American Journalists and China, 1945–1950." Ph.D. dissertation, St. Louis University, 1980.

Although some liberal and conservative journals presented the view that Chiang's government was corrupt and inept and that Mao was offering changes that were winning their support, Americans' traditional view of China, their fear of Communist expansion, and the influence of the China lobby exerted a strong influence on the perceptions of the American public. DAI 41:3161.

2071 Chern, Kenneth S. *Dilemma in China: America's Policy Debate, 1945*. Hamden, CT: Shoe String, 1980.

Chern argues that the vigorous China debate which occurred in 1945 was a critical turning point in U.S. China policy and a determinant of the Sino-American animosity which erupted later. Notes, bibliography, index.

2072 Chern, Kenneth S. "Politics of American China Policy, 1945: Roots of the Cold War in Asia." *Political Science Quarterly* 91 (1976/77): 631–47.

The foreign policy debate in America during 1945 over the question of intervention in the Chinese civil war is reviewed. Notes.

2073 *China White Paper: August 1949*. 2 vols. Stanford: Stanford University Press, 1967.

This collection of documents was originally published by the U.S. Department of State as *United States Relations with China, With Special Reference to the Period 1944–1949* (Washington, DC: G.P.O., 1949). Secretary of State Dean Acheson wrote in the preface that "the ominous result of the civil war in China was beyond the control of the government of the United States."

2074 Cohen, Warren I. "Acheson, His Advisers, and China, 1949–1950." In D. Borg and W. Heinrichs, eds. *Uncertain Years: Chinese-American Relations, 1947–1950*. New York: Columbia University Press, 1980, pp. 13–52.

Cohen examines the views of many advisers, including W. Walton Butterworth, Philip C. Jessup, George F. Kennan, Dean Rusk, and John P. Davies. Acheson was initially a moderating influence on demands for the use of American power. The Korean War ended Acheson's complacency about East Asia. Notes.

2075 Dallek, Robert. "The Truman Era." In Ernest R. May and James C. Thomson, Jr., eds. *American-East Asian Relations: A Survey*. Cambridge: Harvard University Press, 1972, pp. 356–76.

Dallek provides a most useful historiographical survey of the Truman administration's response to China's civil war. No issue in post-World War II American foreign relations—aside from Vietnam—has raised more controversy.

2076 Etzold, Thomas H. "The Far East in American Strategy." In Thomas H. Etzold, ed. *Aspects of Sino-Soviet Relations Since 1784*. New York: New Viewpoints, 1978, pp. 102–26.

The containment of communism was the essential motivating factor in U.S. policy between 1948 and 1951. The Chinese civil war and the Korean War had considerable impact on this policy, leading to unwanted commitments on the Asia mainland. Notes.

2077 Feaver, John H. "The Truman Administration and China, 1945–1950: The Policy of Restrained Intervention." Ph.D. dissertation, University of Oklahoma, 1980.

Feaver argues that for military and strategic reasons related to Soviet expansionism, the Truman administration never seriously considered withdrawing from China prior to the Korean War. DAI 41:1186.

2078 Feis, Herbert. *The China Tangle: The American Effort in China from Pearl Harbor to the Marshall Mission.* Princeton: Princeton University Press, 1953.

Feis examines U.S. efforts in China during the war and in the critical period of peace-making. Notes, index.

2079 Fetzer, James A. "Congress and China, 1941–1950." Ph.D. dissertation, Michigan State University, 1969.

American policy toward China was a source of rancor between Truman and Congress, the major point of contention being the capability and responsibility of the United States to effect a non-Communist regime in China. DAI 31:1187-A.

2080 Fetzer, James A. "Senator Vandenberg and the American Commitment to China, 1945–1950." *Historian* 36 (1974): 283–303.

Vandenberg sought to maintain an American commitment to Chiang Kai-shek's faltering regime during the Chinese civil war. The author shows the political problems confronting any U.S. effort to disengage from the Nationalist government. Notes.

2081 Grasso, June M. "Conflict and Controversy: The United States, Taiwan, and the People's Republic of China, 1946–1950." Ph.D. dissertation, Tufts University, 1981.

This study examines U.S.-Chinese relations from the passage of the China Aid Act in 1948 to the outbreak of the Korean War. DAI 42:3710.

2082 Harris, Scott A. "Domestic Politics and the Formulation of United States China Policy, 1949–1972." Ph.D. dissertation, University of Wisconsin, Madison, 1980.

Harris finds that domestic politics did influence the decision-making process, policy continuity and change, and the specific nature of policy decisions. DAI 42:373-A.

2083 Hawley, Sandra McNair. "The China Myth at Mid-Century: Case of an Illusion." Ph.D. dissertation, Case Western Reserve University, 1974.

The "loss" of China to communism in the late 1940s resulted in a search for those Americans responsible and gave rise to the political climate in which McCarthyism prospered. DAI 35:366-A.

2084 Head, William P. "America's China Sojourn: United States Foreign Policy and its Effects on Sino-American Relations,1942–1948." Ph.D. dissertation, Florida State University, 1980.

Head believes that the foreign policy controversies of the Carter administration are rooted in the U.S. Asian policy of the 1940s,which emphasized European affairs and ignored the importance of the growth of postwar nationalism in Asia. DAI 41:1186.

2085 Hedley, John H. "The Truman Administration and the 'Loss' of China: A Study of Public Attitudes and the President's Policies from the Marshall Mission to the Attack on Korea." Ph.D. dissertation, University of Missouri, 1964.

Mail to the president indicated only that China policy was of comparatively little interest to the letter-writing public. Attitudes ascertained by polls and opinion studies revealed that Truman's conduct of China policy was generally endorsed by the American public. DAI 25:4234.

2086 Kemp, Virginia M. "Congress and China, 1945–1959." Ph.D. dissertation, University of Pittsburgh, 1966.

From 1945 to 1947 Congress expressed no definite policy toward the executive's policy of coalition government; nor was there any partisan conflict. Between 1949 and 1951 China became an intensely partisan issue with Republicans pressing for continued recognition of the Nationalist government, military aid for Formosa, and opposition to Communist China's admission to the United Nations. DAI 27:4314.

2087 Kubek, Anthony. *How the Far East Was Lost: American Policy and the Creation of Communist China, 1941–1949.* Chicago: Regnery, 1963.

Although Patrick J. Hurley, Walter Judd, Freda Utley, and Joseph McCarthy had earlier expressed the thesis that Chiang Kai-shek would have defeated the Chinese Communists except for traitors in Washington, Kubek gives the idea its most sympathetic development. Notes.

2088 Lippmann, Walter. *Commentaries on American Far Eastern Policy.* New York: Institute of Pacific Relations, 1950.

Lippmann's contemporary opinion is that the Truman administration's honest mistakes might have partly contributed to Chiang's defeat. (A similar argument is found in John K. Fairbanks, "Toward a Dynamic Far Eastern Policy," *Far Eastern Survey* 18

[7 September 1949]: 209–12.) This pamphlet reprints selections (from 6 September 1949 to 10 August 1950) from Lippmann's newspaper column in the *New York Herald Tribune*.

2089   May, Ernest R. *The Truman Administration and China, 1945–1949*. New York: Lippincott, 1975.

One of the questions explored in this volume is why the Truman administration did not intervene in China as the Kennedy administration did later in Vietnam. Documents, notes, bibliographical essay, index.

2090   Melby, John F. "The Origins of the Cold War in China." *Pacific Affairs* 41 (1968): 19–33.

This essay reviews various American actions (or inaction) from the time of Marshall's mission to China in 1945 to the Korean War. The author believes that Americans were unable to grasp the realities of the Chinese situation (1945–52).

2091   Newman, Robert P. "Clandestine Chinese Nationalist Efforts to Punish their American Detractors." *Diplomatic History* 7 (1983): 205–22.

Nationalist officials manufactured documents purporting to show that Owen Lattimore, John Stewart Service, John Carter Vincent, John Paton Davies, and a number of other detractors of the Nationalist government had maliciously sought to turn Americans against Chiang Kai-shek and to assist Mao Tse-tung. Notes.

2092   Newman, Robert P. "The Self-Inflicted Wound: The China White Paper of 1949." *Prologue* 14 (1982): 151–56.

The evolution of the 642 pages of documents on U.S.-Chinese relations, 1944–49, is closely examined. Reactions within and without the Truman administration to the document are recounted. Notes, illustrations.

2093   Pickler, Gordon K. "The USAAF in China, 1946–47." *Air University Review* 24 (1973): 69–74.

The army air force airlifted Communist Chinese officials and their staffs and families from Nanking and other Nationalist cities to the Communist capital of Yenan in 1947. Illustrations, notes.

2094   Purifoy, Lewis M. *Harry Truman's China Policy: McCarthyism and the Diplomacy of Hysteria, 1947–51*. New York: New Viewpoints, 1976.

Purifoy views the policy decisions toward China as a foreign policy expression of McCarthyism. Notes, index.

2095   Reardon-Anderson, James B. *Yenan and the Great Powers: The Origins of Chinese Communist Foreign Policy, 1944–46*. New York: Columbia University Press, 1980.

This study covers contacts with the United States through the Dixie mission; negotiations with the Chinese Nationalist government through U.S. Ambassador Patrick Hurley; the CCP Seventh Party Congress; postwar relations with the U.S. Marines in North China and the Red Army in Manchuria; and negotiations with General Marshall up to the outbreak of the civil war.

2096   Rhee, Tong-chin. "Sino-American Relations from 1942 through 1949: A Study of Efforts to Settle the China Problem." Ph.D. dissertation, Clark University, 1967.

The United States was responsible for hastening the collapse of the Nationalist government. American sympathy toward China had decreased because of Chiang's inept military performance against the Japanese, and the military-diplomatic representatives sent to China, especially Stilwell, furthered antagonisms. DAI 28:1774-A.

2097   Roche, George C., III. "Public Opinion and the China Policy of the United States, 1941–1951." Ph.D. dissertation, University of Colorado, 1965.

During the war, public opinion was sympathetic toward China, but the division between Nationalist and Communist China led to a parallel division within American opinion and policy. The Cold War, the fear of internal subversion, the loss of Nationalist China, and the Korean War led to increased inflexibility in American Far Eastern policy. DAI 26:6681.

2098   Shaw, Yu-ming. "John Leighton Stuart and U.S.-Chinese Communist Rapprochement in 1949: Was There Another 'Lost Chance in China'?" *China Quarterly* [Great Britain] (1982): 74–96.

It is unlikely that Stuart's failure to meet personally with Chinese Communist leaders affected the course of U.S.-Chinese relations. Notes.

2099   Sheridan, James. *China in Disintegration: The Republican Era in Chinese History, 1912–1949*. Berkeley: University of California Press, 1975.

Chapters 8 and 9 evaluate the Communist victory in China, and its relationship to nationalism. Notes, index.

2100   Tsou, Tang. *America's Failure in China, 1941–50*. 2 vols. Chicago: University of Chicago Press, 1963.

This study finds middle ground between the *China White Paper*'s apologia and Kubek's radical right denunciation. Tsou argues that America played a limited role in Nationalist China's defeat and that this defeat resulted from honest mistakes. Notes, bibliography.

2101   Tsuan, Tai-hsuan. "An Explanation of the Changes in United States Policy Toward China in

1950." Ph.D. dissertation, University of Pennsylvania, 1969.

Two decisions affecting Sino-American relations were made by the Truman administration in 1950. A "hands-off Taiwan" policy was announced on 5 January, and a "neutralization of Taiwan" was proclaimed on 27 June. DAI 30:3079-A.

2102 Tucker, Nancy Bernkopf. "Nationalist China's Decline and Its Interest In Sino-American Relations, 1949–1960." In D. Borg and W. Heinrichs, eds. *Uncertain Years: Chinese-American Relations, 1947–1950.* New York: Columbia University Press, 1980, pp. 131–71.

This essay examines the military ineffectiveness and political vulnerability of the Nationalists and reviews Chiang's addiction to American support. Notes.

2103 Wedemeyer, Albert C. *Wedemeyer Reports!* New York: Holt, 1958.

General Wedemeyer replaced Stilwell as commander of the China theater and chief of staff to Chiang Kai-shek. Chapters 22 to 25 relate his views on the ending of the war in the Pacific and his displeasure with the Marshall mission. Appendix, bibliography, index.

The United States and China's Civil War

2104 Anderson, Helen E. F. "Through Chinese Eyes: American China Policy, 1945–1947." Ph.D. dissertation, University of Virginia, 1980.

Anderson denies that the insufficiency of American aid to Nationalist China allowed for the Communist takeover. American aid tied the Nationalist regime to a Western imperialist nation, contravened Chinese nationalism and patriotism, and provided the Chinese Communist party with a valuable propaganda weapon. DAI 41:2247.

2105 Bodde, Derk. *Peking Diary: A Year of Revolution.* New York: Schuman, 1950.

Bodde was a Fulbright Fellow in China, 1948–49. This volume contains excerpts from the diary he kept. Illustrations, index.

2106 Chassin, Lionel Max. *The Communist Conquest of China: A History of the Civil War, 1945–1949.* Translated by T. Osato and L. Gelas. Cambridge: Harvard University Press, 1965.

First published in France as *La Conquête de la Chine par Mao Tse-tung* (1952), this study presents a French view of the military aspects of the civil war's final years, 1945–49.

2107 Dobbs, Charles M. "American Marines in North China, 1945–1946." *South Atlantic Quarterly* 76 (1977): 318–31.

In October 1945, 50,000 U.S. Marines were sent to North China to accept the surrender of 500,000 Japanese soldiers. Occupying ports, railroads, and cities, the marines stalled Communist efforts to move into the area; however, soon both Nationalists and Communists began to harass the garrisons. Notes.

2108 Engelhart, Tom. "Long Day's Journey: American Observers in China, 1948–1950." In Bruce Douglass and Ross Terrill, eds. *China and Ourselves.* Boston: Beacon, 1970, pp. 90–121.

The author believes that the Americans in China were largely self-centered and self-satisfied; consequently, they had little understanding of the revolutionary struggle going on there. Notes.

2109 Feng, Chi Jen. "The Politics of Intervention: America's Role in the Chinese Civil War." Ph.D. dissertation, New York University, 1973.

This study examines the forces—commercial, ideological, and political—which formed the principles of America's policy toward China and focuses on the actors, especially Marshall and Hurley, who influenced decisions. DAI 34:4362-A.

2110 Hartgen, Stephen. "How Four U.S. Papers Covered the Communist Chinese Revolt." *Journalism Quarterly* 56 (1979): 175–78.

The coverage of the resignation of Patrick J. Hurley, U.S. ambassador to China, on 27 November 1945, and the battles between Chinese Nationalists and Communists in Manchuria during April–May 1946 are examined in the *Atlanta Constitution*, the *Cleveland Plain Dealer*, the *Louisville Courier-Journal*, and the *Minneapolis Tribune*. Notes.

2111 Houchins, Lee S. "American Naval Involvement in the Chinese Civil War, 1945–1949." Ph.D. dissertation, American University, 1971.

This is a case study of the behavior of U.S. naval commanders in an essentially civil-war environment while faced with the inherent contradictions of the August 1945 national policy directive that required support of the Nationalist government but prohibited involvement in fratricidal war. DAI 32:2163-A.

2112 Melby, John F. *The Mandate of Heaven: Record of a Civil War, 1945–1949.* Toronto: University of Toronto Press, 1968.

Melby, a Foreign Service officer, was reassigned to Chungking after the war. This volume is based on his notes, diaries, personal letters, and the *China White Paper*. Illustrated, notes, index.

2113 Palmer, Thomas A. "The First Confrontation: U.S. Marines in North China, 1945–1947." *Marine Corps Gazette* 54 (1970): 22–28.

Military operations by U.S. Marines against Communist Chinese guerrillas in north China are reviewed.

2114 Pickler, Gordon K. "United States Aid to the Chinese Nationalist Air Force, 1931–1949." Ph.D. dissertation, Florida State University, 1971.

Considerable attention has been focused on the role of General Claire L. Chennault, but others such as Lauchlin Currie, a special assistant to FDR, played a more decisive role in providing U.S. aid to the Chinese air force. U.S. advisers during the civil war assisted the Nationalist Chinese air force. DAI 35:1024-A.

2115 Williams, Frederick B. "The Origins of the Sino-American Conflict, 1949–1952." Ph.D. dissertation, University of Illinois, 1967.

Initially, U.S. policy sought to keep a flexible diplomatic stance toward the Chinese Communist regime, and the administration would not fight to prevent the collapse of the Nationalist government. Policy reversed, however, when the Chinese Communists intervened in Korea. DAI 28:5124-A.

Marshall Mission

See also Chapter 3, *George C. Marshall.*

2116 Clubb, O. Edmund. "Manchuria in the Balance, 1945–1946." *Pacific Historical Review* 26 (1957): 377–90.

Civil war resumed in Manchuria immediately after V-J Day; a U.S. delegation led by George C. Marshall attempted unsuccessfully to arbitrate their differences. Notes.

2117 Levine, Steven I. "A New Look at American Mediation in the Chinese Civil War: The Marshall Mission." *Diplomatic History* 3 (1979): 349–75.

Levine chronicles George C. Marshall's efforts to persuade the Nationalists and Communists to form a single government. He gave up on Kuomintang as a means to reform and hoped that an American-style nonpartisan government comprising reformers from both Chinese factions could be formed. Notes.

2118 Marshall, George C. *Marshall's Mission to China: December 1945–January 1947.* 2 vols. Arlington, VA: University Publications of America, 1976.

This is Marshall's final report. All but twenty-four of the supporting documents appear in the *China White Paper* or the U.S. Foreign Relations series. Reviewed by J. F. Melby in *Pacific Affairs* [Canada] 50 (1977): 272–77.

2119 Smith, Cordell A. "The Marshall Mission: Its Impact upon American Foreign Policy toward China,

1945–1949." Ph.D. dissertation, University of Oklahoma, 1963.

Organized opposition to the Marshall Mission did not occur until long after its termination. Further, opposition to America's China policy beyond the Marshall Mission did not coalesce until a year after Marshall returned to the United States. DAI 24:814.

2120 Wilson, Wesley C. "1946: General George C. Marshall and the United States Army Mediate China's Civil War." Ph.D. dissertation, University of Colorado, 1965.

Despite the failure of the Marshall Mission in bringing peace to China, Wilson finds that the mission had some positive accomplishments: the repatriation of over three million Japanese soldiers and civilians and the return to the United States of over 110,000 military men. DAI 27:739-A.

U.S. Economic and Aid Policies

2121 Aronsen, Lawrence R. "The 'New Frontier': Postwar Perceptions of the China Market, 1943–1950." *Mid-America* 64 (1982): 17–32.

American business tried to expand trade with Nationalist, and then Communist, China to avert a believed impending postwar depression. The outbreak of the Korean War ended the China trade. Notes.

2122 Chen, Chin-Yuen. "American Economic Policy Toward Communist China, 1950–1970." Ph.D. dissertation, Columbia University, 1972.

On the eve of the Communist takeover in China, the United States placed a partial embargo on trade and, after Peking's intervention in the Korean War, a total embargo. This account deals with U.S. efforts to line up allied support for the embargo. DAI 33: 1922-A.

2123 Cosgrove, Julia F. "United States Economic Foreign Policy Toward China, 1943–1946." Ph.D. dissertation, Washington University, 1980.

Cosgrove finds that although the United States was initially successful in pursuing its economic interests in China, its policy from 1943 to 1946 ultimately failed to open the China market and contributed to the thirty-year estrangement between the two nations. DAI 41:3694-A.

2124 Devane, Richard T. "The United States and China: Claims and Assets." *Asian Survey* 18 (1978): 1267–79.

This issue in U.S.-Chinese relations began on 16 December 1950 and was one of a series of American responses to Chinese intervention in the Korean conflict. Table, notes.

2125 Feaver, John H. "The China Aid Bill of 1948: Limited Assistance as a Cold War Strategy." *Diplomatic History* 5 (1981): 107–20.

Contrary to common belief that a loosely knit "China bloc" in Congress pressured the Truman administration to extend aid to the Nationalist regime, new documents suggest that the bill resulted from the administration's assessment of the U.S. global strategic position and the importance of East Asia. Notes.

2126 Kan, Kenneth C. "The Diplomacy of Foreign Aid: China, the United States and Marshall Plan Assistance, 1947–1949." Ph.D. dissertation, Miami University, 1983.

The congressional debates, State Department bureaucratic struggles, and Kuomintang corruption are reviewed. The conclusion is that a Communist triumph could not have been prevented even with additional U.S. aid, for the Kuomintang's political and economic problems were too immense. DAI 44:1550-A.

2127 Leary, William M., Jr. "Aircraft and Anti-Communists: CAT in Action, 1949–52." *China Quarterly* [Great Britain] (1972): 654–69.

Fearing the loss of Civil Air Transport's (CAT) seventy-one Hong Kong-based aircraft, the U.S. government assisted in their transfer to a Panamanian-chartered holding company. Problems of international law, diplomacy, sabotage, and a Nationalist Chinese demand for payment notwithstanding, the planes were saved from the Communist government. Notes.

2128 Page, Richard S. "Aiding Development: The Case of Taiwan, 1949–1965." Ph.D. dissertation, Princeton University, 1967.

This study discusses purposes, roles, effects, and usefulness of aid in advancing democratic political ideas, structures, and processes. A detailed review of U.S. diplomatic relations with Taiwan since 1949 is provided. DAI 28:1869-A.

2129 Tozer, Warren W. "Last Bridge to China: The Shanghai Power Company, The Truman Administration and the Chinese Communists." *Diplomatic History* 1 (1977): 64–78.

This study of the American-owned Shanghai Power Company (1949–50) suggests that the Truman administration refused to deal with the Chinese Communists except on its own terms and thus closed the Open Door to China. Notes.

Missionaries

2130 Adcock, Cynthia Letts. "Revolutionary Faithfulness: The Quaker Search for a Peaceable Kingdom in China, 1939–1951." Ph.D. dissertation, Bryn Mawr College, 1974.

The experience of working in China strongly challenged many Quakers' principles. They learned that "helping" people does not automatically produce

goodwill, and that reconciliation is not a universally admired goal. DAI 36:468-A.

2131 Heininger, Janet E. "The American Board in China: The Missionaries' Experiences and Attitudes, 1911–1952." Ph.D. dissertation, University of Wisconsin, Madison, 1981.

Missionaries had a distorted image of China, identifying with Chiang Kai-shek and his programs of reform. After World War II, they developed a more balanced perspective as they attempted to influence U.S. policy for recognition of the People's Republic. DAI 42:3272.

2132 Long, Charles H. "The Liberation of the Chinese Church: A Memoir of the Revolution from a Missionary Point of View." *History Magazine of the Protestant Episcopal Church* 49 (1980): 249–80.

The liberation of the Church began when the Chinese clergy faced the fact that they could not depend upon American support and took control of the Church themselves: The "greatest obstacle to our coming back to China will not be the Communists but the Chinese Church itself."

2133 Tucker, Nancy Bernkopf. "An Unlikely Peace: American Missionaries and the Chinese Communists, 1948–1950." *Pacific Historical Review* 45 (1976): 97–116.

During this period, the Chinese Communsists followed a policy of religious toleration. American missionaries were not all of one mind toward the Communist regime. Notes.

2134 Unsworth, Virginia C. "American Catholic Missions and Communist China, 1945–1953." Ph.D. dissertation, New York University, 1977.

In 1946 there were 562 American Catholic missionaries in China, but by 1953 this presence had been reduced to twelve men languishing in prisons or under house arrest. The Chinese Communists' policy of religious freedom meant only freedom to believe but not to practice one's faith. DAI 38:2288-A.

U.S. Recognition Policy

2135 Anderson, David. "China Policy and Presidential Politics, 1952." *Presidential Studies Quarterly* 10 (1980): 79–90.

The creation of the Communist People's Republic of China and the Korean War focused much of the 1952 election debate on the issue of who "lost China." A new and uncomfortable notion arose during 1952: The United States was no longer "the omnipotent champion of democracy." Notes.

2136 Appleton, Sheldon. *The Eternal Triangle? Communist China, the United States and the United Nations.* East Lansing: Michigan State University Press, 1961.

Appleton analyzes the question of whether Communist China should be seated in the United Nations as it evolved during its first eleven years. The focus is upon American policy and opinion. Notes, bibliography.

2137 Buhite, Russell D. "Missed Opportunities? American Policy and the Chinese Communists, 1949." *Mid-America* 61 (1979): 179–88.

It has been argued that Zhou Enlai's (Chou En-Lai) overture and an invitation to John Leighton Stuart to visit Beijing (Peking) marked two missed opportunities to establish better relations with the Chinese Communists in 1949. Buhite suggests that, given the constraints on State Department and the Chinese Communist leaders, it is not clear if real opportunities actually existed. Notes.

2138 Chen, Chin-shan. "American Recognition and Non-Recognition Policies in China: A Legal, Historical and Political Analysis." Ph.D. dissertation, Southern Illinois University, 1963.

Chen examines American recognition policy toward various Chinese governments during the past 180 years and concludes that on legal, historical, and political grounds, the United States should not recognize the People's Republic. DAI 24:5520.

2139 Cohen, Warren I., ed. "Ambassador Philip D. Sprouse on the Question of Recognition of the People's Republic of China in 1949 and 1950." *Diplomatic History* 2 (1978): 213–17.

Responding to a 1973 query, Sprouse wrote that the Truman administration recognized the inevitable defeat of the Kuomintang and the futility of continuing aid since it would wind up in Communist hands. Diplomatic recognition of the Communist government was considered, but adverse public opinion, especially congressional opposition, made such action politically hazardous.

2140 Cohen, Warren I, ed. "Consul General O. Edmund Clubb on the 'Inevitability' of Conflict between the United States and the People's Republic of China, 1949–50." *Diplomatic History* 5 (1981): 165–68.

Clubb, American consul general in Peking in 1949, reviews essays by Michael H. Hunt and Steven M. Goldstein in *Uncertain Years: Chinese-American Relations, 1947–1950* (1980). Clubb disagrees with the thesis that Sino-American hostility and breach of relations was inevitable in 1949–50.

2141 Dillard, Hardy C. "The United States and China: The Problem of Recognition." *Yale Review* 44 (1954): 180–95.

This is a historical survey of U.S. recognition policy since Jefferson, with some references to British policy regarding recognition. It is useful for a

background to the Truman policy regarding the Communist Chinese government.

2142 Dinegar, Caroline A. "Some Aspects of the Use of the Recognition of New Governments as an Instrument of United States Foreign Policy, 1900–1960." Ph.D. dissertation, Columbia University, 1963.

Among the cases examined is the sanction element of recognition of China in 1949. Recognition practices under Resolution 35 of the Ninth Inter-American Conference of American States at Bogota, Colombia in 1948 are also discussed. DAI 24:4772.

2143 Dougherty, Patrick T. "Catholic Opinion and United States Recognition Policy." Ph.D. dissertation, University of Missouri, 1963.

Whereas the Vatican values recognition as a procedural device for maintaining its contacts throughout the world, American Catholics view recognition as being equated with collaboration, approval, or fellowship, and thus supported the nonrecognition of Peking. DAI 24:4773.

2144 Dulles, Foster Rhea. *American Policy toward Communist China: The Historical Record, 1949–1969.* New York: Crowell, 1972.

Dulles seeks to understand U.S. policy toward China in light of the Cold War ideology of the 1950s and 1960s, finding that the fear of communism that McCarthy exploited remained the prime mover in American policy. Illustrations, bibliographical notes, index.

2145 Goldstein, Steven M. "Chinese Communist Policy Toward the United States: Opportunities and Constraints, 1944–1950." In D. Borg and W. Heinrichs, eds. *Uncertain Years: Chinese-American Relations, 1947–1950.* New York: Columbia University Press, 1980, pp. 235–78.

Goldstein argues that Mao, much as the Truman administration, was constrained by domestic, political, and, especially, ideological factors from any mutual accommodation. Notes.

2146 Hunt, Michael H. "Mao Tse-tung and the Issue of Accommodation with the United States, 1948–1950." In D. Borg and W. Heinrichs, eds. *Uncertain Years: Chinese-American Relations, 1947–1950.* New York: Columbia University Press, 1980, pp. 184–234.

Hunt believes that there was more room for compromise and accommodation in Mao's policies than has been credited. Notes.

2147 Kerpen, Karen S. "Voices in a Silence: American Organizations That Worked for Diplomatic Recognition of the People's Republic of China by the United States, 1945–1979." Ph.D. dissertation, New York University, 1981.

Kerpen looks at the nature, rationale, and extent of the activities of five organizations. Among the organizations examined in this study is the Committee for a Democratic Far Eastern Policy, which was formed in 1945 and dissolved in 1952. DAI 42:837.

2148 Koen, Ross Y. *The China Lobby in American Politics.* New York: Harper & Row, 1974.

Originally enjoined from distribution when first published by Macmillan in 1960, this volume examines the nature of the China lobby and its effect upon American policy. Notes, bibliography, index.

2149 Paterson, Thomas G. "If Europe, Why Not China? The Containment Doctrine, 1947–1949." *Prologue* 13 (1981): 19–38.

After reviewing Truman's containment policy, Paterson suggests reasons for the inconsistent application of the European policy to China. Illustrations, notes.

2150 Stopsky, Fred H. "An Analysis of the Conflict within the United States Federal Government in the Period 1949–1956 concerning American Policy toward China." Ph.D. dissertation, New York University, 1969.

The origins of the nonrecognition policy are examined. The Korean War was crucial in the "hardening" of America's nonrecognition of the People's Republic of China. DAI 30:2471-A.

2151 Tucker, Nancy Bernkopf. *Patterns in the Dust: Chinese-American Relations and the Recognition Controversy, 1949–1950.* New York: Columbia University Press, 1983.

The factors which influenced Washington policymakers during these critical months comprise the focus of this study. The Korean War brought an abrupt end to the administration's efforts to achieve a reasoned public dialogue regarding the question of recognition. Notes, bibliography, index.

JAPAN

2152 Ballard, Jack S., Jr. "Postwar American Plans for the Japanese Mandated Islands." *Rocky Mountain Social Science Journal* 3 (1966): 109–116.

American policy statements toward the Japanese Pacific mandated islands during World War II and reasons for shifts in policy are reviewed. American officials made a bow toward international cooperation and trusteeship while "realistically expanding her territory and her base power." Notes.

2153 Bell, Roger. "Australian-American Disagreement over the Peace Settlement with Japan, 1944–46." *Australian Outlook* [Australia] 30 (1976): 238–62.

Australia's resistance to America's plan to monopolize the occupation of Japan was largely unsuccessful. Notes.

2154 Blakeslee, George H. *The Far Eastern Commission: A Study in International Cooperation, 1945 to 1952.* Far Eastern Series. No. 5138. Washington, DC: G.P.O., 1953.

The author, a distinguished scholar and adviser to the commission, provides a detailed evaluation of the commission's role in developing the U.S.-Japanese peace treaty. Notes.

2155 Borden, William S. "The Pacific Alliance: The United States and Japanese Trade Recovery, 1947–1954." Ph.D. dissertation, University of Wisconsin, Madison, 1981.

Borden finds that vast purchases of war materials in Japan were instrumental in Japan's industrial modernization and eventual trade recovery, and that American military intervention in Southeast Asia in the 1950s was primarily motivated by the need to satiate Japanese economic needs. DAI 42:2259.

2156 Braibanti, Ralph. "The Ryukyu Islands: Pawns of the Pacific." *American Political Science Review* 48 (1954): 972–98.

While the account reviews the seventeenth to twentieth-century history of the Ryukyu Islands, it focuses on the influence of Japan, China, and the United States, 1940–54. American foreign policy regarding the military occupation and jurisdiction of the islands following World War II is emphasized. Notes.

2157 Dower, John W. "Occupied Japan and the American Lake, 1945–1950." In Edward Friedman and Mark Selden, eds. *America's Asia: Dissenting Essays on Asian-American Relations.* New York: Pantheon, 1971, pp. 146–206.

According to the author, the U.S. occupation policies were motivated by the American desire to dominate the Pacific region. Notes.

2158 Gunther, John. *The Riddle of MacArthur: Japan, Korea, and the Far East.* New York: Harper, 1951.

Gunther's main focus is Japan, which he believes is the pivotal point of American policy in Asia. He credits MacArthur with the successful creation of a new Japan. Index.

2159 Hilgenberg, James F., Jr. "To Enlist an Ally: The American Business Press, Japan, and the Cold War, 1948–1952." *Journal of the West Virginia Historical Association* 31 (1979): 17–29.

This analysis focuses on the relationship of the media and foreign policy.

2160 Kublin, Hyman. "Okinawa: A Key to the Western Pacific." *U.S. Naval Institute Proceedings* 80 (1954): 1359–65.

The history and background of the island and its inhabitants are briefly reviewed within the context of the island's strategic importance. It was considered the most valuable Japanese island occupied by the United States in 1945.

2161 Schaller, Michael. "Securing the Great Crescent: Occupied Japan and the Origins of Containment in Southeast Asia." *Journal of American History* 69 (1982): 392–414.

American policymakers counted on an economically strong, pro-Western Japan to help contain communism in Asia. Notes.

U.S. Occupation

Historiographical essays by J. W. Dower (#2166) and R. A. Moore (#2178) are especially useful, as is the bibliography by R. E. Ward and F. J. Shulman, *The Allied Occupation of Japan, 1945–1952* (#3028).

2162 Baerwald, Hans. *The Purge of Japanese Leaders under the Occupation.* Berkeley: University of California Press, 1959.

The author was an official in the Government Section and has prepared a thorough account of the occupation's major reform effort—new democratic leadership. Notes, index.

2163 Borton, Hugh. *American Presurrender Planning for Postwar Japan.* New York: Columbia University, East Asian Institute, 1967.

The author, historian and policy-planner, relates the State Department's role in establishing the initial direction of the occupation.

2164 Boyle, Michael J. "The Planning of the Occupation of Japan and the American Reform Tradition." Ph.D. dissertation, University of Wyoming, 1979.

Boyle examines the extent of the presurrender planning for postwar Japan and its underlying political philosophy. He finds great continuity in planning because the same few individuals worked on Japanese problems throughout the planning process. DAI 41:769.

2165 Dore, Ronald. *Land Reform in Japan.* London: Oxford University Press, 1959.

One of Britain's leading Japanese specialists has prepared a sound analysis of the occupation's attempts at land reform. Notes, index.

2166 Dower, John W. "Occupied Japan as History and Occupation History as Politics." *Journal of Asian Studies* 34 (1975): 485–504.

One of the few scholars who had used American and Japanese sources, the author challenges the view that the occupation was a success and suggests new criteria for assessing it. Notes.

2167 Duke, Ben C. "American Education Reforms in Japan Twelve Years Later." *Harvard Educational Review* 34 (1964): 525–36.

American educational reforms were modified with the termination of the occupation in 1952. While educational opportunities for girls' and students' academic freedom had been maintained, the American concepts of local school boards, university autonomy, and decentralized curriculum are threatened by the Japanese government's desire for greater central control.

2168 Edwards, Catherine R. "U.S. Policy Towards Japan, 1945–1951: Rejection of Revolution." Ph.D. dissertation, University of California, Los Angeles, 1977.

The author examines the shift in U.S. occupation policies toward Japan and concludes that change was substantial but could not be explained entirely by the development of the Cold War. Such internal factors as the conceptual frameworks of the policymakers, bureaucratic struggles, and domestic political events are necessary to explain the policy shifts of 1947–48. DAI 38:6920-A.

2169 Fearey, Robert T. *Occupation of Japan: Second Phase, 1948–1950.* New York: Macmillan, 1950.

A key adviser to John Foster Dulles attempts a contemporary assessment of the effects of the occupation. He believed that security was a major issue in the peace negotiations.

2170 Goodman, Grant K., comp. *The American Occupation of Japan: A Retrospective View.* Lawrence: University of Kansas, Center for East Asian Studies, 1968.

The essays evaluate the social, political, and economic aspects of U.S. occupation policies.

2171 Hadley, Eleanor M. *Antitrust in Japan.* Princeton, NJ: Princeton University Press, 1970.

A former occupation official in the Government Section and economist has prepared a thorough study of efforts to redirect the Japanese economy and Japanese-American economic relations. Notes, index.

2172 Hata, Ikuhiko. "Japan under the Occupation." *Japan Interpreter* [Japan] 10 (1976): 361–80.

The chief legacies are the Americanization of Japan, the introduction of Midwestern democracy, and the shaping of Japanese education.

2173 Hilgenberg, James F., Jr. "The American Business Press and the Occupation of Japan, 1945–1952." Ph.D. dissertation, West Virginia University, 1978.

This is a study of the positions and the responses of the national business press toward the occupation of postwar Japan. DAI 39:1768-A.

2174 Hollerman, Leon. "International Economic Controls in Occupied Japan." *Journal of Asian Studies* 38 (1979): 707–19.

The author believes that American economic reforms resulted in the concentration of controls in the Japanese government's hands, which not only stifled free trade but created difficulties in subsequent U.S.-Japanese economic relations. Notes.

2175 Kawai, Kazuo. *Japan's American Interlude.* Chicago: University of Chicago Press, 1960.

The former editor of the *Nippon Times* attempts to assess the impact of America's occupation of Japan. Index.

2176 Martin, Edwin M. *The Allied Occupation of Japan.* Stanford: Stanford University Press, 1948.

This dated study examines the "reform" aspects of the occupation with chapters dealing with occupation policy, disarmament and demilitarization, and democratization and pacification. Extensive appendix, index.

2177 Moore, Joe B. "Production Control and the Postwar Crisis of Japanese Capitalism, 1945–1946." Ph.D. dissertation, University of Wisconsin, Madison, 1978.

In the spring of 1946 business and government authority was challenged by factory occupations and popular seizures of food depots, while millions took to the streets to overthrow the Yoshida government and the emperor system, the entire old order. Alarmed, General MacArthur threatened intervention by occupation authorities to control the mass demonstrations and maintain order. It was a revolutionary period, the first year. DAI 39:3755-A.

2178 Moore, Ray A. "Reflections on the Occupation of Japan." *Journal of Asian Studies* 38 (1979): 721–34.

The author offers several comments on the current status of occupation research and suggests additional topics which need study. He emphasizes the influence of wartime perceptions upon occupation policy and its contradictions. Notes.

2179 Nishi, Toshio. *Unconditional Democracy: Education and Politics in Occupied Japan, 1945–1952.* Stanford: Hoover Institution Press, 1982.

Nishi's thesis is that during the occupation of Japan, American forces used education as an instrument to transform Japanese culture from an imperialistic society into a democratic nation. Notes, bibliography, index.

2180 Nomura, Gail M. "The Allied Occupation of Japan: Reform of Japanese Government Labor Policy on Women." Ph.D. dissertation, University of Hawaii, 1978.

The legacy of the occupation was a redefinition of the role of women to one of equality and equal participation. It was the legitimation of this new definition of the proper role of women that was to have a greater significance than the initial paper reforms of the occupation. DAI 39:7475-A.

2181 Oakley, Deborah J. "The Development of Population Policy in Japan, 1945–1952, and American Participation." 2 vols. Ph.D. dissertation, University of Michigan, 1977.

Japanese population policy (1945–52) was a combination of a series of explicit administration and legislative statements of government concern about population growth. DAI 38:1626-A.

2182 Perry, John Curtis. *Beneath the Eagle's Wings: Americans in Occupied Japan.* New York: Dodd, Mead, 1980.

America's occupation of Japan (1945–47) "was one of few instances in which one modern industrial state has entirely occupied another modern industrial state for an extended period . . . trying to change it in some rather basic ways." Notes, illustrations, bibliography, index.

2183 Roberts, John G. "The 'Japan Crowd' and the Zaibatsu Restoration." *Japan Interpreter* [Japan] 12 (1979): 384–415.

The American Council on Japan and the broader Japan lobby originated in Joseph C. Grew's prewar State Department "Japan Crowd." During 1947 to 1950, these individuals managed to completely reverse the established U.S. occupation policy of breaking up Japan's Zaibatsu and purging war-tainted businessmen from positions of economic leadership.

2184 Schonberger, Howard. "American Labor's Cold War in Occupied Japan." *Diplomatic History* 3 (1979): 249–72.

American labor leaders actively participated in the administration of occupied Japan (1945–52) and sought to create an American-styled Japanese labor movement which could offset the economic dominance of the Zaibatsu. Notes.

2185 Schonberger, Howard. "The Japan Lobby in American Diplomacy, 1947–1952." *Pacific Historical Review* 46 (1977): 327–59.

The role of the American Council on Japan in influencing the shift of American occupation policy to make that country "a bulwark against Communism in Asia" is explored. Notes.

2186 Sebald, William J. *With MacArthur in Japan: A Personal History of the Occupation.* New York: Norton, 1965.

As a senior civilian American official of the occupation, Sebald offers his personal view of

MacArthur and the occupation. Illustrations, appendixes, index.

2187 Sugimoto, Yoshio. "Equalization and Turbulence: The Case of the American Occupation of Japan." Ph.D. dissertation, University of Pittsburgh, 1973.

This sociological study examines the relationships between social stratification and mass disturbance. DAI 34:7352-A.

2188 Svensson, Eric H. F. "The Military Occupation of Japan: The First Years: Planning, Policy Formulation, and Reforms." Ph.D. dissertation, University of Denver, 1966.

Policy was initially hampered by delay in determining whether the army or navy would be the executive agent. Firm policy formulation began when the State-War-Navy Coordinating Committee (SWNCC) was formed in 1944, but implementation passed to the Supreme Commander for the Allied Powers (SCAP), which initiated the reform program called for by SWNCC policy. DAI 27:4205.

2189 Williams, Justin. "Completing Japan's Political Reorientation, 1947–1952: Crucial Phase of the Allied Occupation." *American Historical Review* 73 (1968): 1454–69.

U.S. occupation of Japan—from 3 May 1947 when the American-inspired constitution was adopted to 28 April 1952 when full sovereignty was restored—was the crucial period for the transformation of Japan from an authoritarian state to a Western-style democracy. Notes.

2190 Williams, Justin, Sr. *Japan's Political Revolution Under MacArthur; A Participant's Account.* Athens: University of Georgia Press, 1979.

This uncritical account by a participant portrays several of the Americans involved in the occupation—for example, MacArthur, Charles L. Kades, Courtney Whitney, and several others. The author focuses on the drafting of Japan's postwar constitution and the development of the new political system. Notes, bibliography, index.

2191 Wittner, Lawrence S. "MacArthur and the Missionaries: God and Man in Occupied Japan." *Pacific Historical Review* 40 (1971): 77–98.

Despite the official policy of religious freedom in occupied Japan, General MacArthur openly and actively assisted the propagation of the Christian faith to halt communism. In 1947 he vigorously supported a Bible campaign which resulted in the shipment of ten million Bibles to Japan. In spite of this support Christianity failed to grow substantially during the occupation. Notes.

2192 Woodward, William P. *The Allied Occupation of Japan, 1945–1952, and Japanese Religions.* Leiden: Brill, 1972.

The author was an occupation official in the Religious Division, Civil Information and Education Section. He has prepared a thorough account of the occupation's efforts to separate Church and State and to secularize the emperor. Notes, bibliography, index.

War Crimes Trials

John R. Lewis's bibliography (#3026) is most useful for those seeking to examine the impact of the trials.

2193 International Military Tribunal for the Far East. *Record of the Proceedings*, 1946–1948. Microfilm. Washington, DC: Library of Congress, 1947.

This collection of documents and testimony is on thirty-six reels; it is most useful as a source on prewar Japan.

2194 Keenan, Joseph B., and Brown, Brendan F. *Crimes Against International Law.* Washington, DC: Public Affairs Press, 1950.

Both of these men participated in the activities of the International Military Tribunal, Far East (Tokyo Trials), and this volume is based on their experiences. Index.

2195 Lael, Richard L. *The Yamashita Precedent: War Crimes and Command Responsibility.* Wilmington, DE: Scholarly Resources, 1982.

This volume examines the trial and execution of General Yamashita and in so doing challenges a number of myths. General MacArthur receives less blame, Washington officials more. Notes, bibliography, index.

2196 Minear, Richard H. *Victor's Justice: The Tokyo War Crimes Trial.* Princeton, NJ: Princeton University Press, 1971.

This volume is the initial scholarly examination of the Tokyo Trials; however, it is colored by the impact of the Vietnam conflict. Bibliography, notes, index.

2197 Piccigallo, Philip R. *The Japanese on Trial: Allied War Crimes Operations in the East, 1945–1951.* Austin: University of Texas Press, 1980.

The International Military Tribunal sitting at Tokyo (1946–48) tried and sentenced twenty-five "major" Japanese war criminals for plotting and waging the Pacific war. Additionally, some 2,200 lesser trials were held by Allied tribunals. This is the most complete study of all the trials. Notes, bibliography, index.

2198 Potter, John D. *A Soldier Must Hang: The Biography of an Oriental General.* London: Muller, 1963.

This is a biography of General Tomoyuki Yamashita, which focuses on his military exploits during World War II and his trial for war crimes after surrender. Appendix, illustrations.

2199 Riley, Walter L. "The International Military Tribunal for the Far East and the Law of the Tribunal as Revealed by the Judgment and the Concurring and Dissenting Opinions." Ph.D. dissertation, University of Washington, 1957.

The tribunal declared that launching an aggressive war was a crime, a proposition which, if it could have been substantiated, would have represented one of the most momentous developments in the history of international law. The tribunal was only partially successful. DAI 18:1481.

2200 Uyeda, Clifford I. "The Pardoning of 'Tokyo Rose': A Report on the Restoration of American Citizenship to Iva Ikuko Toguri." *Amerasia Journal* 5 (1978): 69–93.

The 1977 presidential pardon of Iva Ikuko Toguri D'Aquino, convicted of treason after World War II as "Tokyo Rose," resulted from the efforts of many individuals.

2201 Ward, David A. "The Unending War of Iva Ikuko Toguri D'Aquino: The Trial and Conviction of 'Tokyo Rose'." *Amerasia Journal* 1 (1971): 26–35.

Although "Tokyo Rose" was apparently a number of different women, Iva D'Aquino was arrested, tried and convicted of treason (1946–56) for her alleged role as the seductive radio announcer.

Peace Treaty

2202 Cohen, Bernard C. *The Political Process and Foreign Policy: The Making of the Japanese Peace Settlement.* Princeton, NJ: Princeton University Press, 1957.

This early study focuses on public opinion, special interest groups, and congressional responses. Bibliography, notes, index.

2203 Dingman, Roger V. "Theories of, and Approaches to, Alliance Politics." In Paul G. Gordon, ed. *Diplomacy: New Approaches in History, Theory, and Policy.* New York: Free Press, 1979, pp. 246–66.

Dingman focuses on the unequal 1951 treaty of alliance negotiated by John Foster Dulles and Yoshida Shigeru between the United States and Japan which allowed U.S. troops stationed in Japan to put down internal disturbances at Japan's request. Notes.

2204 Dunn, Frederick S. *Peacemaking and the Settlement with Japan.* Princeton, NJ: Princeton University Press, 1963.

In this assessment of the Japanese peace treaty, the American adjustment to new Cold War conditions provides the background. Bibliography, notes, index.

2205 Okajima, Eiichi. "The Japanese Peace Treaty and its Implications for Japan's Postwar Foreign Policy." Ph.D. dissertation, New York University, 1956.

The author suggests that the United States wanted to incorporate the security arrangement for Japan into a more general all-embracing anti-Communist Asian pact and that the omission of a provision in the peace treaty forbidding Japan's possession of armed forces also presaged an American hope. DAI 20:360.

2206 Ro, Chun Wang. "The Origins and Interpretation of the 1951 U.S.-Japanese Security Treaty." Ph.D. dissertation, Southern Illinois University, 1977.

The allegation that the treaty represented U.S. "imposition" is unfounded, as it was the Japanese leaders who proposed a bilateral defense pact to the U.S. government. The security treaty of 8 September 1951 was the first time Japan and the United States became military allies. DAI 38:1010-A.

2207 Yoshitsu, Michael M. "Peace and Security for Japan, 1945–1952." Ph.D. dissertation, Columbia University, 1979.

This study examines the San Francisco Peace Treaty and Security Settlement that capped off six years of Allied occupation in Japan. Primary focus is placed upon Japanese decision-making related to the two main accords, as it evolved between 1945 and 1952. DAI 40:5998A.

KOREA

Chapter 10 contains references to the Korean War, 1950–53.

2208 Allen, Richard C. *Korea's Syngman Rhee: An Unauthorized Portrait.* Rutland, VT: Tuttle, 1960.

Rhee as president of South Korea had two great failings: his unwillingness to accept criticism and his obsession with his own infallibility and his advanced age, which underscored his tendencies toward inflexibility and irresponsibility. Illustrations, notes, bibliography, index.

2209 Baek, Jong-Chun. "The Conflictive Behavior Patterns of the Two Koreas in the Northeast Asian International Subsystem, 1948–1978." Ph.D. dissertation, University of North Carolina, Chapel Hill, 1980.

This case study focuses on the conflictive behavior patterns in the interactions between North and South Korea as well as the influence of the United States, the Soviet Union, China, and Japan. DAI 41:3711.

2210 Cumings, Bruce, ed. *Child of Conflict: The Korean-American Relationship, 1943–1953.* Seattle: University of Washington Press, 1983.

This useful collection of essays by Mark Paul, Stephen Pelz, John Merrill, James I. Matray, William Stueck, John Kotch, Barton Bernstein, and Jack Saunders focuses on most of the key political elements of this relationship. Notes, index.

2211 Dae-sook Suh. *The Korean Communist Movement, 1918–1948*. Princeton, NJ: Princeton University Press, 1967.

This able study shows that the roots of the Korean War go far back into the early independence movement, beginning with encounters between Korean Communist and Nationalist factions in the 1920s and 1930s. The last two chapters deal with the rise of Kim Il Sung. Maps, bibliography, index.

2212 Henderson, Gregory. *Korea: The Politics of the Vortex*. Cambridge: Harvard University Press, 1968.

Koreans measure the history of their nation in terms of foreign invasions. Hence, the blame for the failure to maintain its independence, develop democratic traditions, and construct a viable economy is traditionally placed on outside forces. Henderson argues that domestic rather than foreign influences are essentially responsible for Korean affairs. Notes, bibliography, index.

2213 Lee, Ha Woo. "The Korean Polity Under Syngman Rhee: An Analysis of its Culture, Structure, and Elite." Ph.D. dissertation, American University, 1975.

The author stresses the leadership realignment under the Rhee regime and argues that personality, style, and the interactions of leaders overshadowed the constitutional framework. Attention is given to the role played by America during Rhee's regime. DAI 36:1792-A.

2214 McCune, George M., and Grey, Arthur L. Jr. *Korea Today*. Cambridge: Harvard University Press, 1950.

A useful contemporary survey of post-1945 Korea, it deals with both the North and the South. It is still considered a key work by many researchers. Documents, bibliography, tables, notes, index.

2215 Oliver, Robert T. *Syngman Rhee: The Man Behind the Myth*. New York: Dodd, Mead, 1954.

This sympathetic biography covers Rhee's life as a determined Nationalist—from childhood to president of South Korea. Appendix, index.

2216 Slusser, Robert M. "Soviet Far Eastern Policy, 1945–50: Soviet Goals in Korea." In Yonosuke Nagai and Akira Iriye, eds. *The Origins of the Cold War in Asia*. New York: Columbia University Press, 1977, pp. 123–46.

Stalin had certain goals in Korea and the pursuit of these goals helped to explain the record of Soviet policy in Korea during the late 1940s. The author provides an interesting analysis of the outbreak of the Korean War. Notes.

The United States and the Korean Occupation, 1945–49

2217 Baldwin, Frank, ed. *Without Parallel: The American-Korean Relationship Since 1945*. New York: Random House, 1973.

Korea was a watershed of American involvement in Asia, for the United States had no economic or ethnic motives for intervention. This revisionist account argues that intervention was due to post-World War II strategic interests, namely, to halt the spread of communism. Notes, index.

2218 Berger, Carl. *The Korea Knot: A Military-Political History*. Philadelphia: University of Pennsylvania Press, 1957.

Berger finds the roots of the Korean War in U.S. and Soviet military-political decisions during World War II. Bibliography, index.

2219 Caldwell, John C., with Lesley Frost. *The Korea Story*. Chicago: Regnery, 1952.

This is an informative inside look at the U.S. Korean commission (1945–50) which sought to hold elections to unify that divided country. Index.

2220 Cheriyan, C. V. "The United States and Korea: A Historical Study of Relations, 1945–1960." Ph.D. dissertation, University of Kerala, 1970.

This is a study of political, military, and economic relations between the United States and South Korea from September 1945 until April 1960. The principal emphasis is on the period of the Korean War.

2221 Cho, Soon-sung. *Korea in World Politics, 1940–1950: An Evaluation of American Responsibility*. Los Angeles: University of California Press, 1967.

The failure to achieve unification can be traced to (1) the personal diplomacy of Roosevelt together with his and Truman's reliance on the advice of military leaders; (2) the lack of coordination between occupation authorities and Washington; and (3) Korea's presumed remoteness from American national interest. Notes, bibliography, index.

2222 Chung, Yong Hwan. "Repatriation under the United States Army Military Government in Korea, 1945–1948." *Asian Forum* 8 (1976): 25–44.

The impact of the repatriation of Koreans from Manchuria, China, Japan and other areas, as well as North Korea, is examined. Notes.

2223 Cumings, Bruce. *The Origins of the Korean War: Liberation and the Emergence of Separate*

Regimes, 1945–1947. Princeton, NJ: Princeton University Press, 1981.

Cumings uses both Korean and Western language materials to provide a detailed analysis of what the American occupation officials in Korea discovered but apparently did not understand. Extensive bibliography, illustrations, tables, appendixes, notes, subject and name indexes.

2224 Dobbs, Charles M. *The Unwanted Symbol: American Foreign Policy, the Cold War, and Korea, 1945–1950*. Kent, OH: Kent State University Press, 1981.

The Truman administration's views and policies regarding Korea are set down here within the context of the developing Cold War. Dobbs's account surveys policies and events prior to the outbreak of war in June 1950. Notes, bibliographical essay, index.

2225 Gaddis, John Lewis. "Korea in American Politics, Strategy, and Diplomacy, 1945–50." In Yonosuke Nagai and Akira Iriye, eds. *The Origins of the Cold War in Asia*. New York: Columbia University Press, 1977, pp. 277–98.

Gaddis provides a useful survey of American policies and actions in post-1945 Korea. Notes.

2226 Jung, Yong Suk. "The Rise of American National Interest in Korea, 1845–1950." Ph.D. dissertation, Claremont Graduate School, 1970.

Jung divides American policy into two periods: 1845–1942 and 1943–50. The first period was marked by interest in a Korea subordinate to Japan and China; the second stage mirrored a revolutionary period in American-Korean relations. DAI 31:6689-A.

2227 Kang Han Mu. "The United States Military Government in Korea, 1945–1948: An Analysis and Evaluation of Its Policy." Ph.D. dissertation, University of Cincinnati, 1970.

Gen. John R. Hodge, commander of American occupation forces in Korea, faced many problems, including General MacArthur's failure to provide policy guidance or trained personnel during the crucial months of 1945–46. Reviewed also are the U.S.-U.S.S.R. Joint Commission negotiations. DAI 31:4242-A.

2228 Kim, Jinwung. "American Policy and Korean Independence: An Appraisal of Military Occupation Policy in South Korea, 1945–1948." Ph.D. dissertation, Brigham Young University, 1983.

The author believes that U.S. policies, prompted by the Cold War, stemmed a budding Korean revolution and turned South Korean politics toward more conservative goals. DAI 44:844-A.

2229 Kim, Joungwon A. *Divided Korea: The Politics of Development, 1945–1972*. Cambridge: Harvard University Press, 1975.

In comparing the development in the two Koreas, the author emphasizes the roles played by leaders, the contrasting uses of political tools, the relative influence played by factors from both within and without the society, and the contrasting processes of consolidation of power by the new political elites and the institutionalization of two distinct political systems. Notes, bibliography, index.

2230 Kotch, John B. "U.S. Policy Toward Korea, 1945–1953: The Origins and Evolution of American Involvement and the Emergence of a National Security Commitment." Ph.D. dissertation, Columbia University, 1976.

This two-part study examines the origins of U.S. security policy toward Korea and how the existing U.S. security commitment to the Republic of Korea was set into place. DAI 37:1209-A.

2231 Lee, U-Gene. "American Policy Toward Korea, 1942–1947: Formulation and Execution." Ph.D. dissertation, Georgetown University, 1973.

Independence was promised to Korean leaders only as a means of weakening Japan, and Korea was divided into two zones as a military operation to expedite the Japanese surrender. DAI 34:6569-A.

2232 Lee, Young-Woo. "Birth of the Korean Army, 1945–50: Evaluation of the Role of the U.S. Occupation Forces." *Korea & World Affairs* [South Korea] 4 (1980): 639–56.

The U.S. occupation forces laid the groundwork for the modern South Korean army during 1945 to 1950. The American experience is compared with that of the Soviets in North Korea.

2233 Matray, James I. "The Reluctant Crusade: American Foreign Policy in Korea, 1941–1950." Ph.D. dissertation, University of Virginia, 1977.

This study focuses particularly on evaluating the wisdom of American leaders in recognizing the limitations on the power of the United States in formulating policy objectives in Korea. DAI 39:4448-A.

2234 Mauck, Kenneth R. "The Formation of American Foreign Policy in Korea, 1945–1953." Ph.D. dissertation, University of Oklahoma, 1978.

This study explores, at the highest levels of the U.S. government, the formation of U.S. policy toward Korea in this period, which resulted in a bilateral security pact that is still in effect today. DAI 39:6919-A.

2235 Meade, E. Grant. *American Military Government in Korea*. New York: King's Crown Press, 1951.

Meade was an observer and participant in the military government in South Korea during the early months of the occupation. He employed documentation to supplement his personal experiences. This volume is an essential work. Notes, index.

2236 Paik, Seunggi. "United States-South Korean National Security Relationship, 1945–1972." Ph.D. dissertation, Southern Illinois University, 1973.

Paik traces the national security interactions between the United States and South Korea since 1945. DAI 36:1080-A.

2237 Park, Chang Jin. "The Influence of Small States upon the Superpowers: United States-South Korean Relations as a Case Study, 1950–1953." *World Politics* 28 (1975): 97–117.

South Korea tried to influence the United States by employing five techniques: (1) a public call for assistance; (2) a public call for mutual assistance against a common enemy; (3) a calculated policy proposal for bargaining advantage; (4) refusal to cooperate; and (5) moral suasion. Techniques 1 and 2 were effective; 3 and 4 least effective; and 5 was most effective. Notes.

2238 Stueck, William. *The Road to Confrontation: American Policy Toward China and Korea, 1947–1950.* Chapel Hill: University of North Carolina Press, 1981.

American policy in post-World War II Korea is examined by focusing on Washington's response to policies of Communist and Nationalist China. The outbreak of the Korean War is set in a Cold War context. Notes, bibliography, index.

2239 U.S. Department of State. Office of Public Affairs. *Korea, 1945–1948: A Report on Political Developments and Economic Resources with Selected Documents.* Publ. 3305. Far Eastern Series 28. Washington, DC: Division of Publications, 1948.

Contained here are forty pages of narrative describing some eighty pages of appended documents which deal with U.S. occupation policies. Also attached is a chronology of events.

2240 U.S. Department of State. Office of Public Affairs. *Korea's Independence.* Publ. 2933. Far Eastern Series 18. Washington, DC: G.P.O., 1947.

This sixty-page pamphlet surveys U.S. wartime and postwar commitments to Korean independence. It also provides excerpts of documents, particularly exchanges with the Soviets on the issue of unification.

Division and Unification

2241 Cho, Soon-sung. "United States Policy Toward Korean Reunification During the Truman Administration." *Journal of Asiatic Studies* 13 (1970): 79–90.

Although the Soviet Union is responsible for the divided condition of Korea, Presidents Roosevelt and Truman come in for criticism. The remoteness of Korea from Washington and American vital interests hindered efforts to achieve unification.

2242 Chung, Manduk. "The United States In Korea: A Reluctant Participant, 1945–1948." Ph.D. dissertation, Michigan State University, 1975.

This study aims to clarify some aspects of the nature of America's postwar Korean policy. The author finds that mutual distrust between the United States and Soviet Union was the decisive cause of the perpetuation of the division of Korea. DAI 36:8253-A.

2243 Grey, Arthur L., Jr. "The Thirty-Eighth Parallel." *Foreign Affairs* 29 (1951): 482–87.

The division of Korea is reviewed in this early, but still useful essay.

2244 Han, Pyo Wook. "The Problem of Korean Unification: A Study of the Unification Policy of the Republic of Korea, 1948–1960." Ph.D. dissertation, University of Michigan, 1963.

Communist China's intervention in Korea led America to adopt a policy of negotiated settlement to end the war, which the Republic of Korea was reluctant to accept. DAI 26:4776.

2245 Kim, Hak-Joon. "Korean Unification in the Asian Balance of Power." Ph.D. dissertation, University of Pittsburgh, 1972.

The purpose of this study is three-fold: (1) to examine the origins of the division of Korea at the 38th parallel; (2) to analyze the positions of the North and South Korean regimes on unification; and (3) to assess the prospects of Korean unification within the context of the changing East Asian balance of power, 1945–72. DAI 33:4494-A.

2246 Kim, Kwang. "Approaches to the Problem of Korean Unification: A Study in Linkage Politics." Ph.D. dissertation, New York University, 1974.

The linkage and interdependence between international and domestic politics are essential to understanding the problem of Korean unification. DAI 35:3832-A.

2247 Kim, Young J. "Toward a Unified Korea: History and Alternatives." Ph.D. dissertation, University of Tennessee, 1977.

This thesis describes and analyzes the history and the alternatives involved in the movement toward the peaceful unification of Korea, 1940–75. DAI 38:4359-A.

2248 Lee, Chong-sik. *The Politics of Korean Nationalism.* Berkeley: University of California Press, 1963.

The Korean Nationalist movement from 1905 to 1945 is extensively examined. As such it provides a very useful introduction to the problems and issues of divided Korea in the post-1945 years. Notes, index.

2249 Matray, James I. "Captive of the Cold War: The Decision to Divide Korea at the 38th Parallel." *Pacific Historical Review* 50 (1981): 145–68.

The partition of Korea at the 38th parallel resulted from a deterioration of Soviet-American relations in 1945, Truman's desire to prevent Soviet occupation of all Korea, and Stalin's efforts to enhance Russia's position in northeastern Asia. Notes.

2250 McCune, Shannon. "The Thirty-Eighth Parallel in Korea." *World Politics* 1 (1949): 223–32.

This early essay focuses on the political and geographical origins of the demarcation line. Notes.

2251 Morris, William G. "The Korean Trusteeship, 1941–1947: The United States, Russia, and the Cold War."

The Korean trusteeship grew out of the American belief that some peoples needed tutelage in the development of self-government. The Cold War resulted in the 38th parallel becoming a closed frontier. DAI 35:5312-A.

2252 Park, Hong-Kyu. "U.S.-Korean Relations, 1945–1947." *Asian Profile* [Hong Kong] 8 (1980): 45–52.

U.S. negotiations with the Soviet Union to end the division of Korea are reviewed, along with some suggestions as to why these efforts failed. Notes.

2253 Perrin, Kwan Sok. "The Problem of Korean Unification and the United Nations, 1945–1955." Ph.D. dissertation, University of Utah, 1971.

Perrin maintains that in addition to the deeply felt antagonism between the United States and the Soviet Union after the failure to reach agreement over the methods of unifying Korea, the renewed conflict between the two powers over the Korean settlement in the United Nations brought about the permanent division of Korea. DAI 32:2164-A.

2254 U.S. Department of State. Historical Office. *The Record of Korean Unification, 1943–1960: Narrative Summary with Principal Documents.* Publ. 7084. Far Eastern Series 101. Washington, DC: G.P.O., 1960.

This narrative survey covers the major documents regarding the unification of North and South Korea, and includes 200 pages of extracts of pertinent documents.

United Nations' Role

2255 Everett, John T., Jr. "The United Nations and the Korean Situation, 1947–1950: A Study of International Techniques of Pacific Settlement." Ph.D. dissertation, University of Cincinnati, 1955.

In 1947, at the request of the United States, the United Nations attempted to find peaceful solutions to the problems (including unification) which had arisen in Korea after World War II. It failed. DAI 15:1433.

2256 Goodrich, Leland M. *Korea: A Study of U.S. Policy in the United Nations.* New York: Council on Foreign Relations, 1956.

This general survey developed from a Council on Foreign Relations study group which focused on U.S. policy in dealing with the Korean question through the United Nations. Notes, appendix.

2257 Gordenker, Leon. *The United Nations and the Peaceful Unification of Korea: The Politics of Field Operations, 1947–1950.* The Hague: Nijhoff, 1959.

This key work focuses on three U.N. commissions operating in Korea which were charged with bringing about the unification of that nation. Special attention is paid to the 1948 Korean election process, with less attention on troop withdrawals and border incidents. Notes, bibliography, index.

2258 Gordenker, Leon. "The United Nations, the United States Occupation, and the 1948 Election in Korea." *Political Science Quarterly* 73 (1958): 426–50.

U.S. influence with the U.N. commission in Korea is examined here. Notes.

2259 Lee, Kwang Ho. "A Study of the United Nations Commission for the Unification and Rehabilitation of Korea (UNCURK): The Cold War and a United Nations Subsidiary Organ." Ph.D. dissertation, University of Pittsburgh, 1974.

UNCURK was a subsidiary organ of the General Assembly established in 1950 to bring about a unified, independent, and democratic government of all Korea. It was terminated in 1973. DAI 36:425-A.

2260 Yoon, Young Kyo. "United Nations Participants in Korean Affairs, 1945–1954." Ph.D. dissertation, American University, 1959.

The purpose of this study is to review the achievement of the United Nations in the establishment and recognition of the Republic of Korea, and to study the United Nations' collective activities against Communist aggression in the Korean War. DAI 20:2880.

Southeast Asia

2261 Baliga, Bantval M. "The American Approach to Imperialism in Southeast Asia—The Attitude of the United States Government in the Philippines, Indo-China and Indonesia, 1945–1958." Ph.D. dissertation, Southern Illinois University, 1961.

Although the United States emerged as the defender of freedom after the Second World War, she was faced with many problems: The European colonial powers failed to follow a realistic course in their dealings with their colonial possessions; their policies unleashed nationalist and anti-Western forces; and their blunders gave the Soviet Union and Communist China inroads into Southeast Asia. DAI 23:684.

2262 Bernabe, Gilbert A. "Southeast Asia and National Security Objectives: An Examination of 1950 Policies." Ph.D. dissertation, Claremont Graduate School, 1977.

This study examines the beginning of U.S. policy involvement in Southeast Asia and its relationship to the development of U.S. global policy as defined in NSC-68. It is argued that by comparing NSC-64 and NSC-68, a more meaningful and logical rationale can be seen for increased U.S. attention to Southeast Asia and Indochina during early 1950. DAI 38:1005.

2263 Colbert, Evelyn. "The Road Not Taken: Decolonization and Independence in Indonesia and Indochina." *Foreign Affairs* 51 (1973): 608–28.

This comparison of U.S. attitudes and policies toward two different episodes in the late 1940s places its emphasis upon international factors in explaining the different roads taken.

2264 Colbert, Evelyn. *Southeast Asia in International Politics, 1941–1956.* Ithaca, NY: Cornell University Press, 1977.

This wide-sweeping narrative covers the activities of all the major powers, including the United States, in Southeast Asia during the Truman years. It is useful for a perspective. Notes, bibliography, index.

2265 Jordan,. Amos A., Jr. "Foreign Aid and Defense: United States Military and Related Economic Assistance to Southeast Asia." Ph.D. dissertation, Columbia University, 1961.

Jordan investigates the relationships between military and economic assistance: (1) the allocation of counterpart funds; (2) the provision of items used by both the recipient's military forces and its civilian economy; and (3) security forces and economic improvements as alternative means of ensuring internal stability. DAI 22:2865.

2266 Ohn, Byunghoon. "United States and Southeast Asia, 1945–1954: The Evolution of American Policy in Southeast Asia." Ph.D. dissertation, University of Kentucky, 1966.

Part I traces American policies toward Southeast Asia from the middle of World War II to 1949. This cautious attitude was changed in conjunction with the overall revision of the U.S. East Asian policies. DAI 30:3075-A.

2267 Ovendale, Ritchie. "Britain, the United States and the Cold War in South-East Asia, 1949–1950." *International Affairs* [Great Britain] 58 (1982): 447–64.

The British successfully persuaded the United States to change its Southeast Asian policy to support British objectives, especially reduction of Soviet influence. Notes.

2268 Rotter, Andrew J. "The Big Canvas: The United States, Southeast Asia and the World: 1948–1950." Ph.D. dissertation, Stanford University, 1981.

U.S. policy in Southeast Asia was related to a victory over communism. A reduction of the commitment of French resources to the war in Vietnam permitted the return of French forces to Europe and encouraged the integration of West Germany into the anti-Communist alliance. DAI 42:3724.

2269 Tongdhummachart, Kramol. "American Policy in Southeast Asia, With Special Reference to Burma, Thailand and Indochina, 1945–1950." Ph.D. dissertation, University of Virginia, 1962.

As Communist China began to extend its influence in the area in 1949, the United States began to cooperate with the anti-Communist authorities in Southeast Asia and with the colonial powers to resist Communist-inspired revolutions. DAI 24:815.

INDONESIA

2270 Leupold, Robert L. "The United States and Indonesian Independence, 1944–1947: An American Revolution." Ph.D. dissertation, University of Kentucky, 1976.

The author suggests that throughout this period the United States pursued two objectives in the Netherlands East Indies: the establishment of a stable government friendly to the United States and the early restoration of the archipelago's economy on a nondiscriminatory basis. DAI 37:3845-A.

2271 McMahon, Robert J. "Anglo-American Diplomacy and the Reoccupation of the Netherlands East Indies." *Diplomatic History* 2 (1978): 1–24.

This essay sheds considerable light on U.S. attitudes toward colonial questions in the immediate postwar years. Notes.

2272 McMahon, Robert J. *Colonialism and Cold War: The United States and the Struggle for Indonesian Independence, 1945–1949.* Ithaca, NY: Cornell University Press, 1981.

Although the United States initially sought to remain neutral in the Indonesian struggle for independence, mounting opposition to Dutch military action prompted the Truman administration to re-evaluate its position. McMahon attempts to explain Washington's response to the Indonesian revolution within the context of overall U.S. foreign policy objectives and the Cold War. Notes, index.

2273 Taylor, Alastair M. *Indonesian Independence and the United Nations.* Ithaca, NY: Cornell University Press, 1960.

This is the standard account of the overall episode by a member of the U.N. Secretariat. Notes, bibliography, index.

2274 Vaughn, Sandra Y. C. "Foreign Aid: Its Impact on Indonesian Political Development, 1950–1972." Ph.D. dissertation, Howard University, 1978.

Vaughn finds that foreign aid in Indonesia had not been provided in the name of political or economic development, but within the context of the growth of the world capitalist system. As such, it has been counterproductive to development. DAI 42:1782.

PHILIPPINES

2275 Edgerton, Ronald K. "General Douglas MacArthur and the American Military Impact in the Philippines." *Philippine Studies* [Philippines] 25 (1977): 420–40.

Although postwar plans existed for the Philippines, U.S. actions there were largely shaped by General MacArthur (1945–46). Notes.

2276 Kesauan, K. V. "The Attitude of the Philippines Toward the Japanese Peace Treaty." *International Studies* [India] 12 (1973): 222–50.

Philippine President Elpidio Quirino sought a postwar settlement which would provide material reparations and security from a possibly remilitarized Japan. The Japanese eventually paid reparations and the United States agreed to aid the Philippines in the event of a new Japanese threat. The Philippines signed the treaty in September 1951, but did not ratify it until 1956. Notes.

2277 Meyer, Milton W. *A Diplomatic History of the Philippine Republic.* Honolulu: University of Hawaii Press, 1965.

This detailed study (1945–61) focuses largely on U.S.-Philippine relations. Notes, bibliography, index.

2278 Shalom, Stephen R. "Philippine Acceptance of the Bell Trade Act of 1946: A Study of Manipulatory Democracy." *Pacific Historical Review* 49 (1980): 499–517.

The United States continued to dominate the nominally independent Philippine Republic by the U.S.-Philippine Trade Agreement (1946), by the Bell Trade Act or the Philippine Trade Act (1946), by the Philippine Rehabilitation Act (1946), and by an alliance with the Filipino elite. Notes.

2279 Valeriano, N.D., and Bohannon, C. T. R. "The Philippine Experience." *Marine Corps Gazette* 47 (1963): 18–24; 47:42–45, 47:46–51.

This three-part essay examines the methods employed by Philippine battalion combat teams, aided by American advisers, to suppress Communist guerrillas in the Philippines after 1950.

2280 Ventura, Mamerto S. "Philippine Post-War Recovery: A Record of United States-Philippine Cooperation and Cross-Purposes." Ph.D. dissertation, Southern Illinois University, 1966.

Although the United States granted the Philippines independence in 1946 and aided in its postwar recovery, colonial-type arrangements persisted. "Parity rights" extended Americans the same rights as Filipinos in the exploitation of natural resources, and agricultural and industrial development were affected by colonial-type trade arrangements. DAI 27:3500.

2281 Wurfel, David O. D. "The Bell Report and After: A Study of the Political Problems of Social Reform Stimulated by Foreign Aid." Ph.D. dissertation, Cornell University, 1960.

In a time of grave national crisis, the summer of 1950, Truman sent an Economic Survey Mission to the Philippines, headed by Daniel Bell. Its report recommended several administrative and socioeconomic reforms to be prerequisites for expanded U.S. aid. The subsequent agreement, signed in November 1950, found the Philippines pledging immediate enactment of higher taxes and a minimum wage law. DAI 21:228.

THAILAND

2282 Darling, Frank C. "American Influence on the Evolution of Constitutional Government in Thailand." Ph.D. dissertation, American University, 1961.

After World War II, the United States assisted the rise of the liberals and the removal of the military regime. However, the overthrow of the unstable liberal government in 1947 coincided with U.S. efforts to deter Communist aggression, and the United States supported the new military regime. DAI 22:1235.

2283 Fine, Herbert A. "The Liquidation of World War II in Thailand." *Pacific Historial Review* 34 (1965): 65–82.

This essay suggests a rising U.S. interest in Thailand at the end of World War II. Notes.

2284 Neher, Arlene B. "Prelude to Alliance: The Expansion of American Economic Interest in Thailand During the 1940s." Ph.D. dissertation, Northern Illinois University, 1980.

Neher finds that such programs as the Military Assistance Agreement of 1950 and the SEATO pact were not products of the Cold War, but culminated a process of rapprochement which had begun before either nation articulated anti-Communist motives. DAI 41:5222.

INDOCHINA/VIETNAM

2285 Buttinger, Joseph. *Vietnam: A Dragon Embattled*. 2 vols. New York: Praeger, 1967.

In these volumes, Buttinger details Vietnam's history from the French conquest at the end of the nineteenth century to the fall of Ngo Dinh Diem in 1963. Volume 2 discusses the Truman administration's policy toward Vietnam. Notes, appendixes, bibliography, index.

2286 Eggleston, Noel C. "America's First Withdrawal From Indochina." *Research Studies* 44 (1976): 217–28.

Roosevelt had suggested the establishment of a trusteeship for Indochina; however, the Truman administration never gave much support to the idea in 1945. Notes.

2287 Eggleston, Noel C. "The Roots of Commitment: United States Policy Toward Vietnam, 1945–1950." Ph.D. dissertation, University of Georgia, 1977.

Influenced by deteriorating relations with the Soviet Union and the need for France as an ally in Europe, the Truman administration not only allowed the French to return to Indochina, but also supplied them with the weapons to reestablish control. DAI 38:4323-A.

2288 Garfield, Gene J. "The Genesis of Involvement: The Truman Decision to Assist the French in Indochina." Ph.D. dissertation, Southern Illinois University, 1972.

The Truman administration decided to become involved in Indochina because of the Communist victory in China, the need for a strong France in Europe, and the Korean War. Military and economic aid programs are examined. DAI 33:1209-A.

2289 Gelb, Leslie H., with Richard K. Betts. *The Irony of Vietnam: The System Worked*. Washington, DC: Brookings Institution, 1979.

Within this broad survey there is an assessment of the Truman administration's role (pp. 36–50) in U.S. involvement in Vietnam. Notes, index.

2290 Hammer, Ellen. *The Struggle for Indochina*. Stanford, CA: Stanford University Press, 1954.

With the advance of the Red forces in China to the Tonkinese border in 1949, U.S. policy took a new turn. Hammer discusses the background of Vietnam and examines the lining up of the great powers into two opposing camps—Communist and anti-Communist. Notes, bibliography, index.

2291 Hays, Samuel P., ed. *The Beginning of American Aid to Southeast Asia: The Griffin Mission of 1950*. Lexington, MA: Lexington Books, 1971.

This volume reprints the original reports of the Griffin mission which led to American aid to Vietnam, Laos, and Cambodia.

2292 Herring, George C. "The Truman Administration and the Restoration of French Sovereignty in Indochina." *Diplomatic History* 1 (1977): 97–117.

The Truman administration consciously chose "to accept the restoration of French sovereignty in Indochina as a means of enlisting French cooperation in the San Francisco Conference and in opposing Soviet expansion in Europe." Notes.

2293 Hess, Gary R. "The First American Commitment in Indochina: The Acceptance of the 'Bao Dai Solution,' 1950." *Diplomatic History* 2 (1978): 331–50.

The Elysée Agreement of March 1949 created a Vietnamese government which lacked genuine independence under Emperor Bao Dai. In February 1950 the United States recognized Bao Dai; however, the Truman administration was divided on whether to take a more active role in the civil war. Notes.

2294 Hess, Gary R. "United States Policy and the Origins of the French-Viet Minh War, 1945–46." *Peace and Change* 3 (1975): 21–33.

Fearing communism, the United States chose to support the French in this early fighting. Washington failed to establish an effective relationship with the leaders of Vietnamese nationalism. Notes.

2295 Irving, R. E. M. *The First Indochina War: French and American Policy, 1945–54*. London: Croom Helm, 1975.

This volume is essentially a study of French policy in Indochina (1945–54), with particular reference to the role and influence of the political parties. But increasingly, it develops into a study of American policy as well, because by the end of the war the United States was almost as involved in Indochina as France. Notes, bibliography, index.

2296 Kahler, John K. "The Genesis of the American Involvement in Indochina, 1940–1954." Ph.D. dissertation, University of Chicago, 1964.

No abstract available.

2297 Kail, F. M. *What Washington Said: Administration Rhetoric and the Vietnam War.* New York: Harper & Row, 1973.

In an effort to contain communism in Asia, Truman opted to oppose the Viet Minh and aid the French in Vietnam. Kail discusses early policy in Vietnam and its impact on the subsequent Vietnam War. Appendix.

2298 Katz, Mark N. "The Origins of the Vietnam War, 1945–1948." *Review of Politics* 42 (1980): 131–51.

The origins of the Vietnam War lay not in the struggle for and against communism but in the nascent strivings for nationalism. Notes.

2299 Kenney, Henry J. "The Changing Importance of Vietnam in United States Policy, 1949–1969." Ph.D. dissertation, American University, 1974.

Among the major decisions analyzed is Truman's assisting the French in Indochina. DAI 35: 2367-A.

2300 Marvel, W. Macy. "Drift and Intrigue: United States Relations with the Viet-Minh, 1945." *Millennium: Journal of International Studies* [Great Britain] 4 (1975): 10–27.

The author agrees that there is considerable confusion regarding U.S. relations with, and priorities concerning, Vietnam at the end of World War II. Notes.

2301 Melby, John F. "Vietnam, 1950." *Diplomatic History* 6 (1982): 97–109.

The author recalls his experiences as head of the Melby-Erskine Mission (Joint State-Defense Military Defense Assistance Program Survey Mission to Southeast Asia). Although the United States decided to support French efforts to regain control of Indochina, it did so for contradictory reasons. Notes.

2302 Nguyen, Lien V. "American Perceptions of the Chinese Role in Vietnam, 1946–1954." Ph.D. dissertation, University of South Carolina, 1979.

American policies toward Indochina during these years were motivated by perceptions of the Communist Chinese threat to the area which, in turn, were substantially derived from their internal and external operational environment. DAI 40:1673-A.

2303 Rice-Maximin, Edward. "The United States, France, and Vietnam, 1945–1950: The View from the State Department." *Contemporary French Civilization* 7 (1982): 20–40.

The United States reluctantly supported France's efforts to reconquer Indochina because it needed French assistance in Europe. Notes.

2304 Siracusa, Joseph M. "The United States, Vietnam, and the Cold War: A Reappraisal." *Journal of Southeast Asian Studies* [Singapore] 5 (1974): 82–101.

Early U.S. policy toward Vietnam (1945–50) is considered here. Roosevelt's determination to keep the United States out of Indochina and Truman's decision to aid France because of Soviet pressures in Europe form the focus of the essay. Notes.

2305 Welch, Susan K. "Groups and Foreign Policy Decisions: The Case of Indochina, 1950–1956." Ph.D. dissertation, University of Illinois, Urbana-Champaign, 1970.

This thesis applies theories of organizational behavior to the decisions made by the United States to aid the French in Indochina and, subsequently, Diem's government. Welch argues that the administration viewed the Indochina struggle as an anti-Communist versus Communist military struggle and chose as its program of aid that which was successful in Europe. DAI 31:4862-A.

2306 White, David H., Jr. "The United States and Indochina, 1942–1945." Ph.D. dissertation, Tulane University, 1974.

While much of the account deals with Roosevelt's idea of a postwar trusteeship for Indochina, the later chapters develop Truman's abandonment of the idea and refusal to recognize Ho Chi Minh. DAI 35:7855-A.

South Asia

2307 Ahmad, Bashir. "The Politics of the Major Powers Toward the Kashmir Dispute, 1947–1965." Ph.D. dissertation, University of Nebraska, 1972.

The author attempts to provide a comprehensive analysis of the politics of the major powers—the United States, Soviet Union, United Kingdom, France, and the People's Republic of China—toward the Kashmir dispute. Offered here is an historical account and a review of the pertinent proceedings in the U.N. Security Council. DAI 33:2461-A.

2308 Habibuddin, S. M. "American Response to the Emergence of Pakistan, 1940–1947." *Indian Journal of Politics* [India] 13 (1979): 47–62.

America's initial reaction was hostile to the idea of separation; however, during the Truman era American response to the Muslim League's demand for an independent Pakistan was modified by the onset of the Cold War. During the transfer of power from the British and the creation of India and Pakistan, the Americans recognized both nations. Notes.

2309 Khair, Mohammed Abul. "United States Foreign Policy in the Indo-Pakistan Subcontinent, 1940–1955." Ph.D. dissertation, University of California, Berkeley, 1962.

The United States sought friendly relations with both India and Pakistan. India regarded American influence in Asia as a threat to her leadership and opposed American-sponsored defensive alliances, while Pakistan joined in. DAI 24:3710.

2310 Miyasato, Seigen. "American Foreign Policy Toward South Asian Neutralism, 1947–1957." Ph.D. dissertation, Ohio State University, 1961.

American opinion was not favorable toward neutralism. However, there were also favorable forces—anticolonialism, humanitarianism, and pragmatism—which also influenced American policy. During the Truman administration, the tension between the two forces was not yet acute. DAI 22:3729.

INDIA

2311 Abel, Maddela. "American Economic Assistance Program in India: 1950–1961. An Analytical Study of Organization and Operation." Ph.D. dissertation, University of California, Los Angeles, 1963.

American aid programs have enabled the Indian government to maintain political stability, prevented India from succumbing to communism, and exerted a beneficial influence on the decisions of the Indian government. DAI 24:5508.

2312 Chary, Srinivas. "An Analysis of Indo-American Relations: Chester Bowles' Views." *Indian Journal of American Studies*. 10 (1980): 3–9.

This essay compares the Cold War views of Chester Bowles and Jawaharlal Nehru (1949–54) concerning the best way to maintain peace and stability in South Asia. Notes.

2313 Desai, Tripta. "American Role in the Indian Freedom Movement." *Indian Political Science Review* [India] 11 (1977): 1–32.

After World War II, the Truman administration encouraged the British to end the political conflict in India but took no active part in the negotiations among the various groups.

2314 Desai, Tripta. "Indo-American Wheat Negotiations of 1950–51." *Indian Political Science Review* [India] 9 (1975): 119–51.

The background of the Indian food shortage (1950–51) and the congressional debate over aid are reviewed. The India Emergency Food Aid Act (United States, 1951) was passed in June due to humanitarian, political, and ideological considerations.

2315 Hess, Gary R. *America Encounters India, 1941–1947*. Baltimore: Johns Hopkins University Press, 1971.

Official and public response to the political struggle in India is examined. Notes, bibliography, index.

2316 Hope, Ashley G. "The American Role in Indian Independence, 1940–1947." Ph.D. dissertation, Syracuse University, 1967.

America played a significant part in the realization of Indian independence through inspiration, example, direct pressure on the British, and as a leader of anticolonial world opinion. DAI 28:1372-A.

2317 Jauhri, R. C. *American Diplomacy and Independence for India*. Bombay: Vora, 1970.

This volume focuses on the period 1941 to 1947 and is more laudatory toward the Truman than the Roosevelt administration.

2318 Jauhri, R. C. "The American Effort to Avert the Impending Partition of India, 1946–47." *Indian Journal of American Studies* [India] 8 (1978): 1–11.

American officials sought to avoid the division of the Indian subcontinent into hostile Hindu and Moslem countries, but gave up their mediatory efforts after their representatives concluded that partition was inevitable. Notes.

2319 Kshiragar, Shiwaram Krishnarao. "Development of Relations Between India and the United States, 1941–1952." Ph.D. dissertation, American University, 1957.

India has followed a policy of self-determination and nonalignment, while the United States has been most interested in containing communism. In 1951, however, the U.S. Wheat Loan ("The India Emergency Food Aid Act of 1951") helped save millions from famine. DAI 17:2052.

2320 Roy, Ram Mohan. "The India Emergency Food Aid Act of 1951: A Study in Foreign Policy Formation in the United States." Ph.D. dissertation, Claremont Graduate School, 1969.

Through the entire debate on the emergency aid to India, it was a unanimous opinion that food was a weapon in the arsenal of the U.S. foreign policy. DAI 30:5508-A.

2321 Sinha, Bishwanath Prasad. "India's Relations with the United States, 1947–1955." Ph.D. dissertation, University of Missouri, 1956.

While American stock was high in India at the end of World War II, the development of the Cold War found differences arising between the two nations. Basically, it stemmed from India's desire to avoid "entangling alliances" and U.S. pressure to join the West in the Cold War. DAI 16:1483.

2322 Srinivasachary, M. S. "Commerce, Peace and Security: United States Foreign Policy Toward India, 1947–1954." Ph.D. dissertation, Kansas State University, 1975.

This account examines U.S. foreign policy toward India during the Truman administration and continues into the Eisenhower presidency. The author argues that U.S. policy toward India centered on the desire to see that American business could operate and profit without restrictions. DAI 36:3022-A.

2323 Venkataramani, M. S. *Undercurrents in American Foreign Relations: Four Studies*. New York: Asia Publishing House, 1965.

The chapter "The United States and India's Food Crisis, 1946" (pp. 43–92) examines the Truman administration's response to India's postwar famine and its impact on U.S./Indian foreign relations. Notes, index.

Latin America

2324 Barnard, Andrew. "Chilean Communists, Radical Presidents and Chilean Relations with the United States, 1940–1947." *Journal of Latin American Studies* [Great Britain] 13 (1981): 347–74.

The Communist party in Chile believed that when radical Chilean presidents broke ties with them in 1940, 1946, and 1947 it was because of U.S. influence. The first occasions were domestic decisions, while in 1947 the State Department did urge a break. Notes.

2325 Bradshaw, James S. "The 'Lost' Conference: The Economic Issue in United States-Latin American Relations, 1945–1957." Ph.D. dissertation, Michigan State University, 1972.

The decline in the wartime closeness between the United States and Latin America after World War II is traced to the postwar failure to agree on an inter-American economic policy. A conference to develop such a policy was first proposed in 1942, but subsequently and frequently postponed until 1957

when an economic summit failed to reach any agreement. DAI 33:688-A.

2326 Day, Lowell C. "United States Policy toward Pan Americanism: A Decade of Shifting Emphasis, 1949–1959." Ph.D. dissertation, University of Pittsburgh, 1965.

During the Truman years, the initial emphasis was on Pan American economic problems, but with the Korean War, the emphasis shifted toward political and military problems. DAI 27:1885.

2327 DeShazo, Elmer A. "The Peaceful Settlement of Disputes in the Inter-American System since World War II." Ph.D. dissertation, Indiana University, 1957.

The Organization of American States Charter affirms peaceful settlement as a basic principle and requires that disputes be submitted to peaceful procedures. The "Pact of Bogota" is a comprehensive treaty continuing such procedures. DAI 18:280.

2328 Francis, Michael J. "The United States and the Act of Chapultepec." *Southwestern Social Science Quarterly* 45 (1964): 249–57.

The U.S. dissatisfaction with proposals concerning aggression at the Mexico City conference (1945) resulted in the weakening of many sections of the Act of Chapultepec.

2329 Green, David E. *The Containment of Latin America*. Chicago: Quadrangle, 1971.

During the postwar period, inter-American relations deteriorated, with the Good Neighbor Policy giving way to U.S. support of military dictatorships. Yet, Green argues, this antinationalist attitude can be seen in Roosevelt's administration and it was fraught with contradictions and tensions that Truman inherited. Notes, bibliographical essay, index.

2330 Green, David. "The Cold War comes to Latin America." In Barton J. Bernstein, ed. *Politics and Policies of the Truman Administration*. Chicago: Quadrangle, 1970, pp. 149–95.

Green examines the Truman administration's concern about the advance of "communism" in Latin America. The impact of the Korean War on the evolution of military advisory programs in Third World areas is not adequately developed. Notes.

2331 Heston, Thomas J. "Cuba, the United States, and the Sugar Act of 1948: The Failure of Economic Coercion." *Diplomatic History* 6 (1982): 1–21.

Efforts by American diplomats to persuade Cuba to cooperate on a number of economic endeavors failed; therefore, the Sugar Act of 1948 was enacted (cutting Cuba's American quota by a third) in an attempt to force positive Cuban responses. Latin American protests resulted in the Charter of the Organization of American States prohibiting economic coercion. Notes.

2332 Leonard, Thomas M. "The United States and Costa Rica, 1944–1949." *Secolas Annals* 13 (1982): 17–31.

Washington's reaction to the Costa Rican Communist party is examined.

2333 Lommel, Anne W. "United States Efforts to Foster Peace and Stability in Central America, 1923–1954." Ph.D. dissertation, University of Minnesota, 1967.

The policy of the United States has been to foster peace and stability by attempting to change some of the prevailing conditions in the area. World War II stimulated efforts to aid in economic development and saw the growth of the inter-American system for security. DAI 28:3609-A.

2334 Major, John. "Wasting Asset: The U.S. Re-Assessment of the Panama Canal, 1945–1949." *Journal of Strategic Studies* [Great Britain] 3 (1980): 123–46.

While the canal had played a major role in U.S. strategic planning before World War II, the postwar years saw U.S. interests shifting toward Europe and thus lessening the need for the canal. Notes.

2335 Pan American Union. *Economic Survey of Inter-American Agriculture.* 2 vols. Washington, DC: Pan American Union, 1949.

Volume 1 is a narrative report which contains statistical tables of basic crop exports and imports from the 1930s to 1949. Volume 2 deals with national problems concerning agricultural credits, machinery, transportation, and record keeping.

2336 Rabe, Stephen G. "The Elusive Conference: United States Economic Relations with Latin America, 1945–1952." *Diplomatic History* 2 (1978): 279–94.

The idea of a hemispheric conference on postwar economic cooperation, suggested in 1942, was much discussed by the Truman administration, but no meeting took place. The fundamental unresolved question was: Would the U.S. government finance development in Latin America, or should the region's governments seek to attract private American capital? Notes.

2337 Rys, John. "Tensions and Conflicts in Cuba, Haiti, and the Dominican Republic Between 1945 and 1959." Ph.D. dissertation, American University, 1966.

Had the United States and the Organization of American States correctly evaluated the underlying social tensions involved in the Caribbean conflicts of the late 1940s and early 1950s, they could have avoided the later conflicts in which much control passed to the forces of international communism. DAI 26:7434.

2338 Sessions, Gene A. "The Multilateralization of the Monroe Doctrine: The Rio Treaty, 1947." *World Affairs* 136 (1973/74): 259–74.

The United States entered into international peace-keeping arrangements after World War II, but retained the basic tenets of the Monroe Doctrine as U.S. policy for Latin America. Notes.

2339 Slater, Jerome N. *The OAS and the United States Foreign Policy.* Columbus: Ohio State University Press, 1967.

Organized topically, this volume does have scattered materials on the Truman years. Notes, bibliography, index.

2340 Spector, Stephen. "United States Attempts at Regional Security and the Extension of the Good Neighbor Policy in Latin America, 1945–1952." Ph.D. dissertation, New York University, 1970.

Spector argues that the United States had a viable and convincing policy toward Latin America during the period 1945–52, which has frequently been overlooked, and that real failures were to come later. DAI 31:1742-A.

2341 Stokes, William S. "Economic Anti-Americanism in Latin America." *Inter-American Economic Affairs* 11 (1957): 3–22.

Stokes ascribes economic anti-Americanism to a basic hostility toward U.S.-style capitalism, resulting from the mercantilistic traditions inherited from the colonial era, and to later collectivistic theories, including Marxism. Bibliography.

2342 Tillspaugh, James C. "From War to Cold War: United States Policies toward Latin America, 1943–1948." Ph.D. dissertation, Northwestern University, 1973.

After World War II, the United States remained preoccupied with noncontinental problems and allowed the wartime solidarity to dissipate. The United States neither joined in projects for mutual postwar advancement nor tried to mobilize the area in its support. DAI 34:5890-A.

2343 Trask, Roger R. "George F. Kennan's Report On Latin America (1950)." *Diplomatic History* 2 (1978): 307–11.

This report is now available in the State Department's *Foreign Relations* series. Kennan's generally deficient understanding of the region's character is evident, but this is partially offset by his realistic assessment of its importance for the United States. Notes.

2344 Trask, Roger R. "The Impact of the Cold War on United States-Latin American Relations, 1945–1949." *Diplomatic History* 1 (1977): 271–84.

In 1945 the United States favored universal rather than regional organizations, but by 1948 the charter of the Organization of American States had been drawn as a safeguard against Communist intervention in Latin America. However, the massive economic aid expected by Latin Americans was not forthcoming. Notes.

U.S. Military Aid

2345 Baines, John M. "U.S. Military Assistance to Latin America: An Assessment." *Journal of International American Studies and World Affairs* 14 (1972): 469–86.

This essay surveys U.S. military aid to Latin American countries (1938 to the 1970s). Notes.

2346 Francis, Michael J. "Attitudes of the United States Government Toward Collective Military Arrangements with Latin America, 1945–1960." Ph.D. dissertation, University of Virginia, 1963.

Collective hemispheric cooperation evolved from the inter-American conferences of 1947 and 1948, which produced the Rio Treaty of Reciprocal Assistance and the Charter of Bogota to the 1951 Mutual Security Act. DAI 24:2550.

2347 Francis, Michael J. "Military Aid to Latin America in the U.S. Congress." *Journal of Inter-American Studies* 6 (1964): 389–404.

This essay focuses on the shifting justifications for military assistance to Latin America since 1951. In 1951 Congress was told that such aid was required for hemispheric defense. Notes.

2348 Hinson, Billy G. "Plans of the United States for Postwar Military Assistance to Latin America, 1945–1951." Ph.D. dissertation, University of Mississippi, 1977.

The Inter-American Military Cooperation Bill (May 1946) failed to pass in 1946, 1947, 1948; when Congress passed the Mutual Defense Assistance Act of 1949 to aid Europe, it allowed Latin American nations also to purchase arms. Not until 1951 did a formal U.S.-Latin American military assistance program develop. DAI 38:7488-A.

2349 Kaplan, Stephen S. "U.S. Arms Transfers to Latin America, 1945–1974: Rational Strategy, Bureaucratic Politics, and Executive Parameters." *International Studies Quarterly* 19 (1975): 399–431.

The author explores U.S. decisionmaking regarding arms transfers, especially to Brazil and the Dominican Republic. Notes.

2350 Pach, Chester J., Jr. "The Containment of U.S. Military Aid to Latin America, 1944–49." *Diplomatic History* 6 (1982): 225–44.

The Western Hemisphere Defense Program grew from army and navy desires to maintain and extend their wartime influence with Latin American countries. Yet the emerging Cold War found limited U.S. resources available for these nations. Notes.

2351 Van Cleve, John V. "The Political Use of Military Aid: The United States and the Latin American Military, 1945–1965." Ph.D. dissertation, University of California, Irvine, 1976.

Although this study reviews Truman administration policies and programs, it focuses on the methods and short-term goals which changed dramatically in the late 1950s and early 1960s. DAI 37:3862-A.

ARGENTINA

2352 Bowen, Nicholas. "The End of British Economic Hegemony in Argentina: Messersmith and the Eady-Miranda Agreement." *Inter-American Economic Affairs* 28 (1975): 3–24.

U.S. Ambassador George S. Messersmith succeeded in breaking the impasse which had developed in the Eady-Miranda negotiations of 1946 on Argentine-British economic relations. Notes.

2353 Giacalone, Rita A. "From Bad Neighbors to Reluctant Partners: Argentina and the United States, 1946–1950." Ph.D. dissertation, Indiana University, 1977.

This study of U.S.-Argentine relations focuses on the years from the close of World War II to the Korean War, and on the rapprochement between the two governments in 1950 when the United States extended financial assistance and Argentina supported U.S. efforts in Korea. DAI 38:2295-A.

2354 MacDonald, C. A. "The Politics of Intervention: The United States and Argentina, 1941–1946." *Journal of Latin American Studies* [Great Britain] 12 (1980): 365–96.

The United States treated Argentina differently from the other Latin American countries during World War II because it was misinformed about the extent of German influence over the Peron government. This essay provides useful information as a backdrop to the Truman administration's difficulties with Argentina. Notes.

2355 May, Ernest R. "The 'Bureaucratic Politics' Approach: U.S.-Argentine Relations, 1942–47." In Julio Cotler and Richard R. Fagen, eds. *Latin America and the United States: The Changing Political Realities.* Stanford: Stanford University Press, 1974, pp. 129–63.

By employing the "bureaucratic" models used by Graham Allison (*Essence of Decision: Explaining the Cuban Missile Crisis*), May seeks to understand why and how the U.S. policies toward Argentina developed. Comments by Guillermo O'Donnell follow.

2356 Rudgers, David F. "Challenge to the Hemisphere: Argentina Confronts the United States, 1938–1947." Ph.D. dissertation, George Washington University, 1972.

During World War II, the United States mobilized the weapons of diplomatic ostracism and pressure, economic sanctions, and moral suasion to force the Argentines to alter their pro-German leanings. This account also deals with the postwar abandonment of this policy. DAI 33:2266-A.

2357 Vannucci, Albert P. "United States-Argentina Relations, 1943–1948: A Case Study in Confused Foreign Policy-Making." Ph.D. dissertation, New School for Social Research, 1978.

The embarrassment which resulted from our Argentine policy could have been avoided if our policymakers had a deeper knowledge of Argentine history and a more realistic assessment of our national interest and policy objectives. DAI 39:3128-A.

2358 Woods, Randall B. "Conflict or Community? The United States and Argentina's Admission to the United Nations." *Pacific Historical Review* 46 (1977): 361–86.

Contrary to revisionist arguments, the U.S. government did hide its disapproval of the Argentine government (and its World War II record) and support its admission to the United Nations because of the Truman administration's commitment to the principles of nonintervention, internationalism, and respect for national sovereignty. Notes.

BRAZIL

2359 Cordell, Arthur J. "The Brazilian Soluble Coffee Problem: A Review." *Quarterly Review of Economics and Business* 9 (1969): 29–38.

Cordell examines Brazil's instant coffee production and its decreasing market, 1947–69, and summarizes the argument for industrialization of agricultural exports.

2360 Godfrey, Erwina E. "The Influence of Economic Factors on United States-Brazilian Relations, 1940–1960." Ph.D. dissertation, University of Kentucky, 1960.

After the war, the United States was distracted from the economic development of Brazil by her focus upon European recovery and military defense in Europe and Asia. Although this engendered some ill will, it did not damage the U.S.-Brazilian friendship. DAI 26:4784.

2361 Hilton, Stanley E. "The United States, Brazil, and the Cold War, 1945–1960." *Journal of American History* 68 (1981): 599–624.

The author believes that the Truman and Eisenhower administrations' general neglect of Brazil, especially its desire for preferential economic treatment, caused Brazil to end its traditional pro-U.S. relationship. Notes.

2362 Lanoue, Kenneth C. "An Alliance Shaken: Brazil and the United States, 1945–1950." Ph.D. dissertation, Louisiana State University, 1978.

At the beginning of this period, U.S.-Brazilian relations were solid as Brazil had made several sacrifices in World War II and had received special benefits from the United States. By 1950, however, Brazil came to realize that the Truman administration was not willing to provide the aid and special treatment which it had expected, and relations subsequently cooled. DAI 39:5097-A.

MEXICO

2363 Kane, N. Stephen. "The United States and the Development of the Mexican Petroleum Industry, 1945–1950: A Lost Opportunity." *Inter-American Economic Affairs* 35 (1981): 45–72.

The years 1945 to 1950 were transitional ones which provided the possibility for a renewed business relationship, since President Lazaro Cardenas nationalized the industry and expropriated foreign oil properties in 1938. Notes.

2364 Luan-Miller, Patricia D. "U.S. Direct Involvement in Mexico, 1876–1978: An Historical, Theoretical and Empirical Analysis." Ph.D. dissertation, University of Texas, Austin, 1980.

This study examines the historical, theoretical, and empirical dimensions of U.S. direct investment in Mexico, showing how the majority of U.S. funds have shifted from the extractive to manufacturing sectors. DAI 41:3230.

2365 Markus De Kennedy, Anneliese. "The Office of Special Studies: A Study of the Joint Mexican Secretariat of Agriculture-Rockefeller Foundation Program in Agriculture, 1943–1963." Ph.D. dissertation, University of North Carolina, Chapel Hill, 1974.

This study describes the development and impact of a joint venture in technical assistance. The efforts of this activity began to be felt with an increase in food crop production during the 1950s. DAI 35:3643-A.

2366 Smedley, Max J. "Mexican-United States Relations and the Cold War, 1945–1954." Ph.D. dissertation, University of Southern California, 1981.

The strong bond of friendship and cooperation forged during World War II continued well into the postwar period despite serious differences Mexico had with U.S. Cold War policy and strategy. DAI 42:3716.

VENEZUELA

2367   Mohr, Cynthia J. B. "Revolution, Reform, and Counter-Revolution: The United States and Economic Nationalism in Venezuela, 1945–1948." Ph.D. dissertation, University of Denver, 1975.

U.S. ideological concern (with Good Neighbor Policy or fear of communism) had little influence on Washington's policies. The notion that Washington's policies were designed to advance private business interests was too simplistic. Strategic interests, at least until 1948, appear to have been the dominant State Department concern. DAI 37:520-A.

2368   Rabe, Stephen G. *The Road to OPEC: United States Relations with Venezuela, 1919–1976.* Austin: University of Texas Press, 1982.

Chapter 5, "The Trienio, 1945–1949," discusses the coup which gave Venezuela a democratic government. Whereas the United States welcomed a democratic Venezuela, she opposed the proposed economic nationalism which threatened U.S. oil interests. Notes, bibliography, index.

Middle East

2369   Abramson, Arthur C. "The Formulation of American Foreign Policy towards the Middle East during the Truman Administration, 1945–1948." Ph.D. dissertation, University of California, Los Angeles, 1981.

Abramson finds that the prime, guiding motivation behind the Truman administration's policies directed toward the Middle East was national security, not domestic, political, or bureaucratic considerations. DAI 42:371.

2370   Baram, Phillip J. *The Department of State in the Middle East, 1919–1945.* Philadelphia: University of Pennsylvania Press, 1978.

The emphasis is upon 1939 to 1945 in this study, and it provides a useful introduction to the problems confronting the Truman administration. Notes, bibliography, index.

2371   Fields, Harvey J. "Pawn of Empires: A Study of United States-Middle East Policy, 1945–1953." Ph.D. dissertation, Rutgers University, 1975.

Fields examines the factors in U.S.-Middle East policy during the Truman years: (1) the access to oil, and (2) the maintenance of Western hegemony over the area stretching from the eastern Mediterranean to the Persian Gulf and India. DAI 36:3068-A.

2372   Kuniholm, Bruce R. *The Origins of the Cold War in the Near East: Great Power Conflict and Diplomacy in Iran, Turkey and Greece.* Princeton: Princeton University Press, 1980.

The apparent successes of American policy in the Near East (1946–47) led the Truman and later administrations to look upon these policies as models of how to deal with the Soviet Union. Thus Great Power relationships in the Near East cast significant light on the origins of the Cold War. Maps, appendix, extensive bibliography, index.

2373   Perkins, Kenneth J. "North African Propaganda and the United States, 1946–1956." *Towson State Journal of International Affairs* 13 (1979): 97–116.

Since 1945, the North African states, especially Morocco and Tunisia, sought to develop an American public sympathetic to their demands for independence.

2374   Rubin, Barry M. "American Perceptions and Great Power Politics in the Middle East, 1941–1947." Ph.D. dissertation, Georgetown University, 1978.

The wartime crises played a key role in the formulation of the postwar policy, especially Stalin's demands for Turkish territory and control of the Straits, and Soviet support of secessionist movements in Iran. DAI 39:6903-A.

ARAB-ISRAELI CONFLICT

2375   Collins, Larry, and Lapierre, Dominique. *O Jerusalem!* New York: Simon & Schuster, 1972.

Sovereignty over Jerusalem has been a problem since the inception of the state of Israel in 1948. The role of the United States in this Arab/Israeli problem is discussed. Notes, bibliography, index.

2376   Johnson, Joseph E. "Arab vs. Israeli: A Persistent Challenge to Americans." *Middle East Journal* 18 (1964): 1–13.

The president of the Carnegie Endowment for International Peace reviews the problems from 1954 to 1964, and focuses on the Truman years.

2377 Picraux, Danice Kent. "The Relative Roles of Humanitarianism and National Interest in the Formulation of Foreign Policy: American Policy Towards the Jewish State, 1914–1951." Ph.D. dissertation, Claremont Graduate School, 1979.

Humanitarian actions were taken even though they were not in the national interest as defined by the State Department, especially under Presidents Wilson and Truman. DAI 39:6954-A.

Palestine Issue

2378 Aben-Rabbo, Samir A. "Might Does Not Make Right: International Law and the Question of Palestine." Ph.D. dissertation, University of Miami, 1981.

The author argues that the establishment of Israel in 1948 was achieved by force and was not based on legal grounds. DAI 42:1778.

2379 Adler, Frank J. "Review Essay: *Harry S. Truman.*" *American Jewish Historical Review* 62 (1973): 414–25.

Margaret Truman's description of the Palestine partition issue (1946–47) and of the role of Truman's Jewish friend Eddie Jacobson is criticized. Margaret Truman's portrayal of her father's dispassionate stance on the partition issue is not accurate; her mentioning only one White House interview with Jacobson is also inaccurate, as the records show twenty-four appointments. Notes.

2380 Bethell, Nicholas. *The Palestine Triangle: The Struggle for the Holy Land, 1935–1948.* New York: Putnam, 1979.

Bethell surveys the struggle over Palestine between the Zionists, the Arabs, and the British. Illustrations, notes, bibliography, index.

2381 Cohen, Michael J. "The Genesis of the Anglo-American Committee on Palestine, November 1945: A Case-Study in the Assertion of American Hegemony." *Historical Journal* [Great Britain] 22 (1979): 185–207.

The politics surrounding the establishment of this committee reveals the assumption of hegemony by the United States. When Ernest Bevin's government was unable to achieve an understanding with the Truman administration, the British decided to end the Palestinian mandate in 1947. Notes.

2382 Cohen, Michael J. "Truman and Palestine, 1945–1948: Revisionism, Politics and Diplomacy." *Modern Judaism* 2 (1982): 1–22.

Using some of the standard works dealing with this topic, the author examines the differing interpretations of the Truman administration's attitude toward the Palestine question.

2383 Cohen, Michael J. "Truman and the State Department: The Palestine Trusteeship Proposal, March, 1948." *Jewish Social Studies* 43 (1981): 165–87.

By February 1948 Truman had become convinced that the establishment of a Jewish state in Palestine was detrimental to U.S. interests; later he changed his mind. Notes.

2384 Dinnerstein, Leonard. "America, Britain, and Palestine: The Anglo-American Committee of Inquiry and the Displaced Persons, 1945–1946." *Diplomatic History* 4 (1980): 283–301.

When the inquiry recommended that Britain permit 100,000 displaced Jews to settle in Palestine, the British refused for fear of upsetting the Arabs. The United States did not press the issue for domestic reasons. Notes.

2385 Doenecke, Justus D. "Principle and Expediency: The State Department and Palestine, 1948." *Journal of Libertarian Studies* 2 (1978): 343–56.

Doenecke holds claims of Truman's consistent support for Israel's independence suspect; indeed, he suggests that Truman only recognized Israel to secure Jewish votes for his reelection.

2386 Dohse, Michael A. "American Periodicals and the Palestine Triangle, April 1936 to February 1947." Ph.D. dissertation, Mississippi State University, 1966.

News magazines emphasized events throughout the period and tended to be neutral regarding the Arab-British-Jewish struggle. Religious periodicals, such as *Catholic World, Christian Century,* and *Commentary*, were pro-Arab. Secular journals, such as *Nation* and *New Republic*, were strongly pro-Zionist as were the *Atlantic Monthly* and *Harper's*. DAI 27:3395.

2387 Gama, Abid Husni. "The United Nations and the Palestinian Refugees: An Analysis of the United Nations Relief and Works Agency for Palestine Refugees in the Near East, 1 May 1950–30 June 1971." Ph.D. dissertation, University of Arizona, 1972.

The early portion of this dissertation deals with the creation of the United Nations Relief for Palestine Refugees during the Truman years. DAI 33:695-A.

2388 Ganin, Zvi. "The Limits of American Jewish Political Power: America's Retreat from Partition, November 1947–March 1948." *Jewish Social Studies* 39 (1977): 1–36.

Opponents to U.S. commitment to the U.N. partition of Palestine resolution (29 November 1947) within the Truman administration included Secretary of Defense Forrestal, members of the National Security Council, and the Central Intelligence Agency. Notes.

2389 Golding, David. "United States Foreign Policy in Palestine and Israel, 1945–1949." Ph.D. dissertation, New York University, 1961.

Policy vacillated because of conflicting views. The president, Congress, the political parties, and pro-Zionist groups favored establishing a Jewish Commonwealth in Palestine, while the State and Defense Departments and religious and secular anti-Zionist groups feared such a Jewish Commonwealth would damage American national interests. DAI 27:1887.

2390 Haron, Miriam J. "Anglo-American Relations and the Question of Palestine, 1945–1947." Ph.D. dissertation, Fordham University, 1979.

While the two nations generally worked harmoniously during these years, the Palestine question generated considerable discord. This study looks at the basis for this discord. DAI 39:6897-A.

2391 Haron, Miriam J. "The British Decision to Give the Palestine Question to the United Nations." *Middle Eastern Studies* 17 (1981): 241–48.

Britain submitted the question of a Palestinian settlement to the United Nations without any recommendations, despite pressures from many sides to offer them. Notes.

2392 Haron, Miriam J. "Palestine and the Anglo-American Connection." *Modern Judaism* 2 (1982): 199–211.

Truman's Palestine policy is reviewed, with emphasis upon his concern for the survivors of the Holocaust, his desire to secure the Jewish vote, and U.S. relations with Great Britain.

2393 Hyatt, David H. "The United States and the Partition of Palestine." Ph.D. dissertation, Catholic University of America, 1973.

Unable to peacefully administer its mandate over Palestine because of rival claims between the Arabs and Zionists, Great Britain submitted the problem to the United Nations in the spring of 1947. DAI 34:5281-A.

2394 Manuel, Frank E. *The Realities of American-Palestine Relations*. Washington, DC: Public Affairs Press, 1949.

This volume covers the history of U.S. concern with Palestine, from 1832, the time of the first consular appointment of an agent to Jerusalem, to 1949. Notes, index.

2395 Mazuzan, George T. "United States Policy Toward Palestine at the United Nations, 1947–48: An Essay." *Prologue* 7 (1975): 163–76.

The State Department's support of a U.N. trusteeship, its support for partitioning Palestine, its reversal of that decision, and the final recognition of Israel are linked to Washington's perception of Soviet strategy. Notes.

2396 Parzen, Herbert. "President Truman and the Palestine Quandary: His Initial Experience, April-December, 1945." *Jewish Social Studies* 35 (1973): 42–72.

After he became president, Truman at first followed State Department recommendations regarding Palestine; however, his pro-Zionist attitudes became more manifest as he sought a humanitarian solution to the problem of Jewish refugees in Europe. Notes, appendix.

2397 Podet, Allen H. "The Anglo-American Committee of Inquiry (AACI)." Ph.D. dissertation, University of Washington, 1979.

The AACI of 1945–46 was the first international government-level attempt to solve the Palestine problem. The AACI succeeded in fulfilling the charges laid on it, provided a workable solution to the displaced persons' problem, and created a possible basis for a future relation of Palestine Jewry and Britain. DAI 41:351.

2398 Podet, Allen H. "Anti-Zionism in a Key U.S. Diplomat: Loy Henderson at the End of World War II." *American Jewish Archives* 30 (1978): 155–87.

Henderson's role as the "single diplomat most centrally involved in questions of Zionism, of Palestine, and of the world Jewish movement" is seen as essential to understanding State Department policy during the creation of Israel. Notes.

2399 Slonim, Shlomo. "The 1948 American Embargo on Arms to Palestine." *Political Science Quarterly* 94 (1979): 495–514.

Loy Henderson, chief of the Office of Near Eastern and African Affairs, raised the suggestion of an arms embargo. Truman's decision to support the embargo was an anomaly in the otherwise supportive U.S. policy toward the formation of Israel. Notes.

2400 Tschirgi, Robert D. "The Politics of Indecision: American Involvement with the Palestine Problem, 1939–1948." Ph.D. dissertation, University of Toronto, 1976.

This study describes the progressive involvement of the American government with the Palestine problem (1939–48), and assesses what, if any, responsibility may be assigned to the United States for the breakdown of internal order in Palestine during the final months of the British mandate. DAI 39: 2533-A.

2401 Welles, Sumner. *We Need Not Fail*. Boston: Houghton Mifflin, 1948.

In November 1947 the U.N. Assembly proposed the partition of Palestine over Arab objections. Welles urges the United States to grant the United Nations authority to enforce the proposal and regards the Palestine issue as crucial to the future of the United Nations. Index.

2402 Wilson, Evan M. "The American Interest in the Palestine Question and the Establishment of Israel." *Annals of the American Academy of Political and Social Science* (1972): 64–73.

This essay summarizes the issues and episodes from the end of World War II, when Truman urged the British to admit more Jews to Palestine, to his recognition of the new state of Israel on 14 May 1948.

Recognition of Israel

2403 Bickerton, Ian J. "President Truman's Recognition of Israel." *American Jewish Historical Quarterly* 58 (1968): 173–240.

In analyzing the factors which led to Truman's decision to recognize the new state of Israel on 14 May 1948, the author concludes that the critical decision was the one in November 1947 to support the United Nations' proposal for partition. Appendix, notes.

2404 Bickerton, Ian. "President Truman's Recognition of Israel: Two Views." *American Jewish Archives* 33 (1981): 141–52.

Reviewed here are Z. Gavin's *Truman, American Jewry, and Israel* (1979) and E. M. Wilson's *Decision on Palestine: How the U.S. Came to Recognize Israel* (1979); the latter concludes that Truman's action was not in the U.S. best interest.

2405 Bierbrier, Doreen. "The American Zionist Emergency Council: An Analysis of a Pressure Group." *American Jewish Historical Quarterly* 60 (1970): 82–105.

The council, which functioned from 1943 to 1946, served as the political arm of American zionism. A review of the council's activities in mobilizing and channeling Jewish public opinion suggests that it was effective in mobilizing support for Jewish aspirations in Palestine. Notes.

2406 Clifford, Clark M. "Recognizing Israel: The 1948 Story." *American Heritage* 28 (1977): 4–11.

The author, a member of Truman's staff, rejects revisionist charges that Truman's recognition of Israel was based largely on political considerations. Illustrations.

2407 Eban, Abba. "Dewey David Stone: Prototype of an American Zionist." *American Jewish History* 69 (1979): 5–14.

In March 1948 Truman's old Kansas City friend Eddie Jacobson arranged a visit of Dr. Chaim Weizmann to the White House. Stone, whom Eban regards as the prototype of an American Zionist, was the key person in this incident.

2408 Feis, Herbert. *The Birth of Israel: The Tousled Diplomatic Bed.* New York: Norton, 1969.

Although the United States and the Soviet Union were in accord, conflicts between the Arab population and the Jews, with the British, and with the United Nations complicated the attempt to provide the Jews with a homeland. Notes, index.

2409 Ganin, Zvi. *Truman, American Jewry, and Israel, 1945–1948.* New York: Holmes & Meier, 1979.

Ganin attempts to elucidate the major aspects of Truman's attitude toward zionism and his role in the creation of Israel. Notes, bibliography, index.

2410 Jacobson, Edward. "Two Presidents and a Haberdasher—1948." *American Jewish Archives* 20 (1968): 3–15.

In this letter dated 30 March 1952 to Dr. Joseph Cohn, Jacobson recalls his role in President Truman's decision to meet with Chaim Weizmann, future president of Israel, and eventually to recognize the new nation.

2411 Klieman, Aaron S. "President Truman and the Recognition of Israel in 1948." Ph.D. dissertation, Columbia University, 1964.

No abstract available.

2412 Moskovits, Shlomo. "The United States Recognition of Israel in the Context of the Cold War, 1945–1948." Ph.D. dissertation, Kent State University, 1976.

This study seeks to present a balanced picture of the anti-Zionist lobby. The American Zionist Organization, though a recognized political force, was unable to dictate or even influence substantially the U.S. diplomacy toward Palestine. DAI 37:7924-A.

2413 Postal, Bernard, and Levy, Henry W. *And the Hills Shouted for Joy: The Day Israel Was Born.* New York: McKay, 1973.

The authors focus on the crucial events surrounding Israel's independence. Chapter 29 discusses Truman's recognition of Israel. Appendixes, bibliography, index.

2414 Schoenbaum, David. "The United States and the Birth of Israel." *Wiener Library Bulletin* [Great Britain] 31 (1978): 87–100.

The author relates the various pressures brought to bear on Truman and concludes that the president's decision to recognize Israel was "neither an opportunistic nor an incompetent one." Notes.

2415 Snetsinger, John. *Truman, the Jewish Vote, and the Creation of Israel.* Stanford: Hoover Institution Press, 1974.

Truman never followed a straight course regarding Palestine; his wavering reflected in part his concern about the reaction of America's allies and friends in the Middle East. Yet domestic political concerns were important in most of his decisions, including the recognition of Israel as an independent state. Notes, bibliography, index.

2416 Stevens, Richard P. *American Zionism and U.S. Foreign Policy, 1942–1947*. New York: Pageant, 1962.

This documented monograph focuses on Zionist efforts to influence Roosevelt and Truman regarding a "Jewish National Homeland." Notes, appendix, bibliography.

2417 Wilson, Evan M. *Decision on Palestine: How the U.S. Came to Recognize Israel*. Stanford, CA: Hoover Institution Press, 1979.

Wilson served as Palestine desk officer in the State Department during most of 1942–48 when policy was developed. This useful perspective contains personal reflections, policy documents, photos, bibliography, notes, and index.

Israel

2418 Balboni, Alan R. "A Study of the Efforts of the American Zionists to Influence the Formulation and Conduct of United States Foreign Policy During the Roosevelt, Truman, and Eisenhower Administrations." Ph.D. dissertation, Brown University, 1973.

The author analyzes the strategies and tactics employed by the American Zionist lobby in their efforts to influence the formulation and conduct of U.S. foreign relations. DAI 34:6056-A.

2419 Blumberg, Harold M. *Weizmann: His Life and Times*. New York: St. Martin's Press, 1975.

Chaim Weizmann was the first president of the state of Israel. This biography of the Israeli statesman is also a history of the formation of the state of Israel. Illustrations.

2420 Burton, William L. "Protestant America and the Rebirth of Israel." *Jewish Social Studies* 26 (1964): 203–14.

Protestant church periodicals (1946–49) appeared not to be pro-Zionist; some of the articles were strongly hostile. In general, the literature suggested a sense of hopelessness and bafflement regarding the Arab-Israeli fighting. Notes.

2421 DeBivort, Lawrence H. "The Establishment of Israel and the Arab-Israeli Conflict: A Legal Analysis." Ph.D. dissertation, Johns Hopkins University, 1978.

Examined here are the three major challenges—by European powers, by the Zionist movement, and by Palestinian Arabs—made to the status of Palestine during 1918 to 1949. DAI 39:3815-A.

2422 Druks, Herbert. *The U.S. and Israel, 1945–1973: A Diplomatic History*. New York: Robert Speller, 1979.

Truman is seen as an avid supporter of the rebirth of Israel. Chapters 1 to 4 focus on Truman's relationship with Israel. Notes, bibliography, index.

2423 Feldblum, Ester Yolles. "The American Catholic Press and the Jewish State, 1917–1959." Ph.D. dissertation, Columbia University, 1973.

From 1946 to 1948, as the world watched for the possible establishment of a Jewish state, many Catholics viewed the possibility with resentment. Part of this antagonism stemmed from the postwar resentment over the preferred treatment extended Jewish displaced persons vis-à-vis Christian displaced persons. DAI 39:5083-A.

2424 Haber, Julius. *The Odyssey of an American Zionist*. New York: Twayne, 1956.

This is a fifty-year narrative of the growth of zionism in America, Europe, and Israel by a participant in the movement. Index.

2425 Huff, Earl D. "Zionist Influences Upon U.S. Foreign Policy: A Study of American Policy Toward the Middle East From the Time of the Struggle for Israel to the Sinai Conflict." Ph.D. dissertation, University of Idaho, 1971.

This study examines the influence of the American Zionist movement on American Middle East policy from 1946 to 1956. DAI 32:3400-A.

2426 Kagan, Benjamin. *The Secret Battle for Israel*. Cleveland: World, 1966.

Kagan, a reporter who was later to become a colonel in the Israeli air force, was arrested several times by the British in the immediate postwar years. Kagan discusses underground activities, the war for independence, and the development of the Israeli air force.

2427 Lapomarda, Vincent A. "Maurice Joseph Tobin and the American Jewish Community: The Preservation of the State of Israel, 1948–1953." *American Benedictine Review* 32 (1981): 387–98.

Tobin, former governor of Massachusetts and secretary of labor for Truman, supported the emerging state of Israel; in doing so he restored the alliance between American Jews and the Democratic party. Notes.

2428 Lilienthal, Alfred M. *What Price Israel?* Chicago: Regnery, 1953.

Writing as an American Jew, Lilienthal looks at the conflict between spiritual Judaism and political zionism and questions the cost of the state of Israel. Notes, index.

2429 McDonald, James G. *My Mission in Israel, 1948–1951*. New York: Simon & Schuster, 1951.

McDonald was U.S. ambassador to Israel from 1948 to 1951. In this book he recounts his experience and impressions of the first few years of Israel's nationhood. Index.

2430 Oden, David H. "Israel's Foreign Policy in the United States, 1948–1967: Security Aspects." Ph.D. dissertation, University of Pennsylvania, 1970.

Oden suggests that initially Israel formulated its policy goals cautiously in the United Nations, not wanting to make enemies and to gain major power support. Yet Israel never succeeded in cultivating a protracted strategy for peace. DAI 32:522-A.

2431 Rubenberg, Cheryl A. "United States-Israeli Relations, 1947–1974: A Study in the Convergence and Divergence of Interests." Ph.D. dissertation, University of Miami, 1979.

Four case studies are employed, the first one involving the U.N. partition resolution, U.S. recognition of the new state of Israel, and the first Arab-Israeli War (1947–48). DAI 40:2253-A.

2432 Safran, Nadav. *The United States and Israel.* Cambridge: Harvard University Press, 1963.

Considerable attention is paid to the internal characteristics of the state of Israel as well as her interaction with the United States. Chapters 4 ("The United States and the Birth of Israel") and 13 ("The First Period: Crystallization of Factors") are of particular interest. Appendixes, index.

2433 Shechtman, Joseph B. *The United States and the Jewish State Movement: The Crucial Decade, 1939–1949.* New York: Herzl, 1966.

This study assesses the major phases of U.S. policy toward zionism and Palestine. As background the Zionist movement and Soviet and British attitudes as they influenced the United States are surveyed. Notes, bibliography, index.

2434 Silverberg, Robert. *If I Forget Thee, O Jerusalem: American Jews and the State of Israel.* New York: Morrow, 1970.

U.S. policy toward the Middle East has taken careful heed of American Jewish thinking. Silverberg analyzes its impact on the formation of the state of Israel and in subsequent policy. Illustrations, bibliography, index.

2435 Urofsky, Melvin I. "A Cause in Search of Itself: American Zionism After the State." *American Jewish History* 69 (1979): 79–91.

The Zionist Organization of America after the founding of Israel has been searching for a new synthesis of American ideals and meaningful Zionist activities. Notes.

2436 Windmueller, Steven F. "American Jewish Interest Groups: Their Role in Shaping United States Foreign Policy in the Middle East. A Study of Two Time Periods, 1945–1948, 1955–1958." Ph.D. dissertation, University of Pennsylvania, 1973.

This is a study of the relationships of the Jewish community, operating as an interest aggregate, to the foreign policymaking apparatus. DAI 34:5288-A.

Arab States

2437 Burrows, Millar. *Palestine is our Business.* Philadelphia: Westminster, 1949.

Burrows argues that the creation of Israel was "a tragic and inexcusable failure to respect the basic right of the Arab people of Palestine to determine their own way of life and their own government." Since the United States played a major role in this episode, we must assume responsibility for the rehabilitation of the Palestinians.

2438 Godfriend, Nathan. "An American Development Policy for the Third World: A Case Study of the United States and the Arab East, 1942–1949." Ph.D. dissertation, University of Wisconsin, Madison, 1980.

This study examines the regional development policies and activities of private and official Americans in the Arab East, and presents case studies of American involvement in the development of Egypt, Iraq, Syria, Lebanon, Saudi Arabia, and Palestine/Israel. DAI 41:4477.

2439 Laffey, Robert M. "United States Policy Toward and Relations With Syria, 1941–1949." Ph.D. dissertation, University of Notre Dame, 1981.

The Open Door and self-determination were the components of American policy toward Syria until the end of World War II. In the postwar years the United States sought to strengthen its position in the Middle East because of American oil interests and broader Cold War issues. DAI 42:1271.

2440 Masannat, George S. "Aspects of American Foreign Policy in the Arab Middle East, 1947–1957: With Emphasis on United States-Egyptian Relations." Ph.D. dissertation, University of Oklahoma, 1964.

America's foreign policy toward Egypt has been handicapped by U.S. unequivocal support of Israel and the lack of unity and cooperation among the Western Big Three. DAI 25:4803.

2441 Stoff, Michael B. *Oil, War and American Security: The Search for a National Policy on Foreign Oil, 1941–1947.* New Haven: Yale University Press, 1980.

Oil shortages during World War II provoked the first serious effort for the United States to develop a coherent national policy for foreign oil. Stoff examines the formation of this policy during and immediately after the war. Notes, bibliography, index.

IRAN

2442 Arcilesi, Salvatore A. "Development of United States Foreign Policy in Iran, 1949–1960." Ph.D. dissertation, University of Virginia, 1965.

After the war, the United States provided firm diplomatic support to prevent Soviet control of the Iranian government during 1945 to 1947. Through various economic, military, and diplomatic means, the United States continued to assist Iran to maintain her independence and territorial integrity. DAI 26:6144.

2443 Blechman, Barry M., and Hart, Douglas M. "Afghanistan and the 1946 Iran Analogy." *Survival* [Great Britain] 22 (1980): 248–53.

The authors compare the 1980 Soviet invasion of Afghanistan with the Soviet intervention in Iran in 1946, by focusing on the Truman presidency.

2444 Hess, Gary R. "The Iranian Crisis of 1945–46 and the Cold War." *Political Science Quarterly* 89 (1974): 117–46.

American leaders and public opinion came to believe that the Iranian crisis was a test of their resolve in the face of what appeared to be Soviet expansionism. Notes.

2445 Hetrick, Kenneth L. "The United Nations as a National Foreign Policy Instrument: The Iranian Case of 1946." Ph.D. dissertation, Rutgers University, 1979.

This study suggests that the U.N. debate in the Security Council between the United States and the Soviet Union may well have undermined the prospects of the United Nations serving as agent of cooperation. DAI 40:4216-A.

2446 Kovac, John E. "Iran and the Beginning of the Cold War: A Case Study in the Dynamics of International Politics." Ph.D. dissertation, University of Utah, 1970.

This study focuses on the allied competition for Iranian natural resources during the war, and the U.S. attempt to oust the Soviet Union from northern Iran. DAI 31:2467-A.

2447 Lytle, Mark H. "American-Iranian Relations, 1941–1947, and the Redefinition of National Security." Ph.D. dissertation, Yale University, 1973.

By October 1946, the State-War-Navy Coordinating Committee determined that Iran's independence was vital to American national security, and Iran assumed an importance once reserved for Latin America. An unwritten "Monroe Doctrine" was applied to Iran. DAI 34:7159-A.

2448 Mark, Eduard M. "Allied Relations in Iran, 1941–1947: The Origins of a Cold War Crisis." *Wisconsin Magazine of History* 59 (1975): 51–63.

Soviet actions in this area are seen as responses to American initiatives. The Russians could not accept the Anglo-American control of the Iranian economy and its oil reserves. Illustration, notes.

2449 McFarland, Stephen L. "The Crisis in Iran, 1941–1947: A Society in Change and the Peripheral Origins of the Cold War." Ph.D. dissertation, University of Texas, Austin, 1981.

Domestic power struggles within Iran, and competition among the three occupying powers, led to international confrontations between the United States and the Soviet Union, played out in Iran and the United Nations. With American support the Iranian elite restored the monarchy. DAI 42:1272-A.

2450 Partin, Michael W. "United States-Iranian Relations, 1945–1947." Ph.D. dissertation, North Texas State University, 1977.

The United States supported Iran's right to make its decisions free from Soviet pressure. Ambassador George Allen was an important and effective advocate of American policy, and his advice regarding oil concessions was actively solicited and considered by Iranian leaders. DAI 38:4331-A.

2451 Pfau, Richard A. "Containment in Iran, 1946: The Shift to an Active Policy." *Diplomatic History* 1 (1977): 359–72.

After attempting to achieve containment in Iran by verbal means, the U.S. government decided to give Iran sufficient arms and credits to assure its independence and to make American influence paramount. Notes.

2452 Pfau, Richard A. "The United States and Iran, 1941–1947: Origins of Partnership." Ph.D. dissertation, University of Virginia, 1975.

American intervention in Iranian affairs began with the arrival of Ambassador George V. Allen in June 1946. He promptly established a close personal relationship with the young shah. DAI 36:6245-A.

2453 Rosenberg, J. Philip. "The Cheshire Ultimatum: Truman's Message to Stalin in the 1946 Azerbaijan Crisis." *Journal of Politics* 41 (1979): 933–40.

The claim that Truman presented Stalin with an ultimatum regarding the Azerbaijan crisis was created by Truman in 1952, nourished in his memoirs, and perpetuated by scholars. No evidence of such an ultimatum exists. Notes.

2454 Thorpe, James A. "Truman's Ultimatum to Stalin on the 1946 Azerbaijan Crisis: The Making of a Myth." *Journal of Politics* 40 (1978): 188–95.

Thorpe's contention that no ultimatum was issued is refuted by arguing that Truman did present an oral ultimatum. Notes.

SAUDI ARABIA

2455 Anderson, Irvine H. *ARAMCO, the United States and Saudi Arabia: A Study of the Dynamics of Foreign Oil Policy, 1933–1950*. Princeton, NJ: Princeton University Press, 1981.

Nearly one-half of this book focuses on the shaping of an informal coalition comprising government agencies, oil companies, and Ibn Saud which created the foundation of the special relationship between the United States and Saudi Arabia. Appendix, notes, bibliography, index.

2456 Gormly, James L. "Keeping the Door Open in Saudi Arabia: The United States and the Dhahran Airfield, 1945–46." *Diplomatic History* 4 (1980): 189–206.

After World War II, the British and Americans jostled for position and influence in Saudi Arabia. The Americans won and assumed a larger role in Saudi affairs. Notes.

2457 Miller, Aaron D. *Search for Security: Saudi Arabian Oil and American Foreign Policy, 1939–1949*. Chapel Hill: University of North Carolina Press, 1980.

Saudi Arabian oil came to shape American perceptions and policies toward the entire Middle East and charted the course for a more active and involved American policy in the Middle East. Notes, bibliography, index.

2458 Nairab, Mohammad Mahmud. "Petroleum in Saudi-American Relations: The Formative Period, 1932–1948." Ph.D. dissertation, North Texas State University, 1978.

The author reviews the Americans who went to Saudi Arabia, the effect of the oil companies on Saudi-American relations, and the American government's response to oil company actions. DAI 39: 4451-A.

2459 Walt, Joseph L. "Saudi Arabia and the Americans, 1928–1951." Ph.D. dissertation, Northwestern University, 1960.

This account concludes with a chapter on the details of the U.S. Navy's purchases of Aramco oil during and after World War II, which became the subject of a Senate investigation in 1947 and 1948. DAI 21:1548.

TURKEY

2460 Alvarez, David J. "The *Missouri*'s Visit to Turkey: An Alternative Perspective in Cold War Diplomacy." *Balkan Studies* 15 (1974): 225–36.

The author concludes that the decision to send the U.S.S. *Missouri* to traverse the Mediterranean to visit Turkey had little to do with Cold War politics. Notes.

2461 Alvarez, David J. "The United States and Turkey, 1945–1946: The Bureaucratic Determinants of Cold War Diplomacy." Ph.D. dissertation, University of Connecticut, 1975.

The author explores the bureaucratic interaction which took place during these years and which he argues ultimately had greater effect upon U.S. policy toward Turkey than did grander designs. DAI 36:6859-A.

2462 DeLuca, Anthony R. "Soviet-American Politics and the Turkish Straits." *Political Science Quarterly* 92 (1977): 503–24.

In 1946 the United States rebuffed a Soviet proposal for a major revision of the Montreux Convention governing the Straits, one which called for stationing Soviet troops in that key area. Notes.

2463 Esmer, Ahmed Su Kru. "The Straits: Crux of World Politics." *Foreign Affairs* 25 (1947): 290–302.

The Soviet demands in 1946 for partial control of the Turkish Straits are put into historical perspective.

2464 Garrett, James M., III. "Assistance to Turkey as an Instrument of United States Foreign Policy, with emphasis on Military Assistance, 1947–1955." Ph.D. dissertation, Columbia University, 1960.

Military aid of $1.3 billion over eight years resulted in Turkish forces being armed with American equipment of Korean War vintage and well trained in its use. However, the Turkish forces were still weak·in logistics and air defense. DAI 21:1990.

2465 Knight, Jonathan. "American International Guarantees for the Straits: Prelude to the Truman Doctrine." *Middle Eastern Studies* [Great Britain] 13 (1977): 241–50.

Truman proposed internationalization of the Turkish Straits in 1945, believing that free passage would expand trade opportunities. The author develops the reasons for the failure of this suggestion. Notes.

2466 Knight, Jonathan. "American Statecraft and the 1946 Black Sea Straits Controversy." *Political Science Quarterly* 90 (1975): 451–75.

During 1946, the Soviet Union and Turkey found themselves in a major controversy prompted by the Russians' desire to have some joint control of shipping entering the Black Sea. The Truman administration, while strongly supporting Turkey, was also careful to avoid any direct military confrontation with the Soviets. Notes.

2467 Overman, Edwin S. "American Aid and the Economy of Turkey." Ph.D. dissertation, Ohio State University, 1953.

More than $1 billion of American aid of various types was allocated to Turkey from 1947 to 1952. This study analyzes the impact of this aid on the Turkish economy. While basic development—roads, hydroelectric power, etc.—has contributed to Turkey's economy, that nation has developed a huge foreign debt to complete the projects begun with American aid. DAI 19:1587.

2468 Tschirgi, Necla Y. "Laying the Foundations of Contemporary Turkish Foreign Policy, 1945–1952." Ph.D. dissertation, University of Toronto, 1980.

This study traces the evolution of Turkey's foreign policy from armed neutrality to integration into a tightly knit Western alliance. DAI 41:799.

Europe

2469 Craddock, Walter R. "United States Diplomacy and the Saar Dispute, 1949–1955." *Orbis* 12 (1968): 247–67.

Although denying it, American officials frequently undercut France by secretly supporting West Germany's position on the Saar question, leading to some French mistrust of U.S. motives. Notes.

2470 Goldman, Alan R. "United States Foreign Policy Toward the Integration of Western Europe, 1947–1954." Ph.D. dissertation, Brown University, 1971.

American foreign policy toward the unity of Western Europe (1946–54) was inseparable from other major policy objectives such as economic recovery and collective security on the Continent. DAI 32:5319-A.

2471 Lundestad, Geir. *America, Scandinavia, and the Cold War, 1945–1949.* New York: Columbia University Press, 1980.

Lundestad examines several questions concerning not only America's policy toward Scandinavia but American policy in general: What was the American attitude toward left-of-center governments? Did the Marshall Plan provide an opportunity to influence Scandinavia's foreign and domestic policies? Notes, index.

2472 Magusson, Sigurdur A. "Iceland and the American Presence." *Queen's Quarterly* [Canada] 85 (1978): 79–85.

Iceland achieved independence in 1944, but U.S. military presence there was assured by the Keflavik Treaty of 1946. The American presence has created special social and economic problems which affect Icelandic cultural integrity.

2473 Matson, Robert W. "The Helsinki Axioms: U.S.-Finnish Relations and the Origins of the Cold War, 1941–1949." Ph.D. dissertation, University of Oregon, 1981.

This study examines U.S.-Finnish relations during the closing phases of the Second World War and traces the efforts of the two nations to restore normal diplomatic relations thereafter. DAI 42:3721.

2474 Rappaport, Armin. "The United States and European Integration: The First Phase." *Diplomatic History* 5 (1981): 121–50.

The United States fostered unity among the Western European nations and thus aided in the formation of the European Coal and Steel Community (1950). There were many reasons for this change of policy by the United States and nationalistic European nations; two of these were fear of a Soviet invasion and the search for a solution to the German problem. Notes.

2475 Rogers, John M. "The International Authority for the Ruhr." Ph.D. dissertation, American University, 1960.

The International Authority for the Ruhr was created by Belgium, France, Luxembourg, the Netherlands, the United Kingdom, and the United States on 28 April 1949 and existed until the formal establishment of the European Coal and Steel Community on 10 February 1953.

2476 Ruddy, T. Michael. "The Nadir of European Glory: The Impact of the Cold War on Europe, 1945–1949." In Harold T. Parker, ed. *Problems in European History*. Durham, NC: Moore, 1979, pp. 296–306.

The Cold War which arose out of the collapse of the traditional European balance of power was complicated by the new superpowers' ideological differences.

2477 Schnorf, Richard A. "The Baltic States in U.S.-Soviet Relations: From Truman to Johnson." *Lituanus* 14 (1968): 43–60.

2478 Schnorf, Richard A. "The Baltic States in U.S.-Soviet Relations: The Years of Doubt, 1943–1946." *Lituanus* 12 (1966): 58–75.

These essays combine to form an overall review of American policy toward the Baltic States from

World War II to 1962, with the latter essay covering 1946 to 1962.

2479 Serfaty, Simon. "An International Anomaly: The United States and the Communist Parties in France and Italy, 1945–1947." *Studies in Comparative Communism* 8 (1975): 123–46.

The author shows that French and Italian political leaders used American support to further their own ambitions so that both sides were using each other. Notes.

2480 Welsh, Charles J. "The Role of the American Economy in the Western Alliance, 1948–1960." Ph.D. dissertation, University of Pennsylvania, 1963.

The unchallenged postwar position of the American economy was a fundamental factor in making and implementing policy decisions, such as NATO, the Marshall Plan, and the Truman Doctrine. In 1959 serious economic issues in the American economy demanded reappraisal. DAI 24:4278.

FRANCE

See also *Indochina/Vietnam* for additional references.

2481 Benjamin, Mary M. "Fluctuations in the Prestige of the United States in France: A Description of French Attitudes toward the United States and its Policies, 1945–1955." Ph.D. dissertation, Columbia University, 1959.

This account uses two French polling systems—the Institut Français d'Opinion Publique and the Service des Bondages et Statistiques—on questions directly or indirectly relevant to Franco-American relations. DAI 20:4157.

2482 Hamburger, Robert L. "Franco-American Relations, 1940–1962: The Role of U.S. Anticolonialism and Anti-communism in the Formulation of U.S. Policy in the Algerian Question." Ph.D. dissertation, University of Notre Dame, 1970.

The United States was unable to formulate a policy that would at the same time effectively fight both a totalitarian threat and the evils of colonialism. He finds that of the two, anticommunism was a consistently more influential factor in the formulation of policy. DAI 32:519-A.

2483 Lerner, Daniel, and Aron, Raymond, eds. *France Defeats EDC*. New York: Praeger, 1957.

This series of essays is tied together with a fine introduction by Aron which stresses that the issues looked considerably different in Paris and Washington.

2484 Loveland, William A. "Deliverance from Dictatorship: American Diplomacy towards France During the 1940s." Ph.D. dissertation, Rutgers University, 1979.

Truman and State Department officials worked hard toward the reconstruction of France as a powerful nation; indeed, the department led the new president to believe he was adhering strictly to his predecessor's policy toward France, when in fact he was not. DAI 40:1030-A.

2485 Maga, Timothy P. "The United States, France, and the Refugee Problem, 1933–1947." Ph.D. dissertation, McGill University, 1981.

During the interwar years, France and the United States were the major countries of refuge and resettlement. But the overwhelming numbers of refugees tested their tradition of asylum, and both nations failed to find a successful solution to the refugee problem. DAI 42:4555.

2486 McKay, Donald C. *The United States and France*. Cambridge: Harvard University Press, 1951.

This dated account is still useful for outlining Franco-American issues for the years 1945 to 1950.

2487 Sapp, Steven P. "The United States, France and the Cold War: Jefferson Caffery and American-French Relations, 1944–1949." Ph.D. dissertation, Kent State University, 1978.

Beyond an assessment of Caffery's significance, this study examined two questions: (1) How and to what degree were American-French relations affected by the Cold War? and (2) What impact did the French relationship have on America's posture in the Cold War? DAI 39:5683-A.

2488 Sapp, Steven P. "Jefferson Caffery, Cold War Diplomat: American-French Relations, 1944–49." *Louisiana History* 23 (1982): 179–92.

Caffery was U.S. ambassador to France during 1944 to 1949, and he supported French centrist parties against the Communist left and the authoritarian right. Notes.

2489 Sullivan, Alfred B. "Franco-American Relations: Aspects of French Politics under Charles De Gaulle." Ph.D. dissertation, University of Utah, 1967.

Central to the problems of European-American cooperation is the potential of Gaullism as a philosophy of the future. This study discusses U.S. policies toward Vichy and the Committee of National Liberation and endeavors to bring to light General de Gaulle's political tactics. DAI 28:1492-A.

GERMANY

2490 Backer, John H. *The Decision to Divide Germany: American Foreign Policy in Transition*. Durham, NC: Duke University Press, 1978.

This study examines the process by which decisions were made, beginning during the war, to partition Germany. It is the author's thesis that these decisions, contrary to many Cold War accounts, were not guided by any long-term policy objectives either in Moscow or Washington. Appendix, bibliography, index.

2491 Baggaley, Philip A. "Reparations, Security, and the Industrial Disarmament of Germany: Origins of the Potsdam Decisions." 2 vols. Ph.D. dissertation, Yale University, 1980.

Baggaley finds that the most important disagreement regarding German economic issues was not one which separated Russia from the West, but rather one which divided officials within each Allied government. DAI 41:2241-A.

2492 Conover, Denise O'Neal. "James F. Byrnes, Germany, and the Cold War, 1946." Ph.D. dissertation, Washington State University, 1978.

Byrnes's two most important actions concerning Germany were his proposed four-power disarmament and economic merger of July 1946. He alienated the Russians by rejecting their demand for reparations and four-power control of the Ruhr. DAI 39:5100-A.

2493 Frey, Herbert. "The German Guilt Question After the Second World War: An Overview." Ph.D. dissertation, University of Washington, 1979.

The issue began to be debated by Germans as soon as the Allies entered Germany, for initially the Allies, particularly the Americans, vigorously accused the Germans. DAI 40:3476-A.

2494 Gardner, Lloyd C. "America and the German 'Problem', 1945–1949." In Barton J. Bernstein, ed. *Politics and Policies of the Truman Administration.* Chicago: Quadrangle, 1970, pp. 113–48.

In this early revisionist assessment of American policies and programs toward West Germany, Gardner believes that the Truman administration favored the German conservatives over the Socialists and radicals. Notes.

2495 Gareau, Frederick H. "A Critical Examination of United States Policy toward German Industrial Disarmament (1943–1955)." Ph.D. dissertation, American University, 1957.

This study examines a new technique in disarmament, that of dismantling the war-making potential of Germany. DAI 17:1799.

2496 Gimbel, John. "The American Reparations Stop in Germany: An Essay on the Political Use of History." *Historian* 37 (1975): 276–96.

Gen. Lucius D. Clay announced on 3 May 1946 that reparations deliveries from the American

zone in Germany would cease. While almost all historians have interpreted this to have been an anti-Soviet act, it actually was an effort to bring pressure to bear on the French. Notes.

2497 Gimbel, John. "Cold War: German Front." *Maryland Historian* 2 (1971): 41–55.

Gimbel reviews Lloyd Gardner's "America and the German 'Problem', 1945–1949" in Barton J. Bernstein, ed., *Politics and Policies of the Truman Administration* (1970), and Wolfgang Schlauch's "American Policy Toward Germany, 1945," *Journal of Contemporary History* 5 (1970): 113–28.

He contends their revisionist themes are larded with factual mistakes, out-of-context quotations, and blind spots. Notes.

2498 Herschler, David. "Retreat in Germany: The Decision to Withdraw Anglo-American Forces from the Soviet Occupational Zone, 1945." Ph.D. dissertation, Indiana University, 1977.

The thesis agrees with the decision to withdraw the troops and argues that Truman did not initiate the Cold War by changing America's policy toward the Soviet Union from conciliation to confrontation. DAI 2302-A.

2499 Johnk, James D. "Development of United States Policy towards a United Germany." *Towson State Journal of International Affairs* 5 (1971): 73–86.

This essay identifies U.S. policies aimed at German unification between 1947 and 1955.

2500 Kellermann, Henry J. *Cultural Relations as an Instrument of U.S. Foreign Policy: The Educational Exchange Program between the United States and Germany, 1945–1954.* Washington, DC: G.P.O., 1978.

The State Department operated the program. This account sees an increasingly positive image of Germany growing out of the exchanges. Notes, bibliography, index.

2501 Kuklick, Bruce. *American Policy and the Division of Germany: The Clash with Russia over Reparations.* Ithaca, NY: Cornell University Press, 1972.

Kuklick finds that the German issue was a major substantive problem whose resistance to resolution played a major role in the development of the Cold War. Notes, bibliography, index.

2502 Kuklick, Bruce. "The Division of Germany and American Policy on Reparations." *Western Political Quarterly* 23 (1970): 276–93.

The author concludes that the American-dominated international economic system brought about the division of Germany. Notes.

2503 Martin, Laurence W. "The American Decision to Rearm Germany." In Harold Stein, ed. *American Civil-Military Decisions*. University: University of Alabama Press, 1963, pp. 643–63.

Within three month during 1950, the United States reversed its decision regarding rearming Germany. It was the Korean attack which caused the Truman administration to reconsider. Notes.

2504 McGeehan, Robert. *The German Rearmament Question: American Diplomacy and European Defense after World War II*. Urbana: University of Illinois Press, 1971.

Secretary of State Acheson first, and unilaterally, raised the issue of German rearmament after the outbreak of the Korean War. This account traces the development of the idea to reality. Notes, bibliography, index.

2505 Pines, Jerome M. "United States Economic Policy Toward Germany, 1945–1949." Ph.D. dissertation, Columbia University, 1958.

This study examines the presurrender policy determinations, as well as U.S. occupational authorities' concern with the basic problems of governing a country whose economy had been shattered by war and by the refusal of the Soviet Union to treat Germany as an economic unit as proclaimed at Potsdam. DAI 19:66.

2506 Ratchford, B. U., and Rose, William D. *Berlin Reparations Assignments: Round One of the German Peace Settlement*. Chapel Hill: University of North Carolina, 1947.

This first-hand account of the reparations issue, September 1945–March 1946, is an essential source.

2507 Sadler, Charles. "The Americans, East Prussia, and the Oder-Neisse Line." *Mid-America* 61 (1979): 159–77.

Sadler describes the State Department's Advisory Committee on Post-War Foreign Policy activities and its influence on U.S. negotiators at Potsdam. U.S. willingness, as early as 1942, to see East Prussia transferred to Poland prepared the way for acceptance of the more radical Oder-Neisse boundary change. Notes.

2508 Schlauch, Wolfgang. "American Policy Towards Germany, 1945." *Journal of Contemporary History* 5 (1970): 113–28.

The author argues that reassessment of U.S. foreign policy came long before the announcement of the Truman Doctrine in 1947, indeed, that the shift was well established in 1945 with the U.S. Germany policy. The United States came to realize that without German recovery, the recovery of Europe was in doubt. Notes.

2509 Wagner, R. Harrison. "The Decision to Divide Germany and the Origins of the Cold War." *International Studies Quarterly* 25 (1980): 155–90.

The author believes that the division of Germany was not a consequence of the Cold War, but rather its chief cause. The inability of the United States and U.S.S.R. to agree on the future of Germany resulted from their unwillingness to accept the risks of letting go of occupied territory. Notes.

2510 Winter, Francis J. "German Reunification: A Problem for American Foreign Policy." Ph.D. dissertation, University of Iowa, 1979.

American policymakers have found it impossible to devise a strategy for reunifying Germany which keeps their basic European security policies intact. This study (1945–73) has an extended chapter dealing with the issues and negotiations from 1945 to 1959. DAI 40:6415-A.

U.S. Occupation

2511 Backer, John H. *Priming the German Economy: American Occupation Policies, 1945–1948*. Durham, NC: Duke University Press, 1971.

The author suggests that the occupation could have gone on much smoother and German recovery begun some eighteen months earlier if the requested currency reform and loans for raw materials had been granted. Bibliography, notes, index.

2512 Balabkins, Nicholas. *Germany under Direct Controls: Economic Aspects of Industrial Disarmament, 1945–1948*. New Brunswick, NJ: Rutgers University Press, 1964.

This volume examines the development and application of U.S. occupation policies to the German economy. The author is particularly critical of American efforts to hold down production and thus decrease the German standard of living. Notes, index.

2513 Bower, Tom. *The Pledge Betrayed: America and Britain and the Denazification of Postwar Germany*. New York: Doubleday, 1982.

Bower finds that not only did Nazi mass murderers remain at large and undisturbed after the war, but in many instances they returned to their desks and were once again in a position to give orders. Notes, bibliography, index.

2514 Clifton, Denzil T. "Bremen Under U.S. Military Occupation, 1945–1949: The Reform of Education." Ph.D. dissertation, University of Delaware, 1973.

Educational reform, initiated by U.S. military government officials and subsequently approved by referendum, signaled the final demise of National Socialist influence on the educational institutions of the city of Bremen. DAI 34:6559-A.

2515 Dastrup, Boyd L. "U.S. Military Occupation of Nuremberg, Germany: 1945–1949." Ph.D. dissertation, Kansas State University, 1980.

This study examines the daily operations of the military government as it struggled to rebuild a city, restructure local government and the economy, and reorient and reeducate the people. DAI 41:5219.

2516 Debevoise, Eli W. "The Occupation of Germany: United States' Objectives and Participation." *Journal of International Affairs* 8 (1954): 166–84.

This essay describes U.S. planning and coordination of occupation policy from the Berlin Declarations and the Potsdam Protocol to the formation of the Federal Republic of Germany. It concludes that a strong Western Germany and Western Europe have been and should remain U.S. policy. Notes.

2517 Dorn, Walter L. "The Debate over American Occupation Policy in Germany in 1944–45." *Political Science Quarterly* 72 (1957): 481–501.

This is a detailed account of the development of the Joint Chiefs of Staff directive (#1067) which guided initial American occupation policy in Germany. Notes.

2518 Giere, Eggert W. "A Case Study in Institutional Aspects of Foreign Policy Making: The American Policy toward Germany from 1942–1945." Ph.D. dissertation, University of Washington, 1958.

This study contains information useful as a background to U.S. occupation policy and procedure. DAI 19:857.

2519 Gimbel, John. "American Military Government and the Education of a New German Leadership." *Political Science Quarterly* 83 (1968): 248–67.

Gen. Lucius D. Clay, the American military governor in Germany, issued a 1945 policy which was designed to assist German democratic elements in recruiting and maintaining a new democratic leadership. The author concludes that German leadership after 1947 was neither an agent leadership nor a natural leadership, but rather a moderate, pragmatic establishment. Notes.

2520 Gimbel, John. *The American Occupation of Germany: Politics and the Military, 1945–1949.* Stanford, CA: Stanford University Press, 1968.

Gimbel finds that American actions and policy in Germany were governed by a broad range of interests. Besides wanting to denazify, demilitarize, decartelize, democratize, and reorient Germans and Germany, Americans were also interested in promoting their own security, guaranteeing the continuation of the free enterprise system in Germany, and containing the Soviet Union. Notes, index.

2521 Gimbel, John. "The Artificial Revolution in Germany." *Political Science Quarterly* 76 (1961): 88–104.

Gimbel questions whether an outside power can produce a democratic revolution as a response to John D. Montgomery's *Forced to be Free* (1957). Notes.

2522 Gimbel, John. "On the Implementation of the Potsdam Agreement: An Essay on U.S. Postwar German Policy." *Political Science Quarterly* 87 (1972): 242–69.

Gimbel reexamines Secretary of State Byrnes's Stuttgart speech of 6 September 1946 and concludes that it supports few of the conclusions historians have drawn from it. Notes.

2523 Gross, Franz B. "Freedom of the Press Under Military Government in Western Germany (1945–1949): The Origin and the Development of the New German Press." Ph.D. dissertation, Harvard University, 1952.

Having three nations supervising West Germany added greatly to the problems of establishing a unified policy toward the press. DAI 36:6933-A.

2524 Hammond, Paul Y. "Directives for the Occupation of Germany: The Washington Controversy." In Harold Stein, ed. *American Civil-Military Decisions.* University: University of Alabama, 1963, pp. 311–464.

The evolution of the first U.S. directives for the occupation of Germany is discussed in this early study. Notes.

2525 Herz, John H. "The Failure of De-Nazification in Germany." *Political Science Quarterly* 83 (1968): 569–94.

American denazification policy, May 1945–March 1948, is examined. Herz employs military government statistics to demonstrate its failure. Notes.

2526 Johnston, Howard W. "United States Public Affairs Activities in Germany, 1945–1955." Ph.D. dissertation, Columbia University, 1956.

The work of the U.S. government in attempting to democratize and reeducate Germans is explored in terms of the social and political forces operating the occupation. The shift away from reeducation to a program of persuasion and assistance is traced in detail. DAI 16:1274.

2527 Kelly, M. A. "The Reconstruction of the German Trade Union Movement." *Political Science Quarterly* 64 (1949): 24–46.

This contemporary essay examines the role of the Allies in reestablishing the trade union movement under the occupation. Notes.

2528 Libby, Brian A. "Policing Germany: The United States Constabulary, 1946–1952." Ph.D. dissertation, Purdue University, 1977.

This is a history of a 30,000-man force under Maj. Gen. Ernest N. Harmon charged with policing Germany during the occupation. The author concludes that while there were no major threats to stability, the constabulary ensured the peace and order which made German recovery possible. DAI 38: 4302-A.

2529 Litchfield, Edward, ed. *Governing Post-War Germany*. Ithaca, NY: Cornell University Press, 1953.

The former director of civil affairs during the occupation edited this volume of essays which reviews the effect of the occupation's efforts on West Germany's political institutions. Notes, index.

2530 Merritt, Richard L. "American Influences in the Occupation of Germany." *Annals of the American Academy of Political and Social Science* (1976): 91–103.

The author agrees that denazification was successfully carried out, but that democratization was neglected to make Germany militarily stronger.

2531 Mosely, Philip E. "Dismemberment of Germany: The Allied Negotiations from Yalta to Potsdam." *Foreign Affairs* 28 (1950): 487–98.
2532 Mosely, Philip E. "The Occupation of Germany: New Light on How the Zones Were Drawn." *Foreign Affairs* 28 (1950): 580–604.

These essays, really a single two-part article, provide an early assessment of Allied efforts to partition Germany. Notes.

2533 Nelson, Kenneth R. "United States Occupation Policy and the Establishment of a Democratic Newspaper Press in Bavaria, 1945–1949." Ph.D. dissertation, University of Virginia, 1966.

Between 1945 and 1949 the Americans exercised complete control over the licensed press. Because of these controls a strong nucleus of democratically oriented newspapers was established. DAI 27:2122.

2534 Peterson, Edward N. *The American Occupation of Germany: Retreat to Victory*. Detroit: Wayne State University Press, 1978.

This wide-ranging study critically examines general occupation policy as well as its operation at the local level. Notes, bibliography, index.

2535 Reinsch, Ruth H. "Currency Reform and Reconstruction of the West-German Economy, 1948–1949." Ph.D. dissertation, University of Kentucky, 1950.

This broad transformation of the financial and commercial life of tens of millions of persons established legal and functioning markets. The criticisms of the reforms are dealt with. DAI 20:3545.

2536 Schechter, Edmund. "USIS During the Occupation of Germany." *Foreign Service Journal* 53 (1976): 17–20, 26–27.

The U.S. military government's policy toward the German media, 1945–48, is reviewed.

2537 Schlauch, Wolfgang. "Representative William Colmer and Senator James O. Eastland and the Reconstruction of Germany, 1945." *Journal of Mississippi History* 34 (1972): 193–213.

Colmer, chairman of the House Special Committee on Postwar Economic Policy and Planning, and Eastland, who was partly concerned with increasing U.S. cotton exports to Germany, played significant roles in moderating the original harsh policy planned for Germany. Notes.

2538 Schmitt, Hans A., ed. *U.S. Occupation in Europe after World War II:* Papers and Reminiscences from April 23–24, 1976, Conference held at the George C. Marshall Research Foundation, Lexington, Virginia. Lawrence: Regents Press of Kansas, 1978.

Published here are essays on U.S. occupation policies toward Germany and Austria, and Soviet occupation policies toward Germany. These essays contain considerable material on General Clay and Secretary of State James Byrnes. Maps, notes, index.

2539 Slind, Marvin G. "Democratization in Occupied Germany: Pursuit of an American Ideal." Ph.D. dissertation, Washington State University, 1978.

American occupation policies regarding political activities in postwar Germany developed slowly. This study examines the conflicting bureaucratic objectives and General Clay's role in putting directives into operation. DAI 39:1049-A.

2540 Taylor, Graham D. "The Rise and Fall of Anti-Trust in Occupied Germany, 1945–48." *Prologue* 11 (1979): 23–39.

American officials who undertook to decentralize the German economy were motivated more by business than ideological concerns. It was the belief in free competition versus the cartel which was most influential. Notes.

2541 Votzenhart-Viehe, Verena. "The German Reaction to the American Occupation, 1944–1947." Ph.D. dissertation, University of California, Santa Barbara, 1980.

This study finds the German reaction to the occuption both critical and complimentary. Although they liked the stability and economic help in reconstruction, they accused the Americans of ignorance, materialism, and an emphasis on moral rehabilitation. DAI 41:4476-A.

2542 Ziemke, Earl F. *The U.S. Army in the Occupation of Germany, 1944–1946*. Washington, DC: Center of Military History, 1975.

This official history focuses on the army's role in Germany during the early months after the war. Notes, bibliography, maps, index.

2543 Zink, Harold. *The United States in Germany, 1944–55.* Englewood Cliffs, NJ: Van Nostrand, 1957.

The first chief historian of the U.S. High Commission in Germany has prepared a comprehensive account of U.S. occupation policy on a wide range of topics.

War Crimes Trials

John R. Lewis's bibliography (#3026) provides a wide range of sources for those who wish to delve much deeper into this topic.

2544 Biddle, Francis. *In Brief Authority.* Garden City, NY: Doubleday, 1962.

Biddle was the American member of the International Military Tribunal to try the major German war criminals. During the 1950s he was national chairman of Americans for Democratic Action (ADA). Part 4 in this volume discusses his role in the Nuremberg trials. Photographs, index.

2545 Borkin, Joseph. *The Crime and Punishment of I. G. Farben.* New York: Macmillan, 1978.

I. G. Farben, like Krupp, was instrumental in providing the Nazi regime with its warmaking capabilities. The rise of I. G. Farben, its trial at Nuremberg, and its continued influence through successor companies are traced. Notes, photographs, index.

2546 Bosch, William J. *Judgment on Nuremberg: American Attitudes toward the Major German War-Crime Trials.* Chapel Hill: University of North Carolina Press, 1970.

Most individuals surveyed agreed that preexisting assumptions rather than the evidence presented at the trial governed their views. Notes, bibliography, index.

2547 Fisch, Arnold G., Jr. "Field Marshal Wilhelm List and the 'Hostages Case' at Nuremberg: An Historical Reassessment." Ph.D. dissertation, Pennsylvania State University, 1975.

The author suggests that all the evidence was not introduced during the trial and that there is considerable mitigating and exculpatory material relating to List. DAI 36:2360-A.

2548 Mendelsohn, John. "Trial by Document: The Problem of Due Process for War Criminals at Nuremberg." *Prologue* 7 (1975): 227–34.

The Nuremberg trials pioneered the massive use of documents as evidence against large numbers of individuals, many of whom were charged with directing but not executing orders. Illustrations, notes.

2549 Mendelsohn, John. "Trial by Document: The Use of Seized Records in the United States Proceedings at Nuremberg." Ph.D. dissertation, University of Maryland, 1974.

This account reviews the manner in which documents were collected for use during the Nuremberg tribunal. DAI 35:6068-A.

2550 Silverglate, Jesse J. "The Role of the Conspiracy Doctrine in the Nuremberg War Crimes Trials." Ph.D. dissertation, University of Wisconsin, 1969.

The United States pressed the application of the conspiracy doctrine to show posterity that Nazi barbarism and aggression was collective and widespread. Historical and legal criticisms of the trials also are analyzed. DAI 31:1969-A.

2551 Smith, Bradley F. *The American Road to Nuremberg: The Documentary Record, 1944–1945.* Stanford: Hoover Institution Press, 1982.

The fifty-nine documents printed here relate to the intent of those who founded the post-World War II international tribunals and are offered in belief that a reexamination of Nuremberg is needed. Bibliography, index.

2552 Smith, Bradley F. *Reaching Judgment at Nuremberg.* New York: Basic Books, 1976.

Despite the expectations of government leaders, the decisions rendered at Nuremberg were the result of eight men's principles, legal views, and compromises. Notes, bibliographical essay, index.

2553 Smith, Bradley F. *The Road to Nuremberg.* New York: Basic Books, 1981.

The Nuremberg trial system was created almost exclusively in Washington. The system was developed, altered, and redrafted during the last ten months of the European war and presented to the Allies for review at a four-power conference held in London during June–July 1945. Bibliography, notes, index.

2554 Weingartner, James J. *Crossroads of Death: The Story of the Malmedy Massacre and Trial.* Berkeley: University of California Press, 1979.

Over seventy American prisoners of war were killed by German troops during World War II outside the little Belgian town of Malmedy. The massacre took on great significance and its trial became a postwar issue which helped catapult Joseph McCarthy to national prominence. Notes, bibliography, index.

2555 Weir, Patricia Ann Lyons. "The German War-Crimes Trials, 1949 to Present: Repercussions of American Involvement." Ph.D. dissertation, Ball State University, 1973.

This account examines the role of the United States in war-crimes prosecution, relating the role to that of the other occupation powers, and then discovering the specific ways that the United States influenced Germany's conduct of its own trials. DAI 34: 5086-A.

Berlin Crisis

2556 Davison, W. Phillips. *The Berlin Blockade: A Study in Cold War Politics.* Princeton, NJ: Princeton University Press, 1958.

Soviet preparations are compared with American indecisiveness during the early days of the crisis. Davison claims that in the end, the Soviets lost because the crisis drew Germans and Americans closer together. Notes, bibliography, index.

2557 Glines, C. V. "Before the Colors Fade: Berlin Airlift Commander." *American Heritage* 20 (1969): 44–45, 93–96.

Gen. William H. Tunner (USAF) recalls the air force's efforts to mobilize transport aircraft and crews to ferry supplies to Berlin. Illustrated.

2558 Gottlieb, Manuel F. *The German Peace Settlement and the Berlin Crisis.* New York: Paine-Whitman, 1960.

The author looks at the cause of the Berlin crisis and finds much of it in the controversy over currency reform. Notes, index.

2559 Harrell, Edward J. "Berlin: Rebirth, Reconstruction and Division, 1945–1948: A Study of Allied Cooperation and Conflict." Ph.D. dissertation, Florida State University, 1965.

Allied cooperation helped to lay the early foundations for the initial recovery of Berlin, but this cooperation ended and interrupted the progress of recovery in East Berlin while it accelerated the coming of prosperity to West Berlin. DAI 26:4605.

2560 Harrington, Daniel F. "American Policy in the Berlin Crisis of 1948–49." Ph.D. dissertation, Indiana University, 1979.

Truman believed that the airlift would fail but refused to decide on an alternative policy until it was necessary; lucky coincidences—a mild winter, improvements in air traffic control, and the airlift commander's passion for efficiency—combined to provide Truman with an escape from making a hard choice on Berlin. DAI 40:5558-A.

2561 Jessup, Philip C. "Park Avenue Diplomacy: Ending the Berlin Blockade." *Political Science Quarterly* 87 (1972): 377–400.

Jessup, U.S. ambassador to the United Nations, met with Soviet Ambassador Malik at the beginning of the blockade to discuss the establishment of a West German government. Finally, they agreed to the lifting of the blockade, 4 May 1949. Notes.

2562 Loftus, Robert A. "The American Response to the Berlin Blockade: Bureaucratic Politics, Partisan Politics, and Foreign Policy Improvisation." 2 vols. Ph.D. dissertation, Columbia University, 1979.

By default, the airlift became the administration's primary response to the blockade, and this dependence upon the airlift constituted a considerable risk. DAI 40:5582-A.

2563 Lodge, Juliet, and Shlaim, Avi. "The U.S. and the Berlin Blockade." *Jerusalem Journal of International Relations* [Israel] 3 (1978): 51–80.

The authors are interested in perceptions and images which governed American crisis managers in their decisions during the 1948 episode.

2564 Miscamble, Wilson D. "Harry S. Truman, The Berlin Blockade and the 1948 Election." *Presidential Studies Quarterly* 10 (1980): 306–16.

The author examines Truman's actions during the Berlin blockade and fails to find any instances of attempting to manipulate the crisis for domestic political advantage. Notes.

2565 Misse, Fred B. "Truman, Berlin and the 1948 Election." *Missouri Historical Review* 76 (1982): 164–73.

Foreign affairs actually played a larger role in the 1948 election than historians have generally realized. The Marshall Plan and the Berlin airlift, for example, prompted conservative German-Americans to switch their votes to Truman. Notes.

2566 Moll, Kenneth L. "The Berlin Airlift: How Airpower Came of Age in the Cold War." *Air Force and Space Digest* 51 (1968): 68–79.

Moll presents an in-depth study of "Operation Vittles;" the airlift (1948–49) which kept West Berlin supplied with food and coal.

2567 Nelson, Daniel J. *Wartime Origins of the Berlin Dilemma.* University: University of Alabama Press, 1978.

By reconstructing the negotiations among the Four Powers that created the divided city, Nelson sheds some light on the postwar dilemma of the city of Berlin. Notes, bibliography, index.

2568 Paeffgen, Hans-Ludwig. "The Berlin Blockade and Airlift: A Study of American Diplomacy." Ph.D. dissertation, University of Michigan, 1979.

The Soviet Union sought to use the Berlin blockade as a means of gaining a voice in the administration of all of Germany; however, with the success of the airlift, the blockade soon became an embarrassment. DAI 40:5561-A.

2569 Pauw, Alan D. "The Historical Background Relating to Access Rights to Berlin." Ph.D. dissertation, University of Southern California, 1960.

In arranging the zonal occupation of Germany, access rights to Berlin were not considered because a unified Germany was assumed. After the war, access rights became a paramount issue, with the Soviets claiming that the Western powers had lost their right of access because of violations of the Yalta and Potsdam agreements. DAI 26:341.

2570 Raphael, Theodore D. "The Cognitive Complexity of Foreign Policy Elites and Conflict Behavior: Forecasting International Crisis—The Berlin Conflict, 1946–1962." Ph.D. dissertation, American University, 1980.

Two hypotheses are tested in this study which focuses on the conflict-prone relationship between the United States and the Soviet Union in Berlin from 1946 to 1962. DAI 41:5237.

2571 Reuss, Martin. "In Memoriam: The First Berlin Crisis." *Military Review* 59 (1979): 30–38.

This review of the Berlin blockade of 1948 examines the collapse of the wartime East-West alliance and the onset of the Cold War in Germany. The famous Berlin airlift, in which the U.S. Air Force transported food and fuel into West Berlin, actually lifted the standard of living there. Illustrations, notes.

2572 Smith, Jean E. *The Defense of Berlin.* Baltimore: Johns Hopkins University, 1963.

This study examines the struggle over Berlin (1945–62). It does provide a solid treatment of the 1948–49 crisis. Notes, bibliography, index.

2573 Viault, Birdsall S. "America, Germany, and the Cold War, 1945–1949." *Proceedings of the South Carolina Historical Association* (1971): 44–57.

The author believes that neither side achieved victory in the Berlin blockade and that the establishment of West Germany did not resolve the right of access issue. Notes.

GREAT BRITAIN

2574 Anderson, Terry H. *The United States, Great Britain, and the Cold War, 1944–1947.* Columbia: University of Missouri Press, 1981.

This book is concerned with British efforts to influence the Roosevelt and Truman administrations. Especially, Britain sought to keep America involved with European affairs and, in the case of Greece, was influential. Notes, bibliographical essay, index.

2575 Bartlett, Christopher J. *The Long Retreat: A Short History of British Defence Policy, 1945–70.* London: Macmillan, 1972.

The first two chapters deal with British efforts to develop a defense program compatible with their resources and commitments. Covered briefly here are relations with the United States during the founding of NATO and the conduct of the Korean War. Notes, index.

2576 Beloff, Max. *New Dimensions in Foreign Policy: A Study in British Administrative Experience, 1947–59.* New York: Macmillan, 1961.

British actions paralleled (and supported) economic undertakings in Europe, such as the Marshall Plan (Chapter 2) and the North Atlantic Treaty Organization (Chapter 3). Notes, index.

2577 Boyle, Peter G. "The British Foreign Office and American Foreign Policy, 1947–48." *Journal of American Studies* [Great Britain] 16 (1982): 373–89.

Great Britain's grave economic crisis of 1946–47 prompted the British to announce their withdrawal from Greece, which in turn led to Truman's intervention with aid and advisers. Notes.

2578 Boyle, Peter G. "The British Foreign Office View of Soviet-American Relations, 1945–1946." *Diplomatic History* 3 (1979): 307–20.

British officials, aware that world leadership had passed to the United States, saw a naive and inexperienced America, reluctant to accept British advice and experience, following a dangerously benevolent policy toward an aggressive and expansionist U.S.S.R., and changing course only when forced to do so.

2579 Clark, William. *Less Than Kin: A Study of Anglo-American Relations.* Boston: Houghton Mifflin, 1957.

Clark analyzes the history of Anglo-American relations to gain a better understanding of the contemporary problems besetting the Atlantic Alliance.

2580 Collier, Basil. *The Lion and the Eagle: British and Anglo-American Strategy, 1900–1950.* New York: Putnam, 1972.

This era has witnessed the replacement of Great Britain by the United States as the leading Anglo-Saxon power. Collier offers a general history of the strategic background of Anglo-American relations. Notes, bibliography, index.

2581 Duncan, Francis. "Atomic Energy and Anglo-American Relations, 1946–1954." *Orbis* 12 (1969): 1188–1207.

This period, until the passage of the Atomic Energy Act (1954), saw several difficulties in the relationship. The revised U.S. legislation greatly improved mutual understanding. Notes.

2582 Epstein, Leon. *Britain: Uneasy Ally.* Chicago: University of Chicago Press, 1954.

This comprehensive account reviews British responses to U.S. policies (1945–52). The British were most uneasy as to whether the United States would help defend Europe against Soviet aggression. Notes, bibliography, index.

2583 Epstein, Leon S. "The British Labour Left and United States Foreign Policy." *American Political Science Review* 45 (1951): 974–95.

The author focuses on 1945 to 1950 and finds that 1945 and 1946 and the Korean War period were times of distrust. Notes.

2584 Hathaway, Robert M. *Ambiguous Partnership: Britain and America, 1944–1947*. New York: Columbia University Press, 1981.

While the larger half of this volume deals with pre-1945 issues, it does provide an extremely useful backdrop to post-1945 matters which dominated Anglo-American relations. Notes, extensive bibliography, index.

2585 Knight, Wayne S. "The Nonfraternal Association: Anglo-American Relations and the Breakdown of the Grand Alliance, 1945–1947." Ph.D. dissertation, American University, 1979.

The Anglo-American relationship was shaped by the manner in which both nations responded to the Soviet threat and to the related problem of European economic recovery. Also, both governments responded to their domestic pressures. DAI 40:2840-A.

2586 Mallalieu, William. *British Reconstruction and American Policy, 1945–1955*. New York: Scarecrow, 1956.

This study, which began as an examination of the Marshall Plan, evolved into a review of British-American financial and commercial policies. Index.

2587 Nicholas, Herbert G. *Britain and the U.S.A.* Baltimore: Johns Hopkins Press, 1963.

He sees the period of 1947 to 1950 to have been one of vitality and creativity in U.S.-British relations, but it disappeared soon thereafter.

2588 Northedge, Frederick S. *British Foreign Policy: The Process of Readjustment, 1945–1961*. London: Allen & Unwin, 1962.

This volume provides a useful, informed introduction to the basic foreign policy issues confronting the Truman administration. The focus is, naturally, on the European scene. Notes, bibliography, index.

2589 Zupnick, Elliot. "Britain's Post-War Dollar Problem, 1946–1951: A Study in International Disequilibrium." Ph.D. dissertation, Columbia University, 1954.

Factors responsible for Britain's postwar dollar shortage are examined. DAI 14:1578.

American Loan

2590 Dalton, Hugh. *High Tide and After: Memoirs, 1945–1960*. London: Frederick Muller, 1962.

Dalton was Chancellor of the Exchequer in the Attlee government (1946–47) and consequently these memoirs focus on the American loan to Britain (1946–47) and the Marshall Plan. Index.

2591 Hedlund, Richard P. "Congress and the British Loan, 1945–1946: A Congressional Study." Ph.D. dissertation, University of Kentucky, 1976.

The British loan was the most hotly debated issue in American foreign policy between lend-lease in 1941 and the Marshall Plan in 1948. This was the first large peacetime government-to-government loan in U.S. history, and Congress reluctantly approved it. DAI 38:947-A.

2592 Herring, George C. "The United States and British Bankruptcy, 1944–1945." *Political Science Quarterly* 86 (1971): 260–80.

Roosevelt and Truman failed to see Britain's need for late-war and early postwar aid. Americans expected Britain to be a postwar commercial rival. Notes.

GREECE

2593 Amen, Michael M. "American Institutional Penetration into Greek Military and Political Policymaking Structures: June 1947–October 1949." *Journal of the Hellenic Diaspora* 5 (1978): 89–113.

This essay reviews U.S. military involvement prior to 1947 and seeks to interpret American military-related decisions during 1947 to 1949.

2594 Barnet, Richard J. *Intervention and Revolution: The United States in the Third World*. Cleveland: World, 1968.

Chapter 6, "The Truman Doctrine and the Greek Civil War," criticizes the policies and activities of the Truman administration. Notes, index.

2595 Eudes, Dominique. *The Kapetanios: Partisans and Civil War in Greece, 1943–1949*. New York: Monthly Review Press, 1972.

Eudes offers a detailed narrative history of the Greek civil war, focusing upon the two strategies which have dominated the workers' movement. Illustrations, bibliography, index.

2596 Hand, Samuel B., ed. "William E. Brown, Dean of UVM's Medical College, 1945–52: An Oral History." *Vermont History* 41 (1973): 158–72.

In 1944–45 he served as a public health administrator in Greece. Brown obtained scarce equipment and supplies in spite of conflicting British and American policies and civil war in Athens.

2597 Howard, Harry N. "United States Policy Toward Greece in the United Nations, 1946–1950." *Balkan Studies* [Greece] 8 (1967): 263–96.

Howard reviews U.S. policy toward Greek issues in the United Nations during the time when Truman Doctrine assistance was being supplied. Notes.

2598 Iatrides, John O., ed. *Ambassador MacVeagh Reports: Greece, 1933–1947*. Princeton: Princeton University Press, 1980.

MacVeagh was not a major figure in the Truman administration, but his papers are extremely valuable for those students seeking to understand the development of American policy toward the Balkans and the Eastern Mediterranean during the early stages of the Cold War. List of principal names, notes, index.

2599 Iatrides, John O. "From Liberation to Civil War: The United States and Greece, 1944–1946." *Southeastern Europe* 3 (1976): 32–43.

Initially the American position in Greece was one of noninvolvement—either in Greek politics or Britain's actions—but by the end of 1946, the United States began taking a more active position in Greece due to the growing conflict with the Soviet Union. Notes.

2600 Kondis, Basil. "Aspects of Greek-American Relations On the Eve of the Truman Doctrine." *Balkan Studies* [Greece] 19 (1978): 327–43.

Greece's problems were due to the slow recovery of its economy after World War II which resulted from political instability and strife. Notes.

2601 Pederson, James H. "Focal Point of Conflict: The United States and Greece, 1943–1947." Ph.D. dissertation, University of Michigan, 1974.

U.S. wartime policies aimed at the creation of a liberal-democratic-capitalist international climate. In Greece the wartime objectives clashed with the new postwar anticommunism and ultimately (and ironically) succumbed. DAI 35:2912-A.

2602 Roubatis, Yiannis P. "The United States Involvement in the Army and Politics of Greece, 1946–1967." Ph.D. dissertation, Johns Hopkins University, 1981.

U.S. postwar goals in Greece were guided by one prime consideration: that internal stability be established, which would assist American national interests in the Eastern Mediterranean and Middle East. As a result, the Greek military evolved into the ultimate arbiter in the postwar Greek political system. DAI 42:844.

2603 Wittner, Lawrence S. *American Intervention in Greece, 1945–1949*. New York: Columbia University Press, 1982.

This study of American policy toward Greece is an attempt to explain the origins and development of the Cold War, especially since the Greek situation prompted the Truman Doctrine and became the prototype for subsequent U.S. intervention. Notes, bibliography, index.

2604 Xydis, Stephen G. *Greece and the Great Powers, 1944–1947: Prelude to the "Truman Doctrine."* Thessalonica: Institute for Balkan Studies, 1963.

Between 1944 and 1947, Greece served as a testing ground for international politics, first as part of the British theater of operations, then as an object of both the British and Soviet spheres of influence, and finally as part of the U.S. system of Great Power concert. Illustrations, notes, bibliography, index.

U.S. Aid

2605 Davis, Margaret M. "The Role of the American Trade Union Representative in the Aid to Greece Program, 1947–1948." Ph.D. dissertation, University of Washington, 1960.

This study presents an eyewitness account of the work of the two trade unionists who were the labor advisers of the American Mission for Aid to Greece, 1947–48. DAI 21:3839.

2606 Kornaros, Christopher N. "Cooperative Administration Between Greece and the United States, 1947–1959." Ph.D. dissertation, New York University, 1966.

The United States not only granted aid to Greece, but through the United States Mission to Greece administered the major aspects of Greek affairs. In many instances, Greece was a passive partner. DAI 27:1084.

2607 McNeill, William H. *Greece: American Aid in Action, 1947–1956*. New York: Twentieth Century Fund, 1957.

The author argues that both Greek and American efforts improved the Greek economy.

2608 Munkman, C. A. *American Aid to Greece: A Report on the First Ten Years*. New York: Praeger, 1958.

A former member of the American Economic Mission to Greece has prepared an extremely critical account of the manner in which U.S. aid was used in Greece.

ITALY

2609 Black, Gregory D. "The United States and Italy, 1943–1946: The Drift Toward Containment." Ph.D. dissertation, University of Kansas, 1973.

Chapter 5 discusses the growing fear of American diplomats in Italy that communism was a definite threat to Italy and describes Truman's reaction to the threat. DAI 34:7670-A.

2610 Caldwell, William S. "Political Science, International Law and Relations: The Organization and Operations of American Information and Propaganda Activities in Early Postwar Italy." Ph.D. dissertation, University of Minnesota, 1960.

The United States sought to influence Italian voters to vote against the leftist bloc, the Popular Front, in Italy's 1948 election. This effort was carried on by official and unofficial American agencies and consisted both of propaganda by deed and propaganda by word. DAI 22:2056.

2611 Edelman, Eric S. "Incremental Involvement: Italy and United States Foreign Policy, 1943–48." Ph.D. dissertation, Yale University, 1981.

Edelman maintains that the United States had no master plan or grand strategy for containing the left in Italy in 1943. As relations with the Soviets deteriorated, U.S. goals in Italy focused upon establishing a centrist government favorable to U.S. interests in the Mediterranean. DAI 44:2261-A.

2612 Harper, John L. "The United States and the Italian Economy, 1945–1948." Ph.D. dissertation, Johns Hopkins University, 1981.

Several ideological currents competed to formulate American policy toward Italian recovery: Hull's plan for a free market economy, a New Deal inspired plan of a "middle way" based upon controls and social reform, and military preoccupation with security. DAI 42:816.

2613 Kogan, Norman. *Italy and the Allies*. Cambridge: Harvard University Press, 1956.

The author focuses on Italian internal politics; however, the basic issues between Italy and the United States (1944–54) are outlined.

2614 Miller, James E. "Taking Off the Gloves: The United States and the Italian Elections of 1948." *Diplomatic History* 7 (1983): 35–56.

The decisions taken by American officials to intervene in the Italian elections of 1948 are examined here. Notes.

2615 Moyer, James E. "An Analysis of United States Economic Aid to Italy From 1943 to 1949." Ph.D. dissertation, University of Illinois, 1951.

During 1943 to 1949, the United States gave assistance to Italy in forms of grants and loans approximating $2,407.1 million. This aid (prior to Marshall Plan aid) went basically to restore the agricultural and industrial activities of a badly devastated nation. DAI 13:578.

2616 Novak, Bogdan C. "American Policy Toward the Slovenes in Trieste, 1941–1974." *Papers of Slovene Studies* (1977): 1–25.

The Slovenes gained limited recognition of basic national rights during the first two years after World War II from the Allied Military Government headed by Colonel Bowman. The American government favored Italian claims until 1954. Maps, notes.

2617 Platt, Alan A., and Leonardi, Robert. "American Foreign Policy and the Postwar Italian Left." *Political Science Quarterly* 93 (1978): 197–215.

This survey focuss on three critical periods in Italy's postwar history, the first being 1945–48 during Italy's social and economic reconstruction. Notes.

2618 Rossi, Ernest E. "The United States and the 1948 Italian Election." Ph.D. dissertation, University of Pittsburgh, 1964.

American intervention was significant to the outcome of the 1948 election. Specific maneuvers included the proposal to return the Free Territory of Trieste to Italy, Ambassador James C. Dunn's speeches, Myron C. Taylor's trip to Italy, the activity of American propaganda agencies, threats to cut immigration, and threats to stop aid to Italy if the Popular Front won. DAI 26:467.

2619 Smith, Emory T. "The United States, Italy and NATO: American Policy Toward Italy, 1948–1952." Ph.D. dissertation, Kent State University, 1981.

With the development of the Cold War, the United States came to view the security of Italy and its independence from Communist domination as essential to the security of the United States. This study examines the impact of NATO and the Mutual Defense Assistance Program on Italy. DAI 42:3726.

2620 Velde, Robert W. van de. "The Role of U.S. Propaganda in Italy's Return to Political Democracy, 1943–1948." Ph.D. dissertation, Princeton University, 1954.

American "influence" is described within the framework of the evolution in Italy's politicosocioeconomic life. DAI 14:1790.

2621 Woolf, S. J., ed. *The Rebirth of Italy, 1943–1950*. New York: Humanities Press, 1972.

Foreign policy issues confronting Italy and the United States are among the many issues examined in this useful volume.

SPAIN

2622 Dorley, Albert J., Jr. "The Role of Congress in the Establishment of Bases in Spain." Ph.D. dissertation, St. John's University, 1969.

The United States approved of the U.N. refusal to admit Spain as a member in 1945 because of its Fascist nature. However, by 1948 Spain was becoming the beneficiary of the Cold War. In 1951 Truman reluctantly authorized the negotiations which led to the Pact of Madrid (1953). DAI 30:3394-A.

2623 Dura, Juan. "United States Policy Toward Dictatorship and Democracy in Spain, 1936–1953: A Case Study in the Realities of Policy Formation." Ph.D. dissertation, University of California, Berkeley, 1979.

Abstract not available.

2624 Gilmore, Riley W. "The American Foreign Policy-Making Process and the Development of a Post-World War II Spanish Policy, 1945–1953: A Case Study." Ph.D. dissertation, University of Pittsburgh, 1967.

The shift in the international environment from 1945 to 1953 was responsible for changing U.S. policy toward Franco Spain from ostracism to accommodation. As the Cold War intensified, anti-Franco groups even became the object of government harassment. DAI 28:4676-A.

2625 Koenig, Louis W. "Foreign Aid to Spain and Yugoslavia: Harry Truman Does His Duty." In Alan F. Westin, ed. *The Uses of Power*. New York: Harcourt, Brace and World, 1962, pp. 73–116.

While Truman took the initiative in providing aid to Yugoslavia, he was forced by congressional pressure into aiding Spain. Koenig uses these two incidents to probe Truman's view of the presidency. Bibliography.

2626 Lowi, Theodore J. "Bases in Spain." In Harold Stein, ed. *American Civil-Military Decisions*. University: University of Alabama Press, 1963, pp. 666–702.

Although both Truman and Acheson disliked Franco Spain, by 1950 they came to support the decision to negotiate for Spanish bases. Again the Korean conflict had an impact upon U.S. foreign policy. Notes.

2627 Weeks, Stanley B. "United States Defense Policy Toward Spain, 1950–1976." Ph.D. dissertation, American University, 1977.

The most fundamental shifts in U.S. policy toward Spain were the 1950 abandonment of a policy of ostracism of the Franco regime and the 1951 decision to establish U.S. military bases in Spain. The 1951 decision set the pattern for U.S. policy toward Spain until 1976. DAI 38:3716-A.

YUGOSLAVIA

2628 Chase, Harry M. "American-Yugoslavian Relations, 1945–1956: A Study in the Motivation of U.S. Foreign Policy." Ph.D. dissertation, Syracuse University, 1957.

U.S. policy toward Yugoslavia consisted of giving military and economic assistance to that nation. The basis of presidential policy was the maintenance of Yugoslav independence because of its strategic location, and Congress tended to follow executive leadership during the Truman years. DAI 18:279.

2629 Kousoulas, D. George. "The Truman Doctrine and the Stalin-Tito Rift: A Reappraisal." *South Atlantic Quarterly* 72 (1973): 427–39.

Stalin was concerned about Tito's support of the Greek Communist operations in 1946, especially about the prospect of U.S. intervention in Greece. Notes.

2630 Larson, David L. *United States Foreign Policy Toward Yugoslavia, 1943–1963*. Washington, DC: University Press of America, 1979.

Larson divides U.S. policy toward Yugoslavia into three periods: prior to 1949 when there was virtually no policy; 1949–51 when the United States supported the political, economic, and ideological independence of Yugoslavia; 1951–63 when the United States failed to continue its policy of *realpolitik*. Notes, bibliography.

2631 Lees, Lorraine M. "The American Decision to Assist Tito, 1948–1949." *Diplomatic History* 2 (1978): 407–33.

After Tito was expelled by the Cominform in June 1948, the State Department gradually relaxed its export restrictions and by September 1949 authorized the sale of a steel mill. Notes.

2632 Lees, Lorraine M. "American Foreign Policy Toward Yugoslavia, 1941–1949." Ph.D. dissertation, Pennsylvania State University, 1976.

American-Yugoslav relations reached their lowest point throughout 1946 and 1947. Tito, who considered himself Russia's Balkan partner, attacked American aircraft flying over Yugoslavia and continually harassed the American embassy. After Tito and Stalin split in 1948, U.S.-Yugoslavian relations improved with the signing in 1949 of a long-term economic agreement. DAI 37:4565-A.

2633 Markovich, Stephen C. "The Influence of American Foreign Aid on Yugoslav Policies, 1948–1966." Ph.D. dissertation, University of Virginia, 1968.

During the early years of the aid program, there were no differences between the United States and Yugoslavia on the major reason for granting aid, namely, to maintain Yugoslavia's independence. DAI 29:3653-A.

2634 Stefan, Charles G. "The Emergence of the Soviet-Yugoslav Break: A Personal View from the Belgrade Embassy." *Diplomatic History* 6 (1982): 387–404.

On the eve of Marshal Tito's death an American Foreign Service officer recalls the events of 1947 and 1948. The difficulty in learning about developments is reviewed. Notes.

Eastern and Central Europe

2635 Clemens, Walter C., Jr. "American Policy and the Origins of the Cold War in Central Europe, 1945–1947." In Peter J. Potichnyj and Jane P. Shapiro, eds. *From Cold War to Détente.* New York: Praeger, 1976, pp. 3–25.

Western proposals "offered far more to the mutual advantage of all parties than those of the USSR. The tragedy was that Moscow did not respond positively to the Byrnes overtures in 1946, and that the Western governments did not explore more deeply the potential for compromise in Molotov's counterproposal of April 1947." Notes.

2636 Davis, Lynn Etheridge. *The Cold War Begins: Soviet-American Conflict over Eastern Europe.* Princeton, NJ: Princeton University Press, 1974.

The second half of this volume deals with the Truman administration's efforts in 1945 to deal with Eastern European issues. Notes, appendix, bibliography, index.

2637 Domke, Martin. "Assets of East Europeans Impounded in the United States." *American Slavic and Eastern European Review* 18 (1959): 351–60.

Domke discusses American legal statutes governing the proper and complete dispersal of testate funds to beneficiaries residing in Communist countries from 1939 to 1959.

2638 Ethridge, Mark, and Black, C. E. "Negotiating in the Balkans, 1945–1947." In Raymond Dennett and Joseph Johnson, eds. *Negotiating With the*

Russians. Boston: World Peace Foundation, 1951, pp. 171–206.

The United States expected Soviet wartime cooperation to continue in the postwar period. This essay traces the negotiations over the Balkans with the Soviets from the Yalta agreements to the formulation of the Truman Doctrine.

2639 Garrett, Stephen A. "Images and Foreign Policy: The United States, Eastern Europe, and the Beginnings of the Cold War." *World Affairs* 138 (1976): 288–308.

The American-Soviet conflict over policies in Eastern Europe is seen as a major factor in the origins of the Cold War. America's national self-image played an important role in defining the conflict. Notes.

2640 Garson, Robert. "The Role of Eastern Europe in America's Containment Policy, 1945–1948." *Journal of American Studies* [Great Britain] 13 (1979): 73–92.

The Truman administration's adoption of the containment policy resulted when it decided it could not immediately reverse the Soviet Union's hegemony over Eastern European nations. Americans pinned their hopes on East European nationalism eroding away Russia's hold. Notes.

2641 Lundestad, Geir. *The American Non-Policy Towards Eastern Europe, 1943–1947: Universalism in an Area Not of Essential Interest to the United States.* New York: Humanities, 1978.

The subtitle fairly describes the theme of this volume which finds that American policymakers were never quite able to decide how important Eastern Europe was to them. It is a lengthy, balanced, and insightful account. Notes, bibliography, index.

2642 Mares, Vaclav E. "American Policy Toward the East European Satellites." *Current History* 37 (1959): 208–13.

American policy toward the Soviet-dominated East European satellites was one of containment, 1944–59.

2643 Mark, Eduard. "American Policy Toward Eastern Europe and the Origins of the Cold War, 1941–1946: An Alternative Interpretation." *Journal of American History* 68 (1981): 313–36.

The author suggests that U.S. policy did accommodate the influence of the U.S.S.R. in Eastern Europe after World War II; but while the United States was prepared for a Soviet "sphere of influence," it was not willing to accept political/military domination. Notes.

2644 Mark, Eduard. "Charles E. Bohlen and the Acceptable Limits of Soviet Hegemony in Eastern

Europe: A Memorandum of 18 October 1945." *Diplomatic History* 3 (1979): 201–13.

Bohlen's memo suggests that as late as October 1945 the U.S. State Department recognized that the U.S.S.R. had a legitimate right to a secure western frontier and expected Soviet domination of the external affairs of Eastern European nations.

2645 Max, Stanley M. "Cold War on the Danube: The Belgrade Conference of 1948 and Anglo-American Efforts to Reinternationalize the River." *Diplomatic History* 7 (1983): 57–77.

The conference rejected Anglo-American proposals for opening the Danube to all shipping; the Soviet-backed proposals which succeeded excluded all Western traffic and commerce from the waterway. Notes.

2646 Misse, Frederick B., Jr. "The Loss of Eastern Europe, 1938–1946." Ph.D. dissertation, University of Illinois, 1964.

America failed to develop a viable policy toward Eastern Europe and instead relied upon the principles of the Atlantic Charter and the Yalta Declaration. By 1946 the Truman administration had three choices: to fight Russia, to bargain for Russian withdrawal, or to resort to moral criticism. DAI 25:6573.

2647 Mosely, Philip. "Hopes and Failures: American Policy Toward East Central Europe, 1941–1947." *Review of Politics* 17 (1955): 461–85.

Americans gradually came to realize that Soviet aims ran counter to American aspirations for the people in Eastern Europe. Mosely believes that American officials failed during the war to secure positions of power from which the United States could achieve its objectives. Notes.

2648 Quinlan, Paul D. "British and American Policies Toward Romania, 1938–1947." Ph.D. dissertation, Boston College, 1974.

The final chapters detail Western efforts to get the Soviets to live up to their promises. Frustrated over their failure, the United States became directly involved in an effort by Romanians to overthrow the Communist government. DAI 35:2189-A.

2649 Sheehy, Edward J. "The United States Navy in the Mediterranean, 1945–1947." Ph.D. dissertation, George Washington University, 1983.

The growth of the U.S. naval presence in the Mediterranean is examined along with its political and strategic rationale. DAI 44:1551-A.

AUSTRIA

2650 Bader, William B. *Austria Between East and West, 1945–1955*. Stanford, CA: Stanford University Press, 1966.

The first portion of this study deals with the development of Allied occupation policy in the immediate postwar years. Maps, notes, index.

2651 Cox, Charles L. "The Allied Commission and the Creation of the Second Austrian Republic." Ph.D. dissertation, University of Georgia, 1979.

This study focuses on the early years (1943–46) which were the formative ones as far as constructing Allied policy. DAI 40:4181-A.

2652 Eggleston, Patricia B. "The Marshall Plan in Austria: A Study in American Containment of the Soviet Union in the Cold War." Ph.D. dissertation, University of Alabama, 1980.

The United States financed Austria's rehabilitation to ensure that Austria remained independent of the Soviet Union. As a result, though, Austria lost its commercial ties with Eastern Europe, which slowed her recovery program and prolonged dependence on American aid. DAI 41:3685.

CZECHOSLOVAKIA

2653 Steinitz, Mark S. "United States Economic Assistance Policy Toward Czechoslovakia, 1946–1948." *Maryland History* 7 (1976): 21–46.

The author argues that American inflexibility contributed to the undermining of Czech moderates and the reinforced dependence on the Soviet Union. Notes.

2654 Steinitz, Mark S. "The U.S. Propaganda Effort in Czechoslovakia, 1945–48." *Diplomatic History* 6 (1982): 359–86.

The Truman administration sought to conduct the first peacetime propaganda program. This essay focuses on one of these campaigns. Notes.

2655 Ullman, Walter. "Czechoslovakia's Crucial Years, 1945–1948: An American View." *East European Quarterly* 1 (1967): 217–30.

American-Czech relations from 1945 to 1948 are reviewed, emphasizing the possibilities of U.S. assistance in averting a Communist takeover. Ullman draws his narrative from the viewpoint of Laurence A. Steinhardt, the American ambassador in Prague. Notes.

2656 Ullman, Walter. *The United States in Prague, 1945–1958*. East European Monographs, no. 36. Boulder, CO: East European Quarterly, 1978.

Ullman recounts the problems Ambassador Laurence A. Steinhardt had in reestablishing the American embassy at Prague after World War II.

Additionally, this account traces the State Department's view of U.S.-Czech relations up to the coup of 1948. Notes, bibliography, index.

HUNGARY

2657 Max, Stanley M. "The Anglo-American Response to the Sovietization of Hungary, 1945–1948." Ph.D. dissertation, State University of New York, Albany, 1980.

Max compares and contrasts British and American policy toward the issue of Sovietization, finding that, although both Western governments were opposed to the growth of Soviet control in Hungary, the United States resisted the Sovietization process more aggressively than did Britain. DAI 41:756.

2658 Rupprecht, Paul. "The Image of Hungary's International Position in American Foreign Policy-Making, 1937–1947." Ph.D. dissertation, University of Minnesota, 1967.

Hungary's position, and the potentials and advantage offered by it, had only limited relevance to U.S. diplomacy, which precluded the establishment within the postwar international system of small country independence in East-Central Europe. DAI 28:5128-A.

POLAND

2659 Cable, John N. "Arthur Bliss Lane: Cold Warrior in Warsaw, 1945–1947." *Polish American Studies* 30 (1973): 66–82.

Lane's refusal to reconcile himself to a Socialist government in Poland hurt the Polish cause and provided the United States with poor representation. By the time Lane realized that Poland's proximity to Russia made a Socialist government the best the Poles could get, most opportunities had slipped by. Notes.

2660 Cable, John N. "The United States and the Polish Question, 1939–1948." Ph.D. dissertation, Vanderbilt University, 1972.

In 1945 the Truman administration made a "colossal error" in sending Arthur Bliss Lane to Warsaw as U.S. ambassador. His open hostility to the Communist regime made negotiation impossible. DAI 33:1621-A.

2661 Cable, John N. "Vandenberg: The Polish Question and Polish Americans, 1944–1948." *Michigan History* 57 (1973): 296–310.

Republican Senator Arthur H. Vandenberg, who has been remembered for his efforts to create a

bipartisan foreign policy, was only moderately bipartisan on the Polish issue. He had a solid anti-Communist, heavily Polish-American constituency. Illustrations, notes.

2662 Glinka-Janczewski, George H. "American Policy Toward Poland Under the Truman Administration, 1945–1952." Ph.D. dissertation, Georgetown University, 1966.

Truman appeared to follow no prescribed lines or pursue any specific objectives. While the United States adopted a positive and friendly attitude toward the Polish people, it was disapproving toward the Communist regime in power. DAI 27:2985.

2663 Irons, Peter H. " 'The Test is Poland': Polish Americans and the Origins of the Cold War." *Polish American Studies* 30 (1973): 5–63.

Polish-Americans sought to influence U.S. policy toward Poland and the Soviet Union during and after World War II, but although the Roosevelt and Truman administrations rendered some rhetorical support, Polish-Americans failed to exert any substantive influence. Notes.

2664 Lukas, Richard C. *Bitter Legacy: Polish-American Relations in the Wake of World War II.* Lexington: University Press of Kentucky, 1982.

Washington's general clumsiness in dealing with Polish issues during 1945 to 1947 is developed here, especially the matters of relief and rehabilitation, repatriation of Polish nationals, and economic aid. Notes, bibliography, index.

2665 Lukas, Richard C. "The Polish American Congress and the Polish Question, 1944–1947." *Polish American Studies* 38 (1981): 39–53.

The attitude of the Truman administration did little to relieve the anxieties of Polish-Americans, especially their distrust of the pro-Soviet Lubin government. Notes.

2666 Lundestad, Geir. "The American Policy Towards Poland, 1943–1946." *American Studies in Scandinavia* [Sweden] (1972): 5–28.

The author argues Roosevelt's search for postwar cooperation between the major powers and Truman's desire to obtain substantial economic concessions played important roles in the recognition of Poland and the establishment of postwar Polish boundaries. Notes, bibliography.

2667 Orzell, Laurence J. "A 'Painful Problem': Poland in Allied Diplomacy, February–July, 1945." *Mid-America* 59 (1977): 147–70.

Differences regarding Polish issues among the Allies—United States, Britain, and Soviet Union—eventually would lead to the Cold War. In 1945 two different Polish governments existed, each supported by various Allies. Territorial problems also created differences. Notes.

2668 Szymczak, Robert. "The Unquiet Dead: The Katyn Forest Massacre as an Issue in American Diplomacy and Politics." Ph.D. dissertation, Carnegie-Mellon University, 1980.

Eleven years after it happened, the U.S. Congress began the investigation of the massacre of 15,000 Polish officers in the Soviet Union. The massacre became an inflammatory Cold War issue and a weapon in America's propaganda arsenal. DAI 42:825.

2669 Thackrah, J. R. "Aspects of American and British Policy Towards Poland from the Yalta to the Potsdam Conferences, 1945." *Polish Review* 21 (1976): 3–34.

The attempts by both countries to secure a democratically elected state for the Polish people in the first six months of 1945 are reviewed. Notes.

Armed Forces Day Parade, May 20, 1950. L to R: Frank Pace, Jr., General Dwight D. Eisenhower, Louis Johnson, President Truman, Admiral William D. Leahy, and an unidentified man. *Abbie Rowe: National Park Service.*

Military Affairs: Atomic Weapons, Defense Policies, and Arms Control

Military affairs necessarily became a matter requiring considerable attention within an administration which found Truman's first months as president involved with the ending of World War II, while his last months were beset with attempts to conclude the Korean conflict. While both of these particular episodes are discussed in Chapters 7 and 10, respectively, this chapter focuses upon such questions as reorganization, weapons, priorities, manpower allocations, and atomic weaponry. A useful survey of these issues may be found in Chapters 8 through 10 of Paul Y. Hammond, *Organizing for Defense* (#2674).

The military services had been formulating their own postwar plans some time before Truman became president. Vincent Davis, *Postwar Defense Policy and the U.S. Navy, 1943–1946* (#2712), Perry McCoy Smith, *The Air Force Plans for Peace, 1943–1945* (#2714), and Michael S. Sherry, *Preparing for the Next War: American Plans for Postwar Defense, 1941–45* (#2713) present the armed services' hopes and expectations. Truman's decision to reorganize the defense establishment, which involved the unification of the armed forces under a secretary of defense, the creation of the Central Intelligence Agency, and the establishment of the National Security Council, touched off a monumental bureaucratic struggle among the senior officers of the army, navy, and air force. Demetrios Caraley, *The Politics of Military Unification: A Study of Conflict and the Policy Process* (#2722) reviews the unification battle, while Douglas Kinnard, *The Secretary of Defense* (#2727) provides the history of that office.

The establishment of the Central Intelligence Agency and its operation under the Truman administration deserve a thorough historical treatment. Until then, chapters in full-length accounts and journal articles will have to suffice. Thomas F. Troy, *Donovan and the CIA: A History of the Establishment of the Central Intelligence Agency* (#2707) is a useful introduction to the subject.

Atomic energy, especially as it related to weaponry, occupied a central position within the administration's defense posture. Gregg Herken, *The Winning Weapon: The Atomic Bomb in the Cold War, 1945–1950* (#2689) deals with the failure of the administration to develop a coherent nuclear strategy, while Noel F. Parrish, *Behind the Sheltering Bomb* (#2693) follows a similar path. The intense debate which followed the Soviet atomic explosion (1949) and concluded with Truman's decision (1950) to build the H-bomb is reviewed by Herbert F. York, *The Advisors: Oppenheimer, Teller, and the Superbomb* (#2810).

The activities and aspirations of bureaucrats and scientists—sometimes they were the same people—are discussed in a number of accounts; however, Richard G. Hewlett and Oscar E. Anderson, Jr., *A History of the United States Atomic Energy Commission*, Vol. 2: *Atomic Shield, 1947–1952* (#2779) provides the most comprehensive introduction. The impact of the scientific community upon military policy is explored by Robert Gilpin, *American Scientists and Nuclear Weapons Policy* (#2785), and Alice Kimball Smith, *A Peril and a Hope: The Scientists' Movement in America, 1945–47* (#2789).

Efforts to erect international controls of nuclear weapons failed. The issues and events which marked the initial phase of arms control are discussed in Joseph I. Lieberman, *The Scorpion and the Tarantula: The Struggle to Control Atomic Weapons, 1945–1949* (#2814). Lawrence S. Wittner, *Rebels Against War: The American Peace Movement, 1941–1960* (#2830) surveys the efforts of early nuclear pacifists and the fate of conscientious objectors.

Military Policies, Programs, and Strategies

See Chapter 3, *Military Officers* and *Congressional and Political Leaders*; also see *James Forrestal*.

STRATEGY, INTELLIGENCE, AND CIVIL DEFENSE

2670 Colhoun, John H. "The Frustration of Power: United States Military Policy, 1945–60." Ph.D. dissertation, York University [Canada], 1976.

During the early years, the United States developed a policy predicated upon a concept of strategic atomic air power and, consequently, sought to make the political and economic burdens of maintaining such a military force bearable by substituting sophisticated defense technology for costly ground troops. DAI 37:6010-A.

2671 Elzy, Martin I. "The Origins of American Military Policy, 1945–1950." Ph.D. dissertation, Miami University, 1975.

American military policy between World War II and the Korean War relied heavily on air power and atomic weapons at the expense of varied conventional forces. DAI 36:2394-A.

2672 Epstein, Laurence B. "The American Philosophy of War, 1945–1967." Ph.D. dissertation, University of Southern California, 1967.

This study examines six issues in order to determine whether America's philosophy of war has undergone a change: the Nuremberg Trials; the use of atomic bombs on Japan; the policy of containment; the United Nations; Korea; and Vietnam. DAI 28:3092-A.

2673 Halperin, Morton H. "The President and the Military." *Foreign Affairs* 52 (1972): 310–24.

This survey of presidential relations with the military, from FDR to Nixon, reviews military advice, organization, and budget. The author observes that "none of our Presidents has been content with his relations with the military."

2674 Hammond, Paul Y. *Organizing for Defense.* Princeton: Princeton University Press, 1961.

Chapter 8 deals with the unification controversy; Chapter 9 examines defense reorganization under the Truman administration; and Chapter 10 evaluates the effects of unification and organizational changes. Footnotes, index.

2675 *The History of the Joint Chiefs of Staff. The Joint Chiefs of Staff and National Policy.* 4 vols. Wilmington, DE: Michael Glazier, 1979–80.

These recently declassified typescript volumes were prepared by JCS historians. They provide a view of world affairs and U.S. national security from the perspective of the Joint Chiefs from 1947 to 1952. Volume 1 was prepared by James F. Schnabel; volume 2 by Kenneth W. Condit; volume 3 (*The Korean War*) in two parts by James F. Schnabel and Robert J. Watson; and volume 4 by Walter S. Poole. Notes, bibliography.

2676 Huntington, Samuel P. *The Common Defense: Strategic Programs in National Politics.* New York: Columbia University Press, 1961.

While more topical than chronological, the author does discuss the Truman administration's military policies (pp. 14–64). Under more topical themes the early developments of the Truman years are listed, e.g., continental defense, limited war, and domestic influences. Tables, notes, index.

2677 Jennings, Richard M. "U.S.-Soviet Arms Competition, 1945–1972: Aspects of Its Nature, Control, and Results." Ph.D. dissertation, Georgetown University, 1975.

This study clarifies the U.S./Soviet arms relationship by adding a more precise profile of its components. It examines whether the arms competition was a race, to what extent it was quantitative versus qualitative and nuclear versus nonnuclear. DAI 37:587-A.

2678 Joseph, Robert G. "Commitments and Capabilities: United States Foreign and Defense Policy Coordination, 1945 to the Korean War." Ph.D. dissertation, Columbia University, 1978.

The Truman administration conceived and implemented increasingly stringent foreign policy guidelines for dealing with the Kremlin. Compromise and concessions were replaced by "patience with firmness" and the latter by containment. This study examines the increase in commitments and the steady decline in military capabilities. DAI 39:5132-A.

2679 Katzenbach, Edward L., Jr. "Information as a Limitation on Military Legislation: A Problem in National Security." *Journal of International Affairs* 8 (1954): 196–205.

The politics and partisanship of military affairs in Congress are examined.

2680 Mathews, Naiven F. "The Public View of Military Policy, 1945–1950." Ph.D. dissertation, University of Missouri, 1964.

Public opinion played a definite role in influencing military policy after World War II; such as rapid demobilization of the armed forces and a focus on air power and nuclear weapons rather than conventional forces. DAI 25:7217-A.

2681 Millis, Walter; Mansfield, Harvey; and Stein, Harold. *Arms and the State: Civil Military Elements in National Policy*. New York: Twentieth Century Fund, 1958.

This volume offers a historical survey of U.S. civil-military issues (1930–55), with special focus on 1945 through 1955. With atomic weapons, there had been a dramatic change in the ends and means of making national policy and a blurring of the lines between civil and military. Notes, index.

2682 Mrozek, Donald J. "Peace Through Strength: Strategic Air Power and the Mobilization of the United States for the Pursuit of Foreign Policy, 1945–1955." Ph.D. dissertation, Rutgers University, 1972.

This thesis studies the defense mobilization policies and practice of the Truman administration, including a consideration of precedents in the Roosevelt years, and continuities into the Eisenhower presidency. DAI 32:4315-A.

2683 Pinkerton, Sam P. "Aspects of the Military Posture of the United States Influenced by Atomic Energy, 1945–1958." Ph.D. dissertation, New York University, 1960.

The United States emphasized air power to the detriment of other forces and limited its ability to check local aggression. DAI 27:1422.

2684 Weigley, Russell F. *The American Way of War: A History of United States Military Strategy and Policy*. New York: Macmillan, 1973.

Chapters 15 and 16 deal with the search for a national strategy during the immediate post-World War II years and the Korean War. The chapters on military policies of World War II provide an excellent introduction to the Truman period. Notes, bibliography, index.

Atomic Weapons and Strategy

See also *Atomic Arms: Control and Protest*; and Chapter 7, *Decision To Use A-Bombs*.

2685 Benson, Charles D. "The U.S. Armed Services' Examination of Their Role, 1945–1950." Ph.D. dissertation, University of Florida, 1970.

Disagreement within the four branches of the armed services focused on air power: How it would be employed; what degree of effectiveness could be expected; and who would control it. DAI 32:349-A.

2686 Borowski, Harry R. "Air Force Atomic Capability From V-J Day to the Berlin Blockade: Potential or Real?" *Military Affairs* 44 (1980): 105–10.

The stockpile of atomic weapons was limited and the Strategic Air Command was ill-prepared to deliver existing weapons. Not until Gen. Curtis LeMay assumed command of SAC in 1948 did the gap between the real and potential capabilities begin to close. Notes.

2687 Comfort, Kenneth J. "National Security Policy and the Development of Tactical Nuclear Forces, 1948–1958." Ph.D. dissertation, Columbia University, 1970.

Tactical nuclear weapons' development required the rearming, reorganization, and retraining of the army to fight nuclear ground war. DAI 32: 518-A.

2688 Herken, Gregg. "A Most Deadly Illusion: The Atomic Secret and American Nuclear Weapons Policy, 1945–1950." *Pacific Historical Review* 49 (1980): 51–76.

The Truman administration's atomic policy was based on the illusion that America had a monopoly of atomic raw materials and technological expertise. When the Soviets exploded their bomb in 1949, it was immediately assumed that spies and traitors had provided them with the secrets. Notes.

2689 Herken, Gregg. *The Winning Weapon: The Atomic Bomb in the Cold War, 1945–1950*. New York: Knopf, 1981.

Truman's initial response to the A-bomb was "hesitant and even vacillating," but he ultimately sided with the policy of monopoly based upon secrecy which undermined his administration's stated objectives of international controls. Herken finds that interservice bureaucratic rivalries and ideological fixations prevented the development of a coherent nuclear strategy. Notes, bibliography, index.

2690 Mandelbaum, Michael. *The Nuclear Question: The United States and Nuclear Weapons, 1946–1976*. New York: Cambridge University Press, 1979.

The first few chapters deal with nuclear issues during the Truman period. Notes, index.

2691 Millett, Stephen M. "The Capabilities of the American Nuclear Deterrent, 1945–1950." *Aerospace Historian* 27 (1980): 27–32.

Americans did not have a nuclear force sufficient to deter the Soviets in July 1948 but acquired that capability by 1950. Illustrations, notes.

2692 O'Brien, Larry D. "National Security and the New Warfare: Defense Policy, War Planning, and Nuclear Weapons, 1945–1950." Ph.D. dissertation, Ohio State University, 1981.

American nuclear policy (1945–50) was based upon deterrence, yet there was no coherent idea of what to do should deterrence fail. While military planners developed a strategy of preemptive counterforce strikes, civilian policymakers were divided in their views on deterrence and strategy. DAI 42:2263.

2693 Parrish, Noel. *Behind the Sheltering Bomb.* New York: Arno, 1979.

This photographic reproduction of Parrish's 1968 dissertation ("Military Indecision from Alamogordo to Korea") is a solid survey of the early impact of atomic weapons upon American military policy. Notes, bibliography.

2694 Rose, John P. "United States Army Nuclear Doctrinal Developments: The Nuclear Battlefield, 1945–1977." Ph.D. dissertation, University of Southern California, 1978.

This study surveys army doctrine and its shifts. DAI 39:455-A.

2695 Rosenberg, David Alan. "The Origins of Overkill: Nuclear Weapons and American Strategy, 1945–1960." *International Security* 7 (1983): 3–71.

The disparity between war plans and lack of atomic capability due to budget restrictions is examined. Notes.

2696 Rosenberg, David Alan. "Toward Armageddon: The Foundations of United States Nuclear Strategy, 1945–1961." Ph.D. dissertation, University of Chicago, 1983.

The author explores the processes of strategic and operational planning for nuclear war within the context of policy decision at the highest levels. He argues that inadequate communication, guidance, and coordination among American government leaders resulted in the emergence of rigid patterns of operational planning.

2697 Rosenberg, David Alan. "The U.S. Nuclear Stockpile, 1945 to 1950." *The Bulletin of the Atomic Scientists* 38 (1982): 25–30.

By bringing together pieces of recently declassified information the author describes the surprisingly small, but growing nuclear arsenal.

2698 Schneider, Mark B. "Nuclear Weapons and American Strategy, 1945–1953." Ph.D. dissertation, University of Southern California, 1974.

The history of the development of nuclear weapons by the United States sheds light on a variety of subjects besides the development of military strategy: the diplomacy of the termination of World War II, the formation of policies to control nuclear weapons, the role of interservice rivalry, and the impact of nuclear arms on U.S. foreign policy. DAI 35:3655-A.

2699 Scrivner, John H., Jr. "Pioneer Into Space: A Biography of Major General Orvil Arson Anderson." Ph.D. dissertation, University of Oklahoma, 1971.

Anderson headed the military division of the Strategic Bombing Survey in both Europe and the Pacific. He was the first commandant of the Air War College (1946) and became involved with the advocacy of "preventive war" in 1950. DAI 32:2620-A.

2700 Wells, Samuel F., Jr. "The Origins of Massive Retaliation." *Political Science Quarterly* 96 (1981): 31–52.

Although the concept received refinement and popular exposure during the Eisenhower administration, the author shows that both the doctrine and the defense programs that formed the basis of the policy were developed during the Truman years. Notes.

Military and Foreign Policy

2701 Beckman, Peter R. "The Influence of the American Military Establishment on American Foreign Policy, 1946–1970." Ph.D. dissertation, University of Wisconsin, Madison, 1974.

This study speaks to the following questions in quantitative fashion: (1) What accounts for the differences in the description of military influence and the correlates of influence? (2) Is it possible to provide a quantifiable description of the degree of military influence on U.S. foreign policy? and (3) What factors are associated with influence? DAI 35:5495-A.

2702 Bell, Coral. *Negotiation from Strength: A Study in the Politics of Power.* New York: Knopf, 1963.

The continuing Cold War led to a mounting emphasis on military power as the guarantor of peace. Bell reveals both the seductive nature of this argument, both on the Right and Left, and its pitfalls. Bibliography, index.

2703 Berger, William E. "The Role of the Armed Services in International Policy." Ph.D. dissertation, University of Nebraska, 1956.

Military chiefs could not understand that force was only one element of the Truman administration's foreign policy; their doctrine of "instantaneous retaliation" failed to consider economic, political, and moral factors. DAI 16:738.

CIA/Intelligence Operations

See M. J. Smith, *The Secret Wars*, Vol. 2:

Intelligence, Propaganda and Psychological Warfare, Covert Operations, 1945–1980 (#3038) for additional references.

2704 Adler, Emanuel. "Executive Command and Control in Foreign Policy: The CIA's Covert Activities." *Orbis* 23 (1979): 671–96.

Adler evaluated the control and command of the CIA's covert activities by presidents between 1947 and 1979. Notes.

2705 Andrew, Christopher. "Governments and Secret Services: A Historical Perspective." *International Journal* [Canada] 34 (1979): 167–86.

The Truman and Eisenhower administrations let the Central Intelligence Agency develop so that it was not accountable to political controls.

2706 Barnes, Trevor. "The Secret Cold War: The C.I.A. and American Foreign Policy in Europe, 1946–1956." *Historical Journal* [Great Britain] 24 (1981): 399–415.

This overview of the CIA's influence on U.S. policy in Europe and European affairs deals with clandestine activity conducted against Communists in Italy and Greece. Notes.

2707 Troy, Thomas. *Donovan and the CIA: A History of the Establishment of the Central Intelligence Agency.* Frederick, MD: University Publications of America, 1981.

A two-volume classified CIA document has been declassified and reedited into this volume. Troy finds a lineal connection between Donovan of the Office of Strategic Services and the creation of the CIA. Illustrations, notes, bibliography, index.

2708 Wittner, Lawrence S. "When CIA Hearts Were Young and Gay: Planning the Cold War (Spring 1945)." *Peace and Change* 5 (1978): 70–76.

This article reprints memos of 2 April and 5 May 1945 to Presidents Roosevelt and Truman, respectively, from the Office of Strategic Services outlining the nature of Soviet-American relations after World War II.

Civil Defense

2709 Blanchard, Boyce W. "American Civil Defense, 1945–1975: The Evolution of Programs and Policies." Ph.D. dissertation, University of Virginia, 1980.

In surveying U.S. civil defense programs and policies, Blanchard raises several questions, such as, why do we have no comprehensive evacuation plan and no adequate shelter system? DAI 41:1746-A.

2710 Cooling, B. Franklin. "Civil Defense and the Army: The Quest for Responsibility, 1946–1948." *Military Affairs* 36 (1972): 11–13.

Although the army recognized the importance of civil defense after World War II, it wished to avoid full responsibility for it. This essay traces the development of the Office of Civil Defense Planning (1947) and the Federal Civil Defense Administration (1951). Notes.

2711 Tyler, Lyon G., Jr. "Civil Defense: The Impact of the Planning Years, 1945–1950." Ph.D. dissertation, Duke University, 1967.

The army initiated postwar civil defense planning, but it was turned over to civilian control in 1949. Planners clung to methods used in World War II and failed to come up with a realistic and viable program. DAI 29:221.

POSTWAR PLANNING AND REORGANIZATION

2712 Davis, Vincent. *Postwar Defense Policy and the U.S. Navy, 1943–1946.* Chapel Hill: University of North Carolina Press, 1966.

Chapter 9 deals with Secretary Forrestal's leadership in developing the postwar navy. Four factors affected the navy's planning after 1945: (1) pressure for rapid demobilization; (2) growing recognition of Russia as the new enemy; (3) the campaign for service unification and air force autonomy; and (4) the impact of the atomic bomb upon strategy. Notes, bibliography, index.

2713 Sherry, Michael S. *Preparing for the Next War: American Plans for Postwar Defense, 1941–45.* New Haven: Yale University Press, 1977.

This volume is important for understanding the postwar policies and ambitions of the various military services; for example, the origins of the Universal Military Training Program, the postwar preparations drive, the early efforts at measuring the Soviet threat, and the new technological reliance are reviewed. Bibliography, index.

2714 Smith, Perry M. *The Air Force Plans for Peace, 1943–1945.* Baltimore: Johns Hopkins Press, 1970.

Army air force leaders equated postwar "peace" with a large regular air force and service autonomy. This study focuses almost exclusively on air force sources and views. Bibliography, interviews, glossary, index.

2715 Wix, William M. "The Army's Plans For Its Postwar Role, 1943–1945." Ph.D. dissertation, Columbia University, 1976.

The army attempted during World War II to win public and congressional acceptance of the program on which the senior leaders concluded the postwar fate of the army hung—Universal Military Training. DAI 37:6742-A.

Universal Military Training

See also *Pacifism and Pacifists*.

2716 Cunningham, Frank D. "The Army and Universal Military Training, 1942–1948." Ph.D. dissertation, University of Texas, Austin, 1976.

Despite a lack of public interest, the army never gave up on UMT. During 1946 army planners brought their UMT plans to a nearly final structural maturity. Truman's Advisory Committee for Universal Military Training studied the issue and, in 1947, the Towe Bill was introduced to implement UMT. It did not pass. DAI 37:7917-A.

2717 Dunn, Joe P. "UMT: A Historical Perspective." *Military Review* 61 (1981): 11–18.

The post-World War II years offered a basic debate over a one-year period of military and civil training for all young men. The choice fell to one between universal military training or selective service; conscription was chosen. Notes.

2718 Jacobs, Clyde E., and Gallagher, John F. *The Selective Service Act: A Case Study of the Governmental Process*. New York: Dodd, Mead, 1967.

The Selective Service Act (1948) provides the focal point of this case study. Tables, notes, index.

2719 Peterson, F. Ross. "Fighting the Drive Toward War: Glen H. Taylor, the 1948 Progressives, and the Draft." *Pacific Northwest Quarterly* 61 (1970):41–45.

This essay reviews statements by Senator Taylor in opposition to the adoption of peacetime military conscription in 1948.

2720 Swomley, John M., Jr. "A Study of the Universal Military Training Program, 1944–1952." Ph.D. dissertation, University of Colorado, 1959.

In 1944 the War Department launched a campaign for a permanent program of compulsory military training for eighteen-year-old boys. Opposition came from many church, farm, labor, and educational groups as well as support from veteran groups. Universal military training was a major issue until its legislative defeat in 1952, after which it was abandoned. DAI 20:4156.

2721 Ward, Robert D. "The Movement for Universal Military Training in the United States, 1942–1952." Ph.D. dissertation, University of North Carolina, 1957.

No abstract available.

Unification Struggle

2722 Caraley, Demetrios. *The Politics of Military Unification: A Study of Conflict and the Policy Process*. New York: Columbia University Press, 1966.

Intense political conflict took place between 1943 and 1947 over the unification of the military services. This account seeks to analyze that conflict in terms of the actors involved, their goals and perceptions, and their strategies and tactics of influence. Notes, index.

2723 Coletta, Paolo E. "The Defense Unification Battle, 1947–50: The Navy." *Prologue* 7 (1975): 6–17.

The navy suffered from a reduced prestige (loss of Cabinet status) and a reduction of its air arm and the Marine Corps. It was also forced to scrap its plans for a supercarrier. Illustrations, notes.

2724 Coletta, Paolo E. *The United States Navy and Defense Unification, 1947–1953*. Newark: University of Delaware Press, 1981.

The interservice "debates" on unification, the B-36, aircraft carriers, national strategy, and the roles and missions of the services are examined. Illustrations, notes, bibliography, index.

2725 French, Thomas A. "Unification and the American Military Establishment, 1945–1950." Ph.D. dissertation, State University of New York, Buffalo, 1972.

The birth of a military-industrial axis was the product, not the cause, of commitment to atomic arms and advanced weapons technology. This axis was controlled at both poles by civilians in the Defense Department and the weapons industry. DAI 33:1637-A.

2726 Haynes, Richard F. "The Defense Unification Battle, 1947–50: The Army." *Prologue* 7 (1975): 27–31.

The army lost its Cabinet status and its air arm but managed to retain budgetary parity with the other services. Thus the army became larger in size, but suffered a loss of prestige. Illustrations, notes.

2727 Kinnard, Douglas. *The Secretary of Defense*. Lexington: University Press of Kentucky, 1980.

In 1947 the National Security Act established the Cabinet position of Secretary of Defense. Kinnard examines the office and those individuals filling it. Chapter 1 discusses James Forrestal as secretary of defense. Notes, bibliography, index.

2728 Mitchell, Franklin D. "An Act of Presidential Indiscretion: Harry S. Truman, Congressman McDonough, and the Marine Corps Incident of 1950." *Presidential Studies Quarterly* 11 (1981): 565–75.

Truman advocated a diminished role for the Marine Corps in the restructured Defense Department; however, when his ill-advised letter to this effect (sent to Republican McDonough) was published, it provided ammunition to the Corps' supporters. Notes.

2729 Tarr, Curtis W. "Unification of America's Armed Forces: A Century and a Half of Conflict,

1798–1947." Ph.D. dissertation, Stanford University, 1962.

The National Security Act (1947) placed the military establishment under the authority of a single directing head. This study analyzes the developments leading to the passage of the National Security Act. DAI 22:4339.

2730 Trager, Frank N. "The National Security Act of 1947: Its Thirtieth Anniversary." *Air University Review* 29 (1977): 2–15.

The effects of the act upon the U.S. defense establishment are discussed. Notes.

2731 Vendegrift, A. A. "Vicious Infighting." In Peter Karsten, ed. *The Military in America: From Colonial Era to the Present*. New York: Free Press, 1980, pp. 363–69.

The "Collins Plan," introduced in 1946 by Gen. J. Lawton Collins, called for unification of the military under a secretary of defense and armed forces chief of staff, and for the reduction of the role of the Marine Corps. It caused a furor.

2732 Wolk, Herman S. "The Defense Unification Battle, 1947–50: The Air Force." *Prologue* 7 (1975): 18–26.

The air force's demand for autonomy and for large strategic (atomic) forces led ultimately to a struggle with the navy. In the end, the navy suffered budgetary reductions and the secretary of defense gained power. Ilustrations, notes.

DEFENSE ECONOMICS AND RESEARCH

See also Chapter 5, *Science and Technology*.

2733 Kevles, Daniel J. "Scientists, the Military, and the Control of Postwar Defense Research: The Case of the Research Board for National Security, 1944–46." *Technology and Culture* 16 (1975): 20–47.

When the postwar ad hoc Research Board for National Security was established, in conjunction with the National Academy of Sciences, to continue the wartime practice of employing civilian scientific participation in defense research, it was opposed by the Bureau of the Budget and ceased to function. With its death, the military became the major patron of academic research. Notes.

2734 Sigethy, Robert. "The Air Force Organization for Basic Research, 1945–1970." Ph.D. dissertation, American University, 1980.

Sigethy finds that the Air Force Organization for Basic Research helped ensure the pluralistic nature

of federal science activities after World War II. DAI 41:4491.

2735 York, Herbert F., and Greb, G. Allen. "Military Research and Development: A Postwar History." *Bulletin of the Atomic Scientists* 33 (1977):12–26.

This overview of the technological arms race focuses on the development of managerial and supervisory positions, specifically those held by scientists and engineers, 1945–75.

Military Expenditures

2736 Agapos, A. M., and Gallaway, Lowell E. "Defense Profits and the Renegotiation Board in the Aerospace Industry." *Journal of Political Economy* 78 (1970): 1093–1105.

This examination of the aerospace industry's net profits from 1945 to 1969 finds that aerospace firms did not receive excess profits with an increased demand for military hardware, and that contract renegotiations circumvented the Federal Renegotiation Board, rendering it ineffective.

2737 Cypher, James M. "Military Expenditures and the Performance of the Postwar U.S. Economy, 1947–1971." Ph.D. dissertation, University of California, Riverside, 1973.

Military expenditures have created many of the "growth industries" in the postwar economy, and they have been an important source of overall demand, particularly during postwar recessions. DAI 34: 3634-A.

2738 Director, Aaron, ed. *Defense, Controls, and Inflation: A Conference Sponsored by the University of Chicago Law School*. Chicago: University of Chicago Press, 1952.

The participants agreed that the mobilization program should be covered by increased taxes and that the budget should be balanced. The chief area of disagreement centered on whether direct controls were needed as a supplement to or substitute for the market system. Index.

2739 Hill, William S., Jr. "The Business Community and National Defense: Corporate Leaders and the Military, 1943–1950." Ph.D. dissertation, Stanford University, 1980.

At the end of the war, business leaders wanted immediate termination of war production, banking on pent-up consumer demand to bring prosperity. Until 1950, business leaders resisted using any federal expenditure, even military spending, to foster economic expansion. DAI 40:5978-A.

2740 Huzar, Elias. *The Purse and the Sword: Control of the Army by Congress through Military Appropriations, 1933–1950*. Ithaca, NY: Cornell University Press, 1950.

This study was prompted by a concern with effective, efficient civilian control by Congress of the military establishment. Material relating to the Truman years is scattered throughout the volume, as it is organized topically rather than chronologically. Notes, appendix, index.

2741 Kolodziej, Edward A. "Rational Consent and Defense Budgets: The Role of Congress, 1945–1952." *Orbis* 7 (1964): 748–77.

The author's examination of defense budgets with foreign policy objectives suggests that, with some exceptions, Congress since 1945 has not been as responsive as it should to the requirements of U.S. security.

2742 Schilling, Warner. "The Politics of National Defense: Fiscal 1950." In Warner Schilling, Paul Hammond, and Glenn Snyder. *Strategy, Politics and Defense Budgets*. New York: Columbia University Press, 1962, pp. 1–266.

This study focuses on the role economics played in shaping political and, particularly, military decisions during the early Cold War years. Notes, index.

2743 Schrieber, Carl. "The Armed Services Procurement Act of 1947: An Administrative Study." Ph.D. dissertation, American University, 1964.

This act granted authority to the military departments to award contracts, in time of peace as well as in time of war, not only by the traditional method of competitive bidding, but also by the method of negotiation under certain circumstances enumerated in the act. DAI 25:4246.

Stockpiling Strategic Materials

2744 Cashier, Philip F. "Natural Resource Management During the Second World War, 1939–1947." Ph.D. dissertation, State University of New York, Binghamton, 1980.

As the war progressed, American leaders were concerned about future dependency upon other nations for vital raw materials. Consequently, the Strategic Materials Stockpiling Act and the National Security Act in 1947 created the first permanent peacetime agency to stockpile raw materials. DAI 40:6389-A.

2745 Kolodziej, Edward A. *The Uncommon Defense and Congress, 1945–1963*. Columbus: Ohio State University Press, 1966.

This study describes how Congress has participated in shaping defense policy, analyzes its review of defense proposals, and evaluates its annual appropriations bills. Chapters 2 to 4 deal with the Truman years and provide a rather thorough survey of defense issues. Appendix, notes, index.

2746 Lo, Clarence Y. H. "Theories of the State and Business Opposition to Increased Military Expending." *Social Problems* 29 (1982): 424–38.

Lo examines U.S. businessmen's opposition to increased military spending, 1948–53, which ultimately led to reduced expenditures. Notes.

2747 Snyder, Glenn H. "The Stockpiling of Strategic Materials: A Study of Civilian and Military Perspectives in the Formulation and Administration of National Security Policy." Ph.D. dissertation, Columbia University, 1956.

The chief purpose of this study is to compare the views of civilian and military participants in the stockpiling activity. Chapters are devoted to the background of the Stockpiling Act (1946), stockpile procurement (1946–50), organization and administration, the calculation of stockpile goals, and alternative means to raw materials security. DAI 16:2199.

THE ARMED SERVICES

See also Chapter 10, *The Korean War*, and Chapter 6, *Desegregation of Armed Forces*.

2748 Generous, William T. "Swords and Scales: The Development of the Uniform Code of Military Justice." Ph.D. dissertation, Stanford University, 1971.

The emphasis in this study is on the Uniform Code from its inception and enactment (1948–50) through the Supreme Court decision in *O'Callahan* v. *Parker* in June 1969. DAI 32:5174-A.

2749 Springarn, Jerome H. "Arms and Technology." *Current History* 33 (1957): 195–200.

This review of the technological development in weapons, 1946–57, focuses on nuclear arms, missiles, and chemical and biological warfare.

Air Force

2750 Borowski, Harry R. *A Hollow Threat: Strategic Air Power and Containment before Korea*. Westport, CT: Greenwood, 1982.

Air Force organization, training, and planning, from 1945 to 1950, are uncritically examined in this volume. Notes, bibliography, index.

2751 Bourgeois, Harold. "*Lucky Lady's* Secret Flight." *Aviation Quarterly* 6 (1980): 180–91.

The top-secret first around-the-world flight in 1949 by the *Lucky Lady II*, a Strategic Air Command Boeing B-50 under the command of Capt. James G. Gallagher, was made by midair refueling. Notes.

2752 Boyle, James M. "This Dreamboat Can Fly." *Aerospace Historian* 14 (1967): 85–92.

In the beginning of a series of long-distance army air force flights designed to prove the capabilities of U.S. aircraft and to show America's vulnerability to air attack, a B-29 named *Dreamboat* flew from Guam to Washington, DC on 9 November 1945, establishing a new record of 8,198 miles. Illustrations.

2753 Coker, William S. "The Extra-Super Block-buster." *Air University Review* 18 (1967): 61–68.

Coker provides an account of the development of the world's largest bomb (42,000 lbs.) from its inception with the design of the B-36 through its tests. Illustrations, notes.

2754 Davis, Shadrach E. "USAF War Readiness Material, 1946–1966." *Air University Review* 18 (1967): 10–16.

Since the Berlin airlift the air force has taken steps to ensure that ample stocks are prepositioned in units and at bases around the world. Illustrations.

2755 Eastman, James N., Jr. "Flight of the Lucky Lady II." *Aerospace Historian* 16 (1969): 9–11, 33–35.

The *Lucky Lady II* made the first round-the-world nonstop aircraft flight 26 February–2 March 1949. Five inflight refuelings demonstrated that the United States had a strategic bombing capability. The flight was part of the air force-navy battle over strategic airpower versus battleships. Map, illustrations.

2756 Green, Murray. "Stuart Symington and the B-36." Ph.D. dissertation, American University, 1960.

With the National Security Act (1947), Symington became the first secretary of the air force where he devoted his energies to the B-36 program. In December 1948 Symington and the USAF chiefs decided to maintain the Strategic Air Command at full operational level despite the cost to other air force missions. DAI 21:1541.

2757 Gross, Charles J. "Prelude to the Total Force: The Origins and Development of the Air National Guard, 1943–1969." Ph.D. dissertation, Ohio State University, 1979.

Prior to 1950, the Air National Guard failed to develop into a combat-ready force. Indeed, the mobilization fiasco during the Korean War moved the air force to expand its efforts to strengthen the guard. DAI 40:2223-A.

2758 Jacobsen, Meyers K. "The Red-Tailed Beauties of the 7th Bomb Wing." *American Aviation History Society Journal* 24 (1979): 19–40.

Jacobsen reviews the testing and mechanical alterations done by the Strategic Air Command (1946–48) in order to prepare the B-36 intercontinental bombers for duty.

2759 MacIsaac, David. *Strategic Bombing in World War Two: The Story of the United States Strategic Bombing Survey.* New York: Garland, 1976.

This introductory volume summarizes the author's (and the air force's) views of strategic bombing in World War II; it is supplemented with ten volumes of selected survey reports. Notes, bibliography, index.

2760 Miller, Edward A. "The Struggle for an Air Force Academy." *Military Affairs* 27 (1963): 163–73.

Although proposals for an air service academy appeared as early as 1919, it was not until 1948 that the air force began a serious campaign for a separate institution. The proposal met with heavy opposition during the Truman years.

2761 Moody, Walton S. "United States Air Force in Europe and the Beginning of the Cold War." *Aerospace Historian* 23 (1976): 75–85.

In January 1951 the Twelfth Air Force was formed to serve as the U.S. air component in NATO. Before this the function of the U.S. Air Force in Europe was largely property disposal; even the beginning of the Cold War in 1947 had not altered this primary mission. Illustration, notes.

2762 Sherman, Dennis M. "The National Security Act, A Blueprint for the Congressional Role in Weapons Development: A Case Study of the B-70 Bomber." Ph.D. dissertation, University of Wisconsin, 1978.

The creation of the Department of Defense by Congress via the National Security Act (1947) and its subsequent amendments was a major factor in the reduced influence of Congress over critical decisions concerning weapons development and procurement policies. DAI 39:3810-A.

2763 Wilson, Donald E. "The History of President Truman's Air Policy Commission and Its Influence on Air Policy, 1947–1949." Ph.D. dissertation, University of Denver, 1978.

The report dealt with military and civilian air policy and had its most immediate effect upon the former. The commission recommended a five-year seventy-group air force, but Truman trimmed this allocation to forty-eight groups. Many of the proposals for civil aviation were temporarily sidetracked, but most were eventually enacted. DAI 39:7488-A.

Army

2764 Arrington, Leonard J., and Alexander, Thomas G. "Sentinels on the Desert: The Dugway Proving Ground (1942–1963) and Deseret Chemical Depot (1942–1955)." *Utah Historical Quarterly* 32 (1964): 32–43.

These two army installations, built during World War II, were reduced in operation after 1945 only to resume operations (expanded operations at Dugway) at the outbreak of the Korean War.

2765 Lane, David A. "An Army Project in the Duty-Time General Education of Negro Troops in Europe, 1947–1951." *Journal of Negro Education* 32 (1964): 117–24.

The inception, growth, and demise of a U.S. Army special educational program for black troops in Europe is traced.

2766 Paddock, Alfred H., Jr. "Psychological and Unconventional Warfare, 1941–1952: Origins of a 'Special Warfare' Capability for the United States Army." Ph.D. dissertation, Duke University, 1980.

Paddock finds the origins of the Psychological Warfare Center, created in 1952, in the Office of Strategic Services, which had engaged in psychological and unconventional warfare during and after World War II. DAI 41:774.

2767 Paone, Rocco M. "The Last Volunteer Army, 1946–1948." *Military Review* 49 (1969): 9–17.

This essay reviews the use of popular recruitment techniques, and notes the continued decline in American military manpower during the period.

Navy

2768 Bruins, Bernard D. "U.S. Naval Bombardment Missiles, 1940–1958: A Study of the Weapons Innovation Process." Ph.D. dissertation, Columbia University, 1981.

Using hypotheses from several recent studies on technological innovations in advanced military weaponry, Bruins attempts to integrate some of those hypotheses into a framework for the analysis of the navy's bombardment missile programs. DAI 42:4136.

2769 Fick, Alvin S. "The Blue Angels: Diamonds and Deltas in the Sky." *Aviation Quarterly* 6 (1980): 276–304; 6:366–73, 6:384–92.

Part 1 describes the aircraft and personnel of the Blue Angels navy flight demonstration team, which originated as a recruiting and public relations program in 1946.

2770 Freund, James C. "The 'Revolt of the Admirals'." *Airpower Historian* 10 (1963): 1–10; 10:37–42.

This two-part essay focuses on the navy's reaction to Secretary of Defense Louis Johnson's cancellation of the construction of the aircraft carrier *United States* in April 1949. The admirals struck back at the House Armed Services Committee hearings (August to October 1949). At issue was the technique of waging total war. Notes.

2771 Hammond, Paul Y. "Super Carriers and B-36 Bombers: Appropriations, Strategy and Politics." In Harold Stein, ed. *American Civil-Military*

Decisions. Birmingham: University of Alabama Press, 1963, pp. 465–567.

Duplication and overlapping of functions among the armed services became a concern. Also there was conflict between the armed services and the administration over the level of strategic forces and appropriations to maintain those forces. Notes.

2772 Holloway, James L., Jr. "A Gentlemen's Agreement." *U.S. Naval Institute Proceedings* 106 (1980): 71–77.

The author assisted in the formulation of the navy's post-World War II policy to procure naval officers. The "Holloway Plan," reluctantly signed by Truman in August 1946, established 7,000 NROTC students. Illustrations, notes.

2773 McFarland, Keith D. "The 1949 Revolt of the Admirals." *Parameters* 11 (1981): 53–63.

The "mutiny" was the feud between the sea-based air power and the land-based air power which Truman's new secretary of defense, Louis A. Johnson, sparked by canceling the navy's new super aircraft carrier, the U.S.S. *United States*.

2774 Rosenberg, David A. "The U.S. Navy and the Problem of Oil in A Future War: The Outline of a Strategic Dilemma, 1945–1950." *Naval War College Review* 29 (1976): 53–64.

At the end of World War II, U.S. military planners realized that domestic oil supplies would be inadequate in another war, thus they turned their attention to gain access to Middle East oil reserves. Notes.

Atomic Arms: Control and Protest

See also Chapter 7, *Decision To Use A-Bombs;* and *Atomic Weapons and Strategy.*

2775 Duncan, Francis. "Atomic Energy and Anglo-American Relations, 1946–1954." *Orbis* 12 (1969): 1188–1203.

The Atomic Energy Act (McMahon Act) of 1946 had the effect of restricting the exchange of information with Britain, even though the British had been involved in the Manhattan Project. Notes.

2776 Erskins, Hazel G. "The Polls: Atomic Weapons and Nuclear Energy." *Public Opinion Quarterly* 27 (1963): 155–90.

The editor of *Public Opinion Quarterly* reproduces most of the nationally posed questions available on the subject of atomic weapons and nuclear energy (1945–63). Control of atomic energy and the moral aspects of the bomb predominated in the years 1945–50.

2777 Gowing, Margaret. *Independence and Deterrence: Britain and Atomic Energy, 1945–1952.* 2 vols. New York: St. Martin's Press, 1974.

This is an official history of the British atomic energy project, commissioned by the United Kingdom Atomic Energy Authority, and those volumes are a sequel to the author's *Britain and Atomic Energy, 1939–1945* (1964). Volume 1, "Policy Making," relates to the foreign policy issues, especially with the United States. Chronology, notes, index.

2778 Hewlett, Richard G., and Anderson, Oscar E., Jr. *A History of the United States Atomic Energy Commission.* Vol. 1: *The New World, 1939–1946.* University Park: Pennsylvania State University Press, 1962.

This useful official history explores the scientific and administrative background of the wartime development of the A-bomb. It also deals with the initial efforts to achieve international control of atomic weapons—the "Baruch Plan"—and the establishment of the Atomic Energy Commission. Illustrations, sources, notes, appendix (McMahon Bill), index.

2779 Hewlett, Richard G., and Duncan, Francis. *A History of the United States Atomic Energy Commission.* Vol. 2: *Atomic Shield, 1947–1952.* University Park: Pennsylvania State University Press, 1969.

The *Atomic Shield* covers the U.S. Atomic Energy Commission from the day it assumed responsibility for the nation's atomic energy program to detonation of the first thermonuclear device. This official history uses uncited documents, but it provides a glimpse into the commission's classified files, which are still largely unavailable to historians. Notes, table of organization, tables of production facilities, index, illustrations.

2780 Munro, John A., and Inglis, Alex I. "The Atomic Conference 1945 and the Pearson Memoirs." *International Journal* [Canada] 29 (1973/74): 90–109.

Long passages from two documents about Canadian-American discussions on atomic arms are quoted.

2781 Northrop, Robert M. "Administrative Doctrine and Administrative Behavior: the AEC Experience." Ph.D. dissertation, University of Michigan, 1957.

The original administrative doctrine, developed in 1946 by David E. Lilienthal, resulted in certain weaknesses and breakdowns in AEC

administration (1948–49); after several personnel changes (1950–51) doctrine came to be preached less often. DAI 18:1482.

2782 Sherwin, Martin. "The Atomic Bomb as History: An Essay Review." *Wisconsin Magazine of History* 53 (1969–1970): 128–34.

This essay examines Gar Alperovitz, *Atomic Diplomacy* (1965); M. Grodzins and E. Rabinowitch, *The Atomic Age* (1963); and N. P. Davis, *Lawrence and Oppenheimer* (1968).

ATOMIC SCIENTISTS AND POLICY

2783 Alexander, William M. "Influences of the Atomic Scientists on the Enactment of the Atomic Energy Act of 1946." Ph.D. dissertation, University of Oregon, 1963.

Scientists united into the Federation of American Scientists in order to influence legislation regarding atomic energy. Their belief was that atomic energy must be controlled by an international agency. DAI 23:4405.

2784 Cornwell, Clifton, Jr. "A Rhetorical Study of the Spokesmanship of Scientists in the Decade After Hiroshima." Ph.D. dissertation, University of Missouri, 1965.

Scientists drew upon two themes: that science was a proper concern of government, and that government was a proper concern of scientists. DAI 27:1954.

2785 Gilpin, Robert. *American Scientists and Nuclear Weapons Policy.* Princeton, NJ: Princeton University Press, 1962.

Gilpin's focus is on the scientist as a participant in political life and the intrascientific controversy over nuclear weapons. Notes, index.

2786 Nader, Claire M. "American Natural Scientists in the Policy Process: Three Atomic Energy Issues and their Foreign Policy Implications." Ph.D. dissertation, Columbia University, 1964.

The three issues examined are the debate over the Atomic Energy Law of 1946, the decision to build the hydrogen bomb, and the issues of peaceful uses of atomic energy (1955–58). DAI 26:7423.

2787 Nelson, William R. "Case Study of a Pressure Group: The Atomic Scientists." Ph.D. dissertation, University of Colorado, 1965.

Scientists were able successfully to influence defeat of the May-Johnson Bill, which they viewed as an open invitation to a military dictatorship and a disastrous arms race, and obtain passage of their own proposal, the McMahon Bill. However, military control was never really an issue, but was created by the scientists to sway public opinion. DAI 26:7424.

2788 Piccard, Paul J. "Scientists and Public Policy: Los Alamos, August–November, 1945." *Western Political Quarterly* 18 (1965): 251–62.

Soon after the A-bombs were dropped, the scientists at Los Alamos organized the Association of Los Alamos Scientists (ALAS) to inform officials and the public as to the magnitude of the new weapon. Five major ALAS documents are reprinted.

2789 Smith, Alice Kimball. *A Peril and a Hope: The Scientists' Movement in America, 1945–47.* Chicago: University of Chicago Press, 1965.

The Federation of Atomic Scientists was formed to engage in the political efforts to harness the atomic adventure to national and international controls. Appendixes, notes, index.

2790 Strickland, Donald A. *Scientists in Politics: The Atomic Scientists Movement, 1945–46.* West Lafayette, IN: Purdue University Studies, 1968.

This is a study of the reaction of the Manhattan Project scientists to the Truman administration's atomic energy bill in the fall of 1945 and to the attempted mobilization of the scientific community behind Senator Brien McMahon's atomic energy bill during the winter and spring of 1946.

2791 Wilson, R. R. "The Conscience of a Physicist." *Bulletin of the Atomic Scientists* 26 (1970): 30–34.

This essay describes how scientists' attitudes have become morally oriented since the explosion of the first A-bombs in 1945.

Biographies and Memoirs

This is only a sampling of personal accounts.

2792 Blumberg, Stanley A., and Owens, Gwinn. *Energy and Conflict: The Life and Times of Edward Teller.* New York: Putnam's, 1976.

This is a sympathetic biography of Teller; its observations regarding the H-bomb incident should be read in conjunction with Herbert York's *The Advisers* (1976). Illustration, notes, index.

2793 Bush, Vannevar. *Pieces of the Action.* New York: William Morrow, 1970.

Bush was an adviser on scientific matters to FDR and to Truman; however, this memoir (pp. 293–305) has little of great import on the Truman years.

2794 Compton, Arthur H. *Atomic Quest: A Personal Narrative.* New York: Oxford University Press, 1956.

Compton was one of the senior scientists involved in developing the A-bomb; he also suffered through the heart-searching decision on whether or not to use it. Illustrations, index.

2795 Conant, James B. *My Several Lives: Memoirs of a Social Inventor.* New York: Harper & Row, 1970.

Conant was involved in the Manhattan Project to develop an atomic bomb. After the war he served as a member of the General Advisory Committee to the Atomic Energy Commission. Appendixes, index.

2796 Davis, Nuell P. *Lawrence and Oppenheimer.* New York: Simon & Schuster, 1968.

The last one-third of this volume deals with the two scientists, the atomic bomb, and the Truman administration; its focus is upon the growing political and moral awareness of the scientists. Glossary, notes, bibliography, index.

2797 Newman, Steven L. "The Oppenheimer Case: A Reconsideration of the Role of the Defense Department and National Security." Ph.D. dissertation, New York University, 1977.

Few accounts have examined the strategic debates (1948–54) and few have attempted to synthesize these factors. Oppenheimer's major foes were proponents of air power doctrines who saw in him a threat to creating a massive deterrence force. DAI 38:2306-A.

2798 Wolfenstein, Lincoln. "The Tragedy of J. Robert Oppenheimer." *Dissent* 15 (1968): 81–85.

A biographical sketch of Oppenheimer (1929–67) is given, including his career as a scientist, his journey through the political spectrum, and the impact of the 1954 Atomic Energy Commission security hearings on his personality and career.

ATOMIC WEAPONS

2799 Mandelbaum, Michael. "The Bomb, Dread, and Eternity." *International Security* 5 (1980): 3–23.

The psychological impact of nuclear armaments since 1945 and the resulting threat of nuclear annihilation on American society are studied.

2800 Segal, Philip D. "Imaginative Literature and the Atomic Bomb: An Analysis of Representative Novels, Plays, and Films from 1945 to 1972." Ph.D. dissertation, Yeshiva University, 1973.

While before 1945 several writers had anticipated atomic bombs, after the Hiroshima explosion, several novels appeared—including James Hilton's *Nothing So Strange*, Pearl Buck's *Command the Morning*, and Upton Sinclair's *O Shepherd Speak!*

An intense literary protest followed the 1952 H-bomb testing. DAI 34:5993-A.

Atomic Tests

2801 Graybar, Lloyd J. "Bikini Revisited." *Military Affairs* 44 (1980): 118–23.

This analysis of Operation Crossroads, the detonation of two atomic weapons at Bikini Atoll in 1946, shows the origin, conduct, and effect of the tests. Militarily, the operation was a success for the navy (it had not become obsolete). Notes.

2802 Moll, Kenneth L. "Operation Crossroads." *Air Force Magazine* 54 (1971): 62–69.

This is a history of the initial post-World War II atomic bomb experiment conducted by the United States on Bikini Atoll from 1 July to 25 July 1946.

2803 O'Hara, Frederick M., Jr. "Attitudes of American Magazines toward Atmospheric Nuclear Testing, 1945–1965." Ph.D. dissertation, University of Illinois, Urbana-Champaign, 1974.

Some 900 magazine articles were examined in this quantitative study to measure the press's impact upon public policy. DAI 35:7337-A.

2804 Shurcliff, William A. *Bombs at Bikini: The Official Report of Operation Crossroads*. New York: Wise, 1947.

Shurcliff prepared an official account of the navy-sponsored tests on 1 July and 25 July 1946. Appendix and illustrations contain useful information. Index.

2805 Weisgall, Jonathan M. "The Nuclear Nomads of Bikini Atoll." *Foreign Policy* (1980): 74–98.

In 1946 the United States evacuated the Bikini islanders in order to use their homeland as a nuclear arms test site. Since then, the record of American dealings with the refugees has been one of "neglect, thwarted hopes, and unkept promises." Map.

H-Bomb Decision

2806 Eayrs, James. "Apocalypse Then: Aspects of Nuclear Weapons-Acquisition Policy Thirty Years Ago." *Dalhousie Review* [Canada] 59 (1979/80): 635–50.

In an anecdotal narrative of the development of the hydrogen bomb (1950–55), Eayrs emphasizes the opposition within the scientific community to the bomb's development. Notes.

2807 Rosenberg, David A. "American Atomic Strategy and the Hydrogen Bomb Decision." *Journal of American History* 66 (1979): 62–87.

This well-researched essay focuses on the military's role in the H-bomb decision. Truman's budget limitations on conventional alternatives indirectly made the United States virtually dependent upon atomic weapons. Notes.

2808 Schilling, Warner R. "The H-Bomb Decision: How to Decide Without Actually Choosing." *Political Science Quarterly* 76 (1961): 24–46.

This essay contains a good discussion of Truman's role in the decision to build the H-bomb.

2809 Shepley, James R., and Blair, Clay, Jr. *The Hydrogen Bomb: The Men, the Menace, the Mechanism*. Westport, CT: Greenwood, 1954.

The decision to build the H-bomb, especially the political controversies, is reviewed. Index.

2810 York, Herbert F. *The Advisors: Oppenheimer, Teller, and the Superbomb*. San Francisco: Freeman, 1976.

The Soviet atomic explosion in the fall of 1949 stimulated debate about a proper American response. This book examines the intellectual content of the debate, particularly the technical and strategic elements, and the significance of Truman's January 1950 decision to build the H-bomb. Appendix, notes, index.

ARMS CONTROL EFFORTS

See R. D. Burns, *Arms Control and Disarmament* (#3034) for bibliographical materials relating to arms control and disarmament policy.

2811 Bailey, Terrell W. "Inspection and Control of Nuclear Armaments in a Nation-State System: United States-Russian Disarmament Negotiations, 1945–1962." Ph.D. dissertation, University of Florida, 1963.

Disarmament negotiations since World War II have revolved around the issues of inspection and control. This study examines the reasons for the deadlock over these issues. DAI 24:5520.

2812 Bernstein, Barton J. "The Quest For Security: American Foreign Policy and International Control of Atomic Energy, 1942–1946." *Journal of American History* 60 (1974): 1003–44.

FDR made the decision not to share atomic energy secrets with the Soviet Union, although Henry L. Stimson considered promising such secrets in return for an opening of Soviet society. Truman later saw the United States as a trustee for the atomic bomb and, although he listened to Stimson and Acheson suggest a more open and direct approach, he was not inclined to share secrets which might end America's atomic monopoly. The Baruch Plan was designed to retain this monopoly. Notes.

2813 Bresler, Robert J. "American Policy toward International Control of Atomic Energy, 1945–1946." Ph.D. dissertation, Princeton University, 1964.

U.S. policy is traced through several important developments—including the decision not to initiate an exchange of scientific information with the Soviet Union and the failure to specify in the Acheson-Lilienthal-Baruch proposals when the United States would relinquish its atomic deterrent. DAI 26:1750.

2814 Lieberman, Joseph I. *The Scorpion and the Tarantula: The Struggle to Control Atomic Weapons, 1945–1949*. Boston: Houghton Mifflin, 1970.

The issues and events which marked the initial phase of discussions to control atomic weapons are summarized in this account. The United States and the Soviet Union are blamed equally for the resulting failure. Notes, bibliography, index.

Baruch Plan, 1946

See also Chapter 3 for *Dean Acheson* and *Bernard M. Baruch*.

2815 Anderson, Oscar E., Jr. "International Control of the Atom: Roots of a Policy." In *A Festschrift for Frederick B. Artz*. Durham, NC: Duke University Press, 1964, pp. 207–27.

The plan to seek international control of the atom originated with Vannevar Bush and James B. Conant, working behind the scenes. This essay uses the records of the U.S. Atomic Energy Commission to discuss events of 1945 and 1946.

2816 Gerber, Larry G. "The Baruch Plan and the Origins of the Cold War." *Diplomatic History* 6 (1982): 69–85.

Baruch and the Truman administration were moved by security interests and Wilsonian idealism in packaging the first plan for controlling atomic weapons. Fearing Soviet violations, American security interests called for U.S. monopoly until enforceable sanctions were agreed upon. Notes.

2817 Lilienthal, David E. *The Journals of David E. Lilienthal*. Vol. 2: *The Atomic Energy Years, 1945–1950*. New York: Harper & Row, 1964.

Lilienthal was chairman of the special State Department Board of Consultants which developed the basic American plan for international atomic control. Appendixes, index.

2818 Rosebury, Theodor. "Technology and the Failure of Disarmament." *Minority of One* 10 (1968): 23–27.

The author believes the first act of the Cold War was the dropping of the A-bombs on Japan, and that subsequent U.S. disarmament proposals such as the Baruch Plan (1946) were designed to hinder the development of atomic power in the Soviet Union. Illustrations, notes.

2819 U.S. House. Committee on Foreign Affairs. *The Baruch Plan: U.S. Diplomacy Enters the Nuclear Age*. Washington, DC: G.P.O., 1972.

This sixty-seven-page pamphlet provides a useful summary of the development of the first U.S. plan to control atomic weapons. Notes.

Other Arms Control Activities

2820 Landen, Walter J. "Geneva Conventions: The Broken Rules." *U.S. Naval Institute Proceedings* 99 (1973): 34–39.

The author examines the 1949 Geneva Conventions as they applied to naval combat, which are based on the premise that individuals who might become *hors de combat* are to be respected and protected. Illustrations.

2821 Parks, W. Hays. "The 1977 Protocols to the Geneva Convention of 1949." *Naval War College Review* 31 (1978): 17–27.

These recently ratified amendments to the original Convention of 1949 reflect the experiences of the last three decades with the legality of weapons, protection of medical transportation, and internal warfare.

2822 Reppy, Judith. "Military R&D: Institutions, Outputs, and Arms Control." *Policy Studies Journal* 8 (1979): 84–92.

This study traces the development (1940s–1970s) of America's military research and development program. It relates the services' emphasis upon technological superiority.

PACIFISM AND PACIFISTS

2823 Brooks, Jerrold L. "In Behalf of a Just and Durable Peace: The Attitudes of American Protestantism Toward War and Military-Related Affairs Involving the United States, 1945–1953." Ph.D. dissertation, Tulane University, 1977.

Although American Protestants exercised little influence on the development of American military policy during these years, they never ceased in their attempts to do so. They tended to see American civil liberties threatened by military domination of the society. DAI 38:2297-A.

2824 DeBenedetti, Charles. *The Peace Reform in American History*. Bloomington: Indiana University Press, 1980.

Chapter 7 of this survey focuses on the period 1941 to 1961. Notes, index.

2825 Dick, Everett N. "The Adventist Medical Cadet Corps As Seen By Its Founder." *Adventist Heritage* 1 (1974): 18–27.

The Adventist Medical Cadet Corps, founded in 1934, trained Adventist boys to serve in the army medical department, if conscripted, in order to avoid moral difficulties with bearing arms and Sabbath observance on active duty. It covers World War II and Korean War service.

2826 Dunn, Joe P. "The Church and the Cold War: Protestants and Conscription, 1940–1955." Ph.D. dissertation, University of Missouri, Columbia, 1973.

In the postwar years the churches took stands on most Cold War issues and demonstrated decided opposition to the hard-line, anti-Communist foreign and military policies of the Truman and Eisenhower administrations. They managed to defeat the Universal Military Training bill four times during the Truman years. DAI 35:1001-A.

2827 Hentoff, Nat. *Peace Agitator: The Story of A. J. Muste*. New York: Macmillan, 1963.

Muste was one of the leading pacifists during the Truman era. He advocated burning of draft cards, unilateral disarmament, and nonviolent resistance.

2828 Larson, Zell A. "An Unbroken Witness: Conscientious Objection to War, 1948–1953." Ph.D. dissertation, University of Hawaii, 1975.

This study examines the laws governing conscientious objection (1948–52), the treatment of men claiming conscientious scruples against war during the period, and the work of peace agencies on behalf of draft-age pacifists as they confronted another era of conscription and war. DAI 36:6265-A.

2829 Thomas, Norman. *Appeal to the Nations*. New York: Holt, 1947.

The Socialist party leader pleads for disarmament and the renunciation of war. The book is largely concerned with improving the United Nations in order to prevent another war. Notes.

2830 Wittner, Lawrence S. *Rebels Against War: The American Peace Movement, 1941–1960*. New York: Columbia University Press, 1969.

The first half of this volume deals with the American peace movement during World War II and the Truman years. Attention is paid to the fate of conscientious objectors and early nuclear pacifism. Notes, bibliography, index.

US infantrymen moving into the Naktong River area past a line of South Korean refugees, August 1950. *Reproduced courtesy of UPI/Bettmann Archives.*

10

The Korean War

The Korean War, sandwiched as it was between World War II and the Vietnam conflict, is almost a forgotten struggle. Yet its battlefields witnessed as desperately fought battles as any war, and its armistice negotiations were as bitterly contested as any diplomatic engagement in history. While the diplomacy, combat, and politics of the Korean conflict (1950–53) are discussed in this chapter, the preceding years of American occupation of Korea (1945–50) are discussed in Chapter 8, "The United States and the Korean Occupation, 1945–50."

General accounts which survey the conflict include Joseph Lawton Collins, *War in Peacetime: The History and Lessons of Korea* (#2832), written from the vantage point of the Joint Chiefs of Staff; Joseph C. Goulden, *Korea: The Untold Story of the War* (#2837), which emphasizes diplomatic and political events; and Allen Guttmann, ed., *Korea: Cold War and Limited War* (#2838), whose selections focus on issues and personalities. How hostilities were initiated and with whose approval is still a matter of historical inquiry; consequently, R. Swartout, Jr., "American Historians and the Outbreak of the Korean War" (#2858) provides a useful historiographical survey.

The political history of the Korean conflict includes Truman's firing of General MacArthur, the truce negotiations, and the public's opinion of America's involvement in a "limited" war. The Truman-MacArthur relationship has been dealt with in several accounts, but a notable introduction to the issues is John W. Spanier, *The Truman-MacArthur Controversy and the Korean War* (#2906). The controversial Wake Island meeting between the two men is reviewed by John E. Wiltz, "Truman and MacArthur: The Wake Island Meeting" (#2909). The armistice negotiations were complicated, intense, and protracted. C. Turner Joy, *How Communists Negotiate* (#2984), and William H. Vatcher, Jr., *Panmunjom:*

The Story of the Korean Military Armistice Negotiations (#2986) survey the issues.

Domestic politics influenced the conduct of the war and were in turn influenced by the conduct of the war. John E. Wiltz, "The Korean War and American Society" (#2924) reviews the home front, while Ronald J. Caridi, *The Korean War and American Politics: The Republican Party as a Case Study* (#2877) finds the war becoming a partisan issue. Economic measures to control inflation are discussed in Chapter 4, under "Wage Stabilization (Korean War)."

Studies are becoming available on the roles of other nations caught up in the Korean conflict. Robert O'Neill, *Australia in the Korean War, 1950–53*. Vol. 1: *Strategy and Diplomacy* (#2869) discusses how and why the Australian government decided to participate in the conflict, while Denis Stairs, *The Diplomacy of Constraint: Canada, the Korean War, and the United States* (#2872) similarly examines Canada's embroilment in the contest. The Soviet Union and the People's Republic of China were also intimately involved in the Korean War as is demonstrated by Robert R. Simmons, *The Strained Alliance: Peking, P'yŏngyang, Moscow and the Politics of the Korean Civil War* (#2870).

Truman's decision to intervene militarily in the Korean conflict has been much reviewed; however, Glenn D. Paige, *The Korean Decision: June 24–30, 1950* (#2890) provides a useful introduction, while James I. Matray, "America's Reluctant Crusade: Truman's Commitment of Combat Troops in the Korean War" (#2888) takes a broad look at the consequences of this decision. Truman's decision to allow MacArthur to cross the 38th parallel is analyzed in James I. Matray, "Truman's Plan for Victory: National Self-Determination and the Thirty-Eighth Parallel Decision in Korea" (#2899).

There are a number of accounts which survey combat operations. Among those which are solid introductions to issues and events are T. R. Fehren-bach, *This Kind of War: A Study in Unpreparedness* (#2929), Robert Leckie, *Conflict: The History of the Korean War, 1950–1953* (#2934), and David Rees, *Korea: The Limited War* (#2943). Additionally, Matthew B. Ridgway, *The Korean War: How We Met the Challenge* (#2945) provides a view of the fighting from the top echelon. General MacArthur's masterful counterattack at Inchon is described by Robert D. Heinl, Jr., *Victory at High Tide: The Inchon-Seoul Campaign* (#2952).

Contemporary charges of American employ-ment of "germ warfare" and the collaboration of American prisoners of war with their captors have never completely faded away. While American offi-cials repeatedly denied that their forces had intro-duced biological warfare into the Korean conflict, Stephen L. Endicott, "Germ Warfare and 'Plausible Denial': The Korean War, 1952–1953" (#2973) is an example of continuing suggestions that American authorities might not have been fully honest in their denials. A useful introduction to this matter may be found in the Stockholm International Peace Research Institute, *The Problem of Chemical and Biological Warfare* (#2977). The charge that American POWs collaborated with the enemy has been examined by A. D. Biderman, *March to Calumny: The Story of American POWs in the Korean War* (#2988), while W. C. Bradbury, *Mass Behavior in Battle and Cap-tivity: The Communist Soldier in the Korean War* (#2989) reviews the other side's defections.

General Accounts

See also C. Blanchard, *Korean War Bibliog-raphy and Maps of Korea* (#3040); R. W. Leopold, "The Korean War: The Historian's Task" (#3041); and Hong-Kyu Park, *The Korean War* (#3042).

2831   Bell, Coral. "Korea and the Balance of Power." *Political Quarterly* 25 (1954): 17–29.
Truman's decision to fight in Korea is placed in a broader postwar perspective.

2832   Collins, J. Lawton. *War in Peacetime: The History and Lessons of Korea.* Boston: Houghton Mifflin, 1969.
Collins was chief of staff of the U.S. Army and a member of the Joint Chiefs of Staff throughout the Korean War. He presents the war from the view-point of the Joint Chiefs of Staff. Illustrations, bib-liography, index.

2833   Dille, John. *Substitute for Victory.* Garden City, NY: Doubleday, 1954.
A war correspondent seeks to put the "limited" nature of the Korean War in perspective. He finds it a "good war," one that "had to be fought."

2834   Dingman, Roger. "Strategic Planning and the Policy Process: American Plans for War in East Asia, 1945–1950." *Naval War College Review* 32 (1979): 4–21.
Plans developed between World War II and the Korean War influenced strategic thinking about war in East Asia for the next two decades; thus, consideration of how and why they were developed should be instructive to contemporary planners and military professionals.

2835   Fehrenbach, T. R. *The Fight for Korea: From the War of 1950 to the Pueblo Incident.* New York: Grosset & Dunlap, 1969.
In 1968 North Koreans captured the U.S. Navy vessel *Pueblo*. Fehrenbach attempts to explain the 1968 hostilities by examining the origins and devel-opments of the Korean War. Illustrations, index.

2836   Gardner, Lloyd C., ed. *The Korean War.* New York: Quadrangle, 1972.
Gardner presents contemporary essays and government pronouncements which recapture the widespread assumption that the Korean War was the opening of the Communist offensive for world con-quest. Index.

2837   Goulden, Joseph C. *Korea: The Untold Story of the War.* New York: Times Books, 1982.
Untold Story does not deal with military oper-ations in any systematic fashion; however, it does provide a considerable amount of diplomatic and political information regarding the contest between MacArthur and the high command over war policies. Notes, index.

2838   Guttmann, Allen, ed. *Korea: Cold War and Limited War.* 2d ed. Lexington, MA: Heath, 1972.
These edited selections capture the contem-porary and retrospective issues, personalities, and viewpoints. Bibliography.

2839   Heller, Francis H., ed. *The Korean War: A 25-Year Perspective.* Lawrence: Regents Press of Kansas, 1977.
This book is the record of a conference held in May 1975 by the Harry S. Truman Library Institute for the purpose of bringing together as many as pos-sible of the major participants to hear their recollec-tions. A bibliographical/historiographical essay by Richard W. Leopold reviews the writings on the war. Illustrations, list of participants, chronology, index.

2840 Kim, Chum-kon. *The Korean War: The First Comprehensive Account of the Historical Background and Development of the Korean War (1950–53)*. Seoul: Kwangmyong Publishing Co., 1973.

Prepared by a professor of international relations at Kyunghee University, this study shows how difficult it is to escape national ideologies and passions. He has written an account of the war from the South's point of view. Illustrations, appendix.

2841 Lawson, Don. *The United States in the Korean War: Defending Freedom's Frontier*. New York: Abelard-Schuman, 1964.

This popular account benefits very little from earlier research and perceptions; it does, however, contain a list of Medal of Honor winners (131). Chronology, illustrations.

2842 Mitchell, C. Clyde. *Korea: Second Failure in Asia*. Washington, DC: Public Affairs Institute, 1951.

The author of this slight monograph states that the experience of the United States in Korea shows that the advance of Soviet imperialism can be halted.

2843 Oliver, Robert T. *Why War Came in Korea*. New York: Fordham University Press, 1950.

Oliver regards the Korean War as the result of a series of muffed opportunities and an unwillingness to stand up to Russia with strength and determination.

2844 Park, Chang Jin. "American Foreign Policy in Korea and Vietnam: Comparative Case Studies." *Review of Politics* 37 (1975): 20–47.

The United States sought to repel Communist expansion in both Korea and Vietnam by a gradualistic policy of intervention, according to the author. The Nixon-Kissinger team saw the Vietnam War as a conflict of nation-states, rather than of moral forces. Notes.

2845 Park, Chang Jin. "Seoul and Washington: A Study of Intra-Alliance Politics." Ph.D. dissertation, University of Washington, 1972.

This study is confined to the problems of Korea from 1950 to 1953, the duration of the Korean conflict. Particular emphasis is placed upon the complicated policies undertaken by the United States during the war, and to the extremely intricate alliance relationship between the United States and the Republic of Korea. DAI 33:2467-A.

2846 Park, Hong-Kyu. "American-Korean Relations, 1949–1953." Ph.D. dissertation, North Texas State University, 1981.

American policy in Korea initially was to restore South Korea's border. Only after the Inchon landing did the United States decide to cross the 38th parallel, but when faced with Chinese Communist intervention

it gave up the idea of unifying Korea militarily. DAI 42:1285.

2847 Poats, Rutherford M. *Decision in Korea*. New York: McBride, 1954.

This strident defense of Truman's decision to use American military forces in Korea perceives the Korean War within the context of the Cold War. Poats sees America's military response in Korea as a rebuff of the Soviet Union. Maps, appendix, index.

2848 Simmons, Robert S. "The Communist Side: An Exploratory Sketch." In F. H. Heller, ed. *The Korean War: A 25-Year Perspective*. Lawrence: Regents Press of Kansas, 1977, pp. 197–208.

This essay reviews the forces which might have affected the unity of purpose within the Communist bloc. Notes.

2849 Smith, Gaddis. "A History Teacher's Reflections on the Korean War." *Ventures* 8 (1968): 57–65.

The Truman administration succeeded in maintaining military restraint—at least A-bombs were not used, the fighting was contained in Korea, and NATO was established. The Korean venture proved that U.S. military force could alter Soviet and Chinese behavior; the Korean War provided the model President Johnson would apply in Vietnam.

2850 Smith, Robert. *MacArthur in Korea: The Naked Emperor*. New York: Simon & Schuster, 1982.

Smith is critical of the role played by General MacArthur in the Korean War.

2851 Stone, I. F. *The Hidden History of the Korean War*. New York: Monthly Review Press, 1952.

Stone's account is both a contemporary history and a personal statement about the origins of the Korean War and the initial months of the war. Notes, index.

2852 Toner, James H. "Candide as Constable: The American Way of War and Peace in Korea, 1950–1953." Ph.D. dissertation, University of Notre Dame, 1976.

Foreign and military policy must emanate from, and be complementary to that cluster of core values in terms of which the nation articulates its existence. This hypothesis is examined against the background of American involvement in the origins, prosecution, and "settlement" of the Korean War. DAI 37:1211-A.

2853 Warner, Geoffrey. "The Korean War." *International Affairs* [Great Britain] 56 (1980): 98–107.

This retrospective view of the Korean conflict focuses on Sino-Soviet-American involvement.

2854 Whiting, Allen S. *China Crosses the Yalu: The Decision to Enter the Korean War*. New York: Macmillan, 1960.

The Korean War conditioned the manner in which Mao Tse-tung subsequently evaluated the role of China in Asia, the nature of the Sino-Soviet alliance, and relations with the United States. Notes, bibliography, index.

OUTBREAK OF WAR: HISTORIOGRAPHICAL ACCOUNTS

2855 Gupta, Karunakar. "How Did the Korean War Begin?" *China Quarterly* (1972): 699–716.

An historiographical account of various writers' theories and opinions, this essay provides a useful survey. Notes.

2856 Soh, Jin Chull. "Some Causes of the Korean War of 1950: A Case Study of Foreign Policy in Korea (1945–1950) with Emphasis on Sino-Soviet Collaboration." Ph.D. dissertation, University of Oklahoma, 1963.

The North Korean attack was a carefully planned incident in Sino-Soviet expansion and a key to the Communist program for exploitation of the Communist victory in China as a basis for Communist victory in the entire Far East. DAI 24:2551.

2857 Stueck, William. "Cold War Revisionism and the Origins of the Korean Conflict: The Kolko Thesis." *Pacific Historical Review* 42 (1973): 537–60.

The Kolkos argue, in their *The Limits of Power* (1972), that an aggressive President Syngman Rhee provoked the attack by North Korea. Stueck concludes that this thesis "does not stand up well in the face of either the available evidence or rational speculation." Rejoinders (pp. 566–75) by both parties continue the debate. Notes.

2858 Swartout, Robert, Jr. "American Historians and the Outbreak of the Korean War: An Historiographical Essay." *Asia Quarterly* [Belgium] (1979): 65–77.

Historians have divided over who started the Korean War. Allen S. Whiting, Adam B. Ulam, John W. Spanier, and Walter LaFeber head a school which holds that the U.S.S.R. planned and ordered the initial North Korean strike southward on 25 June 1950. A second school, led by I. F. Stone, D. F. Fleming, David Horowitz, and Joyce and Gabriel Kolko, holds that South Korea's strongman Syngman Rhee and Douglas MacArthur were responsible. The author suggests that North Korea's Kim Il-song planned and carried out the invasion.

2859 Temple, Harry. "Deaf Captains, Intelligence, Policy, and the Origins of the Korean War." *International Studies Notes* (1981–82): 19–23.

NSC-68's (see Chapter 7) focus on world views is used as an example of why American leaders ignored the explosive situation building in Korea, 1948–50.

LIMITED WAR CONCEPT

2860 Elowitz, Larry, and Spanier, John W. "Korea and Vietnam: Limited War and the American Political System." *Orbis* 18 (1974): 510–34.

This comparative study surveys Truman's problems in gaining support for the Korean War. Notes.

2861 Halperin, Morton H. *Limited War in the Nuclear Age*. New York: Wiley, 1963.

Chapter 3 examines the concept of "limited" war in the sense of preventing escalation of the fighting from reaching territory beyond Korea or the introduction of atomic weapons. Notes, index.

2862 Lai, Nathan Yu-jen. "United States Policy and the Diplomacy of Limited War in Korea, 1950–1951." Ph.D. dissertation, University of Massachusetts, 1974.

This study focuses on *how* and *why* decisions were made to keep the military operations limited. DAI 35:6221-A.

2863 Marshall, Thomas L. "The Strategy of Conflict in the Korean War." Ph.D. dissertation, University of Virginia, 1969.

Marshall's basic premise is that limited wars are a type of bargaining process in which two things are being bargained for: the conduct of the war and the outcome. DAI 31:1348-A.

2864 Martin, Wayne R. "An Analysis of United States International Relations before and during Limited War." Ph.D. dissertation, University of Southern California, 1970.

Martin concludes that there was not a major change in U.S. international relations associated with its involvement in Korea and Vietnam. DAI 31: 6163-A.

2865 Osgood, Robert E. *Limited War: The Challenge to American Strategy*. Chicago: University of Chicago Press, 1957.

Chapter 8 applies the "lessons" of the Korean conflict to the theory of limited war. Notes, index.

2866 Wood, Hugh G. "American Reaction to Limited War in Asia: Korea and Vietnam, 1950–1968." Ph.D. dissertation, University of Colorado, 1974.

This is an impressionistic study of the evolution of American thought toward the concept of limited war and the policy of containment in Asia. DAI 35:2205-A.

THE UNITED NATIONS AND OTHER GOVERNMENTS' ROLES

2867 Heimsath, Charles H., IV. "India's Role in the Korean War." Ph.D. dissertation, Yale University, 1957.

Heimsath analyzes India's participation in the Korean War and in the prisoner exchange operation under the armistice agreement.

2868 Lyons, Gene M. *Military Policy and Economic Aid: The Korean Case, 1950–1953.* Columbus, OH: Ohio State University Press, 1961.

During the Korean War, the twin policies of military civil relief and economic aid (United Nations Reconstruction Agency) came into conflict as the war protracted. Lyons looks at these two contradictory forces, how they were met, and whether the outcome was in the best interests of the United States. Notes, appendixes, bibliography, index.

2869 O'Neill, Robert. *Australia in the Korean War, 1950–53.* Vol. 1: *Strategy and Diplomacy.* Canberra: Australian War Memorial and Australian Government Publishing Service, 1981.

This is the first volume of a projected series dealing with the contributions and controversies associated with Australian participation in the Korean War. How and why Australia chose to participate is detailed in this volume. Notes, bibliography, index.

2870 Simmons, Robert R. *The Strained Alliance: Peking, P'yŏngyang, Moscow and the Politics of the Korean Civil War.* New York: Free Press, 1975.

While recognizing that both Moscow and Peking were intimately involved in the Korean War, this volume stresses the essential "civil" nature of the conflict. Notes, bibliography, index.

2871 Stairs, Denis. "Canada and the Korean War: The Boundaries of Diplomacy." *International Perspectives* [Canada] (1972): 25–32.

Canadian diplomats sought to alter U.S. policies by working through the United Nations.

2872 Stairs, Denis. *The Diplomacy of Constraint: Canada, the Korean War, and the United States.* Toronto: University of Toronto Press, 1974.

With the U.N. involvement in the Korean War, Canada became embroiled in the war. Stairs looks at Canada's attempt to moderate the exercise of U.S. power. Notes, bibliography, index.

2873 Stairs, Denis. "The United Nations and the Politics of the Korean War." *International Journal* 25 (1970): 302–20.

Stairs argues that the U.S. decision to conduct the Korean War under U.N. auspices altered significantly the decision-making environment in which American policymakers had to operate. Notes.

2874 Wood, Herbert F. *Strange Battleground: Official History of the Canadian Army in Korea.* Ottawa: Queen's Printer, 1966.

The operations of the Canadian Special Service Brigade in Korea are detailed here. It is largely an account of military operations. Notes, bibliography, index.

2875 Yoo, Tae-Lc. *The Korean War and the United Nations: A Legal and Diplomatic Historical Study.* Louvain: Librairie Desbarax, 1965.

The author is concerned with the legal basis for U.N. intervention in Korea, the material and technical problems involved in intervention by the world body, the influence of power politics on U.N. collective security, and various legal questions involved in the participation of U.N. forces in the conflict.

U.S. Politics and Public Opinion

2876 Caridi, Ronald J. "The G.O.P. and the Korean War." *Pacific Historical Review* 37 (1968): 423–43.

The Republicans were generally happy with Truman's initial decision to intervene in Korea to stop Communist aggression; however, the honeymoon period began to change when Communist forces pushed U.N. troops into the Pusan Perimeter. This essay looks at the reasons and motives for subsequent Republican attitudes. Notes.

2877 Caridi, Ronald J. *The Korean War and American Politics: The Republican Party as a Case Study.* Philadelphia: University of Pennsylvania Press, 1968.

This study focuses on the Republican party's response to the Korean War and its use of the war as a political issue. Notes, appendixes, index.

2878 Lo, Clarence Yin Hsieh. "The Truman Administration's Military Budgets During the Korean

War." Ph.D. dissertation, University of California, Berkeley, 1978.

This study examines the causes and consequences of the quadrupling of the U.S. military budget during the Korean War. The fighting in Korea was only a partial explanation, because most of the increase was used to augment the general military strength of the United States and its allies. DAI 40:471-A.

2879 Lofgren, Charles A. "Congress and the Korean Conflict." Ph.D. dissertation, Stanford University, 1966.

Congressmen did not see that the Korean War was a standing challenge to the concept of total war which had dominated American military thinking since World War II. DAI 27:1017.

2880 McLellan, David S. "Dean Acheson and the Korean War." *Political Science Quarterly* 83 (1968): 16–39.

This critical evaluation finds that Acheson miscalculated Peking's motives and intentions, and thus failed to provide Truman with a realistic assessment of the situation in 1950. The author is particularly critical of Acheson's failure to push early for General MacArthur's removal. Notes.

2881 Riggs, James R. "Congress and the Conduct of the Korean War." Ph.D. dissertation, Purdue University, 1972.

Congress debated the issues relating to the conduct of the Korean War (1950–53). The author explores most of the debates, including Truman's proclamation of a national emergency which gave the president extensive powers to control the nation's economy and the "Great Debate" which focused on the decision to send four combat divisions to Europe and the recall of General MacArthur, both in 1951. DAI 33:706-A.

2882 Seltzer, Robert V. "The Truman-Johnson Analog: A Study of Presidential Rhetoric in Limited War." Ph.D. dissertation, Wayne State University, 1976.

This study attempts to discover what characteristics were common to attempts by presidents to justify limited wars to the American public. DAI 37:2500-A.

2883 U.S. Department of State. *United States Policy in the Korean Conflict, July 1950–February 1951.* Office of Public Affairs. Publ. 4263. Far Eastern Series 44. Washington, DC: G.P.O., September 1951.

This pamphlet collects some thirty published documents, including U.N. resolutions. Together with a similar pamphlet, *United States Policy in the Korean Crisis* (Publ. 3922, Far Eastern Series 34) issued in July 1950, this collection covers most of the major announced decisions. It also contains a chronology

of major events from 25 June 1950 to 1 February 1951.

DECISION TO INTERVENE

2884 Bernstein, Barton J. "The Week We Went to War: American Intervention in the Korean Civil War." *Foreign Service Journal* 54 (1977): 6–9, ff.

Truman and Acheson are the focal point of this review of the decision to send U.S. troops to aid South Korea.

2885 George, Alexander L. "American Policy-Making and the North Korean Aggression." *World Politics* 7 (1955): 209–32.

George's essay remains the best brief discussion of Truman's decision to send U.S. armed forces into the Korean conflict. Notes.

2886 Hoyt, Edwin C. "The United States Reaction to the Korean Attack: A Study in the Principles of the United Nations Charter as a Factor in American Policy-Making." *American Journal of International Law* 55 (1961): 45–76.

This case study of the principles of the U.N. charter focuses on those aspects which served as an incentive to the action which resulted in U.S. military intervention in 1950. Notes.

2887 Lofgren, Charles A. "Mr. Truman's War: A Debate and Its Aftermath." *Review of Politics* 31 (1969): 223–41.

In the debate over the legal basis of Truman's commitment of U.S. military forces in Korea on 27 June 1950, the administration seemed to suggest that the president derived at least some of his authority from U.N. Security Council resolutions regarding the Korean fighting. Republican Senators Robert A. Taft, Karl Mundt, Arthur V. Watkins, and others argued that Congress must approve U.S. participation in U.N. wars. Notes.

2888 Matray, James I. "America's Reluctant Crusade: Truman's Commitment of Combat Troops in the Korean War." *Historian* 42 (1980): 437–55.

Truman's decision to use combat troops to meet North Korea's attack marked the beginning of U.S. dependence on military intervention rather than nationalism and indigenous hostility to Soviet domination as the best method for combating international communism. Notes.

2889 May, Ernest R. *"Lessons" of the Past: The Use and Misuse of History in American Foreign Policy.* New York: Oxford University Press, 1973.

Chapter 3, "Korea, 1950: History Overpowering Calculation," deals with Truman's decision to commit U.S. military forces to Korea in June 1950. Notes.

2890 Paige, Glenn D. *The Korean Decision: June 24–30, 1950.* New York: Free Press, 1968.

Paige has woven together a most useful reconstruction of upper echelon decision-making activities within the Truman administration. Notes, bibliography, index. See Paige's own critical review of his book in *American Political Science Review* 71 (1977): 1603–9.

2891 Snyder, Richard C., and Paige, Glenn D. "The United States Decision to Resist Aggression in Korea." In R. C. Snyder, et al. *Foreign Policy Decision Making: An Approach to the Study of International Politics.* New York: Free Press, 1962, pp. 206–49.

The authors are interested in the period from 24 June 1950 to 30 June 1950 when Truman made the decision to commit military power to resist the invasion of South Korea by North Korean forces. They focus on why a decision was made and why this particular decision was made. Notes.

2892 Warner, Albert L. "How the Korean Decision Was Made." *Harper's* (June 1951): 99–106.

The priorities and alternatives facing Truman in June 1950 when he had to decide whether or not to send U.S. forces into Korea are recounted.

DECISION TO CROSS 38TH PARALLEL

2893 Bernstein, Barton J. "The Policy of Risk: Crossing the 38th Parallel and Marching to the Yalu." *Foreign Service Journal* 54 (1977): 16–22, 29.

Foreign policy and military policy are discussed (1950–52), focusing on the actions of Truman, Acheson, and MacArthur.

2894 Flint, Roy K. "The Tragic Flaw: MacArthur, the Joint Chiefs, and the Korean War." Ph.D. dissertation, Duke University, 1976.

The purpose of this study is to determine why, after intervening in a local war against a minor Asian power, the United States and its U.N. allies found themselves in a war with China. Study concludes that Truman's decision to cross the 38th parallel was the decisive act. DAI 37:1143-A.

2895 Krasner, Michael A. "Foreign Policy Stereotypes: The Decision to Cross the 38th Parallel." *Military Review* 52 (1972): 17–26.

The author argues that the Truman administration's decision to permit General MacArthur's U.N. forces to cross the 38th parallel and to unite the Korean people was predicated on the belief that the Chinese

people shared our democratic ideology, were historically allied with the American people, and, consequently, would not take military action.

2896 LaFeber, Walter. "Crossing the 38th Parallel: The Cold War in Microcosm." In Lynn H. Miller and Ronald W. Pruessen, eds. *Reflections on the Cold War: A Quarter Century of American Foreign Policy.* Philadelphia: Temple University Press, 1974, pp. 71–90.

The American decision to cross the 38th parallel with military forces signaled a new, global nature to America's view of the Cold War. Notes.

2897 Lichterman, Martin. *To the Yalu and Back.* Indianapolis: Bobbs-Merrill, 1963.

This study describes the series of civil and military decisions relating to operations in Korea in the fall and winter of 1950–51. Its focus is on the limits placed on the land forces and the extent to which Washington-based authorities determined the policies of the field commanders. Notes. Also in Harold Stein, ed., *American Civil-Military Decisions.* University: University of Alabama Press, 1963, pp. 568–631.

2898 Lo, Clarence Y. H. "Civilian Policy Makers and Military Objectives: A Case Study of the U.S. Offensive to Win the Korean War." *Journal of Political and Military Sociology* 7 (1979): 229–42.

Recently declassified documents do not support the traditional interpretation that attributes the offensive to MacArthur's insubordination and a breakdown of civilian control of the military. Notes.

2899 Matray, James I. "Truman's Plan for Victory: National Self-Determination and the Thirty-Eighth Parallel Decision in Korea." *Journal of American History* 66 (1979): 314–33.

Truman's decision to cross the 38th parallel seemed to guarantee for all Koreans the right of national self-determination and would allow them to choose the U.S. model, not the Soviet, for their future development. A decisive victory in Korea was seen as a major defeat for the Soviets. Notes.

TRUMAN DISMISSES MacARTHUR

See also Chapter 3, *Douglas MacArthur.*

2900 Harris, Merne A. "The MacArthur Dismissal: A Study in Political Mail." Ph.D. dissertation, University of Iowa, 1966.

Mail ran 45 percent pro dismissal and 55 percent con. Those in favor of dismissal felt that the president had affirmed the constitutionally delegated authority of civilian over military leadership, while those who objected took the president's total foreign policy as their point of attack. DAI 27:1319.

2901 Higgins, Trumbull. *Korea and the Fall of MacArthur: A Precis in Limited War.* New York: Oxford University Press, 1960.

Higgins sees MacArthur's failure as resulting not from flaws in his arguments for extending the war, but from his inability as a subordinate to convince the Truman administration of his desired ends. Notes, bibliography, index.

2902 Jessup, Philip C. "The Record of Wake Island: A Correction." *Journal of American History* 67 (1981): 866–70.

William Manchester claims in his *American Caesar: Douglas MacArthur, 1880–1964* that a secretary took secret notes of the meeting between Truman and MacArthur on Wake Island in October 1950. Jessup argues that had Manchester consulted the official record of the meeting he would not have made the error. Notes.

2903 Lowitt, Richard, ed. *The Truman-MacArthur Controversy.* Chicago: Rand McNally, 1967.

Using public documents and published statements issued by MacArthur and Truman, Lowitt presents the controversy which led to the firing of MacArthur. Bibliographical essay.

2904 Rovere, Richard H., and Schlesinger, Arthur M., Jr. *The General and the President; and the Future of American Foreign Policy.* New York: Farrar, Straus and Young, 1951.

Truman's dismissal of MacArthur was one of the most controversial issues during his tenure, prompting Senate hearings on the dismissal. The authors examine the controversy and its effect on American foreign policy. Appendixes, index.

2905 Ryan, Halford R. "Harry S. Truman: A Misdirected Defense for MacArthur's Dismissal." *Presidential Studies Quarterly* 11 (1981): 576–82.

In his speech of 11 April 1951, Truman spent little time justifying his decision to dismiss MacArthur. This was a serious mistake, and an instance in which Truman's persuasive powers fell far short of that needed for strong presidential power. Notes.

2906 Spanier, John W. *The Truman-MacArthur Controversy and the Korean War.* Cambridge, MA: Harvard University Press, 1959.

Spanier examines the Truman-MacArthur controversy by analyzing the basic decisions the American policymakers had to make during the Korean War, most notably the decision to repel the North Korean invasion by force. More fundamentally, the author probes the problems of civil-military relations during a limited war. Notes, bibliography, index.

2907 Thompson, Mark E. "The Truman-MacArthur Controversy: A Bibliographical Essay." *Studies in History and Society* 5 (1974): 66–73.

The reasons why Truman removed MacArthur from his command are examined, as well as the views of the general's supporters and detractors. The author suggests that the controversy clearly reveals the political problems inherent in limited warfare. Notes.

2908 Wiltz, John E. "The MacArthur Hearings of 1951: The Secret Testimony." *Military Affairs* 39 (1975): 167–73.

The secret testimony reveals that military leaders in Washington disagreed with MacArthur's views. Notes.

2909 Wiltz, John E. "Truman and MacArthur: The Wake Island Meeting." *Military Affairs* 42 (1978): 169–76.

The author examines the many accounts of the meeting and points out the historical inaccuracies. Truman considered the meeting a "public relations" affair related to upcoming elections. Notes.

PUBLIC OPINION AND DISSENT

2910 Barham, Patricia, and Cunningham, Frank. *Operation Nightmare: The Story of America's Betrayal in Korea and the United States.* Los Angeles: Sequoia University Press, 1953.

This is a good example of the self-identified Radical Right literature of the 1950s. It covers much more than the Korean War; it indicts American "communists" and "pinkos," and supports General MacArthur. Index.

2911 Bartel, Ronald F. "Attitudes Toward Limited War: An Analysis of Elite and Public Opinion During the Korean Conflict." Ph.D. dissertation, University of Illinois, 1970.

Bartel finds that the Truman administration was unable to define the war goals or the enemy but was successful in convincing congressional and military elites that the fate of the free world rested upon the outcome in Korea. Public attitude toward the conflict was one of confusion and frustration. DAI 31:4867-A.

2912 Caine, Philip D. "The United States in Korea and Vietnam: A Study in Public Opinion." *Air University Review* 20 (1968): 49–55.

Caine finds that unpredictable American public opinion has been even less certain in America's last two wars. Notes.

2913 Elowitz, Larry. "Korea and Vietnam: Limited War and the American Political System." Ph.D. dissertation, University of Florida, 1972.

These two conflicts—the Korean War and the Vietnam War—engendered bitter dissension and frustration domestically and were responsible in large measure for the defeat of the incumbent administrations (Truman and Johnson). DAI 34:374-A.

2914   Gietschier, Steven P. "Limited War and the Home Front: Ohio During the Korean War." Ph.D. dissertation, Ohio State University, 1977.

The author believes that the Korean War ushered in a series of new changes, including the acceptance of a permanent Cold War, government expenditures for armaments rather than public works, curtailment of civil liberties, and a general shift away from public social policies. DAI 38:5003-A.

2915   Henderson, Thomas G. "Editorial Reaction of Selected Major Indiana Daily Newspapers To a National Controversy: The Truman, MacArthur Conflict." Ed.D. dissertation, Ball State University, 1977.

This study, based on a survey of five major daily newspapers, finds that the editorial reaction of the papers was conservative and condemned Truman's foreign policy, especially in the Far East. DAI 426-A.

2916   Herzon, Frederick D.; Kincaid, John; and Dalton, Verne. "Personality & Public Opinion: The Case of Authoritarianism, Prejudice, & Support for the Korean & Vietnam Wars." *Polity* 11 (1978): 92–113.

The authors related the authoritarianism theory developed after World War II and racial prejudice to U.S. public support for the Korean and Vietnam Wars.

2917   Lee, Raymond S. H. "Early Korean War Coverage." *Journalism Quarterly* 55 (1978): 789–92.

In reviewing the *New York Times*, the *Washington Post*, and four South Korean newspapers in 1950, Lee finds that the uncensored American papers were consistently more accurate—even in suggesting that an invasion of the South was imminent. Tables, notes.

2918   Mantell, Matthew E. "Opposition to the Korean War: A Study in American Dissent." Ph.D. dissertation, New York University, 1973.

Opponents of the war were divided into three groups: (1) pacifists; (2) political groups on the Left; and (3) pragmatists who became disillusioned. DAI 34:1213-A.

2919   Modigliani, Andre. "Hawks and Doves, Isolationism and Political Distrust: An Analysis of Public Opinion on Military Policy." *American Political Science Review* 66 (1972): 960–78.

In the Korean War there was no simple hawk-to-dove continuum; some people wanted to disengage and others to escalate the war. This differed in the Vietnam War. Tables, notes.

2920   Oliver, Robert T. *Verdict in Korea*. State College, PA: Bald Eagle Press, 1952.

Oliver extends his support to the U.S. role in the Korean conflict from the vantage point of a close friend and counselor to Syngman Rhee and other South Korean officials. If his opinions are not dispassionate and detached, they carry the authority of an insider's assessment.

2921   Rosenberg, Herbert H. "ODM: A Study of Civil-Military Relations During the Korean Mobilization." Ph.D. dissertation, University of Chicago, 1957.

No abstract available.

2922   Stemons, James S. *The Korean Mess and Some Correctives*. Boston: Chapman & Grimes, 1952.

This slim antiwar tract puts the Korean conflict in a larger perspective—the United States and the Soviet Union ought to adopt a live-and-let-live policy. Index.

2923   Twedt, Michael S. "The War Rhetoric of Harry S. Truman During the Korean Conflict." Ph.D. dissertation, University of Kansas, 1969.

During the Korean conflict, Truman made 136 addresses. The president's war rhetoric was primarily defensive and, for a number of reasons, was inadequate for the task. DAI 30:5555-A.

2924   Wiltz, John E. "The Korean War and American Society." In F. H. Heller, ed. *The Korean War: A 25-Year Perspective*. Lawrence: Regents Press of Kansas, 1977, pp. 112–58.

Wiltz provides a panoramic view of the many issues, large and small, which sought to force themselves upon the American public during these years. His discussion of the resurgence of isolationism, spurred on by Herbert Hoover and Joseph Kennedy, reminds us of the reservations which existed about America's involvement in foreign squabbles.

The Military Dimension

See also Chapter 3, for *Douglas MacArthur* and Mark W. Clark.

GENERAL ACCOUNTS

2925   Detzer, David. *Thunder of the Captains: The Short Summer in 1950*. New York: Crowell, 1977.

In a well-researched popular account, Detzer focuses on how and why Truman arrived at his decision to commit American military forces in the Korean conflict, and the fate of these troops in their early battles. Notes, bibliography, index.

2926 DeWeerd, H. A. "Lessons of the Korean War." *Yale Review* 40 (1951): 592–603.

The lessons suggested in this contemporary essay pertain almost exclusively to military operations and strategy.

2927 Dill, James. "Winter of the Yalu." *American Heritage* 34 (1982): 33–48.

Lt. Dill recounts his march to the Yalu River and back with the 7th Division, following the Inchon landing in September 1950. Illustrations.

2928 Duncan, David Douglas. *This is War! A Photo-Narrative in Three Parts.* New York: Bantam, 1967.

Through narrative and photographs, Duncan portrays the effects of the Korean War on the men who fought there. Photographs.

2929 Fehrenbach, T. R. *This Kind of War: A Study in Unpreparedness.* New York: Macmillan, 1963.

This well-written, general account of military action in Korea is spiced with vignettes of individual or small group encounters with the enemy. Maps, chronology, glossary, index.

2930 Gugeler, Russell A. *Combat Actions in Korea.* Washington, DC: Office of the Chief of Military History, U.S. Army, 1970.

Gugeler writes of small-unit actions on the battlefield rather than major campaigns. The book is directed toward junior officers, noncommissioned officers, and privates. Notes, illustrations, index.

2931 Hermes, Walter G. *Truce Tent and Fighting Front. United States Army in the Korean War.* Washington, DC: Office of the Chief of Military History, U.S. Army, 1966.

This official study covers the last two years of the Korean War. The account "treats the interminable armistice negotiations and the violent but sporadic fighting at the front." Illustrations, charts, maps, appendix, bibliographical note, index.

2932 Higgins, Marguerite. *War in Korea: The Report of a Woman Combat Correspondent.* Garden City, NY: Doubleday, 1951.

Higgins was a combat correspondent covering the war front. Photographs by Carl Mydans illustrate her account of the Korean War.

2933 Jacobs, Bruce. *Korea's Heroes: The Medal of Honor Story.* New York: Berkley Highland Books, 1953.

Jacobs presents a cross section of the army, navy, marine, and air force men who were awarded the Medal of Honor. Index.

2934 Leckie, Robert. *Conflict: The History of the Korean War, 1950–1953.* New York: Putnam, 1962.

Leckie covers the campaigns and the negotiations of the Korean War in this volume. Illustrations, notes, index, bibliography.

2935 Mauldin, William H. *Bill Mauldin in Korea.* New York: Norton, 1952.

The letters from a war correspondent that have been collected in this volume first appeared in *Collier's* magazine. These letters are supplemented with illustrations by the author.

2936 McGovern, James. *To the Yalu: From the Chinese Invasion of Korea to MacArthur's Dismissal.* New York: William Morrow, 1972.

On 15 October 1950 MacArthur met with President Truman to discuss the conduct of the Korean War, maintaining that it would be over by Thanksgiving. McGovern covers developments of the war and MacArthur's conduct of it from this meeting to the ouster of MacArthur in April 1951. Notes, bibliography, index.

2937 Middleton, Harry J. *The Compact History of the Korean War.* New York: Hawthorn, 1965.

Middleton argues that the Korean War was particularly unsettling to a nation which had come to regard victory as the end result of war. Korea was the nation's reluctant acknowledgment of the changing conditions of war. Bibliography, index.

2938 Miller, John, Jr.; Carroll, Owen J.; and Tackley, Margaret E. *Korea, 1951–1953.* Washington, DC: Office of the Chief of Military History, Department of the Army, 1956.

This volume, like its predecessor, *Korea, 1950*, attempts to provide "an accurate outline of events in order to show the U.S. Army veteran of the Korean conflict how the part he played was related to the larger plans and operations of United Nations forces." Illustrations, maps.

2939 Myrick, Howard A. "A Critical Analysis of Thematic Content of the United States Army Orientation Films of the Korean War, with Implications for Formulating Limited War Orientation Objectives." Ph.D. dissertation, University of Southern California, 1968.

Korean war films, except for the inclusion of the limited war themes, were similar in all essential aspects to the orientation films of World War II. Even so, the limited war themes were too often contradicted by total war themes. DAI 29:3200-A.

2940 O'Ballance, Edgar. *Korea: 1950–1953*. Hamden: Archon, 1969.

This account is a brief, but useful military history of the Korean War, written by an experienced British military historian. The appendix includes a brief list of U.N. nations' military contributions. Bibliography, index.

2941 O'Ballance, Edgar. "The MacArthur Plan." *Royal United Service Institution Journal* 110 (1965): 248–53.

The author reviews MacArthur's 1951 plan for a quick victory in Korea by destroying the Red Chinese supply lines with twenty to thirty atomic bombs. The bombs would lay down a radioactive belt trapping nearly one million Chinese troops in Korea, while Chinese Nationalist and U.N. troops would advance northward toward the belt. The plan was not accepted by the United States or United Nations. Illustrations, notes.

2942 Ohm, Chang-Il. "The Joint Chiefs of Staff and U.S. Policy and Strategy Regarding Korea, 1945–1953." Ph.D. dissertation, University of Kansas, 1983.

The JCS had a great deal of difficulty identifying Korea with U.S. strategic interests, which is one reason that it supported a "no-win" or limited war policy during the Korean conflict. DAI 44: 1181-A.

2943 Rees, David. *Korea: The Limited War*. New York: St. Martin's, 1964.

Rees's account focuses on the military dimension of the Korean conflict, although he does bring in relevant political episodes and factors. Appendix, bibliography, index.

2944 Republic of Korea. Ministry of National Defense. *The History of the United Nations in the Korean War*. 5 vols. [Seoul]: Ministry of National Defense, 1972–74.

Although these volumes carry obvious propaganda themes, they do contain much information about U.N. troops who fought or supported this war. Volume 1 contains information about forces from Ethiopia, the Philippines, South Africa, Thailand, Turkey; volume 2, Australia, Canada, India, New Zealand, and the United Kingdom; volume 3, Belgium, Colombia, Denmark, France, Greece, Italy, Luxembourg, the Netherlands, Norway, and Sweden; volume 4, the United States.

2945 Ridgway, Matthew B. *The Korean War: How We Met the Challenge*. Garden City, NY: Doubleday, 1967.

General Ridgway commanded the U.S. Eighth Army in Korea from late 1950 until he replaced General MacArthur in April 1951. The account provides a view of the war from the top echelon, including an interesting personal evaluation of MacArthur. Chronology of Korean War, illustrations, maps, appendixes, bibliography, index.

2946 Riley, John W., Jr., and Schramn, Wilbur. *The Reds Take A City: The Communist Occupation of Seoul; With Eyewitness Accounts*. Westport, CT: Greenwood, 1973.

In this 1951 U.S. Air Force-sponsored account, South Korean anti-Communists view their conquerors. It was written in the classic mold of "atrocity" accounts for obvious propaganda purposes.

2947 Ruetten, Richard T. "General Douglas MacArthur's 'Reconnaissance in Force': The Rationalization of a Defeat in Korea." *Pacific Historical Review* 36 (1967): 79–93.

Despite MacArthur's statement that the 1950 northward advance across the 38th parallel was only a "reconnaissance in force," there can be no doubt but that he, as supreme commander, was responsible for the military debacle of November and December 1950. Notes.

2948 Sawyer, Robert K. *Military Advisors in Korea: KMAG in Peace and War*. Edited by Walter G. Hermes. Washington, DC: Office of the Chief of Military History, Department of the Army, 1962.

A professional soldier (Major Sawyer) and a professional military historian (Dr. Hermes) have pooled their talents to prepare this account of the U.S. Military Advisory Group to the Republic of Korea (KMAG) from 1949 to 1951 to develop, equip, and train a South Korean army. Illustrations, maps, bibliography, index.

2949 Stelmach, Daniel S. "The Influence of Russian Armored Tactics on the North Korean Invasion of 1950." Ph.D. dissertation, St. Louis University, 1973.

Soviet military personnel were directly responsible for the impressive showing made by North Korean tank forces in June, July, and August 1950. DAI 34:5887-A.

Intelligence Operations

2950 DeWeerd, H. A. "Strategic Surprise in the Korean War." *Orbis* 6 (1962): 435–52.

Intelligence operations and analysis were mishandled during the Korean War, especially the failure to predict Chinese intervention. Notes.

2951 Poteat, George H. "Strategic Intelligence and National Security: A Case Study of the Korean Crisis (June 25–November 24, 1950)." Ph.D. dissertation, Washington University, 1973.

The American disaster in Korea, as a result of China's intervention, is a classic case of strategic surprise. This study seeks to explain the surprise by focusing on the attitudes of U.S. officials about various aspects of the Korean War. DAI 34:7845-A.

Inchon-Seoul Campaign

2952 Heinl, Robert D., Jr. *Victory at High Tide: The Inchon-Seoul Campaign.* Philadelphia: Lippincott, 1968.

MacArthur conceived and planned the Inchon-Seoul campaign, but its success also depended on others executing it. This excellent study deals with the political and interservice rivalries, as well as the military operations. Maps, illustrations, notes, bibliography, index.

2953 Sheldon, Walter J. *Hell or High Water: MacArthur's Landing at Inchon.* New York: Macmillan, 1968.

This account deals largely with the military operations. Maps, chronology, bibliography, index.

2954 Tomlinson, H. Pat. "Inchon: The General's Decision." *Military Review* 47 (1967): 28–35.

Outlined here are the plans for the amphibious invasion of Inchon and recapture of Seoul, as developed by MacArthur in 1950.

Air Force

2955 Amody, Francis J. "The Sabre Tooth Cheetahs of Osan." *American Aviation Historical Society Journal* 25 (1980): 42–44.

This is an account of the F-86F Sabres flown by the South African Air Force under U.N. command during the Korean War, 1950–53.

2956 Benson, Larry. "The USAF's Korean War Recruiting Rush . . . And the Great Tent City at Lackland Air Force Base." *Aerospace Historian* 25 (1978): 61–73.

The air force open enlistment quotas and a stampede of enlistees led to Lackland AFB swelling to 70,000 airmen. The resulting unpreparedness to handle so many basic trainees led to congressional investigations. Illustrations, notes.

2957 Coble, Donald W. "Air Support In the Korean War." *Aerospace Historian* 16 (1969): 26–29.

This essay deals with the air force in its first combat role as a separate service and focuses on the activities of its various units, such as the Far East Air Force, Fifth Air Force, Combat Cargo Command. Illustrations, appendix.

2958 Futrell, Robert, et al. *The United States Air Force in Korea, 1950–1953.* New York: Duell, Sloan & Pearce, 1961.

Undertaken by the U.S. Air Force Historical Division, this study on the role of the air force in Korea seeks to document and disseminate the role of the air force as well as the lessons learned in the peculiar circumstance of the limited war in Korea. Illustrations, notes, bibliography, index.

2959 Jackson, Robert. *Air War Over Korea.* New York: Scribner, 1973.

Presented here is essentially the air force's version of its role in the Korean War; the army's frequent complaints about inadequate tactical air support are absent. Appendix (air kills, order of battle, etc.).

Army

2960 Appleman, Roy E. *South to the Naktong, North to the Yalu: June–November 1950.* United States Army in the Korean War. Washington, DC: Office of the Chief of Military History, Department of the Army, 1961.

This is the first volume in the series United States Army in the Korean War, and covers army action in Korea from the outbreak of war to the full-scale intervention of the Chinese Communists. Notes, index, maps.

2961 Marshall, Samuel L. A. *The River and the Gauntlet: Defeat of the Eighth Army by the Chinese Communist Forces, November, 1950, in the Battle of the Chongehon River, Korea.* New York: Morrow, 1953.

Marshall's account of the battle (well described in the subtitle) focuses on the Second Infantry Division's chaotic retreat. Maps, glossary, index.

2962 Politella, Dario. *Operation Grasshopper.* Wichita: R. R. Longo, 1958.

Operation Grasshopper is the story of army aviation in Korea. Army pilots, flying light unarmed planes, sought out and reported the movements of enemy forces and other prime targets for the air force. Illustrations, index.

2963 Schnabel, James F. *Policy and Direction: The First Year.* United States Army in the Korean War. Washington, DC: Office of the Chief of Military History, U.S. Army, 1972.

The third volume in the history of the U.S. Army in the Korean War, this study describes the initial direction and strategy of America's first limited war. Notes, illustrations, index.

2964 Schnabel, James F. "Ridgway in Korea." *Military Review* 44 (1964): 3–13.

A laudatory account, it credits Gen. Matthew B. Ridgway with maintaining the morale of the Eighth Army and repelling the Chinese Communist forces, 1950–51.

2965 Skaggs, David C. "The Katusa Experiment: The Integration of Korean Nationals Into the U.S. Army." *Military Affairs* 38 (1974): 53–58.

KATUSA (Korean Augmentation to the U.S. Army) troops were considered a means of providing filler for the undermanned American units sent to Korea in 1950. Because the Koreans had little training the program failed initially; however, as they acquired training and experience the Koreans became excellent troops. Notes.

2966 Westover, John G. *Combat Support in Korea: The United States Army in the Korean Conflict.* Washington, DC: Combat Forces Press, 1955.

This collection of interviews with members of the armed services was written primarily for the army junior officer. Observations from men of the Corps of Engineers, Transportation, Chemical, Signal, Medical, Ordnance, and Quartermaster Corps are presented. Index.

Marine Corps

2967 Geer, Andrew C. *The New Breed: The Story of the U.S. Marines in Korea.* New York: Harper, 1952.

Geer provides a well-written popular account, in the heroic tradition, of combat in Korea. Illustrations, index.

2968 Montrose, Lynn. *Cavalry of the Sky: The Story of the U.S. Marine Combat Helicopters.* New York: Harper, 1954.

This is the story of the growth of marine helicopter combat tactics and techniques during the Korean War. The main function of these helicopters was to provide troop lifts, supply missions, and command activities. Medical and rescue airlifts were especially innovative activities. Notes, index.

2969 U.S. Marine Corps. *U.S. Marine Operations in Korea, 1950–1953.* 5 vols. Washington, DC: Historical Branch, G-3, Headquarters, U.S. Marine Corps, 1954–72.

Volume 1 deals with *The Pusan Perimeter*; volume 2 with *The Inchon-Seoul Operation*; volume 3 with *The Chosin Reservoir Campaign*; volume 4 with *The East-Central Front*; and volume 5 with *Operations in West Korea*. The focus is expectedly on combat operations. Illustrations, maps, notes, index.

Navy

2970 Cagle, Malcolm W., and Manson, Frank A. *The Sea War in Korea.* Annapolis: U.S. Naval Institute, 1957.

The authors argue that control of the sea was a critical factor in the U.N. decision to intervene in Korea, and that sea power helped to limit the conflict. Illustrations, appendixes, index.

2971 Field, James A., Jr. *History of United States Naval Operations: Korea.* Washington, DC: G.P.O., 1962.

This gracefully written official history covers the years 1950 through 1953. It provides a detailed story of naval operations which complements the other services' accounts. Illustrations, glossary, note on sources, tables, maps, and index.

CHARGES OF BACTERIOLOGICAL WARFARE

2972 Commission of the International Association of Democratic Lawyers. *Report on U.S. Crimes in Korea.* Supplement to *People's China*, 1 June 1952.

This report, issued in English by the association's head office in Brussels, was reprinted by several organs. The reports charge that the United States engaged in bacteriological warfare, employed chemical weapons, and used air bombardment in violation of the laws of warfare. Additionally, U.S. and South Korean troops were charged with torture, murder, and other atrocities.

2973 Endicott, Stephen L. "Germ Warfare and 'Plausible Denial': The Korean War, 1952–1953." *Modern China* 5 (1979): 79–104.

The Chinese and North Korean governments' charges that the United States engaged in bacteriological warfare during the Korean War have never been accepted by most Western authorities. Endicott believes that testimony before the 1976 Senate Select Committee to intelligence operations may lend some credence to these charges. Notes.

2974 Ginneken, Japp van. "Bacteriological Warfare." *Journal of Contemporary Asia* [Sweden] 7 (1977): 130–52.

This account connects America's biological warfare research to Japanese assistance, via Shiro Ishii, to the charges that the United States employed such weapons during the Korean conflict. In the author's view, previous findings are not conclusive and a serious investigation of the charges is needed. Notes.

2975 Gittings, John. "Talks, Bombs and Germs: Another Look at the Korean War." *Journal of Contemporary Asia* [Sweden] 5 (1975): 205–17.

The author argues that U.S. military authorities did not practice restraint against North Korean cities and civilians, and that they made plans to use nerve gas and perhaps germ warfare.

2976 Mayo, C. W. "Germ Warfare Confessions." U.S., Department of State, *Bulletin* (9 November 1953): 641–47.

Here and elsewhere, U.S. government officials denied that there was any validity to the charges that

American military forces in Korea employed biological weapons.

2977 Stockholm International Peace Research Institute. *The Problem of Chemical and Biological Warfare.* 6 vols. New York: Humanities, 1971, 4:196–221; 5:238–58.

These two sections provide a reasonably adequate discussion of the issues. Notes.

TRUCE NEGOTIATIONS

2978 Bacchus, Wilfred A. "The Relationship between Combat and Peace Negotiations: Fighting While Talking in Korea, 1951–1953." *Orbis* 17 (1973): 545–74.

The problems of a limited war strategy on peace negotiations are examined. Notes.

2979 Blumenson, Martin. "Neutrality and Armistice in Korea." *Military Review* 47 (1967): 3–12.

Chronicled here are the major events leading to the Korean Armistice Agreement (1953), supervised by the Neutral Nations Supervisory Commission.

2980 Brazda, Jaroslav J. "The Korean Armistice Agreement: A Comparative Study." Ph.D. dissertation, University of Florida, 1956.

Stalemated wars are difficult to end. The Korean armistice negotiations were long and drawn out because of (1) East Asian political considerations; (2) the tensions of the Cold War; (3) the U.N. involvement; and (4) several departures from previous armistice practices. DAI 16:2506.

2981 Burchett, Wilfred G. *Again Korea.* New York: International Publishers, 1968.

An Australian journalist with close ties to Communist figures and governments reviews (with recollections) the Korean armistice talks. Index.

2982 Drummond, S. "Korea and Vietnam: Some Speculations About the Possible Influences of the Korean War on American Policy in Vietnam." *Army Quarterly and Defense Journal* [Great Britain] 97 (1968): 65–71.

The author suggests that adopting the Korean pattern of aerial bombing in Vietnam without examining its effectiveness made the approach to peace negotiations more difficult than would have been the case if full appraisal had been undertaken.

2983 Hermes, Walter G. "The Military Role in the Korean Truce Negotiations." *Military Review* 44 (1964): 14–23.

The essay pays extensive attention to Communist negotiating techniques and describes the interaction of political and military considerations.

2984 Joy, Charles Turner. *How Communists Negotiate.* New York: Macmillan, 1955.

Admiral Joy participated in the Korean Armistice Conference as the senior Western delegate. Particular attention is focused on the methods used by the Communists at Kaesong and Panmunjom.

2985 U.S. Department of State. *The Korean Problem at the Geneva Conference, April 26–June 15, 1954.* Publ. 5609. Washington, DC: G.P.O., 1954.

It is often overlooked, but the 1954 Geneva Conference did seek to resolve some of the issues still plaguing the Korean armistice—elections, withdrawal of foreign troops, etc. Appendix, list of participants.

2986 Vatcher, William H., Jr. *Panmunjom: The Story of the Korean Military Armistice Negotiations.* New York: Praeger, 1958.

The armistice negotiations at Panmunjom, ending the active phase of the Korean War from the first session of the armistice conference held in July 1951 until the signing of the Armistice Agreement in July 1953, are detailed here.

PRISONER OF WAR ISSUES

2987 Alapatt, George K. "The Legal Implications of the Repatriation of War Prisoners in Relation to the Korean Armistice and in View of the Division of Korea." Ph.D. dissertation, St. Louis University, 1958.

The repatriation of war prisoners became a major issue in the final negotiations of the Korean armistice. A Neutral Nations' Repatriation Commission was created to take custody of the prisoners and to effect their repatriation. DAI 19:3003.

2988 Biderman, Albert D. *March to Calumny: The Story of American POWs in the Korean War.* New York: Macmillan, 1963.

Biderman responds to the charge that American POWs collaborated with their Communist captors and that this misbehavior revealed weaknesses in our national behavior. The author examines how these misconceptions came to be formed. Notes, bibliography, index.

2989 Bradbury, William C. *Mass Behavior in Battle and Captivity: The Communist Soldier in the Korean War.* Chicago: University of Chicago Press, 1968.

At the time of repatriation, 14,325 of the 21,014 Chinese captured refused to return home in contrast to the twenty-two Americans of 4,450. This study seeks an understanding of the Chinese Communist indoctrination system and its influence on prisoner-of-war behavior. Notes, appendixes, bibliography, index.

2990 Burchett, Wilfred G., and Winnington, Alan. *Koje Unscreened.* Peking, 1953.

Allegations were made that over 3,000 prisoners of war were massacred by their American captors at the Koje Island prisoner of war camp. Illustrations.

2991 Kim, Myong Whai. "Prisoners of War as a Major Problem of the Korean Armistice, 1953." Ph.D. dissertation, New York University, 1960.

The U.N. command and the Communists differed in their interpretation of POWs under the 1949 Geneva Convention. The United Nations held that prisoners of war should not be repatriated contrary to their expressed wishes. DAI 23:291.

2992 Murray, J. C. "The Prisoner Issue." *Marine Corps Gazette* 39 (1955): 32–40, 38:28–35.

This essay reviews the plight of American prisoners of war in North Korea during and after the Korean War, of American efforts to obtain their release, and of Communist attitudes toward POWs since 1919.

2993 Pasley, Virginia. *22 Stayed: The Story of the American GI's Who Chose Communist China: Who They Were and Why They Stayed.* London: W. H. Allen, 1955.

In 1954 twenty-one American soldiers and one British soldier who had been held in Korean prison camps chose to remain with their captors. Pasley finds remarkable parallels in the lives of these twenty-two men. Appendix.

2994 Spivey, Delmar T., et al. "The Soldier and the Prisoner." *Marine Corps Gazette* 49 (1965): 36–44.

This report reviews the conduct and rate of U.S. prisoners of war from the Korean War to 1965.

2995 White, William L. *The Captives of Korea: An Unofficial White Paper on the Treatment of War Prisoners; Our Treatment of Theirs, Their Treatment of Ours.* New York: Scribner, 1957.

With the support of the government and the help of Undersecretary of State Herbert Hoover, Jr., White compiled this report on the treatment of prisoners of war. Illustrations, index.

2996 Wills, Morris R. *Turncoat: An American's 12 Years in Communist China. The Story of Morris R. Wills as told to J. Robert Moskin.* Englewood Cliffs, NJ: Prentice-Hall, 1968.

Wills was one of the twenty-one American soldiers, captured by the Chinese during the Korean War, who decided to defect to Communist China rather than return home. In 1965 he returned to the United States. This is the story of captivity and years in China. Index.

2997 Winnington, Alan, and Burchett, Wilfred. *Plain Perfidy.* Peking: 1954.

This account relates their purported personal views of the fate of North Korean and Chinese POWs and Rhee's refusal to send all of them back (including those who apparently did not wish to return).

2998 Witherspoon, John A. "International Law and Practices Concerning Prisoners of War During the Korean Conflict (1950–1954)." Ph.D. dissertation, Duke University, 1968.

North Korea denied delegates from the International Committee of the Red Cross operating under the Geneva Convention to enter North Korea. While the U.N. Command regularly reported data on prisoners of war, the North Koreans failed to do so. DAI 29:2778-A.

2999 Wubben, H. H. "American Prisoners of War in Korea: A Second Look at the 'Something New In History' Theme." *American Quarterly* 22 (1970): 3–19.

This article reexamines the view that American POWs in Korea were more easily "brainwashed" than in other such past American experiences. The author concludes that comparisons with other wartime POW experiences were inaccurate and that there was a greater-than-usual American readiness to believe this myth. Notes.

President Truman in his office at the Truman Library, 1962. *Reproduced courtesy of the* Kansas City Star.

11

General Reference Works

Included here are some of the many reference aids which list materials relating to the Truman years, expanding upon the themes developed in Chapters 1 through 10. Additionally, reference works which have been listed with the previous chapters are often cross-referenced here. Finally, most of the monographs, dissertations, and articles listed in the previous chapters contain bibliographies and notes which the researcher will find useful.

Useful introductions to the general historiography of the Truman era may be found in the two volumes edited by Richard S. Kirkendall, *The Truman Period as a Research Field* (#3001, 3002). The historiographical essays by Robert Griffith, "Truman and the Historians: The Reconstruction of Postwar American History" (#3005), Geoffrey S. Smith, " 'Harry, We Hardly Know You': Revisionism, Politics and Diplomacy, 1945–1954. A Review Essay" (#3008), and R. J. Williams, "Harry S. Truman and the American Presidency" (#3010) expand on many of these themes suggested in the Kirkendall volumes.

The Truman presidency will probably be best remembered for its success in the field of foreign affairs, an area which has been extensively explored by historians. Augmenting the materials contained in Chapters 7 and 8 is Richard Dean Burns, *Guide to American Foreign Relations Since 1700* (#3023) and J. S. Walker, "Historians and Cold War Origins: The New Consensus" (#3033). The third volume in *Foreign Affairs Bibliography: A Selected and Annotated List of Books on International Relations* (#3025) is especially useful in locating contemporary books, while the annual, *The United States in World Affairs, 1931–* (#1576) provides an indispensable introduction to the events and personalities dominating the foreign affairs field during the Truman period.

Domestic affairs are also covered in M. L. Stapleton, *The Truman and Eisenhower Years, 1945–1960* (#3004) and in the included specialized bibliographies. Books containing information relating to the Communist "problem," the labor movement, religion in America, and other themes are listed below. These areas, however, have not been developed as thoroughly as have those dealing with foreign affairs since they are relatively of less importance in the Truman story.

Biographical materials are important sources for both foreign and domestic matters. Many biographies and memoirs have been listed in Chapter 3, which also cross-references such groups as jurists, labor leaders, and those individuals caught up in the loyalty scare. Additionally, Eleanora W. Schoenebaum, *Political Profiles: The Truman Years* (#257) focuses on a broad spectrum of personalities who figured prominently in the Truman era. *The Biographical Directory of the American Congress* (#380) provides a brief sketch of representatives and senators who served during the years that Truman was president.

Bibliographies: General

3000 Furer, Howard B., ed. *Harry S. Truman, 1884– : Chronology, Documents, Bibliographical Aids*. Dobbs Ferry, NY: Oceana, 1970.

The chronology is very extensive and probably the most useful aspect of this volume; the documents are taken from the *Public Papers of the Presidents: Harry S. Truman, 1945–1953*, and the bibliography is slim and dated. Index.

3001 Kirkendall, Richard S., ed. *The Truman Period as a Research Field*. Columbia: University of Missouri Press, 1967.

3002 Kirkendall, Richard S., ed. *The Truman Period as a Research Field: A Reappraisal, 1972.* Columbia: University of Missouri Press, 1974.

The essays in the initial volume examine the "research in the Truman period—exploration of the research already completed or in progress, and suggestions for additional studies." Those in the second volume focus more on the differing interpretations of traditionalists (liberals) and revisionists. Notes, appendix, and index.

3003 Rundell, Walter, Jr. *In Pursuit of American History: Research and Training in the United States.* Norman: University of Oklahoma Press, 1970.

This book surveys research, especially that using primary source materials, on the graduate level. The index is useful for locating Truman era materials. Notes, appendixes, bibliography, index.

3004 Stapleton, Margaret L. *The Truman and Eisenhower Years, 1945–1960: A Selective Bibliography.* Metuchen, NJ: Scarecrow, 1973.

This unannotated bibliography lists over 1,600 items published prior to June 1972, which pertain to events occurring in the years 1945 to 1960. These items are listed by subject categories. Author and title indexes.

Historiographical Essays

3005 Griffith, Robert. "Truman and the Historians: The Reconstruction of Postwar American History." *Wisconsin Magazine of History* 59 (1975): 20–50.

This very informative review focuses on the Truman administration's foreign policy, including changing interpretations and evaluations of the Marshall Plan, Truman Doctrine, Point Four, atomic diplomacy, the Korean War, containment, and the origins of the Cold War. It also deals with Truman's domestic policy, highlighting inflation, internal security, McCarthyism, housing, civil rights, and other programs. Illustrations, notes, bibliography.

3006 McCoy, Donald R. "Trends in Viewing Herbert Hoover, Franklin D. Roosevelt, Harry S. Truman, and Dwight D. Eisenhower." *Midwest Quarterly* 20 (1979): 117–36.

McCoy briefly appraises the historical and biographical writings on the presidents from Hoover to Eisenhower, 1928–74.

3007 Polenberg, Richard. "Historians and the Liberal Presidency: Recent Appraisals of Roosevelt and Truman." *South Atlantic Quarterly* 75 (1976): 20–35.

Revisionists have strongly attacked both presidents for failing to go far enough in reform efforts, especially civil liberties. The author is critical of the assumptions and perceptions of the revisionist historians.

3008 Smith, Geoffrey S. " 'Harry, We Hardly Know You': Revisionism, Politics and Diplomacy, 1945–1954: A Review Essay." *American Political Science Review* 70 (1976): 560–82.

Smith examines in perceptive fashion some twenty books which deal with the Truman administration's foreign and domestic policy. This essay, together with Robert Griffith's, forms a solid basis upon which to begin any survey of historiography of the Truman years. Notes.

3009 Theoharis, Athan. "Ignoring History: HST, the Revisionists, and the Press." *Chicago Journalism Review* (March 1973): 14–15.

The author complains that editors and reporters are either unaware of, or unwilling to include the findings of revisionist historians of the Truman presidency.

3010 Williams, Robert J. "Harry S. Truman and the American Presidency." *Journal of American Studies* [Great Britain] 13 (1979): 393–408.

Williams suggests that analyzing Truman's presidency is made difficult because of the lack of critical biographies, and because of Truman's "elusive private and political personality." The study examines the evidence which accounts for the widely contradictory evaluations of Truman.

Bibliographies: Domestic Affairs

3011 Becker, Harold K., and Felkenes, George T. *Law Enforcement: A Selected Bibliography.* Metuchen, NJ: Scarecrow, 1968.

This topically organized list has a few items which might be useful on the Truman era. Author index.

3012 Burr, Nelson R. *A Critical Bibliography of Religion in America.* 2 vols. Princeton, NJ: Princeton University Press, 1961.

Volume 2 (pp. 1088–92) contains references to studies of Reinhold Niebuhr and his "Neo-Orthodox" or realist philosophy.

3013 Eaton, Clement. "Recent Trends in the Writing of Southern History." *Louisiana Historical Quarterly* 38 (1955): 26–42.

This brief review of the "new look" in the writing of Southern history since 1945 finds a new interest in objective history concerning the South, particularly in relation to blacks, and a trend toward emphasizing economic, social, and cultural history rather than political and military history.

3014 Miller, Elizabeth W., and Fisher, Mary L. *The Negro in America: A Bibliography.* 2nd ed., rev. Cambridge: Harvard University Press, 1970.

Some materials on black Americans during the Truman years are contained in this volume—especially social and cultural data. Bibliographical items are arranged topically. Author index.

3015 Paulsen, David F. *Natural Resources in the Government Process: A Bibliography Selected and Annotated.* Tucson: University of Arizona Press, 1970.

This bibliography may be useful for researchers who have previously identified their topics. Its coverage is general and ranges far beyond the Truman era. Author index.

COMMUNISM IN AMERICA

3016 Corker, Charles. *Bibliography on the Communist Problem in the United States.* New York: Fund for the Republic, 1955.

Books, pamphlets, and magazine articles, ending in 1952, are collected here. This annotated volume is useful as a source of contemporary materials.

3017 Delaney, Robert F. *The Literature of Communism in America: A Selected Reference Guide.* Washington, DC: Catholic University of America Press, 1962.

Books which deal with communism and anti-communism in the United States are arranged by topics. Although the annotations reflect the editor's biases, the volume provides a useful guide to the controversies of the Truman years.

3018 Fried, Richard M. "Communism and Anti-Communism: A Review Essay." *Wisconsin Magazine of History* 63 (1980): 309–21.

Reviewed here are V. Gornick, *The Romance of American Communism* (1978), David Caute, *The Great Fear* (1978), M. S. McAuliffe, *Crisis on the Left* (1978), Donald F. Crosby, *God, Church, and Flag* (1978), and Allen Weinstein, *Perjury* (1978).

3019 Griffith, Robert. "The Politics of Anti-Communism: A Review Article." *Wisconsin Magazine of History* 54 (1971): 299–308.

Griffith examines several books on McCarthyism which interpret the politics of anticommunism from 1950 to 1971.

3020 Seidman, Joel, ed. *Communism in the United States: A Bibliography.* Ithaca, NY: Cornell University Press, 1969.

This volume is a comprehensive expansion of Charles Corker's earlier volume. It contains many items, contemporary and reflective, on the Truman years.

LABOR MOVEMENT

3021 "Annual Bibliography on American Labor History." *Labor History* 1 (1959–).

Beginning in the mid-1960s, these annual bibliographies appearing in the fourth issue each year provide a very useful survey of the year's publications. Any student of labor affairs during the Truman years would profit from examining these bibliographies.

3022 Stroud, Gene S., and Donahue, Gilbert S. *Labor History in the United States: A General Bibliography.* Urbana, IL: Institute of Labor and Industrial Relations, 1961.

This list is difficult to use because it is arranged alphabetically by author. The subject index may be of some value.

Bibliographies: Foreign Affairs

3023 Burns, Richard Dean. *Guide to American Foreign Relations Since 1700.* Santa Barbara, CA: ABC-Clio, 1983.

Chapters 24 to 28 directly relate to the Truman era. However, other chapters, especially topical ones, should be reviewed for additional references. While many references will be duplicated, the guide includes many citations not included here. Indexes.

3024 Christman, Calvin L., comp. "Doctoral Dissertations in U.S. Foreign Affairs." *Diplomatic History* 3 (1979): 231–48.

This up-to-date list is to be an annual contribution. It divides the references into subject categories, but is not annotated.

3025 *Foreign Affairs Bibliography: A Selected and Annotated List of Books on International Relations.* 5 vols. to date. New York: Harper, 1933–.

This third volume, for 1942–52, edited by Henry L. Roberts, provides a useful listing of contemporary accounts under a variety of subject headings. Index.

3026 Lewis, John R. *Uncertain Judgment: A Bibliography of War Crimes Trials.* Santa Barbara, CA: Clio Press, 1979.

Sources are listed in this prize-winning volume for the Nuremberg Trials and the Tokyo Trials; indeed, there are sources listed here for the trials of the lesser "war criminals."

3027 Plischke, Elmer. *U.S. Foreign Relations: A Guide to Information Sources.* Detroit: Gale, 1980.

While this volume contains a wide range of materials, it does list references, especially articles and documents, pertinent to the Truman years under appropriate subheadings. Index.

3028 Ward, Robert E., and Shulman, Frank J., comps. *The Allied Occupation of Japan, 1945–1952: An Annotated Bibliography of Western-Language Materials.* Chicago: American Library Association, 1974.

Over 2,500 books, memoirs, and articles are abstracted. Author index, list of occupation personnel.

3029 Zobrist, Benedict K. "Resources of Presidential Libraries for the History of Post World War II American Military Government in Germany and Japan." *Military Affairs* 42 (1978): 17–19.

Identified here are the collections of papers at various presidential libraries which have significant materials that relate to American occupation policy and activities. Notes.

THE COLD WAR

The literature on the Cold War, and especially the origins of the Cold War, is voluminous. Richard Dean Burns, *Guide to American Foreign Relations Since 1700* (#3023) devotes several chapters to Cold War issues, while specific references to the "origins" issue may be found on pages 709–12. John L. Gaddis, "The Emerging Post-Revisionist Synthesis on the Origins of the Cold War" (#1796) provides footnotes which list additional references.

3030 Graebner, Norman A. "Cold War Origins and the Continuing Debate." *Journal of Conflict Resolution* 13 (1969): 123–32.

The author reviews traditional and revisionist arguments and, in the process, provides a useful bibliography. Notes.

3031 Patterson, David S. "Recent Literature on Cold War Origins: An Essay Review." *Wisconsin Magazine of History* 55 (1972): 320–29.

Six books and their differing interpretations of the origins of the Cold War are examined.

3032 Trister, Toby. "Traditionalists, Revisionists, and the Cold War: A Bibliographical Sketch." In Charles Gati, ed. *Caging the Bear: Containment and the Cold War.* New York: Bobbs-Merrill, 1974, pp. 211–22.

This bibliographical essay, and attached bibliography, are useful in sorting out various views of the origins of the Cold War, 1945–50.

3033 Walker, J. Samuel. "Historians and Cold War Origins: The New Consensus." In G. K. Haines and J. S. Walker, eds. *American Foreign Relations: A Historiographical Review.* Westport, CT: Greenwood Press, 1981, pp. 207–36.

By the late 1970s most historians had come to the view that the United States and the Soviet Union shared the responsibility for the onset of the Cold War. This essay reviews some of the major arguments; it is a useful starting point for the novice. Extended notes.

Bibliographies: Arms Control, Intelligence, and Military Affairs

3034 Burns, Richard Dean. *Arms Control and Disarmament: A Bibliography.* Santa Barbara, CA: ABC-Clio, 1977.

Materials related to the Truman years are scattered under various subject headings throughout the volume; for example, the Baruch Plan is on p. 170; Japanese Constitution (1947), pp. 166–67; and United Nations and Arms Control, pp. 79–82.

3035 Higham, Robin, ed. *Guide to the Sources of United States Military History.* Hamden, CT: Shoe String Press, 1975.

The initial volume and its subsequent updates provide useful bibliographical references to military activities and policies during the Truman years.

3036 Millett, Allan R., and Cooling, B. Franklin, III, eds. *Doctoral Dissertations in Military Affairs: A Bibliography*. Manhattan: Kansas State University Library, 1972.

This volume lists dissertations in military history as well as in related disciplines and, while it covers a much broader spectrum, it does contain items relating to the Truman years. This initial undertaking has been updated annually since 1973 in *Military Affairs*.

3037 O'Neill, James E., and Krauskopf, Robert W. *World War II: An Account of Its Documents*. Washington, DC: Howard University Press, 1976.

This volume contains a bibliography indicating the various guides, inventories, and other finding aids to the records and papers pertaining to the Second World War in the National Archives and several presidential libraries. Notes, illustrations, index.

3038 Smith, Myron J., Jr. *The Secret Wars*. Vol. 2: *Intelligence, Propaganda and Psychological Warfare, Covert Operations, 1945–1980*. Santa Barbara, CA: ABC-Clio, 1981.

This bibliography has scattered references relating to the Truman era. Index.

3039 Zobrist, Benedict K. "Resources of the Presidential Libraries for the History of the Second World War." In James F. O'Neill and Robert K. Krauskopf, eds. *World War II: An Account of its Documents*. Washington, DC: Howard University Press, 1976, pp. 113–23.

This essay may have information of value to one examining the closing months of World War II after Truman had assumed the presidency. Notes.

THE KOREAN WAR

For a discussion regarding the outbreak of this conflict, see Chapter 10, *Outbreak of War: Historiographical Accounts*.

3040 Blanchard, Carroll H. *Korean War Bibliography and Maps of Korea*. Albany, NY: Korean Conflict Research Foundation, 1964.

This useful but out-of-date reference aid is perhaps still most helpful for military operations and for its twenty-five maps.

3041 Leopold, Richard W. "The Korean War: The Historian's Task." In Francis H. Heller, ed. *The Korean War: A 25-Year Perspective*. Lawrence: Regents Press of Kansas, 1977, pp. 209–24.

This bibliographical survey is a useful introduction to basic sources. Leopold employs five books and two essays to explore some of the unanswered

and contested questions yet plaguing the historiography of the Korean War. Notes.

3042 Park, Hong-Kyu. *The Korean War: An Annotated Bibliography*. Marshall, TX: Demmer, 1971.

This twenty-five-page pamphlet contains a brief list of materials, some in Korean.

Biographical Dictionaries and Directories

These biographical reference aids supplement items in Chapter 3, which lists biographies, memoirs, and diaries of individuals who played an important role during the Truman years. *The Biographical Directory of the American Congress* (#380) lists all representatives and senators who served during the Truman administration. Eleanora W. Schoenebaum, *Political Profiles: The Truman Years* (#257) is a rather eclectic, but valuable listing of office holders and biographical sketches; while J. A. Garraty, *Encyclopedia of American Biography* (#256) contains additional materials.

3043 *Current Biography*. New York: Wilson, 1940–.

A most useful source, the annual cumulations from 1945 to 1952 provide two- to three-page sketches of national and international personalities.

3044 *Who's Who in America: A Biographical Dictionary of Notable Living Men and Women, 1899–*. Chicago: Marquis, 1899-.

Published biennially, this source provides basic data relating to many individuals identified with the Truman administration.

Harry S. Truman Library

3045 Brooks, Philip C. "The Harry S. Truman Library: Plans and Reality." *American Archivist* 25 (1962): 25–37.

The former president sought to develop the Truman Library into a research center for the study of the presidency, rather than a library devoted to him and his administration.

3046   Ferrell, Robert H. "The Private Papers of Harry S. Truman." Society for Historians of American Foreign Relations *Newsletter* 11 (1980): 1–7.

Ferrell describes his discovery of a box of Truman's private papers at the Truman Library at Independence, Missouri in 1978. These papers were subsequently published as *Off-the-Record* (1980).

3047   Harry S. Truman Library. *Historical Materials in the Harry S. Truman Library*. 25th Anniversary. Independence, MO: Harry S. Truman Library, January 1982.

This sixty-five-page booklet, which is periodically updated, lists and identifies briefly the materials in the Truman Library's holdings of primary research sources. These consist of manuscript and microfilm holdings and oral history interviews. Inquiries should be addressed to: Harry S. Truman Library, Independence, MO 64050.

3048   Harry S. Truman Library Institute. *Whistle Stop*.

A quarterly publication circulated to honorary fellows of the institute, this newsletter usually pre-sents a feature-length article on President Truman or the Truman Library.

3049   Johnson, Niel M., and Lagerquist, Philip D. "Resources at the Harry S. Truman Library on Western Issues and Programs." *Government Publication Review* 7A (1980): 156–66.

This essay identifies holdings of the Truman Library on federal policy toward Indians, 1945–66; water power and supply, 1945–52; migratory labor, 1950–51; Japanese-American relocation, 1940–45; and political activities involving the president and the Western states during the campaigns of 1948, 1950, and 1952.

3050   Lloyd, David D. "The Harry S. Truman Library." *American Archivist* 18 (1955): 99–110.

Some of the administrative problems related to ownership, disposition, preservation, and public release of the papers and mementos of former presidents are discussed. The author concludes that the Federal Records Act of 1950, which provided for the presidential libraries under the National Archives administration, does seem to satisfy the need of living former presidents to protect confidences, and at the same time makes the material accessible to qualified scholars.

Author Index

Abbot, Charles C., 677
Abel, Elie, 327
Abel, Maddela, 2311
Abell, Tyler, 1299
Abels, Jules, 146, 1234
Aben-Rabbo, Samir A., 2378
Abramowicz, Alfred L., 1002
Abrams, Charles, 1046
Abramson, Arthur C., 2369
Acheson, Dean, 294–97
Adams, Walter, 570
Adcock, Cynthia Letts, 2130
Ader, Emile B., 1262
Adler, Emanuel, 2704
Adler, Frank J., 2379
Adler, Leslie K., 907, 1665, 1666
Agapos, A.M., 2736
Agar, Herbert, 107
Agarossi, Elena, 1738
Aghassi, Marjorie E., 1950
Agnews, James B., 23
Ahmad, Bashir, 2307
Alapatt, George K., 2987
Albertazzie, Ralph, 140
Alberts, Robert C., 374
Alberts, William W., 597
Albion, Robert C., 270
Alexander, Thomas G., 492, 2764
Alexander, William M., 2783
Alexandersson, Gunnar, 571
Alfrange, Dean, Jr., 1521
Allen, Charles R., Jr., 1360
Allen, Louis, 2051
Allen, Richard C., 2208
Allen, Robert S., 108
Allison, Oscar H., 561
Allsup, Vernon C., 1141
Alperovitz, Gar, 1765
Alsop, Joseph, 1300
Alsop, Stewart, 1300
Alvarez, David J., 2460, 2461
Alvord, Ben M., 627
Ambrose, Stephen E., 375
Amen, Michael M., 2593
American Assembly, 2025
Amlund, Curtis A., 173, 211
Amody, Francis J., 2955
Anders, Roger M., 1447
Anderson, Bruce, 885
Anderson, Clinton P., 261
Anderson, David, 2135
Anderson, Helen E.E., 2104

Anderson, Irvine H., 2455
Anderson, Jervis, 1069
Anderson, Joel E., Jr., 445
Anderson, Oscar E., Jr., 2778, 2815
Anderson, Patrick, 258
Anderson, Terry H., 2574
Andrew, Christopher, 2705
Andrew, Jean D., 1636
Andrew, William D., 814
Andrews, Bert, 1369, 1428
Andrews, Peter, 1428
Appleman, Roy E., 2960
Appleton, Sheldon, 2136
Arcilesi, Salvatore A., 2442
Arkes, Hadley, 1886
Armstrong, John P., 432
Arndt, Karl J.R., 1003
Arnold, Peri E., 251
Arnold, Truman, 1500
Aron, Raymond, 2483
Aronsen, Lawrence R., 2041, 2121
Aronson, Bernard, 926
Aronson, James, 865
Arrington, Leonard J., 2764
Asbell, Bernard, 92
Asch, Peter, 672
Ashley, Frank W., 1263
Atkins, Irene Kahn, 898
Atkinson, David N., 1522, 1534, 1558, 1559
Atwell, Cynthia M., 886
Atwell, Mary W., 342, 1653, 1951
Atwood, Rollin S., 1970
Auerbach, Carl A., 706
Auerbach, Doris N., 863
Augus, Henry F., 2042
Aurthur, Robert Alan, 27, 28

Bacchus, Wilfred A., 2978
Bachman, George W., 937
Backer, John H., 2490, 2511
Bader, William B., 2650
Baek, Jong-Chun, 2209
Baerwald, Hans, 2162
Baggaley, Philip A., 2491
Bailey, Harry A., Jr., 1124
Bailey, Percival R., 1319, 1320
Bailey, Robert J., 826
Bailey, Stephen K., 212, 735, 736
Bailey, Terrell W., 2811
Bailey, Thomas A., 174, 175, 1887

Baillie, Hugh, 1301
Baines, John M., 2345
Baker, Carlos, 986
Baker, Donald G., 864
Baker, Liva, 1546
Baker, Paul R., 1740
Balabkins, Nicholas, 2512
Balboni, Alan R., 2418
Baldasty, Gerald J., 1473
Baldwin, David A., 1971
Baldwin, Frank, 2217
Baliga, Bantval M., 2261
Ball, Howard, 1507
Ballard, Jack S., Jr., 493, 2152
Banks, James G., 443
Banks, Larry H., 616
Banks, Melvin J., 1082
Bantell, John F., 1986, 1987
Baram, Phillip J., 2370
Barbash, Jack, 768
Barber, James D., 151, 446, 1235
Barber, Willard F., 1952
Barclay, Glen St. John, 2038
Barham, Patricia, 2910
Barker, Lucius J., 585, 586
Barkley, Alben W., 263
Barnard, Andrew, 2324
Barnard, John W., 799
Barnard, William D., 1190
Barnes, Trevor, 2706
Barnes, William R., 606
Barnet, Richard J., 2594
Barnouw, Erik, 913
Baron, Michael L., 2068
Barrett, Edward L., Jr., 1469
Barrie, Robert W., 609
Barros, James, 1988
Bartel, Ronald F., 2911
Bartels, Andres H., 500
Barth, Alan, 1321, 1322
Bartlett, Christopher, Jr., 2575
Bartley, Ernest R., 587
Bartley, Numan V., 1191
Barto, Harold E., 267
Barton, David, 734
Baruch, Bernard M., 306
Baskauskas, Liucija, 1772
Bass, Harold F., Jr., 152
Batchelder, Robert C., 1741
Bateman, Herman E., 93
Bauer, Boyd H., 376
Baum, Edward, 2026

Schnabel, James F., 2963, 2964
Schnapper, M.B., 59
Schneider, Mark B., 2698
Schneier, Edward B., 1378
Schneir, Miriam, 1458
Schneir, Walter, 1458
Schnorf, Richard A., 2477, 2478
Schoenbaum, David, 2414
Schoenberger, Walter S., 1754
Schoenebaum, Eleanora W., 257
Schonberger, Howard, 1261, 2184, 2185
Schramn, Wilbur, 2946
Schrecker, Ellen, 1001
Schrieber, Carl, 2743
Schriftgiesser, Karl, 228
Schroeder, E.H., 965
Schroeder, Gertrude G., 575
Schubert, Glendon A., 1517
Schulze, Franz, 858
Schwartz, Harvey, 806
Schwartz, Leo W., 1784
Schwartz, Louis, 796
Schwartz, Nancy Lynn, 1412
Schwartz, Robert J., 1948
Schwartz, Ruth E., 1120
Schwarz, Jordan A., 308
Scobie, Ingrid W., 1472
Scott, George W., 1216
Scott, Herbert H., 850
Scott, William B., 1130
Scrivner, John H., Jr., 2699
Scruggs, Otey M., 546
Seaton, Douglas P., 788
Sebald, William J., 2186
Secrest, Donald E., 1587
Segal, Philip D., 2800
Seidman, Joel, 503, 3020
Selcraig, James T., 1467
Seligman, Ben B., 731
Sellen, Albert S., 1646
Selton, Robert W., 1882
Seltzer, Robert V., 2882
Senate Committee on Foreign Relations,
    1575
Serfaty, Simon, 2479
Service, John S., 361
Sessions, Gene A., 2338
Seth, Ronald, 1441
Settel, T.S., 32
Shadegg, Stephen C., 484
Shadoian, Jack, 895
Shain, Russell E., 901, 910, 911
Shalom, Stephen R., 2278
Shannon, David A., 1188
Shannon, William V., 108
Sharp, Bert M., 1770
Shattuck, Henry L., 1357
Shaw, Lonel E., Jr., 1183
Shaw, Yu-ming, 2098
Sheehy, Edward J., 2649
Sheldon, Ted, 60
Sheldon, Walter J., 2953
Shelton, James H., 150
Shepard, David H., 497
Shepley, James R., 2809

Sheridan, James, 2099
Sherman, Dennis M., 2762
Sherrill, Robert, 1162
Sherry, Michael S., 2713
Sherwin, Martin J., 1755, 1756, 2782
Sherwood, Morgan, 1045
Shipley, George C., 229
Shlaim, Avi, 2563
Shogan, Robert, 1251
Shulman, Frank J., 3028
Shulman, Marshall D., 1836
Shurbet, Joanna Healey, 805
Shurcliff, William A., 2804
Siegel, Howard B., 1607
Sies, Dennis E., 195
Sievers, Rodney M., 1285
Sigal, Leon V., 1757
Sigelman, Lee, 1297
Sigethy, Robert, 2734
Silber, Irwin, 1252
Silverberg, Robert, 2434
Silverglate, Jesse J., 2550
Silverman, Corrine, 669
Silverman, Sheldon A., 1652
Sim, Herbert E., 704
Simmons, Jerold L., 1379
Simmons, Robert S., 2848
Simmons, Robert R., 2870
Simpson, James R., 1964
Sims, George E., 1217
Sinha, Bishwanath Prasad, 2321
Siracusa, Joseph M., 1634, 2038, 2304
Sirevag, Torbjorn, 281
Sitkoff, Harvard, 1115, 1253
Sivachev, Nikolai V., 1837
Skaggs, David C., 2965
Skau, George H., 154
Skeels, Jack M., 789
Skinner, James M., 912
Slack, Walter H., 803
Slater, Jerome N., 2339
Slind, Marvin G., 2539
Sloan, Alfred P., Jr., 625
Slonim, Shlomo, 2399
Slusser, Robert M., 2216
Small, Melvin, 1679
Smedley, Max J., 2366
Smerk, George, 620
Smith, A. Merriman, 167
Smith, A. Robert, 485
Smith, Alice Kimball, 2789
Smith, Alonzo N., 833
Smith, Bradley F., 1738, 2551–53
Smith, Charles P., 382
Smith, Cordell A., 2119
Smith, E. Timothy, 1927
Smith, Emory T., 2619
Smith, Gaddis, 304, 1965, 2849
Smith, Geoffrey S., 3008
Smith, Gilbert E., III, 985
Smith, Glenn H., 405
Smith, H. Lafollette, 1588
Smith, J. Malcolm, 657
Smith, Jean E., 365, 366, 2572
Smith, Jesse R., 2005

Smith, John C., 1442
Smith, Malcolm, 1362
Smith, Margaret Chase, 486
Smith, Myron J., Jr., 3038
Smith, Perry M., 2714
Smith, Richard N., 384
Smith, Robert, 2850
Smith, Robert L., 378
Smith, Robert T., 331
Smith, Rodney D., 896
Smith, Tom W., 1298
Smithsonian Institution, 897
Smock, Susan Wanless, 880
Snavely, Guy E., 994
Snell, John L., 1717
Snetsinger, John, 2415
Snowman, Daniel, 1758
Snyder, Glenn H., 1632, 2747
Snyder, Richard C., 2891
Soapes, Thomas F., 1218
Sobell, Morton, 1459
Sochen, June, 902
Soh, Jin Chull, 2856
Solomon, Mark, 2030
Somers, Herman M., 498
Somers, Norman, 796
Sorenson, Dale R., 1468, 1608
Sorkin, Alan L., 699
Sosna, Morton P., 1219
Southern, David W., 1121
Spanier, John W., 2860, 2906
Sparks, Donald T., 1696
Sparrow, John C., 1771
Spector, Bert A., 1346
Spector, Stephen, 2340
Spidle, Jake W., Jr., 1710
Spiller, Robert E., 881
Spivey, Delmar T., 2994
Springarn, Jerome H., 2749
Springer, Fred J., 943
Srinivasachary, M.S., 2322, 2323
Stacy, Bill W., 1254
Stafford, Walter W., 1099
Stairs, Denis, 2871–73
Stamey, Roderick A., Jr., 1966
Stanley, David T., 260
Stapleton, Margaret L., 3004
Starobin, Joseph R., 1189
Steahr, Thomas E., 995
Steamer, Robert J., 1557
Stebbins, Phillip E., 658, 1589
Steel, Ronald, 1307
Steelman, John R., 273
Stefan, Charles G., 2634
Stein, Bruno, 765, 766
Stein, Harold, 1739, 2681
Stein, Herbert, 692, 693
Stein, Roger B., 860
Steinberg, Alfred, 15, 53, 412, 429
Steinberg, Peter L., 1427
Steiner, Arthur, 1763
Steiner, George A., 644
Steinitz, Mark S., 2653, 2654
Steinmeyer, George W., 507
Stelmach, Daniel S., 2949

Subject Index

Mexico, 538–47, 2363–66
Middle East, 2369–74, 2437–41
Migratory labor, 242, 515
Military affairs *see* Department of Defense
Mills, C. Wright, 1166
Minerals, 248, 564, 582
Minorities and blacks: accounts of, 830, 832, 1108–11; aid, 940; antilynching, 1081; armed services, 1102–16; churches, 1013–15; education, 990; foreign affairs, 1661, 2030; Hindus, 953, 955; housing, 598, 1046, 1068; Italians, 1158; Japanese-Americans, 1142, 1144; Jews, 963, 996, 997, 1145, 1776; Mexican-Americans, 1141, 1143, 1146; movies, 899; Native Americans, 1131–36; nonwhite income, 695, 769; Polish-Americans, 1691, 1694, 2665; press, 1089, 1094; Puerto Ricans, 969; radio and television, 920, 976; sports, 1018–20, 1022, 1023; unemployment rates, 831; workers, 830, 832–33; writers, 869, 872–74, 877, 880; *see also* Civil rights; Fair Employment Practice Committee; Women
Minton, Sherman H., 1558–62
Morse, Wayne, 485
Movies: accounts, 898–912, 1401, 1402; blacklists, 1409, 1413, 1414, 1416; Hollywood Ten, 1417–24
Mundt, Karl, 1363
Munoz Marin, Luis, 1493, 1495
Murphy, Frank, 1563–64
Murray, Philip, 798, 812

National Archives, 252
National Association for the Advancement of Colored People (NAACP), 1070, 1072, 1073, 1077
National Labor Relations Board, 726, 729, 763
National Science Foundation, 475, 1041–45
National Security Council: accounts, 1625–30; creation of, 204, 207; NSC-68, 1614, 1631–35
National Security Resources Board, 204
Niebuhr, Reinhold, 1178, 1183, 1184
Nixon, Richard M., 423–26, 489
North Atlantic Treaty Organization (NATO): Canada, 2047; development of, 1913–30, 2009; Italy, 2619; opponents, 409; supporters, 1697; Truman Doctrine and, 1860
Norway, 1930
Nunan, Joseph D., 146

O'Conor, Herbert R., 469
Office of Contract Settlement, 293, 499
Office of Price Administration: Bowles and, 261, 501; operations, 500, 531, 532
Oil: antitrust, 590; depletion allowance, 477; Federal Power Commission, 589; Kerr and, 477; Mexico, 2363; national policy, 594, 2441; natural gas, 592, 593; pipelines, 588; Saudi Arabia, 2455, 2457–59; synthetic liquid fuels, 591, 596; tidelands controversy, 266, 585–87, 595; Venezuela, 2368; *see also* Energy sources
Olds, Leland, 589
Oppenheimer, J. Robert, 2796–98, 2810

Pacifists, 2823–30
Pakistan, 2308, 2309
Palestine issue, 2378–2402
Panama Canal, 2334
Patman, Wright, 639

Patton, James G., 522
Pendergast, Tom, 66, 67, 69, 70–75
Pepper, Claude, 357, 487
Philippines, 2275–81
Poland: Katyn massacre, 1727, 2668; Lane and, 2659; Polish-Americans, 1691, 1694, 2665; postwar government of, 1818, 2659–69
Politics: art and, 854; blacks and, 1047, 1124–30; Church-State issue, 977–84; ideologies, 1169–89; Korean War, 2876–83; national, 1149–65; state and local, 1190–1224
Potsdam Conference, 915, 1598, 1724–33
Pound, Ezra, 890, 891, 893
Presidential commissions and committees, 232–50
Presidential ranking, 173–83
Press *see* Media
Press conferences, 184–95, 286
Public opinion: atomic bomb and, 1760, 1761; foreign affairs, 1656–81, 1690–97, 2097; Korean War, 2876–83, 2910–24; League of Women Voters, 1692; polls, 1247, 1248, 1289, 1290, 1294, 1295; United Nations, 1995
Puerto Rico, 409, 1493–95

Quill, Mike, 813

Randolph, A. Philip, 1069
Rayburn, Sam, 427–29
Reconversion, 475, 492–99
Reed, Stanley, 1565, 1566
Religion: accounts, 1002–12; Baptists, 1011; Catholics, 536, 788, 977–84, 997, 1002, 2016, 2058; Cold War, 1004, 1693, 2143; Congregationalism, 1007; education, 1008; Jehovah's Witnesses, 1009; Lutherans, 1003; Methodists, 994; missionaries, 2130–34, 2191; National Council of Churches, 1005; pacifism, 2826; Presbyterians, 1012; race and, 1013–15; Truman and, 183, 1006
Reuther, Walter, 799–803
Robinson, Jackie, 1018–20, 1022, 1023
Rockfeller, Nelson A., 348
Romania, 2648
Roosevelt, Eleanor, 342–44, 981, 983, 2021
Rosenberg, Julius and Ethel, 1447–59
Rosenman, Samuel I., 287
Ross, Charles G., 286
Rusk, Dean, 2074
Russell, Richard B., 1096
Rutledge, Wiley, 1567, 1568

Saudi Arabia, 2455–59
Sawyer, Charles, 291
Scandals, 146–50
Schlesinger, Arthur M., Jr., 1173, 1176, 1179–82
Science and technology: atomic bomb, 1762–64; computers, 1036–40; cybernetics, 1035; federal policy toward, 1027; government controls, 249, 1024, 1033; history of, 1026; loyalty, 1356; National Science Foundation, 475; physics, 1031; Project Paperclip, 1029, 1030; Velikovsky and, 1025
Service, John C., 330, 350, 361
Smith, H. Alexander, 470
Smith, Horace, 350
Social Security, 942, 946
South Africa, 2032, 2033
Spain, 2622–27